ENGLAND

Football League

Tables and Results

1872 to 1958

Alex Graham

INTRODUCTION

This book features a statistical history of football in England from 1872 (when the F.A. Cup was first played) until 1958. The F.A. Cup (or The Football Association Challenge Cup to give the full title) was the first major competition but the roots of organised English football predate this by almost 10 years. Organised football as we know it began with the formation of the Football Association in a meeting in the Freemason's Tavern in Great Queen Street, London on 26th October 1863. At that time there were no universally accepted rules for the playing of the game of football with a number of variations used in different areas of the country. The first revision of the rules for the modern game was drawn up during a series of six meetings held in the social room of this public house between October and December of 1863 and, with relatively minor alterations, these rules are used worldwide to this day!

The F.A. Cup itself was first suggested by C.W. Alcock, then Secretary of the Football Association, at a meeting on 20th July 1871 and the competition was embodied at a later meeting on 16th October 1871. The F.A. Cup remains the oldest and most prestigious domestic cup competition in the world and the 12 clubs who entered in 1872 could scarcely have believed that the Cup would grow to a competition with so many hundreds of clubs entering each season. The F.A. Cup is still played as a strict knock-out competition with no seeding of clubs and this book lists the results from the Quarter-Final stage onwards including full line-ups and goalscorers for the Final matches themselves.

After the great success of the F.A. Cup, it was inevitable that a League competition would eventually begin and to this end William McGregor, a director of Aston Villa FC, arranged a preliminary meeting on 22nd March 1888 at Anderton's Hotel in Fleet Street. The Football League officially came into existence at a subsequent meeting on 17th April 1888 with 12 members. The Football League is, unsurprisingly, the oldest domestic League competition in the world. Since the first game was played on 8th September 1888, the League has expanded considerably and at it's height has consisted of 4 separate divisions containing a total of 92 professional clubs.

Both the Football League and F.A. Cup were suspended during the two World Wars and a number of regional matches and championships were played in their stead. This book includes tables of the combined results of those wartime matches for each year they ran together with the results of games played in the 1939-40 Football League season which was abandoned due to the onset of War.

In addition to the results of all League matches, Final League tables and the F.A. Cup results, this book also lists the top goal-scorers for each season.

Much of the information in this book is taken from the now defunct "Statistical History of Football" series which were published by Skye Soccer Books. As in the original series, the full names of clubs are used whenever possible with name-changes, mergers etc. shown as and when they occur. The club names are listed in the following format:
   Club Name (Home Town/City/Village).

The information contained in this book has been gathered over a number of years and has come from myriad sources although most was collected through personal contacts. Other sources of information include newspapers, magazines, books etc. and in more recent times the internet. I would like to extend my thanks to all those who helped with the collection of this information. In an attempt to ensure accuracy, the information has been checked and collated. However, if any errors are found, readers are invited to notify the author care of the address below and if possible provide the corrected information.

Alex Graham

British Library Cataloguing in Publication Data

A catalogue record for this book is available from the British Library

ISBN 978-1-86223-256-3

Printed by 4edge Limited

1872

F.A. CUP FINAL   (Kennington Oval, London – 16/03/1872 – 2,000)

THE WANDERERS FC (LONDON)   1-0   Royal Engineers Regiment (Chatham)
Betts

Wanderers: Welch, Bowen, Thompson, Lubbock, Crake, Wollaston, Alcock, Hooman, Betts, Vidal, Bonsor.

Royal Engineers: Merriman, Marindin, Addison, Creswell, Mitchell, Renny-Tailyour, Rich, Goodwyn, Muirhead, Cotter, Bogle.

Semi-finals

Royal Engineers Regiment (Chatham)   0-0, 3-0   Crystal Palace FC (London)
The Wanderers FC (London)   0-0, w/o   Queen's Park FC (Glasgow)
Queen's Park FC withdrew due to difficulty in meeting travel expenses for the replay.

Round 3

Royal Engineers Regiment (Chatham)   3-0   Hampstead Heathens FC (London)
The Wanderers FC (London)   0-0   Crystal Palace FC (London)
(Both teams qualified under rule 8.)
Queen's Park FC (Glasgow) received a bye.

1873

F.A. CUP FINAL   (Amateur Athletic Ground, Lillie Bridge, London – 29/03/1873 – 3,000)

THE WANDERERS FC (LONDON)   2-0   Oxford University FC (Oxford)
Kinnaird, Wollaston   (H.T. 2-0)

Wanderers: Welch, Howell, Bowen, Thompson, Kinnaird, Wollaston, Sturgis, Stewart, Kenyon-Slaney, Kingsford, Bonsor.

Oxford University: Leach, Mackarness, Birley, Kirke-Smith, Ottaway, Longman, Chappell-Madison, Dixon, Paton, Vidal, Sumner.

Semi-finals

Oxford University FC (Oxford)   w/o   Queen's Park FC (Glasgow)
The match was due to be played on the same day as an England vs Scotland international so Oxford decided they could not play. Instead of claiming the tie Queen's Park withdrew allowing Oxford to progress to the final.
The Wanderers FC (London) received a bye

Quarter-finals

Oxford University FC (Oxford)   4-0   Maidenhead FC (Maidenhead)
Queen's Park FC (Glasgow) and The Wanderers FC (London) both received byes.

1874

F.A. CUP FINAL (Kennington Oval, London – 14/04/1874 – 2,000)

OXFORD UNIVERSITY FC (OXFORD)   2-0   Royal Engineers Regiment (Chatham)

Mackarness, Patton

Oxford University: Nepean, Mackarness, Birley, Green, Vidal, Ottaway, Benson, Patton, S.Rawson, Chappell-Madison, Johnson.

Royal Engineers: Merriman, Marindin, Addison, Onslow, Digby, Oliver, Renny-Tailyour, E.Rawson, Blackburn, Wood von Donop.

Semi-finals

Oxford University FC (Oxford)	1-0	Clapham Rovers FC (London)
Royal Engineers Regiment (Chatham)	2-0	The Swifts FC (London)

Quarter-finals

Clapham Rovers FC (London)	2-1	Sheffield FC (Sheffield)
Royal Engineers Regiment (Chatham)	7-0	Maidenhead FC (Maidenhead)
The Wanderers FC (London)	1-1, 0-1	Oxford University FC (Oxford)

The Swifts FC (London) received a bye.

1875

F.A. CUP FINAL (Kennington Oval, London – 16/03/1875 – 3,000)

ROYAL ENGINEERS REGIMENT   1-1 (aet)   Old Etonians FC (London)

Renny-Tailyour   *Bonsor*

Royal Engineers: Merriman, Sim, Onslow, Ruck, von Donop, Wood, Rawson, Stafford, Renny-Tailyour, Mein, Wingfield-Stratford.

Old Etonians: Farmer, Wilson, Thompson, E.Lubbock, Benson, Kenyon-Slaney, Patton, Bonsor, Ottaway, Kinnaird, Stronge.

F.A. CUP FINAL REPLAY (Kennington Oval, London – 16/03/1875 – 3,000)

ROYAL ENGINEERS REGIMENT   2-0   Old Etonians FC (London)

Renny-Tailyour, Stafford

Old Etonians: Drummond-Moray, Farrer, E.Lubbock, Wilson, Hamond, A.Lubbock, Patton, Farmer, Bonsor, Kinnaird, Stronge.

Royal Engineers: Merriman, Sim, Onslow, Ruck, von Donop, Wood, Rawson, Stafford, Renny-Tailyour, Mein, Wingfield-Stratford.

Semi-finals

Old Etonians FC (London)	1-0	Shropshire Wanderers FC (Shrewsbury)
Royal Engineers Regiment (Chatham)	1-1, 1-0 (aet)	Oxford University FC (Oxford)

Quarter-finals

Old Etonians FC (London)	1-0	Maidenhead FC (Maidenhead)
Royal Engineers Regiment (Chatham)	3-2	Clapham Rovers FC (London)
Shropshire Wanderers FC (Shrewsbury)	1-1 (aet), 2-0	Woodford Wells FC
The Wanderers FC (London)	1-2	Oxford University FC (London)

1876

F.A. CUP FINAL   (Kennington Oval, London – 11/03/1876 – 3,000)

THE WANDERERS FC (LONDON)   1-1 (aet)   Old Etonians FC (London)

Edwards   *(H.T. 1-0)*   *Bonsor*

Wanderers: Greig, Stratford, Lindsay, Maddison, Birley, Wollaston, GH Heron, F.Heron, Edwards. Kenrick, Hughes.

Old Etonians: Hogg, Wellson, C.Thompson, E.Lyttleton, A.Lyttleton, Kinnaird, Kenyon-Slaney, CM Thompson, Bonsor, Sturgis, Alleyne.

F.A. CUP FINAL REPLAY   (Kennington Oval, London – 18/03/1876 – 3,500)

THE WANDERERS FC (LONDON)   3-0   Old Etonians FC (London)

Hughes 2, Wollaston   *(H.T. 2-0)*

Old Etonians: Hogg, Lubbock, Farrer, E.Lyttleton, Kinnaird, A.Lyttleton, Kenyon-Stanley, Bonsor, Sturgis, Alleyne, Stronge.

Wanderers: Greig, Stratford, Lindsay, Maddison, Birley, Wollaston, GH Heron, F.Heron, Edwards, Kenrick, Hughes.

Semi-finals

Oxford University FC (Oxford)	0-1	Old Etonians FC (London)
The Wanderers FC (London)	2-1	The Swifts FC (London)

Quarter-finals

Cambridge University FC (Cambridge)	0-4	Oxford University FC (Oxford)
Old Etonians FC (London)	1-0	Clapham Rovers FC (London)
Royal Engineers Regiment (Chatham)	1-3	The Swifts FC (London)
The Wanderers FC (London)	2-0	Sheffield FC (Sheffield)

1877

F.A. CUP FINAL   (Kennington Oval, London – 24/03/1877 – 3,000)

THE WANDERERS FC (LONDON)   2-1 (aet)   Oxford University FC (Oxford)

Kenrick, Lindsay   *(H.T. 0-1)*   *Waddington*

Wanderers: Kinnaird, Lindsay, Stratford, Birley, Green, Hughes, Wollaston, GH Heron, Wace, Kenrick, Denton.

Oxford University: Alington, Dunell, Rawson, Waddington, Savory, Otter, Parry, Bain, Todd, Fernandez, Hills.

Semi-finals

The Wanderers FC (London)	1-0	Cambridge University FC (Cambridge)
Oxford University FC (Oxford) received a bye.		

Quarter-finals

Cambridge University FC (Cambridge)	1-0	Royal Engineers Regiment (Chatham)
Oxford University FC (Oxford)	0-0, 1-0	Upton Park FC (London)
The Wanderers FC (London) received a bye.		

1878

F.A. CUP FINAL (Kennington Oval, London – 23/03/1878 – 4,500)

THE WANDERERS FC (LONDON)   3-1   Royal Engineers Regiment (Chatham)
Kenrick 2, Kinnaird   *(H.T. 1-1)*   *Scorer not known*

Wands.: Kirkpatrick, Stratford, Lindsay, Kinnaird, Green, Wollaston, GH.Heron, Wylie, Wace, Denton, Kenrick.
Royal Engineers: Friend, Cowan, Morris, Mayne, Heath, Lindsay, Barnet, Hedley, Haynes, Bond, Ruck.

Semi-finals

Royal Engineers Regiment (Chatham)   2-1   Old Harrovians FC (London)
The Wanderers FC (London) received a bye.

Quarter-finals

Old Harrovians FC (London)   3-1   Upton Park FC (London)
Royal Engineers Regiment (Chatham)   3-3, 2-2 (aet), 4-2   Oxford University FC (Oxford)
The Wanderers FC (London)   3-0   Sheffield FC (Sheffield)

1879

F.A. CUP FINAL (Kennington Oval, London – 29/03/1879 – 5,000)

OLD ETONIANS FC (LONDON)   1-0   Clapham Rovers FC (London)
Clerke   *(H.T. 0-0)*

Old Eton.: Hawtrey, Christian, Bury, Kinnaird, Lubbock, Clerke, Pares, Goodhart, Whitfield, Chevallier, Beaufoy
Clapham: Birkett, Ogilvie, Field, Bailey, Prinsep, Rawson, Stanley, Scott, Bevington, Growse, Keith-Falconer.

Semi-finals

Old Etonians FC (London)   2-1   Nottingham Forest FC (Nottingham)
Clapham Rovers FC (London) received a bye.

Quarter-finals

Clapham Rovers FC (London)   8-1   The Swifts FC (London)
Nottingham Forest FC (Nottingham)   2-1   Oxford University FC (Oxford)
Old Etonians FC (London)   5-5, 2-2 (aet), 6-2   Darwen FC (Darwen)

1880

F.A. CUP FINAL (Kennington Oval, London – 10/04/1880 – 6,000)

CLAPHAM ROVERS FC (LONDON)   1-0   Oxford University FC (Oxford)
Lloyd-Jones   *(H.T. 0-0)*

Clapham Rovers: Birkett, Ogilvie, Field, Weston, Bailey, Brougham, Stanley, Barry, Sparks, Lloyd-Jones, Ram.
Oxford University: Parr, Wilson, King, Phillips, Rogers, Heygate, Childs, Eyre, Crowdy, Hill, Lubbock.

Semi-finals

Oxford University FC (Oxford)   1-0   Nottingham Forest FC (Nottingham)
Clapham Rovers FC (London) received a bye.

Quarter-finals

Clapham Rovers FC (London)   1-0   Old Etonians FC (London)
Oxford University FC (Oxford)   1-1 (aet), 1-0   Royal Engineers Regiment (Chatham)
Nottingham Forest FC (Nottingham) received a bye.

1881

F.A. CUP FINAL   (Kennington Oval, London – 09/04/1881 – 4,500)

OLD CARTHUSIANS FC (LONDON)   3-0   Old Etonians FC (London)

Wynyard, Parry, Todd   *(H.T. 1-0)*

Old Carthusians: Gillett, Norris, Colvin, Prinsep, Vincent, Hensell, Richards, Page, Wynyard, Parry, Todd.

Old Etonians: Rawlinson, Foley, French, Kinnaird, Farrer, Chevallier, Anderson, Goodhart, Macaulay, Whitfield, Novelli.

Semi-finals

Old Carthusians FC (London)   4-1   Darwen FC (Darwen)
Old Etonians FC (London) received a bye.

Quarter-finals

Darwen FC (Darwen)   15-0   Romford FC (London)
Old Carthusians FC (London)   3-1   Clapham Rovers FC (London)
Stafford Road FC (Wolverhampton)   1-2   Old Etonians FC (London)

1882

F.A. CUP FINAL   (Kennington Oval, London – 25/03/1882 – 6,500)

OLD ETONIANS FC (LONDON)   1-0   Blackburn Rovers FC (Blackburn)

Anderson   *(H.T. 1-0)*

Old Etonians: Rawlinson, French, de Paravicini, Kinnaird, Foley, Anderson, Chevallier, Macauley, Goodhart, Dunn, Novelli.

Blackburn: Howarth, McIntyre, Suter, F. Hargreaves, Sharples, Duckworth, Douglas, Brown, Strachan, Avery, J. Hargreaves,

Semi-finals

Blackburn Rovers FC (Blackburn)   0-0, 5-1   The Wednesday FC (Sheffield)
Old Etonians FC (London)   5-0   Great Marlow FC (London)

Quarter-finals

 Blackburn Rovers FC (Blackburn)   3-1   Wednesbury Old Athletic FC (Wednesbury)
Old Foresters FC (London)   0-0, 0-1   Great Marlow FC (London)
The Wednesday FC (Sheffield)   6-0   Upton Park FC (London)
Old Etonians FC (London) received a bye.

1883

F.A. CUP FINAL   (Kennington Oval, London – 31/03/1883 – 8,000)

BLACKBURN OLYMPIC FC	2-1 (aet)	Old Etonians FC (London)
Matthews, Crossley	*(H.T. 0-1)*	*Goodhart*

Blackburn: Hacking, Ward, Warburton, Gibson, Hunter, Astley, Dewhurst, Matthews, Wilson, Crossley, Yates.
Old Etonians: Rawlinson, de Paravicini, French, Kinnaird, Foley, Anderson, Chevallier, Macaulay, Goodhart, Dunn, Bainbridge.

Semi-finals

Blackburn Olympic FC (Blackburn)	4-0	Old Carthusians FC (London)
Old Etonians FC (London)	2-1	Notts County FC (Nottingham)

Quarter-finals

Blackburn Olympic FC (Blackburn)	4-1	Druids FC (Ruabon)
Hendon FC (London)	2-4	Old Etonians FC (London)
Old Carthusians FC (London)	5-3	Clapham Rovers FC (London)
Notts County FC (Nottingham)	4-3	Aston Villa FC (Birmingham)

1884

F.A. CUP FINAL   (Kennington Oval, London – 29/03/1884 – 14,000)

BLACKBURN ROVERS FC (BLACKBURN)	2-1	Queen's Park FC (Glasgow)
Brown, Forrest	*(H.T. 2-1)*	*Christie*

Blackburn: Arthur, Beverley, Suter, McIntyre, Hargreaves, Forrest, Lofthouse, Douglas, Sowerbutts, Inglis, Brown.
Q.P.R.: Gillespie, Arnott, Macdonald, Campbell, Gow, Anderson, Watt, Smith, Harrower, Allan, Christie.

Semi-finals

Blackburn Rovers FC (Blackburn)	1-0	Notts County FC (Nottingham)
Queen's Park FC (Glasgow)	4-1	Blackburn Olympic FC (Blackburn)

Quarter-finals

Blackburn Olympic FC (Blackburn)	9-1	Northwich Victoria FC (Northwich)
Notts County FC (Nottingham)	1-1, 1-0	The Swifts FC (London)
Old Westminsters FC (London)	0-1	Queen's Park FC (Glasgow)
Upton Park FC (London)	0-3	Blackburn Rovers FC (Blackburn)

1885

F.A. CUP FINAL (Kennington Oval, London – 04/04/1885 – 12,500)

BLACKBURN ROVERS FC (BLACKBURN) 2-0 Queen's Park FC (Glasgow)

Forrest, Brown (H.T. 1-0)

Blackburn: Arthur, Turner, Suter, McIntyre, Haworth, Forrest, Lofthouse, Douglas, Brown, Fecitt, Sowerbutts.
QPR: Gillespie, Arnott, McLeod, Campbell, MacDonald, Hamilton, McWhannel, Anderson, Sellar, Gray, Allan.

Semi-finals

Blackburn Rovers FC (Blackburn)	5-1	Old Carthusians FC (London)
Nottingham Forest FC (Nottingham)	1-1, 0-3	Queen's Park FC (Glasgow)

Quarter-finals

Church FC (Accrington)	0-1	Old Carthusians FC (London)
Notts County FC (Nottingham)	2-2, 1-2	Queen's Park FC (Glasgow)
Old Etonians FC (London)	0-2	Nottingham Forest FC (Nottingham)
West Bromwich Albion FC (West Bromwich)	0-2	Blackburn Rovers FC (Blackburn)

1886

F.A. CUP FINAL (Kennington Oval, London – 03/04/1886 – 15,000)

BLACKBURN ROVERS FC (BLACKBURN) 0-0 West Bromwich Albion FC (West Bromwich)

Blackburn: Arthur, Turner, Suter, Heyes, Forrest, McIntyre, Douglas, Strachan, Sowerbutts, Fecitt, Brown.
West Bromwich: Roberts, H.Green, H.Bell, Horton, Perry, Timmins, Woodhall, T.Green, Bayliss, Loach, G.Bell.

F.A. CUP FINAL REPLAY (County Cricket Ground, Derby – 10/04/1886 – 12,000)

BLACKBURN ROVERS FC (BLACKBURN) 2-0 West Bromwich Albion FC (West Bromwich)

Sowerbutts, Brown (H.T. 1-0)

West Bromwich: Roberts, H.Green, H.Bell, Horton, Perry, Timming, Woodhall, T.Green, Bayliss, Loach, G.Bell.
Blackburn: Arthur, Turner, Suter, Douglas, Forest, McIntyre, Walton, Strachan, Brown, Fecitt, Sowerbutts.

Semi-finals

Blackburn Rovers FC (Blackburn)	2-1	The Swifts FC (London)
West Bromwich Albion FC (West Bromwich)	4-0	Small Heath Alliance FC (Birmingham)

Quarter-finals

Brentwood FC (Brentwood)	1-3	Blackburn Rovers FC (Blackburn)
Small Heath Alliance FC (Birmingham)	2-0	Redcar & Coatham FC (Redcar)
South Shore FC (Blackpool)	1-2	The Swifts FC (London)
West Bromwich Albion FC (West Bromwich)	6-0	Old Westminsters FC (London)

1887

F.A. CUP FINAL   (Kennington Oval, London – 02/04/1887 – 15,534)

| ASTON VILLA FC (BIRMINGHAM) | 2-0 | West Bromwich Albion FC (West Bromwich) |

Hodgetts, Hunter   *(H.T. 0-0)*

Aston Villa: Warner, Coulton, Simmonds, Yates, Dawson, Burton, Davis, Brown, Hunter, Vaughton, Hodgetts.

West Bromwich: Roberts, Aldridge, H.Green, Horton, Perry, Timmins, Woodhall, T.Green, Bayliss, Pearson, Paddock.

Semi-finals

| Aston Villa FC (Birmingham) | 3-1 | Rangers FC (Glasgow) |
| West Bromwich Albion FC (West Bromwich) | 3-1 | Preston North End FC (Preston) |

Quarter-finals

Aston Villa FC (Birmingham)	3-2	Darwen FC (Darwen)
Notts County FC (Nottingham)	1-4	West Bromwich Albion FC (West Bromwich)
Old Carthusians FC (London)	1-2 (aet)	Preston North End FC (Preston)
Rangers FC (Glasgow)	5-1	Old Westminsters FC (London)

1888

F.A. CUP FINAL   (Kennington Oval, London – 24/03/1888 – 18,904)

| WEST BROMWICH ALBION FC | 2-1 | Preston North End FC (Preston) |

Bayliss, Woodhall   *(H.T. 1-0)*   *Dewhurst*

West Bromwich: Roberts, Aldridge, H.Green, Horton, Perry, Timmins, Bassett, Woodhall, Bayliss, Wilson, Pearson.

Preston: Mills-Roberts, Howarth, N.J. Ross, Holmes, Russell, Graham, Gordon, J.D. Ross, Goodall, Dewhurst, Drummond.

Semi-finals

| Preston North End FC (Preston) | 4-0 | Crewe Alexandra FC (Crewe) |
| West Bromwich Albion FC (West Bromwich) | 3-0 | Derby Junction FC (Derby) |

Quarter-finals

Derby Junction FC (Derby)	2-1	Blackburn Rovers FC (Blackburn)
Middlesbrough FC (Middlesbrough)	0-2	Crewe Alexandra FC (Crewe)
The Wednesday FC (Sheffield)	1-3	Preston North End FC (Preston)
West Bromwich Albion FC (West Bromwich)	4-2	Old Carthusians FC (London)

The Football League began in season 1888-89 with a single division of 12 clubs, this was extended to 14 clubs for season 1891-92, a 2nd division was introduced for season 1892-93.

Football League 1888-89 Season	Accrington	Aston Villa	Blackburn Rovers	Bolton Wanderers	Burnley	Derby County	Everton	Notts County	Preston North End	Stoke	W.B.A.	Wolves
Accrington FC	■	1-1	0-2	2-3	5-1	6-2	3-1	1-2	0-0	2-0	2-1	4-4
Aston Villa FC	4-3	■	6-1	6-2	4-2	4-2	2-1	9-1	0-2	5-1	2-0	2-1
Blackburn Rovers FC	5-5	5-1	■	4-4	4-2	3-0	3-0	5-2	2-2	5-2	6-2	2-2
Bolton Wanderers FC	4-1	2-3	3-2	■	3-4	3-6	6-2	7-3	2-5	2-1	1-2	2-1
Burnley FC	2-2	4-0	1-7	4-1	■	1-0	2-2	1-0	2-2	2-1	2-0	0-4
Derby County FC	1-1	5-2	0-2	2-3	1-0	■	2-4	3-2	2-3	2-1	1-2	3-0
Everton FC	2-1	2-0	3-1	2-1	3-2	6-2	■	2-1	0-2	2-1	1-4	1-2
Notts County FC	3-3	2-4	3-3	0-4	6-1	3-5	3-1	■	0-7	0-3	2-1	3-0
Preston North End FC	2-0	1-1	1-0	3-1	5-2	5-0	3-0	4-1	■	7-0	3-0	5-2
Stoke FC	2-4	1-1	2-1	2-2	4-3	1-1	0-0	3-0	0-3	■	0-2	0-1
West Bromwich Albion FC	2-2	3-3	2-1	1-5	4-3	5-0	1-0	4-2	0-5	2-0	■	1-3
Wolverhampton Wanderers FC	4-0	1-1	2-2	3-2	4-1	4-1	4-0	2-1	0-4	4-1	2-1	■

Football League

		Pd	Wn	Dw	Ls	GF	GA	Pts
1.	PRESTON NORTH END FC (PRESTON)	22	18	4	-	74	15	40
2.	Aston Villa FC (Birmingham)	22	12	5	5	61	43	29
3.	Wolverhampton Wanderers FC (Wolverhampton)	22	12	4	6	50	37	28
4.	Blackburn Rovers FC (Blackburn)	22	10	6	6	66	45	26
5.	Bolton Wanderers FC (Bolton)	22	10	2	10	63	59	22
6.	West Bromwich Albion FC (West Bromwich)	22	10	2	10	40	46	22
7.	Accrington FC (Accrington)	22	6	8	8	48	48	20
8.	Everton FC (Liverpool)	22	9	2	11	35	46	20
9.	Burnley FC (Burnley)	22	7	3	12	42	62	17
10.	Derby County FC (Derby)	22	7	2	13	41	61	16
11.	Notts County FC (Nottingham)	22	5	2	15	40	73	12
12.	Stoke FC (Stoke-upon-Trent)	22	4	4	14	26	51	12
		264	110	44	110	586	586	264

Top Goalscorers

1)	John GOODALL	(Preston North End FC)	21
2)	James D. ROSS	(Preston North End FC)	18
3)	Albert ALLEN	(Aston Villa FC)	17
4)	John SOUTHWORTH	(Blackburn Rovers FC)	16
	Harold WOOD	(Wolverhampton Wanderers FC)	16

F.A. CUP FINAL   (Kennington Oval, London – 30/03/1889 – 22,000)

PRESTON NORTH END FC (PRESTON)   3-0   Wolverhampton Wanderers FC

Dewhurst, Ross, Thomson   (H.T. 2-0)

Preston: Mills-Roberts, Howarth, Holmes, Drummond, Russell, Graham, Gordon, J.D. Ross, Goodall, Dewhurst, Thomson.

Wolves: Baynton, Baugh, Mason, Fletcher, Allen, Lowder, Hunter, Wykes, Brodie, Wood, Knight.

Semi-finals

Preston North End FC (Preston)	1-0	West Bromwich Albion FC (West Bromwich)
Wolverhampton Wanderers FC	1-1 (aet), 3-1	Blackburn Rovers FC (Blackburn)

Quarter-finals

Blackburn Rovers FC (Blackburn)	8-1	Aston Villa FC (Birmingham)
Chatham FC (Chatham)	1-10	West Bromwich Albion FC (West Bromwich)
Preston North End FC (Preston)	2-0	Birmingham St. George's FC (Birmingham)
Wolverhampton Wanderers FC (Wolverhampton)	3-0	The Wednesday FC (Sheffield)

1889-90

Football League 1889-90 Season	Accrington	Aston Villa	Blackburn Rovers	Bolton Wanderers	Burnley	Derby County	Everton	Notts County	Preston North End	Stoke	W.B.A.	Wolves
Accrington FC		4-2	2-2	3-1	2-2	6-1	5-3	1-8	2-2	2-1	0-0	6-3
Aston Villa FC	1-2		3-0	1-2	2-2	7-1	1-2	1-1	5-3	6-1	1-0	2-1
Blackburn Rovers FC	3-2	7-0		7-1	7-1	4-2	2-4	9-1	3-4	8-0	5-0	4-3
Bolton Wanderers FC	2-4	2-0	3-2		2-2	7-1	3-4	0-4	2-6	5-0	7-0	4-1
Burnley FC	2-2	2-6	1-2	7-0		2-0	0-1	3-0	0-3	1-3	1-2	1-2
Derby County FC	2-3	5-0	4-0	3-2	4-1		2-2	2-0	2-1	2-0	3-1	3-3
Everton FC	2-2	7-0	3-2	3-0	2-1	3-0		5-3	1-5	8-0	5-1	1-1
Notts County FC	3-1	1-1	1-1	3-5	1-1	3-1	4-3		0-1	3-1	1-2	0-2
Preston North End FC	3-1	3-2	1-1	3-1	6-0	5-0	1-2	4-3		10-0	5-0	0-2
Stoke FC	7-1	1-1	0-3	0-1	3-4	1-1	1-2	1-1	1-2		1-3	2-1
West Bromwich Albion FC	4-1	3-0	3-2	6-3	6-1	2-3	4-1	4-2	2-2	2-1		1-4
Wolverhampton Wanderers FC	2-1	1-1	2-4	5-1	9-1	2-1	2-1	2-0	0-1	2-2	1-1	

	Football League	Pd	Wn	Dw	Ls	GF	GA	Pts	
1.	PRESTON NORTH END FC (PRESTON)	22	15	3	4	71	30	33	
2.	Everton FC (Liverpool)	22	14	3	5	65	40	31	
3.	Blackburn Rovers FC (Blackburn)	22	12	3	7	78	41	27	
4.	Wolverhampton Wanderers FC (Wolverhampton)	22	10	5	7	51	38	25	
5.	West Bromwich Albion FC (West Bromwich)	22	11	3	8	47	50	25	
6.	Accrington FC (Accrington)	22	9	6	7	53	56	24	
7.	Derby County FC (Derby)	22	9	3	10	43	55	21	
8.	Aston Villa FC (Birmingham)	22	7	5	10	43	51	19	
9.	Bolton Wanderers FC (Bolton)	22	9	1	12	54	65	19	
10.	Notts County FC (Nottingham)	22	6	5	11	43	51	17	
11.	Burnley FC (Burnley)	22	4	5	13	36	65	13	
12.	Stoke FC (Stoke-upon-Trent)	22	3	4	15	27	69	10	#
		264	109	46	109	611	611	264	

\# Stoke FC (Stoke-upon-Trent) were not re-elected to the league for the next season and were replaced by the election of Sunderland AFC (Sunderland).

Top Goalscorers

1)	James D. ROSS	(Preston North End FC)	24
2)	John SOUTHWORTH	(Blackburn Rovers FC)	22
3)	Frederick C. GEARY	(Everton FC)	21
4)	Nicholas John ROSS	(Preston North End FC)	16
5)	Harold CAMPBELL	(Blackburn Rovers FC)	15
	James OSWALD	(Notts County FC)	15
	David WYKES	(Wolverhampton Wanderers FC)	15

F.A. CUP FINAL   (Kennington Oval, London – 29/03/1890 – 20,000)

BLACKBURN ROVERS FC (BLACKBURN)   6-1   The Wednesday FC (Sheffield)

Townley 3, John Southworth, Lofthouse, Walton   (H.T. 4-0)   *Mumford*

Blackburn: Horne, James Southworth, Forbes, Barton, Dewar, Forrest, Lofthouse, Campbell, John Southworth, Walton, Townley.

Wednesday: Smith, Brayshaw, Morley, Dungworth, Betts, Walker, Ingram, Woodhouse, Bennett, Cawley, Mumford.

Semi-finals

Blackburn Rovers FC (Blackburn)	1-0	Wolverhampton Wanderers FC (Wolverhampton)
The Wednesday FC (Sheffield)	2-1	Bolton Wanderers FC (Bolton)

Quarter-finals

Bootle FC (Bootle)	0-7	Blackburn Rovers FC (Blackburn)
Preston North End FC (Preston)	2-3	Bolton Wanderers FC (Bolton)
The Wednesday FC (Sheffield)	5-0, 2-3, 2-1	Notts County FC (Nottingham)

(The first two games were replayed after protests.)

Wolverhampton Wanderers FC (Wolverhampton)	3-0, 8-0	Stoke FC (Stoke-upon-Trent)

(The first game was replayed after a protest.)

1890-91

Football League 1890-91 Season	Accrington	Aston Villa	Blackburn Rovers	Bolton Wanderers	Burnley	Derby County	Everton	Notts County	Preston North End	Sunderland	W.B.A.	Wolves
Accrington FC	■	1-3	0-4	2-1	1-1	4-0	1-2	3-2	1-3	4-1	1-0	1-2
Aston Villa FC	3-1	■	2-2	5-0	4-4	4-0	2-2	3-2	0-1	0-0	0-4	6-2
Blackburn Rovers FC	0-0	5-1	■	0-2	5-2	8-0	2-1	1-7	1-0	3-2	2-1	2-3
Bolton Wanderers FC	6-0	4-0	2-0	■	1-0	3-1	0-5	4-2	1-0	2-5	7-1	6-0
Burnley FC	2-0	2-1	1-6	1-2	■	6-1	3-2	0-1	6-2	3-3	5-4	4-2
Derby County FC	1-2	5-4	8-5	1-1	2-4	■	2-6	3-1	1-3	3-1	3-1	9-0
Everton FC	3-2	5-0	3-1	2-0	7-3	7-0	■	4-2	0-1	1-0	2-3	5-0
Notts County FC	5-0	7-1	1-2	3-1	4-0	2-1	3-1	■	2-1	2-1	3-2	1-1
Preston North End FC	1-1	4-1	1-2	1-0	7-0	6-0	2-0	0-0	■	0-0	3-0	5-1
Sunderland AFC	2-2	5-1	3-1	2-0	2-3	5-1	1-0	4-0	3-0	■	1-1	3-4
West Bromwich Albion FC	5-1	0-3	1-0	2-4	3-1	3-4	1-4	1-1	1-3	0-4	■	0-1
Wolverhampton Wanderers FC	3-0	2-1	2-0	1-0	3-1	5-1	0-1	1-1	2-0	0-3	4-0	■

Football League	Pd	Wn	Dw	Ls	GF	GA	Pts	
1. EVERTON FC (LIVERPOOL)	22	14	1	7	63	29	29	
2. Preston North End FC (Preston)	22	12	3	7	44	23	27	
3. Notts County FC (Nottingham)	22	11	4	7	52	35	26	
4. Wolverhampton Wanderers FC (Wolverhampton)	22	12	2	8	39	50	26	
5. Bolton Wanderers FC (Bolton)	22	12	1	9	47	34	25	
6. Blackburn Rovers FC (Blackburn)	22	11	2	9	52	43	24	
7. Sunderland AFC (Sunderland)	22	10	5	7	51	31	23	*
8. Burnley FC (Burnley)	22	9	3	10	52	63	21	
9. Aston Villa FC (Birmingham)	22	7	4	11	45	58	18	
10. Accrington FC (Accrington)	22	6	4	12	28	50	16	
11. Derby County FC (Derby)	22	7	1	14	47	81	15	
12. West Bromwich Albion FC (West Bromwich)	22	5	2	15	34	57	12	
	264	116	32	116	554	554	262	

* Sunderland AFC had 2 points deducted for fielding Ned Doig (signed from Arbroath FC) against West Bromwich Albion FC on 20/10/1890 before his registration had been approved by the Football League.

Note: Darwen FC (Darwen) and Stoke FC (Stoke-upon-Trent) were elected to the league which was extended to 14 clubs from the next season.

Top Goalscorers

1)	John SOUTHWORTH	(Blackburn Rovers FC)	26
2)	Frederick C. GEARY	(Everton FC)	20
3)	John M. CAMPBELL	(Sunderland AFC)	18
4)	Claude LAMBIE	(Burnley FC)	17
5)	Thomas PEARSON	(West Bromwich Albion FC)	15

F.A. CUP FINAL   (Kennington Oval, London – 21/03/1891 – 23,000)

BLACKBURN ROVERS FC (BLACKBURN)   3-1   Notts County FC (Nottingham)

Dewar, Southworth, Townley   (H.T. 3-0)   *Oswald*

Blackburn: Pennington, Brandon, Forbes, Barton, Dewar, Forrest, Lofthouse, Walton, John Southworth, Hall, Townley.

Notts County: Thraves, Ferguson, Hendry, Osborne, Calderhead, Shelton, McGregor, McInnes, Oswald, Locker, Daft.

Semi-finals

Blackburn Rovers FC (Blackburn)	3-2	West Bromwich Albion FC (West Bromwich)
Notts County FC (Nottingham)	3-3, 2-0	Sunderland AFC (Sunderland)

Quarter-finals

Blackburn Rovers FC (Blackburn)	2-0	Wolverhampton Wanderers FC (Wolverhampton)
Notts County FC (Nottingham)	1-0	Stoke FC (Stoke-upon-Trent)
Sunderland AFC (Sunderland)	4-0	Nottingham Forest FC (Nottingham)
The Wednesday FC (Sheffield)	0-2	West Bromwich Albion FC (West Bromwich)

1891-92

Football League 1891-92 Season	Accrington	Aston Villa	Blackburn Rovers	Bolton Wanderers	Burnley	Darwen	Derby County	Everton	Notts County	Preston North End	Stoke	Sunderland	W.B.A.	Wolves
Accrington FC		3-2	1-0	0-3	1-0	1-1	1-1	1-1	2-0	1-3	3-0	3-5	4-2	3-2
Aston Villa FC	12-2		5-1	1-2	6-1	7-0	6-0	3-4	5-1	3-1	2-1	5-3	5-1	3-6
Blackburn Rovers FC	2-2	4-3		4-0	3-3	4-0	0-2	2-2	5-4	2-4	5-3	3-1	3-2	2-0
Bolton Wanderers FC	3-4	1-2	4-2		2-0	1-0	3-1	1-0	2-0	3-0	1-1	4-3	1-1	3-0
Burnley FC	2-1	4-1	3-0	1-2		9-0	2-4	1-0	1-0	2-0	4-1	1-2	3-2	1-1
Darwen FC	5-2	1-5	3-5	1-2	2-6		2-0	3-1	2-3	0-4	9-3	1-7	1-1	1-4
Derby County FC	3-1	4-2	1-1	3-2	0-1	7-0		0-3	3-0	1-2	3-3	0-1	1-1	2-1
Everton FC	3-0	5-1	3-1	2-5	1-1	5-3	1-2		4-0	1-1	1-0	0-4	4-3	2-1
Notts County FC	9-0	5-2	2-2	2-0	5-1	5-0	2-1	1-3		2-0	1-1	1-0	4-0	2-2
Preston North End FC	4-1	0-1	3-2	4-0	5-1	4-0	3-0	4-0	6-0		3-2	3-1	1-0	2-0
Stoke FC	3-1	2-3	0-1	0-1	3-0	5-1	2-1	0-1	1-3	0-1		1-3	1-0	1-3
Sunderland AFC	4-1	2-1	6-1	4-1	2-1	7-0	7-1	2-1	4-0	4-1	4-1		4-0	5-2
West Bromwich Albion FC	3-1	0-3	2-2	0-2	1-0	12-0	4-2	4-0	2-2	1-2	2-2	2-5		4-3
Wolverhampton Wanderers FC	5-0	2-0	6-1	1-2	0-0	2-2	1-3	5-1	2-1	3-0	4-1	1-3	2-1	

	Football League	**Pd**	**Wn**	**Dw**	**Ls**	**GF**	**GA**	**Pts**	
1.	SUNDERLAND AFC (SUNDERLAND)	26	21	-	5	93	36	42	
2.	Preston North End FC (Preston)	26	18	1	7	61	31	37	
3.	Bolton Wanderers FC (Bolton)	26	17	2	7	51	37	36	
4.	Aston Villa FC (Birmingham)	26	15	-	11	89	56	30	
5.	Everton FC (Liverpool)	26	12	4	10	49	49	28	
6.	Wolverhampton Wanderers FC (Wolverhampton)	26	11	4	11	59	46	26	
7.	Burnley FC (Burnley)	26	11	4	11	49	45	26	
8.	Notts County FC (Nottingham)	26	11	4	11	55	51	26	
9.	Blackburn Rovers FC (Blackburn)	26	10	6	10	58	65	26	
10.	Derby County FC (Derby)	26	10	4	12	46	52	24	
11.	Accrington FC (Accrington)	26	8	4	14	40	78	20	
12.	West Bromwich Albion FC (West Bromwich)	26	6	6	14	51	58	18	
13.	Stoke FC (Stoke-upon-Trent)	26	5	4	17	38	61	14	
14.	Darwen FC (Darwen)	26	4	3	19	38	112	11	#
		364	159	46	159	777	777	364	

\# Darwen FC (Darwen) were not re-elected to the League for the next season, but were elected to the newly-formed 12 club Division 2. Newton Heath FC (Manchester), Nottingham Forest FC (Nottingham) and The Wednesday FC (Sheffield) were elected to the re-titled Division 1 which was extended to 16 clubs from the next season.

Note: Royal Arsenal FC (London) changed their club name to Woolwich Arsenal FC (London).

Top Goalscorers

1)	John M. CAMPBELL	(Sunderland AFC)	32
2)	John Henry George DEVEY	(Aston Villa FC)	25
3)	John SOUTHWORTH	(Blackburn Rovers FC)	23
4)	James CASSIDY	(Bolton Wanderers FC)	18
5)	James HANNAH	(Sunderland AFC)	17
	Alexander LATTA	(Everton FC)	17

F.A. CUP FINAL   (Kennington Oval, London – 19/03/1892 – 32,810)

WEST BROMWICH ALBION FC	3-0	Aston Villa FC (Birmingham)

Geddes, Nicholls, Reynolds   *(H.T. 2-0)*

West Bromwich: Reader, Nicholson, McCulloch, Reynolds, Perry, Groves, Bassett, McLeod, Nicholls, Pearson, Geddes.

Aston Villa: Warner, Evans, Cox, HP Devey, Cowan, Baird, Athersmith, JH Devey, Dickson, Campbell, Hodgetts.

Semi-finals

Aston Villa FC (Birmingham)	4-1	Sunderland AFC (Sunderland)
Nottingham Forest FC (Nottingham)	1-1 (aet), 1-1 (aet), 2-6	West Bromwich Albion FC

Quarter-finals

Nottingham Forest FC (Nottingham)	2-0	Preston North End FC (Preston)
Stoke FC (Stoke-upon-Trent)	2-2 (aet), 0-4	Sunderland AFC (Sunderland)
West Bromwich Albion FC (West Bromwich)	2-1	The Wednesday FC (Sheffield)
Wolverhampton Wanderers FC (Wolverhampton)	1-3	Aston Villa FC (Birmingham)

1892-93

Football League Division 1 1892-93 Season	Accrington	Aston Villa	Blackburn Rovers	Bolton Wanderers	Burnley	Derby County	Everton	Newton Heath	Nottingham Forest	Notts County	Preston North End	Stoke	Sunderland	Wednesday	W.B.A.	Wolves
Accrington FC	■	1-1	1-1	1-1	0-4	0-3	0-3	2-2	1-1	4-2	1-2	5-2	0-6	4-2	5-4	4-0
Aston Villa FC	6-4	■	4-1	1-1	1-3	6-1	4-1	2-0	1-0	3-1	3-1	3-2	1-6	5-1	5-2	5-0
Blackburn Rovers FC	3-3	2-2	■	3-0	2-0	2-2	2-2	4-3	0-1	1-0	0-0	3-3	2-2	0-2	2-1	3-3
Bolton Wanderers FC	5-2	5-0	2-1	■	1-0	0-3	4-1	4-1	3-1	4-1	2-4	4-4	2-1	1-0	3-1	3-1
Burnley FC	1-3	0-2	0-0	3-0	■	2-1	3-0	4-1	1-1	3-0	4-2	3-2	2-3	4-0	5-0	2-0
Derby County FC	3-3	2-1	3-0	1-1	1-0	■	1-6	5-1	2-3	4-5	1-2	1-0	1-1	2-2	1-1	2-2
Everton FC	1-1	1-0	4-0	3-0	0-1	5-0	■	6-0	2-2	6-0	6-0	2-2	1-4	3-5	1-0	3-2
Newton Heath FC	3-3	2-0	4-4	1-0	1-1	7-1	3-4	■	1-3	1-3	2-1	1-0	0-5	1-5	2-4	10-1
Nottingham Forest FC	3-0	4-5	0-1	2-0	2-2	1-0	2-1	1-1	■	3-1	1-2	3-4	0-5	2-0	3-4	3-1
Notts County FC	2-0	1-4	0-0	2-2	3-1	1-1	1-2	4-0	3-0	■	3-1	0-1	3-1	0-1	8-1	3-0
Preston North End FC	0-0	4-1	2-1	2-1	2-0	0-1	5-0	2-1	1-0	4-0	■	2-1	1-2	4-1	1-1	4-0
Stoke FC	2-2	0-1	2-2	6-0	4-1	1-3	0-1	7-1	3-0	1-0	2-1	■	0-1	2-0	1-2	2-1
Sunderland AFC	4-2	6-0	5-0	3-3	2-0	3-1	4-3	6-0	1-0	2-2	2-0	3-1	■	4-2	8-1	5-2
The Wednesday FC	5-2	5-3	0-3	4-2	2-0	3-3	0-2	1-0	2-2	3-2	0-5	0-1	3-2	■	6-0	0-1
West Bromwich Albion FC	4-0	3-2	1-2	1-0	7-1	3-1	3-0	0-0	2-2	4-2	0-1	1-2	1-3	3-0	■	2-1
Wolverhampton Wanderers FC	5-3	2-1	4-2	1-2	1-0	2-1	2-4	2-0	2-2	3-0	2-1	1-0	2-0	2-0	1-1	■

Division 1		Pd	Wn	Dw	Ls	GF	GA	Pts	
1.	SUNDERLAND AFC (SUNDERLAND)	30	22	4	4	100	36	48	
2.	Preston North End FC (Preston)	30	17	3	10	57	39	37	
3.	Everton FC (Liverpool)	30	16	4	10	74	51	36	
4.	Aston Villa FC (Birmingham)	30	16	3	11	73	62	35	
5.	Bolton Wanderers FC (Bolton)	30	13	6	11	56	55	32	
6.	Burnley FC (Burnley)	30	13	4	13	51	44	30	
7.	Stoke FC (Stoke-upon-Trent)	30	12	5	13	58	48	29	
8.	West Bromwich Albion FC (West Bromwich)	30	12	5	13	58	69	29	
9.	Blackburn Rovers FC (Blackburn)	30	8	13	9	47	56	29	
10.	Nottingham Forest FC (Nottingham)	30	10	8	12	48	52	28	
11.	Wolverhampton Wanderers FC (Wolverhampton)	30	12	4	14	47	68	28	
12.	The Wednesday FC (Sheffield)	30	12	3	15	55	65	27	
13.	Derby County FC (Derby)	30	9	9	12	52	64	27	
14.	Notts County FC (Nottingham)	30	10	4	16	53	61	24	PO
15.	Accrington FC (Accrington)	30	6	11	13	57	81	23	PO*
16.	Newton Heath FC (Manchester)	30	6	6	18	50	85	18	PO
		480	194	92	194	936	936	480	

Promotion/Relegation Play-offs

Darwen FC (Darwen)	3-2	Notts County FC (Nottingham)
Newton Heath FC (Manchester)	1-1, 5-2	Small Heath FC (Birmingham)
Sheffield United FC (Sheffield)	1-0	Accrington FC (Accrington)

* Accrington FC (Accrington) resigned from the league after being relegated to Division 2.

Top Goalscorers

1)	John M. CAMPBELL	(Sunderland AFC)	31
2)	John Henry George DEVEY	(Aston Villa FC)	20
3)	Frederick C. GEARY	(Everton FC)	19
	James HANNAH	(Sunderland AFC)	19
5)	Robert DONALDSON	(Newton Heath FC)	18
	Alexander LATTA	(Everton FC)	18
	Harold WOOD	(Wolverhampton Wanderers FC)	18

Football League Division 2 1892-93 Season	Ardwick	Bootle	Burslem Port Vale	Burton Swifts	Crewe Alexandra	Darwen	Grimsby Town	Lincoln City	Northwich Victoria	Sheffield United	Small Heath	Walsall Town Swifts
Ardwick FC		7-0	2-0	1-1	3-1	4-2	0-3	3-1	1-1	2-3	2-2	2-0
Bootle FC	5-3		1-1	3-2	2-1	5-1	3-1	4-1	2-5	2-0	1-4	7-1
Burslem Port Vale FC	1-2	0-0		1-0	4-1	2-4	0-1	1-2	4-0	0-10	0-3	3-0
Burton Swifts FC	2-0	2-1	3-3		7-1	0-2	5-1	4-2	2-0	0-3	2-3	3-2
Crewe Alexandra FC	4-1	2-1	5-0	2-4		2-2	1-0	4-1	4-2	0-4	1-3	5-6
Darwen FC	3-1	3-0	4-1	2-3	7-3		6-1	3-1	3-1	3-1	4-3	5-0
Grimsby Town FC	2-0	3-0	2-0	4-0	4-0	0-1		2-2	2-1	0-1	3-2	3-0
Lincoln City FC	2-1	5-1	3-4	5-1	1-1	1-1	1-3		5-1	1-0	3-4	3-1
Northwich Victoria FC	0-3	3-2	2-4	2-1	4-1	1-0	5-3	2-1		1-3	0-6	5-2
Sheffield United FC	2-1	8-3	4-0	3-1	4-0	2-0	2-0	4-2	1-1		2-0	3-0
Small Heath FC	3-2	6-2	5-1	3-2	6-0	3-2	8-3	4-1	6-2	1-1		12-0
Walsall Town Swifts FC	2-4	4-4	3-0	3-2	3-3	1-2	3-1	2-1	2-3	1-1	1-3	

Division 2

		Pd	Wn	Dw	Ls	GF	GA	Pts	
1.	Small Heath FC (Birmingham)	22	17	2	3	90	35	36	PO
2.	Sheffield United FC (Sheffield)	22	16	3	3	62	19	35	PO
3.	Darwen FC (Darwen)	22	14	2	6	60	36	30	POP
4.	Grimsby Town FC (Cleethorpes)	22	11	1	10	42	41	23	
5.	Ardwick FC (Manchester)	22	9	3	10	45	40	21	
6.	Burton Swifts FC (Burton-upon-Trent)	22	9	2	11	47	47	20	
7.	Northwich Victoria FC (Northwich)	22	9	2	11	42	58	20	
8.	Bootle FC (Liverpool)	22	8	3	11	49	63	19	#
9.	Lincoln City FC (Lincoln)	22	7	3	12	45	51	17	
10.	Crewe Alexandra FC (Crewe)	22	6	3	13	42	69	15	
11.	Burslem Port Vale FC (Burslem)	22	6	3	13	30	57	15	
12.	Walsall Town Swifts FC (Walsall)	22	5	3	14	37	75	13	
		264	117	30	117	591	591	264	

Bootle FC (Liverpool) resigned from the league and later disbanded.

Liverpool FC (Liverpool), Middlesbrough Ironopolis FC (Middlesbrough), Newcastle United FC (Newcastle-upon-Tyne), Rotherham Town FC (Rotherham) and Woolwich Arsenal FC (London) were all elected to Division 2 which was extended to 16 clubs then reduced to 15 by the resignation of Bootle FC.

Note: Newcastle West End FC (Newcastle-upon-Tyne) and Newcastle East End FC (Newcastle-upon-Tyne) merged to become Newcastle United FC (Newcastle-upon-Tyne).

F.A. CUP FINAL   (Manchester Athletic Club, Fallowfield, Manchester – 25/03/1893 – 45,000)

WOLVERHAMPTON WANDERERS FC   1-0   Everton FC (Liverpool)

Allen   *(H.T. 0-0)*

Wolves: Rose, Baugh, Swift, Malpass, Allen, Kinsey, Topham, Wykes, Butcher, Wood, Griffin.

Everton: Williams, Kelso, Howarth, Boyle, Holt, Stewart, Latta, Gordon, Maxwell, Chadwick, Milward.

Semi-finals

Everton FC (Liverpool)	2-2 (aet), 0-0 (aet), 2-1	Preston North End FC (Preston)
Wolverhampton Wanderers FC (Wolverhampton)	2-1	Blackburn Rovers FC (Blackburn)

Quarter-finals

Blackburn Rovers FC (Blackburn)	3-0	Sunderland AFC (Sunderland)
Everton FC (Liverpool)	3-0	The Wednesday FC (Sheffield)
Preston North End FC (Preston)	2-2 (aet), 7-0	Middlesbrough Ironopolis FC (Middlesbrough)
Wolverhampton Wanderers FC (Wolverhampton)	5-0	Darwen FC (Darwen)

1893-94

Football League Division 1 1893-94 Season	Aston Villa	Blackburn Rovers	Bolton Wanderers	Burnley	Darwen	Derby County	Everton	Newton Heath	Nottingham Forest	Preston North End	Sheffield United	Stoke	Sunderland	Wednesday	W.B.A.	Wolves
Aston Villa FC	■	2-1	2-3	4-0	9-0	1-1	3-1	5-1	3-1	2-0	4-0	5-1	2-1	3-0	3-2	1-1
Blackburn Rovers FC	2-0	■	0-1	3-2	4-1	0-2	4-3	4-0	6-1	1-0	4-1	5-0	4-3	5-1	3-0	3-0
Bolton Wanderers FC	0-1	2-1	■	2-0	1-0	1-1	0-1	2-0	1-1	0-3	0-1	4-1	2-0	1-1	0-3	2-0
Burnley FC	3-6	1-0	2-1	■	5-1	3-1	2-1	4-1	3-1	4-1	4-1	4-0	1-0	0-1	3-0	4-2
Darwen FC	1-1	2-3	1-3	0-0	■	2-3	3-3	1-0	0-4	2-1	3-3	3-1	0-3	2-1	2-1	3-1
Derby County FC	0-3	5-2	6-1	3-3	2-1	■	7-3	2-0	3-4	2-1	2-1	5-2	1-4	3-3	2-3	4-1
Everton FC	4-2	2-2	3-2	4-3	8-1	1-2	■	2-0	4-0	2-3	2-3	6-2	7-1	8-1	7-1	3-0
Newton Heath FC	1-3	5-1	2-2	3-2	0-1	2-6	0-3	■	1-1	1-3	0-2	6-2	2-4	1-2	4-1	1-0
Nottingham Forest FC	1-2	0-0	1-0	5-0	4-1	4-2	3-2	2-0	■	4-2	1-1	2-0	1-2	1-0	2-3	7-1
Preston North End FC	2-5	0-1	1-0	1-2	4-1	1-0	2-4	2-0	0-2	■	3-0	3-3	1-2	1-0	3-1	1-3
Sheffield United FC	3-0	3-2	4-2	1-0	2-1	1-2	0-3	3-1	0-2	1-1	■	3-3	1-0	1-1	0-2	3-2
Stoke FC	3-3	3-1	5-0	4-2	3-1	3-1	3-1	3-1	2-1	2-1	5-0	■	2-0	4-1	3-1	0-3
Sunderland AFC	1-1	2-3	2-1	2-2	4-0	5-0	1-0	4-1	2-0	6-3	4-1	4-0	■	1-1	2-1	6-0
The Wednesday FC	2-2	4-2	2-1	0-1	5-0	4-0	1-1	0-1	1-0	3-0	1-2	4-1	2-2	■	2-4	1-4
West Bromwich Albion FC	3-6	2-1	5-2	1-1	2-2	0-1	3-1	3-1	3-0	2-0	3-1	4-2	2-3	2-2	■	0-0
Wolverhampton Wanderers FC	3-0	5-1	2-1	1-0	2-1	2-4	2-0	2-0	3-1	0-0	3-4	4-2	2-1	3-1	0-8	■

Division 1

	Division 1	Pd	Wn	Dw	Ls	GF	GA	Pts	
1.	ASTON VILLA FC (BIRMINGHAM)	30	19	6	5	84	42	44	
2.	Sunderland AFC (Sunderland)	30	17	4	9	72	44	38	
3.	Derby County FC (Derby)	30	16	4	10	73	62	36	
4.	Blackburn Rovers FC (Blackburn)	30	16	2	12	69	53	34	
5.	Burnley FC (Burnley)	30	15	4	11	61	51	34	
6.	Everton FC (Liverpool)	30	15	3	12	90	57	33	
7.	Nottingham Forest FC (Nottingham)	30	14	4	12	57	48	32	
8.	West Bromwich Albion FC (West Bromwich)	30	14	4	12	66	59	32	
9.	Wolverhampton Wanderers FC (Wolverhampton)	30	14	3	13	52	63	31	
10.	Sheffield United FC (Sheffield)	30	13	5	12	47	61	31	
11.	Stoke FC (Stoke-upon-Trent)	30	13	3	14	65	79	29	
12.	The Wednesday FC (Sheffield)	30	9	8	13	48	57	26	
13.	Bolton Wanderers FC (Bolton)	30	10	4	16	38	52	24	
14.	Preston North End FC (Preston)	30	10	3	17	44	56	23	PO
15.	Darwen FC (Darwen)	30	7	5	18	37	83	19	PO
16.	Newton Heath FC (Manchester)	30	6	2	22	36	72	14	POR
		480	208	64	208	939	939	480	

Promotion/Relegation Play-offs

Liverpool FC (Liverpool)	2-0	Newton Heath FC (Manchester)
Preston North End FC (Preston)	4-0	Notts County FC (Nottingham)
Small Heath FC (Birmingham)	3-1	Darwen FC (Darwen)

Top Goalscorers

1) John SOUTHWORTH   (Everton FC)   27
2) John Henry George DEVEY   (Aston Villa FC)   21
3) James MILLAR   (Sunderland AFC)   20
4) Stephen BLOOMER   (Derby County FC)   18
    Patrick TURNBULL   (Burnley FC)   18

Football League Division 2 — 1893-94 Season

	Ardwick	Burslem Port Vale	Burton Swifts	Crewe Alexandra	Grimsby Town	Lincoln City	Liverpool	Mid. Iron.	Newcastle United	Northwich Victoria	Notts County	Rotherham Town	Small Heath	Walsall Town Swifts	Woolwich Arsenal
Ardwick FC		8-1	1-4	1-2	4-1	0-1	0-1	6-1	2-3	4-2	0-0	3-2	0-1	3-0	0-1
Burslem Port Vale FC	4-2		3-1	4-2	6-1	5-3	2-2	4-0	1-1	3-2	1-0	2-3	5-0	1-2	2-1
Burton Swifts FC	5-0	5-3		6-1	0-3	1-3	1-1	7-0	3-1	6-2	0-2	4-1	0-2	8-5	6-2
Crewe Alexandra FC	1-1	1-1	1-2		3-3	1-1	0-5	5-0	1-1	3-0	0-2	2-0	3-5	1-1	0-0
Grimsby Town FC	5-0	4-0	2-1	3-2		2-4	0-1	2-1	0-0	7-0	5-2	7-1	2-1	5-2	3-1
Lincoln City FC	6-0	2-2	1-1	6-1	1-2		1-1	2-3	2-1	4-1	0-2	1-1	2-5	0-2	3-0
Liverpool FC	3-0	2-1	3-1	2-0	2-0	4-0		6-0	5-1	4-0	2-1	5-1	3-1	3-0	2-0
Middlesbrough Ironopolis FC	2-0	3-1	2-1	2-0	2-6	0-0	0-2		1-1	2-1	0-0	6-1	3-0	1-1	3-6
Newcastle United FC	2-1	2-1	4-1	2-1	4-1	5-1	0-0	7-2		3-0	3-0	4-0	0-2	2-0	6-0
Northwich Victoria FC	1-4	1-5	1-1	1-2	0-1	0-3	2-3	2-1	5-3		0-1	1-1	0-7	1-0	2-2
Notts County FC	5-0	6-1	6-2	9-1	3-0	1-2	1-1	3-0	3-1	6-1		4-2	3-1	2-0	3-2
Rotherham Town FC	1-3	0-1	2-5	1-4	4-3	2-8	1-4	4-1	2-1	5-4	0-2		2-3	3-2	1-1
Small Heath FC	10-2	6-0	6-1	6-1	5-2	6-0	3-4	2-1	1-4	8-0	3-0	4-3		4-0	4-1
Walsall Town Swifts FC	5-2	0-5	3-4	5-1	5-0	5-2	1-1	1-0	1-2	3-0	2-1	3-0	1-3		1-2
Woolwich Arsenal FC	1-0	4-1	0-2	3-2	3-1	4-0	0-5	1-0	2-2	6-0	1-2	3-0	1-4	4-0	

Division 2

		Pd	Wn	Dw	Ls	GA	GF	Pts	
1.	Liverpool FC (Liverpool)	28	22	6	-	77	18	50	POP
2.	Small Heath FC (Birmingham)	28	21	-	7	103	44	42	PO
3.	Notts County FC (Nottingham)	28	18	3	7	70	31	39	PO
4.	Newcastle United FC (Newcastle-upon-Tyne)	28	15	6	7	66	39	36	
5.	Grimsby Town FC (Cleethorpes)	28	15	2	11	71	58	32	
6.	Burton Swifts FC (Burton-upon-Trent)	28	14	3	11	79	61	31	
7.	Burslem Port Vale FC (Burslem)	28	13	4	11	66	64	30	
8.	Lincoln City FC (Lincoln)	28	11	6	11	59	58	28	
9.	Woolwich Arsenal FC (London)	28	12	4	12	52	55	28	
10.	Walsall Town Swifts FC (Walsall)	28	10	3	15	51	61	23	
11.	Middlesbrough Ironopolis FC (Middlesbrough)	28	8	4	16	37	72	20	#
12.	Crewe Alexandra FC (Crewe)	28	6	7	15	42	73	19	
13.	Ardwick FC (Manchester)	28	8	2	18	47	71	18	
14.	Rotherham Town FC (Rotherham)	28	6	3	19	44	91	15	
15.	Northwich Victoria FC (Northwich)	28	3	3	22	30	98	9	#
		420	182	56	182	894	894	420	

Middlesbrough Ironopolis FC (Middlesbrough) and Northwich Victoria FC (Northwich) resigned from the league at the end of the season.

Burton Wanderers FC (Burton-upon-Trent), Bury FC (Bury) and Leicester Fosse FC (Leicester) were elected to Division 2 which was extended to 16 clubs for next season.

F.A. CUP FINAL   (Goodison Park, Liverpool – 31/03/1894 – 37,000)

NOTTS COUNTY FC (NOTTINGHAM)	4-1	Bolton Wanderers FC (Bolton)
Logan 3, Watson	*(H.T. 2-0)*	*Cassidy*

Notts County: Toone, Harper, Hendry, Bramley, Calderhead, Shelton, Watson, Donnelly, Logan, Bruce, Daft.
Bolton: Sutcliffe, Somerville, Jones, Paton, Hughes, Gardiner, Tannahill, Wilson, Cassidy, Bentley, Dickenson.

Semi-finals

Bolton Wanderers FC (Bolton)	2-1	The Wednesday FC (Sheffield)
Notts County FC (Nottingham)	1-0	Blackburn Rovers FC (Blackburn)

Quarter-finals

Bolton Wanderers FC (Bolton)	3-0	Liverpool FC (Liverpool)
Derby County FC (Derby)	1-4	Blackburn Rovers FC (Blackburn)
Nottingham Forest FC (Nottingham)	1-1 (aet), 1-4	Notts County FC (Nottingham)
The Wednesday FC (Sheffield)	3-2 (aet)	Aston Villa FC (Birmingham)

1894-95

Football League Division 1 1894-95 Season	Aston Villa	Blackburn Rovers	Bolton Wanderers	Burnley	Derby County	Everton	Liverpool	Nottingham Forest	Preston North End	Sheffield United	Small Heath	Stoke	Sunderland	Wednesday	W.B.A.	Wolves
Aston Villa FC		3-0	2-1	5-0	4-0	2-2	5-0	4-1	4-1	5-0	2-1	6-0	1-2	3-1	3-1	2-2
Blackburn Rovers FC	1-3		2-1	1-0	0-0	4-3	1-1	0-0	1-1	3-2	9-1	6-0	1-1	3-1	3-0	5-1
Bolton Wanderers FC	4-3	1-3		1-1	6-0	1-3	1-0	4-1	1-2	6-2	1-2	2-2	4-1	2-2	5-0	6-1
Burnley FC	3-3	2-1	1-0		2-0	2-4	3-3	0-1	2-1	2-4	3-1	1-2	0-3	3-0	2-0	2-1
Derby County FC	0-2	0-0	2-2	0-2		2-2	0-1	4-2	2-1	4-1	4-1	1-1	1-2	1-2	1-1	1-3
Everton FC	4-2	2-1	3-1	3-2	2-3		3-0	6-1	4-2	1-1	5-0	3-0	2-2	3-1	4-1	2-1
Liverpool FC	1-2	2-2	1-2	0-3	5-1	2-2		5-0	2-5	2-2	3-1	2-0	2-3	4-2	4-0	3-3
Nottingham Forest FC	2-1	2-3	3-3	2-1	2-1	2-3	3-0		0-2	3-0	2-0	3-1	2-1	2-1	5-3	0-2
Preston North End FC	0-1	1-1	2-2	4-0	3-2	1-2	2-2	3-1		2-1	0-1	3-0	1-0	3-1	5-0	2-0
Sheffield United FC	2-1	3-0	5-0	2-2	1-4	4-2	2-2	3-2	0-1		0-2	3-0	4-0	1-0	2-1	1-0
Small Heath FC	2-2	1-1	2-0	1-0	3-5	4-4	3-0	1-2	4-4	4-2		4-2	1-1	0-0	1-2	4-3
Stoke FC	4-1	5-1	5-0	5-1	4-1	1-3	3-1	0-3	2-1	1-3	2-2		2-5	0-2	1-1	0-0
Sunderland AFC	4-4	3-2	4-0	3-0	8-0	2-1	3-2	2-2	2-0	2-0	7-1	3-1		3-1	3-0	2-0
The Wednesday FC	1-0	4-1	2-1	4-3	1-1	3-0	5-0	0-0	3-1	2-3	2-0	2-4	1-2		3-2	3-1
West Bromwich Albion FC	3-2	2-0	1-1	0-1	2-2	1-4	5-0	1-0	4-5	1-0	4-1	3-2	0-2	6-0		5-1
Wolverhampton Wanderers FC	0-4	3-3	4-2	1-0	2-2	1-0	3-1	1-1	1-3	0-3	2-1	0-0	1-4	2-0	3-1	

Division 1	Pd	Wn	Dw	Ls	GF	GA	Pts	
1. SUNDERLAND AFC (SUNDERLAND)	30	21	5	4	80	37	47	
2. Everton FC (Liverpool)	30	18	6	6	82	50	42	
3. Aston Villa FC (Birmingham)	30	17	5	8	82	43	39	
4. Preston North End FC (Preston)	30	15	5	10	62	46	35	
5. Blackburn Rovers FC (Blackburn)	30	11	10	9	59	49	32	
6. Sheffield United FC (Sheffield)	30	14	4	12	57	55	32	
7. Nottingham Forest FC (Nottingham)	30	13	5	12	50	56	31	
8. The Wednesday FC (Sheffield)	30	12	4	14	50	55	28	
9. Burnley FC (Burnley)	30	11	4	15	44	56	26	
10. Bolton Wanderers FC (Bolton)	30	9	7	14	61	62	25	
11. Wolverhampton Wanderers FC (Wolverhampton)	30	9	7	14	43	63	25	
12. Small Heath FC (Birmingham)	30	9	7	14	50	74	25	
13. West Bromwich Albion FC (West Bromwich)	30	10	4	16	51	66	24	
14. Stoke FC (Stoke-upon-Trent)	30	9	6	15	50	67	24	PO
15. Derby County FC (Derby)	30	7	9	14	45	68	23	PO
16. Liverpool FC (Liverpool)	30	7	8	15	51	70	22	POR
	480	192	96	192	917	917	480	

Top Goalscorers

1)	John M. CAMPBELL	(Sunderland AFC)	22
2)	William Henry HAMMOND	(Sheffield United FC)	17
3)	Thomas Henry BRADSHAW	(Liverpool FC)	16
	Albert Frederick CARNELLY	(Nottingham Forest FC)	16
	Frank MOBLEY	(Small Heath FC)	16

Promotion/Relegation Play-offs

Bury FC (Bury)	1-0	Liverpool FC (Liverpool)
Derby County FC (Derby)	2-1	Notts County FC (Nottingham)
Stoke FC (Stoke-upon-Trent)	3-0	Newton Heath FC (Manchester)

Football League Division 2 1894-95 Season	Burslem Port Vale	Burton Swifts	Burton W.	Bury	Crewe Alexandra	Darwen	Grimsby Town	Leicester Fosse	Lincoln City	Manchester City	Newcastle United	Newton Heath	Notts County	Rotherham Town	Walsall Town Swifts	Woolwich Arsenal
Burslem Port Vale FC		2-0	1-0	1-2	4-0	0-3	5-0	1-1	7-1	1-2	4-4	2-5	0-3	1-1	1-0	0-1
Burton Swifts FC	1-0		2-2	0-1	4-0	3-0	2-1	0-5	6-1	2-1	5-3	1-2	2-2	2-0	1-2	3-0
Burton Wanderers FC	4-0	1-2		1-2	4-0	2-2	0-0	1-1	4-1	8-0	9-0	1-0	1-0	4-0	7-0	2-1
Bury FC	4-0	2-0	4-0		4-1	1-0	5-1	4-1	4-1	4-2	4-1	2-1	2-1	2-1	4-1	2-0
Crewe Alexandra FC	2-2	1-3	1-2	1-5		2-2	2-1	2-2	1-4	2-3	2-1	0-2	0-3	2-1	2-3	0-0
Darwen FC	2-0	5-0	2-0	0-1	5-0		4-1	8-2	6-0	4-0	5-0	1-1	2-1	4-3	2-0	3-1
Grimsby Town FC	4-1	7-1	7-2	3-2	5-0	2-1		4-3	3-0	2-1	3-0	0-1	4-1	1-0	4-2	
Leicester Fosse FC	2-1	2-2	1-2	1-0	4-0	2-1	1-0		2-1	3-1	4-4	2-3	5-1	4-2	9-1	3-1
Lincoln City FC	6-1	3-2	0-2	1-3	5-2	0-2	1-5	1-2		0-2	3-1	3-0	1-3	2-0	1-0	5-2
Manchester City FC	4-1	4-1	1-1	3-3	4-1	2-4	2-5	1-1	11-3		4-0	2-5	7-1	1-0	6-1	4-1
Newcastle United FC	1-2	6-3	3-1	1-0	6-0	3-2	1-4	2-0	4-2	5-4		3-0	2-2	5-2	7-2	2-4
Newton Heath FC	3-0	5-1	1-1	2-2	6-1	1-1	2-0	2-2	3-0	4-1	5-1		3-3	3-2	9-0	3-3
Notts County FC	10-0	5-1	2-0	2-1	5-1	2-1	3-2	3-0	3-0	1-3	2-1	1-1		4-2	5-0	2-2
Rotherham Town FC	2-1	4-1	1-3	2-3	2-0	4-1	3-2	0-1	5-2	3-2	1-0	2-1	1-2		6-1	1-2
Walsall Town Swifts FC	2-0	4-1	3-1	0-3	4-0	5-1	4-3	1-3	1-2	1-2	2-3	1-2	2-1	1-2		4-1
Woolwich Arsenal FC	7-0	3-0	1-1	4-2	7-0	4-0	1-3	3-3	5-2	4-2	3-2	3-2	2-1	1-1	6-1	

	Division 2	Pd	Wn	Dw	Ls	GF	GA	Pts	
1.	Bury FC (Bury)	30	23	2	5	78	33	48	POP
2.	Notts County FC (Nottingham)	30	17	5	8	75	45	39	PO
3.	Newton Heath FC (Manchester)	30	15	8	7	78	44	38	PO
4.	Leicester Fosse FC (Leicester)	30	15	8	7	72	53	38	
5.	Grimsby Town FC (Cleethorpes)	30	18	1	11	79	52	37	
6.	Darwen FC (Darwen)	30	16	4	10	74	43	36	
7.	Burton Wanderers FC (Burton-upon-Trent)	30	14	7	9	67	39	35	
8.	Woolwich Arsenal FC (London)	30	14	6	10	75	58	34	
9.	Manchester City FC (Manchester)	30	14	3	13	82	72	31	*
10.	Newcastle United FC (Newcastle-upon-Tyne)	30	12	3	15	72	84	27	
11.	Burton Swifts FC (Burton-upon-Trent)	30	11	3	16	52	74	25	
12.	Rotherham Town FC (Rotherham)	30	11	2	17	55	62	24	
13.	Lincoln City FC (Lincoln)	30	10	-	20	52	92	20	
14.	Walsall Town Swifts FC (Walsall)	30	10	-	20	47	92	20	#
15.	Burslem Port Vale FC (Burslem)	30	7	4	19	39	77	18	
16.	Crewe Alexandra FC (Crewe)	30	3	4	23	26	103	10	
		480	210	60	210	1023	1023	480	

* Ardwick FC (Manchester) were declared bankrupt in 1894 and re-formed as Manchester City FC (Manchester).

Walsall Town Swifts FC (Walsall) were not re-elected to the league and changed their name to Walsall FC.

Loughborough Town FC (Loughborough) were elected to Division 2 for the next season.

F.A. CUP FINAL   (Crystal Palace, London – 20/04/1895 – 42,560)

ASTON VILLA FC (BIRMINGHAM)	1-0	West Bromwich Albion FC (West Bromwich)
Devey	*(H.T. 1-0)*	

Aston Villa: Wilkes, Spencer, Walford, Reynolds, Cowan, Russell, Athersmith, Chatt, Devey, Hodgetts, Smith.

West Bromwich: Reader, Horton, Williams, Perry, Higgins, Taggart, Bassett, McLeod, Richards, Hutchinson, Banks.

Semi-finals

Aston Villa FC (Birmingham)	2-1	Sunderland AFC (Sunderland)
West Bromwich Albion FC (West Bromwich)	2-0	The Wednesday FC (Sheffield)

Quarter-finals

Aston Villa FC (Birmingham)	6-2	Nottingham Forest FC (Nottingham)
Sunderland AFC (Sunderland)	2-1	Bolton Wanderers FC (Bolton)
The Wednesday FC (Sheffield)	2-0	Everton FC (Liverpool)
West Bromwich Albion FC (West Bromwich)	1-0	Wolverhampton Wanderers FC (Wolverhampton)

1895-96

Football League Division 1 1895-96 Season	Aston Villa	Blackburn Rovers	Bolton Wanderers	Burnley	Bury	Derby County	Everton	Nottingham Forest	Preston North End	Sheffield United	Small Heath	Stoke	Sunderland	Wednesday	W.B.A.	Wolves
Aston Villa FC		3-1	2-0	5-1	2-0	4-1	4-3	3-1	1-0	2-2	7-3	5-2	2-1	2-1	1-0	4-1
Blackburn Rovers FC	1-1		3-2	1-0	0-2	0-2	2-3	2-0	3-0	1-0	2-1	3-1	2-4	2-1	1-0	3-1
Bolton Wanderers FC	2-2	1-1		1-0	2-4	2-1	3-1	2-1	1-0	4-1	4-1	3-1	1-0	2-0	2-1	4-0
Burnley FC	3-4	6-0	1-2		3-0	2-2	1-1	0-0	1-0	5-0	1-1	2-0	0-0	2-0	3-0	3-1
Bury FC	5-3	2-0	0-3	3-4		1-2	1-1	1-0	1-2	1-0	4-5	0-1	1-2	6-1	3-0	3-0
Derby County FC	2-2	0-0	2-1	5-1	2-1		2-1	4-0	1-0	0-2	8-0	2-1	2-0	3-1	4-1	5-2
Everton FC	2-0	0-2	1-1	2-1	3-2	2-2		6-2	3-2	5-0	3-0	7-2	1-0	2-2	1-1	2-0
Nottingham Forest FC	0-2	4-2	0-0	2-1	5-0	2-5	2-1		0-1	3-1	3-0	4-0	3-1	1-0	2-0	3-2
Preston North End FC	4-3	1-1	1-0	1-1	1-1	1-0	1-1	6-0		4-3	3-2	0-1	4-1	0-1	0-0	4-3
Sheffield United FC	2-1	1-1	1-0	1-1	8-0	1-1	1-2	2-1	2-1		2-0	1-0	1-2	1-1	2-0	2-1
Small Heath FC	1-4	2-1	1-2	1-0	1-0	1-3	0-3	1-0	5-2	2-1		1-2	0-1	1-1	2-2	3-2
Stoke FC	1-2	3-0	2-0	2-1	0-2	2-1	1-2	1-0	4-0	4-0	6-1		5-0	5-0	3-1	4-1
Sunderland AFC	2-1	2-1	1-0	3-0	0-0	2-2	3-0	1-1	4-1	1-1	2-1	4-1		2-1	7-1	2-2
The Wednesday FC	1-3	3-0	1-1	1-0	1-3	0-4	3-1	3-0	1-1	1-0	3-0	2-1	3-0		5-3	3-1
West Bromwich Albion FC	1-1	3-2	2-3	0-2	1-3	0-0	0-3	3-1	1-2	1-0	0-0	1-0	1-1	2-3		2-1
Wolverhampton Wanderers FC	1-2	1-2	5-0	5-1	1-0	2-0	2-3	6-1	2-1	4-1	7-2	1-0	1-3	4-0	1-2	

	Division 1	Pd	Wn	Dw	Ls	GF	GA	Pts	
1.	ASTON VILLA FC (BIRMINGHAM)	30	20	5	5	78	45	45	
2.	Derby County FC (Derby)	30	17	7	6	68	35	41	
3.	Everton FC (Liverpool)	30	16	7	7	66	43	39	
4.	Bolton Wanderers FC (Bolton)	30	16	5	9	49	37	37	
5.	Sunderland AFC (Sunderland)	30	15	7	8	52	41	37	
6.	Stoke FC (Stoke-upon-Trent)	30	15	-	15	56	47	30	
7.	The Wednesday FC (Sheffield)	30	12	5	13	44	53	29	
8.	Blackburn Rovers FC (Blackburn)	30	12	5	13	40	50	29	
9.	Preston North End FC (Preston)	30	11	6	13	44	48	28	
10.	Burnley FC (Burnley)	30	10	7	13	48	44	27	
11.	Bury FC (Bury)	30	12	3	15	50	54	27	
12.	Sheffield United FC (Sheffield)	30	10	6	14	40	50	26	
13.	Nottingham Forest FC (Nottingham)	30	11	3	16	42	57	25	
14.	Wolverhampton Wanderers FC (Wolverhampton)	30	10	1	19	61	65	21	
15.	Small Heath FC (Birmingham)	30	8	4	18	39	79	20	POR
16.	West Bromwich Albion FC (West Bromwich)	30	6	7	17	30	59	19	PO
		480	201	78	201	807	807	480	

Top Goalscorers

1)	Stephen BLOOMER	(Derby County FC)	20
	John CAMPBELL	(Aston Villa FC)	20
3)	John Henry George DEVEY	(Aston Villa FC)	19
4)	Thomas HYSLOP	(Stoke FC)	18
5)	Alfred MILWARD	(Everton FC)	17

Football League Promotion/Relegation Play-offs 1895-96 Season	Liverpool	West Brom. Albion	Small Heath	Manchester City
Liverpool FC		2-0	4-0	---
West Bromwich Albion FC	2-0		---	6-1
Small Heath FC	0-0	---		8-0
Manchester City FC	1-1	3-0	*	

Prom/Relegation Play-offs

		Pd	Wn	Dw	Ls	GF	GA	Pts	
1.	Liverpool FC (Liverpool)	4	2	1	1	6	2	5	P
2.	West Bromwich Albion FC (West Bromwich)	4	2	1	1	9	4	5	--
3.	Small Heath FC (Birmingham)	4	1	1	2	8	7	3	R
4.	Manchester City FC (Manchester)	4	1	1	2	5	15	3	--
		16	6	4	6	28	28	16	

Football League Division 2 1895-96 Season	Burslem Port Vale	Burton Swifts	Burton W.	Crewe Alexandra	Darwen	Grimsby Town	Leicester Fosse	Lincoln City	Liverpool	Loughborough Town	Manchester City	Newcastle United	Newton Heath	Notts County	Rotherham Town	Woolwich Arsenal
Burslem Port Vale FC		1-0	2-2	2-1	3-3	1-4	1-1	0-1	5-4	1-1	0-1	2-0	3-0	0-4	4-0	0-2
Burton Swifts FC	2-1		0-2	1-1	1-2	2-1	0-2	4-0	0-7	1-2	1-4	3-1	4-1	0-0	2-0	3-2
Burton Wanderers FC	2-1	2-1		4-0	3-0	2-1	0-0	4-1	2-1	4-0	4-1	0-3	5-1	1-3	6-1	4-1
Crewe Alexandra FC	3-2	1-3	0-1		3-1	0-1	1-1	2-2	0-7	1-2	0-2	3-0	0-2	5-1	3-2	0-1
Darwen FC	8-2	3-0	3-0	6-1		3-3	4-1	5-0	0-4	1-1	2-3	4-4	3-0	2-0	10-2	1-1
Grimsby Town FC	6-1	3-0	2-1	2-0	5-0		7-1	4-2	1-0	2-0	5-0	2-1	4-2	3-0	4-0	1-1
Leicester Fosse FC	5-0	2-1	1-3	4-1	2-3	1-2		1-3	2-0	5-0	1-2	2-0	3-0	2-1	8-0	1-0
Lincoln City FC	4-2	1-2	1-2	6-2	1-0	2-5	2-3		0-1	4-1	1-2	4-0	2-0	2-3	5-0	1-1
Liverpool FC	5-1	6-1	4-1	6-1	0-0	3-1	3-1	6-1		1-0	3-1	5-1	7-1	3-0	10-1	3-0
Loughborough Town FC	3-0	2-2	1-1	4-1	4-1	0-1	1-4	3-0	2-4		2-4	1-0	3-3	1-3	3-0	2-1
Manchester City FC	1-0	1-1	1-1	4-0	4-1	2-1	2-0	4-0	1-1	5-1		5-2	2-1	2-0	2-0	1-0
Newcastle United FC	4-2	5-0	4-0	6-0	7-2	1-5	1-0	5-0	1-0	3-0	4-1		2-1	5-1	6-1	3-1
Newton Heath FC	2-1	5-0	1-2	5-0	4-0	3-2	2-0	5-5	5-2	2-0	1-1	2-1		3-0	3-0	5-1
Notts County FC	7-2	5-0	1-4	6-0	4-1	5-3	1-2	2-0	2-3	2-0	3-0	0-1	0-2		0-0	3-4
Rotherham Town FC	0-2	1-4	1-6	4-0	3-0	1-0	2-0	2-2	0-5	4-0	2-3	1-1	2-3	1-0		3-0
Woolwich Arsenal FC	2-1	5-0	3-0	7-0	1-3	3-1	1-1	4-0	0-2	5-0	0-1	2-1	2-1	2-0	5-0	

Division 2

	Division 2	Pd	Wn	Dw	Ls	GF	GA	Pts	
1.	Liverpool FC (Liverpool)	30	22	2	6	106	32	46 POP	
2.	Manchester City FC (Manchester)	30	21	4	5	63	38	46 PO	
3.	Grimsby Town FC (Cleethorpes)	30	20	2	8	82	38	42	
4.	Burton Wanderers FC (Burton-upon-Trent)	30	19	4	7	69	40	42	
5.	Newcastle United FC (Newcastle-upon-Tyne)	30	16	2	12	73	50	34	
6.	Newton Heath FC (Manchester)	30	15	3	12	66	57	33	
7.	Woolwich Arsenal FC (London)	30	14	4	12	59	42	32	
8.	Leicester Fosse FC (Leicester)	30	14	4	12	57	44	32	
9.	Darwen FC (Darwen)	30	12	6	12	72	67	30	
10.	Notts County FC (Nottingham)	30	12	2	16	57	54	26	
11.	Burton Swifts FC (Burton-upon-Trent)	30	10	4	16	39	69	24	
12.	Loughborough Town FC (Loughborough)	30	9	5	16	40	67	23	
13.	Lincoln City FC (Lincoln)	30	9	4	17	53	75	22	
14.	Burslem Port Vale FC (Burslem)	30	7	4	19	43	78	18	#
15.	Rotherham Town FC (Rotherham)	30	7	3	20	34	97	17	#
16.	Crewe Alexandra FC (Crewe)	30	5	3	22	30	95	13	#
		480	212	56	212	943	943	480	

Burslem Port Vale FC (Burslem), Crewe Alexandra FC (Crewe) and Rotherham Town FC (Rotherham) were not re-elected to the league for next season.

Blackpool FC (Blackpool), Gainsborough Trinity FC (Gainsborough) and Walsall FC (Walsall) were elected to Division 2 for next season.

F.A. CUP FINAL   (Crystal Palace, London – 18/04/1896 – 48,836)

THE WEDNESDAY FC (SHEFFIELD)	2-1	Wolverhampton Wanderers FC
Spiksley 2	*(H.T. 2-1)*	*Black*

Wednesday: Massey, Earp, Langley, Brandon, Crawshaw, Petrie, Brash, Brady, Bell, Davis, Spiksley.

Wolves: Tennant, Baugh, Dunn, Griffiths, Malpass, Owen, Tonks, Henderson, Beats, Wood, Black.

Semi-finals

The Wednesday FC (Sheffield)	1-1 (aet), 3-1	Bolton Wanderers FC (Bolton)
Wolverhampton Wanderers FC (Wolverhampton)	2-1	Derby County FC (Derby)

Quarter-finals

Bolton Wanderers FC (Bolton)	2-0	Bury FC (Bury)
Derby County FC (Derby)	1-0	West Bromwich Albion FC (West Bromwich)
The Wednesday FC (Sheffield)	4-0	Everton FC (Liverpool)
Wolverhampton Wanderers FC (Wolverhampton)	3-0	Stoke FC (Stoke-upon-Trent)

1896-97

Football League Division 1 1896-97 Season	Aston Villa	Blackburn Rovers	Bolton Wanderers	Burnley	Bury	Derby County	Everton	Liverpool	Nottingham Forest	Preston North End	Sheffield United	Stoke	Sunderland	Wednesday	W.B.A.	Wolves
Aston Villa FC	■	3-0	6-2	0-3	1-1	2-1	1-2	0-0	3-2	3-1	2-2	2-1	2-1	4-0	2-0	5-0
Blackburn Rovers FC	1-5	■	1-0	3-2	1-2	5-2	4-2	1-0	0-0	0-4	1-3	2-1	1-2	4-0	1-2	2-0
Bolton Wanderers FC	1-2	0-0	■	2-1	2-0	1-3	2-0	1-4	0-0	3-1	0-2	4-0	1-0	2-1	2-2	1-2
Burnley FC	3-4	0-1	0-2	■	1-0	2-3	2-1	4-1	2-2	2-2	1-1	1-3	1-1	1-1	5-0	0-3
Bury FC	0-2	3-0	2-2	1-1	■	1-0	3-1	1-2	2-0	0-0	0-1	4-2	1-1	1-1	3-0	3-2
Derby County FC	1-3	6-0	1-0	3-2	7-2	■	0-1	3-2	1-1	2-2	1-3	5-1	1-0	2-1	8-1	4-3
Everton FC	2-3	0-3	2-3	6-0	1-2	5-2	■	2-1	3-1	3-4	1-2	4-2	5-2	2-1	6-3	0-0
Liverpool FC	3-3	4-0	0-2	1-2	3-1	2-0	0-0	■	3-0	0-0	0-0	1-0	3-0	2-2	0-0	3-0
Nottingham Forest FC	2-4	2-1	2-0	4-1	3-0	1-2	3-0	2-0	■	0-0	2-2	4-0	2-1	2-2	0-1	1-2
Preston North End FC	0-1	3-1	2-3	5-3	2-2	0-2	4-1	1-1	3-2	■	1-0	3-0	5-3	2-2	0-0	4-0
Sheffield United FC	0-0	7-0	1-0	1-0	2-2	2-2	1-2	1-1	0-3	0-2	■	1-0	3-0	2-0	0-1	1-3
Stoke FC	0-2	1-0	2-3	3-2	3-0	2-2	2-3	6-1	3-0	2-1	2-0	■	0-1	0-0	2-2	2-1
Sunderland AFC	4-2	0-1	1-1	1-1	0-1	1-2	1-1	4-3	2-2	1-1	0-1	4-1	■	0-0	2-1	0-3
The Wednesday FC	1-3	6-0	0-0	1-0	2-0	2-0	4-1	1-2	3-0	1-0	1-1	4-3	0-0	■	3-1	0-0
West Bromwich Albion FC	3-1	1-0	1-0	3-0	0-0	1-4	1-4	0-1	4-0	1-1	0-1	1-2	1-0	0-2	■	1-0
Wolverhampton Wanderers FC	1-2	1-1	4-0	2-0	1-1	1-0	0-1	1-2	4-1	1-1	1-1	2-0	1-2	0-1	6-1	■

	Division 1	Pd	Wn	Dw	Ls	GF	GA	Pts	
1.	ASTON VILLA FC (BIRMINGHAM)	30	21	5	4	73	38	47	
2.	Sheffield United FC (Sheffield)	30	13	10	7	42	29	36	
3.	Derby County FC (Derby)	30	16	4	10	70	50	36	
4.	Preston North End FC (Preston)	30	11	12	7	55	40	34	
5.	Liverpool FC (Liverpool)	30	12	9	9	46	38	33	
6.	The Wednesday FC (Sheffield)	30	10	11	9	42	37	31	
7.	Everton FC (Liverpool)	30	14	3	13	62	57	31	
8.	Bolton Wanderers FC (Bolton)	30	12	6	12	40	43	30	
9.	Bury FC (Bury)	30	10	10	10	39	44	30	
10.	Wolverhampton Wanderers FC (Wolverhampton)	30	11	6	13	45	41	28	
11.	Nottingham Forest FC (Nottingham)	30	9	8	13	44	49	26	
12.	West Bromwich Albion FC (West Bromwich)	30	10	6	14	33	56	26	
13.	Stoke FC (Stoke-upon-Trent)	30	11	3	16	48	59	25	
14.	Blackburn Rovers FC (Blackburn)	30	11	3	16	35	62	25	
15.	Sunderland AFC (Sunderland)	30	7	9	14	34	47	23	PO
16.	Burnley FC (Burnley)	30	6	7	17	43	61	19	POR
		480	184	112	184	751	751	480	

Top Goalscorers

1)	Stephen BLOOMER	(Derby County FC)	22
2)	George Frederick WHELDON	(Aston Villa FC)	17
3)	George ALLAN	(Liverpool FC)	16
	John BELL	(Everton FC)	16
	John Henry George. DEVEY	(Aston Villa FC)	16
	James William STEVENSON	(Derby County FC)	16

Football League Promotion/Relegation Play-offs 1896-1897 Season	Notts County	Sunderland	Burnley	Newton Heath
Notts County FC		1-0	1-1	---
Sunderland AFC	0-0		---	2-0
Burnley FC	0-1	---		2-0
Newton Heath FC	---	1-1	2-0	

Promotion/Relegation Play-offs

		Pd	Wn	Dw	Ls	GF	GA	Pts	
1.	Notts County FC (Nottingham)	4	2	2	-	3	1	6	P
2.	Sunderland AFC (Sunderland)	4	1	2	1	3	2	4	--
3.	Burnley FC (Burnley)	4	1	1	2	3	4	3	R
4.	Newton Heath FC (Manchester)	4	1	1	2	3	5	3	--
		16	5	6	5	12	12	16	

Football League Division 2 1896-97 Season	Blackpool	Burton Swifts	Burton W.	Darwen	Gainsborough Trinity	Grimsby Town	Leicester Fosse	Lincoln City	Loughborough Town	Manchester City	Newcastle United	Newton Heath	Notts County	Small Heath	Walsall	Woolwich Arsenal
Blackpool FC		3-0	5-0	1-0	1-1	1-0	3-0	3-1	4-1	2-2	4-1	4-2	3-2	1-3	3-2	1-1
Burton Swifts FC	2-2		1-1	2-0	4-0	0-0	2-1	4-0	3-1	5-0	3-0	3-5	1-4	1-1	1-3	1-2
Burton Wanderers FC	3-1	1-0		1-0	3-2	5-1	2-1	2-0	0-1	1-1	0-1	1-2	0-3	2-6	1-0	0-3
Darwen FC	2-3	5-1	3-0		3-2	3-1	4-1	4-1	5-1	3-1	2-1	0-2	2-1	2-0	12-0	4-1
Gainsborough Trinity FC	2-0	4-1	2-1	2-4		1-1	0-2	7-0	2-0	1-1	2-0	2-0	3-2	1-3	2-0	4-1
Grimsby Town FC	2-2	3-0	3-0	4-2	1-1		4-1	3-1	8-1	3-1	3-2	2-0	3-1	2-1	0-1	3-1
Leicester Fosse FC	2-1	3-0	2-1	4-1	0-0	4-2		4-1	4-2	3-3	5-0	1-0	2-3	0-1	4-1	6-3
Lincoln City FC	3-1	1-1	2-3	1-0	0-2	0-3	2-1		0-2	0-1	1-2	1-3	1-1	1-3	2-1	2-3
Loughborough Town FC	4-1	0-2	6-0	4-2	1-0	1-4	0-2	3-0		2-0	3-0	2-0	0-1	2-0	1-2	8-0
Manchester City FC	4-2	3-1	2-1	4-1	4-1	3-1	4-0	3-0	1-1		1-2	0-0	1-4	3-0	5-0	1-1
Newcastle United FC	4-1	2-1	3-0	5-1	1-2	3-0	3-1	2-1	4-1	3-0		2-0	2-2	4-3	2-0	2-0
Newton Heath FC	2-0	1-1	3-0	3-1	2-0	4-2	2-1	3-1	6-0	2-1	4-0		1-1	1-1	2-0	1-1
Notts County FC	3-1	6-1	5-0	4-0	2-0	1-3	6-0	8-0	3-1	3-3	3-1	3-0		1-2	5-2	7-4
Small Heath FC	1-3	1-2	3-2	5-1	2-2	0-1	2-2	1-2	3-0	3-1	3-1	1-0	3-1		3-3	5-2
Walsall FC	2-0	5-2	2-0	4-0	1-1	0-1	1-1	5-0	5-1	3-2	0-2	2-3	1-3	1-6		5-3
Woolwich Arsenal FC	4-2	3-0	3-0	1-0	6-1	4-2	2-1	6-2	2-0	1-2	5-1	0-2	2-3	2-3	1-1	

Division 2		Pd	Wn	Dw	Ls	GF	GA	Pts	
1.	Notts County FC (Nottingham)	30	19	4	7	92	43	42	POP
2.	Newton Heath FC (Manchester)	30	17	5	8	56	34	39	
3.	Grimsby Town FC (Cleethorpes)	30	17	4	9	66	45	38	
4.	Small Heath FC (Birmingham)	30	16	5	9	69	47	37	
5.	Newcastle United FC (Newcastle-upon-Tyne)	30	17	1	12	56	52	35	
6.	Manchester City FC (Manchester)	30	12	8	10	58	50	32	
7.	Gainsborough Trinity FC (Gainsborough)	30	12	7	11	50	47	31	
8.	Blackpool FC (Blackpool)	30	13	5	12	59	56	31	
9.	Leicester Fosse FC (Leicester)	30	13	4	13	59	56	30	
10.	Woolwich Arsenal FC (London)	30	13	4	13	68	70	30	
11.	Darwen FC (Darwen)	30	14	-	14	67	61	28	
12.	Walsall FC (Walsall)	30	11	4	15	53	69	26	
13.	Loughborough Town FC (Loughborough)	30	12	1	17	50	64	25	
14.	Burton Swifts FC (Burton-upon-Trent)	30	9	6	15	46	61	24	
15.	Burton Wanderers FC (Burton-upon-Trent)	30	9	2	19	31	67	20	#
16.	Lincoln City FC (Lincoln)	30	5	2	23	27	85	12	
		480	209	62	209	907	907	480	

\# Burton Wanderers FC (Burton-upon-Trent) were not re-elected to the league and were replaced in Division 2 for next season by Luton Town FC (Luton).

F.A. CUP FINAL   (Crystal Palace, London – 10/04/1897 – 65,891)

ASTON VILLA FC (BIRMINGHAM)	3-2	Everton FC (Liverpool)
Devey, Campbell, Crabtree	*(H.T. 3-2)*	*Bell, Hartley*

Aston Villa: Whitehouse, Spencer, Evans, Reynolds, James Cowan, Crabtree, Athersmith, Devey, Campbell, Wheldon, John Cowan.

Everton: Menham, Meechan, Storrier, Boyle, Holt, Stewart, Taylor, Bell, Hartley, Chadwick, Milward.

Semi-finals

Aston Villa FC (Birmingham)	3-0	Liverpool FC (Liverpool)
Everton FC (Liverpool)	3-2	Derby County FC (Derby)

Quarter-finals

Aston Villa FC (Birmingham)	1-1 (aet), 0-0 (aet), 3-2	Preston North End FC (Preston)
Derby County FC (Derby)	2-0	Newton Heath FC (Manchester)
Everton FC (Liverpool)	2-0	Blackburn Rovers FC (Blackburn)
Nottingham Forest FC (Nottingham)	1-1 (aet), 0-1	Liverpool FC (Liverpool)

1897-98

Football League Division 1 1897-98 Season	Aston Villa	Blackburn Rovers	Bolton Wanderers	Bury	Derby County	Everton	Liverpool	Nottingham Forest	Notts County	Preston North End	Sheffield United	Stoke	Sunderland	Wednesday	W.B.A.	Wolves
Aston Villa FC	■	5-1	3-2	3-1	4-1	3-0	3-1	2-0	4-2	4-0	1-2	1-1	4-3	5-2	4-3	1-2
Blackburn Rovers FC	4-3	■	1-3	1-1	1-1	1-1	2-1	1-1	0-1	1-0	1-1	1-1	2-1	1-1	1-3	2-3
Bolton Wanderers FC	2-0	1-2	■	0-0	3-3	1-0	0-2	2-0	1-0	1-0	0-1	2-1	1-0	0-3	2-0	2-1
Bury FC	1-2	1-0	2-1	■	4-0	0-1	0-2	2-2	0-0	1-0	2-5	3-3	1-0	3-0	3-2	2-1
Derby County FC	3-1	3-1	1-0	2-2	■	5-1	3-1	5-0	1-2	3-1	1-1	4-1	2-2	1-2	3-2	3-2
Everton FC	2-1	1-1	2-1	4-2	3-0	■	3-0	2-0	1-0	1-1	1-4	1-1	2-0	1-0	6-1	3-0
Liverpool FC	4-0	0-1	1-1	2-2	4-2	3-1	■	1-2	2-0	0-0	0-4	4-0	0-2	4-0	1-1	1-0
Nottingham Forest FC	3-1	3-1	2-0	3-1	3-4	2-2	2-3	■	1-1	4-1	1-1	3-1	1-1	1-0	0-1	1-1
Notts County FC	2-3	0-0	1-2	2-1	1-1	3-2	3-2	1-3	■	1-1	1-3	4-0	0-1	0-0	2-2	2-2
Preston North End FC	3-1	1-4	0-0	2-1	5-0	1-1	1-1	3-0	3-1	■	1-3	0-0	2-0	2-0	1-1	1-2
Sheffield United FC	1-0	5-2	4-0	1-1	2-1	0-0	1-2	1-1	0-1	2-1	■	4-3	1-0	1-1	2-0	2-1
Stoke FC	0-0	2-1	2-0	3-1	2-1	2-0	2-1	1-2	2-0	1-2	2-1	■	0-1	2-1	0-0	0-2
Sunderland AFC	0-0	2-1	2-0	2-1	2-1	0-0	1-0	4-0	2-0	1-0	3-1	4-0	■	1-0	0-2	3-2
The Wednesday FC	3-0	4-1	3-0	3-0	3-1	2-1	4-2	3-6	3-1	2-1	0-1	4-0	0-1	■	3-0	2-0
West Bromwich Albion FC	1-1	1-1	2-0	1-0	3-1	2-2	2-1	2-0	0-3	3-1	2-0	2-0	2-2	0-2	■	2-2
Wolverhampton Wanderers FC	1-1	3-2	2-0	3-0	2-0	2-3	2-1	0-0	3-1	3-0	1-1	4-2	4-2	5-0	1-1	■

	Division 1	Pd	Wn	Dw	Ls	GF	GA	Pts	
1.	SHEFFIELD UNITED FC (SHEFFIELD)	30	17	8	5	56	31	42	
2.	Sunderland AFC (Sunderland)	30	16	5	9	43	30	37	
3.	Wolverhampton Wanderers FC (Wolverhampton)	30	14	7	9	57	41	35	
4.	Everton FC (Liverpool)	30	13	9	8	48	39	35	
5.	The Wednesday FC (Sheffield)	30	15	3	12	51	42	33	
6.	Aston Villa FC (Birmingham)	30	14	5	11	61	51	33	
7.	West Bromwich Albion FC (West Bromwich)	30	11	10	9	44	45	32	
8.	Nottingham Forest FC (Nottingham)	30	11	9	10	47	49	31	
9.	Liverpool FC (Liverpool)	30	11	6	13	48	45	28	
10.	Derby County FC (Derby)	30	11	6	13	57	61	28	
11.	Bolton Wanderers FC (Bolton)	30	11	4	15	28	41	26	
12.	Preston North End FC (Preston)	30	8	8	14	35	43	24	
13.	Notts County FC (Nottingham)	30	8	8	14	36	46	24	
14.	Bury FC (Bury)	30	8	8	14	39	51	24	
15.	Blackburn Rovers FC (Blackburn)	30	7	10	13	39	54	24	PO
16.	Stoke FC (Stoke-upon-Trent)	30	8	8	14	35	55	24	PO
		480	183	114	183	724	724	480	

Top Goalscorers

1)	George Frederick WHELDON	(Aston Villa FC)	21
2)	Frederick SPIKESLEY	(Sheffield United FC)	17
3)	Stephen BLOOMER	(Derby County FC)	16
4)	Walter BENNETT	(The Wednesday FC)	13
	Harold WOOD	(Wolverhampton Wanderers FC)	13

Football League Promotion/Relegation Play-offs 1897-98 Season	Stoke City	Burnley	Newcastle United	Blackburn Rovers
Stoke FC	■	0-0	1-0	---
Burnley FC	0-2	■	---	2-0
Newcastle United FC	2-1	---	■	4-0
Blackburn Rovers FC	---	1-3	4-3	■

Promotion/Relegation Play-offs

		Pd	Wn	Dw	Ls	GF	GA	Pts
1.	Stoke FC (Stoke-upon-Trent)	4	2	1	1	4	2	5
2.	Burnley FC (Burnley)	4	2	1	1	5	3	5
3.	Newcastle United FC (Newcastle/Tyne)	4	2	-	2	9	6	4
4.	Blackburn Rovers FC (Blackburn)	4	1	-	3	5	12	2
		16	7	2	7	23	23	16

Division 1 was extended to 18 clubs for next season so all 4 clubs who entered the play-offs played in Division 1 the next season.

Football League Division 2 1897-98 Season	Blackpool	Burnley	Burton Swifts	Darwen	Gainsborough Trinity	Grimsby Town	Leicester Fosse	Lincoln City	Loughborough Town	Luton Town	Manchester City	Newcastle United	Newton Heath	Small Heath	Walsall	Woolwich Arsenal
Blackpool FC	■	1-1	2-1	1-0	5-0	1-1	2-1	5-0	4-0	1-0	0-2	2-3	0-1	4-1	1-1	3-3
Burnley FC	5-1	■	2-0	6-1	1-1	6-0	4-0	2-1	9-3	4-0	3-1	3-0	6-3	4-1	4-1	5-0
Burton Swifts FC	2-1	0-2	■	2-0	1-1	4-0	2-3	1-1	3-0	2-1	0-0	3-1	0-4	1-3	3-2	1-2
Darwen FC	3-1	0-1	1-2	■	2-4	1-0	1-2	3-2	2-1	0-2	2-4	1-3	2-3	1-1	1-2	1-4
Gainsborough Trinity FC	4-1	0-0	3-2	3-1	■	2-0	1-0	4-0	4-0	3-3	1-0	1-3	2-1	0-0	1-1	1-0
Grimsby Town FC	3-0	2-1	7-2	5-0	4-2	■	0-0	4-2	7-0	1-3	3-4	2-0	1-3	3-1	1-2	1-4
Leicester Fosse FC	4-1	0-1	1-1	0-1	3-1	1-0	■	3-1	4-0	1-1	0-0	1-1	1-1	2-0	3-1	2-1
Lincoln City FC	3-2	1-1	3-0	2-2	2-1	1-1	1-4	■	2-3	4-2	2-1	2-3	1-0	1-2	0-2	2-3
Loughborough Town FC	0-2	0-2	3-2	0-1	0-5	2-1	1-1	4-2	■	2-0	0-3	0-1	0-0	0-2	2-1	1-3
Luton Town FC	3-1	2-0	1-1	3-0	4-0	6-0	0-1	9-3	7-0	■	3-0	3-1	2-2	1-2	6-0	0-2
Manchester City FC	3-3	1-1	9-0	5-0	3-0	3-0	2-1	3-1	3-0	2-1	■	1-1	0-1	3-3	3-2	4-1
Newcastle United FC	2-0	0-1	3-1	1-0	5-2	4-0	4-2	3-0	3-1	4-1	2-0	■	2-0	4-0	2-1	4-1
Newton Heath FC	4-0	0-0	4-0	3-2	1-0	2-1	2-0	5-0	5-1	1-2	1-1	0-1	■	3-1	6-0	5-1
Small Heath FC	2-3	2-2	2-1	5-1	4-3	0-2	2-1	4-0	1-0	4-2	0-1	1-0	2-1	■	6-0	2-1
Walsall FC	6-0	1-2	4-0	5-0	3-0	1-1	2-1	3-1	3-0	5-0	2-2	2-3	1-1	1-2	■	3-2
Woolwich Arsenal FC	2-1	1-1	3-0	3-1	4-0	4-1	0-3	2-2	4-0	3-0	2-2	0-0	5-1	4-2	4-0	■

	Division 2	Pd	Wn	Dw	Ls	GF	GA	Pts	
1.	Burnley FC (Burnley)	30	20	8	2	80	24	48	POP
2.	Newcastle United FC (Newcastle-upon-Tyne)	30	21	3	6	64	32	45	POP
3.	Manchester City FC (Manchester)	30	15	9	6	66	36	39	
4.	Newton Heath FC (Manchester)	30	16	6	8	64	35	38	
5.	Woolwich Arsenal FC (London)	30	16	5	9	69	49	37	
6.	Small Heath FC (Birmingham)	30	16	4	10	58	50	36	
7.	Leicester Fosse FC (Leicester)	30	13	7	10	46	35	33	
8.	Luton Town FC (Luton)	30	13	4	13	68	50	30	
9.	Gainsborough Trinity FC (Gainsborough)	30	12	6	12	50	54	30	
10.	Walsall FC (Walsall)	30	12	5	13	58	58	29	
11.	Blackpool FC (Blackpool)	30	10	5	15	49	61	25	
12.	Grimsby Town FC (Cleethorpes)	30	10	4	16	52	62	24	
13.	Burton Swifts FC (Burton-upon-Trent)	30	8	5	17	38	69	21	
14.	Lincoln City FC (Lincoln)	30	6	5	19	43	82	17	
15.	Darwen FC (Darwen)	30	6	2	22	31	76	14	
16.	Loughborough Town FC (Loughborough)	30	6	2	22	24	87	14	
		480	200	80	200	860	860	480	

Barnsley St. Peter's FC (Barnsley), Burslem Port Vale FC (Burslem), Glossop North End FC (Glossop) and New Brighton Tower FC (Wallasey) were elected to Division 2 which was extended to 18 clubs for next season.

Automatic promotion/relegation started from the next season.

F.A. CUP FINAL (Crystal Palace, London – 16/04/1898 – 62,017)

NOTTINGHAM FOREST FC (NOTTINGHAM)   3-1   Derby County FC (Derby)

Capes 2, McPherson   *(H.T. 2-1)*   *Bloomer*

Nottingham Forest: Allsop, Ritchie, Scott, Forman, McPherson, Wragg, McInnes, Richards, Benbow, Capes, Spouncer.

Derby: Fryer, Methven, Leiper, Cox, Goodall, Turner, Goodall, Bloomer, Boag, Stevenson, McQueen.

Semi-finals

Derby County FC (Derby)   3-1   Everton FC (Liverpool)

Southampton FC (Southampton)   1-1 (aet), 0-2   Nottingham Forest FC (Nottingham)

Quarter-finals

Burnley FC (Burnley)   1-3   Everton FC (Liverpool)

Liverpool FC (Liverpool)   1-1 (aet), 1-5   Derby County FC (Derby)

Southampton FC (Southampton)   0-0 (aet), 4-0   Bolton Wanderers FC (Bolton)

West Bromwich Albion FC (West Bromwich)   2-3   Nottingham Forest FC (Nottingham)

1898-99

Football League Division 1 1898-99 Season	Aston Villa	Blackburn Rovers	Bolton Wanderers	Burnley	Bury	Derby County	Everton	Liverpool	Newcastle United	Nottingham Forest	Notts County	Preston North End	Sheffield United	Stoke	Sunderland	Wednesday	W.B.A.	Wolves
Aston Villa FC		3-1	2-1	4-0	3-2	7-1	3-0	5-0	1-0	3-0	6-1	4-2	1-1	3-1	2-0	3-1	7-1	1-1
Blackburn Rovers FC	0-0		4-1	0-2	0-0	3-0	1-3	1-3	4-2	3-3	6-0	2-2	2-1	4-1	3-2	2-0	4-1	2-2
Bolton Wanderers FC	0-0	0-2		2-0	0-1	2-1	2-4	2-1	0-0	0-2	0-1	2-2	3-0	0-2	6-1	0-0	3-3	2-1
Burnley FC	2-4	2-0	2-0		2-1	2-1	0-0	2-1	2-1	0-0	0-0	3-1	1-0	1-1	1-0	5-0	1-1	4-2
Bury FC	2-1	3-2	3-1	1-1		0-0	3-1	3-0	1-1	2-0	2-0	3-1	1-3	5-2	1-2	0-0	1-1	0-2
Derby County FC	1-1	0-0	1-1	2-1	1-2		5-5	1-0	3-1	2-0	4-2	1-0	1-0	1-1	4-2	9-0	4-1	6-2
Everton FC	1-1	2-1	1-0	4-0	0-1	1-2		1-2	3-0	1-3	1-2	1-0	2-0	0-0	2-0	1-0	2-1
Liverpool FC	0-3	2-0	2-0	2-0	1-0	4-0	2-0		3-2	0-1	0-0	3-1	2-1	1-0	0-0	4-0	2-2	1-0
Newcastle United FC	1-1	1-0	4-1	4-1	2-0	2-0	2-2	3-0		0-1	1-2	2-1	1-2	3-0	0-1	2-2	3-0	2-4
Nottingham Forest FC	1-0	0-1	1-2	0-1	1-2	3-3	0-0	0-3	2-0		0-0	2-2	2-1	2-1	1-1	1-1	3-0	3-0
Notts County FC	1-0	5-3	2-1	2-2	4-1	2-2	0-1	1-1	3-1	2-2		1-0	2-2	2-0	5-2	1-0	0-0	0-2
Preston North End FC	2-0	1-1	0-1	1-1	3-1	3-1	0-0	1-2	1-0	1-0	2-0		1-0	4-2	2-3	1-1	4-0	2-1
Sheffield United FC	1-3	1-1	3-1	1-1	4-1	2-1	1-1	0-2	2-2	2-2	2-2	1-1		1-1	2-0	2-1	5-0	1-0
Stoke FC	3-0	0-1	2-3	4-1	1-1	2-0	2-1	2-1	0-0	2-1	1-1	2-1	4-1		1-0	1-0	2-1	2-4
Sunderland AFC	4-2	0-1	0-0	0-1	3-0	1-0	2-1	1-0	2-3	1-1	1-1	1-0	1-0	2-0		2-0	2-0	3-0
The Wednesday FC	4-1	1-2	1-0	1-0	3-2	3-1	1-2	0-3	1-3	2-1	1-1	2-1	1-1	1-3	0-1		1-2	3-0
West Bromwich Albion FC	0-1	6-2	1-0	0-1	2-0	1-1	3-0	1-1	2-0	2-0	2-0	2-0	3-0	0-1	1-0	2-0		1-2
Wolverhampton Wanderers FC	4-0	2-1	1-0	4-0	1-2	2-2	1-2	0-0	0-0	0-2	1-0	0-0	4-1	3-2	2-0	0-0	5-1	

	Division 1	Pd	Wn	Dw	Ls	GF	GA	Pts	
1.	ASTON VILLA FC (BIRMINGHAM)	34	19	7	8	76	40	45	
2.	Liverpool FC (Liverpool)	34	19	5	10	49	33	43	
3.	Burnley FC (Burnley)	34	15	9	10	45	47	39	
4.	Everton FC (Liverpool)	34	15	8	11	48	41	38	
5.	Notts County FC (Nottingham)	34	12	13	9	47	51	37	
6.	Blackburn Rovers FC (Blackburn)	34	14	8	12	60	52	36	
7.	Sunderland AFC (Sunderland)	34	15	6	13	41	41	36	
8.	Wolverhampton Wanderers FC (Wolverhampton)	34	14	7	13	54	48	35	
9.	Derby County FC (Derby)	34	12	11	11	62	57	35	
10.	Bury FC (Bury)	34	14	7	13	48	49	35	
11.	Nottingham Forest FC (Nottingham)	34	11	11	12	42	42	33	
12.	Stoke FC (Stoke-upon-Trent)	34	13	7	14	47	52	33	
13.	Newcastle United FC (Newcastle-upon-Tyne)	34	11	8	15	49	48	30	
14.	West Bromwich Albion FC (West Bromwich)	34	12	6	16	42	57	30	
15.	Preston North End FC (Preston)	34	10	9	15	44	47	29	
16.	Sheffield United FC (Sheffield)	34	9	11	14	45	51	29	
17.	Bolton Wanderers FC (Bolton)	34	9	7	18	37	51	25	R
18.	The Wednesday FC (Sheffield)	34	8	8	18	32	61	24	R
		612	232	148	232	868	868	612	

Top Goalscorers

1)	Stephen BLOOMER	(Derby County FC)	23
2)	John Henry George DEVEY	(Aston Villa FC)	21
3)	William S. MAXWELL	(Stoke FC)	17
	Jack H. PEDDIE	(Newcastle United FC)	17
5)	Daniel J. HURST	(Blackburn Rovers FC)	15

Football League Division 2 — 1898-99 Season

	Barnsley	Blackpool	Burslem Port Vale	Burton Swifts	Darwen	Gainsborough Trin.	Glossop	Grimsby Town	Leicester Fosse	Lincoln City	Loughborough Tn.	Luton Town	Manchester City	New Brighton	Newton Heath	Small Heath	Walsall	Woolwich Arsenal
Barnsley St. Peter's FC	■	2-1	2-1	2-0	6-0	1-0	1-1	2-2	3-4	1-0	9-0	2-1	1-1	2-1	0-2	7-2	1-1	2-1
Blackpool FC	3-1	■	0-4	3-0	6-0	4-0	1-2	3-6	2-2	3-0	2-1	2-3	2-4	1-2	0-1	1-1	1-2	1-1
Burslem Port Vale FC	2-0	6-1	■	4-1	3-1	2-1	1-2	2-0	0-2	2-1	3-0	4-1	1-1	0-0	1-0	1-0	0-1	3-0
Burton Swifts FC	5-0	3-1	2-0	■	4-0	2-1	1-2	1-2	1-1	2-1	1-1	1-1	3-3	1-1	5-1	2-6	0-2	1-2
Darwen FC	1-1	0-2	1-3	0-2	■	0-3	0-2	0-2	3-0	1-2	0-1	4-1	0-2	2-4	1-1	1-1	1-1	1-4
Gainsborough Trinity FC	2-0	7-0	3-2	1-2	2-2	■	2-4	5-1	4-0	2-2	3-0	2-3	3-1	3-1	0-2	1-1	0-0	0-1
Glossop FC	1-0	4-1	0-0	5-0	5-0	5-1	■	4-2	1-3	2-0	4-0	5-0	1-2	5-0	1-2	1-2	2-0	2-0
Grimsby Town FC	0-1	2-1	3-1	1-3	9-2	0-2	1-1	■	1-0	1-1	5-0	1-2	2-2	3-0	2-0	2-1	1-0	
Leicester Fosse FC	3-1	4-0	1-1	1-0	4-0	1-0	4-2	2-0	■	3-2	1-0	1-1	1-1	4-1	1-0	0-0	2-2	2-1
Lincoln City FC	1-0	0-0	1-0	1-1	2-0	1-0	2-2	1-6	3-1	■	6-0	2-0	3-1	1-2	2-0	2-2	1-1	2-0
Loughborough Town FC	2-0	1-3	0-3	1-0	10-0	0-0	1-3	1-3	0-3	2-4	■	4-1	1-3	6-0	0-1	1-1	1-1	1-0
Luton Town FC	4-1	3-2	0-1	3-0	8-1	4-2	0-2	3-1	1-6	2-0	2-2	■	0-3	2-3	0-1	2-3	3-2	0-1
Manchester City FC	5-0	4-1	3-1	6-0	10-0	4-0	0-2	7-2	3-1	3-1	5-0	2-0	■	1-1	4-0	2-0	2-0	3-1
New Brighton Tower FC	2-1	4-0	1-0	2-2	7-0	3-2	2-2	2-0	1-0	4-1	3-0	4-0	0-1	■	0-3	4-0	6-0	3-1
Newton Heath FC	0-0	3-1	2-1	2-2	9-0	6-1	3-2	2-2	1-0	6-1	5-0	3-0	1-2		■	2-0	1-0	2-2
Small Heath FC	3-1	5-0	1-2	4-1	8-0	6-1	1-1	2-1	0-3	4-1	6-0	9-0	4-1	3-2	4-1	■	2-1	4-1
Walsall FC	1-1	6-0	1-1	7-1	10-0	6-1	2-0	4-1	1-1	3-2	7-0	6-0	1-1	1-1	2-0	2-0	■	4-1
Woolwich Arsenal FC	3-0	6-0	1-0	2-1	6-0	5-1	3-0	1-1	4-0	4-2	3-1	6-2	0-1	4-0	5-1	2-0	0-0	■

Division 2

		Pd	Wn	Dw	Ls	GF	GA	Pts	
1.	Manchester City FC (Manchester)	34	23	6	5	92	35	52	P
2.	Glossop FC (Glossop)	34	20	6	8	76	38	46	P *
3.	Leicester Fosse FC (Leicester)	34	18	9	7	64	42	45	
4.	Newton Heath FC (Manchester)	34	19	5	10	67	43	43	
5.	New Brighton Tower FC (Wallasey)	34	18	7	9	71	52	43	
6.	Walsall FC (Walsall)	34	15	12	7	79	36	42	
7.	Woolwich Arsenal FC (London)	34	18	5	11	72	41	41	
8.	Small Heath FC (Birmingham)	34	17	7	10	85	50	41	
9.	Burslem Port Vale FC (Burslem)	34	17	5	12	56	34	39	
10.	Grimsby Town FC (Cleethorpes)	34	15	5	14	71	60	35	
11.	Barnsley St. Peter's FC (Barnsley)	34	12	7	15	52	56	31	*
12.	Lincoln City FC (Lincoln)	34	12	7	15	51	56	31	
13.	Burton Swifts FC (Burton-upon-Trent)	34	10	8	16	51	70	28	
14.	Gainsborough Trinity FC (Gainsborough)	34	10	5	19	56	72	25	
15.	Luton Town FC (Luton)	34	10	3	21	51	95	23	
16.	Blackpool FC (Blackpool)	34	8	4	22	49	90	20	# *
17.	Loughborough Town FC (Loughborough)	34	6	6	22	38	92	18	
18.	Darwen FC (Darwen)	34	2	5	27	22	141	9	#
		612	250	112	250	1103	1103	612	

developed for the footnotes

\# Blackpool FC (Blackpool) and Darwen FC (Darwen) were not re-elected to the league for next season and were replaced in Division 2 by Chesterfield FC (Chesterfield) and Middlesbrough FC (Middlesbrough).

* Barnsley St. Peter's FC (Barnsley) changed the club name to Barnsley FC (Barnsley) and Blackpool FC (Blackpool) merged with South Shore FC (Blackpool) as Blackpool FC (Blackpool) for the next season. Glossop FC (Glossop) changed their club name from Glossop North End FC (Glossop) prior to the start of this season.

F.A. CUP FINAL   (Crystal Palace, London – 15/04/1899 – 73,833)

SHEFFIELD UNITED FC (SHEFFIELD)   4-1   Derby County FC (Derby)

Bennett, Beer, Almond, Priest   *(H.T. 0-1)*   *Boag*

Sheffield United: Foulke, Thicket, Boyle, Johnson, Morren, Needham, Bennett, Beer, Hedley, Almond, Priest.
Derby: Fryer, Methven, Staley, Cox, Paterson, May, Arkesden, Bloomer, Boag, McDonald, Allan.

Semi-finals

Derby County FC (Derby)	3-1	Stoke FC (Stoke-upon-Trent)
Sheffield United FC (Sheffield)	2-2 (aet), 4-4 (aet), 0-1, 1-0	Liverpool FC (Liverpool)

(The third match was abandoned after the crowd encroached on the field of play.)

Quarter-finals

Nottingham Forest FC (Nottingham)	0-1	Sheffield United FC (Sheffield)
Southampton FC (Southampton)	1-2	Derby County FC (Derby)
Stoke FC (Stoke-upon-Trent)	4-1	Tottenham Hotspur FC (London)
West Bromwich Albion FC (West Bromwich)	0-2	Liverpool FC (Liverpool)

1899-1900

Football League Division 1 1899-1900 Season	Aston Villa	Blackburn Rovers	Burnley	Bury	Derby County	Everton	Glossop	Liverpool	Manchester City	Newcastle United	Nottingham Forest	Notts County	Preston North End	Sheffield United	Stoke	Sunderland	W.B.A.	Wolves
Aston Villa FC		3-1	2-0	2-1	3-2	1-1	9-0	1-0	2-1	2-1	2-2	6-2	3-1	1-1	4-1	4-2	0-2	0-0
Blackburn Rovers FC	0-4		2-0	3-2	2-0	3-1	2-2	2-0	4-3	2-3	2-1	6-0	3-0	3-3	3-0	1-2	2-0	2-1
Burnley FC	1-2	1-0		1-0	1-2	3-1	3-1	2-1	2-0	1-3	2-2	3-0	0-1	1-0	2-2	3-1	2-0	0-1
Bury FC	2-0	2-0	1-1		1-1	4-1	2-1	2-1	1-4	2-1	2-1	0-1	2-0	2-1	0-1	2-0	1-0	3-0
Derby County FC	2-0	0-2	4-1	3-0		2-1	4-1	3-2	0-0	2-1	2-2	0-1	2-0	0-1	2-0	2-0	4-1	0-2
Everton FC	1-2	0-0	2-0	2-0	3-0		4-1	3-1	4-0	3-2	2-1	0-2	1-0	1-2	2-0	1-0	1-3	0-1
Glossop FC	1-0	4-2	2-0	0-0	1-3	1-1		1-2	0-2	0-0	3-0	0-0	0-2	2-2	1-2	0-2	1-1	2-3
Liverpool FC	3-3	3-1	0-1	2-0	0-2	1-2	5-2		5-2	2-0	1-0	3-1	1-0	2-2	0-0	0-2	2-0	1-1
Manchester City FC	0-2	1-1	1-0	2-2	4-0	1-2	4-1	0-1		1-0	2-0	5-1	3-1	1-2	1-0	2-1	4-0	1-1
Newcastle United FC	3-2	4-1	2-0	2-1	2-0	2-0	1-0	1-1	0-0		3-1	6-0	0-0	0-0	2-2	2-4	4-2	0-1
Nottingham Forest FC	1-1	3-2	4-0	2-2	4-1	4-2	5-0	1-0	2-0	1-0		0-3	3-1	4-0	1-0	1-3	6-1	0-0
Notts County FC	1-4	5-1	6-1	2-2	0-0	2-2	0-0	2-1	1-1	0-0	1-2		3-0	1-2	1-3	3-1	1-2	0-0
Preston North End FC	0-5	2-0	1-1	1-0	0-0	1-1	1-0	1-3	0-2	4-1	3-0	4-3		0-1	3-0	0-1	5-2	2-0
Sheffield United FC	2-1	3-0	0-0	4-0	1-1	5-0	4-0	1-2	3-0	3-1	3-0	1-1	1-0		1-0	2-2	1-1	5-2
Stoke FC	0-2	2-0	3-0	2-0	1-1	1-1	1-0	3-2	1-0	2-2	0-0	1-0	3-1	1-1		1-2	1-0	1-3
Sunderland AFC	0-1	1-0	2-1	1-0	2-0	1-0	0-0	3-1	1-2	1-0	5-0	1-0	1-1	3-0			3-1	1-2
West Bromwich Albion FC	0-2	1-0	2-0	0-1	0-0	0-0	3-3	2-0	0-0	1-1	8-0	0-0	1-0	1-2	4-0	1-0		3-2
Wolverhampton Wanderers FC	0-1	4-0	3-0	1-0	3-0	2-1	4-0	0-1	1-1	1-1	2-2	2-2	1-3	1-2	0-2	1-0	2-0	

Division 1

		Pd	Wn	Dw	Ls	GF	GA	Pts	
1.	ASTON VILLA FC (BIRMINGHAM)	34	22	6	6	77	35	50	
2.	Sheffield United FC (Sheffield)	34	18	12	4	63	33	48	
3.	Sunderland AFC (Sunderland)	34	19	3	12	50	35	41	
4.	Wolverhampton Wanderers FC (Wolverhampton)	34	15	9	10	48	37	39	
5.	Newcastle United FC (Newcastle-upon-Tyne)	34	14	10	11	53	43	36	
6.	Derby County FC (Derby)	34	14	8	12	45	43	36	
7.	Manchester City FC (Manchester)	34	13	8	13	50	44	34	
8.	Nottingham Forest FC (Nottingham)	34	13	8	13	56	55	34	
9.	Stoke FC (Stoke-upon-Trent)	34	13	8	13	37	45	34	
10.	Liverpool FC (Liverpool)	34	14	5	15	49	45	33	
11.	Everton FC (Liverpool)	34	13	7	14	47	49	33	
12.	Bury FC (Bury)	34	13	6	15	40	44	32	
13.	West Bromwich Albion FC (West Bromwich)	34	11	8	15	43	51	30	
14.	Blackburn Rovers FC (Blackburn)	34	13	4	17	49	61	30	
15.	Notts County FC (Nottingham)	34	9	11	14	46	60	29	
16.	Preston North End FC (Preston)	34	12	4	18	38	48	28	
17.	Burnley FC (Burnley)	34	11	5	18	34	54	27	R
18.	Glossop FC (Glossop)	34	4	10	20	31	74	18	R
		612	240	132	240	856	856	612	

Top Goalscorers

1)	William GARRATY	(Aston Villa FC)	27
2)	Stephen BLOOMER	(Derby County FC)	19
3)	John CALVEY	(Nottingham Forest FC)	17
4)	Walter BENNETT	(Sheffield United FC)	15
	Jack H. PEDDIE	(Newcastle United FC)	15

Football League Division 2 1899-1900 Season	Barnsley	Bolton Wanderers	Burslem Port Vale	Burton Swifts	Chesterfield	Gainsborough Trinity	Grimsby Town	Leicester Fosse	Lincoln City	Loughborough Town	Luton Town	Middlesbrough	New Brighton	Newton Heath	Small Heath	Walsall	Wednesday	Woolwich Arsenal
Barnsley FC		1-6	3-0	4-1	0-0	5-0	0-1	1-2	0-4	7-0	2-1	5-2	1-1	0-0	1-1	2-2	1-0	3-2
Bolton Wanderers FC	2-0		5-0	5-0	3-0	3-0	1-2	2-2	4-0	7-0	3-0	3-0	2-1	2-1	1-1	2-0	1-0	1-0
Burslem Port Vale FC	3-1	0-2		2-1	2-0	1-0	2-3	0-2	2-0	3-1	1-0	3-1	1-1	1-0	3-0	1-0	0-3	1-1
Burton Swifts FC	4-0	2-5	2-2		2-1	1-1	1-2	2-0	0-0	3-1	3-1	5-0	2-2	0-0	0-3	2-1	0-5	2-0
Chesterfield FC	2-1	3-3	0-4	0-4		3-1	3-1	0-0	2-2	1-0	2-0	7-1	5-2	2-1	0-0	1-3	1-0	3-1
Gainsborough Trinity FC	1-0	1-1	4-0	4-1	3-5		2-3	3-0	3-1	4-2	2-2	5-0	1-1	0-1	1-4	2-0	0-2	1-1
Grimsby Town FC	8-1	0-0	1-1	6-0	0-3	3-0		6-1	5-2	3-3	2-0	1-2	0-7	2-0	4-2	1-2	1-0	
Leicester Fosse FC	1-0	0-0	2-0	1-0	2-2	5-0	3-0		2-0	5-0	2-2	4-1	1-2	2-0	2-0	2-1	0-0	0-0
Lincoln City FC	1-1	1-0	1-1	3-0	2-0	2-1	1-1	2-0		3-2	2-0	3-0	0-0	1-0	0-0	3-1	1-2	5-0
Loughborough Town FC	0-0	2-3	1-2	2-1	0-4	1-2	0-0	0-2	0-1		1-1	1-1	1-2	0-2	1-2	0-0	0-0	2-3
Luton Town FC	3-0	0-2	1-1	5-2	0-3	4-0	0-4	0-0	0-2	4-0		1-1	1-4	0-1	1-2	4-0	0-1	1-2
Middlesbrough FC	3-0	0-3	1-0	8-1	0-1	0-0	1-0	0-1	1-1	3-0	0-0		5-2	2-0	1-3	1-1	1-2	1-0
New Brighton Tower FC	6-2	3-1	2-0	5-0	2-3	5-0	2-1	2-2	3-0	3-0	5-1	1-1		1-4	2-2	0-1	2-2	0-2
Newton Heath FC	3-0	1-2	3-0	4-0	2-1	2-2	1-0	3-2	1-0	4-0	5-0	2-1	2-1		3-2	5-0	1-0	2-0
Small Heath FC	5-0	0-0	2-1	2-0	5-3	8-1	0-1	4-1	5-0	6-0	3-0	5-1	2-0	1-0		3-2	4-1	3-1
Walsall FC	4-2	2-2	0-1	2-0	6-3	1-0	1-1	1-2	3-1	1-0	7-3	1-1	2-1	0-0	1-0		1-1	2-0
The Wednesday FC	5-1	2-1	4-0	6-0	5-1	5-1	2-1	2-0	1-0	5-0	6-0	3-0	4-0	2-1	4-0	2-0		3-1
Woolwich Arsenal FC	5-1	0-1	1-0	1-1	2-0	2-1	2-0	0-2	2-1	12-0	3-1	3-0	5-0	2-1	3-0	3-1	1-2	

	Division 2	Pd	Wn	Dw	Ls	GF	GA	Pts	
1.	The Wednesday FC (Sheffield)	34	25	4	5	84	22	54	P
2.	Bolton Wanderers FC (Bolton)	34	22	8	4	79	25	52	P
3.	Small Heath FC (Birmingham)	34	20	6	8	78	38	46	
4.	Newton Heath FC (Manchester)	34	20	4	10	63	27	44	
5.	Leicester Fosse FC (Leicester)	34	17	9	8	53	36	43	
6.	Grimsby Town FC (Cleethorpes)	34	17	6	11	67	46	40	
7.	Chesterfield FC (Chesterfield)	34	16	6	12	65	60	38	
8.	Woolwich Arsenal FC (London)	34	16	4	14	61	43	36	
9.	Lincoln City FC (Lincoln)	34	14	8	12	46	43	36	
10.	New Brighton Tower FC (Wallasey)	34	13	9	12	66	58	35	
11.	Burslem Port Vale FC (Burslem)	34	14	6	14	39	49	34	
12.	Walsall FC (Walsall)	34	12	8	14	50	55	32	
13.	Gainsborough Trinity FC (Gainsborough)	34	9	7	18	47	75	25	
14.	Middlesbrough FC (Middlesbrough)	34	8	8	18	39	69	24	
15.	Burton Swifts FC (Burton-upon-Trent)	34	9	6	19	43	84	24	
6.	Barnsley FC (Barnsley)	34	8	7	19	46	79	23	
17.	Luton Town FC (Luton)	34	5	8	21	40	75	18	#
18.	Loughborough Town FC (Loughborough)	34	1	6	27	18	100	8	#
		612	246	120	246	984	984	612	

Loughborough Town FC (Loughborough) and Luton Town FC (Luton) were not re-elected to the league for next season and were replaced by Blackpool FC (Blackpool) and Stockport County FC (Stockport).

F.A. CUP FINAL   (Crystal Palace, London – 21/04/1900 – 68,945)

BURY FC (BURY)   4-0   Southampton FC (Southampton)

McLuckie 2, Wood, Plant

Bury: Thompson, Darroch, Davidson, Pray, Leeming, Ross, Richards, Wood, McLuckie, Sagar, Plant.

Southampton: Robinson, Meehan, Durber, Meston, Chadwick, Petrie, Turner, Yates, Farrell, Wood, Milward.

Semi-finals

Nottingham Forest FC (Nottingham)	1-1 (aet), 2-3 (aet)	Bury FC (Bury)
Southampton FC (Southampton)	0-0 (aet), 3-0	Millwall Athletic FC (London)

Quarter-finals

Millwall Athletic FC (London)	1-1 (aet), 0-0 (aet), 2-1	Aston Villa FC (Birmingham)
Preston North End FC (Preston)	0-0 (aet), 0-1	Nottingham Forest FC (Nottingham)
Sheffield United FC (Sheffield)	2-2 (aet), 0-2	Bury FC (Bury)
Southampton FC (Southampton)	2-1	West Bromwich Albion FC (West Bromwich)

1900-01

Football League Division 1 1900-1901 Season	Aston Villa	Blackburn Rovers	Bolton Wanderers	Bury	Derby County	Everton	Liverpool	Manchester City	Newcastle United	Nottingham Forest	Notts County	Preston North End	Sheffield United	Stoke	Sunderland	Wednesday	W.B.A.	Wolves
Aston Villa FC		3-3	3-0	1-0	2-1	1-2	0-2	7-1	2-2	2-1	1-2	4-0	0-0	2-0	2-2	2-1	0-1	0-0
Blackburn Rovers FC	2-2		2-0	0-2	1-0	2-1	3-1	1-0	0-0	1-3	0-2	3-1	1-0	3-2	0-1	2-2	1-1	2-0
Bolton Wanderers FC	1-0	1-0		3-2	0-1	1-0	1-0	0-0	3-2	4-2	0-1	1-1	0-0	1-0	0-0	1-1	3-2	1-0
Bury FC	3-1	0-1	3-0		2-1	3-0	0-0	4-0	1-0	0-1	1-0	2-1	1-1	3-2	0-0	2-0	6-1	0-1
Derby County FC	3-0	4-0	4-2	5-2		0-1	2-3	2-0	1-1	0-0	2-1	0-0	4-0	4-1	1-1	3-1	4-0	4-5
Everton FC	2-1	0-0	2-3	3-3	2-0		1-1	5-2	0-1	4-1	0-1	4-1	3-1	3-1	1-0	1-1	1-0	5-1
Liverpool FC	5-1	3-0	2-1	1-0	0-0	1-2		3-1	3-0	2-0	1-0	3-2	1-2	3-1	1-2	1-1	5-0	1-0
Manchester City FC	4-0	1-3	1-1	1-0	2-0	1-0	3-4		2-1	1-0	2-0	3-1	2-1	2-0	1-1	2-2	1-0	3-2
Newcastle United FC	3-0	1-0	3-0	0-0	2-1	1-0	1-1	2-1		0-0	2-0	3-5	3-0	2-1	0-2	0-0	1-1	3-1
Nottingham Forest FC	3-1	0-1	3-0	1-1	1-0	2-1	0-0	4-2	1-2		5-0	4-1	2-0	1-1	0-0	1-0	2-3	2-1
Notts County FC	2-0	2-1	3-1	1-0	2-1	3-2	3-0	0-0	3-1	1-0		6-1	2-4	2-4	2-2	2-0	1-0	4-1
Preston North End FC	0-2	4-1	1-3	3-1	3-2	1-2	2-2	0-4	0-1	1-1	0-1		3-1	4-2	1-1	3-2	2-3	1-1
Sheffield United FC	2-2	2-1	0-2	0-3	2-1	2-1	0-2	1-1	2-0	0-1	4-2	2-1		0-4	2-0	1-0	1-1	1-1
Stoke FC	0-0	2-0	2-1	1-2	0-1	0-2	1-2	2-1	2-0	0-3	1-1	5-0	0-1		0-0	2-1	2-0	3-0
Sunderland AFC	0-0	2-0	5-1	4-1	2-1	2-0	0-1	3-0	1-1	0-1	1-1	3-1	3-0	6-1		1-0	3-0	7-2
The Wednesday FC	3-2	1-1	1-0	1-2	2-1	3-1	3-2	4-1	2-2	4-1	4-1	0-1	1-0	4-0	1-0		2-1	2-0
West Bromwich Albion FC	0-1	1-1	7-2	1-2	1-1	1-2	0-1	3-2	0-1	1-6	1-0	0-1	0-2	2-2	1-0	1-1		1-2
Wolverhampton Wanderers FC	0-0	2-2	1-1	1-1	0-0	1-1	2-1	1-0	1-0	1-0	3-2	2-2	3-0	0-2	2-2	1-1	0-0	

	Division 1	Pd	Wn	Dw	Ls	GF	GA	Pts	
1.	LIVERPOOL FC (LIVERPOOL)	34	19	7	8	59	35	45	
2.	Sunderland AFC (Sunderland)	34	15	13	6	57	26	43	
3.	Notts County FC (Nottingham)	34	18	4	12	54	46	40	
4.	Nottingham Forest FC (Nottingham)	34	16	7	11	53	36	39	
5.	Bury FC (Bury)	34	16	7	11	53	37	39	
6.	Newcastle United FC (Newcastle-upon-Tyne)	34	14	10	10	42	37	38	
7.	Everton FC (Liverpool)	34	16	5	13	55	42	37	
8.	The Wednesday FC (Sheffield)	34	13	10	11	52	42	36	
9.	Blackburn Rovers FC (Blackburn)	34	12	9	13	39	47	33	
10.	Bolton Wanderers FC (Bolton)	34	13	7	14	39	55	33	
11.	Manchester City FC (Manchester)	34	13	6	15	48	58	32	
12.	Derby County FC (Derby)	34	12	7	15	55	42	31	
13.	Wolverhampton Wanderers FC (Wolverhampton)	34	9	13	12	39	55	31	
14.	Sheffield United FC (Sheffield)	34	12	7	15	35	52	31	
15.	Aston Villa FC (Birmingham)	34	10	10	14	45	51	30	
16.	Stoke FC (Stoke-upon-Trent)	34	11	5	18	46	57	27	
17.	Preston North End FC (Preston)	34	9	7	18	49	75	25	R
18.	West Bromwich Albion FC (West Bromwich)	34	7	8	19	35	62	22	R
		612	235	142	235	855	855	612	

* Burton Swifts FC (Burton-upon-Trent) merged with Burton Wanderers FC (Burton-upon-Trent) as Burton United FC (Burton-upon-Trent) for next season.

Top Goalscorers

1) Stephen BLOOMER   (Derby County FC)   23
2) Samuel RAYBOULD   (Liverpool FC)   17
3) MORRIS   (Notts County FC)   16

Football League Division 2 1900-1901 Season	Barnsley	Blackpool	Burnley	Burslem Port Vale	Burton Swifts	Chesterfield	Gainsborough Trinity	Glossop	Grimsby Town	Leicester Fosse	Lincoln City	Middlesbrough	New Brighton	Newton Heath	Small Heath	Stockport County	Walsall	Woolwich Arsenal
Barnsley FC	■	0-1	2-1	1-3	3-2	4-1	1-3	2-2	2-3	1-0	0-0	3-1	1-1	6-2	1-2	2-0	2-1	3-0
Blackpool FC	1-1	■	0-1	2-1	2-0	1-1	1-1	0-0	0-1	1-0	2-0	3-0	1-2	1-2	0-0	3-0	1-0	1-1
Burnley FC	4-0	4-0	■	1-0	2-1	5-1	2-1	5-1	3-0	0-0	1-0	2-0	2-1	1-0	1-0	3-1	0-0	3-0
Burslem Port Vale FC	3-2	4-0	1-0	■	4-0	5-1	1-1	0-0	0-0	2-0	0-2	1-3	2-0	2-2	0-1	2-2	1-0	
Burton Swifts FC	1-1	1-2	1-0	0-2	■	0-4	1-0	1-3	1-2	0-1	0-0	0-0	1-0	3-1	0-2	3-2	2-1	1-0
Chesterfield FC	1-2	2-0	1-3	1-1	2-0	■	2-2	0-1	3-3	1-0	2-0	2-3	0-1	2-1	1-1	4-2	1-1	0-1
Gainsborough Trinity FC	4-2	1-3	3-0	2-1	2-1	2-3	■	1-1	0-1	0-0	1-1	1-1	4-1	0-1	1-2	2-0	1-0	1-0
Glossop FC	2-1	6-0	0-1	1-2	3-0	1-1	3-1	■	0-0	3-1	2-0	2-0	0-1	1-0	2-0	6-0	2-0	0-1
Grimsby Town FC	1-0	2-0	2-1	6-1	5-2	5-2	0-0	1-0	■	4-1	4-0	2-0	5-2	2-0	1-1	5-1	0-0	1-0
Leicester Fosse FC	2-0	3-1	1-1	0-0	5-2	1-3	1-0	1-2	4-0	■	0-2	1-0	1-1	1-0	1-1	2-2	5-0	1-0
Lincoln City FC	3-0	3-0	2-0	2-2	2-1	2-0	6-0	1-1	0-1	1-0	■	1-2	2-0	3-1	4-0	2-0		3-3
Middlesbrough FC	3-0	3-1	0-0	4-0	3-1	2-0	9-2	2-2	0-0	2-1	2-0	■	2-1	1-2	0-1	2-0	2-1	1-1
New Brighton Tower FC	2-0	0-0	2-1	1-1	1-1	1-1	3-2	1-0	5-0	0-0	2-0	3-1	■	2-0	0-0	3-0	5-1	1-0
Newton Heath FC	1-0	4-0	0-1	4-0	1-1	1-0	0-0	3-0	1-0	2-3	4-1	4-0	1-0	■	0-1	3-1	1-1	1-0
Small Heath FC	3-1	10-1	0-1	2-1	2-0	0-0	6-0	1-0	2-1	0-0	2-0	2-1	4-0	1-0	■	2-0	2-1	2-1
Stockport County FC	2-1	0-1	3-2	1-1	2-0	3-1	1-2	1-3	0-1	3-1	1-0	0-1	0-5	1-0	0-0	■	4-1	3-1
Walsall FC	3-0	1-2	2-0	2-1	1-5	2-2	3-3	2-1	0-0	2-0	3-0	0-0	3-3	1-1	2-2	1-3	■	1-0
Woolwich Arsenal FC	1-2	3-1	3-1	3-0	3-1	1-0	2-1	2-0	1-1	0-0	1-0	2-1	2-1	1-0	2-0	1-1		■

Division 2

		Pd	Wn	Dw	Ls	GF	GA	Pts	
1.	Grimsby Town FC (Cleethorpes)	34	20	9	5	60	33	49	P
2.	Small Heath FC (Birmingham)	34	19	10	5	57	24	48	P
3.	Burnley FC (Burnley)	34	20	4	10	53	29	44	
4.	New Brighton Tower FC (Wallasey)	34	17	8	9	57	38	42	#
5.	Glossop FC (Glossop)	34	15	8	11	51	33	38	
6.	Middlesbrough FC (Middlesbrough)	34	15	7	12	50	40	37	
7.	Woolwich Arsenal FC (London)	34	15	6	13	39	35	36	
8.	Lincoln City FC (Lincoln)	34	13	7	14	43	39	33	
9.	Burslem Port Vale FC (Burslem)	34	11	11	12	45	47	33	
10.	Newton Heath FC (Manchester)	34	14	4	16	42	38	32	
11.	Leicester Fosse FC (Leicester)	34	11	10	13	39	37	32	
12.	Blackpool FC (Blackpool)	34	12	7	15	33	58	31	
13.	Gainsborough Trinity FC (Gainsborough)	34	10	10	14	45	60	30	
14.	Chesterfield FC (Chesterfield)	34	9	10	15	46	58	28	
15.	Barnsley FC (Barnsley)	34	11	5	18	47	60	27	
16.	Walsall FC (Walsall)	34	7	13	14	40	56	27	#
17.	Stockport County FC (Stockport)	34	11	3	20	38	68	25	
18.	Burton Swifts FC (Burton-upon-Trent)	34	8	4	22	34	66	20	*
		612	238	136	238	819	819	612	

New Brighton Tower FC (Wallasey) resigned from the league at the end of the season.
Walsall FC (Walsall) were not re-elected to the league for the next season.

Bristol City FC (Bristol) and Doncaster Rovers FC (Doncaster) were elected to Division 2 for next season.

F.A. CUP FINAL   (Crystal Palace, London – 20/04/1901 – 114,815)

TOTTENHAM HOTSPUR FC (LONDON)	2-2	Sheffield United FC (Sheffield)
Brown 2	*(H.T. 1-1)*	*Priest, Bennett*

Tottenham: Clawley, Erentz. Tait, Morris, Hughes, Jones, Smith, Cameron, Brown, Copeland, Kirwan.
Sheffield United: Foulke, Thickett, Boyle, Johnson, Morren, Needham, Bennett, Field, Hedley, Priest, Lipsham.

F.A. CUP FINAL REPLAY   (Burnden Park, Bolton – 27/04/1901 – 20,470)

TOTTENHAM HOTSPUR FC (LONDON)	3-1	Sheffield United FC (Sheffield)
Cameron, Smith, Brown	*(H.T. 0-1)*	*Priest*

Tottenham: Clawley, Erentz. Tait, Morris, Hughes, Jones, Smith, Cameron, Brown, Copeland, Kirwan.
Sheffield United: Foulke, Thickett, Boyle, Johnson, Morren, Needham, Bennett, Field, Hedley, Priest, Lipsham.

Semi-finals

Sheffield United FC (Sheffield)	2-2, 3-0	Aston Villa FC (Birmingham)
Tottenham Hotspur FC (London)	4-0	West Bromwich Albion FC (West Bromwich)

Quarter-finals

Middlesbrough FC (Middlesbrough)	0-1	West Bromwich Albion FC (West Bromwich)
Reading FC (Reading)	1-1, 0-3	Tottenham Hotspur FC (London)
Small Heath FC (Birmingham)	0-0, 0-1	Aston Villa FC (Birmingham)
Wolverhampton Wanderers FC (Wolverhampton)	0-4	Sheffield United FC (Sheffield)1901-02

1901-02

Football League Division 1 1901-1902 Season	Aston Villa	Blackburn Rovers	Bolton Wanderers	Bury	Derby County	Everton	Grimsby Town	Liverpool	Manchester City	Newcastle United	Nottingham Forest	Notts County	Sheffield United	Small Heath	Stoke	Sunderland	Wednesday	Wolves
Aston Villa FC	■	1-1	1-0	2-0	3-2	1-1	4-1	0-1	2-2	0-0	3-0	2-0	1-2	1-0	0-0	0-1	4-1	2-1
Blackburn Rovers FC	4-0	■	2-0	0-3	3-1	3-1	2-0	1-1	1-4	0-0	1-0	4-2	2-1	3-1	6-1	0-1	2-0	2-0
Bolton Wanderers FC	2-2	4-0	■	2-2	2-1	1-3	4-0	1-0	3-3	3-1	3-0	1-1	1-0	4-0	2-1	0-0	3-1	2-2
Bury FC	0-0	2-0	2-2	■	2-0	1-0	1-1	0-0	3-0	4-0	1-1	3-0	1-2	2-0	4-2	1-0	2-0	2-1
Derby County FC	1-0	1-1	1-2	1-0	■	3-1	2-0	1-1	2-0	1-0	1-1	2-0	3-1	0-0	1-0	1-0	2-2	3-1
Everton FC	2-3	0-2	1-0	1-1	2-0	■	0-1	4-0	3-1	0-0	1-0	0-1	2-1	1-0	1-0	2-0	5-0	6-1
Grimsby Town FC	4-1	2-1	4-1	2-0	1-1	0-2	■	1-1	3-2	3-0	1-0	0-1	1-0	1-2	3-3	3-1	3-0	
Liverpool FC	1-0	1-0	1-1	1-0	0-2	2-2	2-2	■	4-0	0-1	0-2	0-1	1-0	3-1	7-0	0-1	1-2	4-1
Manchester City FC	1-0	1-1	1-0	2-0	0-0	2-0	3-0	2-3	■	2-0	3-1	1-0	4-0	1-4	2-2	0-3	0-3	3-0
Newcastle United FC	2-1	0-3	4-1	1-1	0-1	1-1	5-1	1-0	3-0	■	3-0	8-0	1-1	2-0	5-1	0-1	2-1	3-1
Nottingham Forest FC	1-1	3-0	4-1	2-1	3-1	4-0	0-1	1-1	3-1	0-2	■	1-0	1-1	1-2	2-0	2-1	1-1	2-0
Notts County FC	0-3	3-0	2-1	2-1	3-2	0-2	3-0	2-2	2-0	0-2	3-0	■	4-0	6-1	1-1	2-0	6-1	5-3
Sheffield United FC	6-0	4-1	2-0	3-1	3-0	0-0	2-2	2-1	5-0	1-0	2-2	3-0	■	1-4	1-1	0-1	3-0	0-0
Small Heath FC	0-2	2-0	2-0	1-0	5-1	0-1	6-0	0-0	1-0	3-1	1-1	0-0	5-1	■	1-1	2-3	1-1	1-2
Stoke FC	1-0	2-2	4-0	1-2	1-1	1-2	2-0	1-0	3-0	0-0	1-1	3-0	3-2	1-0	■	3-0	1-2	3-0
Sunderland AFC	1-0	3-2	2-1	3-0	1-0	2-4	3-1	1-1	1-0	0-0	4-0	2-1	3-1	1-1	2-0	■	1-2	2-0
The Wednesday FC	1-0	0-1	5-1	4-1	2-0	1-1	3-1	1-1	2-1	0-0	0-2	4-0	1-0	1-2	3-1	1-1	■	1-1
Wolverhampton Wanderers FC	0-2	3-1	1-2	1-0	0-0	2-1	2-0	3-1	0-0	3-0	2-0	3-1	1-1	2-1	4-1	4-2	1-0	■

Division 1

	Division 1	Pd	Wn	Dw	Ls	GF	GA	Pts	
1.	SUNDERLAND AFC (SUNDERLAND)	34	19	6	9	50	35	44	
2.	Everton FC (Liverpool)	34	17	7	10	53	35	41	
3.	Newcastle United FC (Newcastle-upon-Tyne)	34	14	9	11	48	34	37	
4.	Blackburn Rovers FC (Blackburn)	34	15	6	13	52	48	36	
5.	Nottingham Forest FC (Nottingham)	34	13	9	12	43	43	35	
6.	Derby County FC (Derby)	34	13	9	12	39	41	35	
7.	Bury FC (Bury)	34	13	8	13	44	38	34	
8.	Aston Villa FC (Birmingham)	34	13	8	13	42	40	34	
9.	The Wednesday FC (Sheffield)	34	13	8	13	48	52	34	
10.	Sheffield United FC (Sheffield)	34	13	7	14	53	48	33	
11.	Liverpool FC (Liverpool)	34	10	12	12	42	38	32	
12.	Bolton Wanderers FC (Bolton)	34	12	8	14	51	56	32	
13.	Notts County FC (Nottingham)	34	14	4	16	51	57	32	
14.	Wolverhampton Wanderers FC (Wolverhampton)	34	13	6	15	46	57	32	
15.	Grimsby Town FC (Cleethorpes)	34	13	6	15	44	60	32	
16.	Stoke FC (Stoke-upon-Trent)	34	11	9	14	45	55	31	
17.	Small Heath FC (Birmingham)	34	11	8	15	47	45	30	R
18.	Manchester City FC (Manchester)	34	11	6	22	42	58	28	R
		612	238	136	238	840	840	612	

Top Goalscorer

1) James SETTLE   (Everton FC)   18

Football League Division 2 1901-1902 Season	Barnsley	Blackpool	Bristol City	Burnley	Burslem Port Vale	Burton United	Chesterfield	Doncaster Rovers	Gainsborough Trinity	Glossop	Leicester Fosse	Lincoln City	Middlesbrough	Newton Heath	Preston North End	Stockport County	W.B.A.	Woolwich Arsenal
Barnsley FC		2-0	2-2	2-2	4-0	3-2	3-2	3-0	2-0	1-4	2-3	2-2	2-7	3-2	0-4	3-1	0-2	2-0
Blackpool FC	2-1		0-2	2-1	1-0	1-0	0-0	3-1	3-0	1-1	4-0	3-0	0-2	2-4	1-4	1-0	2-2	1-3
Bristol City FC	3-1	3-0		1-0	4-0	0-2	5-2	3-0	4-0	2-0	2-1	1-1	1-0	4-0	2-0	3-0	1-2	0-3
Burnley FC	2-0	2-0	0-1		4-1	0-0	0-0	7-0	6-0	1-1	1-0	1-0	2-2	1-0	0-3	3-0	0-0	0-0
Burslem Port Vale FC	2-1	0-1	3-0	1-1		2-1	4-2	2-2	1-1	1-0	3-0	1-2	1-1	1-1	0-0	1-1	2-3	1-0
Burton United FC	2-1	1-1	2-2	5-2	3-0		0-1	1-1	5-0	1-1	2-0	0-6	3-2	0-0	1-1	3-2	1-3	2-0
Chesterfield FC	1-2	3-1	1-0	3-0	4-3	3-1		0-0	2-0	1-0	3-3	0-1	0-0	3-0	2-0	8-1	0-3	1-3
Doncaster Rovers FC	0-1	4-3	3-0	3-0	3-3	2-0	4-1		3-0	1-2	2-1	1-0	0-0	4-0	4-0	2-0	2-0	1-0
Gainsborough Trinity FC	0-0	3-0	2-0	1-1	2-3	1-4	0-0	4-1		2-1	3-3	2-2	1-4	1-1	0-1	1-1	1-1	2-2
Glossop FC	1-1	3-1	1-2	0-0	0-1	2-1	3-1	3-1	0-0		1-1	1-1	1-0	0-0	3-1	2-1	1-2	0-1
Leicester Fosse FC	2-0	1-0	0-1	2-1	0-1	4-0	3-0	1-0	2-0	1-1		3-1	0-2	3-2	1-0	1-1	0-3	2-1
Lincoln City FC	1-1	0-0	1-0	1-0	1-1	0-0	4-0	0-0	3-0	1-0	2-0		2-1	2-0	2-1	5-0	1-0	0-0
Middlesbrough FC	2-1	2-1	2-0	3-0	3-0	5-0	7-1	6-0	3-1	5-0	5-0	0-0		5-0	2-1	6-0	1-2	1-0
Newton Heath FC	1-0	0-1	1-0	2-0	1-0	3-1	2-0	6-0	3-0	1-0	2-0	0-0	1-2		0-2	3-3	1-2	0-1
Preston North End FC	4-0	1-1	0-0	3-1	2-0	1-0	5-0	3-0	4-1	2-2	5-0	8-0	0-3	5-1		4-0	1-2	2-0
Stockport County FC	2-3	3-1	1-1	1-2	4-2	2-0	3-0	1-2	2-1	0-0	2-0	2-1	1-3	1-0	0-2		0-2	0-0
West Bromwich Albion FC	3-1	7-2	2-2	3-0	3-1	2-1	4-0	2-2	7-0	0-1	1-0	4-1	2-0	4-0	3-1	3-0		2-1
Woolwich Arsenal FC	2-1	0-0	2-0	4-0	3-1	0-1	3-2	1-0	5-0	4-0	2-0	0-3	2-0	2-0	0-0	3-0	2-1	

Division 2

		Pd	Wn	Dw	Ls	GF	GA	Pts	
1.	West Bromwich Albion FC (West Bromwich)	34	25	5	4	82	29	55	P
2.	Middlesbrough FC (Middlesbrough)	34	23	5	6	90	24	51	P
3.	Preston North End FC (Preston)	34	18	6	10	71	32	42	
4.	Woolwich Arsenal FC (London)	34	18	6	10	50	26	42	
5.	Lincoln City FC (Lincoln)	34	14	13	7	45	35	41	
6.	Bristol City FC (Bristol)	34	17	6	11	52	35	40	
7.	Doncaster Rovers FC (Doncaster)	34	13	8	13	49	58	34	
8.	Glossop FC (Glossop)	34	10	12	12	36	40	32	
9.	Burnley FC (Burnley)	34	10	10	14	41	45	30	
10.	Burton United FC (Burton-upon-Trent)	34	11	8	15	46	54	30	
11.	Barnsley FC (Barnsley)	34	12	6	16	51	63	30	
12.	Burslem Port Vale FC (Burslem)	34	10	9	15	43	59	29	
13.	Blackpool FC (Blackpool)	34	11	7	16	40	56	29	
14.	Leicester Fosse FC (Leicester)	34	12	5	17	38	56	29	
15.	Newton Heath FC (Manchester)	34	11	6	17	38	53	28	*
16.	Chesterfield FC (Chesterfield)	34	11	6	17	47	68	28	
17.	Stockport County FC (Stockport)	34	8	7	19	36	72	23	
18.	Gainsborough Trinity FC (Gainsborough)	34	4	11	19	30	80	19	
		612	238	136	238	885	885	612	

* Newton Heath FC (Manchester) were declared bankrupt and re-formed as Manchester United FC (Manchester)

F.A. CUP FINAL   (Crystal Palace, London – 19/04/1902 – 76,914)

SHEFFIELD UNITED FC (SHEFFIELD)   1-1   Southampton FC (Southampton)

Common   *(H.T. 0-0)*   *Wood*

Sheffield: Foulke, Thickett, Boyle, Johnson, Wilkinson, Needham, Bennett, Common, Hedley, Priest, Lipsham.

Southampton: Robinson, Fry, Molyneux, Meston, Bowman, Lee, A.Turner, Wood, Brown, Chadwick, J.Turner.

F.A. CUP FINAL REPLAY   (Crystal Palace, London – 26/04/1902 – 33,068)

SHEFFIELD UNITED FC (SHEFFIELD)   2-1   Southampton FC (Southampton)

Hedley, Barnes   *(H.T. 1-0)*   *Brown*

Sheffield: Foulke, Thickett, Boyle, Johnson, Wilkinson, Needham, Barnes, Common, Hedley, Priest, Lipsham.

Southampton: Robinson, Fry, Molyneux, Meston, Bowman, Lee, A.Turner, Wood, Brown, Chadwick, J.Turner.

Semi-finals

Sheffield United FC (Sheffield)	1-1, 1-1 (aet), 1-0	Derby County FC (Derby)
Southampton FC (Southampton)	3-1	Nottingham Forest FC (Nottingham)

Quarter-finals

Bury FC (Bury)	2-3	Southampton FC (Southampton)
Derby County FC (Derby)	0-0, 6-3	Portsmouth FC (Portsmouth)
Newcastle United FC (Newcastle-upon-Tyne)	1-1, 1-2	Sheffield United FC (Sheffield)
Nottingham Forest FC (Nottingham)	2-0	Stoke FC (Stoke-upon-Trent)

1902-03

Football League Division 1 1902-1903 Season	Aston Villa	Blackburn Rovers	Bolton Wanderers	Bury	Derby County	Everton	Grimsby Town	Liverpool	Middlesbrough	Newcastle United	Nottingham Forest	Notts County	Sheffield United	Stoke	Sunderland	Wednesday	W.B.A.	Wolves
Aston Villa FC		5-0	4-2	2-2	0-0	2-1	2-2	1-2	5-0	7-0	3-1	2-1	4-2	2-0	0-1	1-0	0-3	3-1
Blackburn Rovers FC	0-2		4-2	0-3	2-4	3-2	2-0	3-1	0-1	3-1	2-2	1-2	2-0	1-1	0-2	2-1	1-0	1-0
Bolton Wanderers FC	0-1	1-2		1-0	2-0	1-3	0-1	1-1	2-1	0-2	1-1	0-1	1-0	2-3	2-0	0-2	0-1	4-1
Bury FC	0-1	1-1	3-0		1-0	4-2	2-1	3-1	3-1	1-0	3-1	3-1	3-1	2-1	3-1	4-0	1-2	4-0
Derby County FC	2-0	1-0	5-0	2-0		0-1	2-2	2-1	3-2	0-0	0-1	4-1	1-0	2-0	5-2	1-0	1-0	3-1
Everton FC	0-1	0-3	3-1	3-0	2-1		4-2	3-1	3-0	0-1	1-1	2-0	1-0	0-1	0-3	1-1	3-1	2-1
Grimsby Town FC	0-2	4-1	1-1	2-1	4-1	0-0		3-1	2-2	1-0	0-1	1-1	1-2	2-2	2-4	0-1	4-0	1-2
Liverpool FC	2-1	5-2	5-1	2-0	3-1	0-0	9-2		5-0	3-0	2-1	0-2	2-4	1-1	1-1	4-2	0-2	4-1
Middlesbrough FC	1-2	4-0	4-3	1-1	3-1	1-0	2-0	0-2		1-0	2-0	2-1	0-2	1-1	0-1	2-1	1-1	2-0
Newcastle United FC	2-0	1-0	2-0	1-0	2-1	3-0	1-0	1-2	0-1		0-2	6-1	0-0	5-0	1-0	3-0	1-0	2-4
Nottingham Forest FC	2-0	2-0	1-2	3-0	2-3	2-2	2-1	1-0	1-0	3-2		0-0	2-2	1-3	5-2	1-4	3-1	2-0
Notts County FC	2-1	4-0	1-3	1-0	2-1	2-0	0-1	1-2	2-0	2-2	1-1		1-1	3-0	0-0	0-3	3-1	0-0
Sheffield United FC	2-4	2-1	7-1	1-0	3-2	0-2	3-0	2-0	1-3	2-1	2-0	3-0		1-3	1-0	2-3	1-2	3-0
Stoke FC	1-0	0-2	2-0	1-0	2-0	2-0	1-1	1-0	0-2	5-0	3-2	0-2	0-1		1-1	4-0	3-0	3-0
Sunderland AFC	1-0	2-2	3-1	3-1	2-0	2-1	5-1	2-1	2-1	0-0	0-1	2-1	0-0	0-0		0-1	0-0	3-0
The Wednesday FC	4-0	0-0	3-0	2-0	0-1	4-1	1-1	3-1	2-0	3-0	1-0	2-0	0-1	1-0	1-0		3-1	1-1
West Bromwich Albion FC	1-2	5-3	2-1	1-3	3-0	2-1	1-0	1-2	1-0	6-1	2-0	3-2	3-3	2-1	0-3	2-3		2-2
Wolverhampton Wanderers FC	2-1	2-0	3-1	3-2	3-0	1-1	3-0	0-2	2-0	3-0	2-1	2-0	1-3	1-0	3-3	2-1	1-2	

	Division 1	Pd	Wn	Dw	Ls	GF	GA	Pts	
1.	THE WEDNESDAY FC (SHEFFIELD)	34	19	4	11	54	36	42	
2.	Aston Villa FC (Birmingham)	34	19	3	12	61	40	41	
3.	Sunderland AFC (Sunderland)	34	16	9	9	51	36	41	
4.	Sheffield United FC (Sheffield)	34	17	5	12	58	44	39	
5.	Liverpool FC (Liverpool)	34	17	4	13	68	49	38	
6.	Stoke FC (Stoke-upon-Trent)	34	15	7	12	46	38	37	
7.	West Bromwich Albion FC (West Bromwich)	34	16	4	14	54	53	36	
8.	Bury FC (Bury)	34	16	3	15	54	43	35	
9.	Derby County FC (Derby)	34	16	3	15	50	47	35	
10.	Nottingham Forest FC (Nottingham)	34	14	7	13	49	47	35	
11.	Wolverhampton Wanderers FC (Wolverhampton)	34	14	5	15	48	57	33	
12.	Everton FC (Liverpool)	34	13	6	15	45	47	32	
13.	Middlesbrough FC (Middlesbrough)	34	14	4	16	41	50	32	
14.	Newcastle United FC (Newcastle-upon-Tyne)	34	14	4	16	41	51	32	
15.	Notts County FC (Nottingham)	34	12	7	15	41	49	31	
16.	Blackburn Rovers FC (Blackburn)	34	12	5	17	44	63	29	
17.	Grimsby Town FC (Cleethorpes)	34	8	9	17	43	62	25	R
18.	Bolton Wanderers FC (Bolton)	34	8	3	23	37	73	19	R
		612	260	92	260	885	885	612	

Top Goalscorer

1)   Sam RAYBOULD   (Liverpool FC)   31

Football League Division 2 — 1902-1903 Season

	Barnsley	Blackpool	Bristol City	Burnley	Burslem Port Vale	Burton United	Chesterfield	Doncaster Rovers	Gainsborough Trinity	Glossop	Leicester Fosse	Lincoln City	Manchester City	Manchester United	Preston North End	Small Heath	Stockport County	Woolwich Arsenal
Barnsley FC	■	6-0	2-0	3-0	1-0	4-0	2-2	2-0	2-3	0-1	1-2	0-0	0-3	0-0	3-0	3-0	2-1	1-1
Blackpool FC	3-3	■	0-1	2-0	2-5	3-3	2-1	4-0	4-0	2-2	2-0	2-3	0-3	2-0	2-2	0-1	2-0	0-0
Bristol City FC	3-3	0-1	■	3-0	3-0	3-1	2-1	4-2	1-0	1-1	6-1	0-2	3-2	3-1	2-1	1-1	7-1	1-0
Burnley FC	1-2	1-1	0-0	■	3-3	4-1	1-1	1-1	3-2	2-1	1-3	1-0	1-1	0-2	1-1	2-1	3-2	0-3
Burslem Port Vale FC	2-0	1-1	2-0	3-1	■	4-2	2-1	3-0	3-1	1-0	2-0	5-1	1-4	1-1	0-0	2-2	3-1	1-1
Burton United FC	1-1	2-0	0-3	0-0	0-0	■	1-0	1-0	2-1	2-3	2-2	0-5	3-1	2-1	0-1	5-1	2-1	
Chesterfield FC	3-0	1-1	3-0	2-0	3-0	1-0	■	1-1	0-1	10-0	5-0	1-0	0-1	2-0	4-2	1-1	4-1	2-2
Doncaster Rovers FC	2-0	3-0	0-0	2-1	3-2	1-1	3-4	■	0-0	4-1	0-0	2-1	1-2	2-2	1-2	1-0	2-0	0-1
Gainsborough Trinity FC	1-2	0-0	2-1	3-0	1-1	3-1	3-2	3-0	■	1-1	5-1	4-0	0-3	0-1	1-0	1-0	0-0	0-1
Glossop FC	2-2	1-0	0-2	2-0	2-1	3-0	0-3	3-0	4-2	■	1-2	2-0	0-1	1-3	1-0	3-1	1-2	
Leicester Fosse FC	1-2	2-1	2-2	2-1	2-0	0-1	0-2	0-1	4-1	3-2	■	0-0	1-1	1-1	1-1	1-3	0-2	0-2
Lincoln City FC	1-3	0-2	1-1	4-1	4-1	4-0	0-0	4-2	1-0	1-0	1-2	■	1-0	1-3	2-3	0-1	3-1	2-2
Manchester City FC	3-2	2-0	2-2	6-0	7-1	2-0	4-2	4-1	9-0	5-2	3-1	3-1	■	0-2	1-0	4-0	5-0	4-1
Manchester United FC	2-1	2-2	1-2	4-0	2-1	1-0	2-1	4-0	3-1	1-1	5-1	1-2	1-1	■	0-1	0-1	0-0	3-0
Preston North End FC	3-0	3-1	1-0	5-0	5-1	1-1	1-1	5-0	0-0	0-0	2-0	0-1	0-2	3-1	■	2-1	6-1	2-2
Small Heath FC	2-1	5-1	2-0	3-0	5-1	2-0	2-1	12-0	1-0	3-1	4-3	3-1	4-0	2-1	3-1	■	2-0	2-0
Stockport County FC	4-1	4-0	0-1	3-0	0-4	0-2	2-2	1-0	1-1	2-3	2-2	3-1	0-2	2-1	1-1	1-2	■	0-1
Woolwich Arsenal FC	4-0	2-1	2-1	5-1	3-0	3-0	3-0	3-0	6-1	0-0	0-0	2-1	1-0	0-1	3-1	6-1	3-1	■

44

	Division 2	Pd	Wn	Dw	Ls	GF	GA	Pts	
1.	Manchester City FC (Manchester)	34	25	4	5	95	29	54	P
2.	Small Heath FC (Birmingham)	34	24	3	7	74	36	51	P
3.	Woolwich Arsenal FC (London)	34	20	8	6	66	30	48	
4.	Bristol City FC (Bristol)	34	17	8	9	59	38	42	
5.	Manchester United FC (Manchester)	34	15	8	11	53	38	38	
6.	Chesterfield FC (Chesterfield)	34	14	9	11	67	40	37	
7.	Preston North End FC (Preston)	34	13	10	11	56	40	36	
8.	Barnsley FC (Barnsley)	34	13	8	13	55	51	34	
9.	Burslem Port Vale FC (Burslem)	34	13	8	13	57	62	34	
10.	Lincoln City FC (Lincoln)	34	12	6	16	46	53	30	
11.	Glossop FC (Glossop)	34	11	7	16	43	58	29	
12.	Gainsborough Trinity FC (Gainsborough)	34	11	7	16	41	59	29	
13.	Burton United FC (Burton-upon-Trent)	34	11	7	16	39	59	29	
14.	Blackpool FC (Blackpool)	34	9	10	15	44	59	28	
15.	Leicester Fosse FC (Leicester)	34	10	8	16	41	65	28	
16.	Doncaster Rovers FC (Doncaster)	34	9	7	18	35	72	25	#
17.	Stockport County FC (Stockport)	34	7	6	21	39	74	20	
18.	Burnley FC (Burnley)	34	6	8	20	30	77	20	
		612	240	132	240	940	940	612	

Doncaster Rovers FC (Doncaster) were not re-elected to the league for the next season and were replaced in Division 2 by Bradford City AFC (Bradford).

F.A. CUP FINAL   (Crystal Palace, London – 18/04/1903 – 63,102)

BURY FC (BURY)	6-0	Derby County FC (Derby)

Ross, Sagar, Leeming 2, Wood, Plant   *(H.T. 1-0)*

Bury: Monteith, Lindsay, McEwen, Johnston, Thorpe, Ross, W.Richards, Wood, Sagar, Leeming, Plant.

Derby: Fryer, Methven, Morris, Warren, Goodall, May, Warrington, York, Boag, G. Richards, Davis.

Semi-finals

Aston Villa FC (Birmingham)	0-3	Bury FC (Bury)
Derby County FC (Derby)	3-0	Millwall Athletic FC (London)

Quarter-finals

Bury FC (Bury)	1-0	Notts County FC (Nottingham)
Derby County FC (Derby)	3-0	Stoke FC (Stoke-upon-Trent)
Millwall Athletic FC (London)	1-0	Everton FC (Liverpool)
Tottenham Hotspur FC (London)	2-3	Aston Villa FC (Birmingham)

1903-04

Football League Division 1 1903-1904 Season	Aston Villa	Blackburn Rovers	Bury	Derby County	Everton	Liverpool	Manchester City	Middlesbrough	Newcastle United	Nottingham Forest	Notts County	Sheffield United	Small Heath	Stoke	Sunderland	Wednesday	W.B.A.	Wolves
Aston Villa FC	■	2-3	0-2	3-0	3-1	2-1	0-1	2-1	3-1	3-1	4-0	6-1	1-1	3-1	2-0	2-1	3-1	2-0
Blackburn Rovers FC	0-3	■	2-2	2-1	0-2	2-3	2-5	1-1	4-0	3-1	3-0	3-0	1-1	2-0	1-3	0-0	2-0	1-1
Bury FC	2-2	3-0	■	2-2	0-0	2-2	1-3	1-1	0-3	2-2	3-0	0-1	1-0	2-2	3-1	1-0	2-1	0-0
Derby County FC	2-2	3-0	2-2	■	0-1	2-0	2-3	2-2	1-3	2-6	0-1	3-5	4-1	5-0	7-2	0-2	4-2	2-1
Everton FC	1-0	3-1	2-1	0-1	■	5-2	1-0	2-0	4-1	0-2	3-1	2-0	5-1	0-1	0-1	2-0	4-0	2-0
Liverpool FC	1-1	1-2	3-0	3-1	2-2	■	2-2	1-0	1-0	0-0	2-1	3-0	0-2	0-0	2-1	1-3	1-3	1-2
Manchester City FC	1-0	1-0	3-0	2-1	1-3	3-2	■	1-1	1-3	0-0	3-0	0-1	4-0	2-2	2-1	1-1	6-3	4-1
Middlesbrough FC	2-1	0-2	1-0	0-0	3-0	1-0	6-0	■	1-3	1-1	1-0	4-1	3-1	2-0	2-3	0-1	2-2	1-2
Newcastle United FC	1-1	2-1	3-2	0-0	1-0	1-1	1-0	2-1	■	3-1	4-1	0-1	3-1	1-0	1-3	4-0	1-0	3-0
Nottingham Forest FC	3-7	0-1	2-2	5-1	0-4	2-1	0-3	1-1	1-0	■	0-1	1-1	0-1	4-2	3-0	0-1	2-0	5-0
Notts County FC	0-0	4-2	0-0	2-2	0-3	4-2	0-3	3-2	3-2	1-3	■	2-1	2-0	1-0	2-1	1-0	2-3	0-2
Sheffield United FC	1-2	2-2	0-0	3-2	2-1	2-1	5-3	3-0	2-2	2-0	3-1	■	1-1	1-1	1-2	1-1	4-0	7-2
Small Heath FC	2-2	2-1	1-0	1-0	1-1	1-2	0-3	2-2	3-0	3-3	2-0	1-3	■	1-0	2-1	0-0	0-1	3-0
Stoke FC	2-0	6-2	4-1	1-1	2-3	5-2	1-2	0-0	2-3	2-3	0-2	3-4	1-0	■	3-1	3-1	5-0	5-1
Sunderland AFC	6-1	2-0	6-0	0-3	2-0	1-1	1-1	3-1	1-1	3-1	4-1	2-1	3-1	3-0	■	0-1	1-1	2-1
The Wednesday FC	4-2	3-1	1-1	1-0	1-0	2-1	1-0	4-1	1-1	2-1	2-0	3-0	3-2	1-0	0-0	■	1-0	4-0
West Bromwich Albion FC	1-3	2-1	3-2	0-0	0-0	2-2	2-1	0-0	1-2	1-1	0-2	2-2	0-1	3-0	1-1	0-1	■	1-2
Wolverhampton Wanderers FC	3-2	1-0	0-0	2-2	2-2	4-2	1-6	2-2	3-2	3-2	1-1	1-0	1-0	0-0	2-1	2-1	1-0	■

Division 1

		Pd	Wn	Dw	Ls	GF	GA	Pts	
1.	THE WEDNESDAY FC (SHEFFIELD)	34	20	7	7	48	28	47	
2.	Manchester City FC (Manchester)	34	19	6	9	71	45	44	
3.	Everton FC (Liverpool)	34	19	5	10	59	32	43	
4.	Newcastle United FC (Newcastle-upon-Tyne)	34	18	6	10	58	45	42	
5.	Aston Villa FC (Birmingham)	34	17	7	10	70	48	41	
6.	Sunderland AFC (Sunderland)	34	17	5	12	63	49	39	
7.	Sheffield United FC (Sheffield)	34	15	8	11	62	57	38	
8.	Wolverhampton Wanderers FC (Wolverhampton)	34	14	8	12	44	66	36	
9.	Nottingham Forest FC (Nottingham)	34	11	9	14	57	57	31	
10.	Middlesbrough FC (Middlesbrough)	34	9	12	13	46	47	30	
11.	Small Heath FC (Birmingham)	34	11	8	15	39	52	30	
12.	Bury FC (Bury)	34	7	15	12	40	53	29	
13.	Notts County FC (Nottingham)	34	12	5	17	37	61	29	
14.	Derby County FC (Derby)	34	9	10	15	58	60	28	
15.	Blackburn Rovers FC (Blackburn)	34	11	6	17	48	60	28	
16.	Stoke FC (Stoke-upon-Trent)	34	10	7	17	54	57	27	
17.	Liverpool FC (Liverpool)	34	9	8	17	49	62	26	R
18.	West Bromwich Albion FC (West Bromwich)	34	7	10	17	36	60	24	R
		612	235	142	235	939	939	612	

Top Goalscorer

1) Stephen BLOOMER   (Derby County FC)   20

Football League Division 2 1903-1904 Season	Barnsley	Blackpool	Bolton Wanderers	Bradford City	Bristol City	Burnley	Burslem Port Vale	Burton United	Chesterfield	Gainsborough Trinity	Glossop	Grimsby Town	Leicester Fosse	Lincoln City	Manchester United	Preston North End	Stockport County	Woolwich Arsenal
Barnsley FC	■	2-2	1-0	1-2	2-0	1-1	1-0	2-1	0-0	2-0	4-0	3-1	1-1	2-1	0-2	1-0	0-0	2-1
Blackpool FC	0-2	■	1-4	0-1	0-1	0-5	1-0	4-1	0-0	2-1	3-2	3-0	1-2	2-1	2-1	0-3	4-1	2-2
Bolton Wanderers FC	5-1	3-0	■	1-0	1-1	1-1	5-0	3-0	4-0	5-0	0-1	4-0	3-1	1-2	0-0	0-2	0-1	2-1
Bradford City AFC	3-1	0-2	3-3	■	1-0	3-0	1-1	3-0	2-6	1-3	2-1	1-0	4-0	2-1	3-3	1-1	0-0	0-3
Bristol City FC	2-0	5-0	2-0	1-1	■	6-0	2-1	4-0	3-2	2-1	5-0	4-0	4-0	3-1	1-1	3-1	6-0	0-4
Burnley FC	2-2	1-4	0-0	3-2	2-3	■	1-0	2-1	2-1	2-0	2-4	2-0	2-1	3-1	2-0	2-1	2-0	1-0
Burslem Port Vale FC	3-0	5-0	2-3	5-2	3-1	2-2	■	3-1	3-0	3-0	1-1	1-2	6-2	2-2	1-0	0-1	2-0	2-3
Burton United FC	1-1	1-1	2-1	0-2	2-3	1-2	0-0	■	4-0	2-1	2-0	1-0	0-0	5-2	2-2		7-0	3-1
Chesterfield FC	1-0	2-1	1-1	1-1	1-0	0-0	1-1	2-1	■	6-1	0-0	0-1	2-0	0-1	0-2	0-1	4-1	1-0
Gainsborough Trinity FC	4-2	3-1	3-1	3-0	3-1	1-2	3-0	1-2	1-0	■	0-1	4-2	4-0	0-0	0-1	2-0	2-2	0-2
Glossop FC	7-0	0-1	3-3	2-0	1-1	6-2	4-1	0-1	0-2	0-2	■	1-1	5-0	5-0	0-5	2-2	5-1	1-3
Grimsby Town FC	5-1	4-0	0-0	2-0	2-0	0-0	3-1	4-0	3-1	2-0		■	4-3	1-1	3-1	1-1	2-1	2-2
Leicester Fosse FC	2-0	5-1	2-2	1-2	1-0	0-0	1-1	1-3	0-0	2-2	4-2	1-1	■	2-2	0-1	1-4	3-0	0-0
Lincoln City FC	0-0	0-0	1-0	1-0	2-6	3-1	3-2	1-0	0-2	0-1	3-1	2-1	6-1	■	0-0	0-0	3-1	0-2
Manchester United FC	4-0	3-1	0-0	3-1	2-2	3-1	2-0	2-0	3-1	4-2	3-1	2-0	5-2	2-0	■	0-2	3-1	1-0
Preston North End FC	1-1	1-0	3-1	4-0	3-0	2-0	3-1	4-0	2-1	2-0	3-0	2-0	4-3	2-1	1-1	■	1-1	0-0
Stockport County FC	2-2	2-1	3-2	2-0	1-1	2-2	1-1	1-1	2-0	1-4	3-0	1-1	2-0	4-0	0-3	1-5	■	0-0
Woolwich Arsenal FC	3-0	3-0	3-0	4-1	2-0	4-0	0-0	8-0	6-0	6-0	2-1	5-1	8-0	4-0	4-0	0-0	5-2	■

	Division 2	Pd	Wn	Dw	Ls	GF	GA	Pts	
1.	Preston North End FC (Preston)	34	20	10	4	62	24	50	P
2.	Woolwich Arsenal FC (London)	34	21	7	6	91	22	49	P
3.	Manchester United FC (Manchester)	34	20	8	6	65	33	48	
4.	Bristol City FC (Bristol)	34	18	6	10	73	41	42	
5.	Burnley FC (Burnley)	34	15	9	10	50	55	39	
6.	Grimsby Town FC (Cleethorpes)	34	14	8	12	50	49	36	
7.	Bolton Wanderers FC (Bolton)	34	12	10	12	59	41	34	
8.	Barnsley FC (Barnsley)	34	11	10	13	38	57	32	
9.	Gainsborough Trinity FC (Gainsborough)	34	14	3	17	53	60	31	
10.	Bradford City AFC (Bradford)	34	12	7	15	45	59	31	
11.	Chesterfield FC (Chesterfield)	34	11	8	15	37	45	30	
12.	Lincoln City FC (Lincoln)	34	11	8	15	41	58	30	
13.	Burslem Port Vale FC (Burslem)	34	10	9	15	54	52	29	
14.	Burton United FC (Burton-upon-Trent)	34	11	7	16	45	61	29	
15.	Blackpool FC (Blackpool)	34	11	5	18	40	67	27	
16.	Stockport County FC (Stockport)	34	8	11	15	40	72	27	#
17.	Glossop FC (Glossop)	34	10	6	18	57	64	26	
18.	Leicester Fosse FC (Leicester)	34	6	10	18	42	82	22	
		612	235	142	235	942	942	612	

Stockport County FC (Stockport) were not re-elected to the league for the next season and were replaced in Division 2 by Doncaster Rovers FC (Doncaster).

F.A. CUP FINAL   (Crystal Palace, London – 23/04/1904 – 61,374)

MANCHESTER CITY FC (MANCHESTER)   1-0   Bolton Wanderers FC (Bolton)

Meredith

Man. City: Hillman, McMahon, Burgess, Frost, Hynds, Ashworth, Meredith, Livingstone, Gillespie, Turnbull, Booth.

Bolton: Davies, Brown, Struthers, Clifford, Greenhaigh, Freebairn, Stokes, Marsh, Yenson, White, Taylor.

Semi-finals

| Bolton Wanderers FC (Bolton) | 1-0 | Derby County FC (Derby) |
| Manchester City FC (Manchester) | 3-0 | The Wednesday FC (Sheffield) |

Quarter-finals

Derby County FC (Derby)	2-1	Blackburn Rovers FC (Blackburn)
Manchester City FC (Manchester)	0-0, 3-1	Middlesbrough FC (Middlesbrough)
Sheffield United FC (Sheffield)	0-2	Bolton Wanderers FC (Bolton)
Tottenham Hotspur FC (London)	1-1, 0-2	The Wednesday FC (Sheffield)

1904-05

Football League Division 1 1904-1905 Season	Aston Villa	Blackburn Rovers	Bury	Derby County	Everton	Manchester City	Middlesbrough	Newcastle United	Nottingham Forest	Notts County	Preston North End	Sheffield United	Small Heath	Stoke	Sunderland	Wednesday	Wolves	Woolwich Arsenal
Aston Villa FC	■	3-0	2-0	0-2	1-0	3-2	0-0	0-1	2-0	4-2	1-2	3-0	2-1	3-0	2-2	0-2	3-0	3-1
Blackburn Rovers FC	4-0	■	0-2	3-1	1-0	3-1	0-2	2-0	0-0	1-0	1-1	2-4	1-4	4-0	2-1	0-1	3-0	1-1
Bury FC	2-3	0-2	■	2-0	1-2	2-4	1-0	2-4	5-1	2-0	0-1	7-1	1-1	3-1	1-0	1-4	3-1	1-1
Derby County FC	0-2	1-1	3-2	■	1-2	0-1	4-2	1-1	3-2	1-1	3-1	2-3	3-0	3-0	1-0	1-0	2-1	0-0
Everton FC	3-2	1-0	2-0	0-0	■	0-0	1-0	2-1	5-1	5-1	1-0	2-0	2-1	4-1	0-1	5-2	2-1	1-0
Manchester City FC	2-1	2-1	3-2	6-0	2-0	■	3-2	3-2	1-1	2-1	6-1	1-1	2-1	1-0	5-2	1-1	5-1	1-0
Middlesbrough FC	3-1	2-1	2-2	2-0	1-0	0-1	■	0-3	0-0	2-5	1-1	1-1	2-1		1-3	1-3	1-3	1-0
Newcastle United FC	2-0	1-0	3-1	2-0	3-2	2-0	3-0	■	5-1	1-0	1-0	1-1	0-1	4-1	1-3	6-2	3-0	3-0
Nottingham Forest FC	1-1	5-2	5-1	0-1	0-2	2-1	1-1	1-3	■	2-1	0-1	1-2	0-2	0-1	2-3	2-1	2-2	0-3
Notts County FC	1-2	2-1	0-1	0-0	1-2	1-1	0-0	0-3	1-2	■	1-3	1-5	0-0	0-0	2-2	3-4	1-5	
Preston North End FC	2-3	0-0	0-0	2-0	1-1	0-1	2-0	1-0	0-1	3-1	■	4-0	2-2	2-1	3-1	1-0	2-2	3-0
Sheffield United FC	0-3	3-1	4-0	3-1	1-0	0-3	0-1	1-3	4-0	2-1	1-0	■	2-1	5-2	1-0	4-2	4-2	4-0
Small Heath FC	0-3	2-0	5-0	2-0	1-2	3-1	2-1	2-1	1-2	1-2	2-0	2-0	■	0-1	1-1	2-1	4-1	2-1
Stoke FC	1-4	4-0	2-0	1-2	2-2	3-1	1-0	0-0	0-2	1-1	2-1	1-0		■	1-3	2-1	2-1	1-0
Sunderland AFC	2-3	2-1	2-1	3-0	2-3	0-0	1-1	3-1	1-0	5-0	3-2	2-1	1-4	3-1	■	3-0	3-0	1-1
The Wednesday FC	3-2	1-2	4-0	1-1	5-5	2-1	5-0	1-3	2-0	1-0	2-0	1-3	3-1	3-0	1-1	■	4-0	0-3
Wolverhampton Wanderers FC	1-1	2-0	2-0	2-0	0-3	0-3	5-3	1-3	3-2	3-1	0-0	4-2	0-1	1-3	1-0	1-0	■	4-1
Woolwich Arsenal FC	1-0	2-0	2-1	0-0	2-1	1-0	1-1	0-2	0-3	1-2	0-0	1-0	1-1	2-1	0-0	3-0	2-0	■

Division 1	Pd	Wn	Dw	Ls	GF	GA	Pts
1. NEWCASTLE UNITED FC (NEWCASTLE/TYNE)	34	23	2	9	72	33	48
2. Everton FC (Liverpool)	34	21	5	8	63	36	47
3. Manchester City FC (Manchester)	34	20	6	8	66	37	46
4. Aston Villa FC (Birmingham)	34	19	4	11	63	43	42
5. Sunderland AFC (Sunderland)	34	16	8	10	60	44	40
6. Sheffield United FC (Sheffield)	34	19	2	13	64	56	40
7. Small Heath FC (Birmingham)	34	17	5	12	54	38	39
8. Preston North End FC (Preston)	34	13	10	11	42	37	36
9. The Wednesday FC (Sheffield)	34	14	5	15	61	57	33
10. Woolwich Arsenal FC (London)	34	12	9	13	36	40	33
11. Derby County FC (Derby)	34	12	8	14	37	48	32
12. Stoke FC (Stoke-upon-Trent)	34	13	4	17	40	58	30
13. Blackburn Rovers FC (Blackburn)	34	11	5	18	40	51	27
14. Wolverhampton Wanderers FC (Wolverhampton)	34	11	4	19	47	73	26
15. Middlesbrough FC (Middlesbrough)	34	9	8	17	36	56	26
16. Nottingham Forest FC (Nottingham)	34	9	7	18	40	61	25
17. Bury FC (Bury)	34	10	4	20	47	67	24
18. Notts County FC (Nottingham)	34	5	8	21	36	69	18
	612	254	104	254	904	904	612

Divisions 1 & 2 were both extended to 20 clubs for the next season. As a result of this, no clubs were relegated from Division 1 for this season.

Top Goalscorer

1) A. BROWN (Sheffield United FC) 22

Football League Division 2 1904-1905 Season	Barnsley	Blackpool	Bolton Wanderers	Bradford City	Bristol City	Burnley	Burslem Port Vale	Burton United	Chesterfield	Doncaster Rovers	Gainsborough Trinity	Glossop	Grimsby Town	Leicester Fosse	Lincoln City	Liverpool	Manchester United	W.B.A.
Barnsley FC	■	2-1	2-1	1-0	1-0	1-2	3-0	7-0	1-0	2-1	2-1	0-0	2-2	2-1	2-1	0-2	0-0	1-1
Blackpool FC	6-0	■	0-2	2-0	2-4	2-0	3-0	1-0	1-1	1-0	2-2	4-1	1-1	0-0	1-0	0-3	0-1	0-0
Bolton Wanderers FC	2-1	3-0	■	2-0	3-1	4-0	3-1	7-1	4-3	2-0	5-1	4-0	4-1	0-1	4-1	2-0	2-4	2-1
Bradford City AFC	1-2	3-1	2-1	■	2-3	4-1	2-1	3-1	0-1	4-1	3-1	1-1	0-0	0-0	0-0	2-4	1-1	3-1
Bristol City FC	3-0	2-0	3-4	1-0	■	0-0	4-2	5-0	2-1	4-1	1-1	2-0	5-0	3-0	2-0	0-1	1-1	2-1
Burnley FC	3-0	0-1	0-1	2-1	2-3	■	5-0	1-1	2-0	4-3	1-3	3-1	1-0	2-0	2-1	0-2	2-0	1-4
Burslem Port Vale FC	0-2	2-2	1-2	1-1	3-2	3-1	■	4-2	0-0	2-0	3-2	0-1	2-0	1-3	0-1	1-2	2-2	3-2
Burton United FC	1-2	0-0	0-1	1-0	2-0	3-1	2-3	■	0-3	1-0	1-3	2-2	1-0	0-3	2-1	2-1	2-3	0-6
Chesterfield FC	2-0	2-0	1-0	0-0	0-3	1-1	2-1	6-0	■	4-1	3-2	1-2	0-0	0-0	0-0	1-1	2-0	1-0
Doncaster Rovers FC	2-0	2-0	0-4	0-1	0-2	0-2	2-2	1-3	0-2	■	1-5	2-1	0-2	0-2	0-2	1-4	0-1	0-1
Gainsborough Trinity FC	4-0	1-1	0-4	3-2	4-1	3-1	1-0	2-0	1-1	2-0	■	0-0	2-1	2-0	2-0	1-2	0-0	4-2
Glossop FC	5-0	0-0	1-2	3-1	0-1	0-0	0-0	1-1	0-1	2-0	3-1	■	2-0	0-0	3-2	0-2	1-2	2-1
Grimsby Town FC	0-0	2-0	2-2	0-2	4-0	1-0	0-3	1-0	3-1	2-1	0-0	3-0	■	2-0	1-0	0-1	0-1	1-3
Leicester Fosse FC	2-0	3-1	2-4	1-2	2-1	2-2	3-0	2-0	1-1	3-2	1-1	0-2	5-1	■	0-1	0-3	0-3	3-1
Lincoln City FC	2-0	1-0	0-2	1-1	1-3	2-0	3-3	3-1	0-0	3-0	4-1	3-0	0-0	5-1	■	0-2	3-0	0-2
Liverpool FC	2-1	5-0	1-1	4-1	3-1	3-0	8-1	2-0	6-1	1-0	6-1	2-2	5-0	4-0	1-1	■	4-0	3-2
Manchester United FC	4-0	3-1	1-2	7-0	4-1	1-0	6-1	5-0	3-0	6-0	3-1	4-1	2-1	4-1	2-0	3-1	■	2-0
West Bromwich Albion FC	4-1	4-2	0-1	0-2	0-0	1-1	0-1	4-0	0-2	6-1	4-3	1-0	0-2	2-0	2-0	0-2		■

	Division 2	Pd	Wn	Dw	Ls	GF	GA	Pts	
1.	Liverpool FC (Liverpool)	34	27	4	3	93	25	58	P
2.	Bolton Wanderers FC (Bolton)	34	27	2	5	87	32	56	P
3.	Manchester United FC (Manchester)	34	24	5	5	81	30	53	
4.	Bristol City FC (Bristol)	34	19	4	11	66	45	42	
5.	Chesterfield FC (Chesterfield)	34	14	11	9	44	35	39	*
6.	Gainsborough Trinity FC (Gainsborough)	34	14	8	12	61	58	36	
7.	Barnsley FC (Barnsley)	34	14	5	15	38	56	33	
8.	Bradford City AFC (Bradford)	34	12	8	14	45	49	32	
9.	Lincoln City FC (Lincoln)	34	12	7	15	42	40	31	
10.	West Bromwich Albion FC (West Bromwich)	34	13	4	17	56	48	30	
11.	Burnley FC (Burnley)	34	12	6	16	43	52	30	
12.	Glossop FC (Glossop)	34	10	10	14	37	46	30	
13.	Grimsby Town FC (Cleethorpes)	34	11	8	15	33	46	30	
14.	Leicester Fosse FC (Leicester)	34	11	7	16	40	55	29	
15.	Blackpool FC (Blackpool)	34	9	10	15	36	48	28	
16.	Burslem Port Vale FC (Burslem)	34	10	7	17	47	72	27	
17.	Burton United FC (Burton-upon-Trent)	34	8	4	22	30	84	20	
18.	Doncaster Rovers FC (Doncaster)	34	3	2	29	23	81	8	#
		612	250	112	250	902	902	612	

* Chesterfield FC (Chesterfield) changed their club name to Chesterfield Town FC (Chesterfield) for the next season.

Doncaster Rovers FC (Doncaster) were not re-elected to the league for the next season.

Chelsea FC (London), Clapton Orient FC (London), Hull City AFC (Kingston-upon-Hull), Leeds City AFC (Leeds) and Stockport County FC (Stockport) were elected to Division 2 which was extended to 20 clubs for the next season.

F.A. CUP FINAL   (Crystal Palace, London – 15/04/1905 – 101,117)

ASTON VILLA FC (BIRMINGHAM)   2-0   Newcastle United FC (Newcastle-upon-Tyne)

Hampton 2

Aston Villa: George, Spencer, Miles, Pearson, Leake, Windmill, Brown, Garratty, Hampton, Bache, Hall.
Newcastle: Lawrence, McCombie, Carr, Gardner, Aitken, McWilliam, Rutherford, Howie, Appleyard, Veitch, Gosnell.

Semi-finals

Everton FC (Liverpool)	1-1, 1-2	Aston Villa FC (Birmingham)
Newcastle United FC (Newcastle-upon-Tyne)	1-0	The Wednesday FC (Sheffield)

Quarter-finals

Aston Villa FC (Birmingham)	5-0	Fulham FC (London)
Bolton Wanderers FC (Bolton)	0-2	Newcastle United FC (Newcastle-upon-Tyne)
Everton FC (Liverpool)	4-0	Southampton FC (Southampton)
Preston North End FC (Preston)	1-1, 0-3	The Wednesday FC (Sheffield)

1905-06

Football League Division 1 1905-1906 Season	Aston Villa	Birmingham	Blackburn Rvs.	Bolton Wands.	Bury	Derby County	Everton	Liverpool	Manchester City	Middlesbrough	Newcastle Utd.	Nottingham For.	Notts County	Preston N.E.	Sheffield United	Stoke	Sunderland	Wednesday	Wolves	Wool. Arsenal
Aston Villa FC		1-3	0-1	1-1	3-3	6-0	4-0	5-0	2-1	4-1	0-3	3-1	2-1	0-1	4-1	3-0	2-1	3-0	6-0	2-1
Birmingham FC	2-0		3-0	2-5	0-3	3-1	1-0	1-0	3-2	7-0	0-1	5-0	4-2	1-1	2-0	2-0	3-0	5-1	3-3	2-1
Blackburn Rovers FC	1-1	5-1		4-1	3-0	3-0	1-2	0-0	1-1	1-1	1-0	1-1	1-3	1-2	2-1	3-0	0-3	1-0	3-1	2-0
Bolton Wanderers FC	4-1	0-1	1-0		4-0	5-0	3-2	3-2	1-3	2-1	1-1	6-0	2-0	1-2	1-2	1-2	6-2	1-0	3-2	6-1
Bury FC	0-1	1-0	5-0	2-1		0-2	3-2	0-0	2-4	1-1	1-4	2-1	0-0	1-1	2-5	3-0	3-1	2-2	0-1	2-0
Derby County FC	1-0	0-0	1-2	0-1	3-1		0-0	0-3	1-2	1-1	2-1	2-2	1-1	3-0	1-0	1-0	1-0	2-1	2-0	5-1
Everton FC	4-2	1-2	3-2	3-1	1-2	2-1		4-2	0-3	4-1	1-2	4-1	6-2	1-0	3-2	0-3	3-1	2-2	2-2	0-1
Liverpool FC	3-0	2-0	1-3	2-2	3-1	4-1	1-1		0-1	6-1	3-0	4-1	2-0	1-1	3-1	23-1	2-0	2-1	4-0	3-0
Manchester City FC	1-4	4-1	1-1	3-1	5-2	1-2	1-0	0-1		4-0	1-4	5-0	5-1	0-1	0-2	2-0	5-1	2-1	4-0	1-2
Middlesbrough FC	1-2	1-0	1-1	4-4	5-1	1-0	0-0	1-5	6-1		1-0	2-0	4-1	1-2	0-1	5-0	2-2	2-2	3-1	2-0
Newcastle United FC	3-1	2-2	3-0	2-1	3-1	0-1	4-2	2-3	2-2	4-1		3-2	3-1	1-0	2-1	5-0	1-0	0-3	8-0	1-1
Nottingham Forest FC	2-2	2-1	1-2	4-0	3-2	0-0	4-3	1-2	0-1	2-1	2-1		1-2	0-1	4-1	3-1	1-2	3-4	3-1	1-1
Notts County FC	2-1	0-0	1-1	3-3	2-2	1-0	0-0	3-0	3-0	1-1	1-0	1-1		2-2	2-3	1-1	4-1	1-3	5-2	1-0
Preston North End FC	2-0	3-0	1-1	3-0	1-0	3-1	1-1	1-2	2-0	2-1	0-0	3-1	4-1		1-1	2-0	1-1	0-1	3-2	2-2
Sheffield United FC	1-1	3-0	0-2	5-2	1-1	1-0	3-2	1-2	1-3	1-0	2-0	1-4	1-0	0-0		1-1	4-1	0-2	4-1	3-1
Stoke FC	0-1	2-2	3-0	1-2	4-2	2-2	2-2	2-1	0-0	1-1	1-0	4-0	3-0	3-0	2-1		1-0	4-0	4-0	2-1
Sunderland AFC	2-0	3-1	3-0	3-3	2-2	2-0	2-1	2-1	2-1	3-2	0-1	3-1	2-0	2-0	2-0	1-0		2-0	7-2	2-2
The Wednesday FC	2-2	4-2	0-1	1-2	1-1	1-0	3-1	3-2	1-0	3-0	1-1	1-0	3-1	1-1	1-0	2-0	3-3		5-1	4-2
Wolverhampton Wanderers FC	4-1	0-0	2-1	2-0	2-2	7-0	2-5	0-2	2-3	0-0	0-2	2-1	6-1	2-3	1-1	1-2	5-2	0-0		0-2
Woolwich Arsenal FC	2-1	5-0	3-2	0-0	4-0	1-0	1-2	3-1	2-0	2-2	4-3	3-1	1-1	2-2	5-1	1-2	2-0	0-2	2-1	

Division 1

		Pd	Wn	Dw	Ls	GF	GA	Pts	
1.	LIVERPOOL FC (LIVERPOOL)	38	23	5	10	79	46	51	
2.	Preston North End FC (Preston)	38	17	13	8	54	39	47	
3.	The Wednesday FC (Sheffield)	38	18	8	12	63	52	44	
4.	Newcastle United FC (Newcastle-upon-Tyne)	38	18	7	13	74	48	43	
5.	Manchester City FC (Manchester)	38	19	5	14	73	54	43	
6.	Bolton Wanderers FC (Bolton)	38	17	7	14	81	67	41	
7.	Birmingham FC (Birmingham)	38	17	7	14	65	59	41	*
8.	Aston Villa FC (Birmingham)	38	17	6	15	72	56	40	
9.	Blackburn Rovers FC (Blackburn)	38	16	8	14	54	52	40	
10.	Stoke FC (Stoke-upon-Trent)	38	16	7	15	54	55	39	
11.	Everton FC (Liverpool)	38	15	7	16	70	66	37	
12.	Woolwich Arsenal FC (London)	38	15	7	16	62	64	37	
13.	Sheffield United FC (Sheffield)	38	15	6	17	57	62	36	
14.	Sunderland AFC (Sunderland)	38	15	5	18	61	70	35	
15.	Derby County FC (Derby)	38	14	7	17	39	58	35	
16.	Notts County FC (Nottingham)	38	11	12	15	55	71	34	
17.	Bury FC (Bury)	38	11	10	17	57	74	32	
18.	Middlesbrough FC (Middlesbrough)	38	10	11	17	56	71	31	
19.	Nottingham Forest FC (Nottingham)	38	13	5	20	58	79	31	R
20.	Wolverhampton Wanderers FC (Wolverhampton)	38	8	7	23	58	99	23	R
		760	305	150	305	1242	1242	760	

* Birmingham FC (Birmingham) changed their club name pre-season from Small Heath FC (Birmingham).

Top Goalscorer

1)   W. WHITE   (Bolton Wanderers FC)   26

Football League Division 2 1905-1906 Season	Barnsley	Blackpool	Bradford City	Bristol City	Burnley	Bursl. Port Vale	Burton United	Chelsea	Chesterfield	Clapton Orient	Gainsborough T.	Glossop	Grimsby Town	Hull City	Leeds City	Leicester Fosse	Lincoln City	Manchester Utd.	Stockport Co.	W.B.A.
Barnsley FC	■	1-1	0-1	2-2	1-2	4-0	3-0	1-2	8-1	4-1	2-1	1-1	2-0	2-0	3-0	0-0	4-2	0-3	4-0	3-0
Blackpool FC	0-0	■	2-2	1-3	0-1	2-1	2-0	0-1	2-1	3-0	2-2	1-0	2-0	1-2	0-3	0-1	2-0	0-1	2-0	0-3
Bradford City AFC	0-0	2-1	■	1-2	0-1	2-0	1-0	1-1	1-0	3-0	1-2	2-0	0-1	0-2	1-0	3-3	2-2	1-5	0-1	0-1
Bristol City FC	3-0	2-1	1-0	■	2-0	4-0	4-0	2-1	3-1	1-0	2-0	2-1	2-0	2-1	2-0	1-2	1-0	1-1	7-0	1-0
Burnley FC	2-1	4-1	0-0	2-2	■	1-3	1-0	2-0	1-1	3-0	1-0	1-0	0-0	1-3	4-3	0-2	2-1	1-3	0-1	0-2
Burslem Port Vale FC	1-2	1-2	2-1	0-1	2-2	■	4-1	3-2	4-3	2-1	1-0	3-3	2-2	1-3	2-0	2-0	3-1	1-0	0-1	2-2
Burton United FC	4-1	1-1	0-1	0-1	1-3	1-0	■	2-4	4-0	1-0	3-1	1-0	0-3	1-1	1-0	2-0	3-1	1-0	2-2	2-2
Chelsea FC	6-0	6-0	4-2	0-0	1-0	7-0	3-0	■	0-1	6-1	1-3	0-0	2-0	5-1	4-0	3-3	4-2	1-1	4-2	1-0
Chesterfield Town FC	2-0	2-0	1-1	1-2	3-0	2-0	1-0	0-2	■	1-1	0-0	3-1	1-4	1-2	0-2	3-3	1-2	1-0	3-1	0-3
Clapton Orient FC	0-0	0-0	4-2	0-2	0-1	1-3	0-1	0-3	3-3	■	1-0	2-0	1-2	0-1	0-0	3-0	0-1	1-0	1-0	0-2
Gainsborough Trinity FC	1-0	0-1	2-3	1-3	0-1	4-0	5-2	0-2	4-0	2-1	■	2-0	1-0	3-1	4-1	1-0	2-3	2-2	0-0	2-1
Glossop FC	2-2	4-1	2-3	1-5	1-1	3-2	2-0	2-4	2-0	5-0	1-0	■	2-0	3-1	1-2	0-2	2-1	1-2	1-0	1-3
Grimsby Town FC	2-1	1-1	1-0	1-1	2-0	5-0	1-0	1-1	2-0	4-1	2-0	1-1	■	1-0	1-1	1-1	2-2	0-1	2-0	3-2
Hull City AFC	4-1	2-2	5-2	0-3	1-1	1-1	4-3	3-0	3-1	2-0	1-2	0-1	0-1	■	0-0	0-0	0-1	0-1	3-0	4-0
Leeds City AFC	3-2	3-0	0-2	1-1	1-1	3-1	2-1	0-0	3-0	6-1	1-0	1-0	3-0	3-1	■	4-1	2-2	1-3	1-1	0-2
Leicester Fosse FC	1-0	2-0	2-4	1-2	2-0	2-1	1-1	0-1	2-1	4-0	2-1	2-0	1-2	0-1	0-1	■	3-1	2-5	2-0	1-0
Lincoln City FC	4-1	1-1	5-0	0-3	5-0	5-1	5-1	1-4	0-1	2-3	4-1	3-1	1-4	1-2	3-1	1-2	■	2-3	2-0	1-2
Manchester United FC	5-1	2-1	0-0	5-1	1-0	3-0	6-0	0-0	4-1	2-0	2-0	5-2	5-0	5-0	0-3	3-2	2-1	■	3-1	0-0
Stockport County FC	0-0	2-1	1-0	2-3	3-1	3-0	2-0	1-0	1-3	3-3	0-0	5-0	2-2	2-1	2-1	1-1	3-0	0-1	■	2-2
West Bromwich Albion FC	5-3	5-0	6-1	1-3	1-2	4-1	3-0	1-1	3-0	1-1	4-0	6-0	2-0	1-1	2-1	3-0	1-1	1-0	3-1	■

	Division 2	**Pd**	**Wn**	**Dw**	**Ls**	**GF**	**GA**	**Pts**	
1.	Bristol City FC (Bristol)	38	30	6	2	83	28	66	P
2.	Manchester United FC (Manchester)	38	28	6	4	90	28	62	P
3.	Chelsea FC (London)	38	22	9	7	90	37	53	
4.	West Bromwich Albion FC (West Bromwich)	38	22	8	8	79	36	52	
5.	Hull City FC (Kingston-upon-Hull)	38	19	6	13	67	54	44	
6.	Leeds City AFC (Leeds)	38	17	9	12	59	47	43	
7.	Leicester Fosse FC (Leicester)	38	15	12	11	53	48	42	
8.	Grimsby Town FC (Cleethorpes)	38	15	10	13	46	46	40	
9.	Burnley FC (Burnley)	38	15	8	15	42	53	38	
10.	Stockport County FC (Stockport)	38	13	9	16	44	56	35	
11.	Bradford City AFC (Bradford)	38	13	8	17	46	60	34	
12.	Barnsley FC (Barnsley)	38	12	9	17	60	62	33	
13.	Lincoln City FC (Lincoln)	38	12	6	20	69	72	30	
14.	Blackpool FC (Blackpool)	38	10	9	19	37	62	29	
15.	Gainsborough Trinity FC (Gainsborough)	38	12	4	22	44	57	28	
16.	Glossop FC (Glossop)	38	10	8	20	49	71	28	
17.	Burslem Port Vale FC (Burslem)	38	12	4	22	49	82	28	
18.	Chesterfield Town FC (Chesterfield)	38	10	8	20	40	72	28	
19.	Burton United FC (Burton-upon-Trent)	38	10	6	22	34	67	26	
20.	Clapton Orient FC (London)	38	7	7	24	35	78	21	
		760	304	152	304	1116	1116	760	

F.A. CUP FINAL   (Crystal Palace, London – 21/04/1906 – 75,609)

EVERTON FC (LIVERPOOL)	1-0	Newcastle United FC (Newcastle-upon-Tyne)

Young

Everton: Scott, Crelley, Balmer, Makepeace, Taylor, Abbott, Sharp, Bolton, Young, Settle, Hardman.
Newcastle: Lawrence, McCombie, Carr, Gardner, Aitken, McWilliam, Rutherford, Howie, Orr, Veitch, Gosnell.

Semi-finals

Everton FC (Liverpool)	2-0	Liverpool FC (Liverpool)
Woolwich Arsenal FC (London)	0-2	Newcastle United FC (Newcastle-upon-Tyne)

Quarter-finals

Birmingham FC (Birmingham)	2-2, 0-3	Newcastle United FC (Newcastle-upon-Tyne)
Everton FC (Liverpool)	4-3	The Wednesday FC (Sheffield)
Liverpool FC (Liverpool)	3-0	Southampton FC (Southampton)
Manchester United FC (Manchester)	2-3	Woolwich Arsenal FC (London)

1906-07

Football League Division 1 1906-1907 Season	Aston Villa	Birmingham	Blackburn Rovers	Bolton Wanderers	Bristol City	Bury	Derby County	Everton	Liverpool	Manchester City	Manchester United	Middlesbrough	Newcastle United	Notts County	Preston North End	Sheffield United	Stoke	Sunderland	Wednesday	Woolwich Arsenal
Aston Villa FC	■	4-1	4-2	0-2	3-2	3-1	2-0	2-1	4-0	4-1	2-0	2-3	0-0	0-0	3-0	5-1	1-0	2-2	8-1	2-2
Birmingham FC	3-2	■	2-0	4-2	2-2	3-1	2-1	1-0	2-1	4-0	1-1	0-0	2-4	2-0	3-0	0-0	2-1	2-0	1-1	5-1
Blackburn Rovers FC	2-1	1-0	■	2-3	0-1	4-1	5-1	2-1	1-1	4-0	2-4	4-1	4-0	0-2	1-1	1-1	3-1	2-1	0-2	2-3
Bolton Wanderers FC	1-2	2-3	5-2	■	1-2	1-0	1-0	1-3	3-0	1-1	0-1	1-0	4-2	0-0	3-0	6-1	1-1	1-0	0-0	3-0
Bristol City FC	2-4	0-0	3-0	1-2	■	2-0	3-0	2-1	3-1	2-0	1-2	3-0	2-1	1-0	1-0	3-3	4-0	1-1	2-0	1-3
Bury FC	0-3	1-0	0-0	2-3	1-1	■	1-0	1-2	1-3	3-1	1-2	1-1	3-2	3-0	2-0	2-1	2-0	2-3	0-0	4-1
Derby County FC	0-1	1-1	2-3	0-1	1-3	2-1	■	5-2	0-1	2-2	2-2	1-0	0-0	3-0	3-0	2-1	1-1	1-0	0-0	
Everton FC	1-2	3-0	2-0	1-0	2-0	1-0	2-0	■	0-0	9-1	3-0	5-1	3-0	2-2	1-0	4-2	3-0	4-1	2-0	2-1
Liverpool FC	5-2	2-0	0-2	0-2	2-4	2-2	2-0	1-2	■	5-4	0-1	2-4	4-1	5-1	6-1	2-2	1-0	1-2	1-2	4-0
Manchester City FC	4-2	1-0	0-0	1-1	0-1	2-2	2-2	3-1	1-0	■	3-0	3-1	1-1	2-1	1-1	0-2	2-2	2-3	0-1	1-4
Manchester United FC	1-0	2-1	1-1	1-2	0-0	2-4	1-1	3-0	0-0	1-1	■	3-1	1-3	0-0	3-0	2-0	4-1	2-0	5-0	1-0
Middlesbrough FC	1-0	1-0	0-1	0-0	1-0	3-1	4-1	2-2	0-1	2-3	2-0	■	0-3	2-0	2-1	0-1	5-0	2-1	1-3	5-3
Newcastle United FC	3-2	2-0	3-1	4-0	3-0	3-2	2-0	1-0	2-0	5-0	4-0		■	4-3	2-1	0-0	1-0	4-2	5-1	1-0
Notts County FC	1-1	2-2	1-2	0-0	2-3	1-2	4-0	0-1	2-0	0-0	3-0	2-2	1-0	■	0-0	4-0	2-2	0-0	2-2	4-1
Preston North End FC	2-0	2-0	1-0	3-1	3-1	3-2	1-0	1-1	3-1	1-3	2-0	4-2	2-2	0-0	■	2-1	2-2	2-0	1-0	0-3
Sheffield United FC	0-0	2-0	3-0	2-1	1-1	3-0	2-0	4-1	1-0	1-4	0-2	1-1	0-0	2-1	3-1	■	2-0	3-2	2-1	4-2
Stoke FC	0-2	3-0	1-1	3-0	0-3	3-1	2-1	2-0	1-1	3-0	1-2	0-2	1-2	1-1	0-2	1-1	■	2-2	1-1	2-0
Sunderland AFC	2-1	4-1	1-0	1-2	3-3	3-5	0-2	1-0	5-5	1-1	4-1	4-2	2-0	3-1	1-0	1-2	3-1	■	1-1	2-3
The Wednesday FC	2-1	0-1	3-1	2-0	3-0	1-2	1-1	1-1	2-3	3-1	5-2	0-2	2-2	1-3	2-1	2-2	0-1	2-1	■	1-1
Woolwich Arsenal FC	3-1	2-1	2-0	2-2	1-2	3-1	3-2	3-1	2-1	4-1	4-0	2-0	1-0	1-0	0-1	2-1	0-1	1-0		■

Division 1

		Pd	Wn	Dw	Ls	GF	GA	Pts	
1.	NEWCASTLE UNITED FC (NEWCASTLE/TYNE)	38	22	7	9	74	46	51	
2.	Bristol City FC (Bristol)	38	20	8	10	66	47	48	
3.	Everton FC (Liverpool)	38	20	5	13	70	46	45	
4.	Sheffield United FC (Sheffield)	38	17	11	10	57	55	45	
5.	Aston Villa FC (Birmingham)	38	19	6	13	78	52	44	
6.	Bolton Wanderers FC (Bolton)	38	18	8	12	59	47	44	
7.	Woolwich Arsenal FC (London)	38	20	4	14	66	59	44	
8.	Manchester United FC (Manchester)	38	17	8	13	53	56	42	
9.	Birmingham FC (Birmingham)	38	15	8	15	52	52	38	
10.	Sunderland AFC (Sunderland)	38	14	9	15	65	66	37	
11.	Middlesbrough FC (Middlesbrough)	38	15	6	17	56	63	36	
12.	Blackburn Rovers FC (Blackburn)	38	14	7	17	56	59	35	
13.	The Wednesday FC (Sheffield)	38	12	11	15	49	60	35	
14.	Preston North End FC (Preston)	38	14	7	17	44	57	35	
15.	Liverpool FC (Liverpool)	38	13	7	18	64	65	33	
16.	Bury FC (Bury)	38	13	6	19	58	68	32	
17.	Manchester City FC (Manchester)	38	10	12	16	53	77	32	
18.	Notts County FC (Nottingham)	38	8	15	15	46	50	31	
19.	Derby County FC (Derby)	38	9	9	20	41	59	27	R
20.	Stoke FC (Stoke-upon-Trent)	38	8	10	20	41	64	26	R
		760	298	164	298	1148	1148	760	

Top Goalscorer

1) A. YOUNG   (Everton FC)   28

Football League Division 2 1906-1907 Season	Barnsley	Blackpool	Bradford City	Burnley	Burslem Port Vale	Burton United	Chelsea	Chesterfield	Clapton Orient	Gainsborough Trinity	Glossop	Grimsby Town	Hull City	Leeds City	Leicester Fosse	Lincoln City	Nottingham Forest	Stockport County	W.B.A.	Wolves
Barnsley FC		3-2	3-1	5-0	3-2	6-1	3-1	2-1	3-2	6-0	3-0	1-1	4-2	3-0	2-2	6-2	0-1	3-1	0-1	0-1
Blackpool FC	2-3		1-0	2-0	0-1	1-1	0-0	0-0	1-3	1-0	4-1	4-3	1-1	1-0	1-0	2-0	1-2	0-1	2-1	1-2
Bradford City AFC	2-0	3-0		3-1	3-2	2-3	6-3	1-0	5-2	1-1	2-1	1-0	1-0	2-2	3-1	3-0	1-2	1-0	4-0	2-3
Burnley FC	2-2	2-1	0-1		6-0	4-0	1-1	0-0	3-0	1-0	1-1	2-0	4-2	1-2	5-0	5-1	2-1	3-0	0-1	3-0
Burslem Port Vale FC	2-2	3-0	2-3	4-4		0-0	2-0	2-2	3-2	1-0	4-1	3-2	2-1	1-2	1-2	4-2	4-2	5-0	2-1	0-0
Burton United FC	1-1	0-0	1-0	0-1	2-0		2-1	3-1	2-1	0-0	1-2	2-3	1-2	0-2	0-1	3-4	0-2	0-1	2-0	4-1
Chelsea FC	2-1	3-0	5-1	2-0	2-1	1-0		7-1	2-1	4-1	9-2	2-0	3-0	2-0	1-0	2-0	0-0	2-0	2-0	4-0
Chesterfield Town FC	3-2	0-1	3-4	0-1	4-2	2-0	0-0		2-1	7-0	1-3	1-3	3-1	1-0	2-1	1-0	1-1	0-2	2-2	3-2
Clapton Orient FC	1-0	0-0	1-1	2-1	1-1	1-0	0-1	1-2		3-1	3-0	1-0	2-1	1-1	1-0	1-1	0-1	1-1	1-1	4-0
Gainsborough Trinity FC	1-1	2-0	4-1	0-2	2-0	2-0	1-1	1-0	3-1		2-1	2-1	1-1	1-0	1-2	2-1	2-3	3-1	2-4	1-0
Glossop FC	2-1	0-0	1-2	1-0	4-0	2-2	0-1	3-1	3-0	3-1		1-0	2-4	2-0	2-2	2-1	0-2	2-3	0-0	2-1
Grimsby Town FC	1-0	0-0	0-2	1-0	2-0	1-1	2-1	3-1	1-2	2-0	2-1		1-3	4-0	0-1	4-0	3-1	3-1	2-1	2-1
Hull City AFC	2-0	3-0	0-3	1-1	4-1	3-0	0-1	2-0	2-0	2-4	5-0	4-2		2-1	1-1	1-2	1-2	3-0	0-1	5-1
Leeds City AFC	2-1	1-1	1-1	0-1	2-0	3-1	0-1	1-0	3-2	4-0	1-4	4-3	2-2		1-1	1-1	1-4	6-1	3-2	2-0
Leicester Fosse FC	2-1	5-1	1-0	2-0	4-1	3-0	1-1	2-0	2-1	3-1	2-2	2-0	3-0	2-2		3-0	1-2	1-0	3-0	2-0
Lincoln City FC	1-0	0-1	0-2	1-2	4-0	2-0	0-5	1-0	3-0	4-0	2-1	2-1	0-1	1-1	2-2		1-2	3-1	2-1	0-4
Nottingham Forest FC	0-0	3-0	3-0	2-0	2-2	2-0	3-1	3-1	4-0	3-1	2-0	0-3	2-1	3-0	2-1	3-1		2-1	3-1	1-0
Stockport County FC	0-0	0-0	2-1	2-1	3-0	2-0	1-2	1-1	1-1	1-2	5-0	3-0	1-1	2-2	1-0	1-0	0-0		0-1	0-0
West Bromwich Albion FC	3-1	3-0	3-0	3-2	3-0	5-1	1-2	5-2	5-0	5-0	5-1	6-1	3-0	5-0	0-1	2-1	3-1	1-1		1-1
Wolverhampton Wanderers FC	5-1	1-1	1-1	3-0	6-2	3-0	1-2	2-1	6-1	1-0	4-0	5-0	1-1	3-2	1-0	3-0	2-0	1-1	0-3	

54

	Division 2	Pd	Wn	Dw	Ls	GF	GA	Pts	
1.	Nottingham Forest FC (Nottingham)	38	28	4	6	74	36	60	P
2.	Chelsea FC (London)	38	26	5	7	80	34	57	P
3.	Leicester Fosse FC (Leicester)	38	20	8	10	62	39	48	
4.	West Bromwich Albion FC (West Bromwich)	38	21	5	12	83	45	47	
5.	Bradford City AFC (Bradford)	38	21	5	12	70	53	47	
6.	Wolverhampton Wanderers FC (Wolverhampton)	38	17	7	14	66	53	41	
7.	Burnley FC (Burnley)	38	17	6	15	62	47	40	
8.	Barnsley FC (Barnsley)	38	15	8	15	73	55	38	
9.	Hull City AFC (Kingston-upon-Hull)	38	15	7	16	65	57	37	
10.	Leeds City AFC (Leeds)	38	13	10	15	55	63	36	
11.	Grimsby Town FC (Cleethorpes)	38	16	3	19	57	62	35	
12.	Stockport County FC (Stockport)	38	12	11	15	42	52	35	
13.	Blackpool FC (Blackpool)	38	11	11	16	33	51	33	
14.	Gainsborough Trinity FC (Gainsborough)	38	14	5	19	45	72	33	
15.	Glossop FC (Glossop)	38	13	6	19	53	79	32	
16.	Burslem Port Vale FC (Burslem)	38	12	7	19	60	83	31	#
17.	Clapton Orient FC (London)	38	11	8	19	45	67	30	
18.	Chesterfield Town FC (Chesterfield)	38	11	7	20	50	66	29	
19.	Lincoln City FC (Lincoln)	38	12	4	22	46	73	28	
20.	Burton United FC (Burton-upon-Trent)	38	8	7	23	34	68	23	#
		760	313	134	313	1155	1155	760	

Burslem Port Vale FC (Burslem) resigned from the league at the end of the season.
Burton United (Burton-upon-Trent) were not re-elected to the league for next season.

Fulham FC (London) and Oldham Athletic AFC (Oldham) were elected to Division 2 for next season.

F.A. CUP FINAL   (Crystal Palace, London – 20/04/1907 – 84,594)

THE WEDNESDAY FC (SHEFFIELD)	2-1	Everton FC (Liverpool)
Stewart, Simpson		*Sharp*

Wednesday: Lyall, Layton, Burton, Brittleton, Crawshaw, Bartlett, Chapman, Bradshaw, Wilson, Stewart, Simpson.

Everton: Scott, W.Balmer, R.Balmer, Makepeace, Taylor, Abbott, Sharp, Bolton, Young, Settle, Hardman.

Semi-finals

West Bromwich Albion FC (West Bromwich)	1-2	Everton FC (Liverpool)
Woolwich Arsenal FC (London)	1-3	The Wednesday FC (Sheffield)

Quarter-finals

Barnsley FC (Barnsley)	1-2	Woolwich Arsenal FC (London)
Crystal Palace FC (London)	1-1, 0-4	Everton FC (Liverpool)
The Wednesday FC (Sheffield)	1-0	Liverpool FC (Liverpool)
West Bromwich Albion FC (West Bromwich)	3-1	Notts County FC (Nottingham)

1907-08

Football League Division 1 1907-1908 Season	Aston Villa	Birmingham	Blackburn Rovers	Bolton Wanderers	Bristol City	Bury	Chelsea	Everton	Liverpool	Manchester City	Manchester United	Middlesbrough	Newcastle United	Nottingham Forest	Notts County	Preston North End	Sheffield United	Sunderland	Wednesday	Woolwich Arsenal
Aston Villa FC	■	2-3	1-1	2-0	4-4	2-2	0-0	0-2	5-1	2-2	1-4	6-0	3-3	4-0	5-1	3-0	1-0	1-0	5-0	0-1
Birmingham FC	2-3	■	1-1	2-1	0-4	0-1	1-1	2-1	1-1	2-1	3-4	1-4	1-1	1-0	0-0	2-0	0-0	0-2	2-1	1-2
Blackburn Rovers FC	2-0	1-0	■	3-2	4-1	1-0	2-0	2-0	1-3	0-0	1-5	2-0	1-1	3-3	1-1	1-1	3-3	4-2	2-0	1-1
Bolton Wanderers FC	3-1	1-0	3-1	■	1-2	3-6	1-2	3-0	0-4	2-0	2-2	1-1	4-0	1-0	2-0	1-1	2-3	2-1	3-1	
Bristol City FC	2-2	0-0	2-2	2-0	■	1-1	0-0	3-2	2-0	2-1	1-1	0-1	1-1	3-0	2-1	1-3	3-2	3-0	0-2	1-2
Bury FC	2-1	1-0	1-1	2-2	1-1	■	1-1	3-0	3-1	0-0	0-1	1-4	1-2	0-0	0-0	5-1	3-2	2-1	0-2	3-2
Chelsea FC	1-3	2-2	1-0	1-3	4-1	3-4	■	2-1	0-2	2-2	1-4	1-0	2-0	0-4	1-2	0-0	2-4	2-1	3-1	2-1
Everton FC	1-0	4-1	4-1	2-1	0-0	6-1	0-3	■	2-4	3-3	1-3	2-1	2-0	1-0	2-1	2-1	0-3	0-0	1-1	
Liverpool FC	5-0	3-4	2-0	1-0	3-1	2-1	1-4	0-0	■	0-1	7-4	1-5	0-0	6-0	1-2	3-0	1-0	3-0	4-1	
Manchester City FC	3-2	2-1	2-0	1-0	0-0	2-2	0-3	4-2	1-1	■	0-0	2-1	1-0	4-2	2-1	5-0	0-2	0-0	3-2	4-0
Manchester United FC	1-2	1-0	1-2	2-1	2-1	2-1	4-1	4-3	4-0	3-1	■	2-1	1-1	4-0	0-1	2-1	2-1	3-0	4-1	4-2
Middlesbrough FC	0-1	1-0	3-0	0-1	0-2	0-2	3-1	0-2	3-1	2-0	2-1	■	2-1	1-1	3-1	1-0	2-0	3-1	6-1	0-0
Newcastle United FC	2-5	8-0	3-0	3-0	2-0	3-0	1-0	2-1	3-1	1-1	1-6	1-1	■	3-0	1-1	2-0	2-3	1-3	2-1	2-1
Nottingham Forest FC	2-2	1-1	3-2	1-0	3-1	1-2	6-0	5-2	3-1	3-1	2-0	0-3	0-0	■	2-0	2-2	1-1	4-1	2-2	1-0
Notts County FC	0-3	0-0	0-2	0-1	3-1	2-1	2-1	2-1	2-2	1-0	1-1	2-0	0-1	2-0	■	0-1	3-0	4-0	1-2	2-0
Preston North End FC	3-0	1-1	1-1	2-0	3-0	3-1	2-4	2-2	2-4	0-0	1-1	2-0	0-1	1-0	■	0-0	3-2	1-1	3-0	
Sheffield United FC	1-1	1-0	4-2	1-0	2-0	0-2	0-3	2-0	0-0	1-2	2-0	0-0	1-1	2-2	0-1	2-0	■	5-3	1-3	2-2
Sunderland AFC	3-0	1-0	4-0	1-2	3-3	6-2	3-0	1-2	1-0	2-5	1-2	0-0	2-4	7-2	4-3	4-1	4-1	■	1-2	5-2
The Wednesday FC	2-3	1-4	2-0	5-2	5-3	2-0	3-1	1-2	1-2	5-1	2-0	3-2	3-1	2-1	2-0	1-0	2-0	2-2	■	6-0
Woolwich Arsenal FC	0-1	1-1	2-0	1-1	0-4	0-0	0-0	2-1	2-1	2-1	1-0	4-1	2-2	3-1	1-1	1-1	5-1	4-0	1-1	■

Division 1

		Pd	Wn	Dw	Ls	GF	GA	Pts	
1.	MANCHESTER UNITED FC (MANCHESTER)	38	23	6	9	81	48	52	
2.	Aston Villa FC (Birmingham)	38	17	9	12	77	59	43	
3.	Manchester City FC (Manchester)	38	16	11	11	62	54	43	
4.	Newcastle United FC (Newcastle-upon-Tyne)	38	15	12	11	65	54	42	
5.	The Wednesday FC (Sheffield)	38	19	4	15	73	64	42	
6.	Middlesbrough FC (Middlesbrough)	38	17	7	14	54	45	41	
7.	Bury FC (Bury)	38	14	11	13	58	61	39	
8.	Liverpool FC (Liverpool)	38	16	6	16	68	61	38	
9.	Nottingham Forest FC (Nottingham)	38	13	11	14	59	62	37	
10.	Bristol City FC (Bristol)	38	12	12	14	58	61	36	
11.	Everton FC (Liverpool)	38	15	6	17	58	64	36	
12.	Preston North End FC (Preston)	38	12	12	14	47	53	36	
13.	Chelsea FC (London)	38	14	8	16	53	62	36	
14.	Blackburn Rovers FC (Blackburn)	38	12	12	14	51	63	36	
14.	Woolwich Arsenal FC (London)	38	12	12	14	51	63	36	
16.	Sunderland AFC (Sunderland)	38	16	3	19	78	75	35	
17.	Sheffield United FC (Sheffield)	38	12	11	15	52	58	35	
18.	Notts County FC (Nottingham)	38	13	8	17	39	51	34	
19.	Bolton Wanderers FC (Bolton)	38	14	5	19	52	58	33	R
20.	Birmingham FC (Birmingham)	38	9	12	17	40	60	30	R
		760	291	178	291	1176	1176	760	

Top Goalscorer

1)   E. WEST   (Nottingham Forest FC)   27

Football League Division 2 1907-1908 Season	Barnsley	Blackpool	Bradford City	Burnley	Chesterfield	Clapton Orient	Derby County	Fulham	Gainsborough T.	Glossop	Grimsby Town	Hull City	Leeds City	Leicester Fosse	Lincoln City	Oldham Athletic	Stockport Co.	Stoke	W.B.A.	Wolves
Barnsley FC		0-0	1-2	2-3	5-2	2-2	2-4	6-0	1-2	4-1	2-1	4-2	1-3	1-3	2-1	2-1	0-0	0-1	1-3	5-0
Blackpool FC	1-1		2-1	1-0	2-0	5-0	1-0	2-1	0-1	4-0	3-0	1-1	2-3	2-2	4-3	1-0	1-3	1-0	0-1	0-2
Bradford City AFC	2-0	3-0		2-0	8-1	1-0	3-1	1-3	7-1	2-1	1-1	2-1	5-0	1-5	2-0	1-0	5-0	6-0	0-0	6-2
Burnley FC	4-1	2-1	2-1		1-1	3-0	2-2	0-1	2-0	1-0	5-1	5-0	1-0	4-1	1-2	2-1	4-0	3-1	1-1	1-0
Chesterfield Town FC	1-3	3-2	1-1	2-4		1-1	0-2	1-1	2-2	3-7	0-0	1-2	4-3	2-2	2-1	1-2	4-1	2-4	1-0	2-0
Clapton Orient FC	2-0	1-1	0-3	0-1	5-1		1-0	0-1	2-0	0-0	2-1	1-0	0-0	1-0	2-0	2-0	4-1	3-0	2-2	1-1
Derby County FC	3-0	2-1	2-3	1-0	0-0	4-0		0-1	5-2	2-0	4-0	4-1	6-1	1-2	4-0	1-0	3-0	3-0	3-0	3-2
Fulham FC	2-0	3-0	0-2	2-1	5-0	4-0	0-0		6-0	6-1	0-1	0-1	2-0	5-1	6-1	1-2	0-1	5-1	1-1	2-1
Gainsborough Trinity	0-1	2-1	1-5	2-0	2-1	0-0	1-4	3-3		1-0	3-2	1-2	2-1	1-1	5-1	1-1	3-2	2-0	1-2	0-1
Glossop FC	3-1	2-2	2-2	3-1	3-2	2-1	2-3	1-2	1-0		1-2	5-1	0-2	2-3	3-1	0-0	1-1	2-0	2-1	1-1
Grimsby Town FC	4-1	2-2	0-1	0-1	4-3	0-0	1-0	0-4	1-4	4-0		1-1	2-0	1-1	0-2	2-0	2-1	1-0	2-2	0-1
Hull City AFC	2-0	3-2	0-2	3-1	2-0	5-0	4-0	1-2	0-1	3-2	4-2		4-1	3-2	5-3	3-2	0-0	3-4	4-2	2-0
Leeds City AFC	1-1	1-1	0-1	2-2	0-0	5-2	5-1	0-1	0-0	2-1	4-1	3-2		0-0	2-1	1-2	3-0	0-0		3-1
Leicester Fosse FC	4-0	2-1	2-1	3-1	3-1	0-2	1-3	2-3	3-0	3-1	1-1	3-2	2-2		1-0	4-1	2-1	1-0	3-0	1-0
Lincoln City FC	0-2	2-0	2-4	1-3	4-0	2-2	1-0	2-4	2-0	0-1	1-0	0-1	5-0	0-3		0-2	1-1	1-2	0-2	3-1
Oldham Athletic AFC	1-0	3-2	4-0	1-1	4-0	4-1	3-1	3-3	4-1	0-0	2-0	3-0	4-2	1-1	4-0		5-0	3-1	2-1	2-0
Stockport County FC	2-0	1-1	1-1	1-3	1-0	6-1	2-1	2-0	1-1	3-2	0-2	2-3	2-1	2-1	1-1	2-3		1-2	1-2	1-3
Stoke FC	4-0	3-1	3-0	0-0	1-1	3-0	0-3	6-1	5-0	4-0	5-0	1-1	2-1	0-1	3-0	1-3	1-0		1-1	0-0
West Bromwich Albion FC	1-1	3-0	3-2	5-0	4-0	3-0	1-0	3-1	0-1	1-1	1-2	1-0	1-0	1-1	5-2	1-2	2-0	1-0		1-0
Wolverhampton Wanderers FC	0-1	1-0	0-0	5-1	0-0	2-2	2-2	2-0	1-0	5-0	5-1	1-2	2-0	0-0	3-0	2-1	0-1	2-0	1-2	

Division 2

	Division 2	Pd	Wn	Dw	Ls	GF	GA	Pts	
1.	Bradford City AFC (Bradford)	38	24	6	8	90	42	54	P
2.	Leicester Fosse FC (Leicester)	38	21	10	7	72	47	52	P
3.	Oldham Athletic AFC (Oldham)	38	22	6	10	76	42	50	
4.	Fulham FC (London)	38	22	5	11	82	49	49	
5.	West Bromwich Albion FC (West Bromwich)	38	19	9	10	61	39	47	
6.	Derby County FC (Derby)	38	21	4	13	77	45	46	
7.	Burnley FC (Burnley)	38	20	6	12	67	50	46	
8.	Hull City AFC (Kingston-upon-Hull)	38	21	4	13	73	62	46	
9.	Wolverhampton Wanderers FC (Wolverhampton)	38	15	7	16	50	45	37	
10.	Stoke FC (Stoke-upon-Trent)	38	16	5	17	57	52	37	#
11.	Gainsborough Trinity FC (Gainsborough)	38	14	7	17	47	71	35	
12.	Leeds City AFC (Leeds)	38	12	8	18	53	65	32	
13.	Stockport County FC (Stockport)	38	12	8	18	48	67	32	
14.	Clapton Orient FC (London)	38	11	10	17	40	65	32	
15.	Blackpool FC (Blackpool)	38	11	9	18	51	58	31	
16.	Barnsley FC (Barnsley)	38	12	6	20	54	68	30	
17.	Glossop FC (Glossop)	38	11	8	19	54	74	30	
18.	Grimsby Town FC (Cleethorpes)	38	11	8	19	43	71	30	
19.	Chesterfield Town FC (Chesterfield)	38	6	11	21	46	92	23	
20.	Lincoln City FC (Lincoln)	38	9	3	26	46	83	21	#
		760	310	140	310	1187	1187	760	

\# Stoke FC (Stoke-upon-Trent) resigned from the league at the end of the season.
Lincoln City FC (Lincoln) were not re-elected to the league for next season.

Bradford Park Avenue FC (Bradford) & Tottenham Hotspur FC (London) were elected to Division 2 for next season.

F.A. CUP FINAL (Crystal Palace, London – 25/04/1908 – 74,697)

WOLVERHAMPTON WANDERERS FC 3-1 Newcastle United FC (Newcastle-upon-Tyne)
Hunt, Hedley, Harrison *Howie*

Wolves: Lunn, Jones, Collins, Hunt, Wooldridge, Bishop, Harrison, Shelton, Hedley, Radford, Pedley.
Newcastle: Lawrence, McCracken, Pudan, Gardner, Veitch, McWilliam, Rutherford, Howie, Appleyard, Speedie, Wilson.

Semi-finals

Newcastle United FC (Newcastle-upon-Tyne)	6-0	Fulham FC (London)
Wolverhampton Wanderers FC (Wolverhampton)	2-0	Southampton FC (Southampton)

Quarter-finals

Everton FC (Liverpool)	0-0, 2-3	Southampton FC (Southampton)
Fulham FC (London)	2-1	Manchester United FC (Manchester)
Newcastle United FC (Newcastle-upon-Tyne)	5-1	Grimsby Town FC (Cleethorpes)
Stoke FC (Stoke-upon-Trent)	0-1	Wolverhampton Wanderers FC (Wanderers)

1908-09

Football League Division 1 1908-1909 Season	Aston Villa	Blackburn Rvs.	Bradford City	Bristol City	Bury	Chelsea	Everton	Leicester Fosse	Liverpool	Manchester City	Manchester Utd.	Middlesbrough	Newcastle United	Nottingham For.	Notts County	Preston N.E.	Sheffield United	Sunderland	Wednesday	Woolw. Arsenal
Aston Villa FC	■	1-1	1-3	1-1	3-0	0-0	3-1	1-1	1-1	2-1	3-1	0-3	3-0	1-2	1-1	2-4	3-0	2-0	1-1	2-1
Blackburn Rovers FC	3-1	■	1-1	1-1	0-1	2-0	0-0	3-0	1-0	3-2	1-3	0-0	2-4	0-3	0-2	1-1	0-1	8-1	2-2	1-3
Bradford City AFC	1-1	0-2	■	0-1	4-1	3-0	1-1	4-1	0-2	0-0	1-0	0-2	1-2	1-1	2-2	2-0	3-1	0-2	0-0	4-1
Bristol City FC	0-0	1-4	0-1	■	4-2	1-0	0-2	1-1	1-0	1-0	0-0	1-1	3-3	2-1	1-0	2-3	1-1	2-4	1-1	2-1
Bury FC	1-2	1-1	2-1	1-2	■	2-1	2-2	2-2	2-1	1-0	2-2	2-1	1-1	3-2	3-1	0-1	1-2	4-2	4-2	1-1
Chelsea FC	0-2	1-1	1-1	3-1	4-1	■	3-3	1-0	3-0	1-2	1-1	3-0	1-2	2-1	3-2	0-0	1-1	2-0	2-2	1-2
Everton FC	3-1	4-4	0-1	5-2	4-0	3-2	■	4-2	5-0	6-3	3-2	1-1	0-1	3-3	0-1	5-1	4-0			0-3
Leicester Fosse FC	4-2	2-4	1-4	1-1	2-5	5-2	0-2	■	3-2	3-1	3-2	1-1	0-4	0-3	0-2	0-0	1-1	4-3	1-1	1-1
Liverpool FC	3-2	1-1	4-0	1-2	2-2	2-1	0-1	4-1	■	1-3	3-1	1-2	2-1	1-1	1-1	2-1	2-1	3-0	1-2	2-2
Manchester City FC	2-0	3-3	4-3	5-1	6-1	1-2	4-0	5-2	4-0	■	1-2	0-0	0-2	2-1	1-0	4-1	1-3	1-0	4-0	2-2
Manchester United FC	0-2	0-3	2-0	0-1	2-1	0-1	2-2	4-2	3-2	3-1	■	6-3	1-0	2-2	4-3	0-2	2-1	2-2	3-1	1-4
Middlesbrough FC	1-0	1-0	1-0	4-0	0-1	1-4	2-3	6-2	1-0	3-0	5-0	■	0-0	4-0	1-2	4-2	1-2	0-3	2-1	1-1
Newcastle United FC	0-2	2-0	1-0	2-1	3-1	1-3	3-0	2-0	0-1	2-0	2-1	1-0	■	1-1	1-0	2-0	4-0	1-9	1-0	3-1
Nottingham Forest FC	1-2	2-1	2-1	1-1	0-2	2-1	1-2	12-0	5-1	0-2	2-0	4-1	0-4	■	1-0	1-1	0-2	4-0	1-2	0-1
Notts County FC	1-1	2-3	1-1	0-1	3-2	3-0	0-0	2-3	1-2	5-1	0-1	3-2	0-4	3-0	■	1-0	3-1	0-0	1-0	2-1
Preston North End FC	3-2	2-0	0-0	2-1	0-2	6-0	3-3	0-1	2-0	3-0	0-3	1-1	0-1	1-1	0-0	■	1-1	1-0	4-1	0-0
Sheffield United FC	3-1	0-0	3-0	3-1	2-2	1-3	1-5	2-1	0-2	4-0	0-0	2-0	1-1	3-2	2-1		■	0-2	2-1	1-1
Sunderland AFC	4-3	0-1	2-1	0-2	3-1	1-2	2-0	3-1	1-4	2-0	6-1	2-0	3-1	2-1	0-1	2-1	3-1	■	4-2	1-0
The Wednesday FC	4-2	1-2	0-2	2-0	4-3	5-1	2-0	3-1	2-3	3-1	2-0	3-2	2-0	3-0	2-0	1-0	1-0	2-5	■	6-2
Woolwich Arsenal FC	0-1	0-1	1-0	1-1	4-0	0-0	0-4	2-1	5-0	3-0	0-1	1-1	1-2	1-2	1-0	1-0	1-0	0-4	2-0	■

Division 1	Pd	Wn	Dw	Ls	GF	GA	Pts	
1. NEWCASTLE UNITED FC (NEWCASTLE/TYNE)	38	24	5	9	65	41	53	
2. Everton FC (Liverpool)	38	18	10	10	82	57	46	
3. Sunderland AFC (Sunderland)	38	21	2	15	78	63	44	
4. Blackburn Rovers FC (Blackburn)	38	14	13	11	61	50	41	
5. The Wednesday FC (Sheffield)	38	17	6	15	67	61	40	
6. Woolwich Arsenal FC (London)	38	14	10	14	52	49	38	
7. Aston Villa FC (Birmingham)	38	14	10	14	58	56	38	
8. Bristol City FC (Bristol)	38	13	12	13	45	58	38	
9. Middlesbrough FC (Middlesbrough)	38	14	9	15	59	53	37	
10. Preston North End FC (Preston)	38	13	11	14	48	44	37	
11. Chelsea FC (London)	38	14	9	15	56	61	37	
12. Sheffield United FC (Sheffield)	38	14	9	15	51	59	37	
13. Manchester United FC (Manchester)	38	15	7	16	58	68	37	
14. Nottingham Forest FC (Nottingham)	38	14	8	16	66	57	36	
15. Notts County FC (Nottingham)	38	14	8	16	51	48	36	
16. Liverpool FC (Liverpool)	38	15	6	17	57	65	36	
17. Bury FC (Bury)	38	14	8	16	63	77	36	
18. Bradford City AFC (Bradford)	38	12	10	16	47	47	34	
19. Manchester City FC (Manchester)	38	15	4	19	67	69	34	R
20. Leicester Fosse FC (Leicester)	38	8	9	21	54	102	25	R
	760	297	166	297	1185	1185	760	

Top Goalscorer

1) B. FREEMAN   (Everton FC)   38

Football League Division 2 1908-1909 Season	Barnsley	Birmingham	Blackpool	Bolton Wanderers	Bradford Park Ave.	Burnley	Chesterfield	Clapton Orient	Derby County	Fulham	Gainsborough Tr.	Glossop	Grimsby Town	Hull City	Lincoln City	Oldham Athletic	Stockport County	Tottenham Hotspur	W.B.A.	Wolves
Barnsley FC		3-1	4-0	0-1	3-1	1-2	4-0	3-0	1-0	1-2	2-2	1-3	3-1	2-1	2-1	2-0	2-0	1-1	0-2	1-1
Birmingham FC	2-1		2-2	2-0	3-1	2-0	3-0	1-0	1-1	1-3	2-2	1-2	3-1	1-2	1-0	2-0	4-2	3-3	0-0	1-1
Blackpool FC	1-1	2-0		1-2	2-1	0-0	2-2	1-3	2-2	2-0	3-0	2-1	2-2	2-3	1-0	1-0	2-1	1-1	0-2	3-1
Bolton Wanderers FC	3-0	2-1	3-1		0-1	2-1	4-0	2-0	1-0	0-0	4-0	2-0	2-0	1-0	2-0	3-0	4-1	0-1	1-1	1-1
Bradford Park Avenue	3-2	1-2	4-3	1-2		2-3	1-0	0-1	2-0	1-1	4-1	1-0	0-2	1-0	2-0	3-4	0-1	0-2	0-0	4-1
Burnley FC	3-2	1-1	1-1	1-2	3-3		0-1	0-1	2-0	1-3	5-2	3-2	2-0	1-0	0-0	1-0	5-1	1-2	0-2	3-5
Chesterfield Town FC	1-0	4-2	3-1	0-2	2-1	1-0		2-0	2-4	2-1	2-1	1-2	0-4	0-1	1-1	1-2	1-3	2-2		1-1
Clapton Orient FC	1-1	3-2	1-1	0-2	2-0	0-1	1-1		2-0	1-1	2-2	0-2	2-1	1-2	0-0	2-0	5-0	0-0	1-0	1-3
Derby County FC	0-0	1-2	1-1	1-0	3-1	1-0	1-1	1-0		2-1	5-0	4-0	2-1	0-0	5-1	1-0	5-0	1-1	2-1	2-1
Fulham FC	2-2	1-1	3-0	1-2	3-0	3-0	0-0	1-2	1-2		4-0	2-3	5-2	0-3	0-1	3-2	5-1	2-3	2-0	1-1
Gainsborough Trinity	4-1	1-3	1-0	2-1	2-1	1-0	3-0	2-0	0-0	1-1		3-1	0-3	2-0	1-1	1-4	3-2	0-2	2-0	1-0
Glossop FC	3-0	3-1	3-0	0-2	1-1	1-2	2-0	4-0	3-1	0-0	2-2		1-0	2-1	0-0	2-1	3-0	1-1	1-3	3-2
Grimsby Town FC	0-0	0-3	2-1	1-0	1-1	0-1	1-0	1-0	2-0	2-2	1-2	2-0		0-0	0-1	2-0	3-0	1-2	1-1	3-0
Hull City AFC	4-0	4-1	2-0	2-0	2-3	3-2	1-0	3-2	4-0	2-0	5-1	0-0	0-1		4-1	1-0	4-1	1-0	2-2	0-1
Leeds City AFC	2-0	2-0	1-0	1-2	0-3	1-1	3-0	0-0	2-5	2-0	0-2	3-1	4-1	2-0		3-0	2-1	1-0	1-1	5-2
Oldham Athletic AFC	0-0	2-0	3-1	1-1	2-0	4-1	2-0	2-0	1-1	1-0	2-0	2-1	4-0	2-2	6-0		0-1	1-0	2-0	2-1
Stockport County FC	2-1	3-2	1-0	1-0	0-1	2-1	2-0	1-1	1-0	1-2	0-1	4-2	0-1	3-1	1-0	1-3		1-3	0-0	1-0
Tottenham Hotspur FC	4-0	4-0	4-1	2-1	3-0	4-2	4-0	0-1	0-0	1-0	1-1	3-3	2-0	0-0	3-0	3-0	0-0		1-3	3-0
West Bromwich Albion FC	1-1	1-1	5-1	2-0	1-0	0-0	2-2	1-0	2-0	1-1	2-0	1-0	7-0	1-0	2-1	1-0	2-0	3-0		0-2
Wolverhampton Wanderers FC	2-0	2-0	2-2	1-2	1-1	2-1	3-0	5-1	1-1	0-1	4-0	0-0	0-0	3-0	2-1	1-1	2-0	1-0	0-1	

Division 2	Pd	Wn	Dw	Ls	GF	GA	Pts	
1. Bolton Wanderers FC (Bolton)	38	24	4	10	59	28	52	P
2. Tottenham Hotspur FC (London)	38	20	11	7	67	32	51	P
3. West Bromwich Albion FC (West Bromwich)	38	19	13	6	56	27	51	
4. Hull City AFC (Kingston-upon-Hull)	38	19	6	13	63	39	44	
5. Derby County FC (Derby)	38	16	11	11	55	41	43	
6. Oldham Athletic AFC (Oldham)	38	17	6	15	55	43	40	
7. Wolverhampton Wanderers FC (Wolverhampton)	38	14	11	13	56	48	39	
8. Glossop FC (Glossop)	38	15	8	15	57	53	38	
9. Gainsborough Trinity FC (Gainsborough)	38	15	8	15	49	70	38	
10. Fulham FC (London)	38	13	11	14	58	48	37	
11. Birmingham FC (Birmingham)	38	14	9	15	58	61	37	
12. Leeds City AFC (Leeds)	38	14	7	17	43	53	35	
13. Grimsby Town FC (Cleethorpes)	38	14	7	17	41	54	35	
14. Burnley FC (Burnley)	38	13	7	18	51	58	33	
15. Clapton Orient FC (London)	38	12	9	17	37	49	33	
16. Bradford Park Avenue FC (Bradford)	38	13	6	19	51	59	32	
17. Barnsley FC (Barnsley)	38	11	10	17	48	57	32	
18. Stockport County FC (Stockport)	38	14	3	21	39	71	31	
19. Chesterfield Town FC (Chesterfield)	38	11	8	19	37	67	30	#
20. Blackpool FC (Blackpool)	38	9	11	18	46	68	29	
	760	297	166	297	1026	1026	760	

Chesterfield Town FC (Chesterfield) were not re-elected to the league for next season and subsequently changed their club name to Chesterfield FC (Chesterfield).

Lincoln City FC (Lincoln) were elected to Division 2 for next season.

F.A. CUP FINAL   (Crystal Palace, London – 24/04/1909 – 71,401)

MANCHESTER UNITED FC (MANCHESTER)   1-0   Bristol City FC (Bristol)

A.Turnbull

Man. United: Moger, Stacey, Hayes, Duckworth, Roberts, Bell, Meredith, Halse, J.Turnbull, A.Turnbull, Wall.

Bristol City: Clay, Annan, Cottle, Hanlin, Wedlock, Spear, Staniforth, Hardy, Gilligan, Burton, Hilton.

Semi-finals

Bristol City FC (Bristol)	1-1, 2-1	Derby County FC (Derby)
Manchester United FC (Manchester)	1-0	Newcastle United FC (Newcastle-upon-Tyne)

Quarter-finals

Burnley FC (Burnley)	1-0, 2-3	Manchester United FC (Manchester)
	(The first match was abandoned after 72 minutes.)	
Derby County FC (Derby)	3-0	Nottingham Forest FC (Nottingham)
Glossop FC (Glossop)	0-0, 0-1	Bristol City FC (Bristol)
Newcastle United FC (Newcastle-upon-Tyne)	2-2, 3-0	Sunderland AFC (Sunderland)

1909-10

Football League Division 1 1909-1910 Season	Aston Villa	Blackburn Rovers	Bolton Wanderers	Bradford City	Bristol City	Bury	Chelsea	Everton	Liverpool	Manchester United	Middlesbrough	Newcastle United	Nottingham Forest	Notts County	Preston North End	Sheffield United	Sunderland	Wednesday	Tottenham Hotspur	Woolwich Arsenal
Aston Villa FC	■	4-3	3-1	3-1	1-0	4-1	4-1	3-1	3-1	7-1	4-2	4-0	0-0	1-1	3-0	2-1	3-2	5-0	3-2	5-1
Blackburn Rovers FC	3-2	■	4-2	2-0	5-2	5-1	1-0	2-1	1-1	3-2	1-1	2-0	2-2	2-0	2-2	3-1	0-0	0-0	2-0	7-0
Bolton Wanderers FC	1-2	1-2	■	1-1	4-2	1-3	5-2	0-1	1-2	2-3	1-1	0-4	2-1	3-4	3-1	1-0	2-1	0-1	0-2	3-0
Bradford City AFC	1-2	2-0	1-0	■	3-1	0-0	4-1	2-0	1-2	0-2	4-1	3-3	1-1	2-1	2-0	2-0	3-1	2-0	5-1	0-1
Bristol City FC	0-0	2-2	1-0	2-0	■	1-1	1-0	3-1	0-1	2-1	4-1	0-3	4-0	3-1	2-0	0-2	2-3	1-1	0-0	0-1
Bury FC	0-2	2-1	1-2	3-4	1-2	■	4-2	2-2	1-2	1-1	2-1	1-2	4-1	1-1	3-1	2-0	0-1	3-2	3-1	1-2
Chelsea FC	0-0	3-1	3-2	0-3	4-1	2-0	■	0-1	2-1	1-1	2-1	2-1	0-1	2-2	2-0	2-2	1-4	4-1	2-1	0-1
Everton FC	0-0	0-2	3-1	1-1	1-0	3-0	2-2	■	2-3	3-3	1-1	1-4	0-4	2-0	1-2	2-1	1-1	4-2	1-0	
Liverpool FC	2-0	3-1	3-0	1-0	0-1	2-2	5-1	0-1	■	3-2	0-0	6-5	7-3	2-1	2-0	0-0	1-4	3-1	2-0	5-1
Manchester United FC	2-0	2-0	5-0	1-0	2-1	2-0	2-0	3-2	3-4	■	4-1	1-1	2-6	2-1	1-1	1-0	2-0	0-3	5-0	1-0
Middlesbrough FC	3-2	1-3	1-2	3-7	0-0	0-5	0-1	1-1	2-2	1-2	■	1-1	2-1	2-0	1-0	2-0	3-2	4-0	4-3	5-2
Newcastle United FC	1-0	4-1	1-0	1-0	3-1	2-2	1-0	1-2	1-3	3-4	2-0	■	1-2	1-3	5-2	0-0	1-0	3-1	1-0	1-1
Nottingham Forest FC	1-4	0-4	2-0	1-1	0-0	3-3	0-0	1-0	1-4	2-0	0-1	0-1	■	2-1	0-0	2-3	1-3	0-6	2-2	1-1
Notts County FC	2-3	2-2	0-0	3-2	0-2	3-1	2-1	2-3	3-1	3-2	2-1	2-2	4-1	■	3-1	1-2	1-1	0-0	3-0	5-1
Preston North End FC	1-0	3-2	1-0	2-2	3-0	2-0	0-1	2-0	1-0	0-0	4-0	0-1	4-0		■	1-1	1-0	1-0	4-1	3-4
Sheffield United FC	0-1	3-0	2-2	1-2	4-0	2-0	0-0	3-0	4-2	0-1	2-0	4-0	1-4	2-2	5-1	■	3-0	3-3	1-1	2-0
Sunderland AFC	1-1	0-0	3-0	3-0	4-0	2-3	4-0	0-1	2-1	3-0	2-2	0-2	2-1	0-3	2-1	1-0	■	2-0	3-1	6-2
The Wednesday FC	3-2	2-1	0-0	2-1	2-0	1-4	4-1	1-3	3-0	4-1	1-5	3-1	4-3	0-0	4-1	1-3	1-0	■	1-1	1-1
Tottenham Hotspur FC	1-1	4-0	1-1	0-0	3-2	1-0	2-1	3-0	1-0	2-2	1-3	0-4	2-2	1-3	2-1	5-1	3-0	1-1	■	1-1
Woolwich Arsenal FC	1-0	0-1	2-0	0-1	2-2	0-0	3-2	1-0	1-1	0-0	3-0	0-3	0-1	1-2	1-3	0-0	1-2	0-1	1-0	■

Division 1

		Pd	Wn	Dw	Ls	GF	GA	Pts	
1.	ASTON VILLA FC (BIRMINGHAM)	38	23	7	8	84	42	53	
2.	Liverpool FC (Liverpool)	38	21	6	11	78	57	48	
3.	Blackburn Rovers FC (Blackburn)	38	18	9	11	73	55	45	
4.	Newcastle United FC (Newcastle-upon-Tyne)	38	19	7	12	70	56	45	
5.	Manchester United FC (Manchester)	38	19	7	12	69	61	45	
6.	Sheffield United FC (Sheffield)	38	16	10	12	62	41	42	
7.	Bradford City AFC (Bradford)	38	17	8	13	64	47	42	
8.	Sunderland AFC (Sunderland)	38	18	5	15	66	51	41	
9.	Notts County FC (Nottingham)	38	15	10	13	67	59	40	
10.	Everton FC (Liverpool)	38	16	8	14	51	56	40	
11.	The Wednesday FC (Sheffield)	38	15	9	14	60	63	39	
12.	Preston North End FC (Preston)	38	15	5	18	52	58	35	
13.	Bury FC (Bury)	38	12	9	17	62	66	33	
14.	Nottingham Forest FC (Nottingham)	38	11	11	16	54	72	33	
15.	Tottenham Hotspur FC (London)	38	11	10	17	53	69	32	
16.	Bristol City FC (Bristol)	38	12	8	18	45	60	32	
17.	Middlesbrough FC (Middlesbrough)	38	11	9	18	56	73	31	
18.	Woolwich Arsenal FC (London)	38	11	9	18	37	67	31	
19.	Chelsea FC (London)	38	11	7	20	47	70	29	R
20.	Bolton Wanderers FC (Bolton)	38	9	6	23	44	71	24	R
		760	300	160	300	1194	1194	760	

Top Goalscorer

1) J. PARKINSON   (Liverpool FC)   30

Football League Division 2 1909-1910 Season	Barnsley	Birmingham	Blackpool	Bradford Park Ave.	Burnley	Clapton Orient	Derby County	Fulham	Gainsborough Trin.	Glossop	Grimsby Town	Hull City	Leeds City	Leicester Fosse	Lincoln City	Manchester City	Oldham Athletic	Stockport County	W.B.A.	Wolves
Barnsley FC	■	5-1	1-0	4-0	0-0	2-1	5-1	2-1	4-1	3-0	2-1	1-2	1-1	3-1	2-1	1-1	2-1	1-0	2-1	7-1
Birmingham FC	2-1	■	1-2	0-1	2-1	1-2	1-3	1-1	5-0	2-2	2-4	0-2	1-2	2-1	1-0	1-1	2-2	3-0	0-1	1-0
Blackpool FC	0-0	2-0	■	0-0	2-3	2-2	1-1	1-1	0-2	1-1	1-0	1-2	3-1	0-1	3-0	0-0	1-3	2-0	2-1	2-0
Bradford Park Avenue	2-0	5-0	2-1	■	3-1	3-1	1-2	3-0	2-0	3-3	6-1	0-1	4-2	1-3	4-0	2-0	1-6	2-4	1-0	2-3
Burnley FC	2-0	2-0	5-1	1-0	■	2-0	1-2	2-0	2-1	0-1	3-1	0-1	3-0	5-2	3-0	3-3	1-2	2-2	2-3	4-2
Clapton Orient FC	4-0	3-0	2-1	1-0	2-1	■	0-2	0-0	2-0	0-0	0-0	0-0	0-2	3-0	1-2	3-2	1-2	2-0	1-3	1-0
Derby County FC	2-1	3-1	2-1	1-2	5-2	1-0	■	3-1	2-2	2-1	6-0	4-0	1-0	0-1	2-0	3-1	1-1	1-0	2-1	5-0
Fulham FC	3-0	0-0	0-1	3-1	2-1	0-0	0-0	■	0-1	2-0	3-2	3-1	5-1	2-0	1-1	1-1	1-1	2-0	0-2	0-0
Gainsborough Trinity	0-0	1-0	3-1	3-1	2-0	0-1	2-4	2-0	■	1-3	1-1	0-1	2-0	0-1	0-0	1-3	0-2	1-0	3-1	0-2
Glossop FC	3-0	4-1	2-3	3-1	2-0	3-1	1-1	0-1	4-0	■	3-1	2-1	2-1	1-0	0-1	0-3	6-2	1-0	3-2	2-0
Grimsby Town FC	7-0	0-2	0-1	0-1	5-3	2-0	1-1	0-2	2-1	4-0	■	2-3	3-1	0-0	1-2	0-1	0-0	0-1	3-0	1-0
Hull City AFC	1-0	7-0	1-2	2-1	3-2	3-0	0-0	3-2	5-1	4-2	5-1	■	3-1	2-1	0-0	1-2	4-0	1-1	5-1	2-2
Leeds City AFC	0-7	2-1	3-2	2-3	1-0	2-1	2-1	2-2	0-0	1-2	3-1	1-1	■	1-1	5-0	1-3	3-5	0-2	0-1	1-0
Leicester Fosse FC	1-1	3-1	3-2	3-0	1-1	4-0	6-0	2-3	9-1	3-1	3-1	3-1	6-2	■	4-1	1-3	3-0	1-0	2-1	2-1
Lincoln City FC	2-1	3-2	2-2	1-1	0-0	4-0	2-3	2-2	4-0	1-2	0-0	1-3	0-0	3-1	■	0-2	0-2	1-0	0-3	1-0
Manchester City FC	0-0	3-0	1-2	3-1	4-0	2-1	2-1	3-1	3-1	3-3	2-0	3-0	3-0	2-0	6-2	■	0-2	2-1	3-2	6-0
Oldham Athletic AFC	5-0	1-1	2-0	1-1	1-0	5-0	4-0	0-1	2-0	1-0	4-1	3-0	2-1	2-1	6-1	1-0	■	3-0	1-2	3-0
Stockport County FC	5-0	1-1	2-0	2-1	1-1	3-0	1-1	0-2	3-0	5-0	2-1	1-5	0-0	6-2	1-1	1-2	2-0	■	0-2	1-1
West Bromwich Albion FC	4-3	3-1	0-3	1-0	1-2	3-0	0-0	3-2	5-0	0-0	4-3	0-2	3-1	1-2	1-0	0-0	1-1	0-1	■	0-1
Wolverhampton Wanderers FC	1-0	4-2	2-1	0-2	3-1	3-1	2-3	1-1	0-0	3-1	8-1	2-2	5-0	4-1	4-2	3-2	1-0	2-1	3-1	■

	Division 2	Pd	Wn	Dw	Ls	GF	GA	Pts	
1.	Manchester City FC (Manchester)	38	23	8	7	81	40	54	P
2.	Oldham Athletic FC (Oldham)	38	23	7	8	79	39	53	P
3.	Hull City AFC (Kingston-upon-Hull)	38	23	7	8	80	46	53	
4.	Derby County FC (Derby)	38	22	9	7	72	47	53	
5.	Leicester Fosse FC (Leicester)	38	20	4	14	79	58	44	
6.	Glossop FC (Glossop)	38	18	7	13	64	57	43	
7.	Fulham FC (London)	38	14	13	11	51	43	41	
8.	Wolverhampton Wanderers FC (Wolverhampton)	38	17	6	15	64	63	40	
9.	Barnsley FC (Barnsley)	38	16	7	15	62	59	39	
10.	Bradford Park Avenue FC (Bradford)	38	17	4	17	64	59	38	
11.	West Bromwich Albion FC (West Bromwich)	38	16	5	17	58	56	37	
12.	Blackpool FC (Blackpool)	38	14	9	16	50	52	36	
13.	Stockport County FC (Stockport)	38	13	8	17	50	47	34	
14.	Burnley FC (Burnley)	38	14	6	18	62	61	34	
15.	Lincoln City FC (Lincoln)	38	10	11	17	42	69	31	
16.	Clapton Orient FC (London)	38	12	6	20	37	60	30	
17.	Leeds City AFC (Leeds)	38	10	7	21	46	80	27	
18.	Gainsborough Trinity FC (Gainsborough)	38	10	6	22	33	75	26	
19.	Grimsby Town FC (Cleethorpes)	38	9	6	23	50	77	24	#
20.	Birmingham FC (Birmingham)	38	8	7	23	42	78	23	
		760	309	142	309	1166	1166	760	

\# Grimsby Town FC (Cleethorpes) were not re-elected to the league for the next season and were replaced in Division 2 by Huddersfield Town AFC (Huddersfield).

F.A. CUP FINAL   (Crystal Palace, London – 23/04/1910 – 77,747)

NEWCASTLE UNITED FC   1-1   Barnsley FC (Barnsley)

Rutherford   *Tuffnell*

Newcastle: Lawrence, McCracken, Carr, Veitch, Low, McWilliam, Rutherford, Howie, Shepherd, Wilson, Higgins.
Barnsley: Mearns, Downs, Ness, Glendinning, Boyle, Utley, Bartrop, Gadsby, Lilycrop, Tuffnell, Forman.

F.A. CUP FINAL REPLAY   (Goodison Park, Liverpool – 28/04/1910 – 69,000)

NEWCASTLE UNITED FC   2-0   Barnsley FC (Barnsley)

Shepherd 2 (1 pen)

Newcastle: Lawrence, McCracken, Carr, Veitch, Low, McWilliam, Rutherford, Howie, Shepherd, Wilson, Whitson.
Barnsley: Mearns, Downs, Ness, Glendinning, Boyle, Utley, Bartrop, Gadsby, Lilycrop, Tuffnell, Forman.

Semi-finals

Barnsley FC (Barnsley)	0-0, 3-0	Everton FC (Liverpool)
Newcastle United FC (Newcastle-upon-Tyne)	2-0	Swindon Town FC (Swindon)

Quarter-finals

Barnsley FC (Barnsley)	1-0	Queen's Park Rangers FC (London)
Coventry City FC (Coventry)	0-2	Everton FC (Liverpool)
Newcastle United FC (Newcastle-upon-Tyne)	3-0	Leicester Fosse FC (Leicester)
Swindon Town FC (Swindon)	2-0	Manchester City FC (Manchester)

1910-11

Football League Division 1 1910-1911 Season	Aston Villa	Blackburn Rovers	Bradford City	Bristol City	Bury	Everton	Liverpool	Manchester City	Manchester United	Middlesbrough	Newcastle United	Nottingham Forest	Notts County	Oldham Athletic	Preston North End	Sheffield United	Sunderland	Wednesday	Tottenham Hotspur	Woolwich Arsenal
Aston Villa FC	■	2-2	4-1	2-0	4-1	2-1	1-1	2-1	4-2	5-0	3-2	3-1	3-1	1-1	0-2	3-0	2-1	4-0	2-1	3-0
Blackburn Rovers FC	0-0	■	3-0	2-0	6-2	0-1	1-2	2-0	1-0	5-1	3-1	4-1	1-1	1-0	0-1	1-2	0-1	3-0	6-1	1-0
Bradford City AFC	1-2	1-0	■	3-1	2-2	3-1	1-3	1-0	1-0	1-0	1-0	2-1	0-1	1-2	1-0	0-1	3-0	3-0	5-2	3-0
Bristol City FC	1-2	1-0	0-2	■	2-0	0-1	1-1	2-1	0-1	3-2	1-0	5-1	1-0	3-2	0-0	1-1	0-2	1-1	2-2	0-1
Bury FC	1-0	2-2	0-1	2-1	■	0-0	3-0	5-2	0-3	4-2	1-1	1-0	0-2	2-2	1-1	0-0	2-1	1-1	1-1	1-1
Everton FC	0-1	6-1	0-0	4-3	2-1	■	0-1	1-0	1-0	2-0	1-5	2-1	5-0	1-0	2-0	1-0	2-2	2-0	1-1	2-0
Liverpool FC	3-1	2-2	1-2	4-0	2-0	0-2	■	1-1	3-2	3-0	2-3	1-0	3-0	2-0	1-2	1-2	3-0			1-1
Manchester City FC	1-1	0-0	1-3	1-2	5-1	2-1	1-2	■	1-1	2-1	2-0	1-0	0-1	2-0	0-2	0-4	3-3	2-1	1-2	1-1
Manchester United FC	2-0	3-2	1-0	3-1	3-2	2-2	2-0	2-1	■	1-2	2-0	4-2	0-0	0-0	5-0	1-1	5-1	3-2	3-2	5-0
Middlesbrough FC	0-1	2-3	3-2	3-0	2-1	1-0	2-2	0-0	2-2	■	0-2	2-2	4-1	1-2	2-0	3-1	1-0	0-1	0-1	1-1
Newcastle United FC	1-0	2-2	6-1	0-1	5-1	1-0	6-1	3-3	0-1	0-0	■	4-1	2-0	3-0	1-1	1-1	1-1	1-1		0-1
Nottingham Forest FC	3-1	5-2	3-3	1-2	1-4	2-0	0-0	2-1	1-1	0-1		■	0-2	4-1	1-3	1-2	1-3	1-2	2-3	
Notts County FC	1-2	2-0	1-1	2-0	1-0	0-0	1-0	0-1	1-0	1-0	2-2	1-1	■	1-0	3-3	0-3	1-1	1-0	2-0	0-2
Oldham Athletic AFC	1-1	2-0	1-0	1-0	0-0	2-0	3-1	1-1	1-3	1-1	0-2	2-0	2-1	■	2-1	3-0	2-1	2-0	1-0	3-0
Preston North End FC	0-1	0-0	2-0	4-0	2-0	0-2	2-1	1-0	0-2	1-1	2-1	0-2	1-1	0-2	■	1-1	0-2	2-0	1-3	4-1
Sheffield United FC	2-1	1-1	0-1	0-4	3-0	0-1	2-0	2-2	2-0	2-1	0-0	0-1	0-2	1-2	5-0	■	1-2	3-0	0-1	3-2
Sunderland AFC	3-2	2-2	1-1	3-1	4-1	4-0	4-0	4-0	1-2	3-1	2-1	2-2	1-1	2-1	1-1	0-2	■	4-0	1-2	2-2
The Wednesday FC	3-2	2-1	2-1	2-0	1-4	1-3	3-0		4-1	1-5	3-1	4-3	0-0		4-1	1-3	1-0	■	1-1	1-1
Tottenham Hotspur FC	1-0	1-0	2-1	2-1	1-0	0-2	1-0		4-1	1-0		2-0	5-2	1-3	2-0	1-1	2-1		■	0-0
Woolwich Arsenal FC	1-1	4-1	0-0	3-0	3-2	1-0	0-0	0-1	1-2	0-2	1-2	3-2	2-1	0-0	2-0	0-0	0-0	2-0	1-0	■

Division 1

		Pd	Wn	Dw	Ls	GF	GA	Pts	
1.	MANCHESTER UNITED FC (MANCHESTER)	38	22	8	8	72	40	52	
2.	Aston Villa FC (Birmingham)	38	22	7	9	69	41	51	
3.	Sunderland AFC (Sunderland)	38	15	15	8	67	48	45	
4.	Everton FC (Liverpool)	38	19	7	12	50	36	45	
5.	Bradford City AFC (Bradford)	38	20	5	13	51	42	45	
6.	The Wednesday FC (Sheffield)	38	17	8	13	47	48	42	
7.	Oldham Athletic AFC (Oldham)	38	16	9	13	44	41	41	
8.	Newcastle United FC (Newcastle-upon-Tyne)	38	15	10	13	61	43	40	
9.	Sheffield United FC (Sheffield)	38	15	8	15	49	43	38	
10.	Woolwich Arsenal FC (London)	38	13	12	13	41	49	38	
11.	Notts County FC (Nottingham)	38	14	10	14	37	45	38	
12.	Blackburn Rovers FC (Blackburn)	38	13	11	14	62	54	37	
13.	Liverpool FC (Liverpool)	38	15	7	16	53	53	37	
14.	Preston North End FC (Preston)	38	12	11	15	40	49	35	
15.	Tottenham Hotspur FC (London)	38	13	6	19	52	63	32	
16.	Middlesbrough FC (Middlesbrough)	38	11	10	17	49	63	32	
17.	Manchester City FC (Manchester)	38	9	13	16	43	58	31	
18.	Bury FC (Bury)	38	9	11	18	43	71	29	
19.	Bristol City FC (Bristol)	38	11	5	22	43	66	27	R
20.	Nottingham Forest FC (Nottingham)	38	9	7	22	55	75	25	R
		760	290	180	290	1028	1028	760	

Top Goalscorer

1) A. SHEPHERD   (Newcastle United FC)   25

Football League Division 2 1910-1911 Season	Barnsley	Birmingham	Blackpool	Bolton Wanderers	Bradford Park Ave.	Burnley	Chelsea	Clapton Orient	Derby County	Fulham	Gainsborough Trin.	Glossop	Huddersfield Town	Hull City	Leeds City	Leicester Fosse	Lincoln City	Stockport County	W.B.A.	Wolves
Barnsley FC		2-3	1-2	0-0	7-0	0-1	3-2	1-2	0-2	4-2	2-2	4-0	1-2	0-1	4-0	1-1	2-2	1-1	1-1	2-2
Birmingham FC	1-0		2-0	2-1	1-0	1-1	2-1	0-1	2-0	1-1	1-1	1-2	2-1	1-0	2-1	1-0	0-1	1-3	1-1	1-3
Blackpool FC	1-0	3-1		1-1	4-1	1-0	0-2	1-1	0-1	1-2	1-1	1-0	1-1	2-0	1-2	2-0	5-1	2-1	0-0	2-0
Bolton Wanderers FC	4-0	5-1	1-0		1-0	1-1	2-0	2-0	2-1	2-0	3-0	4-0	3-1	2-1	3-0	6-2	3-1	2-2	3-1	4-1
Bradford Park Avenue	2-3	2-2	1-0	1-1		1-1	2-1	3-0	2-1	1-0	5-0	6-0	0-1	2-0	0-2	3-1	6-0	3-2	3-3	1-0
Burnley FC	0-0	2-2	1-1	1-3	1-1		1-1	2-0	2-1	1-0	1-1	0-0	2-1	0-0	4-1	2-1	3-1	5-3	2-0	1-1
Chelsea FC	3-1	2-2	0-0	3-0	3-0	3-0		1-0	3-2	2-0	3-0	2-0	2-0	4-1	2-0	7-0	2-0	2-1	2-0	
Clapton Orient FC	3-0	2-1	2-1	0-0	1-0	0-2	0-0		1-0	1-0	4-0	1-1	1-1	0-1	1-0	2-1	1-0	0-0		3-1
Derby County FC	5-1	1-0	1-1	2-2	4-2	3-0	1-4	3-1		2-2	4-0	2-1	1-1	2-3	2-2	3-0	5-0	4-1	1-3	2-0
Fulham FC	0-2	3-0	2-1	2-0	4-0	3-0	1-0	1-1	3-1		1-0	2-2	0-1	2-1	3-1	0-0	6-2	0-1	0-1	
Gainsborough Trinity	1-1	1-0	2-0	1-0	1-2	1-2	3-1	3-1	0-0	0-1		3-0	3-1	1-1	1-2	2-0	1-0	0-0	1-1	1-3
Glossop FC	1-1	2-1	3-1	1-2	0-1	1-1	2-1	1-3	2-2	2-1	3-1		5-2	0-0	2-1	1-0	0-0		0-2	5-1
Huddersfield Town AFC	2-0	7-1	2-2	1-1	0-0	0-1	3-1	2-0	0-3	1-2	2-1	1-0		2-0	3-2	1-2	1-1	4-1	0-2	3-1
Hull City AFC	5-1	4-1	1-1	1-1	2-2	3-0	1-1	1-2	2-0	0-0	3-2	1-0	2-2		1-1	2-2	2-1	4-1	1-1	2-2
Leeds City AFC	0-0	1-1	1-2	1-0	0-0	3-3	1-0	3-2	3-1	4-0	0-2	5-2	1-0			2-3	1-0	4-0	3-1	1-0
Leicester Fosse FC	1-1	2-0	2-0	5-0	2-0	1-1	1-0	2-1	1-2	3-2	1-0	1-1	2-1	0-2	2-1		2-0	5-1	2-3	2-3
Lincoln City FC	1-0	0-1	0-1	1-3	1-0	1-0	0-0	0-0	0-2	1-0	0-0	2-2	2-2	1-4	1-1	2-0		2-0	1-2	1-5
Stockport County FC	2-2	3-1	1-3	0-1	1-0	4-2	2-2	0-3	3-2	1-1	2-1	1-0	1-1	0-4	1-0	3-2			0-1	1-0
West Bromwich Albion FC	3-3	1-0	0-1	2-0	2-1	2-1	1-3	3-0	1-1	2-1	3-1	1-0	0-2	2-0	5-1	3-0	4-2			2-1
Wolverhampton Wanderers FC	1-0	3-1	0-3	3-0	0-0	1-0	0-0	1-0	1-2	5-1	1-1	2-0	0-3	0-0	3-1	1-0	2-1	0-0	2-3	

	Division 2	Pd	Wn	Dw	Ls	GF	GA	Pts	
1.	West Bromwich Albion FC (West Bromwich)	38	22	9	7	67	41	53	P
2.	Bolton Wanderers FC (Bolton)	38	21	9	8	69	40	51	P
3.	Chelsea FC (London)	38	20	9	9	71	35	49	
4.	Clapton Orient FC (London)	38	19	7	12	44	35	45	
5.	Hull City AFC (Kingston-upon-Hull)	38	14	16	8	55	39	44	
6.	Derby County FC (Derby)	38	17	8	13	73	52	42	
7.	Blackpool FC (Blackpool)	38	16	10	12	49	38	42	
8.	Burnley FC (Burnley)	38	13	15	10	45	45	41	
9.	Wolverhampton Wanderers FC (Wolverhampton)	38	15	8	15	51	52	38	
10.	Fulham FC (London)	38	15	7	16	52	48	37	
11.	Leeds City AFC (Leeds)	38	15	7	16	58	56	37	
12.	Bradford Park Avenue FC (Bradford)	38	14	9	15	53	55	37	
13.	Huddersfield Town AFC (Huddersfield)	38	13	8	17	57	58	34	
14.	Glossop FC (Glossop)	38	13	8	17	48	62	34	
15.	Leicester Fosse FC (Leicester)	38	14	5	19	52	62	33	
16.	Birmingham FC (Birmingham)	38	12	8	18	42	64	32	
17.	Stockport County FC (Stockport)	38	11	8	19	47	79	30	
18.	Gainsborough Trinity FC (Gainsborough)	38	9	11	18	37	55	29	
19.	Barnsley FC (Barnsley)	38	7	14	17	52	62	28	
20.	Lincoln City FC (Lincoln)	38	7	10	21	28	72	24	#
		760	287	186	287	1050	1050	760	

Lincoln City FC (Lincoln) were not re-elected to the league for the next season and were replaced in Division 2 by Grimsby Town FC (Cleethorpes).

Burslem Port Vale FC (Burslem) re-formed as a Limited Company under the name of Port Vale FC (Stoke-on-Trent) the town of Burslem having been merged in 1910 with the towns of Fenton, Hanley, Longton, Stoke-upon-Trent and Tunstall as the city of Stoke-on-Trent.

F.A. CUP FINAL   (Crystal Palace, London – 22/04/1911 – 69,098)

BRADFORD CITY AFC (BRADFORD)   0-0   Newcastle United FC (Newcastle-upon-Tyne)

Bradford: Mellors, Campbell, Taylor, Robinson, Gildea, McDonald, Logan, Spiers, O'Rourke, Devine, Thompson.

Newcastle: Lawrence, McCracken, Whitson, Veitch, Low, Willis, Rutherford, Jobey, Stewart, Higgins, Wilson.

F.A. CUP FINAL REPLAY   (Old Trafford, Manchester – 26/04/1911 – 58,000)

BRADFORD CITY AFC (BRADFORD)   1-0   Newcastle United FC (Newcastle-upon-Tyne)

Speirs

Bradford: Mellors, Campbell, Taylor, Robinson, Torrance, McDonald, Logan, Spiers, O'Rourke, Devine, Thompson.

Newcastle: Lawrence, McCracken, Whitson, Veitch, Low, Willis, Rutherford, Jobey, Stewart, Higgins, Wilson.

Semi-finals

Bradford City AFC (Bradford)	3-0	Blackburn Rovers FC (Blackburn)
Newcastle United FC (Newcastle-upon-Tyne)	3-0	Chelsea FC (London)

Quarter-finals

Bradford City AFC (Bradford)	1-0	Burnley FC (Burnley)
Chelsea FC (London)	3-1	Swindon Town FC (Swindon)
Newcastle United FC (Newcastle-upon-Tyne)	4-0	Derby County FC (Derby)
West Ham United FC (London)	2-3	Blackburn Rovers FC (Blackburn)

1911-12

Football League Division 1 1911-1912 Season	Aston Villa	Blackburn Rovers	Bolton Wanderers	Bradford City	Bury	Everton	Liverpool	Manchester City	Manchester United	Middlesbrough	Newcastle United	Notts County	Oldham Athletic	Preston North End	Sheffield United	Sunderland	Wednesday	Tottenham Hotspur	W.B.A.	Woolwich Arsenal
Aston Villa FC		0-3	0-1	0-0	5-2	3-0	5-0	3-1	6-0	2-1	2-0	5-1	6-1	1-0	1-0	2-3	1-3	2-2	0-3	4-1
Blackburn Rovers FC	3-1		2-0	3-1	2-0	2-1	1-0	2-0	2-2	2-1	1-1	0-0	1-0	3-0	1-0	2-2	0-0	0-0	4-1	4-0
Bolton Wanderers FC	3-0	2-0		2-0	1-0	1-2	2-1	2-1	1-1	1-0	0-2	3-0	2-1	3-0	0-3	3-0	4-2	1-0	2-0	2-2
Bradford City AFC	2-1	1-0	1-0		1-0	1-0	0-2	4-1	0-1	2-1	1-1	2-3	0-0	0-1	2-1	2-1	5-1	3-0	4-1	1-1
Bury FC	1-1	1-2	1-3	2-0		1-2	2-2	1-2	0-1	0-2	2-1	0-1	1-1	0-0	3-1	0-2	2-2	2-1	1-0	3-1
Everton FC	1-1	1-3	1-0	1-0	1-1		2-1	1-0	4-0	1-0	2-0	1-1	1-1	1-0	3-2	1-0	1-0	2-2	3-0	1-0
Liverpool FC	1-2	1-2	1-0	1-0	1-1	1-3		2-2	3-2	1-1	0-1	3-0	1-0	0-1	2-0	2-1	1-1	1-2	1-3	4-1
Manchester City FC	2-6	3-0	3-1	4-0	2-0	4-0	2-3		0-0	2-0	1-1	4-0	1-3	0-0	0-0	2-0	4-0	2-1	0-2	3-3
Manchester United FC	3-1	3-1	2-0	0-1	0-0	2-1	1-1	0-0		3-4	0-2	2-0	3-1	0-0	1-0	2-2	3-1	1-2	1-2	2-0
Middlesbrough FC	1-2	2-1	1-0	1-0	1-1	0-0	3-2	3-1	3-0		1-1	4-0	3-0	4-2	1-1	3-3	1-1	2-0	1-0	0-2
Newcastle United FC	6-2	4-2	5-2	0-2	3-2	2-0	1-1	1-0	2-3	0-1		3-2	1-1	1-0	2-2	3-1	0-2	2-0	0-0	1-1
Notts County FC	2-0	1-3	3-2	0-0	2-0	0-1	0-0	0-1	0-1	2-1	1-4		1-1	1-2	2-0	3-1	1-0	2-2	2-2	3-1
Oldham Athletic AFC	1-2	0-1	3-1	3-0	2-0	3-0	0-1	4-1	2-2	2-0	2-4	1-2		1-0	2-3	0-0	1-0	2-1	3-1	0-0
Preston North End FC	4-1	2-2	1-2	2-2	1-0	2-1	2-1	2-1	0-0	0-3	2-1	2-1	0-1		3-0	0-3	2-3	0-1	1-1	0-1
Sheffield United FC	0-1	1-1	0-5	7-3	4-0	2-1	3-1	6-2	6-1	1-1	2-1	1-3	4-0	4-2		1-2	1-1	1-2	1-2	2-1
Sunderland AFC	2-2	3-0	0-1	1-1	1-0	4-0	1-2	1-1	5-0	1-0	1-2	5-0	4-2	3-0	0-0		0-0	1-1	3-2	1-0
The Wednesday FC	3-0	1-1	0-1	4-2	2-1	1-3	2-2	3-0	3-0	0-2	1-2	3-0	1-0	0-1	1-1	8-0		4-0	4-1	3-0
Tottenham Hotspur FC	2-1	0-2	1-0	2-3	2-1	0-1	2-0	0-2	1-1	2-1	1-2	2-2	4-0	6-2	1-1	0-0	3-1		1-0	5-0
West Bromwich Albion FC	2-2	2-0	0-0	0-0	2-0	1-0	1-0	1-1	1-0	3-1	3-1	2-1	0-0	0-2	1-0	1-0	1-5	2-0		1-1
Woolwich Arsenal FC	2-2	5-1	3-0	2-0	1-0	0-1	2-2	2-0	2-1	3-1	2-0	0-3	1-1	4-1	3-1	3-0	0-2	3-1	0-2	

Division 1

		Pd	Wn	Dw	Ls	GF	GA	Pts	
1.	BLACKBURN ROVERS FC (BLACKBURN)	38	20	9	9	60	43	49	
2.	Everton FC (Liverpool)	38	20	6	12	46	42	46	
3.	Newcastle United FC (Newcastle-upon-Tyne)	38	18	8	12	64	50	44	
4.	Bolton Wanderers FC (Bolton)	38	20	3	15	54	43	43	
5.	The Wednesday FC (Sheffield)	38	16	9	13	69	49	41	
6.	Aston Villa FC (Birmingham)	38	17	7	14	76	63	41	
7.	Middlesbrough FC (Middlesbrough)	38	16	8	14	56	45	40	
8.	Sunderland AFC (Sunderland)	38	14	11	13	58	51	39	
9.	West Bromwich Albion FC (West Bromwich)	38	15	9	14	43	47	39	
10.	Woolwich Arsenal FC (London)	38	15	8	15	55	59	38	
11.	Bradford City AFC (Bradford)	38	15	8	15	46	50	38	
12.	Tottenham Hotspur FC (London)	38	14	9	15	53	53	37	
13.	Manchester United FC (Manchester)	38	13	11	14	45	60	37	
14.	Sheffield United FC (Sheffield)	38	13	10	15	63	56	36	
15.	Manchester City FC (Manchester)	38	13	9	16	56	58	35	
16.	Notts County FC (Nottingham)	38	14	7	17	46	63	35	
17.	Liverpool FC (Liverpool)	38	12	10	16	49	55	34	
18.	Oldham Athletic AFC (Oldham)	38	12	10	16	46	54	34	
19.	Preston North End FC (Preston)	38	13	7	18	40	57	33	R
20.	Bury FC (Bury)	38	6	9	23	32	59	21	R
		760	296	168	296	1057	1057	760	

Top Goalscorers

1) H. HAMPTON   (Aston Villa FC)   25
    G. HOLLEY   (Sunderland AFC)   25
    D. McLEAN   (The Wednesday FC)   25

Football League Division 2 1911-1912 Season	Barnsley	Birmingham	Blackpool	Bradford Park Avenue	Bristol City	Burnley	Chelsea	Clapton Orient	Derby County	Fulham	Gainsborough Trinity	Glossop	Grimsby Town	Huddersfield Town	Hull City	Leeds City	Leicester Fosse	Nottingham Forest	Stockport County	Wolves
Barnsley FC	■	1-0	1-0	1-0	4-1	1-1	0-2	2-1	0-2	2-2	4-0	1-0	2-2	0-0	1-2	3-4	0-0	1-0	2-1	2-1
Birmingham FC	1-3	■	2-1	2-3	0-0	4-0	1-4	4-0	0-4	1-3	2-2	2-0	2-2	1-0	5-1	4-3	4-0	4-2	2-0	3-1
Blackpool FC	0-0	1-0	■	0-4	1-0	0-0	1-0	1-0	1-0	3-1	0-0	2-0	1-2	3-1	3-2	3-0	1-1	2-0	0-1	1-0
Bradford Park Avenue	1-0	3-0	0-0	■	0-1	2-1	1-1	2-1	0-1	0-2	5-0	1-1	4-1	3-1	3-1	1-1	1-1	2-1	1-0	0-1
Bristol City FC	0-1	2-1	2-0	1-0	■	0-3	1-1	1-0	1-1	1-0	2-0	2-0	3-0	3-2	0-0	4-1	0-1	2-2	2-1	0-3
Burnley FC	3-0	1-1	1-1	3-1	4-2	■	2-2	1-0	0-0	5-1	2-0	4-0	1-1	3-0	5-1	4-2	3-0	2-0	4-1	2-1
Chelsea FC	2-1	0-2	4-1	1-0	2-2	0-2	■	3-0	1-0	1-0	1-0	1-0	4-1	3-1	1-0	4-2	2-1	2-0	0-0	4-0
Clapton Orient FC	2-0	2-0	2-0	2-0	4-0	1-2	1-4	■	3-0	4-0	3-0	2-1	1-0	2-1	4-0	2-1	4-1	0-2	4-2	1-0
Derby County FC	0-0	0-1	5-1	1-0	3-0	2-0	2-0	5-1	■	6-1	4-0	5-0	2-1	4-2	2-3	5-2	5-0	1-0	2-0	1-1
Fulham FC	2-2	2-1	3-0	2-0	2-1	3-4	0-1	0-2	0-0	■	7-1	0-2	1-3	3-1	0-1	7-2	4-1	2-0	3-1	1-1
Gainsborough Trinity	1-2	0-0	0-0	0-0	2-3	1-0	0-2	0-2	1-1	0-1	■	1-1	2-3	5-0	0-3	2-1	0-1	1-2	0-0	1-0
Glossop FC	0-2	2-0	1-1	0-0	3-0	1-3	1-2	3-3	3-1	1-1	1-1	■	5-2	2-3	1-1	2-1	6-0	0-0	1-1	0-1
Grimsby Town FC	0-0	1-0	1-0	0-0	3-0	1-0	2-1	2-1	0-3	1-0	3-3	0-0	■	1-2	1-0	1-2	4-0	1-4	2-2	0-0
Huddersfield Town AFC	2-1	3-2	4-0	3-1	1-2	1-1	1-3	0-0	0-0	2-0	2-2	3-1	2-0	■	0-2	1-2	1-2	1-2	2-0	1-1
Hull City AFC	0-0	4-0	3-0	5-1	3-0	4-1	1-0	0-2	0-0	2-3	1-1	2-0	1-0	0-1	■	1-0	4-1	2-1	0-2	3-0
Leeds City AFC	3-2	0-0	1-0	1-2	3-1	1-5	0-0	0-2	0-1	0-2	0-0	2-1	1-2	2-0	0-0	■	2-1	3-1	1-1	1-1
Leicester Fosse FC	0-0	5-2	4-0	3-0	2-0	3-2	2-0	2-0	0-1	2-5	2-0	1-0	0-2	0-2	3-0	2-1	■	1-1	1-1	1-1
Nottingham Forest FC	0-2	0-1	2-1	2-1	2-0	0-1	2-3	3-0	1-3	1-1	2-0	0-1	1-0	3-0	0-0	2-1	4-1	■	1-2	0-0
Stockport County FC	1-1	2-0	1-2	1-0	1-0	0-1	0-1	1-1	4-0	2-1	0-3	3-0	3-0	3-1	1-1	3-3	2-3	2-2	■	1-2
Wolverhampton Wanderers FC	5-0	1-0	3-0	1-1	3-1	2-0	3-1	0-1	0-1	0-0	1-0	1-1	1-2	1-2	8-0	5-0	1-0	1-0	4-0	■

	Division 2	Pd	Wn	Dw	Ls	GF	GA	Pts	
1.	Derby County FC (Derby)	38	23	8	7	74	28	54	P
2.	Chelsea FC (London)	38	24	6	8	64	34	54	P
3.	Burnley FC (Burnley)	38	22	8	8	77	41	52	
4.	Clapton Orient FC (London)	38	21	3	14	61	44	45	
5.	Wolverhampton Wanderers FC (Wolverhampton)	38	16	10	12	57	33	42	
6.	Barnsley FC (Barnsley)	38	15	12	11	45	42	42	
7.	Hull City AFC (Kingston-upon-Hull)	38	17	8	13	54	51	42	
8.	Fulham FC (London)	38	16	7	15	66	58	39	
9.	Grimsby Town FC (Cleethorpes)	38	15	9	14	48	55	39	
10.	Leicester Fosse FC (Leicester)	38	15	7	16	49	66	37	
11.	Bradford Park Avenue FC (Bradford)	38	13	9	16	44	45	35	
12.	Birmingham FC (Birmingham)	38	14	6	18	55	59	34	
13.	Bristol City FC (Bristol)	38	14	6	18	41	60	34	
14.	Blackpool FC (Blackpool)	38	13	8	17	32	52	34	
15.	Nottingham Forest FC (Nottingham)	38	13	7	18	46	48	33	
16.	Stockport County FC (Stockport)	38	11	11	16	47	54	33	
17.	Huddersfield Town AFC (Huddersfield)	38	13	6	19	50	64	32	
18.	Glossop FC (Glossop)	38	8	12	18	42	56	28	
19.	Leeds City AFC (Leeds)	38	10	8	20	50	78	28	
20.	Gainsborough Trinity FC (Gainsborough)	38	5	13	20	30	64	23	#
		760	298	164	298	1032	1032	760	

Gainsborough Trinity FC (Gainsborough) were not re-elected to the league for next season and were replaced in Division 2 by Lincoln City FC (Lincoln).

F.A. CUP FINAL   (Crystal Palace, London – 20/04/1912 – 54,556)

BARNSLEY FC (BARNSLEY)　　　　0-0 (aet)　　　　West Bromwich Albion FC

Barnsley: Copper, Downs, Taylor, Glendinning, Bratley, Utley, Bartrop, Tuffnell, Lillycrop, Travers, Moore.

West Bromwich: Pearson, Cook, Pennington, Baddeley, Buck, McNeal, Jephcott, Wright, Pailor, Bowser, Shearman.

F.A. CUP FINAL REPLAY   (Bramall Lane, Sheffield – 24/04/1912 – 38,555)

BARNSLEY FC (BARNSLEY)　　　　1-0　　　West Bromwich Albion FC (West Bromwich)

Tuffnell

Barnsley: Copper, Downs, Taylor, Glendinning, Bratley, Utley, Bartrop, Tuffnell, Lillycrop, Travers, Moore.

West Bromwich: Pearson, Cook, Pennington, Baddeley, Buck, McNeal, Jephcott, Wright, Pailor, Bowser, Shearman.

Semi-finals

Blackburn Rovers FC (Blackburn)	0-0, 0-1	West Bromwich Albion FC (West Bromwich)
Swindon Town FC (Swindon)	0-0, 0-1	Barnsley FC (Barnsley)

Quarter-finals

Barnsley FC (Barnsley)	0-0, 0-0, 0-0, 3-2	Bradford City AFC (Bradford)
Manchester United FC (Manchester)	1-1, 2-4	Blackburn Rovers FC (Blackburn)
Swindon Town FC (Swindon)	2-1	Everton FC (Liverpool)
West Bromwich Albion FC (West Bromwich)	3-0	Fulham FC (London)

1912-13

Football League Division 1 1912-1913 Season	Aston Villa	Blackburn Rovers	Bolton Wanderers	Bradford City	Chelsea	Derby County	Everton	Liverpool	Manchester City	Manchester United	Middlesbrough	Newcastle United	Notts County	Oldham Athletic	Sheffield United	Sunderland	Wednesday	Tottenham Hotspur	W.B.A.	Woolwich Arsenal
Aston Villa FC	■	1-1	1-1	3-1	1-0	5-1	1-1	1-3	2-0	4-2	5-1	3-1	1-0	7-1	4-2	1-1	10-0	1-0	2-4	4-1
Blackburn Rovers FC	2-2	■	6-0	5-0	1-1	0-1	1-2	5-1	2-2	0-0	5-2	2-0	2-1	7-1	3-1	4-0	0-1	6-1	2-4	1-1
Bolton Wanderers FC	2-3	1-1	■	2-0	1-0	1-1	0-0	1-1	2-2	2-1	3-2	1-2	0-0	3-0	4-2	1-3	3-0	2-0	2-1	5-1
Bradford City AFC	1-1	0-2	4-1	■	2-2	2-3	4-1	2-0	2-1	1-0	1-2	2-0	1-0	0-0	3-1	1-5	0-0	3-1	1-1	3-1
Chelsea FC	1-2	1-6	2-3	0-3	■	3-1	1-3	1-2	2-1	1-4	2-3	1-0	5-1	1-1	4-2	2-0	0-4	1-0	0-2	1-1
Derby County FC	0-1	1-1	3-3	4-0	3-1	■	1-4	4-2	2-0	2-1	0-2	2-1	1-0	1-2	5-1	0-3	1-4	5-0	1-2	4-1
Everton FC	0-1	2-1	2-3	2-1	1-0	2-2	■	0-2	0-0	4-1	1-0	0-6	4-0	2-3	0-1	0-4	3-1	1-2	1-3	3-0
Liverpool FC	2-0	4-1	5-0	2-1	1-2	2-1	2-2	■	1-2	0-2	4-2	2-1	0-0	2-0	2-2	2-5	2-1	4-1	2-1	3-0
Manchester City FC	1-0	3-1	2-0	1-3	2-0	1-1	1-0	4-1	■	0-2	3-0	0-1	4-0	2-0	3-0	1-0	2-2	2-2	2-1	0-1
Manchester United FC	4-0	1-1	2-1	2-0	4-2	4-0	2-0	3-1	0-1	■	2-3	3-0	2-1	0-4	4-0	1-3	2-0	0-1	1-1	2-0
Middlesbrough FC	1-1	0-0	4-0	1-1	0-3	4-1	0-0	3-4	0-0	3-2	■	0-0	1-1	2-2	4-1	0-2	0-2	1-1	3-1	2-0
Newcastle United FC	2-3	0-1	2-1	1-1	3-2	2-4	0-0	0-1	1-3	3-1	0-0	■	4-1	1-2	1-1	1-0	3-1	1-0	1-1	3-1
Notts County FC	1-1	3-1	1-0	1-1	0-0	0-1	0-1	3-0	0-1	1-2	1-3	0-1	■	2-1	0-1	2-1	1-2	0-1	1-1	2-1
Oldham Athletic AFC	2-2	0-0	2-3	0-0	3-2	2-2	2-0	3-1	2-1	0-0	1-0	1-0	4-0	■	2-0	3-0	2-0	4-1	0-0	0-0
Sheffield United FC	3-2	0-0	0-2	3-2	3-3	4-1	4-1	4-1	1-2	1-0	1-1	2-0	1-1	1-1	■	1-3	0-2	4-0	1-0	1-3
Sunderland AFC	3-1	2-4	2-1	1-0	4-0	0-2	3-1	7-0	1-0	3-1	4-0	2-0	4-0	1-1	1-0	■	0-2	2-2	3-1	4-1
The Wednesday FC	1-1	2-1	2-2	6-0	3-2	3-3	1-2	1-0	1-0	3-3	3-1	1-2	3-1	5-0	1-2	1-2	■	2-1	3-2	2-0
Tottenham Hotspur FC	3-3	0-1	0-1	2-1	1-0	1-2	0-2	1-0	4-0	1-1	5-3	1-0	0-3	1-0	1-2	2-4		■	3-1	1-1
West Bromwich Albion FC	2-2	1-1	2-2	1-1	0-1	0-0	0-0	3-1	0-2	1-2	2-0	1-0	2-0	2-3	3-1	3-1	1-1	4-1	■	2-1
Woolwich Arsenal FC	0-3	0-1	1-2	1-1	0-1	1-2	0-0	1-1	0-4	0-0	1-1	1-1	0-0	0-0	1-3	1-3	2-5	0-3	1-0	■

Division 1

		Pd	Wn	Dw	Ls	GF	GA	Pts	
1.	SUNDERLAND AFC (SUNDERLAND)	38	25	4	9	86	43	54	
2.	Aston Villa FC (Birmingham)	38	19	12	7	86	52	50	
3.	The Wednesday FC (Sheffield)	38	21	7	10	75	55	49	
4.	Manchester United FC (Manchester)	38	19	8	11	69	43	46	
5.	Blackburn Rovers FC (Blackburn)	38	16	13	9	79	43	45	
6.	Manchester City FC (Manchester)	38	18	8	12	53	37	44	
7.	Derby County FC (Derby)	38	17	8	13	69	66	42	
8.	Bolton Wanderers FC (Bolton)	38	16	10	12	62	63	42	
9.	Oldham Athletic AFC (Oldham)	38	14	14	10	50	55	42	
10.	West Bromwich Albion FC (West Bromwich)	38	13	12	13	57	50	38	
11.	Everton FC (Liverpool)	38	15	7	16	48	54	37	
12.	Liverpool FC (Liverpool)	38	16	5	17	61	71	37	
13.	Bradford City AFC (Bradford)	38	12	11	15	50	60	35	
14.	Newcastle United FC (Newcastle-upon-Tyne)	38	13	8	17	47	47	34	
15.	Sheffield United FC (Sheffield)	38	14	6	18	56	70	34	
16.	Middlesbrough FC (Middlesbrough)	38	11	10	17	55	69	32	
17.	Tottenham Hotspur FC (London)	38	12	6	20	45	72	30	
18.	Chelsea FC (London)	38	11	6	21	51	73	28	
19.	Notts County FC (Nottingham)	38	7	9	22	28	56	23	R
20.	Woolwich Arsenal FC (London)	28	3	12	23	26	74	18	R
		760	292	176	292	1153	1153	760	

Top Goalscorer

1) D. McLEAN   (The Wednesday FC)   30

Football League Division 2 1912-1913 Season	Barnsley	Birmingham	Blackpool	Bradford Park A.	Bristol City	Burnley	Bury	Clapton Orient	Fulham	Glossop	Grimsby Town	Huddersfield T.	Hull City	Leeds City	Leicester Fosse	Lincoln City	Nottingham For.	Preston N.E.	Stockport County	Wolves
Barnsley FC	■	1-0	5-3	4-0	7-1	1-4	4-3	0-0	2-1	2-1	3-0	2-0	2-1	2-0	1-0	4-0	1-0	1-1	1-1	3-2
Birmingham FC	3-1	■	3-2	1-1	3-0	3-0	1-2	1-1	2-1	0-0	2-1	3-2	3-1	2-2	5-1	4-1	2-0	0-1	1-1	0-0
Blackpool FC	0-1	2-0	■	0-2	1-1	0-2	2-1	2-0	2-0	1-1	2-1	2-1	1-2	0-3	2-1	1-1	2-1	0-1	1-1	1-2
Bradford Park Avenue	0-0	0-0	4-2	■	4-1	2-3	3-1	3-0	2-3	5-0	3-0	2-1	2-0	0-1	2-2	3-0	3-1	0-0	4-2	5-1
Bristol City FC	3-0	0-3	0-0	0-0	■	3-3	1-5	1-0	2-1	3-3	2-2	0-0	1-1	1-1	2-0	1-2	1-1		7-2	3-1
Burnley FC	0-1	3-0	4-0	5-1	2-2	■	3-1	5-0	5-0	2-1	3-2	4-0	0-0	2-2	5-1	3-1	3-5	2-2	3-2	4-2
Bury FC	2-0	3-0	1-1	2-0	0-1	1-1	■	0-0	1-0	4-1	4-2	0-2	3-0	1-1	2-2	0-3	2-0	0-0	2-0	1-0
Clapton Orient FC	2-2	0-2	1-0	1-0	0-0	2-0	1-2	■	2-1	1-0	1-3	1-1	2-1	2-0	1-1	1-2	2-2	1-2	4-1	0-0
Fulham FC	1-1	3-2	4-2	3-1	0-0	4-2	3-1	1-1	■	2-0	0-1	2-0	2-0	4-0	1-1	3-1	0-0	3-1	7-0	4-2
Glossop FC	1-0	0-2	2-0	4-3	3-1	1-3	1-1	3-0	2-0	■	2-0	1-0	0-3	2-1	3-0	0-1	4-3	2-3	2-2	1-3
Grimsby Town FC	1-1	2-2	1-1	3-0	3-0	2-0	4-0	1-2	2-1	0-0	■	0-0	3-2	2-0	0-0	0-0	2-0	0-0	4-1	2-1
Huddersfield Town AFC	2-0	0-0	3-0	2-0	5-0	1-0	4-0	0-0	5-1	6-0	0-2	■	5-2	1-0	5-1	1-1	1-1	3-3	2-1	
Hull City AFC	0-1	1-2	4-1	5-0	3-1	0-0	2-0	2-1	0-1	2-0	5-0	1-3	■	6-2	2-1	2-0	2-1	2-2	3-2	0-1
Leeds City AFC	2-0	4-0	0-2	2-0	1-1	4-1	4-2	3-1	2-3	4-0	1-2	0-3	1-0	■	5-1	2-2	1-0	5-1	2-1	2-2
Leicester Fosse FC	1-0	1-2	5-1	3-0	3-1	2-3	3-0	1-0	1-0	1-4	1-0	0-0	3-2	1-1	■	1-0	3-1	0-3	4-1	2-1
Lincoln City AFC	2-0	0-1	1-0	1-1	2-0	1-3	0-1	1-1	3-0	0-0	3-0	3-1	1-1	3-3	3-0	■	2-1	0-0	3-2	2-1
Nottingham Forest FC	2-0	3-1	1-1	1-2	4-1	2-1	1-1	0-0	2-4	3-2	1-2	0-1	5-0	1-2	4-2	1-2	■	0-2	2-1	2-0
Preston North End FC	4-0	1-0	2-1	4-2	5-1	1-1	2-0	0-1	1-0	2-0	2-0	2-1	1-0	3-2	1-0	0-0	1-1	■	1-1	1-1
Stockport County FC	0-3	0-1	2-0	1-0	0-1	0-1	1-2	2-0	1-1	1-1	1-1	3-1	3-3	6-0	1-2	2-4	2-1	1-1	■	5-1
Wolverhampton Wanderers FC	3-0	2-2	4-0	0-0	1-1	0-2	3-1	1-1	2-1	3-1	3-0	2-0	0-1	2-2	1-1	2-0	2-3	2-0	1-0	■

	Division 2	**Pd**	**Wn**	**Dw**	**Ls**	**GF**	**GA**	**Pts**	
1.	Preston North End FC (Preston)	38	19	15	4	56	33	53	P
2.	Burnley FC (Burnley)	38	21	8	9	88	53	50	P
3.	Birmingham FC (Birmingham)	38	18	10	10	59	44	46	
4.	Barnsley FC (Barnsley)	38	19	7	12	57	47	45	
5.	Huddersfield Town AFC (Huddersfield)	38	17	9	12	66	40	43	
6.	Leeds City AFC (Leeds)	38	15	10	13	70	64	40	
7.	Grimsby Town FC (Cleethorpes)	38	15	10	13	51	50	40	
8.	Lincoln City FC (Lincoln)	38	15	10	13	50	52	40	
9.	Fulham FC (London)	38	17	5	16	65	55	39	
10.	Wolverhampton Wanderers FC (Wolverhampton)	38	14	10	14	56	54	38	
11.	Bury FC (Bury)	38	15	8	15	53	57	38	
12.	Hull City AFC (Kingston-upon-Hull)	38	15	6	17	60	56	36	
13.	Bradford Park Avenue FC (Bradford)	38	14	8	16	60	60	36	
14.	Clapton Orient FC (London)	38	10	14	14	34	47	34	
15.	Leicester Fosse FC (Leicester)	38	13	7	18	50	65	33	
16.	Bristol City FC (Bristol)	38	9	15	14	46	72	33	
17.	Nottingham Forest FC (Nottingham)	38	12	8	18	58	59	32	
18.	Glossop FC (Glossop)	38	12	8	18	49	68	32	
19.	Stockport County FC (Stockport)	38	8	10	20	56	78	26	
20.	Blackpool FC (Blackpool)	38	9	8	21	39	69	26	
		760	287	186	287	1123	1123	760	

F.A. CUP FINAL   (Crystal Palace, London – 19/04/1913 – 121,919)

ASTON VILLA FC (BIRMINGHAM)	1-0	Sunderland AFC (Sunderland)

Barber

Aston Villa: Hardy, Lyons, Weston, Barber, Harrop, Leach, Wallace, Halse, Hampton, Stephenson, Bache.
Sunderland: Butler, Gladwin, Ness, Cuggy, Thomson, Low, Mordue, Buchan, Richardson, Holley, Martin.

Semi-finals

Aston Villa FC (Birmingham)	1-0	Oldham Athletic AFC (Oldham)
Sunderland AFC (Sunderland)	0-0, 3-2	Burnley FC (Burnley)

Quarter-finals

Blackburn Rovers FC (Blackburn)	0-1	Burnley FC (Burnley)
Bradford Park Avenue FC (Bradford)	0-5	Aston Villa FC (Birmingham)
Everton FC (Liverpool)	0-1	Oldham Athletic AFC (Oldham)
Sunderland AFC (Sunderland)	0-0, 2-2, 3-0	Newcastle United FC (Newcastle-upon-Tyne)

1913-14

Football League Division 1 1913-1914 Season	Aston Villa	Blackburn Rovers	Bolton Wanderers	Bradford City	Burnley	Chelsea	Derby County	Everton	Liverpool	Manchester City	Manchester United	Middlesbrough	Newcastle United	Oldham Athletic	Preston North End	Sheffield United	Sunderland	Wednesday	Tottenham Hotspur	W.B.A.
Aston Villa FC	■	1-3	1-0	0-1	1-0	1-2	3-2	3-1	2-1	1-1	3-1	1-3	1-3	0-0	3-0	3-0	5-0	2-0	3-3	2-0
Blackburn Rovers FC	0-0	■	3-2	0-0	0-0	3-1	3-1	6-0	6-2	2-1	0-1	6-0	3-0	2-1	5-0	3-2	3-1	3-2	1-1	2-0
Bolton Wanderers FC	3-0	1-0	■	3-0	0-0	1-1	3-1	0-0	2-1	3-0	6-1	1-1	3-1	6-2	0-3	3-1	2-1	0-1	3-0	1-0
Bradford City AFC	0-0	0-2	5-1	■	1-1	0-0	0-0	0-1	1-0	3-2	1-1	2-3	2-0	0-1	0-0	2-1	0-2	3-1	2-1	1-0
Burnley FC	4-0	1-2	2-2	2-2	■	6-1	5-1	2-0	5-2	2-0	1-2	1-2	1-0	2-0	3-4	0-0	1-1	3-0	1-1	0-0
Chelsea FC	0-3	2-0	2-1	2-1	0-0	■	2-1	2-0	3-0	1-0	0-2	3-2	0-1	2-1	2-0	2-0	1-1	2-1	1-3	1-1
Derby County FC	0-2	2-3	3-3	3-1	3-1	0-1	■	1-0	1-1	2-4	4-2	2-2	2-0	1-2	0-1	3-5	1-1	1-1	4-0	1-2
Everton FC	1-4	0-0	1-1	1-1	1-1	0-0	5-0	■	1-2	1-0	5-0	2-0	2-0	0-2	2-0	5-0	1-5	1-1	1-1	2-0
Liverpool FC	0-1	3-3	2-1	0-1	1-1	3-0	1-0	1-2	■	4-2	1-2	2-1	0-0	0-3	3-1	2-1	1-3	1-2	2-1	0-0
Manchester City FC	3-1	1-2	0-1	1-0	4-1	2-1	1-2	1-1	1-0	■	0-2	1-1	0-1	2-1	1-1	2-1	3-1	1-2	2-1	2-3
Manchester United FC	0-6	0-0	0-1	1-1	0-1	0-1	3-3	0-1	3-0	0-1	■	0-1	2-2	4-1	3-0	2-1	3-1	2-1	3-1	1-0
Middlesbrough FC	5-2	3-0	2-3	1-1	2-1	2-0	3-2	2-0	4-0	2-0	3-1	■	3-0	0-0	4-1	2-3	3-4	5-2	6-0	3-0
Newcastle United FC	2-2	0-0	4-3	0-0	3-1	1-0	1-1	0-1	1-2	0-1	0-1	1-0	■	0-0	2-0	2-1	2-1	3-1	2-0	3-3
Oldham Athletic AFC	0-1	1-1	2-0	3-1	1-1	3-2	0-0	2-0	2-2	1-3	2-2	3-0	3-0	■	1-0	1-2	2-1	2-0	3-0	2-0
Preston North End FC	3-2	1-5	1-1	2-1	3-3	2-0	1-0	0-1	2-2	4-2	4-1	4-1	0-1		■	2-4	2-2	5-0	1-2	0-2
Sheffield United FC	3-0	1-1	2-0	1-1	5-0	3-2	2-2	4-1	0-1	1-3	2-0	3-1	2-0	2-1	2-0	■	1-0	0-1	1-4	1-1
Sunderland AFC	2-0	2-1	3-2	0-1	1-1	2-0	1-0	5-2	1-2	0-0	2-0	4-2	1-2	2-0	3-1	1-2	■	0-1	2-0	0-0
The Wednesday FC	2-3	3-1	1-1	1-3	2-6	3-0	1-3	2-2	4-1	2-2	1-3	2-0	0-0	1-2	2-1	2-1	2-1	■	2-0	1-4
Tottenham Hotspur FC	0-2	3-3	3-0	0-0	2-0	1-2	1-1	4-1	0-0	3-1	2-1	0-1	0-0	3-1	1-0	2-1	1-4	1-1	■	3-0
West Bromwich Albion FC	1-0	2-0	1-1	2-1	4-1	3-1	2-1	1-1	0-1	0-0	2-1	2-1	1-1	2-2	1-0	2-1	2-1	1-1	1-1	■

Division 1

		Pd	Wn	Dw	Ls	GF	GA	Pts	
1.	BLACKBURN ROVERS FC (BLACKBURN)	38	20	11	7	78	42	51	
2.	Aston Villa FC (Birmingham)	38	19	6	13	65	50	44	
3.	Middlesbrough FC (Middlesbrough)	38	19	5	14	77	60	43	
4.	Oldham Athletic AFC (Oldham)	38	17	9	12	55	45	43	
5.	West Bromwich Albion FC (West Bromwich)	38	15	13	10	46	42	43	
6.	Bolton Wanderers FC (Bolton)	38	16	10	12	65	52	42	
7.	Sunderland AFC (Sunderland)	38	17	6	15	63	52	40	
8.	Chelsea FC (London)	38	16	7	15	46	55	39	
9.	Bradford City AFC (Bradford)	38	12	14	12	40	40	38	
10.	Sheffield United FC (Sheffield)	38	16	5	17	63	60	37	
11.	Newcastle United FC (Newcastle-upon-Tyne)	38	13	11	14	39	48	37	
12.	Burnley FC (Burnley)	38	12	12	14	61	53	36	
13.	Manchester City FC (Manchester)	38	14	8	16	51	53	36	
14.	Manchester United FC (Manchester)	38	15	6	17	52	62	36	
15.	Everton FC (Liverpool)	38	12	11	15	46	55	35	
16.	Liverpool FC (Liverpool)	38	14	7	17	46	62	35	
17.	Tottenham Hotspur FC (London)	38	12	10	16	50	62	34	
18.	The Wednesday FC (Sheffield)	38	13	8	17	53	70	34	
19.	Preston North End FC (Preston)	38	12	6	20	52	69	30	R
20.	Derby County FC (Derby)	38	8	11	19	55	71	27	R
		760	292	176	292	1103	1103	760	

Top Goalscorer

1) G. ELLIOTT   (Middlesbrough FC)   32

Football League Division 2 1913-1914 Season	Barnsley	Birmingham	Blackpool	Bradford Park Ave.	Bristol City	Bury	Clapton Orient	Fulham	Glossop	Grimsby Town	Huddersfield Town	Hull City	Leeds City	Leicester Fosse	Lincoln City	Nottingham Forest	Notts County	Stockport County	Wolves	Woolwich Arsenal
Barnsley FC		1-1	2-1	1-2	3-0	2-0	2-1	1-0	2-0	3-1	2-1	0-2	1-4	3-0	1-0	5-0	0-1	1-0	2-1	1-0
Birmingham FC	0-0		0-0	1-2	2-2	1-0	2-0	0-1	6-0	1-2	1-4	1-1	0-2	1-0	2-0	2-0	2-1	3-2	4-1	2-0
Blackpool FC	3-1	2-2		2-1	0-1	0-1	0-0	1-1	1-1	1-1	0-1	2-2	2-2	1-0	2-1	2-1	0-0	2-2	2-0	1-1
Bradford Park Avenue	1-1	5-1	4-1		4-3	3-1	1-0	1-0	2-1	3-0	2-1	2-0	3-1	3-2	3-0	4-0	0-3	0-2	1-0	2-3
Bristol City FC	1-1	1-2	1-0	2-0		2-0	3-0	0-1	4-1	1-0	1-0	2-1	1-1	1-0	4-1	1-0	1-1	5-0	0-0	1-1
Bury FC	4-0	3-1	1-0	0-0	3-1		0-0	1-0	1-0	3-1	2-1	2-0	1-1	1-1	1-0	1-0	3-3	1-0	1-4	1-1
Clapton Orient FC	1-0	2-2	2-0	1-0	5-2	1-0		1-0	5-1	0-0	0-0	3-0	3-1	1-0	5-1	3-1	1-0	1-1	2-2	1-0
Fulham FC	1-2	1-0	0-0	1-6	3-1	1-1	2-0		2-1	2-2	1-0	0-1	0-1	1-2	4-0	2-0	1-2	2-0	1-0	6-1
Glossop FC	5-1	4-1	1-2	2-1	1-1	2-1	0-3	0-1		3-0	2-3	2-1	1-1	0-2	4-0	3-0	0-1	1-1	1-2	0-2
Grimsby Town FC	1-1	0-2	2-0	0-0	1-0	1-0	2-0	0-3	3-0		2-1	1-3	0-1	3-0	1-3	3-0	0-0	2-0	1-0	1-1
Huddersfield Town AFC	3-1	7-0	1-0	0-1	1-2	1-1	1-0	3-1	2-1	1-2		0-3	1-1	1-2	1-1	2-1	0-2	0-0	0-0	1-2
Hull City AFC	0-1	0-0	0-0	1-3	0-1	0-1	2-0	1-1	3-0	2-1	4-1		1-0	0-0	1-1	1-0	2-0	3-0	7-1	1-2
Leeds City AFC	3-0	3-2	2-1	5-1	1-0	2-1	0-0	2-1	3-0	4-1	5-1	1-2		2-1	1-0	8-0	2-4	5-1	5-0	0-0
Leicester Fosse FC	0-2	0-0	0-1	2-3	3-0	0-0	1-0	3-0	1-3	2-0	0-1	0-4	5-1		2-0	5-1	0-2	2-5	2-3	1-2
Lincoln City AFC	2-2	1-1	1-2	0-3	2-1	1-0	0-0	0-1	1-5	1-3	3-0	0-0	1-0	3-0		1-0	0-0	0-3	1-0	5-2
Nottingham Forest FC	0-2	3-1	3-0	1-0	1-1	1-1	1-1	1-1	1-2	4-1	1-1	1-2	2-1	1-3	2-1		1-0	2-2	1-3	0-0
Notts County FC	3-1	5-1	2-0	2-3	4-0	2-0	3-0	4-0	2-2	4-0	3-0	4-1	4-0	4-1	2-1	2-2		2-1	2-0	1-0
Stockport County FC	1-1	2-0	0-0	3-1	5-1	3-0	0-1	1-3	1-1	2-2	2-1	2-1	3-0	2-3	2-1	1-2			0-0	2-0
Wolverhampton Wanderers FC	0-1	1-0	1-0	1-0	0-2	3-0	2-1	1-0	1-0	4-1	2-2	1-0	1-3	2-1	1-0	4-1	4-1	3-1		1-2
Woolwich Arsenal FC	1-0	1-0	2-1	2-0	1-1	0-1	2-2	2-0	2-0	0-1	0-0	1-0	2-1	3-0	3-2	3-0	4-0	3-1		

	Division 2	Pd	Wn	Dw	Ls	GF	GA	Pts	
1.	Notts County FC (Nottingham)	38	23	7	8	77	36	53	P
2.	Bradford Park Avenue FC (Bradford)	38	23	3	12	71	47	49	P
3.	Woolwich Arsenal FC (London)	38	20	9	9	54	38	49	*
4.	Leeds City AFC (Leeds)	38	20	7	11	76	46	47	
5.	Barnsley FC (Barnsley)	38	19	7	12	51	45	45	
6.	Clapton Orient FC (London)	38	16	11	11	47	35	43	
7.	Hull City AFC (Kingston-upon-Hull)	38	16	9	13	53	37	41	
8.	Bristol City FC (Bristol)	38	16	9	13	52	50	41	
9.	Wolverhampton Wanderers FC (Wolverhampton)	38	18	5	15	51	52	41	
10.	Bury FC (Bury)	38	15	10	13	39	40	40	
11.	Fulham FC (London)	38	16	6	16	46	43	38	
12.	Stockport County FC (Stockport)	38	13	10	15	55	57	36	
13.	Huddersfield Town AFC (Huddersfield)	38	13	8	17	47	53	34	
14.	Birmingham FC (Birmingham)	38	12	10	16	48	60	34	
15.	Grimsby Town FC (Cleethorpes)	38	13	8	17	42	58	34	
16.	Blackpool FC (Blackpool)	38	9	14	15	33	44	32	
17.	Glossop FC (Glossop)	38	11	6	21	51	67	28	
18.	Leicester Fosse FC (Leicester)	38	11	4	23	45	61	26	
19.	Lincoln City FC (Lincoln)	38	10	6	22	36	66	26	
20.	Nottingham Forest FC (Nottingham)	38	7	9	22	37	76	23	
		760	301	158	301	1011	1011	760	

* Woolwich Arsenal FC (London) changed their club name to The Arsenal FC (London) for next season.

F.A. CUP FINAL   (Crystal Palace, London – 25/04/1914 – 72,778)

BURNLEY FC (BURNLEY)	1-0	Liverpool FC (Liverpool)

Freeman

Burnley: Sewell, Bamford, Taylor, Halley, Boyle, Watson, Nesbitt, Lindley, Freeman, Hodgson, Mosscrop.

Liverpool: Campbell, Longworth, Pursell, Fairfoul, Ferguson, MacKinlay, Sheldon, Metcalfe, Miller, Lacey, Nicholl.

Semi-finals

Aston Villa FC (Birmingham)	0-2	Liverpool FC (Liverpool)
Sheffield United FC (Sheffield)	0-0, 0-1	Burnley FC (Burnley)

Quarter-finals

Liverpool FC (Liverpool)	2-1	Queen's Park Rangers FC (London)
Manchester City FC (Manchester)	0-0, 0-0 (aet), 0-1	Sheffield United FC (Sheffield)
Sunderland AFC (Sunderland)	0-0, 1-2	Burnley FC (Burnley)
The Wednesday FC (Sheffield)	0-1	Aston Villa FC (Birmingham)

1914-15

Football League Division 1 1914-1915 Season	Aston Villa	Blackburn Rovers	Bolton Wanderers	Bradford City	Bradford Park Avenue	Burnley	Chelsea	Everton	Liverpool	Manchester City	Manchester United	Middlesbrough	Newcastle United	Notts County	Oldham Athletic	Sheffield United	Sunderland	Wednesday	Tottenham Hotspur	W.B.A.
Aston Villa FC		2-1	1-7	0-0	1-2	3-3	2-1	1-5	6-2	4-1	3-3	5-0	2-1	2-1	0-0	1-0	1-3	0-0	3-1	2-1
Blackburn Rovers FC	1-2		2-2	2-1	2-2	6-0	3-2	2-1	4-2	0-1	3-3	4-0	2-3	5-1	4-1	1-2	3-1	1-1	4-1	2-1
Bolton Wanderers FC	2-2	3-2		3-5	3-2	3-1	3-1	0-0	0-1	2-3	3-0	4-0	0-0	1-2	2-0	0-1	1-1	0-3	4-2	1-1
Bradford City AFC	3-0	3-0	4-2		3-2	0-0	2-2	0-1	3-2	0-0	4-2	1-1	1-1	3-1	1-0	1-1	3-1	1-0	2-2	5-0
Bradford Park Avenue	2-2	1-2	1-2	3-0		2-2	3-0	1-2	1-0	3-1	5-0	2-0	1-0	3-1	1-1	2-0	2-1	1-1	5-1	1-4
Burnley FC	2-1	3-2	5-0	0-1	2-0		2-0	1-0	3-0	1-2	3-0	4-0	0-0	2-3	1-2	2-1	1-2	2-3	3-1	0-2
Chelsea FC	3-1	1-3	2-1	2-0	0-1	1-4		2-0	3-1	0-0	1-3	2-2	0-3	4-1	2-2	1-1	3-0	0-0	1-1	4-1
Everton FC	0-0	1-3	5-3	1-1	4-1	0-2	2-2		1-3	4-1	4-2	2-3	3-0	4-0	3-4	0-0	7-1	0-1	1-1	2-1
Liverpool FC	3-6	3-0	4-3	2-1	2-1	3-0	3-3	0-5		3-2	1-1	1-1	2-2	1-1	1-2	2-1	2-1	2-1	7-2	3-1
Manchester City FC	1-0	1-3	2-1	4-1	2-3	1-0	2-1	0-1	1-1		1-1	1-1	1-1	0-0	0-0	0-0	2-0	4-0	2-1	4-0
Manchester United FC	1-0	2-0	4-1	1-0	1-2	0-2	2-2	1-2	2-0	0-0		2-2	1-0	2-2	1-3	1-2	3-0	2-0	1-1	0-0
Middlesbrough FC	1-1	1-4	0-0	3-0	1-3	1-1	3-0	5-1	3-0	1-0	1-1		1-1	1-0	4-1	2-2	2-3	3-1	7-5	2-0
Newcastle United FC	3-0	2-1	1-2	1-1	1-0	1-2	0-1	0-0	2-1	2-0	1-2			1-1	1-2	4-3	2-5	0-0	4-0	1-2
Notts County FC	1-1	1-1	0-0	0-0	1-2	0-0	2-0	0-0	3-1	0-2	4-2	5-1	1-0		2-1	3-1	2-1	1-2	1-2	1-1
Oldham Athletic AFC	3-3	3-2	5-3	1-0	6-2	1-2	0-0	1-1	0-2	0-0	1-0	5-1	1-0	2-0		3-0	4-5	5-2	4-1	1-1
Sheffield United FC	3-0	1-2	3-1	1-1	3-2	1-0	1-1	1-0	2-1	0-0	3-1	1-0	1-0	3-0			1-1	0-1	1-1	2-0
Sunderland AFC	4-0	5-1	4-3	1-1	3-3	2-1	2-1	0-3	2-2	0-2	4-1	2-4	3-1	1-2	3-2			3-1	5-0	1-2
The Wednesday FC	5-2	1-1	7-0	3-3	6-0	0-0	3-2	1-4	2-1	2-1	1-0	3-1	2-1	0-0	2-2	1-1	1-2		3-2	0-0
Tottenham Hotspur FC	0-2	0-4	4-2	0-0	3-0	1-3	1-1	1-3	1-1	2-2	2-0	3-3	0-0	2-0	1-0	1-1	0-6	6-1		2-0
West Bromwich Albion FC	2-0	0-0	3-0	3-0	1-0	3-0	2-0	1-2	4-0	0-1	0-0	1-0	2-0	4-1	0-0	1-1	1-2	0-0	3-2	

Division 1

		Pd	Wn	Dw	Ls	GF	GA	Pts	
1.	EVERTON FC (LIVERPOOL)	38	19	8	11	76	47	46	
2.	Oldham Athletic AFC (Oldham)	38	17	11	10	70	56	45	
3.	Blackburn Rovers FC (Blackburn)	38	18	7	13	83	61	43	
4.	Burnley FC (Burnley)	38	18	7	13	61	47	43	
5.	Manchester City FC (Manchester)	38	15	13	10	49	39	43	
6.	Sheffield United FC (Sheffield)	38	15	13	10	49	41	43	
7.	The Wednesday FC (Sheffield)	38	15	13	10	61	54	43	
8.	Sunderland AFC (Sunderland)	38	18	5	15	81	72	41	
9.	Bradford Park Avenue FC (Bradford)	38	17	7	14	69	65	41	
10.	Bradford City AFC (Bradford)	38	13	14	11	55	49	40	
11.	West Bromwich Albion FC (West Bromwich)	38	15	10	13	49	43	40	
12.	Middlesbrough FC (Middlesbrough)	38	13	12	13	62	74	38	
13.	Aston Villa FC (Birmingham)	38	13	11	14	62	72	37	
14.	Liverpool FC (Liverpool)	38	14	9	15	65	75	37	
15.	Newcastle United FC (Newcastle-upon-Tyne)	38	11	10	17	46	48	32	
16.	Notts County FC (Nottingham)	38	9	13	16	41	57	31	
17.	Bolton Wanderers FC (Bolton)	38	11	8	19	68	84	30	
18.	Manchester United FC (Manchester)	38	9	12	17	46	62	30	
19.	Chelsea FC (London)	38	8	13	17	51	65	29	#
20.	Tottenham Hotspur FC (London)	38	8	12	18	57	90	28	#
		760	276	208	276	1201	1201	760	

Top Goalscorer

1) Robert PARKER   (Everton FC)   35

Football League Division 2 1914-1915 Season	Barnsley	Birmingham	Blackpool	Bristol City	Bury	Clapton Orient	Derby County	Fulham	Glossop	Grimsby Town	Huddersfield Town	Hull City	Leeds City	Leicester Fosse	Lincoln City	Nottingham Forest	Preston North End	Stockport County	The Arsenal	Wolves
Barnsley FC		2-1	1-2	2-1	2-0	1-0	1-0	2-2	2-0	0-0	1-0	1-0	2-1	1-0	3-1	3-0	2-1	2-0	1-0	2-1
Birmingham FC	2-0		3-0	1-1	1-0	1-0	0-2	1-0	11-1	3-0	1-0	2-2	6-3	2-0	2-0	3-0	1-1	0-1	3-0	1-2
Blackpool FC	1-1	3-1		2-0	3-4	5-1	2-1	2-2	3-0	5-0	3-2	1-2	1-0	1-2	0-0	3-0	0-2	4-2	0-2	1-0
Bristol City FC	3-1	2-3	2-1		1-0	3-0	2-3	0-0	3-1	7-0	0-1	5-2	1-0	1-0	2-1	1-2	4-0	0-2	1-1	0-1
Bury FC	1-2	1-3	2-2	2-1		3-0	2-0	1-0	5-0	2-2	3-1	0-1	0-0	3-1	1-1	4-2	0-0	2-1	3-1	4-1
Clapton Orient FC	4-2	1-1	2-0	2-0	2-2		0-1	2-1	5-2	2-1	3-1	0-3	2-0	2-0	3-1	0-0	1-1	3-0	1-0	1-1
Derby County FC	7-0	1-0	5-0	1-0	2-1	0-3		1-1	1-1	1-1	1-0	4-1	1-2	1-0	3-0	1-0	2-0	1-0	4-0	3-1
Fulham FC	2-0	2-3	0-1	1-2	6-3	4-0	2-0		2-0	2-1	2-3	4-1	1-0	1-0	3-1	2-1	0-2	1-0	0-1	0-1
Glossop FC	0-1	3-3	1-3	2-1	3-0	3-1	1-1	1-0		0-0	2-2	0-5	0-3	2-3	1-2	1-0	1-1	1-0	0-4	0-2
Grimsby Town FC	2-3	1-0	2-0	2-3	1-0	2-1	1-2	1-1	1-0		0-0	1-1	2-5	1-0	5-1	4-0	2-2	6-1	1-0	1-4
Huddersfield Town AFC	1-0	0-0	5-0	5-3	0-1	1-1	0-0	2-2	0-1	3-1		1-0	1-0	3-1	0-1	4-0	3-1	2-1	3-0	2-0
Hull City AFC	2-1	0-0	1-3	1-1	3-1	1-0	2-0	2-0	4-1	0-4	2-1		2-6	2-1	6-1	3-1	0-1	1-0	1-0	5-1
Leeds City AFC	0-2	2-0	2-0	1-1	2-1	0-1	3-5	0-1	3-0	5-0	1-0	2-3		7-2	3-1	4-0	0-0	1-3	2-2	2-3
Leicester Fosse FC	0-1	1-0	2-2	1-3	1-3	1-1	0-6	0-2	3-2	2-0	1-2	1-1	5-1		2-2	3-1	2-3	5-4	1-4	0-3
Lincoln City AFC	3-0	0-1	0-1	3-1	2-3	1-0	0-0	2-1	2-1	1-1	0-3	0-1	2-3	2-3		2-1	3-1	2-2	1-0	2-2
Nottingham Forest FC	2-1	1-1	2-1	0-1	1-1	0-1	2-2	2-2	1-0	4-2	3-2	1-0	3-1	1-3	3-2		1-1	1-1	1-1	3-1
Preston North End FC	5-2	2-0	1-0	4-1	2-0	2-2	1-3	2-1	1-0	3-0	1-1	2-1	2-0	1-0	0-0	2-2		2-0	3-0	5-3
Stockport County FC	1-2	3-1	0-2	2-2	1-0	2-0	3-2	0-2	2-1	1-1	2-1	3-0	3-1	3-0	1-0	1-0	2-1		1-1	2-2
The Arsenal FC	1-0	1-0	2-0	3-0	3-1	2-1	1-2	3-0	6-0	0-3	2-1	2-0	6-0	1-1	7-0	1-1	1-2	3-1		5-1
Wolverhampton Wanderers FC	4-1	0-0	2-0	2-2	1-1	0-0	0-1	2-0	4-0	0-1	4-1	1-2	5-1	7-0	3-1	5-1	2-0	4-1	1-0	

Division 2	**Pd**	**Wn**	**Dw**	**Ls**	**GF**	**GA**	**Pts**	
1. Derby County FC (Derby)	38	23	7	8	71	33	53	P
2. Preston North End FC (Preston)	38	20	10	8	61	42	50	P
3. Barnsley FC (Barnsley)	38	22	3	13	51	51	47	
4. Wolverhampton Wanderers FC (Wolverhampton)	38	19	7	12	77	52	45	
5. Birmingham FC (Birmingham)	38	17	9	12	62	39	43	
6. The Arsenal FC (London)	38	19	5	14	69	41	43	#
7. Hull City AFC (Kingston-upon-Hull)	38	19	5	14	65	54	43	
8. Huddersfield Town AFC (Huddersfield)	38	17	8	13	61	42	42	
9. Clapton Orient FC (London)	38	16	9	13	50	48	41	
10. Blackpool FC (Blackpool)	38	17	5	16	58	57	39	
11. Bury FC (Bury)	38	15	8	15	61	56	38	
12. Fulham FC (London)	38	15	7	16	53	47	37	
13. Bristol City FC (Bristol)	38	15	7	16	62	56	37	
14. Stockport County FC (Stockport)	38	15	7	16	54	60	37	
15. Leeds City AFC (Leeds)	38	14	4	20	65	64	32	
16. Lincoln City FC (Lincoln)	38	11	9	18	46	65	31	
17. Grimsby Town FC (Cleethorpes)	38	11	9	18	48	76	31	
18. Nottingham Forest FC (Nottingham)	38	10	9	19	43	77	29	
19. Leicester Fosse FC (Leicester)	38	10	4	24	47	88	24	
20. Glossop FC (Glossop)	38	6	6	26	31	87	18	##
	760	311	138	311	1135	1135	760	

Glossop FC (Glossop) resigned from the league at the end of the season.

The league was suspended due to World War 1 and did not resume until season 1919-20 when Divisions 1 & 2 were both extended to 22 clubs. As a result of this Chelsea FC (London) and The Arsenal FC (London) were both elected to Division 1 for season 1919-20, however Tottenham Hotspur FC (London) were relegated to Division 2.

Coventry City FC (Coventry), Rotherham County FC (Rotherham), South Shields FC (South Shields), Stoke FC (Stoke-on-Trent) and West Ham United FC (London) were elected to Division 2 for the 1919-20 season.

F.A. CUP FINAL (Old Trafford, Manchester – 24/04/1915 – 49,557)

SHEFFIELD UNITED FC (SHEFFIELD)	3-0	Chelsea FC (London)

Simmons, Fazackerley, Kitchen

Sheffield United: Gough, Cook, English, Sturgess, Brelsford, Utley, Simmons, Fazackerley, Kitchen, Masterman, Evans.

Chelsea: Molyneux, Bettridge, Harrow, Taylor, Logan, Walker, Ford, Halse, Thompson, Croal, McNeil.

Semi-finals

Chelsea FC (London)	2-0	Everton FC (Liverpool)
Sheffield United FC (Sheffield)	2-1	Bolton Wanderers FC (Bolton)

Quarter-finals

Bolton Wanderers FC (Bolton)	4-2	Hull City AFC (Kingston-upon-Hull)
Bradford City AFC (Bradford)	0-2	Everton FC (Liverpool)
Chelsea FC (London)	1-1 (aet), 1-0	Newcastle United FC (Newcastle-upon-Tyne)
Oldham Athletic AFC (Oldham)	0-0 (aet), 0-3	Sheffield United FC (Sheffield)

1915-16

	Lancashire (Principal)	Pd	Wn	Dw	Ls	GF	GA	Pts
1.	Manchester City FC (Manchester)	26	16	3	7	61	35	35
2.	Burnley FC (Burnley)	26	14	5	7	71	43	33
3.	Blackpool FC (Blackpool)	26	14	3	9	54	41	31
4.	Everton FC (Liverpool)	25	15	-	10	59	42	30
5.	Oldham Athletic AFC (Oldham)	25	13	3	9	52	44	29
6.	Liverpool FC (Liverpool)	26	11	7	8	48	42	29
7.	Stockport County FC (Stockport)	26	13	3	10	47	43	29
8.	Stoke FC (Stoke-on-Trent)	26	10	7	9	43	46	27
9.	Southport Central FC (Southport)	26	9	6	11	41	41	24
10.	Bury FC (Bury)	26	10	3	13	46	52	23
11.	Manchester United FC (Manchester)	26	7	8	11	41	51	22
12.	Bolton Wanderers FC (Bolton)	26	9	3	14	48	65	21
13.	Rochdale AFC (Rochdale)	26	7	5	14	34	56	19
14.	Preston North End FC (Preston)	26	4	2	20	23	67	10
		362	152	58	152	668	668	362

	Lancashire (Subsidiary – North)	Pd	Wn	Dw	Ls	GF	GA	Pts
1.	Burnley FC (Burnley)	10	8	-	2	29	12	16
2.	Blackpool FC (Blackpool)	10	8	-	2	24	13	16
3.	Preston North End FC (Preston)	10	4	2	4	22	19	10
4.	Bolton Wanderers FC (Bolton)	10	4	1	5	16	22	9
5.	Bury FC (Bury)	10	3	-	7	17	26	6
6.	Southport Central FC (Southport)	10	1	1	8	12	28	3
		60	28	4	28	120	120	60

Lancashire (Subsidiary – South)

		Pd	Wn	Dw	Ls	GF	GA	Pts
1.	Manchester City FC (Manchester)	10	5	3	2	23	19	13
2.	Everton FC (Liverpool)	10	6	1	3	19	16	13
3.	Liverpool FC (Liverpool)	10	4	2	4	21	13	10
4.	Oldham Athletic AFC (Oldham)	10	4	2	4	17	21	10
5.	Stockport County FC (Stockport)	10	4	1	5	19	18	9
6.	Manchester United FC (Manchester)	10	2	1	7	12	24	5
		60	25	10	25	111	111	60

Midland (Principal)

		Pd	Wn	Dw	Ls	GF	GA	Pts
1.	Nottingham Forest FC (Nottingham)	26	15	5	6	48	25	35
2.	Sheffield United FC (Sheffield)	26	12	7	7	51	36	31
3.	Huddersfield Town AFC (Huddersfield)	26	12	5	9	43	36	29
4.	Bradford City AFC (Bradford)	26	12	4	10	52	32	28
5.	Leicester Fosse FC (Leicester)	26	11	6	9	42	34	28
6.	Barnsley FC (Barnsley)	26	12	4	10	46	55	28
7.	The Wednesday FC (Sheffield)	26	11	5	10	46	43	27
8.	Notts County FC (Nottingham)	26	10	6	10	39	36	26
9.	Lincoln City FC (Lincoln)	26	12	2	12	54	54	26
10.	Leeds City AFC (Leeds)	26	10	5	11	39	43	25
11.	Hull City AFC (Kingston-upon-Hull)	26	10	3	13	42	58	23
12.	Bradford Park Avenue FC (Bradford)	26	9	4	13	46	46	22
13.	Grimsby Town FC (Cleethorpes)	26	7	6	13	31	46	20
14.	Derby County FC (Derby)	26	7	2	17	39	74	16
		364	150	64	150	618	618	364

Midland (Subsidiary – North)

		Pd	Wn	Dw	Ls	GF	GA	Pts
1.	Leeds City AFC (Leeds)	10	7	1	2	21	13	15
2.	Bradford Park Avenue FC (Bradford)	10	6	-	4	27	17	12
3.	Huddersfield Town AFC (Huddersfield)	10	4	3	3	19	15	11
4.	Bradford City AFC (Bradford)	10	4	1	5	18	20	9
5.	Rochdale AFC (Rochdale)	10	4	1	5	15	21	9
6.	Barnsley FC (Barnsley)	10	2	-	8	13	27	4
		60	27	6	27	113	113	60

Midland (Subsidiary – Midland)

		Pd	Wn	Dw	Ls	GF	GA	Pts
1.	Grimsby Town FC (Cleethorpes)	10	5	2	3	25	10	12
2.	Sheffield United FC (Sheffield)	10	4	3	3	17	11	11
3.	Rotherham County FC (Rotherham)	10	5	1	4	20	24	11
4.	Hull City AFC (Kingston-upon-Hull)	10	5	-	5	18	27	10
5.	The Wednesday FC (Sheffield)	10	3	3	4	10	13	9
6.	Lincoln City FC (Lincoln)	10	2	3	5	17	22	7
		60	24	12	24	107	107	60

Midland (Subsidiary – South)

		Pd	Wn	Dw	Ls	GF	GA	Pts
1.	Nottingham Forest FC (Nottingham)	10	7	-	3	28	12	14
2.	Notts County FC (Nottingham)	10	5	3	2	16	12	13
3.	Leicester Fosse FC (Leicester)	10	3	3	4	15	19	9
4.	Stoke FC (Stoke-on-Trent)	10	4	-	6	21	18	8
5.	Derby County FC (Derby)	10	4	-	6	23	28	8
6.	Chesterfield FC (Chesterfield)	10	3	2	5	15	29	8
		60	26	8	26	118	118	60

London (Principal)

		Pd	Wn	Dw	Ls	GF	GA	Pts
1.	Chelsea FC (London)	22	17	3	2	71	18	37
2.	Millwall Athletic FC (London)	22	12	6	4	46	24	30
3.	The Arsenal FC (London)	22	10	5	7	43	46	25
4.	West Ham United FC (London)	22	10	4	8	47	35	24
5.	Fulham FC (London)	22	10	4	8	45	37	24
6.	Tottenham Hotspur FC (London)	22	8	8	6	38	35	24
7.	Brentford FC (London)	22	6	8	8	36	40	20
8.	Queen's Park Rangers FC (London)	22	8	3	11	27	41	19
9.	Crystal Palace FC (London)	22	8	3	11	35	55	19
10.	Watford FC (Watford)	22	8	1	13	37	46	17
11.	Clapton Orient FC (London)	22	4	6	12	22	44	14
12.	Croydon Common FC (London)	22	3	5	14	24	50	11
		264	104	56	104	471	471	264

London (Principal)

		Pd	Wn	Dw	Ls	GF	GA	Pts
1.	Chelsea FC (London)	14	10	1	3	50	15	21
2.	West Ham United FC (London)	14	9	2	3	32	16	20
3.	Tottenham Hotspur FC (London)	14	8	3	3	32	22	19
4.	Fulham FC (London)	14	9	-	5	38	19	18
5.	Millwall Athletic FC (London)	14	8	2	4	30	22	18
6.	Crystal Palace FC (London)	14	8	2	4	41	29	18
7.	Watford FC (Watford)	14	5	3	6	22	20	13
8.	Brentford FC (London)	14	5	2	7	29	33	12
9.	Croydon Common FC (London)	14	4	3	7	28	27	11
10.	Clapton Orient FC (London)	14	3	4	7	17	27	10
11.	The Arsenal FC (London)	14	3	4	7	19	31	10
12.	Luton Town FC (Luton)	14	4	1	9	31	44	9
13.	Queen's Park Rangers FC (London)	14	2	5	7	14	37	9
14.	Reading FC (Reading)	14	2	4	8	23	64	8
		196	80	36	80	406	406	196

South-West Combination

		Pd	Wn	Dw	Ls	GF	GA	Pts
1.	Portsmouth FC (Portsmouth)	12	9	-	3	29	11	18
2.	Southampton FC (Southampton)	12	8	1	3	37	19	17
3.	Cardiff City AFC (Cardiff)	12	7	-	5	21	18	14
4.	Bristol Rovers FC (Bristol)	12	5	3	4	17	20	13
5.	Bristol City FC (Bristol)	12	5	1	6	13	16	11
6.	Swindon Town FC (Swindon)	11	2	2	7	12	17	6
7.	Newport County AFC (Newport)	11	1	1	9	8	32	3
		82	37	8	37	138	133	82

1916-17

Lancashire (Principal)	Pd	Wn	Dw	Ls	GF	GA	Pts
1. Liverpool FC (Liverpool)	30	19	8	3	62	26	46
2. Stockport County FC (Stockport)	30	18	7	5	61	31	43
3. Stoke FC (Stoke-on-Trent)	30	16	7	7	64	36	39
4. Manchester City FC (Manchester)	30	14	9	7	49	29	37
5. Everton FC (Liverpool)	30	15	7	8	62	41	37
6. Burnley FC (Burnley)	30	15	4	11	73	56	34
7. Manchester United FC (Manchester)	30	13	6	11	48	54	32
8. Rochdale AFC (Rochdale)	30	12	5	13	47	54	29
9. Southport Central FC (Southport)	30	10	8	12	40	43	28
10. Bolton Wanderers FC (Bolton)	30	9	6	15	59	65	24
11. Blackburn Rovers FC (Blackburn)	30	10	4	16	52	66	24
12. Preston North End FC (Preston)	30	8	7	15	47	65	23
13. Bury FC (Bury)	30	7	8	15	40	63	22
14. Oldham Athletic AFC (Oldham)	30	8	6	16	36	65	22
15. Port Vale FC (Stoke-on-Trent)	30	7	7	16	50	60	21
16. Blackpool FC (Blackpool)	30	6	7	17	44	80	19
	480	187	106	187	834	834	480

Lancashire (Subsidiary – Group "A")	Pd	Wn	Dw	Ls	GF	GA	Pts
1. Burnley FC (Burnley)	6	4	1	1	14	9	9
2. Preston North End FC (Preston)	6	2	2	2	8	7	6
3. Blackpool FC (Blackpool)	6	2	1	3	10	12	5
4. Blackburn Rovers FC (Blackburn)	6	2	-	4	11	15	4
	24	10	4	10	43	43	24

Lancashire (Subsidiary – Group "B")	Pd	Wn	Dw	Ls	GF	GA	Pts
1. Rochdale AFC (Rochdale)	6	5	1	-	15	6	11
2. Bolton Wanderers FC (Bolton)	6	3	-	3	12	12	6
3. Oldham Athletic AFC (Oldham)	6	2	1	3	9	8	5
4. Bury FC (Bury)	6	1	-	5	6	16	2
	24	11	2	11	42	42	24

Lancashire (Subsidiary – Group "C")	Pd	Wn	Dw	Ls	GF	GA	Pts
1. Manchester United FC (Manchester)	6	4	-	2	15	9	8
2. Stoke FC (Stoke-on-Trent)	6	3	-	3	11	6	6
3. Port Vale FC (Stoke-on-Trent)	6	2	1	3	9	12	5
4. Manchester City FC (Manchester)	6	2	1	3	3	11	5
	24	11	2	11	38	38	24

Lancashire (Subsidiary – Group "D")	Pd	Wn	Dw	Ls	GF	GA	Pts
1. Everton FC (Liverpool)	6	4	1	1	16	5	9
2. Stockport County FC (Stockport)	6	2	3	1	6	10	7
3. Liverpool FC (Liverpool)	6	2	1	3	13	10	5
4. Southport Central FC (Southport)	6	1	1	4	5	15	3
	24	9	6	9	40	40	24

London (Combination)

		Pd	Wn	Dw	Ls	GF	GA	Pts
1.	West Ham United FC (London)	40	30	5	5	110	45	65
2.	Millwall Athletic FC (London)	40	26	6	8	85	48	58
3.	Chelsea FC (London)	40	24	5	11	93	48	53
4.	Tottenham Hotspur FC (London)	40	24	5	11	112	64	53
5.	The Arsenal FC (London)	40	19	10	11	62	47	48
6.	Fulham FC (London)	40	21	3	16	102	63	45
7.	Luton Town FC (Luton)	39	20	3	16	101	82	43
8.	Crystal Palace FC (London)	38	14	7	17	68	72	35
9.	Southampton FC (Southampton)	39	13	8	18	57	80	34
10.	Queen's Park Rangers FC (London)	39	10	9	20	48	86	29
11.	Watford FC (Watford)	39	8	9	22	69	115	25
12.	Brentford FC (London)	40	9	7	24	56	99	25
13.	Portsmouth FC (Portsmouth)	40	9	4	27	58	117	22
14.	Clapton Orient FC (London)	40	6	7	27	49	104	19
		554	233	88	233	1070	1070	554

Midland (Principal)

		Pd	Wn	Dw	Ls	GF	GA	Pts
1.	Leeds City AFC (Leeds)	30	18	10	2	68	29	46
2.	Barnsley FC (Barnsley)	30	15	8	7	65	41	38
3.	Birmingham FC (Birmingham)	30	14	9	7	56	38	37
4.	Huddersfield Town AFC (Huddersfield)	30	15	6	9	41	31	36
5.	Bradford Park Avenue FC (Bradford)	30	14	6	10	51	32	34
6.	Nottingham Forest FC (Nottingham)	30	14	5	11	57	39	33
7.	Notts County FC (Nottingham)	30	13	6	11	47	52	32
8.	Bradford City FC (Bradford)	30	12	7	11	41	41	31
9.	Rotherham County FC (Rotherham)	30	12	6	12	53	52	30
10.	Sheffield United FC (Sheffield)	30	11	7	12	43	47	29
11.	Hull City AFC (Kingston-upon-Hull)	30	10	7	13	36	57	27
12.	Chesterfield FC (Chesterfield)	30	11	4	15	59	62	26
13.	The Wednesday FC (Sheffield)	30	9	6	15	36	48	24
14.	Grimsby Town FC (Cleethorpes)	30	8	6	16	38	71	22
15.	Leicester Fosse FC (Leicester)	30	6	7	17	29	53	19
16.	Lincoln City FC (Lincoln)	30	5	6	19	38	65	16
		480	187	106	187	758	758	480

Midland (Subsidiary – Group "A")

		Pd	Wn	Dw	Ls	GF	GA	Pts
1.	Sheffield United FC (Sheffield)	6	4	-	2	12	7	8
2.	The Wednesday FC (Sheffield)	6	2	2	2	12	12	6
3.	Barnsley FC (Barnsley)	6	1	3	2	8	9	5
4.	Rotherham County FC (Rotherham)	6	2	1	3	9	13	5
		24	9	6	9	41	41	24

Midland (Subsidiary – Group "B")

		Pd	Wn	Dw	Ls	GF	GA	Pts
1.	Birmingham FC (Birmingham)	6	3	2	1	17	12	8
2.	Leicester Fosse FC (Leicester)	6	4	-	2	12	12	8
3.	Notts County FC (Nottingham)	6	1	2	3	9	12	4
4.	Nottingham Forest FC (Nottingham)	6	1	2	3	12	14	4
		24	9	6	9	50	50	24

Midland (Subsidiary – Group "C")	Pd	Wn	Dw	Ls	GF	GA	Pts
1. Bradford Park Avenue FC (Bradford)	6	3	2	1	10	5	8
2. Huddersfield Town AFC (Huddersfield)	6	3	1	2	6	4	7
3. Leeds City AFC (Leeds)	6	2	2	2	8	7	6
4. Bradford City AFC (Bradford)	6	-	3	3	5	13	3
	24	8	8	8	29	29	24

Midland (Subsidiary – Group "D")	Pd	Wn	Dw	Ls	GF	GA	Pts
1. Chesterfield FC (Chesterfield)	6	4	-	2	15	16	8
2. Grimsby Town FC (Cleethorpes)	6	2	2	2	12	11	6
3. Hull City AFC (Kingston-upon-Hull)	6	2	2	2	13	12	6
4. Lincoln City FC (Lincoln)	6	1	2	3	11	12	4
	24	9	6	9	51	51	24

1917-18

Lancashire (Principal)	Pd	Wn	Dw	Ls	GF	GA	Pts
1. Stoke FC (Stoke-on-Trent)	30	22	4	4	109	27	48
2. Liverpool FC (Liverpool)	30	21	6	3	101	26	48
3. Everton FC (Liverpool)	30	19	6	5	92	36	44
4. Manchester City FC (Manchester)	30	15	8	7	57	28	38
5. Stockport County FC (Stockport)	30	17	3	10	59	32	37
6. Rochdale AFC (Rochdale)	30	14	9	7	78	51	37
7. Bolton Wanderers FC (Bolton)	30	13	4	13	68	70	30
8. Manchester United FC (Manchester)	30	11	8	11	45	49	30
9. Oldham Athletic AFC (Oldham)	30	11	6	13	50	59	28
10. Preston North End FC (Preston)	30	12	3	15	38	53	27
11. Port Vale FC (Stoke-on-Trent)	30	9	8	13	47	58	26
12. Blackpool FC (Blackpool)	30	10	5	15	46	70	25
13. Southport Central FC (Southport)	30	8	6	16	33	69	22
14. Bury FC (Bury)	30	8	5	17	46	64	21
15. Burnley FC (Burnley)	30	5	4	21	32	104	14
16. Blackburn Rovers FC (Blackburn)	30	2	1	27	22	127	5
	480	197	86	197	923	923	480

Lancashire (Subsidiary – Group "A")	Pd	Wn	Dw	Ls	GF	GA	Pts
1. Preston North End FC (Preston)	6	4	1	1	10	8	9
2. Blackpool FC (Blackpool)	6	4	-	2	18	9	8
3. Burnley FC (Burnley)	6	2	1	3	10	11	5
4. Blackburn Rovers FC (Blackburn)	6	1	-	5	3	13	2
	24	11	2	11	41	41	24

Lancashire (Subsidiary – Group "B")	Pd	Wn	Dw	Ls	GF	GA	Pts
1. Bolton Wanderers FC (Bolton)	6	3	1	2	11	9	7
2. Oldham Athletic AFC (Oldham)	6	3	1	2	9	9	7
3. Rochdale AFC (Rochdale)	6	3	-	3	13	8	6
4. Bury FC (Bury)	6	1	2	3	8	15	4
	24	10	4	10	41	41	24

Lancashire (Subsidiary – Group "C")

		Pd	Wn	Dw	Ls	GF	GA	Pts
1.	Manchester City FC (Manchester)	6	4	1	1	11	4	9
2.	Manchester United FC (Manchester)	6	3	1	2	6	7	7
3.	Stoke FC (Stoke-on-Trent)	6	2	2	2	10	5	6
4.	Port Vale FC (Stoke-on-Trent)	6	1	-	5	4	15	2
		24	10	4	10	31	31	24

Lancashire (Subsidiary – Group "D")

		Pd	Wn	Dw	Ls	GF	GA	Pts
1.	Liverpool FC (Liverpool)	6	5	-	1	24	7	10
2.	Everton FC (Liverpool)	6	5	-	1	19	7	10
3.	Stockport County FC (Stockport)	6	2	-	4	6	13	4
4.	Southport Central FC (Southport)	6	-	-	6	1	23	-
		24	12	-	12	50	50	24

London (Combination)

		Pd	Wn	Dw	Ls	GF	GA	Pts
1.	Chelsea FC (London)	36	21	8	7	82	39	50
2.	West Ham United FC (London)	36	20	9	7	103	51	49
3.	Fulham FC (London)	36	20	7	9	75	60	47
4.	Tottenham Hotspur FC (London)	36	22	2	12	86	56	46
5.	The Arsenal FC (London)	36	16	5	15	76	57	37
6.	Brentford FC (London)	36	16	3	17	81	94	35
7.	Crystal Palace FC (London)	36	13	4	19	54	83	30
8.	Queen's Park Rangers FC (London)	36	14	2	20	48	73	30
9.	Millwall Athletic FC (London)	36	12	4	20	52	74	28
10.	Clapton Orient FC (London)	36	2	4	30	34	104	8
		360	156	48	156	691	691	360

Midland (Principal)

		Pd	Wn	Dw	Ls	GF	GA	Pts
1.	Leeds City AFC (Leeds)	28	23	1	4	75	23	47
2.	Sheffield United FC (Sheffield)	28	20	1	7	66	27	41
3.	Birmingham FC (Birmingham)	28	14	6	8	59	38	34
4.	Hull City AFC (Kingston-upon-Hull)	28	15	4	9	67	50	34
5.	Nottingham Forest FC (Nottingham)	28	13	4	11	41	28	30
6.	Bradford Park Avenue FC (Bradford)	28	13	4	11	40	29	30
7.	Leicester Fosse FC (Leicester)	28	13	3	12	52	43	29
8.	Huddersfield Town AFC (Huddersfield)	28	12	2	14	49	46	26
9.	Rotherham County FC (Rotherham)	28	8	9	11	42	52	25
10.	Notts County FC (Nottingham)	28	7	9	12	43	54	23
11.	The Wednesday FC (Sheffield)	28	9	5	14	45	59	23
12.	Grimsby Town FC (Cleethorpes)	28	5	11	12	24	62	21
13.	Bradford City AFC (Bradford)	28	8	4	16	34	55	20
14.	Lincoln City FC (Lincoln)	28	7	5	16	25	62	19
15.	Barnsley FC (Barnsley)	28	8	2	18	40	74	18
		420	175	70	175	702	702	420

Midland (Subsidiary – Group "A")

		Pd	Wn	Dw	Ls	GF	GA	Pts
1.	The Wednesday FC (Sheffield)	6	3	2	1	15	8	8
2.	Barnsley FC (Barnsley)	6	3	1	2	14	12	7
3.	Sheffield United FC (Sheffield)	6	2	1	3	9	12	5
4.	Rotherham County FC (Rotherham)	6	1	2	3	4	10	4
		24	9	6	9	42	42	24

Midland (Subsidiary – Group "B")	Pd	Wn	Dw	Ls	GF	GA	Pts
1. Notts County FC (Nottingham)	6	4	-	2	19	9	8
2. Birmingham FC (Birmingham)	6	2	2	2	6	9	6
3. Leicester Fosse FC (Leicester)	6	2	1	3	6	10	5
4. Nottingham Forest FC (Nottingham)	6	2	1	3	4	7	5
	24	10	4	10	35	35	24

Midland (Subsidiary – Group "C")	Pd	Wn	Dw	Ls	GF	GA	Pts
1. Leeds City AFC (Leeds)	6	3	2	1	8	6	8
2. Huddersfield Town AFC (Huddersfield)	6	3	1	2	13	11	7
3. Bradford City AFC (Bradford)	6	1	4	1	8	8	6
4. Bradford Park Avenue FC (Bradford)	6	1	1	4	8	12	3
	24	8	8	8	37	37	24

Midland (Subsidiary – Group "D")	Pd	Wn	Dw	Ls	GF	GA	Pts
1. Grimsby Town FC (Cleethorpes)	6	4	1	1	13	3	9
2. Hull City AFC (Kingston-upon-Hull)	6	3	2	1	12	9	8
3. Lincoln City FC (Lincoln)	6	3	1	2	11	8	7
4. Gainsborough Trinity FC (Gainsborough)	6	-	-	6	3	19	-
	24	10	4	10	39	39	24

1918-19

Football League Championship Play-off

Nottingham Forest FC (Nottingham)   0-0, 1-0   Everton FC (Liverpool)

Lancashire (Principal)	Pd	Wn	Dw	Ls	GF	GA	Pts
1. Everton FC (Liverpool)	30	27	2	1	108	26	56
2. Stoke FC (Stoke-on-Trent)	30	20	3	7	84	36	43
3. Liverpool FC (Liverpool)	30	19	4	7	82	33	42
4. Bolton Wanderers FC (Bolton)	30	15	6	9	58	58	36
5. Manchester City FC (Manchester)	30	15	3	12	57	36	33
6. Southport Vulcan FC (Southport)	30	15	3	12	49	53	33
7. Preston North End FC (Preston)	30	12	6	12	41	51	30
8. Stockport County FC (Stockport)	30	11	7	12	48	52	29
9. Manchester United FC (Manchester)	30	11	5	14	51	50	27
10. Rochdale AFC (Rochdale)	30	11	5	14	56	61	27
11. Blackpool FC (Blackpool)	30	10	5	15	45	61	25
12. Port Vale FC (Stoke-on-Trent)	30	10	4	16	39	77	24
13. Burnley FC (Burnley)	30	10	3	17	54	76	23
14. Bury FC (Bury)	30	7	6	17	27	58	20
15. Oldham Athletic AFC (Oldham)	30	7	4	19	39	62	18
16. Blackburn Rovers FC (Blackburn)	30	5	4	21	35	83	14
	480	205	70	205	873	873	480

Lancashire (Subsidiary – Group "A")	Pd	Wn	Dw	Ls	GF	GA	Pts
1. Blackpool FC (Blackpool)	6	3	2	1	13	7	8
2. Burnley FC (Burnley)	6	3	1	2	15	8	7
3. Preston North End FC (Preston)	6	3	1	2	6	7	7
4. Blackburn Rovers FC (Blackburn)	6	-	2	4	6	18	2
	24	9	6	9	40	40	24

Lancashire (Subsidiary – Group "B")	Pd	Wn	Dw	Ls	GF	GA	Pts
1. Oldham Athletic AFC (Oldham)	6	5	-	1	17	4	10
2. Bolton Wanderers FC (Bolton)	6	5	-	1	16	9	10
3. Rochdale AFC (Rochdale)	6	1	-	5	5	13	2
4. Bury FC (Bury)	6	1	-	5	4	16	2
	24	12	-	12	42	42	24

Lancashire (Subsidiary – Group "C")	Pd	Wn	Dw	Ls	GF	GA	Pts
1. Manchester City FC (Manchester)	6	5	1	-	14	4	11
2. Stoke FC (Stoke-on-Trent)	6	2	2	2	9	10	6
3. Manchester United FC (Manchester)	6	2	-	4	9	14	4
4. Port Vale FC (Stoke-on-Trent)	6	1	1	4	9	13	3
	24	10	4	10	41	41	24

Lancashire (Subsidiary – Group "D")	Pd	Wn	Dw	Ls	GF	GA	Pts
1. Liverpool FC (Liverpool)	6	4	2	-	13	6	10
2. Stockport County FC (Stockport)	6	3	1	2	7	6	7
3. Southport Vulcan FC (Southport)	6	2	-	4	9	12	4
4. Everton FC (Liverpool)	6	1	1	4	5	10	3
	24	10	4	10	34	34	24

Lancashire Cup Final

Liverpool FC (Liverpool)	3-0	Oldham Athletic AFC (Oldham)

Semi-finals

Blackpool FC (Blackpool)	0-1	Liverpool FC (Liverpool)
Manchester City FC (Manchester)	0-1	Oldham Athletic AFC (Oldham)

London Victory Cup

Chelsea FC (London)	3-0	Fulham FC (London)

Semi-finals

Chelsea FC (London)	4-0	Crystal Palace FC (London)
Tottenham Hotspur FC (London)	0-2	Fulham FC (London)

Midland (Principal)	Pd	Wn	Dw	Ls	GF	GA	Pts
1. Nottingham Forest FC (Nottingham)	30	18	6	6	59	31	42
2. Birmingham FC (Birmingham)	30	20	1	9	72	36	41
3. Notts County FC (Nottingham)	30	16	9	5	65	38	41
4. Leeds City AFC (Leeds)	30	17	4	9	53	38	38
5. Bradford Park Avenue FC (Bradford)	30	15	7	8	53	41	37
6. Huddersfield Town AFC (Huddersfield)	30	13	8	9	45	45	34
7. Hull City AFC (Kingston-upon-Hull)	30	12	7	11	48	42	31
8. Sheffield United FC (Sheffield)	30	12	6	12	56	47	30
9. Coventry City FC (Coventry)	30	13	4	13	55	59	30
10. Leicester Fosse FC (Leicester)	30	13	3	14	53	53	29
11. The Wednesday FC (Sheffield)	30	11	6	13	49	49	28
12. Lincoln City FC (Lincoln)	30	10	4	16	38	59	24
13. Bradford City AFC (Bradford)	30	9	4	17	48	56	22
14. Barnsley FC (Barnsley)	30	9	3	18	45	79	21
15. Grimsby Town FC (Cleethorpes)	30	7	6	17	40	69	20
16. Rotherham County FC (Rotherham)	30	2	8	20	23	60	12
	480	197	86	197	802	802	480

Midland (Subsidiary – Group "A")	Pd	Wn	Dw	Ls	GF	GA	Pts
1. Sheffield United FC (Sheffield)	6	5	1	-	14	3	11
2. The Wednesday FC (Sheffield)	6	3	1	2	11	10	7
3. Barnsley FC (Barnsley)	6	1	1	4	13	18	3
4. Rotherham County FC (Rotherham)	6	1	1	4	11	18	3
	24	10	4	10	49	49	24

Midland (Subsidiary – Group "B")	Pd	Wn	Dw	Ls	GF	GA	Pts
1. Birmingham FC (Birmingham)	6	5	-	1	13	7	10
2. Leicester Fosse FC (Leicester)	6	3	-	3	10	13	6
3. Notts County FC (Nottingham)	6	2	-	4	13	13	4
4. Nottingham Forest FC (Nottingham)	6	2	-	4	7	10	4
	24	12	-	12	43	43	24

Midland (Subsidiary – Group "C")	Pd	Wn	Dw	Ls	GF	GA	Pts
1. Bradford Park Avenue FC (Bradford)	6	3	2	1	13	6	8
2. Huddersfield Town AFC (Huddersfield)	6	2	3	1	7	4	7
3. Leeds City AFC (Leeds)	6	3	-	3	10	9	6
4. Bradford City FC (Bradford)	6	1	1	4	4	15	3
	24	9	6	9	34	34	24

Midland (Subsidiary – Group "D")	Pd	Wn	Dw	Ls	GF	GA	Pts
1. Hull City AFC (Kingston-upon-Hull)	6	4	-	2	11	7	8
2. Coventry City FC (Coventry)	6	3	2	1	7	6	8
3. Grimsby Town FC (Cleethorpes)	6	2	1	3	8	10	5
4. Lincoln City FC (Lincoln)	6	1	1	4	6	9	3
	24	10	4	10	32	32	24

London (Combination)	Pd	Wn	Dw	Ls	GF	GA	Pts
1. Brentford FC (London)	36	20	9	7	94	48	49
2. The Arsenal FC (London)	36	20	5	11	85	56	45
3. West Ham United FC (London)	36	17	7	12	65	51	41
4. Fulham FC (London)	36	17	6	13	70	55	40
5. Queen's Park Rangers FC (London)	36	16	7	13	69	60	39
6. Chelsea FC (London)	36	13	11	12	70	53	37
7. Crystal Palace FC (London)	36	14	6	16	66	73	34
8. Tottenham Hotspur FC (London)	36	13	8	15	52	72	34
9. Millwall Athletic FC (London)	36	10	9	17	50	67	29
10. Clapton Orient FC (London)	36	3	6	27	35	123	12
	360	143	74	143	656	658	360

1919-20

Football League Division 1 1919-1920 Season	Aston Villa	Blackburn R.	Bolton Wands.	Bradford City	Bradford P.A.	Burnley	Chelsea	Derby County	Everton	Liverpool	Man. City	Man. United	Middlesbro'	Newcastle U.	Notts County	Oldham Ath.	Preston N.E.	Sheffield U.	Sunderland	The Arsenal	Wednesday	W.B.A.
Aston Villa FC		1-2	3-6	3-1	1-0	2-2	5-2	2-2	2-2	0-1	0-1	2-0	5-3	4-0	3-1	3-0	2-4	4-0	0-3	2-1	3-1	2-4
Blackburn Rovers FC	5-1		2-2	4-1	3-3	2-3	3-1	2-0	3-2	0-2	1-4	5-0	0-2	2-0	1-1	0-1	4-0	4-0	3-0	2-2	1-0	1-5
Bolton Wanderers FC	2-1	2-1		1-1	1-2	1-1	1-2	3-0	0-2	0-3	6-2	3-5	2-1	0-3	1-0	1-0	4-1	1-0	1-0	2-2	2-0	1-2
Bradford City AFC	3-1	3-1	0-1		0-0	2-1	3-1	3-1	3-3	1-3	1-0	2-1	0-1	1-0	3-4	1-1	2-2	1-2	2-0	1-1	1-1	3-0
Bradford Park Avenue	6-1	5-2	2-0	0-0		0-1	1-0	1-1	0-2	1-2	2-1	1-4	1-1	0-1	2-0	3-3	1-2	2-2	0-0	3-0		0-4
Burnley FC	0-0	3-1	2-1	1-1	2-6		2-3	2-0	5-0	1-2	2-0	2-1	5-3	1-0	2-1	2-1	1-1	2-2	2-1	2-1	2-0	2-2
Chelsea FC	2-1	2-1	2-3	1-0	4-0	0-1		0-0	0-1	1-0	1-0	1-0	3-1	0-0	1-0	4-0	1-1	2-0	3-1	1-1		2-0
Derby County FC	1-0	0-0	1-2	3-0	0-0	0-2	5-0		2-1	3-0	0-0	1-1	1-2	3-1	1-1	2-0	5-1	3-1	2-1	1-2		0-4
Everton FC	1-1	3-0	3-3	4-1	2-0	2-2	2-3	4-0		0-0	0-0	5-2	4-0	1-2	0-2	0-1	3-0	1-3	2-3	1-1		2-5
Liverpool FC	2-1	3-0	2-0	2-1	3-3	0-1	0-1	3-0	3-1		1-0	0-0	1-0	1-1	3-0	2-2	1-2	2-0	3-2	2-3	1-0	0-0
Manchester City FC	2-2	8-2	1-4	1-0	4-1	3-1	1-0	3-1	1-1	2-1		3-3	1-0	0-0	4-1	3-1	1-0	3-3	1-0	4-1	4-2	2-3
Manchester United FC	1-2	1-1	1-1	0-0	0-1	0-2	0-2	1-0	0-0	1-0		1-1	2-1	0-0	1-1	5-1	3-4	2-2	0-1	0-0	1-2	
Middlesbrough FC	1-4	2-2	1-3	4-0	1-2	4-0	0-0	2-0	1-1	3-2	0-2	1-1		0-1	5-2	1-0	4-1	1-0	0-2	1-0	3-0	0-0
Newcastle United FC	2-0	0-0	0-1	0-1	4-0	1-0	3-0	0-0	3-0	3-0	3-0	2-1	0-0		2-1	1-0	2-1	2-3	3-1	1-1		0-2
Notts County FC	2-1	5-0	2-2	5-2	0-2	2-0	0-1	2-2	1-1	1-0	4-1	0-2	1-1	0-0		2-1	1-2	2-2	2-2	2-2	3-1	2-0
Oldham Athletic AFC	0-3		2-0	0-0	2-2	1-0	4-1	1-1	1-3	0-3	1-2	1-0	0-0				4-1	4-0	2-1	3-0	1-0	2-1
Preston North End FC	3-0	0-0	1-1	1-5	0-3	0-1	3-1	1-1	1-1	2-1	1-1	2-3	3-1	2-3	2-0	2-1		2-0	5-2	1-1	3-0	0-1
Sheffield United FC	1-2	2-0	3-2	0-0	2-2	1-3	0-1	0-1	3-2	3-1	2-2	5-1	2-2	3-0	1-0	2-1			3-1	2-0	3-0	1-0
Sunderland AFC	2-1	2-0	2-0	2-0	2-0	3-0	3-2	2-1	2-3	0-1	3-0	1-1	3-0	1-0	3-0	1-0	3-2			1-1	2-1	4-1
The Arsenal FC	0-1	0-1	2-2	1-2	3-0	2-0	1-1	1-1	1-1	1-0	2-2	0-3	2-1	0-1	3-1	3-2	0-0	3-0	3-2		3-1	1-0
The Wednesday FC	0-1	0-0	0-2	1-0	0-1	3-1	1-1	2-0	1-0	2-2	0-0	1-3	0-1	0-1	0-0	1-0	0-1	2-1	0-2	1-2		0-3
West Bromwich Albion FC	1-2	5-2	4-1	4-1	3-1	4-1	4-0	3-0	4-3	1-1	2-0	2-1	4-1	3-0	8-0	3-1	4-1	0-2	4-0	1-0	1-3	

Division 1

		Pd	Wn	Dw	Ls	GF	GA	Pts	
1.	WEST BROMWICH ALBION FC (W. BROMWICH)	42	28	4	10	104	47	60	
2.	Burnley FC (Burnley)	42	21	9	12	65	59	51	
3.	Chelsea FC (London)	42	22	5	15	56	51	49	
4.	Liverpool FC Liverpool)	42	19	10	13	59	44	48	
5.	Sunderland AFC (Sunderland)	42	22	4	16	72	59	48	
6.	Bolton Wanderers FC (Bolton)	42	19	9	14	72	65	47	
7.	Manchester City FC (Manchester)	42	18	9	15	71	62	45	
8.	Newcastle United FC (Newcastle-upon-Tyne)	42	17	9	16	44	39	43	
9.	Aston Villa FC (Birmingham)	42	18	6	18	75	73	42	
10.	The Arsenal FC (London)	42	15	12	15	56	58	42	
11.	Bradford Park Avenue FC (Bradford)	42	15	12	15	60	63	42	
12.	Manchester United FC (Manchester)	42	13	14	15	54	50	40	
13.	Middlesbrough FC (Middlesbrough)	42	15	10	17	61	65	40	
14.	Sheffield United FC (Sheffield)	42	16	8	18	59	69	40	
15.	Bradford City AFC (Bradford)	42	14	11	17	54	63	39	
16.	Everton FC (Liverpool)	42	12	14	16	69	68	38	
17.	Oldham Athletic AFC (Oldham)	42	15	8	19	49	52	38	
18.	Derby County FC (Derby)	42	13	12	17	47	57	38	
19.	Preston North End FC (Preston)	42	14	10	18	57	73	38	
20.	Blackburn Rovers FC (Blackburn)	42	13	11	18	64	77	37	
21.	Notts County FC (Nottingham)	42	12	12	18	56	74	36	R
22.	The Wednesday FC (Sheffield)	42	7	9	26	28	64	23	R
		924	358	208	358	1332	1332	924	

Grimsby Town FC (Cleethorpes) and Lincoln City FC (Lincoln) were not re-elected to the league for next season and were replaced in Division 2 by Cardiff City AFC (Cardiff) and Leeds United AFC (Leeds) (who were founded after Leeds City AFC was disbanded – see below for further details of this).

Top Goalscorer

1)   Fred MORRIS   (West Bromwich Albion FC)   37

A new Division 3 began the next season and was formed by the promotion of Southern League Division 1 clubs plus Grimsby Town FC

Football League Division 2 1919-1920 Season	Barnsley	Birmingham	Blackpool	Bristol City	Bury	Clapton Orient	Coventry City	Fulham	Grimsby Town	Huddersfield Town	Hull City	Leeds City	Leicester City	Lincoln City	Nottingham Forest	Port Vale	Rotherham County	South Shields	Stockport County	Stoke	Tottenham Hotspur	West Ham United	Wolves
Barnsley FC	■	0-5	1-1	0-0	1-3	2-1	1-0	4-1	0-1	3-3	2-3	---	0-1	5-2	2-2	1-0	4-0	0-1	0-0	1-2	3-0	7-0	4-1
Birmingham FC	0-0	■	4-2	1-0	0-2	2-1	4-1	2-0	4-0	4-2	4-1	---	0-1	7-0	8-0	3-0	2-2	4-0	1-1	2-1	0-1	0-1	2-0
Blackpool FC	0-2	3-0	■	0-0	1-0	3-0	2-0	1-1	2-0	0-3	2-1	4-2	3-0	6-0	3-2	---	5-1	0-3	1-0	3-1	0-1	0-0	1-1
Bristol City FC	3-1	1-1	0-0	■	1-0	1-1	1-0	0-3	3-1	2-1	2-2	---	0-0	6-0	0-0	1-1	2-1	3-1	1-0	1-2	1-2	0-0	1-1
Bury FC	2-0	1-0	1-2	0-1	■	3-0	2-2	2-2	1-1	2-0	2-0	---	1-0	3-0	1-1	2-1	4-1	2-1	0-2	1-0	2-1	1-0	2-0
Clapton Orient FC	2-0	2-1	3-0	1-0	2-1	■	2-2	0-1	3-0	0-1	2-2	---	3-0	1-0	1-0	2-1	1-2	4-0	2-1	2-1	0-4	1-0	0-0
Coventry City FC	1-0	1-3	0-0	0-0	2-1	0-0	■	0-1	2-0	0-2	0-1	0-4	1-2	2-0	4-2	---	1-1	1-1	1-1	3-2	0-5	0-0	1-0
Fulham FC	1-1	1-2	1-2	1-1	1-0	2-1	0-0	■	2-1	2-2	1-0	---	5-0	3-0	1-0	4-0	3-0	1-0	4-1	0-0	1-4	1-2	1-1
Grimsby Town FC	1-1	0-3	1-1	2-2	1-2	2-0	0-1	0-2	■	1-0	2-1	---	1-2	2-2	1-0	2-0	0-1	3-1	0-3	2-0	2-0	0-1	0-1
Huddersfield Town AFC	4-1	0-0	1-3	1-0	5-0	2-1	5-0	3-0	3-0	■	2-0	---	0-0	4-2	2-1	4-1	7-1	2-2	5-0	3-0	1-1	2-0	2-0
Hull City AFC	3-1	0-0	0-1	0-0	4-2	3-1	0-1	2-0	4-1	1-4	■	1-1	5-1	5-2	2-0	---	1-0	3-0	4-1	3-0	1-3	1-1	10-3
Leeds City AFC	---	---	1-0	---	---	---	3-0	---	---	---	1-2	■	---	---	---	---	---	---	---	---	---	---	1-1
Leicester City FC	0-0	1-0	2-3	2-1	0-5	1-1	1-0	3-2	2-0	0-4	3-2	---	■	4-0	0-0	0-1	1-1	0-0	0-2	3-1	2-4	0-0	1-2
Lincoln City AFC	0-4	2-2	0-3	0-0	2-1	2-1	4-1	0-1	2-0	1-3	2-0	---	0-3	■	1-4	0-0	0-0	1-1	2-0	2-1	1-1	1-4	4-0
Nottingham Forest FC	0-1	1-2	2-0	1-2	1-0	2-1	2-1	0-3	2-0	1-2	0-2	---	0-0	2-1	■	0-1	4-1	0-0	1-1	0-2	1-1	2-1	1-0
Port Vale FC	0-2	1-3	---	3-1	2-2	4-2	---	3-4	2-1	0-0	---	---	1-2	1-0	4-1	■	4-2	1-0	2-0	0-3	0-1	1-0	
Rotherham County FC	1-0	0-3	1-2	2-2	1-2	3-1	4-3	1-1	3-1	1-3	1-2	---	1-0	3-0	2-0	2-2	■	1-0	1-0	1-3	1-1	0-1	2-0
South Shields FC	0-0	1-0	6-0	0-2	0-0	2-0	1-0	2-0	2-0	1-2	7-1	---	2-0	2-2	5-2	2-0	6-2	■	3-2	2-2	0-3	3-0	0-0
Stockport County FC	1-0	2-1	0-0	2-3	1-1	3-1	1-1	2-1	1-2	1-2	3-1	---	0-2	3-0	0-0	0-4	4-1	1-0	■	3-1	1-2	1-0	4-1
Stoke FC	2-0	0-1	2-0	2-0	1-1	2-0	6-1	1-0	3-0	0-1	3-1	---	3-0	1-3	0-2	0-0	3-0	0-0	2-1	■	1-3	2-1	3-0
Tottenham Hotspur FC	4-0	0-0	2-2	2-0	2-1	2-1	4-1	4-0	3-1	2-0	4-0	---	4-0	6-1	5-2	2-0	2-0	2-0	2-0	2-0	■	2-0	4-2
West Ham United FC	0-2	1-2	1-0	2-0	1-0	0-1	2-0	0-1	1-0	1-1	2-1	---	1-0	1-1	5-1	3-1	2-1	1-0	3-0	1-1	2-1	■	4-0
Wolverhampton Wands.	2-4	0-2	0-3	3-1	0-1	1-2	2-0	2-1	6-1	2-3	4-2	2-4	1-1	4-0	4-0	---	0-1	0-0	2-2	4-0	1-3	1-1	■

	Division 2	Pd	Wn	Dw	Ls	GF	GA	Pts	
1.	Tottenham Hotspur FC (London)	42	32	6	4	102	32	70	P
2.	Huddersfield Town AFC (Huddersfield)	42	28	8	6	97	38	64	P
3.	Birmingham FC (Birmingham)	42	24	8	10	85	34	56	
4.	Blackpool FC (Blackpool)	42	21	10	11	65	47	52	
5.	Bury FC (Bury)	42	20	8	14	60	44	48	
6.	Fulham FC (London)	42	19	9	14	61	50	47	
7.	West Ham United FC (London)	42	19	9	14	47	40	47	
8.	Bristol City FC (Bristol)	42	13	17	12	46	43	43	
9.	South Shields FC (South Shields)	42	15	12	15	58	48	42	
10.	Stoke FC (Stoke-on-Trent)	42	18	6	18	60	54	42	
11.	Hull City AFC (Kingston-upon-Hull)	42	18	6	18	78	72	42	
12.	Barnsley FC (Barnsley)	42	15	10	17	61	55	40	
13.	Port Vale FC (Stoke-on-Trent)	42	16	8	18	59	62	40	*
14.	Leicester City FC (Leicester)	42	15	10	17	41	61	40	
15.	Clapton Orient FC (London)	42	16	6	20	51	59	38	
16.	Stockport County FC (Stockport)	42	14	9	19	52	61	37	
17.	Rotherham County FC (Rotherham)	42	13	8	21	51	83	34	
18.	Nottingham Forest FC (Nottingham)	42	11	9	22	43	73	31	
19.	Wolverhampton Wanderers FC (Wolverhampton)	42	10	10	22	55	80	30	
20.	Coventry City FC (Coventry)	42	9	11	22	35	73	29	
21.	Lincoln City FC (Lincoln)	42	9	9	24	44	101	27	
22.	Grimsby Town FC (Cleethorpes)	42	10	5	27	34	75	25	
		924	365	194	365	1285	1285	924	

* Port Vale FC (Stoke-on-Trent) took the place of Leeds City AFC (Leeds) who were expelled from the league for refusing to submit their club accounts to Football League inspection after allegations of financial misconduct.

Leeds City AFC (Leeds) playing record	8	4	2	2	17	10	10
Port Vale FC (Stoke-on-Trent) playing record	34	12	6	16	42	52	30

F.A. CUP FINAL   (Stamford Bridge, London – 24/04/1920 – 50,018)

ASTON VILLA FC (BIRMINGHAM)   1-0 (aet)   Huddersfield Town AFC (Huddersfield)
Kirton

Aston Villa: Hardy, Smart, Weston, Ducat, Barson, Moss, Wallace, Kirton, Walker, Stephenson, Dorrell.
Huddersfield: Mutch, Wood, Bullock, Slade, Wilson, Watson, Richardson, Mann, Taylor, Swan, Islip.

Semi-finals

Aston Villa FC (Birmingham)	3-1	Chelsea FC (London)
Bristol City FC (Bristol)	1-2	Huddersfield Town AFC (Huddersfield)

Quarter-finals

Bristol City FC (Bristol)	2-0	Bradford City AFC (Bradford)
Chelsea FC (London)	4-1	Bradford Park Avenue FC (Bradford)
Huddersfield Town AFC (Huddersfield)	2-1	Liverpool FC (Liverpool)
Tottenham Hotspur FC (London)	0-1	Aston Villa FC (Birmingham)

Football League Division 1 1920-1921 Season	Aston Villa	Blackburn R.	Bolton Wands.	Bradford City	Bradford P.A.	Burnley	Chelsea	Derby County	Everton	Liverpool	Huddersfield T.	Man. City	Man. United	Middlesbro'	Newcastle Utd.	Oldham Ath.	Preston N.E.	Sheffield Utd.	Sunderland	The Arsenal	Tottenham H.	W.B.A.
Aston Villa FC	■	3-0	2-0	1-2	4-1	0-0	3-0	1-0	1-3	0-0	0-2	3-1	3-4	0-1	0-0	3-0	1-0	4-0	1-5	5-0	4-2	0-0
Blackburn Rovers FC	0-1	■	2-2	2-3	1-0	1-3	0-0	2-0	0-0	1-2	1-1	0-2	2-0	3-2	3-3	5-1	2-2	1-1	1-2	2-2	1-1	5-1
Bolton Wanderers FC	5-0	2-1	■	1-1	2-0	1-1	3-1	1-0	4-2	3-1	1-0	3-0	1-1	6-2	3-1	1-1	3-0	2-2	6-2	1-1	1-0	3-0
Bradford City AFC	3-0	3-4	2-2	■	2-1	2-0	1-1	2-2	2-2	0-2	0-0	1-2	1-1	0-1	1-1	1-3	6-2	4-0	2-2	3-1	1-0	1-1
Bradford Park Avenue	4-0	1-1	2-1	1-2	■	1-3	0-2	2-1	3-3	1-1	1-3	1-2	2-4	3-0	0-2	2-1	1-3	2-0	1-1	0-1	1-1	0-3
Burnley FC	7-1	4-1	3-1	1-4	1-0	■	4-0	2-1	1-1	3-0	1-0	2-1	1-0	2-1	3-1	7-1	2-0	6-0	2-2	1-0	2-0	1-1
Chelsea FC	5-1	1-2	1-0	3-1	4-1	1-1	■	1-1	0-1	1-1	1-1	2-1	1-2	1-1	2-0	1-1	1-1	2-1	3-1	1-2	0-4	3-0
Derby County FC	2-3	0-1	0-0	1-1	1-0	0-0	0-0	■	2-4	2-1	0-0	3-0	1-1	0-1	3-3	1-1	1-1	0-1	1-1	2-2	1-1	
Everton FC	1-1	2-1	2-3	2-2	1-1	1-1	5-1	3-1	■	0-0	0-3	3-0	2-0	2-1	3-1	5-2	0-1	3-0	1-1	2-4	0-0	2-2
Huddersfield Town AFC	1-0	0-0	0-0	1-0	0-0	1-0	2-0	2-0	0-1	■	1-2	0-1	5-2	0-1	1-3	3-1	1-0	1-0	0-0	0-45	2-0	5-1
Liverpool FC	4-1	2-0	2-3	2-1	0-1	0-0	2-1	1-1	1-0	4-1	■	4-2	2-0	0-0	2-1	5-2	6-0	2-2	0-0	3-0	1-1	0-0
Manchester City FC	3-1	1-0	3-1	1-0	1-0	3-0	1-0	0-0	2-0	3-2	3-2	■	3-0	2-1	3-1	5-1	3-1	3-1	3-1	2-0	1-0	4-0
Manchester United FC	1-3	0-1	2-3	1-1	5-1	0-3	3-1	3-0	1-2	2-0	1-1	1-1	■	0-1	2-0	4-1	1-0	2-1	3-0	1-1	0-1	1-4
Middlesbrough FC	1-4	1-1	4-1	2-1	2-1	0-0	0-0	1-1	3-1	2-0	0-1	3-1	2-4	■	0-0	1-2	0-0	2-2	2-0	2-1	1-0	0-1
Newcastle United FC	2-1	1-2	1-0	4-0	2-1	1-2	1-0	0-1	2-0	1-0	2-0	1-1	6-3	2-0	■	1-2	4-2	3-0	6-1	1-1	1-1	1-1
Oldham Athletic AFC	1-1	1-0	0-0	2-0	1-0	2-2	1-2	2-1	0-1	1-2	0-0	2-0	2-2	3-3	0-0	■	0-2	0-0	2-1	1-1	2-5	0-3
Preston North End FC	6-1	4-2	1-2	1-1	3-3	0-3	0-1	2-1	1-0	0-1	2-3	0-1	0-0	2-0	3-2	4-0	■	2-0	1-1	0-1	4-1	2-1
Sheffield United FC	0-0	1-1	2-2	4-1	2-0	1-1	1-1	2-0	1-0	1-1	1-1	0-0	1-1	0-3	3-0	1-0		■	1-1	1-1	1-1	0-2
Sunderland AFC	0-1	2-0	0-0	0-0	5-1	1-0	1-0	3-0	1-1	2-0	1-0	2-3	1-2	2-1	1-1	2-2	3-1		■	5-1	0-1	3-0
The Arsenal FC	0-1	2-0	0-0	1-2	2-1	1-1	1-1	2-0	1-1	2-0	0-0	2-1	2-0	2-2	1-1	2-2	2-1	2-6	1-2	■	3-2	2-1
Tottenham Hotspur FC	1-2	1-2	5-2	2-0	2-0	1-2	5-0	2-0	2-0	1-0	1-0	2-0	4-1	2-2	2-0	5-1	1-2	4-1	0-0	2-1	■	1-0
West Bromwich Albion FC	2-1	1-1	2-1	2-0	0-1	2-0	1-1	3-0	1-2	3-0	1-1	2-2	0-2	0-1	0-0	0-0	0-3	1-1	4-1	3-4	3-1	■

Division 1

		Pd	Wn	Dw	Ls	GF	GA	Pts	
1.	BURNLEY FC (BURNLEY)	42	23	13	6	79	36	59	
2.	Manchester City FC (Manchester)	42	24	6	12	70	50	54	
3.	Bolton Wanderers FC (Bolton)	42	19	14	9	77	53	52	
4.	Liverpool FC (Liverpool)	42	18	15	9	63	35	51	
5.	Newcastle United FC (Newcastle-upon-Tyne)	42	20	10	12	66	45	50	
6.	Tottenham Hotspur FC (London)	42	19	9	14	70	48	47	
7.	Everton FC (Liverpool)	42	17	13	12	66	55	47	
8.	Middlesbrough FC (Middlesbrough)	42	17	12	13	53	53	46	
9.	The Arsenal FC (London)	42	15	14	13	59	63	44	
10.	Aston Villa FC (Birmingham)	42	18	7	17	63	70	43	
11.	Blackburn Rovers FC (Blackburn)	42	13	15	14	57	59	41	
12.	Sunderland AFC (Sunderland)	42	14	13	15	57	60	41	
13.	Manchester United FC (Manchester)	42	15	10	17	64	68	40	
14.	West Bromwich Albion FC (West Bromwich)	42	13	14	15	54	58	40	
15.	Bradford City AFC (Bradford)	42	12	15	15	61	63	39	
16.	Preston North End FC (Preston)	42	15	9	18	61	65	39	
17.	Huddersfield Town AFC (Huddersfield)	42	15	9	18	42	49	39	
18.	Chelsea FC (London)	42	13	13	16	48	58	39	
19.	Oldham Athletic AFC (Oldham)	42	9	15	18	49	86	33	
20.	Sheffield United FC (Sheffield)	42	6	18	18	42	68	30	
21.	Derby County FC (Derby)	42	5	16	21	32	58	26	R
22.	Bradford Park Avenue FC (Bradford)	42	8	8	26	43	76	24	R
		924	328	268	328	1276	1276	924	

Top Goalscorer

1) Joe SMITH   (Bolton Wanderers FC)   38

Football League Division 2 1920-1921 Season	Barnsley	Birmingham	Blackpool	Bristol City	Bury	Cardiff City	Clapton Orient	Coventry City	Fulham	Hull City	Leeds United	Leicester City	Nottingham Forest	Notts County	Port Vale	Rotherham County	South Shields	Stockport County	Stoke	Wednesday	West Ham United	Wolves
Barnsley FC		1-1	0-1	1-1	5-0	0-2	1-0	2-2	3-1	0-0	1-1	2-1	0-0	2-2	3-0	2-1	1-1	2-0	1-0	0-0	1-1	3-2
Birmingham FC	1-3		3-0	0-0	4-0	1-1	0-0	3-2	1-0	5-1	1-0	5-0	3-0	2-1	4-0	3-2	1-1	5-0	3-0	4-0	2-1	4-1
Blackpool FC	1-0	3-0		1-2	0-1	2-4	2-2	4-0	1-0	1-2	1-0	2-0	1-0	0-2	1-0	0-1	3-2	1-1	3-1	1-1	1-0	3-0
Bristol City FC	1-0	0-1	1-1		1-0	0-0	2-0	2-0	2-0	2-1	0-0	1-0	1-0	0-1	3-0	2-4	4-2	5-1	5-0	0-1	1-0	2-0
Bury FC	0-0	0-1	2-2	2-0		3-1	0-1	2-0	1-1	0-0	1-1	4-0	2-2	0-1	1-0	1-0	1-0	1-1	3-0	1-1	1-0	3-1
Cardiff City AFC	3-2	2-1	0-0	1-0	2-1		0-0	0-1	3-0	0-0	1-0	2-0	3-0	1-1	1-2	1-0	1-0	3-0	0-1	1-0	0-0	2-0
Clapton Orient FC	3-2	1-1	0-0	0-0	1-0	2-0		0-0	3-0	1-1	1-0	2-0	2-1	3-0	0-0	2-0	1-0	5-0	3-2	1-0	0-1	0-1
Coventry City FC	3-1	0-4	0-2	2-1	1-0	2-4	1-1		0-2	3-2	1-1	1-0	0-0	1-1	0-0	0-1	1-0	1-1	1-0	2-3	0-1	4-0
Fulham FC	1-0	5-0	1-2	3-0	0-0	0-3	1-0	2-0		3-0	1-0	1-1	2-1	3-1	1-0	1-0	0-0	3-1	1-3	2-0	0-0	2-0
Hull City AFC	3-0	1-0	2-1	2-0	1-1	2-0	3-0	1-1	0-0		0-1	1-1	0-3	1-1	1-1	1-1	0-2	1-1	1-1	1-1	2-1	0-1
Leeds United AFC	0-0	1-0	2-0	0-1	1-0	1-2	2-1	4-0	0-0	1-1		3-1	1-1	3-0	3-1	1-0	1-2	0-2	0-0	2-0	1-2	3-0
Leicester City FC	2-0	3-0	0-1	0-0	4-0	2-0	2-1	0-1	1-1	0-0	1-1		2-0	0-3	0-0	1-1	2-0	0-0	3-1	2-1	1-0	0-0
Nottingham Forest FC	0-0	1-1	3-1	0-1	4-2	1-2	0-0	0-2	5-1	2-0	1-0	1-2		1-0	1-4	6-1	1-2	1-1	2-2	4-2	1-0	1-1
Notts County FC	1-0	0-0	1-2	2-2	2-1	1-2	3-1	1-1	2-1	4-1	1-2	1-1	2-0		0-1	1-0	2-0	3-0	3-0	3-0	1-1	2-1
Port Vale FC	1-1	0-2	0-1	0-2	3-0	0-0	4-0	0-0	0-0	4-0	2-0	0-0	0-1	1-2		1-1	0-2	6-1	2-1	1-0	1-2	2-3
Rotherham County FC	1-0	1-1	0-2	0-0	0-5	2-0	0-0	2-3	2-0	1-1	0-2	1-1	0-0	0-0	1-1		5-4	1-0	1-1	2-0	2-0	1-0
South Shields FC	3-2	3-0	1-0	0-0	2-0	0-1	3-0	4-1	3-0	0-0	3-0	4-3	0-1	6-1	1-0			3-1	1-1	2-3	0-0	1-2
Stockport County FC	3-2	0-3	2-2	0-2	-2	2-5	6-0	3-0	1-1	2-2	3-1	0-0	1-0	1-0	0-0	0-1	0-0		2-0	0-1	2-0	1-2
Stoke FC	3-2	1-2	1-1	0-0	0-1	0-0	0-1	4-1	1-2	1-3	4-0	1-1	4-0	1-0	0-1	2-0	0-0	1-0		0-1	1-0	1-0
The Wednesday FC	0-0	1-2	0-1	2-2	2-0	0-1	1-1	3-0	3-0	3-0	2-0	0-0	0-0	1-1	1-0	2-0	1-1	2-1	1-3		0-1	6-0
West Ham United FC	2-1	1-1	1-1	1-0	0-1	1-1	1-0	7-0	2-0	1-1	3-0	0-1	3-0	0-2	1-1	1-0	2-1	5-0	1-0	4-0		1-0
Wolverhampton Wanderers FC	1-1	0-3	3-1	0-0	2-1	1-3	0-2	1-0	1-0	1-3	3-0	3-0	2-1	1-0	2-2	3-0	3-0	2-0	3-3	1-2	1-2	

Division 2		Pd	Wn	Dw	Ls	GF	GA	Pts	
1.	Birmingham FC (Birmingham)	42	24	10	8	79	38	58	P
2.	Cardiff City AFC (Cardiff)	42	24	10	8	59	32	58	P
3.	Bristol City FC (Bristol)	42	19	13	10	49	29	51	
4.	Blackpool FC (Blackpool)	42	20	10	12	54	42	50	
5.	West Ham United FC (London)	42	19	10	13	51	30	48	
6.	Notts County FC (Nottingham)	42	18	11	13	55	40	47	
7.	Clapton Orient FC (London)	42	16	13	13	43	42	45	
8.	South Shields FC (South Shields)	42	17	10	15	61	46	44	
9.	Fulham FC (London)	42	16	10	16	43	47	42	
10.	The Wednesday FC (Sheffield)	42	15	11	16	48	48	41	
11.	Bury FC (Bury)	42	15	10	17	45	49	40	
12.	Leicester City FC (Leicester)	42	12	16	14	39	46	40	
13.	Hull City AFC (Kingston-upon-Hull)	42	10	20	12	43	53	40	
14.	Leeds United AFC (Leeds)	42	14	10	18	40	45	38	
15.	Wolverhampton Wanderers FC (Wolverhampton)	42	16	6	20	49	66	38	
16.	Barnsley FC (Barnsley)	42	10	16	16	48	50	36	
17.	Port Vale FC (Stoke-on-Trent)	42	11	14	17	43	49	36	
18.	Nottingham Forest FC (Nottingham)	42	12	12	18	48	55	36	
19.	Rotherham County FC (Rotherham)	42	12	12	18	37	53	36	
20.	Stoke FC (Stoke-on-Trent)	42	12	11	19	46	56	35	
21.	Coventry City FC (Coventry)	42	12	11	19	39	70	35	
22.	Stockport County FC (Stockport)	42	9	12	21	42	75	30	R
		924	333	258	333	1061	1061	924	

Football League Division 3 1920-1921 Season	Brentford	Brighton	Bristol Rovers	Crystal Palace	Exeter City	Gillingham	Grimsby Town	Luton Town	Merthyr Town	Millwall Athletic	Newport County	Northampton	Norwich City	Plymouth Argyle	Portsmouth	Q.P.R.	Reading	Southampton	Southend United	Swansea Town	Swindon Town	Watford
Brentford FC		2-0	0-0	0-4	0-0	3-3	5-0	1-0	0-0	1-0	2-2	1-1	3-1	0-0	1-2	0-2	3-2	1-1	2-2	1-2	0-1	1-0
Brighton & Hove Albion	4-0		2-0	0-2	1-1	1-0	1-3	1-1	0-0	1-0	3-2	2-0	1-0	3-0	2-1	2-2	1-1	1-0	1-1	1-1	0-3	0-3
Bristol Rovers FC	2-1	3-1		2-1	5-0	2-0	2-0	5-0	1-1	1-2	3-2	4-2	2-2	2-0	2-2	3-0	3-2	1-2	2-1	1-2	3-1	2-0
Crystal Palace FC	4-2	3-2	3-0		2-1	4-1	2-0	2-1	3-0	3-2	2-0	5-1	1-0	0-0	3-0	0-0	2-0	1-1	2-3	0-1	1-0	2-2
Exeter City FC	3-0	1-0	1-0	1-1		2-1	1-1	1-0	3-3	4-0	0-1	4-0	1-1	1-1	0-1	0-1	0-1	0-0	1-2	1-0	1-1	1-2
Gillingham FC	1-3	1-0	1-0	0-1	2-1		2-1	0-0	0-0	1-4	2-5	0-0	1-1	1-2	1-0	1-1	2-1	1-1	2-1	1-1	1-1	1-1
Grimsby Town FC	2-0	2-2	3-1	1-0	2-0	2-0		0-1	1-1	0-2	1-1	2-0	1-1	1-1	0-3	2-1	2-0	3-0	1-0	0-2	3-0	3-0
Luton Town FC	2-0	3-2	1-2	2-2	3-0	5-0	3-1		1-0	0-0	2-2	3-1	4-0	1-1	2-2	2-1	6-0	1-1	4-0	3-0	2-1	1-0
Merthyr Town FC	3-1	4-1	2-2	2-1	7-1	6-1	3-1	4-1		0-1	1-0	1-0	0-0	1-1	2-1	3-1	1-1	1-0	1-1	0-3	2-2	1-0
Millwall Athletic FC	0-0	0-1	2-0	0-1	2-0	4-0	0-1	0-0	0-0		1-0	1-0	2-0	0-0	1-1	2-0	0-1	2-0	0-1	4-2	0-2	5-0	1-0
Newport County AFC	3-1	0-4	0-2	0-1	2-0	1-0	2-1	2-0	0-3	3-1		1-1	2-0	0-0	1-1	1-3	0-1	0-0	1-1	1-1	0-1	0-2
Northampton Town	6-2	1-0	1-2	2-2	3-3	2-0	4-1	1-0	2-2	0-2	0-2		1-0	1-1	0-3	1-0	2-0	1-0	2-0	1-2	1-2	0-1
Norwich City FC	0-0	3-0	1-1	0-0	0-0	2-1	0-0	3-0	0-0	2-0	3-0	3-3		0-0	2-2	2-0	0-1	3-1	1-1	3-2	1-1
Plymouth Argyle FC	1-0	5-0	2-1	0-1	3-1	0-0	2-1	0-2	5-1	0-2	1-1		2-0	1-0	1-0	0-0	1-0	0-0	0-2
Portsmouth FC	0-2	3-0	1-0	0-0	2-1	2-2	2-1	3-0	0-0	0-2	2-0	2-1	1-1		0-0	2-2	0-1	3-0	3-0	1-1	1-0
Queen's Park Rangers	1-0	4-0	2-1	3-0	2-1	0-1	2-0	4-1	4-2	0-0	2-0	1-2	2-0	4-0	0-0		2-0	2-0	1-1	1-0	1-2
Reading FC	2-1	0-1	2-1	1-0	0-1	1-2	4-1	0-1	2-0	0-1	2-1	0-1	1-1	0-0		0-4	1-1	1-3	2-3	0-0
Southampton FC	3-0	1-0	4-0	1-1	3-0	3-0	0-1	1-1	5-0	1-1	3-1	1-0	1-0	2-2	1-2		3-0	3-0	4-0	4-1
Southend United FC	4-1	2-0	1-0	0-2	0-0	3-1	1-1	0-1	1-2	1-2	3-1	2-1	1-0	1-0	1-0		1-2	1-3	4-1
Swansea Town AFC	1-1	0-0	2-2	0-0	2-0	3-1	1-1	1-0	0-0	1-2	2-2	5-2	3-0	0-0	1-3	2-1	1-1	2-0		1-1	2-1
Swindon Town FC	1-0	2-0	2-1	1-3	1-1	1-1	0-0	9-1	3-0	4-1	5-0	2-1	4-2	1-1	5-2	0-1	2-0	3-2	3-0	0-0		2-0
Watford FC	1-0	1-0	2-1	1-1	0-0	3-1	4-2	1-0	1-0	1-0	5-1	7-1	2-0	1-1	3-2	0-2	1-2	0-0	3-0	3-0	0-1	

92

	Division 3	Pd	Wn	Dw	Ls	GF	GA	Pts	
1.	Crystal Palace FC (London)	42	24	11	7	70	34	59	P
2.	Southampton FC (Southampton)	42	19	16	7	64	28	54	
3.	Queen's Park Rangers FC (London)	42	22	9	11	61	32	53	
4.	Swindon Town FC (Swindon)	42	21	10	11	73	49	52	
5.	Swansea Town AFC (Swansea)	42	18	15	9	56	45	51	
6.	Watford FC (Watford)	42	20	8	14	59	44	48	
7.	Millwall Athletic FC (London)	42	18	11	13	42	30	47	
8.	Merthyr Town FC (Merthyr Tydfil)	42	15	15	12	60	49	45	
9.	Luton Town FC (Luton)	42	16	12	14	61	56	44	
10.	Bristol Rovers FC (Bristol)	42	18	7	17	68	57	43	
11.	Plymouth Argyle FC (Plymouth)	42	11	21	10	35	34	43	
12.	Portsmouth FC (Portsmouth)	42	12	15	15	46	48	39	
13.	Grimsby Town FC (Cleethorpes)	42	15	9	18	49	59	39	T
14.	Northampton Town FC (Northampton)	42	15	8	19	59	75	38	
15.	Newport County AFC (Newport)	42	14	9	19	43	64	37	
16.	Norwich City FC (Norwich)	42	10	16	16	44	53	36	
17.	Southend United FC (Southend-on-Sea)	42	14	8	20	44	61	36	
18.	Brighton & Hove Albion FC (Hove)	42	14	8	20	42	61	36	
19.	Exeter City FC (Exeter)	42	10	15	17	39	54	35	
20.	Reading FC (Reading)	42	12	7	23	42	59	31	
21.	Brentford FC (London)	42	8	12	21	42	67	30	
22.	Gillingham FC (Gillingham)	42	8	12	22	34	74	28	
		924	335	254	335	1133	1133	924	

T: Grimsby Town FC (Cleethorpes) were transferred to the newly-formed Division 3 (North) for next season

Promoted: Charlton Athletic FC (London), Aberdare Athletic FC (Aberdare)

Division 3 was changed to Division 3 (South) for the next season and a new Division 3 (North) was inaugurated with the following clubs as members: Accrington Stanley FC, Ashington FC, Barrow AFC, Chesterfield FC, Crewe Alexandra FC, Darlington FC, Durham City FC, Halifax Town AFC, Hartlepools United FC, Lincoln City FC, Nelson FC, Rochdale AFC, Southport FC, Stalybridge Celtic FC, Tranmere Rovers FC, Walsall FC, Wigan Borough FC, Wrexham AFC + Grimsby Town FC (Cleethorpes) transferred from Division 3 + Stockport County FC relegated from Division 2.

F.A. CUP FINAL (Stamford Bridge, London – 23/04/1921 – 72,805)

TOTTENHAM HOTSPUR FC (LONDON)   1-0   Wolverhampton Wanderers FC (Wolverhampton)

Dimmock

Tottenham: Hunter, Clay, McDonald, Smith, Walters, Grimsdell, Banks, Seed, Cantrell, Bliss, Dimmock.

Wolves: George, Woodward, Marshall, Gregory, Hodnett, Riley, Lea, Burrill, Edmonds, Potts, Brooks.

Semi-finals

Tottenham Hotspur FC (London)	2-1	Preston North End FC (Preston)
Wolverhampton Wanderers FC	0-0, 3-1	Cardiff City AFC (Cardiff)

Quarter-finals

Cardiff City AFC (Cardiff)	1-0	Chelsea FC (London)
Everton FC (Liverpool)	0-1	Wolverhampton Wanderers FC (Wolverhampton)
Hull City AFC (Kingston-upon-Hull)	0-0, 0-1	Preston North End FC (Preston)
Tottenham Hotspur FC (London)	1-0	Aston Villa FC (Birmingham)

1921-22

Football League Division 1, 1921-1922 Season

Column key: AV = Aston Villa, Bir = Birmingham, BR = Blackburn R., BW = Bolton Wands., BC = Bradford City, Bur = Burnley, CC = Cardiff City, Che = Chelsea, Ev = Everton, HT = Huddersfield T., Liv = Liverpool, MC = Man. City, MU = Man. United, Mid = Middlesbro', NU = Newcastle Utd., OA = Oldham Ath., PNE = Preston N.E., SU = Sheffield Utd., Sun = Sunderland, Ars = The Arsenal, TH = Tottenham H., WBA = W.B.A.

	AV	Bir	BR	BW	BC	Bur	CC	Che	Ev	HT	Liv	MC	MU	Mid	NU	OA	PNE	SU	Sun	Ars	TH	WBA
Aston Villa FC	■	1-1	1-1	2-1	7-1	2-0	2-1	1-4	2-1	2-0	1-1	4-0	3-1	6-2	1-0	2-0	2-0	5-3	2-0	2-0	2-1	0-1
Birmingham FC	1-0	■	1-0	1-1	1-0	2-3	0-1	5-1	1-1	0-2	0-2	3-1	0-1	4-3	0-4	3-0	0-2	2-1	1-0	0-1	0-3	0-2
Blackburn Rovers FC	1-2	1-1	■	1-2	3-1	3-2	1-3	1-1	2-2	2-0	0-0	3-1	3-0	2-2	0-2	3-2	3-0	2-3	1-2	0-1	1-1	2-3
Bolton Wanderers FC	1-0	1-2	1-1	■	3-3	0-1	1-2	0-2	1-0	3-1	1-3	5-0	1-0	4-2	3-2	5-1	2-2	3-1	1-1	1-0	1-1	2-0
Bradford City AFC	3-2	1-2	1-1	4-3	■	0-4	1-0	0-1	3-1	4-0	0-0	1-2	2-1	0-2	2-3	3-0	1-0	1-0	0-0	0-2	0-4	1-1
Burnley FC	2-1	3-1	1-2	2-0	4-0	■	1-1	5-0	2-0	1-0	1-1	5-2	4-2	3-1	2-0	1-0	3-3	2-1	2-0	1-0	1-0	4-2
Cardiff City AFC	0-4	3-1	1-3	1-2	6-3	4-2	■	2-0	2-1	0-0	2-0	0-2	3-1	3-1	1-0	0-1	3-0	1-1	2-0	4-3	0-1	2-0
Chelsea FC	1-0	1-2	1-0	0-3	1-0	4-1	1-0	■	1-0	0-0	0-0	1-1	1-1	1-0	0-0	0-2	1-0	2-0	0-2	1-0	1-2	1-1
Everton FC	3-2	2-1	2-0	1-0	2-0	2-0	0-1	2-3	■	6-2	1-1	2-2	5-0	4-1	2-3	2-2	1-0	3-0	1-1	0-0	1-0	2-0
Huddersfield Town AFC	1-0	1-0	3-0	3-0	1-2	1-0	0-1	2-0	1-2	■	0-1	2-0	1-1	2-1	1-0	6-0	1-1	1-2	2-0	1-1	2-0	
Liverpool FC	2-0	1-0	2-0	0-2	2-1	2-1	5-1	1-1	1-1	2-0	■	3-2	2-1	4-0	1-0	2-0	4-0	1-1	2-1	4-0	1-1	1-2
Manchester City FC	2-1	2-1	1-1	2-3	3-2	2-0	1-1	0-0	2-1	2-1	1-1	■	4-1	2-2	1-0	2-1	2-0	2-0	3-0	3-3	6-1	
Manchester United FC	1-0	1-1	0-1	0-1	1-1	0-1	1-1	2-1	1-1	0-0	3-1		■	3-5	0-1	0-3	1-1	3-2	3-1	1-0	2-1	2-3
Middlesbrough FC	5-0	1-1	0-1	4-2	1-2	4-1	0-0	0-1	3-1	5-1	3-1	4-1	2-0	■	1-1	1-1	1-0	1-1	3-0	4-2	0-0	3-2
Newcastle United FC	1-2	0-1	2-0	2-1	1-2	2-1	0-1	1-0	2-1	1-2	5-1	3-0	0-0		■	1-1	3-1	2-2	3-1	0-2		
Oldham Athletic AFC	3-1	0-1	1-1	0-0	0-0	1-0	2-1	0-3	0-1	1-1	0-1	0-0			2-0	■	1-0	2-0	3-1	2-1	1-0	1-0
Preston North End FC	1-0	2-2	2-1	3-1	2-1	2-1	1-1	2-0	1-0	1-1	1-1	1-0	3-2	1-1	2-0	0-0	■	3-0	1-1	3-2	1-2	0-3
Sheffield United FC	2-3	1-2	0-1	1-0	1-0	0-1	0-2	1-2	1-0	1-1	0-1	1-1	3-0	6-1	1-1	1-0	3-0	■	4-1	4-1	1-0	2-2
Sunderland AFC	1-4	2-1	3-1	6-2	0-0	3-2	4-1	1-2	2-3	2-0	2-3	2-1	1-1	0-0	5-1	1-0	1-0		■	1-0	2-1	5-0
The Arsenal FC	2-0	5-2	1-1	1-1	1-0	0-0	0-0	1-1	1-3	1-0	0-1	3-1	2-2	2-1	1-0	1-0	1-2	1-2		■	1-0	2-2
Tottenham Hotspur FC	3-1	2-1	2-1	1-2	1-0	1-1	4-1	0-0	2-0	1-0	0-1	3-1	2-2	2-4	4-0	3-1	5-0	2-1	1-0	2-0	■	2-0
West Bromwich Albion FC	0-1	1-0	0-2	0-1	1-1	2-0	2-2	2-2	1-1	3-2	1-4	2-0	0-0	0-0	1-2	0-1	2-0	3-0	2-1	0-3	3-0	■

Division 1

		Pd	Wn	Dw	Ls	GF	GA	Pts	
1.	LIVERPOOL FC (LIVERPOOL)	42	22	13	7	63	36	57	
2.	Tottenham Hotspur FC (London)	42	21	9	12	65	39	51	
3.	Burnley FC (Burnley)	42	22	5	15	72	54	49	
4.	Cardiff City AFC (Cardiff)	42	19	10	13	61	53	48	
5.	Aston Villa FC (Birmingham)	42	22	3	17	74	55	47	
6.	Bolton Wanderers FC (Bolton)	42	20	7	15	68	59	47	
7.	Newcastle United FC (Newcastle-upon-Tyne)	42	18	10	14	59	45	46	
8.	Middlesbrough FC (Middlesbrough)	42	16	14	12	79	69	46	
9.	Chelsea FC (London)	42	17	12	13	40	43	46	
10.	Manchester City FC (Manchester)	42	18	9	15	65	70	45	
11.	Sheffield United FC (Sheffield)	42	15	10	17	59	54	40	
12.	Sunderland AFC (Sunderland)	42	16	8	18	60	62	40	
13.	West Bromwich Albion FC (West Bromwich)	42	15	10	17	51	63	40	
14.	Huddersfield Town AFC (Huddersfield)	42	15	9	18	53	54	39	
15.	Blackburn Rovers FC (Blackburn)	42	13	12	17	54	57	38	
16.	Preston North End FC (Preston)	42	13	12	17	42	65	38	
17.	The Arsenal FC (London)	42	15	7	20	47	56	37	
18.	Birmingham FC (Birmingham)	42	15	7	20	48	60	37	
19.	Oldham Athletic AFC (Oldham)	42	13	11	18	38	50	37	
20.	Everton FC (Liverpool)	42	12	12	18	57	55	36	
21.	Bradford City AFC (Bradford)	42	11	10	21	48	72	32	R
22.	Manchester United FC (Manchester)	42	8	12	22	41	73	28	R
		924	356	212	356	1244	1244	924	

Top Goalscorer

1) Andrew WILSON (Middlesbrough FC) 31

Football League Division 2 1921-1922 Season	Barnsley	Blackpool	Bradford Park Avenue	Bristol City	Bury	Clapton Orient	Coventry City	Crystal Palace	Derby County	Fulham	Hull City	Leeds United	Leicester City	Nottingham Forest	Notts County	Port Vale	Rotherham County	South Shields	Stoke	Wednesday	West Ham United	Wolves
Barnsley FC	■	3-2	2-0	1-1	3-0	4-0	0-1	3-1	2-1	2-1	4-1	2-2	0-0	2-0	3-0	3-2	0-1	2-1	2-2	2-0	1-1	2-1
Blackpool FC	1-0	■	1-1	2-0	0-1	2-0	2-1	1-3	4-2	0-2	0-1	1-3	2-0	2-1	1-2	0-1	3-1	4-0	3-2	0-2	3-1	1-3
Bradford Park Avenue	2-3	0-0	■	2-1	1-1	3-1	1-2	0-0	5-1	1-2	1-1	0-1	0-1	1-0	2-1	2-0	4-2	1-0	2-4	2-1	2-0	0-0
Bristol City FC	3-0	0-1	1-0	■	2-0	2-1	0-2	1-2	1-2	1-0	1-0	0-0	1-1	0-1	2-2	2-1	1-2	0-1	2-0	3-1	0-1	2-0
Bury FC	1-2	3-0	2-2	5-0	■	0-0	3-2	1-2	2-0	1-0	4-0	2-1	0-1	1-2	1-0	5-2	0-0	1-0	0-1	1-2	0-1	2-1
Clapton Orient FC	2-1	3-0	1-0	0-1	3-1	■	4-0	0-0	3-2	4-2	0-2	4-2	0-0	1-2	2-1	2-0	1-2	0-1	1-0	1-1	0-0	1-0
Coventry City FC	0-1	0-1	2-2	1-1	1-2	1-2	■	1-1	1-2	2-0	2-0	1-0	0-1	4-2	4-1	4-0	0-1	0-1	2-2	2-0	3-1	
Crystal Palace FC	0-1	1-0	1-1	1-1	4-1	1-0	1-1	■	3-1	2-0	0-2	1-2	1-0	4-1	1-0	0-0	2-0	1-2	0-2	2-2	1-2	1-1
Derby County FC	1-0	1-0	1-3	5-1	1-0	3-0	1-0	2-0	■	1-1	0-0	2-0	0-1	1-2	1-1	3-2	4-0	0-2	2-4	0-1	3-1	2-3
Fulham FC	0-0	1-0	2-1	0-0	0-1	2-0	5-0	1-1	2-2	■	6-0	0-1	0-0	2-0	4-1	1-0	4-0	3-0	2-1	3-1	2-0	1-0
Hull City AFC	1-3	2-0	3-0	1-0	1-1	2-1	2-0	1-0	1-1	2-1	■	1-0	5-2	0-1	2-0	2-0	0-1	1-1	7-1	0-0	2-0	0-0
Leeds United AFC	4-0	0-0	3-0	3-0	2-0	2-0	5-2	0-0	2-1	2-0	0-2	■	3-0	0-0	1-1	2-1	0-2	0-0	1-2	1-1	0-0	0-0
Leicester City FC	1-0	1-0	2-1	4-1	0-0	1-0	1-1	2-0	1-1	1-2	0-1	0-0	■	2-2	3-0	3-0	1-0	1-0	3-4	1-1	2-1	0-1
Nottingham Forest FC	1-1	0-0	4-1	1-0	1-2	2-0	1-0	2-1	3-0	0-0	3-2	1-0	0-0	■	0-1	1-1	1-0	1-0	3-1	2-0	2-0	1-0
Notts County FC	1-4	2-1	3-0	0-2	1-1	0-0	1-1	3-2	1-2	3-0	2-0	4-1	0-0	1-1	■	1-2	2-0	2-0	0-0	2-0	1-1	4-0
Port Vale FC	2-3	1-0	1-0	3-1	5-2	3-0	1-2	3-0	1-1	1-1	1-0	0-1	1-1	0-2	0-0	■	1-0	1-1	0-1	1-0	2-1	0-2
Rotherham County FC	0-0	0-1	2-0	0-0	1-1	2-0	0-0	1-1	2-0	1-0	2-0	1-0	0-0	0-1	3-0	0-1	■	1-1	0-0	0-0	0-1	1-0
South Shields FC	5-2	2-1	1-0	2-0	1-1	1-1	2-1	1-1	3-1	1-0	1-0	0-1	1-0	0-0	0-1	1-0	2-0	■	1-1	0-0	1-0	0-2
Stoke FC	1-0	1-1	0-1	3-0	1-0	0-0	2-2	5-1	1-1	3-0	0-0	3-0	1-1	1-1	0-0	0-0	1-1	2-1	■	1-1	2-0	3-0
The Wednesday FC	2-3	5-1	2-1	1-0	4-1	0-0	3-2	1-0	1-1	1-4	0-0	2-1	1-0	0-4	2-0	1-0	0-3	0-1		■	2-1	3-1
West Ham United FC	4-0	0-2	1-0	3-0	3-2	1-2	3-0	2-0	3-1	1-0	1-1	1-1	1-0	1-0	2-1	3-0	1-2	1-1	3-0	2-0	■	2-0
Wolverhampton Wanderers FC	2-0	4-0	5-0	2-2	1-1	0-2	1-0	0-1	0-3	0-0	0-2	0-0	1-1	2-0	1-2	2-0	3-1	3-2	1-1	0-0	0-1	■

Division 2

		Pd	Wn	Dw	Ls	GF	GA	Pts	
1.	Nottingham Forest FC (Nottingham)	42	22	12	8	51	30	56	P
2.	Stoke FC (Stoke-on-Trent)	42	18	16	8	60	44	52	P
3.	Barnsley FC (Barnsley)	42	22	8	12	67	52	52	
4.	West Ham United FC (London)	42	20	8	14	52	39	48	
5.	Hull City AFC (Kingston-upon-Hull)	42	19	10	13	51	41	48	
6.	South Shields FC (South Shields)	42	17	12	13	43	38	46	
7.	Fulham FC (London)	42	18	9	15	57	38	45	
8.	Leeds United AFC (Leeds)	42	16	13	13	48	38	45	
9.	Leicester City FC (Leicester)	42	14	17	11	39	34	45	
10.	The Wednesday FC (Sheffield)	42	15	14	13	47	50	44	
11.	Bury FC (Bury)	42	15	10	17	54	55	40	
12.	Derby County FC (Derby)	42	15	9	18	60	64	39	
13.	Notts County FC (Nottingham)	42	12	15	15	47	51	39	
14.	Crystal Palace FC (London)	42	13	13	16	45	51	39	
15.	Clapton Orient FC (London)	42	15	9	18	43	50	39	
16.	Rotherham County FC (Rotherham)	42	14	11	17	32	43	39	
17.	Wolverhampton Wanderers FC (Wolverhampton)	42	13	11	18	44	49	37	
18.	Port Vale FC (Stoke-on-Trent)	42	14	8	20	43	57	36	
19.	Blackpool FC (Blackpool)	42	15	5	22	44	57	35	
20.	Coventry City FC (Coventry)	42	12	10	20	51	60	34	
21.	Bristol City FC (Bristol)	42	12	9	21	37	58	33	R
22.	Bradford Park Avenue FC (Bradford)	42	12	9	21	46	62	33	R
		924	343	238	343	1061	1061	924	

Football League Division 3 (N) 1921-1922 Season	Accrington Stanley	Ashington	Barrow	Chesterfield	Crewe Alexandra	Darlington	Durham City	Grimsby Town	Halifax Town	Hartlepools United	Lincoln City	Nelson	Rochdale	Southport	Stalybridge Celtic	Stockport County	Tranmere Rovers	Walsall	Wigan Borough	Wrexham
Accrington Stanley FC	■	3-0	3-0	3-1	2-0	1-0	5-1	1-0	1-2	4-1	2-0	4-1	4-0	1-2	4-1	1-3	3-0	3-3	4-0	1-0
Ashington FC	2-1	■	0-2	1-0	0-1	1-0	1-0	1-0	3-1	4-1	4-2	4-0	7-3	2-2	2-3	2-0	1-0	2-3	3-1	2-2
Barrow AFC	3-1	2-0	■	1-0	1-2	0-2	0-1	2-2	1-1	0-1	0-2	0-2	1-0	2-1	2-1	0-2	2-0	3-0	2-0	5-2
Chesterfield FC	0-1	0-1	2-0	■	1-1	0-3	2-1	4-1	2-0	2-1	3-0	1-2	2-1	2-1	4-0	0-1	3-0	1-0	1-1	3-0
Crewe Alexandra FC	2-1	1-2	2-1	1-2	■	7-3	3-2	1-2	2-1	2-0	0-2	2-1	2-0	1-0	5-1	0-1	1-1	2-0	2-1	3-0
Darlington FC	3-0	5-0	3-0	7-0	0-1	■	2-2	2-0	2-0	0-0	4-2	0-1	2-1	3-0	3-0	1-0	4-0	5-0	3-0	3-0
Durham City FC	3-1	1-0	2-0	3-1	4-2	3-7	■	1-2	3-1	0-1	2-0	0-2	0-2	2-0	3-1	0-2	3-0	2-0	6-0	3-1
Grimsby Town FC	2-1	6-1	4-0	2-2	3-0	3-1	5-2	■	4-1	2-0	3-1	3-1	3-0	0-0	1-1	2-1	5-1	3-1	1-1	2-0
Halifax Town AFC	2-1	2-0	3-2	1-2	5-5	5-1	3-2	2-0	■	3-0	1-2	3-1	1-1	1-1	2-3	1-0	0-2	1-3	1-2	0-0
Hartlepools United FC	2-1	2-1	3-1	7-0	1-0	0-0	0-1	0-0	4-0	■	1-1	6-1	5-3	1-0	0-1	0-0	1-0	0-0	0-0	0-1
Lincoln City FC	1-1	4-1	1-0	2-1	2-3	0-2	3-0	0-2	3-1	1-1	■	0-2	1-2	3-1	2-0	0-1	4-1	1-0	3-0	1-0
Nelson FC	0-1	0-2	1-1	2-0	1-2	1-1	3-5	3-0	0-0	0-4	0-0	■	4-1	3-2	1-0	2-2	0-1	1-0	1-2	4-0
Rochdale AFC	6-3	2-1	0-1	0-1	2-0	0-2	1-0	0-2	3-3	0-1	0-2	2-2	■	0-1	2-1	0-1	2-1	7-0	4-2	3-0
Southport FC	1-1	0-0	1-0	3-0	3-1	1-1	7-1	3-0	3-0	0-0	0-1	2-1	■		5-1	2-1	1-1	3-0	1-1	1-2
Stalybridge Celtic FC	3-1	2-0	3-0	6-0	2-2	1-0	4-3	3-0	2-1	1-3	2-0	2-0	1-0	0-0	■		0-4	2-0	0-0	4-1
Stockport County FC	2-1	3-2	2-0	2-1	1-1	1-0	4-0	0-1	0-0	1-0	2-2	3-0	3-0	2-1	4-0	■	0-0	3-1	3-0	0-0
Tranmere Rovers FC	2-4	2-3	2-2	2-0	4-1	0-1	3-3	2-2	2-2	1-2	4-0	4-0	0-1	4-1	0-2		■	0-1	2-0	0-0
Walsall FC	6-1	6-2	3-1	2-1	1-0	0-1	2-0	2-1	4-1	3-1	2-0	4-0	4-1	2-2	0-2	2-0		■	4-1	2-2
Wigan Borough FC	0-1	1-1	1-2	1-2	2-0	3-3	2-0	1-1	4-3	1-0	3-1	1-4	3-2	3-2	0-2	0-1	0-0	4-2	■	2-1
Wrexham AFC	2-1	2-0	0-0	6-1	1-0	1-1	3-1	0-1	5-1	0-2	3-1	4-2	1-1	2-0	2-0	0-0	1-3	4-0	3-2	■

Division 3 (North)

		Pd	Wn	Dw	Ls	GF	GA	Pts	
1.	Stockport County FC (Stockport)	38	24	8	6	60	21	56	P
2.	Darlington FC (Darlington)	38	22	6	10	81	37	50	
3.	Grimsby Town FC (Cleethorpes)	38	21	8	9	72	47	50	
4.	Hartlepools United FC (Hartlepool)	38	17	8	13	52	39	42	
5.	Accrington Stanley FC (Accrington)	38	19	3	16	73	57	41	
6.	Crewe Alexandra FC (Crewe)	38	18	5	15	60	56	41	
7.	Stalybridge Celtic FC (Stalybridge)	38	18	5	15	62	63	41	
8.	Walsall FC (Walsall)	38	18	3	17	66	65	39	
9.	Southport FC (Southport)	38	14	10	14	55	44	38	
10.	Ashington FC (Ashington)	38	17	4	17	59	66	38	
11.	Durham City FC (Durham)	38	17	3	18	68	67	37	
12.	Wrexham AFC (Wrexham)	38	14	9	15	51	56	37	
13.	Chesterfield FC (Chesterfield)	38	16	3	19	48	67	35	
14.	Lincoln City FC (Lincoln)	38	14	6	18	48	59	34	
15.	Barrow AFC (Barrow-in-Furness)	38	14	5	19	42	54	33	
16.	Nelson FC (Nelson)	38	13	7	18	48	66	33	
17.	Wigan Borough FC (Wigan)	38	11	9	18	46	72	31	
18.	Tranmere Rovers FC (Birkenhead)	38	9	11	18	51	61	29	
19.	Halifax Town AFC (Halifax)	38	10	9	19	56	76	29	
20.	Rochdale AFC (Rochdale)	38	11	4	23	52	77	26	
		760	317	126	317	1150	1150	760	

Football League Division 3 (S) 1921-1922 Season	Aberdare Athletic	Brentford	Brighton	Bristol Rovers	Charlton Athletic	Exeter City	Gillingham	Luton Town	Merthyr Town	Millwall Athletic	Newport County	Northampton	Norwich City	Plymouth Argyle	Portsmouth	Q.P.R.	Reading	Southampton	Southend United	Swansea Town	Swindon Town	Watford
Aberdare Athletic FC		2-0	2-0	2-0	3-3	0-2	6-1	2-0	0-0	0-0	3-0	4-2	1-2	0-0	0-0	4-2	0-1	0-1	1-1	2-1	3-2	3-0
Brentford FC	2-1		4-0	4-2	0-2	5-2	0-1	0-2	0-1	1-0	1-0	1-0	2-1	3-1	2-2	5-1	2-0	1-0	1-0	3-0	3-0	1-1
Brighton & Hove Albion	1-2	2-1		3-1	2-0	3-1	0-1	1-1	1-3	0-1	3-0	7-0	0-2	1-1	3-0	2-1	1-1	0-1	0-0	0-0	2-1	1-1
Bristol Rovers FC	5-1	0-0	1-2		4-2	1-3	0-3	2-0	2-0	0-0	3-4	2-0	4-2	1-3	1-1	1-1	2-0	1-0	0-0	1-1	1-1	1-1
Charlton Athletic FC	2-1	1-1	1-0	2-0		1-0	0-0	0-1	1-0	2-1	1-1	2-2	2-1	0-0	1-2	1-1	0-1	1-2	4-0	1-0	4-5	1-0
Exeter City FC	0-1	1-0	0-3	2-2	1-0		1-1	0-1	1-0	1-0	2-2	2-0	0-2	1-4	0-1	1-3	0-0	4-1	1-1	1-4	1-3	
Gillingham FC	3-1	0-0	1-2	3-2	2-0	3-0		0-1	5-0	0-1	0-2	3-2	5-2	1-2	1-2	1-2	2-0	2-0	1-0	0-0	2-2	1-1
Luton Town FC	1-2	3-0	2-0	1-2	2-0	4-0	7-0		3-0	1-0	4-0	3-0	2-1	1-0	0-1	3-1	0-1	1-0	3-0	3-0	2-1	1-1
Merthyr Town FC	0-1	2-0	2-1	0-2	1-0	0-0	2-0	2-0		3-1	2-1	2-1	3-0	0-1	2-1	2-0	2-2	1-0	1-0	4-1	1-2	
Millwall Athletic FC	0-0	1-1	3-0	4-1	0-1	1-0	1-0	1-1	4-0		1-1	0-0	2-2	1-1	1-1	0-0	3-0	0-1	0-1	0-0	0-0	0-0
Newport County AFC	1-0	2-1	0-1	0-1	2-1	1-1	1-1	2-2	0-2	1-0		2-2	1-0	0-0	0-1	1-0	0-1	2-1	2-3	4-0	0-0	
Northampton Town	2-0	2-0	2-0	2-2	1-0	2-3	3-1	2-0	2-0	0-3	2-0		3-0	1-3	0-0	2-1	2-0	0-2	0-1	0-1	2-1	1-0
Norwich City FC	0-0	0-0	1-1	0-1	2-0	2-0	2-0	2-0	3-1	2-2	2-0		1-1	2-1	0-0	4-1	2-2	1-1	3-2	1-2	1-1	
Plymouth Argyle FC	3-0	4-1	3-1	1-0	3-0	0-0	3-0	2-0	0-0	2-0	1-0	2-0	1-1		0-0	4-0	2-0	1-0	4-0	3-1	1-0	3-0
Portsmouth FC	2-2	1-0	0-0	1-0	1-0	2-0	4-1	1-1	2-1	2-2	4-3	1-1	0-1	3-1		1-0	1-0	6-0	3-0	1-3	2-0	
Queen's Park Rangers	1-0	1-1	3-0	1-2	3-1	2-1	1-0	1-0	6-1	2-1	4-0	2-0	2-0	1-1		1-1	2-2	1-0	1-0	0-0		
Reading FC	0-1	0-3	0-0	4-0	1-2	0-0	2-1	5-0	1-0	1-0	2-1	0-1	1-1	0-1		0-1	4-0	2-0	1-1	2-1		
Southampton FC	1-0	0-0	3-0	1-0	6-0	2-0	2-0	2-1	1-1	4-2	5-0	8-0	2-0	0-0	1-1	0-0		5-0	1-1	3-1	2-0	
Southend United FC	3-2	1-1	1-2	3-0	1-1	0-1	0-1	2-1	1-0	0-1	1-1	1-0	1-2	1-2	2-0	0-0		1-0	1-2	1-4		
Swansea Town AFC	1-2	1-0	2-1	8-1	0-0	2-1	2-0	1-0	3-2	3-0	2-2	2-2	1-1	3-0	2-2	1-0	0-0	1-0	1-1		1-3	3-0
Swindon Town FC	2-2	2-1	1-0	0-1	0-0	1-1	0-0	1-1	3-0	1-1	3-2	4-2	6-1	1-2	0-0	2-0	4-0	2-3	6-1	1-0		0-3
Watford FC	3-0	0-0	1-0	1-0	2-2	0-0	1-0	4-1	4-1	0-1	1-0	2-2	4-2	0-1	0-3	2-2	2-2	1-1	4-1	0-0	2-2	

Division 3 (South)	Pd	Wn	Dw	Ls	GF	GA	Pts	
1. Southampton FC (Southampton)	42	23	15	4	68	21	61	P
2. Plymouth Argyle FC (Plymouth)	42	25	11	6	63	24	61	
3. Portsmouth FC (Portsmouth)	42	18	17	7	62	39	53	
4. Luton Town FC (Luton)	42	22	8	12	64	35	52	
5. Queen's Park Rangers FC (London)	42	18	13	11	53	44	49	
6. Swindon Town FC (Swindon)	42	16	13	13	72	60	45	
7. Watford FC (Watford)	42	13	18	11	54	48	44	
8. Aberdare Athletic FC (Aberdare)	42	17	10	15	57	51	44	
9. Brentford FC (London)	42	16	11	15	52	43	43	
10. Swansea Town AFC (Swansea)	42	13	15	14	50	47	41	
11. Merthyr Town FC (Merthyr Tydfil)	42	17	6	19	45	56	40	
12. Millwall Athletic FC (London)	42	10	18	14	38	42	38	
13. Reading FC (Reading)	42	14	10	18	40	47	38	
14. Bristol Rovers FC (Bristol)	42	14	10	18	52	67	38	
15. Norwich City FC (Norwich)	42	12	13	17	50	62	37	
16. Charlton Athletic FC (London)	42	13	11	18	43	56	37	
17. Northampton Town FC (Northampton)	42	13	11	18	47	71	37	
18. Gillingham FC (Gillingham)	42	14	8	20	47	60	36	
19. Brighton & Hove Albion FC (Hove)	42	13	9	20	45	51	35	
20. Newport County AFC (Newport)	42	11	12	19	44	61	34	
21. Exeter City FC (Exeter)	42	11	12	19	38	59	34	
22. Southend United FC (Southend-on-Sea)	42	8	11	23	34	74	27	
	924	331	262	331	1118	1118	924	

F.A. CUP FINAL   (Stamford Bridge, London – 29/04/1922 – 53,000)

HUDDERSFIELD TOWN AFC   1-0   Preston North End FC (Preston)

Smith

Huddersfield: Mutch, Wood, Wadsworth, Slade, Wilson, Watson, Richardson, Mann, Islip, Stephenson, W.H. Smith.

Preston: J.F. Mitchell, Hamilton, Doolan, Duxbury, McCall, Williamson, Rawlings, Jefferies, Roberts, Woodhouse, Quinn.

Semi-finals

Huddersfield Town AFC (Huddersfield)	3-1	Notts County FC (Nottingham)
Preston North End FC (Preston)	2-1	Tottenham Hotspur FC (London)

Quarter-finals

Cardiff City AFC (Cardiff)	1-1, 1-2	Tottenham Hotspur FC (London)
Huddersfield Town AFC (Huddersfield)	3-0	Millwall Athletic FC (London)
Notts County FC (Nottingham)	2-2, 4-3	Aston Villa FC (Birmingham)
The Arsenal FC (London)	1-1, 1-2	Preston North End FC (Preston)

1922-23

1922-1923 Season	Aston Villa	Birmingham	Blackburn R.	Bolton Wands.	Burnley	Cardiff City	Chelsea	Everton	Huddersfield T.	Liverpool	Man. City	Middlesbro'	Newcastle Utd.	Nottingham F.	Oldham Ath.	Preston N.E.	Sheffield Utd.	Stoke	Sunderland	The Arsenal	Tottenham H.	W.B.A.
Aston Villa FC		3-0	2-0	2-0	3-1	1-3	1-0	3-0	2-1	0-1	2-0	2-2	1-1	4-0	3-0	1-0	0-1	6-0	1-0	1-1	2-0	2-0
Birmingham FC	1-0		1-1	2-0	1-0	0-0	0-1	1-1	0-0	0-1	0-1	2-0	0-2	2-0	2-3	1-0	4-2	2-0	1-2	3-2	2-1	0-2
Blackburn Rovers FC	4-2	1-1		1-0	2-1	3-1	0-0	5-1	0-0	1-0	0-0	2-0	1-1	2-0	1-0	1-1	1-0	1-5	0-0	0-5	1-0	5-1
Bolton Wanderers FC	3-0	3-0	3-0		2-1	0-0	1-1	0-2	1-0	1-1	2-1	1-1	1-0	4-2	3-1	1-1	1-1	1-1	4-1	0-2	2-1	3-0
Burnley FC	1-1	0-2	3-1	2-1		1-5	1-0	0-1	0-2	2-0	2-0	3-0	0-0	8-2	1-1	2-0	1-4	3-2	2-0	4-1	0-1	3-0
Cardiff City AFC	3-0	1-1	5-0	1-0	2-2		6-1	0-2	0-1	3-0	3-1	2-0	5-0	3-1	2-1	1-0	2-1	2-4	4-1	2-3	3-0	3-0
Chelsea FC	1-1	1-1	1-1	3-0	0-1	1-1		3-1	2-2	0-1	1-1	3-0	2-2	4-0	0-1	0-0	3-2	1-3	0-0	0-0	0-0	2-2
Everton FC	2-1	2-1	2-0	1-1	1-0	3-1	3-1		0-3	0-1	0-0	5-3	3-2	4-2	0-1	5-1	4-0	1-1	1-0	3-1	1-0	0-1
Huddersfield Town AFC	3-5	4-0	0-2	0-2	2-0	1-0	3-0	1-0		0-0	0-0	0-2	2-0	2-1	3-0	2-1	1-0	0-1	4-0	1-0	1-0	4-1
Liverpool FC	3-0	0-0	3-0	3-0	3-0	3-1	1-0	5-1	1-1		2-0	2-0	0-2	2-1	2-1	5-2	2-1	1-0	5-1	5-2	0-0	2-0
Manchester City FC	1-1	0-1	2-1	2-0	1-0	5-1	3-0	2-1	3-1	1-0		1-1	0-0	1-1	3-2	2-1	3-3	2-1	1-0	0-0	3-0	1-1
Middlesbrough FC	2-2	2-1	1-2	1-2	4-1	0-1	2-4	2-2	0-2	5-0	1-1		4-0	2-1	1-3	3-2	3-1	4-2	4-0	1-2	4-0	2-1
Newcastle United FC	0-0	0-0	5-1	1-0	0-2	3-1	0-0	2-0	1-0	0-1	3-1	1-1		1-0	1-0	3-0	1-0	2-1	1-1	1-1	1-1	2-0
Nottingham Forest FC	3-1	1-1	1-0	1-1	1-0	3-2	0-4	2-1	0-1	1-3	2-0	2-1	0-1		1-0	3-0	1-0	0-1	1-0	2-1	0-1	0-4
Oldham Athletic AFC	0-2	2-0	1-0	3-1	1-1	3-1	2-0	1-0	0-2	0-3	0-2	0-3	0-0	2-0		2-1	0-2	4-1	0-0	0-0	0-3	0-3
Preston North End FC	3-2	2-3	1-0	3-1	3-1	3-0	0-1	3-1	1-0	1-3	0-2	1-2	1-0	2-2	5-1		2-3	4-2	2-0	1-2	2-0	0-0
Sheffield United FC	1-1	7-1	1-1	2-2	2-1	0-0	0-2	0-1	0-2	4-1	2-0	4-1	2-0	0-0	2-2	2-2		2-0	3-1	2-1	2-0	3-1
Stoke FC	1-1	0-0	1-1	2-0	0-1	3-1	1-2	4-1	2-2	0-0	1-1	0-0	1-1	2-2	4-2	4-0	1-2		1-0	1-0	1-0	0-2
Sunderland AFC	2-0	5-3	4-3	5-1	3-1	2-1	3-1	1-1	1-1	1-1	0-0	0-0	0-0	2-0	2-0	1-0	2-0	3-5		2-0	3-3	1-1
The Arsenal FC	2-0	1-0	1-1	5-0	1-1	2-1	3-1	1-2	1-1	1-0	1-0	3-0	1-2	2-0	2-0	1-0	3-0	2-3	3-2		0-2	3-1
Tottenham Hotspur FC	1-2	2-0	2-0	0-1	1-3	1-1	3-1	2-0	0-0	2-4	3-1	2-0	0-1	2-1	3-0	1-1	2-1	3-1	0-1	1-2		3-1
West Bromwich Albion FC	3-0	1-0	3-0	1-1	2-1	3-0	0-0	0-2	0-0	2-0	1-0	2-1	0-0	1-0	2-2	4-0	0-1	1-1	7-0	5-1	0-0	

Division 1

		Pd	Wn	Dw	Ls	GF	GA	Pts	
1.	LIVERPOOL FC (LIVERPOOL)	42	26	8	8	70	31	60	
2.	Sunderland AFC (Sunderland)	42	22	10	10	72	54	54	
3.	Huddersfield Town AFC (Huddersfield)	42	21	11	10	60	32	53	
4.	Newcastle United FC (Newcastle-upon-Tyne)	42	18	12	12	45	37	48	
5.	Everton FC (Liverpool)	42	20	7	15	63	59	47	
6.	Aston Villa FC (Birmingham)	42	18	10	14	64	51	46	
7.	West Bromwich Albion FC (West Bromwich)	42	17	11	14	58	49	45	
8.	Manchester City FC (Manchester)	42	17	11	14	50	49	45	
9.	Cardiff City AFC (Cardiff)	42	18	7	17	73	59	43	
10.	Sheffield United FC (Sheffield)	42	16	10	16	68	64	42	
11.	The Arsenal FC (London)	42	16	10	16	61	62	42	
12.	Tottenham Hotspur FC (London)	42	17	7	18	50	50	41	
13.	Bolton Wanderers FC (Bolton)	42	14	12	16	50	58	40	
14.	Blackburn Rovers FC (Blackburn)	42	14	12	16	47	62	40	
15.	Burnley FC (Burnley)	42	16	6	20	58	59	38	
16.	Preston North End FC (Preston)	42	13	11	18	60	64	37	
17.	Birmingham FC (Birmingham)	42	13	11	18	41	57	37	
18.	Middlesbrough FC (Middlesbrough)	42	13	10	19	57	63	36	
19.	Chelsea FC (London)	42	9	18	15	45	53	36	
20.	Nottingham Forest FC (Nottingham)	42	13	8	21	41	70	34	
21.	Stoke FC (Stoke-on-Trent)	42	10	10	22	47	67	30	R
22.	Oldham Athletic AFC (Oldham)	42	10	10	22	35	65	30	R
		924	351	222	351	1215	1215	924	

Top Goalscorer

1) Charles BUCHAN   (Sunderland AFC)   30

Football League Division 2 1922-1923 Season	Barnsley	Blackpool	Bradford City	Bury	Clapton Orient	Coventry City	Crystal Palace	Derby County	Fulham	Hull City	Leeds United	Leicester City	Manchester United	Notts County	Port Vale	Rotherham County	Southampton	South Shields	Stockport County	Wednesday	West Ham United	Wolves
Barnsley FC	■	2-2	3-1	2-1	2-1	6-2	1-2	5-0	0-1	1-0	1-0	0-1	2-2	1-0	0-1	2-2	3-0	5-0	1-1	2-4	2-0	1-0
Blackpool FC	0-1	■	3-0	5-1	0-0	0-1	4-0	3-2	3-0	0-0	1-0	1-2	1-0	1-1	0-2	1-0	1-2	3-0	0-0	3-0	4-1	3-1
Bradford City AFC	2-0	0-2	■	4-0	1-2	4-0	1-1	0-0	2-1	2-1	0-2	2-2	1-1	1-2	2-0	0-1	0-0	1-0	2-0	1-1	0-1	1-1
Bury FC	2-1	3-0	1-0	■	5-1	1-1	2-1	4-1	0-1	1-0	1-1	2-0	2-2	2-2	2-0	1-0	0-0	1-0	2-0	4-0	2-5	3-0
Clapton Orient FC	0-1	0-1	1-0	0-2	■	0-0	3-1	0-0	0-2	2-0	3-0	2-0	1-1	2-1	0-0	5-1	1-0	0-0	0-2	2-2	0-2	4-1
Coventry City FC	3-0	1-2	2-1	3-0	2-1	■	2-1	1-0	1-0	0-1	1-2	1-1	2-0	1-2	1-2	2-1	2-0	0-2	1-0	1-1	1-3	7-1
Crystal Palace FC	2-0	1-1	2-0	1-1	2-0	0-0	■	2-2	0-0	1-1	1-0	0-1	2-3	0-1	2-0	4-0	1-0	1-1	3-0	2-0	1-5	5-0
Derby County FC	0-1	1-0	0-2	1-0	0-0	4-0	6-0	■	2-0	0-2	0-1	2-0	1-1	0-0	1-2	1-0	0-2	1-0	1-2	1-1	2-1	1-1
Fulham FC	0-1	1-1	0-0	3-0	0-0	4-0	2-1	3-1	■	0-0	3-0	2-0	0-0	2-1	1-1	1-2	1-1	0-1	3-0	1-0	0-2	2-0
Hull City AFC	2-1	0-0	0-0	2-2	2-1	1-1	1-1	4-2	1-0	■	3-1	1-3	2-1	0-2	3-0	2-3	1-3	2-0	1-0	0-0	1-1	0-0
Leeds United AFC	1-1	1-1	1-0	0-0	0-0	1-0	4-1	1-0	1-1	2-2	■	0-0	0-1	3-0	2-1	2-0	1-0	0-1	2-0	0-0	3-1	1-0
Leicester City FC	2-2	1-2	2-0	2-0	2-0	2-1	3-0	0-1	1-1	0-1	2-1	■	0-1	2-1	3-0	3-0	2-1	3-0	2-0	3-1	0-6	7-0
Manchester United FC	1-0	2-1	1-1	0-1	0-0	2-1	2-1	0-0	1-1	3-2	0-0	0-2	■	1-1	1-2	3-0	1-2	3-0	1-0	1-0	1-2	1-0
Notts County FC	1-0	2-0	0-0	1-0	3-1	2-0	0-4	1-2	1-0	0-1	1-0	1-0	1-6	■	1-0	2-0	1-0	2-0	2-0	1-0	2-0	4-1
Port Vale FC	1-1	2-0	1-2	2-0	3-1	0-1	2-0	2-3	0-1	1-0	1-2	0-0	1-0	0-0	■	0-0	0-0	3-0	0-2	2-2	1-3	1-0
Rotherham County FC	1-1	1-0	0-2	0-0	0-0	2-0	4-1	3-0	1-3	0-1	3-1	0-0	1-1	1-0	3-1	■	0-0	2-1	2-1	1-2	2-2	3-2
Southampton FC	2-2	1-1	2-0	0-3	2-0	3-0	0-2	0-4	2-0	2-1	0-1	0-0	0-0	0-1	3-1	4-2	■	0-2	1-0	1-1	2-0	3-0
South Shields FC	2-0	1-0	0-0	0-2	3-0	0-0	2-0	3-1	2-0	0-0	0-2	2-1	0-0	0-3	1-0	3-1	2-0	■	3-0	1-1	0-0	1-1
Stockport County FC	3-1	2-2	1-0	1-0	0-2	5-1	2-2	2-1	0-2	1-1	2-1	4-5	1-0	0-0	0-2	1-0	3-0	1-1	■	0-1	2-1	1-1
The Wednesday FC	2-3	2-3	2-2	2-0	4-1	3-0	3-1	0-0	1-0	1-0	3-1	2-1	1-0	0-1	2-0	1-0	0-0	2-0	4-1	■	0-2	1-0
West Ham United FC	0-0	2-0	1-2	0-0	1-0	1-0	1-1	0-0	1-0	3-0	0-0	2-2	0-2	0-1	0-0	4-0	1-1	1-0	0-1	2-1	■	1-0
Wolverhampton Wanderers FC	3-3	3-4	4-1	1-1	1-3	1-2	1-0	0-1	0-0	3-0	0-1	1-2	0-1	1-0	3-0	3-2	0-0	1-0	3-1	2-0	1-4	■

Division 2

		Pd	Wn	Dw	Ls	GF	GA	Pts	
1.	Notts County FC (Nottingham)	42	23	7	12	46	34	53	P
2.	West Ham United FC (London)	42	20	11	11	63	38	51	P
3.	Leicester City FC (Leicester)	42	21	9	12	65	44	51	
4.	Manchester United FC (Manchester)	42	17	14	11	51	36	48	
5.	Blackpool FC (Blackpool)	42	18	11	13	60	43	47	
6.	Bury FC (Bury)	42	18	11	13	55	46	47	
7.	Leeds United AFC (Leeds)	42	18	11	13	43	36	47	
8.	The Wednesday FC (Sheffield)	42	17	12	13	54	47	46	
9.	Barnsley FC (Barnsley)	42	17	11	14	62	51	45	
10.	Fulham FC (London)	42	16	12	14	43	32	44	
11.	Southampton FC (Southampton)	42	14	14	14	40	40	42	
12.	Hull City AFC (Kingston-upon-Hull)	42	14	14	14	43	45	42	
13.	South Shields FC (South Shields)	42	15	10	17	35	44	40	
14.	Derby County FC (Derby)	42	14	11	17	46	50	39	
15.	Bradford City AFC (Bradford)	42	12	13	17	41	45	37	
16.	Crystal Palace FC (London)	42	13	11	18	54	62	37	
17.	Port Vale FC (Stoke-on-Trent)	42	14	9	19	39	51	37	
18.	Coventry City FC (Coventry)	42	15	7	20	46	63	37	
19.	Clapton Orient FC (London)	42	12	12	18	40	50	36	
20.	Stockport County FC (Stockport)	42	14	8	20	43	58	36	
21.	Rotherham County FC (Rotherham)	42	13	9	20	44	63	35	R
22.	Wolverhampton Wanderers FC (Wolverhampton)	42	9	9	24	42	77	27	R
		924	344	236	344	1055	1055	924	

Football League Division 3 (N) 1922-1923 Season	Accrington Stanley	Ashington	Barrow	Bradford P.A.	Chesterfield	Crewe Alexandra	Darlington	Durham City	Grimsby Town	Halifax Town	Hartlepools United	Lincoln City	Nelson	Rochdale	Southport	Stalybridge Celtic	Tranmere Rovers	Walsall	Wigan Borough	Wrexham
Accrington Stanley FC		4-1	3-4	4-3	0-4	0-0	2-1	3-1	4-0	4-1	2-1	1-0	0-1	2-1	3-1	1-0	4-1	2-1	0-0	1-0
Ashington FC	2-5		2-6	2-1	2-0	2-4	3-1	0-0	2-1	3-2	4-2	0-2	0-2	2-0	1-1	0-3	3-1	3-0	2-1	1-1
Barrow AFC	5-2	3-0		1-2	3-1	2-0	0-1	2-1	2-0	0-1	0-0	1-3	1-0	4-1	2-0	0-1	2-1	0-0	2-3	1-0
Bradford Park Avenue	5-1	3-0	3-0		1-0	3-0	2-1	4-1	2-1	2-2	1-1	4-1	6-2	3-0	5-1	1-0	3-0	2-2	1-1	0-1
Chesterfield FC	3-1	2-2	2-1	2-2		2-1	0-0	3-1	3-2	3-0	1-1	3-3	1-2	4-0	3-0	1-0	5-0	6-0	3-1	2-1
Crewe Alexandra FC	1-1	3-1	1-0	0-1	2-0		3-0	4-0	3-0	2-1	2-1	3-1	1-0	0-1	1-0	4-1	1-0	0-0	0-1	0-0
Darlington FC	4-0	1-1	3-2	2-0	4-1	5-0		1-0	1-3	0-1	4-0	0-0	2-3	1-1	2-1	1-0	2-0	2-0	2-0	4-1
Durham City FC	4-1	1-1	4-1	0-0	1-1	2-0	0-0		0-3	2-2	3-2	7-1	0-1	1-1	1-1	0-0	1-0	0-2	2-2	2-0
Grimsby Town FC	7-1	7-4	2-0	0-1	3-1	2-3	0-1	1-0		0-1	1-0	1-0	0-2	1-1	2-1	3-0	0-0	1-2	0-0	4-0
Halifax Town AFC	0-0	0-0	3-0	3-0	2-0	1-0	2-1	1-3	1-0		3-0	3-1	2-2	1-0	0-1	2-1	3-1	1-2	0-1	1-1
Hartlepools United FC	0-0	3-1	2-0	0-1	5-0	1-1	1-0	2-1	2-0	3-2		2-0	5-1	0-2	1-1	4-0	0-1	2-2	0-0	1-1
Lincoln City FC	0-0	2-0	1-1	0-0	0-0	1-0	1-1	3-1	1-2	0-0	2-1		1-0	0-1	2-0	1-1	2-0	0-2	2-1	2-0
Nelson FC	2-1	1-3	2-1	1-0	4-0	0-0	3-0	4-0	1-1	2-0	4-1	2-1		1-2	2-0	1-0	1-0	3-0	1-0	2-0
Rochdale AFC	1-1	2-0	3-1	0-3	0-2	1-1	2-2	2-0	0-1	1-0	4-0	1-1	0-3		3-2	2-0	0-2	3-2	3-2	5-0
Southport FC	1-2	1-0	0-0	0-0	0-2	2-0	2-1	1-0	3-1	1-3	1-0	3-0	0-1	0-1		0-0	0-0	2-1	1-0	1-0
Stalybridge Celtic FC	1-0	2-1	2-0	1-0	1-2	0-1	4-2	1-0	3-2	4-3	1-1	0-1	2-0	0-0	1-0		4-1	2-0	0-2	3-2
Tranmere Rovers FC	4-1	1-0	3-0	0-0	2-3	1-2	2-2	5-1	3-2	2-1	1-1	0-2	2-0	2-0	1-1			2-3	4-2	4-0
Walsall FC	0-2	2-1	3-1	1-0	0-1	1-1	2-2	2-0	1-0	2-1	2-2	2-0	5-0	0-0	2-1	2-1			3-1	1-0
Wigan Borough FC	2-0	6-1	2-1	3-2	1-0	1-1	3-0	0-2	1-0	0-1	9-1	3-1	6-0	1-0	3-0	0-0	1-0			1-1
Wrexham AFC	2-0	0-0	0-0	3-0	3-1	2-1	0-0	1-0	1-1	2-1	2-0	0-2	2-1	3-1	1-1	2-1	2-1	1-0	2-1	

Division 3 (North)	Pd	Wn	Dw	Ls	GF	GA	Pts	
1. Nelson FC (Nelson)	38	24	3	11	61	41	51	P
2. Bradford Park Avenue FC (Bradford)	38	19	9	10	67	38	47	
3. Walsall FC (Walsall)	38	19	8	11	51	44	46	
4. Chesterfield FC (Chesterfield)	38	19	7	12	68	52	45	
5. Wigan Borough FC (Wigan)	38	18	8	12	64	39	44	
6. Crewe Alexandra FC (Crewe)	38	17	9	12	48	38	43	
7. Halifax Town AFC (Halifax)	38	17	7	14	53	46	41	
8. Accrington Stanley FC (Accrington)	38	17	7	14	59	65	41	
9. Darlington FC (Darlington)	38	15	10	13	59	46	40	
10. Wrexham AFC (Wrexham)	38	14	10	14	38	48	38	
11. Stalybridge Celtic FC (Stalybridge)	38	15	6	17	42	47	36	#
12. Rochdale AFC (Rochdale)	38	13	10	15	42	53	36	
13. Lincoln City FC (Lincoln)	38	13	10	15	39	55	36	
14. Grimsby Town FC (Cleethorpes)	38	14	5	19	55	52	33	
15. Hartlepools United FC (Hartlepool)	38	10	12	16	48	54	32	
16. Tranmere Rovers FC (Birkenhead)	38	12	8	18	49	59	32	
17. Southport FC (Southport)	38	12	7	19	32	46	31	
18. Barrow AFC (Barrow-in-Furness)	38	13	4	21	50	60	30	
19. Ashington FC (Ashington)	38	11	8	19	51	77	30	
20. Durham City FC (Durham)	38	9	10	19	43	59	28	
	760	301	158	301	1019	1019	760	

\# Stalybridge Celtic FC (Stalybridge) resigned from the league at the end of the season.

Elected: Doncaster Rovers FC (Doncaster) and New Brighton FC (Wallasey)

Division 3 (North) was extended to 22 clubs for next season

Football League Division 3 (S) — 1922-1923 Season

Results grid (home team in rows, away team in columns). Shaded diagonal cells shown as ■.

Home \ Away	Aberdare Athletic	Brentford	Brighton	Bristol City	Bristol Rovers	Charlton Athletic	Exeter City	Gillingham	Luton Town	Merthyr Town	Millwall Athletic	Newport County	Northampton	Norwich City	Plymouth Argyle	Portsmouth	Q.P.R.	Reading	Southend United	Swansea Town	Swindon Town	Watford
Aberdare Athletic FC	■	0-0	0-1	0-1	0-0	3-1	3-1	2-0	2-1	0-0	0-1	6-2	0-2	0-3	2-2	0-2	0-0	0-0	1-1	0-1	3-3	3-1
Brentford FC	0-1	■	1-2	4-0	0-1	0-3	0-1	2-0	3-2	3-1	1-1	0-0	2-1	1-4	2-0	1-0	1-3	1-1	0-0	0-1	3-0	2-1
Brighton & Hove Albion	3-1	2-1	■	2-1	2-1	1-0	3-0	3-0	0-1	0-0	2-0	2-1	1-0	0-0	1-0	7-1	2-0	3-1	0-1	1-3	1-1	3-0
Bristol City FC	0-0	1-1	3-1	■	0-1	3-1	1-1	2-1	1-0	3-0	1-1	2-0	1-0	4-0	2-0	2-1	3-2	2-1	5-0	0-1	3-1	3-1
Bristol Rovers FC	1-0	1-1	0-0	1-2	■	1-1	3-3	1-0	1-1	3-0	0-0	3-1	0-0	3-2	0-1	0-1	1-3	1-1	2-0	0-0	2-0	1-2
Charlton Athletic FC	1-1	1-1	0-1	1-0	0-0	■	0-0	3-1	2-1	0-1	0-2	6-0	2-0	3-0	1-0	0-2	1-1	1-0	5-1	3-1	3-1	0-0
Exeter City FC	1-0	0-2	1-0	0-0	0-0	0-0	■	0-1	1-2	2-1	2-1	4-0	1-2	2-0	0-0	2-3	1-2	4-0	2-1	1-0	2-1	1-2
Gillingham FC	4-0	2-0	2-0	1-1	0-1	2-2	2-1	■	1-0	2-0	3-0	3-0	0-3	5-0	4-2	0-1	2-1	1-0	2-2	0-0		1-4
Luton Town FC	4-1	4-0	1-1	1-1	1-0	2-2	6-0	2-0	■	2-1	2-2	1-0	2-1	4-0	2-1	0-2	1-0	1-2	2-0	6-1	3-2	0-1
Merthyr Town FC	0-2	1-0	2-0	0-1	1-1	3-0	3-1	1-0	0-1	■	1-1	1-0	3-0	0-1	3-0	0-1	1-2	2-1	2-1	1-1	2-3	
Millwall Athletic FC	1-0	1-1	2-1	1-1	1-0	1-1	3-0	3-1	0-0	1-0	■	0-0	2-0	3-0	0-0	1-3	0-0	0-0	1-1	0-2	0-2	5-1
Newport County AFC	0-0			4-1	4-0	6-2	0-2	0-3	1-1	0-0		■	1-1	1-3	1-0	0-0	0-2	1-2	2-2	1-1		
Northampton Town	3-1	1-1	0-0	2-1	1-0	0-0	3-0	1-0	2-0	1-1	2-1	2-1	■	1-1	0-0	4-2	5-0	5-2	1-3	1-2	1-1	
Norwich City FC	1-4	0-2	1-0	2-2	0-0	2-3	6-0	1-1	1-2	1-1	3-2	1-1	1-0	■	0-2	1-1	2-1	1-4	0-0	2-0		
Plymouth Argyle FC	2-0	3-0	2-2	5-1	3-0	2-0	5-1	2-0	4-0	1-0	1-0	1-1	1-0	1-1	■	2-0	3-0	1-1	2-0	3-1	1-1	2-0
Portsmouth FC	1-0	3-0	1-2	1-2	0-0	3-0	3-4	6-1	1-2	1-1	2-0	0-0	0-0	2-1	1-2	■	1-1	1-0	0-0	0-3	4-1	2-3
Queen's Park Rangers	4-1	1-1	0-0	1-2	3-1	1-2	2-0	2-1	4-0	2-3	1-1	3-2	2-0	2-3	0-1		■	1-0	1-0	2-1	0-2	1-2
Reading FC	1-0	0-0	0-1	0-0	0-1	1-3	1-1	3-0	1-0	1-2	2-0	4-1	0-0	1-1	0-0		0-0	■	1-1	4-4	1-0	1-1
Southend United FC	4-0			0-3		0-0	5-0	1-3		3-1	2-0	3-1	1-2	2-0	3-1	2-0	3-1		■	0-1	2-0	2-1
Swansea Town AFC	5-1	0-0	0-0	4-1	0-1	3-2	5-1	1-0	1-0	1-1	0-1	5-1	4-0	3-1	1-1	2-1	3-0	2-2	1-0	■	5-0	0-0
Swindon Town FC	5-4	3-0	3-0	0-1	1-0	2-1	2-1	0-1	1-1	4-0	0-0	2-2	2-0	1-2	2-1	3-0	1-0	3-1	3-0	2-1	■	1-1
Watford FC	6-0	2-0	1-2	1-1	0-1	2-2	4-0	5-2	2-1	1-1	0-0	2-1	0-0	2-1	1-0	2-3	0-3	1-0	1-1	2-1	0-3	■

Division 3 (South)	**Pd**	**Wn**	**Dw**	**Ls**	**GF**	**GA**	**Pts**	
1. Bristol City FC (Bristol)	42	24	11	7	66	40	59	P
2. Plymouth Argyle FC (Plymouth)	42	23	7	12	61	29	53	
3. Swansea Town AFC (Swansea)	42	22	9	11	78	45	53	
4. Brighton & Hove Albion FC (Brighton)	42	20	11	11	52	34	51	
5. Luton Town FC (Luton)	42	21	7	14	68	49	49	
6. Portsmouth FC (Portsmouth)	42	19	8	15	58	52	46	
7. Millwall Athletic FC (London)	42	14	18	10	45	40	46	
8. Northampton Town FC (Northampton)	42	17	11	14	54	44	45	
9. Swindon Town FC (Swindon)	42	17	11	14	62	56	45	
10. Watford FC (Watford)	42	17	10	15	57	54	44	
11. Queen's Park Rangers FC (London)	42	16	10	16	54	49	42	
12. Charlton Athletic FC (London)	42	14	14	14	55	51	42	
13. Bristol Rovers FC (Bristol)	42	13	16	13	35	36	42	
14. Brentford FC (London)	42	13	12	17	41	51	38	
15. Southend United FC (Southend-on-Sea)	42	12	13	17	49	54	37	
16. Gillingham FC (Gillingham)	42	15	7	20	51	59	37	
17. Merthyr Town FC (Merthyr Tydfil)	42	11	14	17	39	48	36	
18. Norwich City FC (Norwich)	42	13	10	19	51	71	36	
19. Reading FC (Reading)	42	10	14	18	36	55	34	
20. Exeter City FC (Exeter)	42	13	7	22	47	84	33	
21. Aberdare Athletic FC (Aberdare)	42	9	11	22	42	70	29	
22. Newport County AFC (Newport)	42	8	11	23	40	70	27	
	924	341	242	341	1141	1141	924	

F.A. CUP FINAL   (Wembley Stadium, London – 28/04/1923 – 126,047)

BOLTON WANDERERS FC (BOLTON)	2-0	West Ham United FC (London)

Jack, JR Smith

Bolton: Pym, Haworth, Finney, Nuttall, Seddon, Jennings, Butler, Jack, JR Smith, J.Smith, Vizard.

West Ham: Hufton, Henderson, Young, Bishop, Kay, Tresadern, Richards, Brown, V.Watson, Moore, Ruffell.

Semi-finals

Bolton Wanderers FC (Bolton)	1-0	Sheffield United FC (Sheffield)
West Ham United FC (London)	5-2	Derby County FC (Derby)

Quarter-finals

Charlton Athletic FC (London)	0-1	Bolton Wanderers FC (Bolton)
Queen's Park Rangers FC (London)	0-1	Sheffield United FC (Sheffield)
Southampton FC (Southampton)	1-1, 1-1, 0-1	West Ham United FC (London)
Tottenham Hotspur FC (London)	0-1	Derby County FC (Derby)

1923-24

Football League Division 1 1923-1924 Season	Aston Villa	Birmingham	Blackburn Rovers	Bolton Wanderers	Burnley	Cardiff City	Chelsea	Everton	Huddersfield Town	Liverpool	Manchester City	Middlesbrough	Newcastle United	Nottingham Forest	Notts County	Preston North End	Sheffield United	Sunderland	The Arsenal	Tottenham Hotspur	W.B.A.	West Ham United
Aston Villa FC	■	0-0	1-0	1-0	1-1	2-1	0-0	1-1	3-1	0-0	2-0	0-0	6-1	2-0	0-0	5-1	2-2	0-1	2-1	0-0	4-0	1-1
Birmingham FC	3-0	■	1-1	0-3	2-1	0-0	1-0	0-1	0-1	2-1	3-0	2-1	4-1	0-2	0-0	2-0	0-1	0-2	0-2	3-2	0-0	2-0
Blackburn Rovers FC	3-1	4-1	■	3-1	1-1	2-1	3-0	2-0	1-0	0-0	0-1	2-0	2-1	1-1	4-1	2-0	1-1	3-2	2-0	0-1	4-0	0-0
Bolton Wanderers FC	1-0	1-1	3-0	■	0-0	2-2	4-0	2-0	3-4	4-1	0-0	2-0	0-1	4-0	7-1	0-0	4-2	1-0	1-2	3-1	2-0	1-1
Burnley FC	1-2	1-2	1-2	1-0	■	1-2	2-0	2-2	1-1	2-0	3-2	0-0	3-2	2-4	1-1	1-0	2-0	0-3	4-1	2-2	4-0	5-1
Cardiff City AFC	0-2	2-0	2-0	3-2	2-0	■	1-1	0-0	0-0	2-0	1-1	1-0	1-0	4-1	0-2	1-1	3-1	2-1	4-0	2-1	3-0	1-0
Chelsea FC	0-0	1-1	2-0	0-0	3-2	1-2	■	1-1	0-1	2-1	3-1	2-0	1-0	1-1	0-6	1-2	1-1	4-1	0-0	0-1	0-0	0-0
Everton FC	2-0	2-0	0-0	2-2	3-3	0-0	2-0	■	1-1	1-0	6-1	1-0	2-2	2-1	3-0	1-1	2-0	2-3	3-1	4-2	2-0	2-1
Huddersfield Town AFC	1-0	1-0	1-0	1-0	1-0	2-0	0-1	2-0	■	3-1	1-1	1-0	1-1	3-0	0-0	4-0	1-0	3-2	6-1	2-1	0-0	1-1
Liverpool FC	0-1	6-2	0-0	3-1	1-0	0-2	3-1	1-2	1-1	■	0-0	3-1	0-1	4-2	1-0	3-1	2-3	4-2	0-0	1-0	0-0	2-0
Manchester City FC	1-2	1-0	3-1	1-1	2-2	1-1	1-0	2-1	1-0	0-1	■	3-2	1-1	1-3	1-0	2-2	2-1	4-1	1-0	1-0	3-3	2-1
Middlesbrough FC	0-2	0-1	2-0	1-2	3-0	0-1	2-0	1-1	2-0	1-1	1-1	■	1-0	5-2	2-3	1-2	0-1	1-3	0-0	0-1	0-1	2-1
Newcastle United FC	4-1	2-1	2-1	1-0	2-0	1-1	2-1	3-1	0-1	2-1	4-1	3-2	■	4-0	1-2	3-1	2-2	0-2	1-0	2-2	1-1	0-0
Nottingham Forest FC	0-0	1-1	1-0	1-0	0-0	0-1	2-0	1-0	0-1	1-2	3-1	0-0		■	1-0	1-1	1-2	1-2	2-1	0-0	1-1	2-1
Notts County FC	0-1	1-1	3-0	1-1	2-1	1-0	0-1	1-1	1-0	1-2	2-0	1-0	1-0	2-1	■	0-0	0-2	1-2	1-2	0-0	1-0	1-1
Preston North End FC	2-2	1-0	0-1	0-2	5-0	3-1	1-1	0-1	1-3	0-1	4-1	4-0	1-2	3-1	2-1	■	1-1	1-2	0-2	2-2	1-2	2-1
Sheffield United FC	2-1	0-2	4-0	0-0	2-1	1-1	1-0	4-0	0-1	1-1	3-0	0-1	2-1	0-0	3-1	4-0	■	1-1	3-1	6-2	2-0	0-2
Sunderland AFC	2-0	1-1	5-1	2-2	0-1	0-3	2-0	3-0	2-1	0-0	5-2	3-2	3-2	1-0	1-1	2-1	2-2	■	1-1	1-0	2-0	1-0
The Arsenal FC	0-1	0-0	2-2	0-0	2-0	1-2	1-0	0-1	1-3	3-1	1-2	2-1	1-4	1-0	0-0	1-2	1-3	2-0	■	1-1	1-0	4-1
Tottenham Hotspur FC	2-3	1-1	2-1	0-0	1-0	1-1	0-1	2-5	1-0	1-1	4-1	2-1	2-0	3-0	1-3	2-0	1-1	1-1	3-0	■	0-0	0-1
West Bromwich Albion FC	1-0	0-0	3-3	0-5	0-3	2-4	2-2	5-0	2-4	2-0	2-1	1-1	0-0	3-2	5-0	1-2	3-1	3-1	4-0	4-1	■	0-0
West Ham United FC	1-0	4-1	0-1	0-1	0-0	0-0	2-0	2-1	2-3	1-0	1-2	1-1	1-0	3-2	1-1	3-1	2-2	0-1	1-0	0-0	1-0	■

	Division 1	Pd	Wn	Dw	Ls	GF	GA	Pts	
1.	HUDDERSFIELD TOWN AFC (HUDDERSFIELD)	42	23	11	8	60	33	57	
2.	Cardiff City AFC (Cardiff)	42	22	13	7	61	34	57	
3.	Sunderland AFC (Sunderland)	42	22	9	11	71	54	53	
4.	Bolton Wanderers FC (Bolton)	42	18	14	10	68	34	50	
5.	Sheffield United FC (Sheffield)	42	19	12	11	69	49	50	
6.	Aston Villa FC (Birmingham)	42	18	13	11	52	37	49	
7.	Everton FC (Liverpool)	42	18	13	11	62	53	49	
8.	Blackburn Rovers FC (Blackburn)	42	17	11	14	54	50	45	
9.	Newcastle United FC (Newcastle-upon-Tyne)	42	17	10	15	60	54	44	
10.	Notts County FC (Nottingham)	42	14	14	14	44	49	42	
11.	Manchester City FC (Manchester)	42	15	12	15	54	71	42	
12.	Liverpool FC (Liverpool)	42	15	11	16	49	48	41	
13.	West Ham United FC (London)	42	13	15	14	40	43	41	
14.	Birmingham FC (Birmingham)	42	13	13	16	41	49	39	
15.	Tottenham Hotspur FC (London)	42	12	14	16	50	56	38	
16.	West Bromwich Albion FC (West Bromwich)	42	12	14	16	51	62	38	
17.	Burnley FC (Burnley)	42	12	12	18	55	60	36	
18.	Preston North End FC (Preston)	42	12	10	20	52	67	34	
19.	The Arsenal FC (London)	42	12	9	21	40	63	33	
20.	Nottingham Forest FC (Nottingham)	42	10	12	20	42	64	32	
21.	Chelsea FC (London)	42	9	14	19	31	53	32	R
22.	Middlesbrough FC (Middlesbrough)	42	7	8	27	37	60	22	R
		924	330	264	330	1143	1143	924	

Top Goalscorer

1)	W. CHADWICK	(Everton FC)	28

Football League Division 2 1923-1924 Season	Barnsley	Blackpool	Bradford City	Bristol City	Bury	Clapton Orient	Coventry City	Crystal Palace	Derby County	Fulham	Hull City	Leeds United	Leicester City	Man. United	Nelson	Oldham Ath.	Port Vale	Southampton	South Shields	Stockport Co.	Stoke	Wednesday
Barnsley FC	■	3-1	2-1	3-1	2-0	1-0	1-1	5-2	1-3	2-1	0-0	1-3	3-1	1-0	0-0	4-1	3-0	1-1	1-0	0-0	0-0	0-0
Blackpool FC	0-2	■	2-1	2-0	3-1	3-0	5-0	2-0	4-0	3-0	0-0	1-1	3-1	1-0	1-1	2-2	6-1	2-0	1-1	0-0	1-1	1-0
Bradford City AFC	3-2	0-2	■	1-1	2-2	0-0	0-0	0-1	1-2	1-0	2-1	0-0	2-2	0-0	0-2	2-1	2-0	2-1	0-1	0-1	2-1	4-1
Bristol City FC	1-1	1-1	0-1	■	4-1	0-2	2-2	0-0	0-8	0-1	1-0	0-1	1-2	1-0	0-0	0-0	1-1	1-0	3-0	1-1		2-3
Bury FC	1-1	2-0	3-0	6-0	■	0-0	5-0	1-1	1-0	2-1	1-0	3-0	2-0	2-0	2-2	0-0	1-0	0-1	2-1	1-0	5-0	
Clapton Orient FC	2-1	1-0	1-1	2-0	1-0	■	4-0	1-0	2-0	0-0	0-1	1-0	1-0	5-1	1-2	1-1	0-0	3-0	1-1	0-2	0-0	
Coventry City FC	2-3	3-1	1-0	1-1	1-0	1-1	■	0-0	3-0	0-2	2-1	2-4	1-1	4-0	5-2	1-3	0-0	1-0	0-0	1-2	5-1	
Crystal Palace FC	3-1	3-1	3-0	1-0	1-0	2-1	3-1	■	0-1	1-1	0-0	1-1	4-3	1-1	2-3	1-2	0-0	1-0	1-1	5-1	3-0	
Derby County FC	2-1	2-0	0-0	2-3	0-2	1-0	1-0	5-0	■	3-3	4-1	2-0	4-0	3-0	6-0	2-1	2-0	1-0	6-1	4-1	1-1	1-1
Fulham FC	3-0	2-3	1-1	1-1	0-2	0-0	1-1	1-0	3-2	■	1-1	0-2	1-0	3-1	0-0	0-0	3-2	2-3	1-0	3-0	4-1	
Hull City AFC	1-2	2-1	2-0	5-0	0-1	2-2	3-2	2-2	0-1	4-2	■	1-2	1-1	2-1	0-0	1-2	0-0	1-1	2-0	1-1		
Leeds United AFC	3-1	0-0	1-0	0-0	1-2	1-0	3-1	3-0	1-1	3-0	5-2	■	1-2	0-0	5-0	3-0	3-0	2-1	4-0	0-0	1-0	
Leicester City FC	2-0	1-2	0-1	5-1	3-0	1-2	2-0	1-0	3-0	2-1	1-1	2-0	■	2-2	3-1	1-1	2-0	0-1	4-1	1-1	5-0	2-1
Manchester United FC	1-2	0-0	3-0	2-1	0-1	2-2	1-2	5-1	0-0	0-0	1-1	3-1	3-0	■	0-1	2-0	5-0	1-1	1-1	3-0	2-2	2-0
Nelson FC	4-3	2-3	1-1	2-1	0-5	1-1	3-0	4-2	2-1	1-1	1-1	3-1	1-1	0-2	■	2-1	1-3	0-0	0-2	1-1	2-0	1-1
Oldham Athletic AFC	1-1	1-1	0-0	0-0	0-0	1-0	1-1	1-0	2-0	2-1	0-0	2-2	0-0	3-2	1-0	■	2-0	1-3	1-0	3-1	0-0	2-0
Port Vale FC	4-1	2-6	2-2	0-2	2-1	1-1	1-1	3-4	2-0	3-1	2-2	0-1	2-1	0-1	0-0	3-0	■	1-0	1-1	0-1	2-4	2-0
Southampton FC	6-0	3-2	2-0	1-0	3-0	5-0	1-3	1-0	0-0	1-0	2-0	1-0	0-0	3-0	1-1			■	0-1	3-0		
South Shields FC	2-0	1-0	0-0	1-1	1-0	1-1	4-2	2-0	3-2	1-0	0-1	3-0	1-2	1-0	3-0	2-0	3-3	1-2	■	3-1	1-0	1-1
Stockport County FC	1-1	2-1	1-2	0-0	3-2	2-0	0-0	2-2	0-0	5-1	3-1	3-2	1-0	0-0	2-3	3-2				■	0-1	1-0
Stoke FC	2-0	2-2	2-0	3-0	0-0	0-1	2-1	1-1	1-1	0-0	1-0	1-0	3-0	4-0	1-1	1-0	1-0	0-0	0-0		■	1-1
The Wednesday FC	1-0	2-2	0-0	1-0	1-1	1-0	2-0	6-0	1-0	2-1	1-0	0-0	2-1	2-0	5-0	1-2	2-1	1-1	5-0	3-0	3-0	■

Division 2

		Pd	Wn	Dw	Ls	GF	GA	Pts	
1.	Leeds United AFC (Leeds)	42	21	12	9	61	35	54	P
2.	Bury FC (Bury)	42	21	9	12	63	35	51	P
3.	Derby County FC (Derby)	42	21	9	12	75	42	51	
4.	Blackpool FC (Blackpool)	42	18	13	11	72	47	49	
5.	Southampton FC (Southampton)	42	17	14	11	52	31	48	
6.	Stoke FC (Stoke-on-Trent)	42	14	18	10	44	42	46	
7.	Oldham Athletic AFC (Oldham)	42	14	17	11	45	52	45	
8.	The Wednesday FC (Sheffield)	42	16	12	14	54	51	44	
9.	South Shields FC (South Shields)	42	17	10	15	49	50	44	
10.	Clapton Orient FC (London)	42	14	15	13	40	36	43	
11.	Barnsley FC (Barnsley)	42	16	11	15	57	61	43	
12.	Leicester City FC (Leicester)	42	17	8	17	64	54	42	
13.	Stockport County FC (Stockport)	42	13	16	13	44	52	42	
14.	Manchester United FC (Manchester)	42	13	14	15	52	44	40	
15.	Crystal Palace FC (London)	42	13	13	16	53	65	39	
16.	Port Vale FC (Stoke-on-Trent)	42	13	12	17	50	66	38	
17.	Hull City AFC (Kingston-upon-Hull)	42	10	17	15	46	51	37	
18.	Bradford City AFC (Bradford)	42	11	15	16	35	48	37	
19.	Coventry City FC (Coventry)	42	11	13	18	52	68	35	
20.	Fulham FC (London)	42	10	14	18	45	56	34	
21.	Nelson FC (Nelson)	42	10	13	19	40	74	33	R
22.	Bristol City FC (Bristol)	42	7	15	20	32	65	29	R
		924	317	290	317	1125	1125	924	

Football League Division 3 (N) — 1923-1924 Season

	Accrington S.	Ashington	Barrow	Bradford P.A.	Chesterfield	Crewe Alex.	Darlington	Doncaster R.	Durham City	Grimsby Town	Halifax Town	Hartlepools Utd.	Lincoln City	New Brighton	Rochdale	Rotherham Co.	Southport	Tranmere Rvrs.	Walsall	Wigan Boro'	Wolves	Wrexham
Accrington Stanley FC	■	0-1	3-1	2-2	2-0	1-1	2-0	0-0	5-4	2-0	1-2	2-0	3-1	0-0	0-1	3-2	2-0	3-1	0-3	2-2	1-0	1-0
Ashington FC	1-1	■	2-0	1-0	1-1	3-0	2-1	3-1	2-1	1-0	4-0	0-0	2-1	5-0	1-0	1-2	2-0	3-3	3-1	3-0	1-7	0-2
Barrow AFC	0-0	2-2	■	1-1	2-0	1-2	1-0	0-0	1-2	3-1	1-0	1-2	2-1	2-1	1-2	1-2	1-3	1-1	0-1	2-1	2-2	0-0
Bradford Park Avenue FC	1-1	3-1	3-0	■	2-1	1-1	1-0	4-2	3-0	2-1	1-0	4-0	3-1	1-1	4-2	2-0	2-0	2-0	5-0	4-0	0-1	2-0
Chesterfield FC	3-0	2-0	2-1	2-3	■	2-1	5-1	2-1	1-1	4-2	1-1	5-1	2-1	1-0	1-1	3-1	4-0	5-0	7-0	1-0	1-0	1-0
Crewe Alexandra FC	1-2	1-3	2-0	1-1	0-1	■	2-1	0-2	0-2	0-0	2-2	2-1	1-2	2-0	0-2	1-0	1-1	1-1	2-0	0-2	0-0	1-1
Darlington FC	2-1	3-2	5-1	3-1	2-1	1-1	■	1-1	3-2	1-0	0-0	5-0	1-0	3-1	2-2	1-0	3-1	4-1	4-2	3-1	1-1	3-0
Doncaster Rovers FC	1-2	2-1	2-2	1-1	0-2	4-1	1-0	■	2-1	7-0	3-1	3-2	2-0	0-0	0-1	3-0	4-0	3-0	0-0	0-2		
Durham City FC	3-0	4-0	1-2	2-0	1-1	3-1	3-2	2-1	■	0-1	2-2	3-0	1-0	2-0	0-0	3-2	0-1	1-1	1-0	2-2	2-3	4-3
Grimsby Town FC	2-0	4-0	5-0	2-0	0-0	2-0	3-0	1-1	1-0	■	1-1	0-1	2-2	0-0	1-1	1-0	0-0	1-0	1-1	2-0	0-0	
Halifax Town AFC	3-0	3-0	1-0	0-0	2-0	2-0	1-4	0-1	2-1	1-3	■	1-0	1-0	2-1	0-1	0-2	1-0	0-0	3-0	1-2	2-2	0-0
Hartlepools United FC	3-0	0-1	1-0	0-0	2-3	2-2	0-1	1-1	0-0	1-1	1-3	■	1-1	0-1	1-2	2-5	0-1	2-1	0-1	0-0	0-1	0-1
Lincoln City FC	0-2	2-0	4-1	2-3	0-1	0-0	2-0	1-1	3-1	1-3	1-1	1-1	■	1-0	0-2	2-1	1-1	1-1	2-1	1-0		4-2
New Brighton FC	1-2	1-1	5-0	1-0	0-0	2-1	1-1	2-0	2-0	0-0	2-0	0-0	3-1	■	1-1	1-2	0-0	1-0	1-0	5-0	0-1	
Rochdale AFC	4-1	1-0	3-1	3-0	3-0	1-0	0-0	2-0	2-0	4-2	3-0	1-0	1-0	6-2	■	1-0	2-2	1-0	1-0	1-0	0-0	
Rotherham County FC	2-0	1-0	2-0	1-0	1-2	0-1	2-0	3-0	5-1	2-1	3-2	5-0	2-0	3-1	0-0	■	1-1	5-1	0-2	4-0	1-1	2-1
Southport FC	1-0	2-0	2-0	1-0	1-0	1-0	1-0	2-2	1-0	3-0	3-0	2-2	3-2	3-0	1-0	0-0	■	1-1	1-1	1-1	0-0	1-0
Tranmere Rovers FC	2-0	2-4	3-0	2-1	0-0	1-1	1-4	3-0	1-0	2-1	3-0	2-0	1-3	1-2	2-1	0-1	1-1	■	3-1	1-0	0-0	1-1
Walsall FC	2-0	1-1	1-1	2-3	0-1	1-1	5-2	1-1	2-0	1-1	2-1	1-0	2-1	1-0	1-1	0-1	0-4		■	3-0	2-1	1-2
Wigan Borough FC	2-0	1-1	4-0	0-1	3-1	3-0	2-2	1-0	0-1	4-1	0-0	1-0	3-0	3-1	1-2	2-1				■	1-1	3-1
Wolverhampton Wanderers	5-1	1-0	3-0	2-0	2-1	1-0	2-0	1-1	2-1	4-1	4-0	2-1	3-0	5-1			3-0	2-1	3-0	3-3	■	3-0
Wrexham AFC	1-0	4-0	2-0	2-2	0-0	1-0	0-1	2-2	0-0	1-1	0-1	1-0	2-1	0-0	1-1	3-0	1-1	0-0	0-0	2-2		■

Division 3 (North)

		Pd	Wn	Dw	Ls	GF	GA	Pts	
1.	Wolverhampton Wanderers FC (Wolverhampton)	42	24	15	3	76	27	63	P
2.	Rochdale AFC (Rochdale)	42	25	12	5	60	26	62	
3.	Chesterfield FC (Chesterfield)	42	22	10	10	70	39	54	
4.	Rotherham County FC (Rotherham)	42	23	6	13	70	43	52	
5.	Bradford Park Avenue FC (Bradford)	42	21	1-	11	69	43	52	
6.	Darlington FC (Darlington)	42	20	8	14	70	53	48	
7.	Southport FC (Southport)	42	16	14	12	44	42	46	
8.	Ashington FC (Ashington)	42	18	8	16	59	61	44	
9.	Doncaster Rovers FC (Doncaster)	42	15	12	15	59	53	42	
10.	Wigan Borough FC (Wigan)	42	14	14	14	55	53	42	
11.	Grimsby Town FC (Cleethorpes)	42	14	13	15	49	47	41	
12.	Tranmere Rovers FC (Birkenhead)	42	13	15	14	51	60	41	
13.	Accrington Stanley FC (Accrington)	42	16	8	18	48	61	40	
14.	Halifax Town AFC (Halifax)	42	15	10	17	42	59	40	
15.	Durham City FC (Durham)	42	15	9	18	59	60	39	
16.	Wrexham AFC (Wrexham)	42	10	18	14	37	44	38	
17.	Walsall FC (Walsall)	42	14	8	20	44	59	36	
18.	New Brighton FC (Wallasey)	42	11	13	18	40	53	35	
19.	Lincoln City FC (Lincoln)	42	10	12	20	48	59	32	
20.	Crewe Alexandra FC (Crewe)	42	7	13	22	32	58	27	
21.	Hartlepools United FC (Hartlepool)	42	7	11	24	33	70	25	
22.	Barrow AFC (Barrow-in-Furness)	42	8	9	25	35	80	25	
		924	338	248	338	1150	1150	924	

Football League Division 3 (S) — 1923-1924 Season

Result grid (home team in rows, away team in columns). Team order: Aberdare Athletic (ABE), Bournemouth (BOU), Brentford (BRE), Brighton (BHA), Bristol Rovers (BRO), Charlton Athletic (CHA), Exeter City (EXE), Gillingham (GIL), Luton Town (LUT), Merthyr Town (MER), Millwall (MIL), Newport County (NEW), Northampton (NTH), Norwich City (NRW), Plymouth Argyle (PLY), Portsmouth (POR), Q.P.R. (QPR), Reading (REA), Southend United (SOU), Swansea Town (SWA), Swindon Town (SWI), Watford (WAT).

	ABE	BOU	BRE	BHA	BRO	CHA	EXE	GIL	LUT	MER	MIL	NEW	NTH	NRW	PLY	POR	QPR	REA	SOU	SWA	SWI	WAT
Aberdare Athletic FC		1-0	1-2	3-1	2-0	4-1	0-0	1-1	0-1	0-0	1-1	2-0	2-2	0-0	1-2	0-0	1-1	1-0	5-2	4-2	2-2	4-0
Bournemouth & B. Athletic	0-1		2-4	1-0	0-1	1-0	1-0	0-0	2-3	3-3	2-0	0-1	2-1	1-2	0-0	0-1	3-1	0-0	0-1	0-0	0-0	1-1
Brentford FC	1-1	2-0		1-2	1-2	0-0	1-0	3-2	2-1	0-0	1-3	0-0	1-0	3-0	1-1	1-1	0-1	4-1	3-1	2-2	2-2	4-1
Brighton & Hove Albion	5-0	5-0	2-0		2-1	3-0	1-0	2-2	4-0	0-0	2-2	4-0	2-0	3-0	4-1	0-4	3-0	4-0	2-0	4-1	1-1	3-0
Bristol Rovers FC	2-0	3-4	2-0	2-0		2-0	0-0	4-1	0-0	4-1	0-0	1-1	3-1	1-1	0-1	2-1	0-0	3-1	2-0	0-1		4-2
Charlton Athletic FC	3-1	1-2	3-1	0-2	1-3		1-0	0-0	1-1	1-0	0-1	2-1	0-0	0-0	1-1	3-0	0-0	4-1	1-3	3-1	1-1	
Exeter City FC	1-1	0-2	1-0	0-1	3-1	0-0		2-1	2-1	1-0	2-0	5-0	2-1	1-2	0-4	0-0	3-0	3-2	2-0	1-0	3-1	1-1
Gillingham FC	3-1	1-0	6-0	1-1	1-0	0-1	1-1		0-0	2-1	0-2	2-1	1-1	3-1	1-0	0-2	1-0	3-2	0-1	1-0		0-0
Luton Town FC	1-0	6-2	2-1	0-0	0-0	0-1	1-0	1-1		1-1	2-0	1-1	2-1	0-2	4-1	2-0	2-0	4-4	1-2	3-2		
Merthyr Town FC	0-0	4-2	2-0	2-1	1-1	2-1	3-0	0-2	0-0		1-0	3-3	0-0	2-3	1-1	2-2	2-0	1-1	3-2	0-0	2-0	2-1
Millwall Athletic FC	2-0	4-2	4-1	0-0	1-0	1-0	3-1	5-0	0-1	6-0		2-1	4-3	2-1	1-0	2-0	3-0	0-0	0-0	2-1	1-0	2-0
Newport County AFC	0-0	2-0	3-2	0-0	0-1	2-0	2-1	1-0	4-4	2-1	1-1		1-0	1-2	2-1	2-1	2-0	5-0	4-1	0-0	1-1	1-2
Northampton Town	1-2	3-1	2-3	3-0	0-0	1-0	1-0	2-0	2-0	3-0	2-1	0-0		1-0	1-0	4-0	3-0	3-1	8-0	2-0	1-1	1-2
Norwich City FC	5-0	1-1	2-3	1-0	3-1	2-2	4-0	1-0	2-0	2-0	1-1	3-1	1-4		0-1	3-1	5-0	2-2	3-1	2-0	2-0	0-0
Plymouth Argyle FC	2-0	4-0	4-1	3-0	2-2	1-1	4-0	3-0	0-0	1-1	1-1	3-2	0-0	2-0		1-2	2-0	2-1	7-1	2-0	1-3	1-0
Portsmouth FC	4-0	3-0	3-0	1-3	1-1	0-0	4-0	3-0	3-0	0-1	5-0	1-3	4-0	2-1			7-0	1-1	3-0	3-0	4-1	4-0
Queen's Park Rangers	3-0	0-1	1-0	1-0	1-2	0-0	2-0	1-1	0-2	3-0	1-1	0-3	3-2	2-1	3-2	0-2		1-4	0-0	2-2	2-2	2-1
Reading FC	0-1	1-2	1-0	0-1	3-2	3-1	1-0	4-0	0-1	3-0	2-0	1-1	1-0	3-0	1-2	1-4	4-0		1-0	3-4	1-0	1-1
Southend United FC	1-1	1-1	3-1	1-0	1-0	2-2	0-0	3-2	1-1	3-1	0-0	2-0	5-1	1-0	2-1	0-1	4-2	2-1		0-0	0-0	1-0
Swansea Town AFC	1-0	1-0	4-0	1-0	3-1	1-0	1-0	1-0	5-1	1-2	2-1	2-1	1-0	1-0	0-0	2-0	5-1	2-1			1-1	1-0
Swindon Town FC	3-1	3-1	2-1	4-0	0-0	1-1	0-1	4-1	3-2	3-0	1-0	3-0	2-0	4-2	0-1	0-0	0-0	1-0	3-0	1-0		0-0
Watford FC	2-0	0-0	0-1	0-0	4-0	1-0	4-1	1-1	0-0	4-0	1-1	8-2	0-2	0-0	0-0	2-3	0-2	2-1	4-1	2-2	0-0	

Division 3 (South)

		Pd	Wn	Dw	Ls	GF	GA	Pts	
1.	Portsmouth FC (Portsmouth)	42	24	11	7	87	30	59	P
2.	Plymouth Argyle FC (Plymouth)	42	23	9	10	70	34	55	
3.	Millwall Athletic FC (London)	42	22	10	10	64	38	54	
4.	Swansea Town AFC (Swansea)	42	22	8	12	60	48	52	
5.	Brighton & Hove Albion FC (Hove)	42	21	9	12	68	37	51	
6.	Swindon Town FC (Swindon)	42	17	13	12	58	44	47	
7.	Luton Town FC (Luton)	42	16	14	12	50	44	46	
8.	Northampton Town FC (Northampton)	42	17	11	14	64	47	45	
9.	Bristol Rovers FC (Bristol)	42	15	13	14	52	46	43	
10.	Newport County AFC (Newport)	42	17	9	16	56	64	43	
11.	Norwich City FC (Norwich)	42	16	8	18	60	59	40	
12.	Aberdare Athletic FC (Aberdare)	42	12	14	16	45	58	38	
13.	Merthyr Town FC (Merthyr Tydfil)	42	11	16	15	45	65	38	
14.	Charlton Athletic FC (London)	42	11	15	16	38	45	37	
15.	Gillingham FC (Gillingham)	42	12	13	17	43	58	37	
16.	Exeter City FC (Exeter)	42	15	7	20	37	52	37	
17.	Brentford FC (London)	42	14	8	20	54	71	36	
18.	Reading FC (Reading)	42	13	9	20	51	57	35	
19.	Southend United FC (Southend-on-Sea)	42	12	10	20	53	84	34	
20.	Watford FC (Watford)	42	9	15	18	45	54	33	
21.	Bournemouth & Boscombe Athletic FC (Bournemouth)	42	11	11	20	40	65	33	
22.	Queen's Park Rangers FC (London)	42	11	9	22	37	77	31	
		924	341	242	341	1177	1177	924	

F.A. CUP FINAL (Wembley Stadium, London – 26/04/1924 – 91,695)

NEWCASTLE UNITED FC   2-0   Aston Villa FC (Birmingham)

Harris, Seymour

Newcastle: Gradle, Hampson, Hudspeth, Mooney, Spencer, Gibson, Low, Cowan, Harris, McDonald, Seymour.

Aston Villa: Jackson, Smart, Mort, Moss, Milne, Blackburn, York, Kirton, Capewell, Walker, Dorrell.

Semi-finals

Aston Villa FC (Birmingham)	3-0	Burnley FC (Burnley)
Newcastle United FC (Newcastle-upon-Tyne)	2-0	Manchester City FC (Manchester)

Quarter-finals

Manchester City FC (Manchester)	0-0, 1-0 (aet)	Cardiff City AFC (Cardiff)
Newcastle United FC (Newcastle-upon-Tyne)	1-0	Liverpool FC (Liverpool)
Swindon Town FC (Swindon)	1-1, 1-3	Burnley FC (Burnley)
West Bromwich Albion FC (West Bromwich)	0-2	Aston Villa FC (Birmingham)

1924-25

Football League Division 1 — 1924-1925 Season

	Aston Villa	Birmingham	Blackburn Rovers	Bolton Wanderers	Burnley	Bury	Cardiff City	Everton	Huddersfield Town	Leeds United	Liverpool	Manchester City	Newcastle United	Nottingham Forest	Notts County	Preston North End	Sheffield United	Sunderland	The Arsenal	Tottenham Hotspur	W.B.A.	West Ham United
Aston Villa FC	■	1-0	4-3	2-2	3-0	3-3	1-2	3-1	1-1	2-1	1-4	2-1	0-0	2-0	0-0	1-0	1-1	1-4	4-0	0-1	1-0	1-1
Birmingham FC	1-0	■	1-1	1-0	1-0	0-1	2-1	2-2	0-1	0-0	5-2	2-1	1-1	1-1	1-0	3-0	1-1	2-1	2-1	0-2	0-0	1-1
Blackburn Rovers FC	1-1	7-1	■	0-2	0-3	0-1	3-1	3-0	2-3	2-3	3-1	3-1	1-1	0-0	0-2	0-1	2-2	1-1	1-0	1-1	1-0	0-1
Bolton Wanderers FC	4-0	3-0	6-0	■	5-0	3-3	3-0	1-0	1-0	1-0	2-0	4-2	3-2	1-0	1-0	6-1	3-1	1-2	4-1	3-0	1-1	5-0
Burnley FC	1-1	3-2	3-5	0-0	■	4-0	0-0	0-0	1-5	1-1	2-1	1-0	1-3	0-0	1-1	1-0	1-1	1-2	1-0	1-4	0-1	5-4
Bury FC	4-3	1-4	1-1	1-0	1-0	■	4-1	1-0	0-1	1-0	0-0	0-2	0-0	3-0	2-1	1-1	1-0	3-0	2-0	5-2	0-2	4-2
Cardiff City AFC	2-1	1-0	3-0	1-2	4-0	4-1	■	2-1	2-2	3-0	1-3	0-2	3-0	2-0	1-1	0-0	1-1	2-0	1-1	0-2	0-1	2-1
Everton FC	2-0	2-1	1-0	2-2	3-2	0-0	1-2	■	0-2	1-0	0-1	3-1	0-1	3-1	1-0	0-0	1-1	0-3	2-3	1-0	1-0	1-0
Huddersfield Town AFC	4-1	0-1	0-0	0-0	2-0	2-0	0-0	2-0	■	2-0	1-1	1-1	0-0	3-0	0-0	1-0	2-1	4-0	4-0	1-2	1-1	1-2
Leeds United AFC	6-0	0-1	1-1	2-1	0-2	1-0	0-0	1-0	1-1	■	4-1	0-3	1-1	1-1	1-1	4-0	1-1	1-0	1-0	0-1	0-1	2-1
Liverpool FC	2-4	1-1	0-0	0-0	3-0	4-0	1-2	3-1	2-3	1-0	■	5-3	1-1	3-0	1-0	3-1	4-1	3-1	2-1	1-1	1-2	2-0
Manchester City FC	1-0	2-2	1-3	2-2	3-3	0-0	2-2	2-2	1-1	4-2	5-0	■	3-1	4-2	2-1	2-1	1-3	2-0	1-0	1-2	3-1	3-1
Newcastle United FC	4-1	4-0	4-0	0-1	3-0	2-2	1-2	1-1	1-3	4-1	0-0	2-0	■	4-1	1-0	3-1	0-0	2-0	2-2	1-1	0-1	4-1
Nottingham Forest FC	0-2	1-1	0-2	1-1	0-0	2-0	2-1	0-1	0-1	4-0	0-1	0-3	1-1	■	0-0	2-3	1-1	0-2	1-1	0-1	0-1	2-1
Notts County FC	0-0	0-1	0-0	0-1	2-0	1-1	3-0	3-1	1-1	1-0	1-2	2-0	2-0	0-0	■	1-0	2-0	4-1	2-1	0-0	0-2	4-1
Preston North End FC	3-2	1-0	3-2	1-0	0-2	1-1	1-3	1-1	1-4	1-4	4-0	2-3	0-1	3-1	0-1	■	0-1	1-2	2-0	0-3	1-2	3-2
Sheffield United FC	2-2	4-3	2-3	2-0	4-0	0-1	1-0	1-1	1-1	1-1	1-1	0-5	1-2	1-2	2-0	3-0	■	2-1	2-1	2-0	2-0	1-1
Sunderland AFC	1-1	4-0	1-0	1-1	1-1	1-1	4-1	1-1	2-1	3-0	3-2	1-1	3-1	0-1	2-0	0-1	2-0	■	2-0	4-1	3-0	1-1
The Arsenal FC	1-1	0-1	1-0	1-0	5-0	0-1	1-1	3-1	0-5	6-1	2-0	1-0	0-2	2-1	0-1	4-0	2-0	0-0	■	1-0	2-0	1-2
Tottenham Hotspur FC	1-3	0-1	5-0	3-0	1-1	1-1	1-1	0-0	1-2	2-1	1-1	1-1	3-0	1-0	1-1	2-0	4-1	1-0	2-0	■	0-1	1-1
West Bromwich Albion FC	4-1	1-1	1-1	0-0	1-4	1-1	1-0	3-0	3-1	2-0	5-1	1-2	2-1	2-1	2-0	2-0	2-0	2-0	2-0	2-0	■	4-1
West Ham United FC	2-0	0-1	2-0	1-1	2-0	1-1	3-2	4-1	0-0	0-0	0-1	4-0	0-0	0-0	3-0	1-0	6-2	4-1	1-0	1-1	2-1	■

	Division 1	Pd	Wn	Dw	Ls	GF	GA	Pts	
1.	HUDDERSFIELD TOWN AFC (HUDDERSFIELD)	42	21	16	5	69	28	58	
2.	West Bromwich Albion FC (West Bromwich)	42	23	10	9	58	34	56	
3.	Bolton Wanderers FC (Bolton)	42	22	11	9	76	34	55	
4.	Liverpool FC Liverpool)	42	20	10	12	63	55	50	
5.	Bury FC (Bury)	42	17	15	10	54	51	49	
6.	Newcastle United FC (Newcastle-upon-Tyne)	42	16	16	10	61	42	48	
7.	Sunderland AFC (Sunderland)	42	19	10	13	64	51	48	
8.	Birmingham FC (Birmingham)	42	17	12	13	49	53	46	
9.	Notts County FC (Nottingham)	42	16	13	13	42	31	45	
10.	Manchester City FC (Manchester)	42	17	9	16	76	68	43	
11.	Cardiff City AFC (Cardiff)	42	16	11	15	56	51	43	
12.	Tottenham Hotspur FC (London)	42	15	12	15	52	43	42	
13.	West Ham United FC (London)	42	15	12	15	62	60	42	
14.	Sheffield United FC (Sheffield)	42	13	13	16	55	63	39	
15.	Aston Villa FC (Birmingham)	42	13	13	16	58	71	39	
16.	Blackburn Rovers FC (Blackburn)	42	11	13	18	53	66	35	
17.	Everton FC (Liverpool)	42	12	11	19	40	60	35	
18.	Leeds United AFC (Leeds)	42	11	12	19	46	59	34	
19.	Burnley FC (Burnley)	42	11	12	19	46	75	34	
20.	The Arsenal FC (London)	42	14	5	23	46	58	33	
21.	Preston North End FC (Preston)	42	10	6	26	37	74	26	R
22.	Nottingham Forest FC (Nottingham)	42	6	12	24	29	65	24	R
		924	335	254	335	1192	1192	924	

Top Goalscorer

1)	F. ROBERTS	(Manchester City FC)	31

Football League Division 2 — 1924-1925 Season

	Barnsley	Blackpool	Bradford City	Chelsea	Clapton Orient	Coventry City	Crystal Palace	Derby County	Fulham	Hull City	Leicester City	Man. United	Middlesbro'	Oldham Ath.	Portsmouth	Port Vale	Southampton	South Shields	Stockport Co.	Stoke	Wednesday	Wolves
Barnsley FC	■	2-4	3-1	3-3	1-1	3-1	3-0	3-0	1-0	1-2	1-1	0-0	1-0	0-0	1-4	1-3	1-1	1-0	0-1	1-1	3-0	0-0
Blackpool FC	1-2	■	1-2	1-2	1-0	3-1	0-1	5-1	4-1	0-0	2-1	1-1	1-1	1-2	1-1	4-1	1-0	5-0	0-1	1-2	2-2	2-4
Bradford City AFC	1-0	1-0	■	2-0	0-0	1-0	0-0	0-3	1-1	4-1	1-1	0-1	0-1	1-1	2-0	1-1	1-2	1-0	3-0	1-0	2-0	3-1
Chelsea FC	0-1	3-0	3-0	■	1-1	1-0	2-2	1-1	0-0	1-0	4-0	0-0	2-0	4-1	2-3	1-0	1-0	1-1	1-1	2-1	0-0	1-0
Clapton Orient FC	0-0	1-0	0-0	0-0	■	1-2	3-0	0-1	3-0	0-0	0-1	0-1	0-1	5-1	1-1	3-1	1-0	0-0	1-1	0-2	1-0	2-1
Coventry City FC	3-2	2-1	0-0	0-3	1-0	■	1-4	0-0	0-1	0-0	4-2	1-0	2-2	5-1	2-1	0-0	1-0	0-1	4-2	3-1	1-1	2-4
Crystal Palace FC	0-1	1-2	4-1	1-0	0-1	0-0	■	2-0	1-2	0-2	2-1	2-2	0-1	1-2	0-0	3-1	0-0	3-0	0-1	0-1	2-1	
Derby County FC	1-1	2-2	2-0	1-0	3-0	5-1	3-0	■	5-1	4-0	0-3	1-0	3-1	1-0	6-1	4-1	3-0	0-0	2-0	1-2	2-1	0-1
Fulham FC	1-2	1-0	1-1	1-2	0-2	2-0	3-1	0-2	■	4-0	2-2	1-0	0-0	1-0	0-0	1-1	1-0	1-1	2-0	1-0	2-1	1-0
Hull City AFC	5-2	1-1	0-0	1-0	2-1	4-1	5-0	1-1	3-0	■	2-1	0-1	0-0	1-0	5-0	2-1	1-1	0-1	3-0	0-0	4-2	0-1
Leicester City FC	6-0	0-2	1-0	4-0	4-2	5-1	3-1	0-0	4-0	1-0	■	3-0	0-0	3-0	4-0	7-0	0-0	1-1	4-0	0-1	6-1	2-0
Manchester United FC	1-0	0-0	3-0	1-0	4-2	5-1	1-0	1-1	2-0	2-0	1-0	■	2-0	0-1	4-0	1-1	1-0	2-0	2-0	2-0	2-0	3-0
Middlesbrough FC	2-0	4-1	1-0	1-1	1-1	1-1	0-0	1-3	1-3	0-1	1-5	1-1	■	0-0	1-1	0-1	1-1	1-1	1-2	1-0	0-0	2-0
Oldham Athletic AFC	2-0	4-1	1-3	0-5	2-1	5-0	0-2	0-1	0-0	1-0	0-0	0-3	0-0	■	0-2	1-1	1-0	0-0	2-0	1-1	1-1	2-0
Portsmouth FC	0-0	1-1	5-0	0-0	0-2	1-0	0-0	1-1	3-0	2-0	1-1	1-1	3-1	2-2	■	2-0	1-1	1-0	1-1	0-0	1-1	2-2
Port Vale FC	2-0	1-2	1-0	1-1	4-2	4-0	3-0	2-1	0-1	1-1	1-2	2-1	2-1	1-0	0-2	■	1-1	0-0	4-1	2-0	1-0	1-3
Southampton FC	3-1	2-1	2-0	0-0	2-0	3-0	2-0	2-0	1-0	2-2	0-0	0-2	1-1	0-0	0-0	1-0	■	1-1	2-1	3-0	1-0	1-1
South Shields FC	5-2	1-3	1-0	1-1	2-0	4-1	1-1	1-0	2-1	2-0	1-1	0-1	0-0	0-2	3-0	1-1	0-1	■	4-0	0-1	3-3	
Stockport County FC	1-0	1-0	3-0	4-0	0-1	1-1	1-0	4-1	0-2	0-2	2-1	1-1	2-0	1-2	0-2	1-1	0-0		■	2-0	1-0	1-1
Stoke FC	1-1	3-1	0-0	1-0	0-1	4-1	1-1	1-1	1-1	0-1	0-1	0-1	2-1	0-1	0-0	2-1	0-1	2-0	0-0	■	0-2	0-3
The Wednesday FC	1-0	2-6	3-3	2-1	0-0	2-0	0-1	0-1	3-1	5-0	1-4	1-1	2-0	1-0	5-2	0-1	1-0	1-0	3-0	2-1	■	2-0
Wolverhampton Wanderers FC	0-1	2-0	2-0	0-1	1-2	3-1	3-1	0-4	2-1	2-1	0-1	0-0	1-0	2-0	0-5	1-0	3-0	2-1	3-0	1-0	1-0	■

	Division 2	Pd	Wn	Dw	Ls	GF	GA	Pts	
1.	Leicester City FC (Leicester)	42	24	11	7	90	32	59	P
2.	Manchester United FC (Manchester)	42	23	11	8	57	23	57	P
3.	Derby County FC (Derby)	42	22	11	9	71	36	55	
4.	Portsmouth FC (Portsmouth)	42	15	18	9	58	50	48	
5.	Chelsea FC (London)	42	16	15	11	51	37	47	
6.	Wolverhampton Wanderers FC (Wolverhampton)	42	20	6	16	55	51	46	
7.	Southampton FC (Southampton)	42	13	18	11	40	36	44	
8.	Port Vale FC (Stoke-on-Trent)	42	17	8	17	48	56	42	
9.	South Shields FC (South Shields)	42	12	17	13	42	38	41	
10.	Hull City AFC (Kingston-upon-Hull)	42	15	11	16	50	49	41	
11.	Clapton Orient FC (London)	42	14	12	16	42	42	40	
12.	Fulham FC (London)	42	15	10	17	41	56	40	
13.	Middlesbrough FC (Middlesbrough)	42	10	19	13	36	44	39	
14.	The Wednesday FC (Sheffield)	42	15	8	19	50	56	38	
15.	Barnsley FC (Barnsley)	42	13	12	17	46	59	38	
16.	Bradford City AFC (Bradford)	42	13	12	17	37	50	38	
17.	Blackpool FC (Blackpool)	42	14	9	19	65	61	37	
18.	Oldham Athletic AFC (Oldham)	42	13	11	18	35	51	37	
19.	Stockport County FC (Stockport)	42	13	11	18	37	57	37	
20.	Stoke FC (Stoke-on-Trent)	42	12	11	19	34	46	35	*
21.	Crystal Palace FC (London)	42	12	10	20	38	54	34	R
22.	Coventry City FC (Coventry)	42	11	9	22	45	84	31	R
		924	332	260	332	1068	1068	924	

* Stoke FC (Stoke-on-Trent) changed their club name to Stoke City FC (Stoke-on-Trent) from the next season.

Football League Division 3 (N) 1924-1925 Season	Accrington St.	Ashington	Barrow	Bradford P.A.	Chesterfield	Crewe Alex.	Darlington	Doncaster R.	Durham City	Grimsby Town	Halifax Town	Hartlepools U.	Lincoln City	Nelson	New Brighton	Rochdale	Rotherham U.	Southport	Tranmere R.	Walsall	Wigan Boro'	Wrexham
Accrington Stanley FC	■	2-2	1-2	2-2	2-2	1-0	2-0	3-2	6-0	0-3	2-0	4-1	0-2	2-0	0-1	2-2	2-0	5-1	2-1	1-1	3-1	1-0
Ashington FC	1-2	■	5-2	1-0	2-1	1-1	4-2	2-0	0-2	0-2	2-0	0-3	2-1	1-1	1-1	4-3	3-1	2-0	1-0	6-1	1-1	2-0
Barrow AFC	3-1	3-2	■	2-1	1-0	2-0	0-4	4-0	2-0	3-2	2-1	1-1	1-2	3-0	1-1	1-0	3-1	1-0	1-1	3-2	0-1	2-2
Bradford Park Avenue FC	3-0	7-1	1-1	■	3-0	6-1	0-0	4-1	4-1	0-1	2-1	3-0	4-0	1-1	5-2	0-0	3-0	1-0	5-1	2-0	2-2	3-0
Chesterfield FC	1-0	1-1	1-1	1-1	■	1-0	0-1	2-1	6-0	2-0	1-3	4-0	2-0	0-1	3-0	2-0	3-2	1-2	4-1	1-0	3-1	3-0
Crewe Alexandra FC	4-2	1-0	3-1	2-1	1-1	■	0-5	1-1	3-0	3-1	1-1	3-1	1-1	2-1	1-0	2-0	3-1	1-1	0-2	1-1	1-1	1-2
Darlington FC	2-1	2-1	3-0	2-1	3-3	5-1	■	1-1	0-0	3-0	0-0	1-1	0-0	3-1	2-0	4-0	2-1	2-1	3-0	5-0	3-1	2-0
Doncaster Rovers FC	4-1	7-3	0-0	1-0	0-1	1-1	0-2	■	0-0	2-2	0-1	1-0	2-1	1-1	1-0	2-1	4-1	0-1	2-0	2-1	5-0	1-0
Durham City FC	2-0	0-0	6-0	1-0	1-1	4-1	2-1	1-0	■	6-1	1-2	0-1	5-0	3-1	0-0	3-2	1-1	0-0	0-3	0-2	1-1	1-0
Grimsby Town FC	4-0	1-3	2-1	2-0	0-0	0-0	0-2	1-1	1-1	■	1-1	2-1	1-2	2-0	2-3	1-1	3-1	3-1	6-1	2-1	4-0	0-1
Halifax Town AFC	2-2	0-0	2-0	1-3	1-0	2-2	1-1	2-0	3-0	1-0	■	2-0	1-0	2-4	1-2	3-1	4-0	2-1	1-3	1-1	1-2	3-1
Hartlepools United FC	3-0	0-1	1-0	2-2	1-0	2-0	1-1	2-2	1-0	2-1	1-1	■	1-1	2-4	0-2	1-1	0-0	1-2	2-1	3-1	1-0	1-1
Lincoln City FC	3-0	5-0	2-1	0-4	3-1	4-1	0-1	2-0	3-0	0-0	1-1	2-1	■	2-1	1-0	1-2	3-1	1-1	3-2	0-1	1-1	1-1
Nelson FC	4-1	4-0	2-0	2-2	1-1	7-0	1-1	3-0	7-1	1-0	2-1	2-0	1-0	■	5-0	1-0	4-1	2-1	4-1	2-1	1-0	2-4
New Brighton FC	4-0	4-4	3-0	0-0	2-1	3-0	1-0	0-2	4-0	3-2	3-1	2-0	4-1	5-0	■	5-0	3-1	1-1	1-0	3-2	3-0	2-1
Rochdale AFC	0-1	0-0	5-1	2-2	2-1	5-0	2-1	5-2	3-0	2-1	3-1	3-0	0-1	2-0	■	4-1	1-0	2-1	3-0	3-2	3-1	—
Rotherham United FC	1-1	1-4	0-1	1-1	1-3	1-3	1-1	3-0	1-2	0-0	1-2	1-1	1-0	2-1	1-3	1-3	■	1-3	2-0	2-0	3-4	2-0
Southport FC	3-1	3-0	5-0	3-0	0-2	2-0	1-0	3-0	1-1	3-1	3-1	0-0	4-0	1-0	2-0	2-0	2-0	■	1-0	1-0	0-1	1-0
Tranmere Rovers FC	2-1	5-4	4-1	2-0	5-1	2-2	0-1	1-2	1-1	2-3	0-2	4-3	0-0	2-0	1-3	3-1	1-0	1-0	■	0-1	2-3	2-0
Walsall FC	1-1	1-0	1-0	0-2	0-0	0-0	2-1	4-0	2-2	0-2	1-1	2-0	1-2	2-1	0-2	0-1	0-0	2-0	2-0	■	3-1	3-0
Wigan Borough FC	1-2	2-0	2-0	1-0	0-0	3-4	1-1	2-2	0-0	3-1	2-0	0-0	4-1	1-0	0-1	4-1	2-3	4-1	2-0	4-0	■	5-0
Wrexham AFC	1-0	3-1	3-0	1-3	0-0	2-1	0-2	2-0	3-1	1-2	0-0	3-1	0-1	1-1	0-0	1-0	3-1	2-3	4-0	1-1	6-2	■

Division 3 (North)

		Pd	Wn	Dw	Ls	GF	GA	Pts	
1.	Darlington FC (Darlington)	42	24	10	8	78	33	58	P
2.	Nelson FC (Nelson)	42	23	7	12	79	50	53	
3.	New Brighton FC (Wallasey)	42	23	7	12	75	50	53	
4.	Southport FC (Southport)	42	22	7	13	59	37	51	
5.	Bradford Park Avenue FC (Bradford)	42	19	12	11	84	42	50	
6.	Rochdale AFC (Rochdale)	42	21	7	14	75	53	49	
7.	Chesterfield FC (Chesterfield)	42	17	11	14	60	44	45	
8.	Lincoln City FC (Lincoln)	42	18	8	16	53	58	44	
9.	Halifax Town AFC (Halifax)	42	16	11	15	56	52	43	
10.	Ashington FC (Ashington)	42	16	10	16	68	76	42	
11.	Wigan Borough FC (Wigan)	42	15	11	16	62	65	41	
12.	Grimsby Town FC (Cleethorpes)	42	15	9	18	60	60	39	
13.	Durham City FC (Durham)	42	13	13	16	50	68	39	
14.	Barrow AFC (Barrow-in-Furness)	42	16	7	19	51	74	39	
15.	Crewe Alexandra FC (Crewe)	42	13	13	16	53	78	39	
16.	Wrexham AFC (Wrexham)	42	15	8	19	53	61	38	
17.	Accrington Stanley FC (Accrington)	42	15	8	19	60	72	38	
18.	Doncaster Rovers FC (Doncaster)	42	14	10	18	54	65	38	
19.	Walsall FC (Walsall)	42	13	11	18	44	53	37	
20.	Hartlepools United FC (Hartlepool)	42	12	11	19	45	63	35	
21.	Tranmere Rovers FC (Birkenhead)	42	14	4	24	59	78	32	
22.	Rotherham County FC (Rotherham)	42	7	7	28	42	88	21	*
		924	361	202	361	1320	1320	924	

112

* Rotherham County FC merged with Rotherham Town FC to become Rotherham United FC from the next season.

Football League Division 3 (S) 1924-1925 Season	Aberdare Ath.	Bournemouth	Brentford	Brighton	Bristol City	Bristol Rovers	Charlton Ath.	Exeter City	Gillingham	Luton Town	Merthyr Town	Millwall Ath.	Newport Co.	Northampton	Norwich City	Plymouth A.	Q.P.R.	Reading	Southend U.	Swansea Town	Swindon Town	Watford
Aberdare Athletic FC	■	4-2	2-1	1-2	1-2	2-1	2-0	3-1	2-1	1-1	2-0	0-1	1-3	1-1	2-1	3-1	1-1	3-0	3-0	3-1	1-1	2-0
Bournemouth & B. Athletic	3-1	■	2-0	0-0	1-3	0-1	2-1	1-1	3-0	2-1	2-0	0-1	0-0	1-2	0-0	0-1	0-2	0-0	1-0	0-2	0-0	2-1
Brentford FC	2-2	1-2	■	2-4	1-0	1-1	1-0	2-5	2-1	3-0	2-2	1-0	2-0	1-3	1-1	1-0	0-1	0-1	2-2	3-1	0-0	0-0
Brighton & Hove Albion	4-1	0-1	4-1	■	1-0	1-0	0-0	2-0	2-0	2-1	3-1	3-3	4-1	0-1	3-1	2-3	5-0	0-1	2-1	0-0	3-1	2-0
Bristol City FC	0-1	2-1	3-0	2-1	■	2-0	1-1	0-1	2-1	1-0	4-1	2-0	1-0	2-0	2-2	5-0	3-0	5-0		0-0	0-0	1-1
Bristol Rovers FC	1-0	1-0	2-0	1-2	0-0	■	4-0	0-1	0-0	1-1	1-0	1-1	0-2	3-0	1-1	3-0	1-1	1-3	3-0	1-1	0-1	
Charlton Athletic FC	5-1	2-2	3-0	1-0	0-1	1-1	■	1-0	2-0	2-0	3-0	0-2	1-0	3-2	2-1	2-0	1-2	0-0	0-0	1-0	1-1	
Exeter City FC	3-1	2-1	5-1	2-0	0-2	1-1	2-1	■	3-3	0-1	2-1	0-0	4-3	0-1	3-0	1-3	1-0	0-1	2-0	1-0	4-0	
Gillingham FC	2-0	0-0	1-0	2-0	1-1	0-0	2-0	1-1	■	4-1	2-1	1-0	0-1	3-1	1-0	0-3	1-0	0-1	3-1	1-0	1-1	0-0
Luton Town FC	0-0	0-2	3-1	3-1	3-0	1-1	1-0	1-0	0-0	■	6-0	1-1	2-2	2-0	0-0	1-1	3-0	1-0	4-0	0-0	2-2	0-3
Merthyr Town FC	3-1	3-1	4-0	1-2	2-3	2-1	2-1	0-1	0-0	0-0	■	2-1	1-0	0-2	0-2	1-2	2-3	1-0	1-0	0-2	1-5	0-1
Millwall Athletic FC	2-1	3-1	3-0	1-1	3-1	0-0	1-0	2-0	2-0	2-2	3-1	■	3-0	0-0	0-0	3-0	0-1	2-0	1-2	1-2	1-2	1-0
Newport County AFC	1-0	2-0	1-0	0-0	0-2	4-1	2-1	2-0	2-0	1-1	3-0	2-3	■	1-0	3-0	0-0	1-1	1-1	3-0	3-1	3-1	3-1
Northampton Town	5-0	3-0	0-2	1-0	1-2	5-0	2-1	2-1	1-0	1-0	2-0	0-2	0-2	■	1-1	5-2	1-0	2-0	0-1	1-3	0-0	1-1
Norwich City FC	1-1	6-3	3-0	2-2	0-0	1-1	2-1	0-1	0-0	1-1	1-0	2-2	2-1	4-0	■	1-1	5-0	0-2	0-1	2-0	4-0	2-1
Plymouth Argyle FC	2-0	2-0	7-1	1-0	7-1	3-2	3-2	1-1	2-4	2-0	1-1	2-1	2-1	5-0		■	1-0	6-0	1-1	2-0	1-0	
Queen's Park Rangers	4-1	0-2	1-0	2-0	3-0	1-2	0-0	1-4	1-1	1-1	1-1	0-0	4-3	2-0	1-2	0-1	■	1-0	3-1	0-0	1-0	
Reading FC	2-0	0-1	3-1	0-0	0-1	4-1	0-0	1-1	0-1	3-0	1-1	1-2	0-1	0-1	0-0	0-0	2-1	■	2-2	2-0	1-1	3-0
Southend United FC	2-1	3-0	6-1	2-0	2-0	2-1	0-3	3-0	4-0	2-1			0-3	1-0	3-0		1-0	3-0	■	1-0	0-0	0-4
Swansea Town AFC	2-2	1-0	7-0	1-0	1-1	2-2	6-1	2-1	2-1	2-2	2-0	2-1	2-0	2-0	2-0	1-0	4-0			■	2-0	3-1
Swindon Town FC	2-0	4-0	2-0	3-0	3-0	3-0	2-2	1-0	2-0	4-1	5-1	1-0	2-2	5-0	1-0	1-0	5-3	2-1	3-0	0-2	■	0-1
Watford FC	0-0	2-1	3-1	0-1	1-0	1-0	0-0	3-0	1-2	1-1	3-1	1-0	0-5	1-0	0-2	1-0	1-0	1-0	0-3	1-3	1-0	■

Division 3 (South)

		Pd	Wn	Dw	Ls	GF	GA	Pts	
1.	Swansea Town AFC (Swansea)	42	23	11	8	68	35	57	P
2.	Plymouth Argyle FC (Plymouth)	42	23	10	9	77	38	56	
3.	Bristol City FC (Bristol)	42	22	9	11	60	41	53	
4.	Swindon Town FC (Swindon)	42	20	11	11	66	38	51	
5.	Millwall Athletic FC (London)	42	18	13	11	58	38	49	*
6.	Newport County AFC (Newport)	42	20	9	13	62	42	49	
7.	Exeter City FC (Exeter)	42	19	9	14	59	48	47	
8.	Brighton & Hove Albion FC (Hove)	42	19	8	15	59	45	46	
9.	Northampton Town FC (Northampton)	42	20	6	16	51	44	46	
10.	Southend United FC (Southend-on-Sea)	42	19	5	18	51	61	43	
11.	Watford FC (Watford)	42	17	9	16	38	47	43	
12.	Norwich City FC (Norwich)	42	14	13	15	53	51	41	
13.	Gillingham FC (Gillingham)	42	13	14	15	35	44	40	
14.	Reading FC (Reading)	42	14	10	18	37	38	38	
15.	Charlton Athletic FC (London)	42	13	12	17	46	48	38	
16.	Luton Town FC (Luton)	42	10	17	15	49	57	37	
17.	Bristol Rovers FC (Bristol)	42	12	13	17	42	49	37	
18.	Aberdare Athletic FC (Aberdare)	42	14	9	19	54	67	37	
19.	Queen's Park Rangers FC (London)	42	14	8	20	42	63	36	
20.	Bournemouth & Boscombe Athletic FC (Bournemouth)	42	13	8	21	40	58	34	
21.	Brentford FC (London)	42	9	7	26	38	91	25	
22.	Merthyr Town FC (Merthyr Tydfil)	42	8	5	29	35	77	21	
		924	354	216	354	1120	1120	924	

* Millwall Athletic FC (London) changed their club name to Millwall FC (London) from the next season.

F.A. CUP FINAL   (Wembley Stadium, London – 25/04/1925 – 91,763)

SHEFFIELD UNITED FC (SHEFFIELD)　　　　1-0　　　　　　　Cardiff City AFC (Cardiff)

Tunstall

Sheffield United: Sutcliffe, Cook, Milton, Pantling, King, Green, Mercer, Boyle, Johnson, Gillespie, Tunstall.

Cardiff City: Farqurharson, Nelson, Blair, Wake, Keenor, Hardy, W.Davies, Gill, Nicholson, Beadles, J.Evans.

Semi-finals

Cardiff City AFC (Cardiff)	3-1	Blackburn Rovers FC (Blackburn)
Sheffield United FC (Sheffield)	2-0	Southampton FC (Southampton)

Quarter-finals

Blackburn Rovers FC (Blackburn)	1-0	Blackpool FC (Blackpool)
Cardiff City AFC (Cardiff)	2-1	Leicester City FC (Leicester)
Sheffield United FC (Sheffield)	2-0	West Bromwich Albion FC (West Bromwich)
Southampton FC (Southampton)	1-0	Liverpool FC (Liverpool)

1925-26

Football League Division 1 — 1925-1926 Season

	Aston Villa	Birmingham	Blackburn Rovers	Bolton Wanderers	Burnley	Bury	Cardiff City	Everton	Huddersfield Town	Leeds United	Leicester City	Liverpool	Manchester City	Manchester United	Newcastle United	Notts County	Sheffield United	Sunderland	The Arsenal	Tottenham Hotspur	W.B.A.	West Ham United
Aston Villa FC		3-3	1-2	2-2	10-0	1-1	0-2	3-1	3-0	3-1	2-2	3-0	3-1	2-2	2-2	2-1	2-2	4-2	3-0	3-0	2-1	2-0
Birmingham FC	2-1		2-0	0-1	1-7	2-3	3-2	3-1	1-3	2-1	1-1	2-0	1-0	2-1	1-1	0-1	2-0	2-1	1-0	3-1	3-0	1-0
Blackburn Rovers FC	3-1	4-4		3-0	6-3	1-2	6-3	2-2	2-1	2-2	0-0	1-1	3-3	7-0	1-2	4-1	3-1	3-0	2-3	4-2	1-2	1-0
Bolton Wanderers FC	1-3	5-3	2-2		4-2	3-2	0-1	0-2	6-1	1-0	2-2	0-1	5-1	3-1	2-2	2-1	2-1	3-2	1-1	1-1	2-2	1-0
Burnley FC	2-3	3-1	1-3	1-1		2-2	4-1	1-3	1-1	6-3	4-0	2-1	1-2	0-1	1-0	0-0	1-1	5-2	2-2	1-2	3-4	2-2
Bury FC	2-3	2-1	3-1	0-5	8-1		4-1	1-0	0-0	0-2	4-0	0-1	6-5	1-3	1-1	3-1	7-4	2-2	2-2	3-0	2-0	4-1
Cardiff City AFC	2-0	2-0	4-1	0-1	2-3	3-2		2-1	1-2	0-0	5-2	2-2	2-2	0-2	2-1	0-1	0-1	0-0	3-2	1-0		
Everton FC	1-1	2-2	3-0	2-1	1-1	1-1	1-1		2-3	4-2	1-0	3-3	1-1	1-3	3-0	3-0	2-2	2-1	2-3	1-1	4-0	2-0
Huddersfield Town AFC	5-1	4-1	3-1	3-0	2-1	2-1	1-1	3-0		3-1	3-0	0-0	2-2	5-0	0-1	2-0	4-1	1-1	2-2	2-1	1-1	2-1
Leeds United AFC	2-2	0-0	2-1	2-1	2-2	2-3	1-0	1-1	0-4		1-0	1-1	3-4	2-0	2-0	2-1	2-0	0-2	4-2	4-1	0-1	5-2
Leicester City FC	1-2	1-0	2-1	5-2	3-2	0-2	1-2	1-1	2-0	1-3		3-1	2-3	1-3	3-2	1-0	2-2	4-1	0-1	5-3	3-0	1-1
Liverpool FC	3-1	2-2	2-2	2-2	3-2	0-1	0-2	5-1	1-2	1-1	0-3		2-1	5-0	6-3	2-0	2-2	2-2	3-0	0-0	2-0	1-0
Manchester City FC	4-2	2-4	0-1	1-1	8-3	0-2	3-2	4-4	1-5	2-1	5-1	1-1		1-1	2-2	1-1	2-4	4-1	2-5	0-0	3-1	2-0
Manchester United FC	3-0	3-1	2-0	2-1	6-1	0-1	1-0	0-0	1-1	2-1	3-2	3-3	1-6		2-1	0-1	1-2	5-1	0-1	0-0	3-2	2-1
Newcastle United FC	2-2	1-3	1-7	5-1	1-3	4-0	0-1	3-3	0-2	3-0	3-2	3-0	3-2	4-1		6-3	3-1	0-0	7-0	3-1	3-0	4-1
Notts County FC	1-0	3-0	1-1	3-0	0-1	4-1	2-4	0-3	4-2	1-0	2-2	1-2	1-0	0-3	1-3		2-0	2-0	4-1	4-2	0-0	1-1
Sheffield United FC	4-1	4-1	1-1	2-0	6-1	3-1	11-2	1-1	2-3	2-0	2-4	3-1	8-3	2-0	4-3	3-0		4-1	4-0	2-3	3-2	1-1
Sunderland AFC	3-2	3-1	6-2	2-1	2-2	1-0	1-3	7-3	4-1	1-3	3-0	3-2	5-3	2-1	2-2	3-1	6-1		2-1	3-0	4-0	4-1
The Arsenal FC	2-0	3-0	4-2	2-3	1-2	6-1	5-0	4-1	3-1	4-1	2-2	1-1	1-0	3-2	3-0	3-0	4-0	2-0		0-1	1-0	3-2
Tottenham Hotspur FC	2-2	2-1	4-2	2-3	0-2	4-2	1-2	1-1	5-5	3-2	1-3	3-1	1-0	0-1	1-0	4-0	3-2	0-2	1-1		3-2	4-2
West Bromwich Albion FC	1-1	5-1	1-1	0-3	5-3	4-0	3-0	1-1	2-2	3-0	3-1	0-3	4-1	5-1	4-0	4-4	2-0	2-5	2-1	1-0		7-1
West Ham United FC	5-2	2-2	2-1	6-0	2-0	0-2	3-1	1-0	2-3	4-2	1-1	1-2	3-1	1-0	1-0	1-0	1-3	3-2	0-4	3-1	3-0	

	Division 1	Pd	Wn	Dw	Ls	GF	GA	Pts	
1.	HUDDERSFIELD TOWN AFC (HUDDERSFIELD)	42	23	11	8	92	60	57	
2.	The Arsenal FC (London)	42	22	8	12	87	63	52	
3.	Sunderland AFC (Sunderland)	42	21	6	15	96	80	48	
4.	Bury FC (Bury)	42	20	7	15	85	77	47	
5.	Sheffield United FC (Sheffield)	42	19	8	15	102	82	46	
6.	Aston Villa FC (Birmingham)	42	16	12	14	86	76	44	
7.	Liverpool FC (Liverpool)	42	14	16	12	70	63	44	
8.	Bolton Wanderers FC (Bolton)	42	17	10	15	75	76	44	
9.	Manchester United FC (Manchester)	42	19	6	17	66	73	44	
10.	Newcastle United FC (Newcastle-upon-Tyne)	42	16	10	16	84	75	42	
11.	Everton FC (Liverpool)	42	12	18	12	72	70	42	
12.	Blackburn Rovers FC (Blackburn)	42	15	11	16	91	80	41	
13.	West Bromwich Albion FC (West Bromwich)	42	16	8	18	79	78	40	
14.	Birmingham FC (Birmingham)	42	16	8	18	66	81	40	
15.	Tottenham Hotspur FC (London)	42	15	9	18	66	79	39	
16.	Cardiff City AFC (Cardiff)	42	16	7	19	61	76	39	
17.	Leicester City FC (Leicester)	42	14	10	18	70	80	38	
18.	West Ham United FC (London)	42	15	7	20	63	76	37	
19.	Leeds United AFC (Leeds)	42	14	8	20	64	76	36	
20.	Burnley FC (Burnley)	42	13	10	19	85	108	36	
21.	Manchester City FC (Manchester)	42	12	11	19	89	100	35	R
22.	Notts County FC (Nottingham)	42	13	7	22	54	74	33	R
		924	358	208	358	1703	1703	924	

Top Goalscorer

1) Ted HARPER   (Blackburn Rovers FC)   43

Football League Division 2 — 1925-1926 Season

Results grid (home team in rows, away team in columns). Column abbreviations: Bar = Barnsley, Bla = Blackpool, BrC = Bradford City, Che = Chelsea, CO = Clapton Orient, Dar = Darlington, DC = Derby County, Ful = Fulham, Hul = Hull City, Mid = Middlesbrough, NF = Nottingham Forest, OA = Oldham Athletic, Por = Portsmouth, PV = Port Vale, PNE = Preston North End, Sou = Southampton, SS = South Shields, StC = Stockport County, Sto = Stoke, Swa = Swansea Town, Wed = The Wednesday, Wol = Wolverhampton Wanderers.

	Bar	Bla	BrC	Che	CO	Dar	DC	Ful	Hul	Mid	NF	OA	Por	PV	PNE	Sou	SS	StC	Sto	Swa	Wed	Wol
Barnsley FC	■	2-0	0-0	2-3	3-1	1-1	0-1	2-2	2-1	0-1	4-1	3-4	2-2	3-0	2-0	2-0	2-1	1-1	2-1	2-0	1-1	1-1
Blackpool FC	4-0	■	3-0	0-0	3-0	0-1	1-2	2-0	2-2	2-3	3-0	2-1	2-2	2-2	3-1	2-1	1-0	4-1	0-0	0-0	1-0	4-0
Bradford City AFC	4-1	1-0	■	4-2	0-3	2-0	0-0	0-0	0-1	2-0	0-1	1-1	0-1	2-0	2-0	0-5	1-1	2-2	2-1	3-1	1-4	1-2
Chelsea FC	3-2	2-3	2-0	■	1-3	5-2	2-1	4-0	4-0	0-1	0-0	3-0	0-0	3-1	5-0	0-0	0-0	3-2	1-1	1-3	0-0	3-3
Clapton Orient FC	4-0	2-2	3-1	1-2	■	1-2	0-1	1-1	0-0	1-0	0-1	1-2	1-1	1-2	1-1	2-1	1-2	2-1	4-0	2-0	0-0	2-1
Darlington FC	2-2	1-3	1-3	1-1	6-0	■	3-0	1-2	1-2	0-2	0-1	7-1	4-0	1-1	3-1	4-1	3-2	1-2	3-3	5-1	3-4	1-2
Derby County FC	4-0	5-2	0-0	4-2	3-1	0-2	■	3-1	3-1	2-0	2-0	1-0	2-0	2-2	2-0	4-0	7-3	5-0	4-0	7-3	5-0	2-0
Fulham FC	2-2	1-1	2-0	0-3	0-2	4-0	1-1	■	1-1	2-0	0-2	2-1	2-3	3-3	2-1	1-1	2-1	1-0	2-4	0-1	3-0	1-2
Hull City AFC	2-2	1-2	5-0	0-1	2-0	1-1	0-0	1-0	■	1-2	4-1	1-2	1-0	3-0	1-1	4-0	1-3	4-0	1-0	4-2	0-1	3-1
Middlesbrough FC	5-0	3-2	2-5	1-2	1-2	3-2	1-2	4-0	3-3	■	2-0	1-0	2-1	4-1	3-1	5-1	3-0	1-2	4-0	3-0	0-3	4-1
Nottingham Forest FC	4-2	1-1	0-0	1-5	1-0	2-0	1-2	2-2	4-0	1-0	■	1-1	3-1	2-0	4-0	1-2	4-1	2-0	2-0	2-0	2-0	1-2
Oldham Athletic AFC	2-1	3-2	3-0	1-1	1-1	0-1	2-0	4-0	2-1	4-1	8-3	■	1-3	3-2	3-2	1-0	2-1	3-0	7-2	0-1	1-1	1-2
Portsmouth FC	1-2	2-0	3-1	4-0	3-2	2-0	2-2	0-0	2-2	1-5	5-1	0-2	■	2-0	3-2	5-2	1-2	4-2	2-0	0-0	1-2	3-0
Port Vale FC	3-0	5-0	2-0	0-6	4-2	6-1	0-1	0-1	3-1	4-0	1-1	3-0	1-1	■	3-0	1-1	2-0	2-0	3-0	3-0	4-3	3-0
Preston North End FC	4-2	6-4	3-1	3-1	4-1	0-0	2-1	2-1	4-0	1-0	2-0	2-1	3-2	4-0	■	2-2	0-4	5-3	2-0	4-2	0-3	1-0
Southampton FC	0-0	2-2	1-2	0-1	2-0	4-1	2-1	2-0	0-2	3-1	3-1	3-1	1-3	2-3	2-0	■	0-1	3-0	4-1	1-2	1-2	4-2
South Shields FC	3-0	3-4	1-3	0-0	1-0	2-4	0-0	5-2	1-3	2-2	3-1	0-0	5-1	5-2	1-1	2-0	■	4-2	5-1	3-1	0-2	3-1
Stockport County FC	1-1	4-3	1-1	0-0	3-2	1-1	3-0	1-2	0-1	3-3	2-2	1-1	1-2	4-1	2-1	1-3	0-2	■	1-2	2-1	1-3	0-2
Stoke FC	1-2	1-3	1-0	1-3	0-0	6-1	0-1	5-0	3-1	1-0	2-1	0-3	1-3	1-1	0-1	3-0	1-1	3-0	■	1-1	0-1	0-0
Swansea Town AFC	3-0	6-1	1-0	0-0	0-0	1-1	2-0	6-0	2-0	4-0	3-3	1-0	1-0	4-1	3-1	1-2	4-0	1-1	3-0	■	2-2	2-4
The Wednesday FC	3-0	2-0	5-1	4-1	3-0	4-0	1-4	3-0	2-0	2-0	5-1	4-2	0-2	5-1	2-1	1-0	6-2	2-0	3-1	3-0	■	2-1
Wolverhampton Wanderers FC	7-1	0-0	1-1	0-0	3-0	1-0	2-0	0-1	3-1	3-1	4-0	2-1	4-1	3-1	3-0	4-1	2-0	5-1	5-1	2-3	1-2	■

Division 2

		Pd	Wn	Dw	Ls	GF	GA	Pts	
1.	The Wednesday FC (Sheffield)	42	27	6	9	88	48	60	P
2.	Derby County FC (Derby)	42	25	7	10	77	42	57	P
3.	Chelsea FC (London)	42	19	14	9	76	49	52	
4.	Wolverhampton Wanderers FC (Wolverhampton)	42	21	7	14	84	60	49	
5.	Swansea Town AFC (Swansea)	42	19	11	12	84	57	49	
6.	Blackpool FC (Blackpool)	42	17	11	14	76	69	45	
7.	Oldham Athletic AFC (Oldham)	42	18	8	16	74	62	44	
8.	Port Vale FC (Stoke-on-Trent)	42	19	6	17	79	69	44	
9.	South Shields FC (South Shields)	42	18	8	16	74	65	44	
10.	Middlesbrough FC (Middlesbrough)	42	21	2	19	77	68	44	
11.	Portsmouth FC (Portsmouth)	42	17	10	15	79	74	44	
12.	Preston North End FC (Preston)	42	18	7	17	71	84	43	
13.	Hull City AFC (Kingston-upon-Hull)	42	16	9	17	63	61	41	
14.	Southampton FC (Southampton)	42	15	8	19	63	63	38	
15.	Darlington FC (Darlington)	42	14	10	18	72	77	38	
16.	Bradford City AFC (Bradford)	42	13	10	19	47	66	36	
17.	Nottingham Forest FC (Nottingham)	42	14	8	20	51	73	36	
18.	Barnsley FC (Barnsley)	42	12	12	18	58	84	36	
19.	Fulham FC (London)	42	11	12	19	46	77	34	
20.	Clapton Orient FC (London)	42	12	9	21	50	65	33	
21.	Stoke City FC (Stoke-on-Trent)	42	12	8	22	54	77	32	R
22.	Stockport County FC (Stockport)	42	8	9	25	51	97	25	R
		924	366	192	366	1487	1487	924	

	Accrington St.	Ashington	Barrow	Bradford P.A.	Chesterfield	Coventry City	Crewe Alexandra	Doncaster Rovers	Durham City	Grimsby Town	Halifax Town	Hartlepools Utd.	Lincoln City	Nelson	New Brighton	Rochdale	Rotherham Utd.	Southport	Tranmere Rovers	Walsall	Wigan Borough	Wrexham
Accrington Stanley FC	■	2-1	2-0	1-4	2-0	3-1	2-0	2-3	3-1	1-0	0-1	1-2	3-1	3-2	0-2	1-3	2-3	4-3	4-3	5-2	4-0	4-2
Ashington FC	3-1	■	1-4	1-1	0-0	2-0	2-0	6-1	0-1	4-2	0-1	2-0	4-1	5-1	1-1	0-1	4-2	1-1	1-0	2-0	3-3	2-2
Barrow AFC	1-2	2-3	■	0-1	0-3	1-4	0-1	0-2	1-4	0-3	1-2	1-4	3-0	1-0	2-3	1-3	1-2	0-3	3-3	5-2	1-1	4-3
Bradford Park Avenue	3-0	1-0	3-0	■	1-0	3-0	3-0	2-0	2-1	0-1	2-2	4-0	4-1	3-0	1-0	3-1	6-1	6-1	3-0	8-0	6-1	1-1
Chesterfield FC	7-2	6-1	3-1	1-1	■	4-3	4-2	2-2	2-0	2-0	1-0	5-2	2-0	3-1	3-0	1-2	6-1	3-0	4-0	4-0	4-0	3-1
Coventry City FC	2-1	2-0	2-0	2-2	2-4	■	2-1	4-0	3-1	1-1	4-1	5-2	3-2	1-0	0-0	2-2	7-0	0-0	1-2	2-0	0-0	2-0
Crewe Alexandra FC	3-0	2-1	4-1	1-2	2-0	2-1	■	2-2	2-0	1-1	0-1	2-1	3-1	1-4	4-1	3-2	3-1	0-1	1-1	2-1	3-1	2-0
Doncaster Rovers FC	6-2	2-1	0-1	0-3	3-0	8-1	5-2	■	4-1	1-4	2-2	1-0	1-1	2-0	2-2	0-0	6-1	4-0	1-1	1-1	1-1	
Durham City FC	5-1	0-0	2-1	2-1	5-2	4-1	1-1	3-0	■	0-0	2-0	0-0	3-2	0-2	0-0	0-2	5-1	3-2	2-1	4-1	2-0	2-1
Grimsby Town FC	5-2	3-1	4-0	3-0	1-0	2-0	2-0	3-0	3-1	■	1-0	4-0	3-0	1-0	3-0	3-0	3-2	8-0	5-1	1-1	1-0	
Halifax Town AFC	1-1	0-0	3-2	1-2	2-0	1-0	1-0	0-3	2-1	0-2	■	2-1	0-2	1-1	1-1	5-1	1-1	5-0	1-1	5-0	2-0	2-1
Hartlepools United FC	5-1	2-1	2-0	0-3	2-1	3-2	0-0	2-1	1-1	1-1	1-1	■	4-2	2-0	6-1	4-2	2-1	5-0	3-2	9-3	0-0	5-0
Lincoln City FC	3-1	2-0	4-3	1-1	2-1	0-3	2-2	3-1	1-0	4-1	0-1	2-1	■	1-0	3-1	0-2	0-3	3-0	1-3	5-1	2-1	3-2
Nelson FC	1-0	2-2	3-3	2-2	3-3	4-1	2-1	5-3	4-0	1-1	1-1	5-2	5-2	■	1-1	1-3	3-0	3-3	7-0	2-0	7-0	5-1
New Brighton FC	4-1	1-1	2-1	1-1	1-2	5-1	2-3	2-1	1-2	1-4	3-2	5-0	0-0		■	3-0	5-1	1-0	3-2	3-2	4-2	2-2
Rochdale AFC	3-2	1-3	2-1	2-0	2-4	4-1	2-0	4-1	5-0	5-2	2-1	6-0	0-1	2-0	2-1	■	2-2	3-1	3-2	2-0	2-1	1-2
Rotherham United FC	3-1	5-1	2-1	2-3	0-1	2-1	2-2	1-1	2-0	2-1	1-1	1-0	1-3	1-3	1-0	0-4	■	5-2	2-0	4-1	1-0	6-2
Southport FC	1-3	1-1	2-0	2-1	1-3	1-2	0-0	3-3	6-1	0-1	3-1	1-1	3-2	2-1	3-2	1-7	1-1	■	2-1	1-1	3-1	1-0
Tranmere Rovers FC	2-2	1-4	3-0	3-2	0-4	2-1	1-0	2-1	0-0	3-1	2-0	4-2	0-1	3-5	3-1	1-0			■	2-1	5-1	4-1
Walsall FC	3-3	2-0	1-2	3-1	3-1	4-1	0-3	2-1	0-1	2-2	3-1	1-2	0-0	0-2	3-1	1-5	4-1	2-2	1-3	■	0-1	5-1
Wigan Borough FC	5-0	0-2	4-1	1-3	2-0	5-1	3-1	0-1	4-1	1-0	1-0	3-3	5-0	3-1	2-2	0-1	3-1	2-2	2-0		■	6-0
Wrexham AFC	5-6	2-3	0-0	4-2	1-1	3-1	1-1	0-2	3-0	4-1	2-0	2-2	1-1	3-2	1-2	1-0	2-2	3-2	0-2	0-1	1-0	■

Division 3 (North)

		Pd	Wn	Dw	Ls	GF	GA	Pts	
1.	Grimsby Town FC (Cleethorpes)	42	26	9	7	91	40	61	P
2.	Bradford Park Avenue FC (Bradford)	42	26	8	8	101	43	60	
3.	Rochdale AFC (Rochdale)	42	27	5	10	104	58	59	
4.	Chesterfield FC (Chesterfield)	42	25	5	12	100	54	55	
5.	Halifax Town AFC (Halifax)	42	17	11	14	53	50	45	
6.	Hartlepools United FC (Hartlepool)	42	18	8	16	82	73	44	
7.	Tranmere Rovers FC (Birkenhead)	42	19	6	17	73	83	44	
8.	Nelson FC (Nelson)	42	16	11	15	89	71	43	
9.	Ashington FC (Ashington)	42	16	11	15	70	62	43	
10.	Doncaster Rovers FC (Doncaster)	42	16	11	15	80	72	43	
11.	Crewe Alexandra FC (Crewe)	42	17	9	16	63	61	43	
12.	New Brighton FC (Wallasey)	42	17	8	17	69	67	42	
13.	Durham City FC (Durham)	42	18	6	18	63	70	42	
14.	Rotherham United FC (Rotherham)	42	17	7	18	69	92	41	
15.	Lincoln City FC (Lincoln)	42	17	5	20	66	82	39	
16.	Coventry City FC (Coventry)	42	16	6	20	73	82	38	T
17.	Wigan Borough FC (Wigan)	42	13	11	18	68	74	37	
18.	Accrington Stanley FC (Accrington)	42	17	3	22	81	105	37	
19.	Wrexham AFC (Wrexham)	42	11	10	21	63	92	32	
20.	Southport FC (Southport)	42	11	10	21	62	92	32	
21.	Walsall FC (Walsall)	42	10	6	26	58	107	26	
22.	Barrow AFC (Barrow-in-Furness)	42	7	4	31	50	98	18	
		924	377	170	377	1628	1628	924	

T: Coventry City FC (Coventry) were transferred to Division 3 (South) from the next season.

Football League Division 3 (S) 1925-1926 Season	Aberdare Ath.	Bournemouth	Brentford	Brighton	Bristol City	Bristol Rovers	Charlton Ath.	Crystal Palace	Exeter City	Gillingham	Luton Town	Merthyr Town	Millwall	Newport Co.	Northampton	Norwich City	Plymouth Arg.	Q.P.R.	Reading	Southend Utd.	Swindon Town	Watford
Aberdare Athletic FC	▓	3-3	3-0	2-2	3-3	0-1	3-1	2-0	5-0	0-1	2-5	0-0	1-2	2-0	1-0	3-1	6-1	1-0	2-2	2-0	1-1	8-1
Bournemouth & B. Athletic	3-0	▓	3-2	0-3	1-1	2-0	4-1	6-1	2-1	1-2	2-2	2-1	0-0	0-2	4-2	2-2	1-2	4-1	1-1	1-2	2-0	3-4
Brentford FC	1-0	0-2	▓	1-6	2-1	4-1	4-0	3-2	2-0	0-0	1-0	1-1	2-0	3-3	3-4	5-1	2-2	1-2	1-0	1-3	3-1	4-3
Brighton & Hove Albion	6-2	3-4	3-2	▓	0-0	2-3	1-0	3-2	1-3	1-2	2-0	3-1	3-1	2-1	2-2	1-1	1-2	2-1	2-2	3-2	3-1	3-1
Bristol City FC	1-0	5-0	3-0	1-0	▓	0-0	4-0	1-0	1-0	4-0	5-1	2-1	1-1	1-2	1-1	0-1	2-1	3-1	0-1	1-4	5-1	1-0
Bristol Rovers FC	0-3	7-2	1-2	4-0	0-1	▓	4-1	3-1	0-1	2-0	2-2	0-0	0-1	-2	1-2	2-2	2-3	5-0	4-2	2-0	1-2	2-1
Charlton Athletic FC	1-0	5-0	0-2	1-1	3-1	0-1	▓	1-1	1-0	1-0	0-0	1-4	0-0	3-3	3-0	0-5	1-2	5-0	2-0	1-1		
Crystal Palace FC	0-1	3-1	2-0	2-1	5-2	0-2	4-1	▓	3-2	0-2	3-0	3-0	1-2	4-2	1-0	2-0	5-5	1-0	3-0	3-0	1-0	4-0
Exeter City FC	4-0	0-1	6-1	2-4	1-1	3-0	5-3	0-1	▓	2-1	2-2	6-2	3-1	2-1	1-0	0-1	4-0	3-0	3-2	0-1	1-2	6-1
Gillingham FC	0-1	1-2	1-3	3-1	0-1	6-3	0-0	1-1	2-0	▓	2-1	3-1	0-0	2-0	1-1	2-0	3-0	4-1	3-1	0-1	0-1	
Luton Town FC	2-1	4-1	4-2	3-3	4-1	1-0	1-0	3-2	1-1	5-3	▓	4-0	2-2	4-2	3-2	3-2	1-1	4-0	0-1	2-0	4-1	5-0
Merthyr Town FC	1-1	0-2	6-0	0-1	3-2	2-3	0-1	4-0	3-1	0-0	2-1	▓	0-2	4-1	5-3	3-1	1-1	1-0	5-2	5-1	2-1	4-1
Millwall FC	4-2	0-1	2-1	2-0	3-0	0-0	1-1	1-0	3-0	0-0	7-0	1-1	▓	3-3	4-1	3-1	0-0	3-0	1-0	8-1	3-0	3-0
Newport County AFC	0-0	1-2	2-3	4-3	1-0	3-1	0-0	2-3	3-0	4-0	2-1	3-1	1-0	▓	3-0	1-1	0-3	4-1	1-1	1-0	0-4	3-3
Northampton Town	3-2	1-1	6-1	1-2	1-2	2-0	2-1	4-0	2-1	1-2	0-1	4-1	3-1	2-0	▓	3-2	2-1	3-2	0-1	3-3	2-0	2-2
Norwich City FC	2-3	3-1	1-0	1-2	1-3	1-0	3-0	4-3	3-1	1-0	2-2	1-0	0-0	2-1		▓	0-3	1-1	3-1	1-2	2-2	1-1
Plymouth Argyle FC	7-2	7-2	4-0	5-3	3-1	1-2	1-0	6-2	2-2	2-1	4-3	3-0	2-0	3-0	2-4	6-3	▓	3-1	1-3	6-2	1-1	2-1
Queen's Park Rangers FC	1-3	2-2	1-1	0-2	0-2	2-1	2-2	1-3	0-0	0-1	1-0	1-1	3-0	0-2	3-2	0-1	0-4	▓	1-2	2-2	1-1	2-0
Reading FC	2-1	5-2	7-1	0-0	1-1	3-0	1-1	2-1	3-2	1-0	3-0	1-1	2-0	2-1	4-2	2-0	1-1	2-1	▓	1-0	2-0	4-1
Southend United FC	0-1	3-0	3-1	4-0	1-2	3-1	1-2	5-1	3-1	1-1	2-0	5-1	0-2	4-1	6-1	0-1	2-0	2-1	2-2	▓	3-0	0-1
Swindon Town FC	2-1	8-2	2-1	1-0	1-3	4-2	3-0	3-1	2-1	2-0	0-2	1-1	2-1	1-2	3-1	2-0	2-0	1-1	2-0		▓	5-3
Watford FC	2-0	0-0	2-2	3-3	2-2	2-1	1-1	3-0	3-1	3-1	2-0	6-1	0-1	5-1	3-2	3-1	0-1	3-1	0-1	1-4	3-2	▓

Division 3 (South)

		Pd	Wn	Dw	Ls	GF	GA	Pts	
1.	Reading FC (Reading)	42	23	11	8	77	52	57	P
2.	Plymouth Argyle FC (Plymouth)	42	24	8	10	107	67	56	
3.	Millwall FC (London)	42	21	11	10	73	39	53	
4.	Bristol City FC (Bristol)	42	21	9	12	72	51	51	
5.	Brighton & Hove Albion FC (Hove)	42	19	9	14	84	73	47	
6.	Swindon Town FC (Swindon)	42	20	6	16	69	64	46	
7.	Luton Town FC (Luton)	42	18	7	17	80	75	43	
8.	Bournemouth & Boscombe Athletic FC (Bournemouth)	42	17	9	16	75	91	43	
9.	Aberdare Athletic FC (Aberdare)	42	17	8	17	74	66	42	
10.	Gillingham FC (Gillingham)	42	17	8	17	53	49	42	
11.	Southend United FC (Southend-on-Sea)	42	19	4	19	78	73	42	
12.	Northampton Town FC (Northampton)	42	17	7	18	82	80	41	
13.	Crystal Palace FC (London)	42	19	3	20	75	79	41	
14.	Merthyr Town FC (Merthyr Tydfil)	42	14	11	17	69	75	39	
15.	Watford FC (Watford)	42	15	9	18	73	89	39	
16.	Norwich City FC (Norwich)	42	15	9	18	58	73	39	
17.	Newport County AFC (Newport)	42	14	10	18	64	74	38	
18.	Brentford FC (London)	42	16	6	20	69	94	38	
19.	Bristol Rovers FC (Bristol)	42	15	6	21	66	69	36	
20.	Exeter City FC (Exeter)	42	15	5	22	72	70	35	
21.	Charlton Athletic FC (London)	42	11	13	18	48	68	35	
22.	Queen's Park Rangers FC (London)	42	6	9	27	37	84	21	
		924	373	178	373	1155	1155	924	

F.A. CUP FINAL (Wembley Stadium, London – 24/04/1926 – 91,447)

BOLTON WANDERERS FC (BOLTON)   1-0   Manchester City FC (Manchester)

Jack

Bolton: Pym, Haworth, Greenhaugh, Nuttall, Seddon, Jennings, Butler, Jack, JR Smith, J.Smith, Vizard.

Man. City: Goodchild, Cookson, McCloy, Pringle, Cowen, McMullan, Austin, Browell, Roberts, Johnson, Hicks.

Semi-finals

Bolton Wanderers FC (Bolton)	3-0	Swansea Town AFC (Swansea)
Manchester City FC (Manchester)	3-0	Manchester United FC (Manchester)

Quarter-finals

Clapton Orient FC (London)	1-6	Manchester City FC (Manchester)
Fulham FC (London)	1-2	Manchester United FC (Manchester)
Nottingham Forest FC (Nottingham)	2-2, 0-0, 0-1	Bolton Wanderers FC (Bolton)
Swansea Town AFC (Swansea)	2-1	The Arsenal FC (London)

1926-27

Football League Division 1 1926-1927 Season	Aston Villa	Birmingham	Blackburn Rovers	Bolton Wanderers	Burnley	Bury	Cardiff City	Derby County	Everton	Huddersfield Town	Leeds United	Leicester City	Liverpool	Manchester United	Newcastle United	Sheffield United	Sunderland	The Arsenal	The Wednes.	Tottenham Hotspur	W.B.A.	West Ham United
Aston Villa FC		4-2	4-3	3-4	1-1	1-2	0-0	3-1	5-3	3-0	5-1	2-0	1-1	2-0	1-2	4-0	3-1	2-3	2-2	2-3	2-0	1-5
Birmingham FC	1-2		3-1	6-1	1-0	2-2	1-2	1-0	1-0	1-3	2-0	2-1	3-0	4-0	2-0	2-3	2-0	0-0	0-0	1-0	1-0	0-2
Blackburn Rovers FC	0-2	3-2		0-3	1-5	2-2	1-0	4-4	3-3	4-2	4-1	2-1	2-1	1-2	3-4	0-2	1-2	2-2	1-0	0-0		4-1
Bolton Wanderers FC	0-2	1-0	5-1		3-1	2-2	2-0	3-1	5-0	4-0	3-0	2-0	2-1	4-0	2-1	4-1	2-2	2-2	3-2	2-2	1-1	2-0
Burnley FC	6-3	0-2	3-1	4-3		0-0	4-3	1-0	5-1	2-2	3-2	1-1	4-0	1-0	3-3	2-5	4-2	2-0	1-0	5-0	2-1	2-1
Bury FC	0-1	3-1	0-2	2-0	3-3		2-3	1-2	5-2	2-2	4-2	0-0	0-3	3-2	4-4	1-2	3-2	2-0	0-0	7-3		1-2
Cardiff City AFC	2-3	1-0	0-1	1-0	0-0	2-1		2-0	1-0	2-0	3-1	0-1	2-0	0-2	1-1	3-0	2-0	3-2	1-2	1-1		1-2
Derby County FC	2-3	4-1	4-5	2-0	4-1	2-0	6-3		0-0	4-4	1-0	4-1	2-1	2-2	1-1	1-0	4-2	0-2	8-0	4-1	2-1	3-0
Everton FC	2-2	3-1	1-0	1-1	3-2	2-2	0-1	3-2		0-0	2-1	3-4	1-0	0-0	1-3	5-4	3-1	2-1	1-2	0-0		0-3
Huddersfield Town AFC	0-0	0-2	5-0	1-0	3-1	0-0	4-2	0-0	4-1		5-3	1-0	1-0	0-2	0-0	3-3	4-3	2-0	4-1	2-1		
Leeds United AFC	3-1	2-1	4-1	2-5	0-2	4-1	0-0	1-0	1-3	1-1		1-1	0-0	3-1	1-1	1-2	4-1	4-1	1-1	3-1		6-3
Leicester City FC	5-1	5-2	4-0	0-1	0-3	1-1	3-1	1-1	6-2	2-4	3-2		3-2	2-3	2-1	2-2	2-1	2-1	5-3	2-2	5-0	3-0
Liverpool FC	2-1	2-1	2-2	3-2	2-2	2-2	5-0	3-2	1-0	2-3	2-4	1-0		4-2	1-2	5-1	3-0	3-0	1-0	2-1		0-0
Manchester United FC	2-1	0-1	2-0	0-0	2-1	1-2	1-1	2-1	2-1	0-0	0-2	1-0	0-1		3-1	5-0	0-0	2-2	0-0	2-1		0-3
Newcastle United FC	4-0	5-1	6-1	1-0	1-5	3-1	5-0	3-0	7-3	1-0	1-0	1-1	1-0	4-2		2-0	1-0	6-1	2-1	3-2	5-2	2-0
Sheffield United FC	3-1	4-3	5-3	1-1	2-2	2-0	3-1	1-0	3-3	3-3	1-0	0-3	1-4	2-2	2-1		2-0	4-0	2-0	3-3	2-1	0-2
Sunderland AFC	1-1	4-1	2-5	6-2	7-1	3-0	2-2	1-2	3-2	1-1	6-2	3-0	2-1	6-0	2-0	3-0		5-1	4-1	3-2	4-1	2-3
The Arsenal FC	2-1	3-0	2-2	1-1	6-2	1-0	3-2	1-2	1-2	0-2	1-0	2-2	2-0	1-0	2-2	1-1	2-3		6-2	2-4	4-1	2-2
The Wednesday FC	3-1	4-4	0-3	2-1	2-1	1-3	3-0	2-1	4-0	1-1	1-0	2-2	3-2	2-0	3-2	2-3	4-1	4-2		3-1	2-1	1-0
Tottenham Hotspur FC	0-1	6-1	1-1	1-0	4-1	1-0	4-1	3-2	2-1	3-3	4-1	2-2	1-2	1-1	1-3	3-1	0-2	0-4	7-3		3-0	1-3
West Bromwich Albion FC	6-2	1-2	2-0	1-1	4-2	3-1	1-2	3-1	3-2	2-2	2-4	0-1	0-1	2-2	4-2	1-0	3-0	1-3	2-2	5-0		1-3
West Ham United FC	5-1	1-0	1-5	4-4	2-1	1-2	2-2	1-2	2-1	3-2	3-2	3-3	3-3	4-0	1-1	3-0	1-2	7-0	1-1	1-2	1-2	

	Division 1	Pd	Wn	Dw	Ls	GF	GA	Pts	
1.	NEWCASTLE UNITED FC (NEWCASTLE/TYNE)	42	25	6	11	96	58	56	
2.	Huddersfield Town AFC (Huddersfield)	42	17	17	8	76	60	51	
3.	Sunderland AFC (Sunderland)	42	21	7	14	98	70	49	
4.	Bolton Wanderers FC (Bolton)	42	19	10	13	84	62	48	
5.	Burnley FC (Burnley)	42	19	9	14	91	80	47	
6.	West Ham United FC (London)	42	19	8	15	86	70	46	
7.	Leicester City FC (Leicester)	42	17	12	13	85	70	46	
8.	Sheffield United FC (Sheffield)	42	17	10	15	74	86	44	
9.	Liverpool FC (Liverpool)	42	18	7	17	69	61	43	
10.	Aston Villa FC (Birmingham)	42	18	7	17	81	83	43	
11.	The Arsenal FC (London)	42	17	9	16	77	86	43	*
12.	Derby County FC (Derby)	42	17	7	18	86	73	41	
13.	Tottenham Hotspur FC (London)	42	16	9	17	76	78	41	
14.	Cardiff City AFC (Cardiff)	42	16	9	17	55	65	41	
15.	Manchester United FC (Manchester)	42	13	14	15	52	64	40	
16.	The Wednesday FC (Sheffield)	42	15	9	18	75	92	39	
17.	Birmingham FC (Birmingham)	42	17	4	21	64	73	38	
18.	Blackburn Rovers FC (Blackburn)	42	15	8	19	77	96	38	
19.	Bury FC (Bury)	42	12	12	18	68	77	36	
20.	Everton FC (Liverpool)	42	12	10	20	64	90	34	
21.	Leeds United AFC (Leeds)	42	11	8	23	69	88	30	R
22.	West Bromwich Albion FC (West Bromwich)	42	11	8	23	65	86	30	R
		924	362	200	362	1668	1668	924	

* The Arsenal FC (London) changed their club name to Arsenal FC (London) from the next season.

Top Goalscorer

1) James TROTTER   (The Wednesday FC)   37

Football League Division 2 — 1926-1927 Season

	Barnsley	Blackpool	Bradford City	Chelsea	Clapton Orient	Darlington	Fulham	Grimsby Town	Hull City	Man. City	Middlesbrough	Nottingham For.	Notts County	Oldham Ath.	Portsmouth	Port Vale	Preston N.E.	Reading	Southampton	South Shields	Swansea Town	Wolves
Barnsley FC		6-1	1-0	3-0	4-2	3-2	5-0	2-1	1-2	1-1	1-1	0-2	4-4	0-1	2-0	2-0	3-0	2-2	5-1	6-1	1-1	4-1
Blackpool FC	6-1		3-0	3-1	6-0	1-1	0-0	6-2	4-0	2-4	2-2	2-2	5-0	2-0	2-0	2-2	2-3	3-1	3-2	6-1	3-1	2-3
Bradford City AFC	1-1	4-1		0-1	1-3	0-1	1-0	2-2	1-2	4-3	0-1	1-1	1-2	0-1	1-2	1-2	0-1	1-1	2-0	3-1	5-0	1-2
Chelsea FC	4-2	1-1	5-2		2-1	2-2	2-2	2-0	1-0	0-0	3-0	2-0	2-0	1-0	0-0	2-0	2-1	0-0	2-3	4-1	2-2	1-0
Clapton Orient FC	0-1	1-0	1-1	3-0		0-4	2-3	2-4	1-2	6-1	2-3	2-2	2-1	3-1	4-5	1-2	1-1	5-1	1-0	1-0	1-0	2-0
Darlington FC	3-3	1-3	3-0	2-2	2-1		5-0	2-3	1-3	2-2	1-4	4-2	4-2	0-1	0-4	4-3	0-1	4-2	1-2	8-2	3-1	3-1
Fulham FC	1-0	1-0	1-1	1-2	2-0	2-1		0-5	3-1	2-5	0-3	2-1	3-0	1-1	0-0	6-2	0-1	1-2	3-0	2-2	4-3	4-1
Grimsby Town FC	1-3	2-1	4-2	0-0	2-2	2-1	2-0		0-1	2-2	4-7	1-1	1-4	2-5	0-0	4-4	5-2	0-1	0-1	1-1	0-1	6-0
Hull City AFC	5-1	3-0	4-0	0-1	4-0	2-0	2-0	2-3		3-2	3-3	1-2	0-2	1-2	2-1	0-0	3-1	1-1	0-0	2-0	2-1	1-0
Manchester City FC	1-1	2-1	8-0	1-0	6-1	7-0	4-2	2-0	2-2		3-5	1-1	4-1	3-0	4-0	4-1	1-0	3-0	3-4	1-2	3-1	2-1
Middlesbrough FC	5-1	4-4	4-3	0-0	6-0	4-1	6-1	3-0	2-0	2-1		1-0	4-2	3-1	7-3	5-2	0-2	5-0	3-1	5-0	7-1	2-0
Nottingham Forest FC	3-1	2-0	3-0	4-1	1-1	5-1	2-0	1-1	3-1	3-3	4-3		2-0	1-1	0-3	7-0	0-3	1-1	4-2	2-2	1-1	
Notts County FC	1-1	2-3	4-0	5-0	2-1	3-1	4-0	3-0	1-0	1-0	2-2	1-2		1-2	2-3	2-1	1-1	2-0	0-1	4-1	1-3	2-2
Oldham Athletic AFC	0-4	1-3	2-1	1-2	5-2	3-2	2-3	3-1	1-1	1-2	2-1	3-3	5-2		1-0	1-3	5-1	3-1	1-1	3-2	5-2	2-0
Portsmouth FC	1-2	5-0	1-0	2-3	1-1	0-0	5-2	2-0	2-1	0-1	0-0	9-1	7-2			4-0	5-1	1-1	0-1	1-1	1-0	2-1
Port Vale FC	3-2	2-4	0-0	0-0	3-0	3-2	7-1	6-1	0-0	0-2	3-1	0-2	6-2	3-0	2-3		2-0	1-1	4-2	4-0	2-0	1-1
Preston North End FC	2-1	4-1	3-2	0-2	2-2	4-1	2-2	3-2	1-0	2-4	2-2	4-1	5-2	1-2	4-4			3-1	1-0	4-0	4-0	2-0
Reading FC	3-2	0-1	2-3	2-1	0-1	4-2	2-0	1-1	0-1	1-0	0-1	4-0	7-1	6-1	1-1	2-0	3-0		1-0	2-1	3-0	1-2
Southampton FC	3-1	5-3	0-0	1-1	1-2	3-1	4-1	1-0	1-1	2-1	1-0	2-0	0-1	0-2	2-2	1-1	1-0	4-0		6-2	1-1	1-2
South Shields FC	7-1	2-2	3-3	5-1	1-0	1-1	1-1	3-2	1-2	2-2	0-0	1-1	5-0	4-1	1-0	3-3	1-1	3-0	1-2		0-1	1-2
Swansea Town AFC	5-2	2-0	1-0	2-1	3-2	5-1	4-2	1-1	1-0	1-3	0-1	2-1	0-1	3-0	1-1	2-2	0-0	3-0	2-2	2-0		4-1
Wolverhampton Wanderers FC	9-1	4-1	7-2	0-3	5-0	2-1	2-1	3-4	5-2	4-1	1-2	2-0	0-1	1-1	0-1	1-2	1-2	1-1	2-2	2-0	2-2	

Division 2

		Pd	Wn	Dw	Ls	GF	GA	Pts	
1.	Middlesbrough FC (Middlesbrough)	42	27	8	7	122	60	62	P
2.	Portsmouth FC (Portsmouth)	42	23	8	11	87	49	54	P
3.	Manchester City FC (Manchester)	42	22	10	10	108	61	54	
4.	Chelsea FC (London)	42	20	12	10	62	52	50	
5.	Nottingham Forest FC (Nottingham)	42	18	14	10	80	55	50	
6.	Preston North End FC (Preston)	42	20	9	13	74	72	49	
7.	Hull City AFC (Kingston-upon-Hull)	42	20	7	15	63	52	47	
8.	Port Vale FC (Stoke-on-Trent)	42	16	13	13	88	78	45	
9.	Blackpool FC (Blackpool)	42	18	8	16	95	80	44	
10.	Oldham Athletic AFC (Oldham)	42	19	6	17	74	84	44	
11.	Barnsley FC (Barnsley)	42	17	9	16	88	87	43	
12.	Swansea Town AFC (Swansea)	42	16	11	15	68	72	43	
13.	Southampton FC (Southampton)	42	15	12	15	60	62	42	
14.	Reading FC (Reading)	42	16	8	18	64	72	40	
15.	Wolverhampton Wanderers FC (Wolverhampton)	42	14	7	21	73	75	35	
16.	Notts County FC (Nottingham)	42	15	5	22	70	96	35	
17.	Grimsby Town FC (Cleethorpes)	42	11	12	19	74	91	34	
18.	Fulham FC (London)	42	13	8	21	58	92	34	
19.	South Shields FC (South Shields)	42	11	11	20	71	96	33	
20.	Clapton Orient FC (London)	42	12	7	23	60	96	31	
21.	Darlington FC (Darlington)	42	12	6	24	79	98	30	R
22.	Bradford City AFC (Bradford)	42	7	9	26	50	88	23	R
		924	362	200	362	1668	1668	924	

Football League Division 3 (N) 1926-1927 Season	Accrington St.	Ashington	Barrow	Bradford P.A.	Chesterfield	Crewe Alexandra	Doncaster R.	Durham City	Halifax Town	Hartlepools Utd.	Lincoln City	Nelson	New Brighton	Rochdale	Rotherham Utd.	Southport	Stockport Co.	Stoke City	Tranmere R.	Walsall	Wigan Borough	Wrexham
Accrington Stanley FC	■	3-0	0-1	2-3	2-1	3-1	2-0	3-0	4-2	7-2	1-1	0-5	2-3	0-1	3-1	2-2	2-4	0-1	2-3	3-5	3-1	1-1
Ashington FC	2-1	■	3-0	2-2	2-1	4-1	1-1	3-1	3-0	1-0	1-2	1-1	2-3	2-2	4-4	4-1	1-1	0-2	4-3	0-2	1-1	1-1
Barrow AFC	1-1	2-2	■	0-3	1-0	3-1	0-1	2-1	1-1	1-3	0-3	0-1	0-3	2-3	2-2	1-4	1-3	0-0	2-1	1-0	2-2	0-5
Bradford Park Avenue	6-1	2-0	1-0	■	5-0	2-0	7-3	3-0	2-1	4-1	3-1	2-2	1-1	5-1	2-2	6-2	3-1	3-0	5-3	5-1	2-1	5-0
Chesterfield FC	1-1	4-1	8-1	3-2	■	3-0	1-1	7-1	2-0	1-0	4-2	1-1	3-1	2-3	5-2	5-1	3-0	1-1	3-1	2-0	5-2	1-3
Crewe Alexandra FC	4-0	2-1	5-0	1-1	0-0	■	1-3	2-1	1-2	0-1	3-3	2-1	3-2	4-0	2-2	1-0	3-2	0-2	4-1	1-1	2-4	5-1
Doncaster Rovers FC	2-0	3-1	7-0	4-1	0-3	0-2	■	5-1	2-0	1-3	6-0	2-2	3-2	2-2	3-1	1-2	3-1	4-1	2-2	4-1	2-2	
Durham City FC	2-0	0-2	1-1	2-1	2-1	1-2	2-2	■	0-1	2-1	4-2	3-3	2-2	1-3	0-1	4-2	1-5	1-2	0-3	3-0	3-1	1-0
Halifax Town AFC	4-3	1-1	5-1	2-0	3-1	3-1	2-1	1-2	■	2-1	2-1	4-1	2-2	1-0	4-1	1-1	4-1	2-2	2-0	1-1	0-0	0-1
Hartlepools United FC	3-1	0-1	1-1	2-4	1-2	1-1	3-0	4-0	0-1	■	1-1	3-2	4-0	3-2	3-1	2-0	1-2	1-3	2-1	2-2	2-1	4-0
Lincoln City FC	4-0	4-0	3-1	5-1	3-1	3-3	0-0	5-0	3-1	1-2	■	1-4	4-1	2-3	1-2	1-1	1-3	1-3	1-2	3-3	2-0	2-2
Nelson FC	7-0	4-0	3-0	1-0	0-3	7-1	5-1	1-1	0-0	6-2	2-1	■	2-0	3-1	5-3	1-2	6-1	1-0	1-1	0-2	3-1	3-1
New Brighton FC	0-1	4-0	3-1	3-1	1-0	3-0	0-2	3-1	0-3	2-1	1-1	7-2	■	1-2	3-0	4-1	1-2	5-0	0-0	3-1	3-1	1-1
Rochdale AFC	2-1	5-0	5-1	3-0	8-1	3-1	7-2	1-3	2-0	3-0	7-3	2-1	1-1	■	2-1	1-0	2-0	4-0	3-1	4-4	4-1	3-1
Rotherham United FC	1-1	5-0	2-0	1-1	0-4	2-1	1-3	3-1	2-4	5-3	2-4	2-3	0-0	1-1	■	1-2	1-2	2-2	2-2	4-1	2-0	0-1
Southport FC	2-1	4-1	3-0	2-1	2-1	2-2	2-0	4-5	0-0	3-4	7-2	1-1	2-0			■	2-2	0-3	1-6	3-1	6-1	2-6	6-0
Stockport County FC	3-3	6-2	7-0	1-2	4-0	3-1	1-0	4-0	1-3	3-3	3-3	4-1	1-0	3-0	3-1	2-4	■	2-2	2-1	0-2	4-1	3-2
Stoke City FC	1-0	7-0	4-0	0-0	3-2	0-0	4-0	5-1	2-0	4-1	1-1	3-1	4-1	4-0	0-1			■	2-0	4-1	2-0	2-0
Tranmere Rovers FC	2-1	2-1	7-2	1-2	3-1	1-0	1-1	8-3	0-0	1-1	2-3	4-1	0-0	4-0	3-0	0-0	1-1		■	6-0	3-1	3-2
Walsall FC	5-1	0-0	1-0	1-0	0-1	2-3	1-0	1-1	0-1	2-2	1-2	4-1	0-1	4-1	3-2	1-1	1-0	0-1	5-1	■	3-2	0-1
Wigan Borough FC	3-0	1-4	8-0	1-2	1-2	2-2	1-1	3-0	1-1	3-0	3-2	2-1	3-2	0-3	0-0	3-1	2-0	0-3	1-1	5-2	■	1-1
Wrexham AFC	5-0	1-1	0-2	1-0	3-1	3-1	0-1	3-1	1-2	4-0	1-1	2-2	2-2	2-2	3-0	3-0	2-1	2-6	0-1	1-2	2-0	■

Division 3 (North)

		Pd	Wn	Dw	Ls	GF	GA	Pts	
1.	Stoke City FC (Stoke-on-Trent)	42	27	9	6	92	40	63	P
2.	Rochdale AFC (Rochdale)	42	26	6	10	105	65	58	
3.	Bradford Park Avenue FC (Bradford)	42	24	7	11	101	59	55	
4.	Halifax Town AFC (Halifax)	42	21	11	10	70	53	53	
5.	Nelson FC (Nelson)	42	22	7	13	104	75	51	
6.	Stockport County FC (Stockport)	42	22	7	13	93	69	49	-2
7.	Chesterfield FC (Chesterfield)	42	21	5	16	92	68	47	
8.	Doncaster Rovers FC (Doncaster)	42	18	11	13	81	65	47	
9.	Tranmere Rovers FC (Birkenhead)	42	19	8	15	85	67	46	
10.	New Brighton FC (Wallasey)	42	18	10	14	79	67	46	
11.	Lincoln City FC (Lincoln)	42	15	12	15	90	78	42	
12.	Southport FC (Southport)	42	15	9	18	80	85	39	
13.	Wrexham AFC (Wrexham)	42	14	10	18	65	73	38	
14.	Walsall FC (Walsall)	42	14	10	18	68	81	38	T
15.	Crewe Alexandra FC (Crewe)	42	14	9	19	71	81	37	
16.	Ashington FC (Ashington)	42	12	12	18	60	90	36	
17.	Hartlepools United FC (Hartlepool)	42	14	6	22	66	81	34	
18.	Wigan Borough FC (Wigan)	42	11	10	21	66	83	32	
19.	Rotherham United FC (Rotherham)	42	10	12	20	70	92	32	
20.	Durham City FC (Durham)	42	12	6	24	58	105	30	
21.	Accrington Stanley FC (Accrington)	42	10	7	25	62	98	27	
22.	Barrow AFC (Barrow-in-Furness)	42	7	8	27	34	117	22	
		924	366	192	366	1692	1692	922	

Note: Stockport County FC had 2 points deducted for fielding ineligible player Joe Smith on 26/03/1927 during the away match against Rotherham United FC. T: Walsall FC were transferred to Division 3 (South) from next season.

Football League Division 3 (S) 1926-1927 Season

	Aberdare Ath.	Bournemouth	Brentford	Brighton	Bristol City	Bristol Rovers	Charlton Ath.	Coventry City	Crystal Palace	Exeter City	Gillingham	Luton Town	Merthyr Town	Millwall	Newport Co.	Northampton	Norwich City	Plymouth Arg.	Q.P.R.	Southend Utd.	Swindon Town	Watford
Aberdare Athletic FC		2-1	3-1	2-2	3-7	2-1	0-0	0-7	2-3	3-1	2-1	0-1	1-2	1-3	0-1	6-1	1-2	5-6	0-2	1-0	1-4	3-2
Bournemouth & B. Athletic	3-0		3-1	1-0	2-0	0-1	0-3	1-2	1-1	4-3	4-2	2-0	1-1	0-1	2-1	3-1	0-1	6-2	6-2	3-0	1-2	6-0
Brentford FC	1-4	0-0		4-0	3-0	2-0	2-0	7-3	3-0	6-1	0-0	2-2	1-1	0-0	1-1	1-1	3-0	0-0	4-2	3-1	2-2	3-0
Brighton & Hove Albion	3-1	0-2	1-1		3-0	7-0	3-2	1-1	1-1	5-2	3-2	1-1	4-0	3-1	1-0	2-0	3-2	1-2	4-1	2-1	9-3	4-1
Bristol City FC	2-1	2-0	1-0	0-2		3-1	4-1	3-0	5-4	3-2	9-4	6-0	3-0	4-1	4-1	4-3	1-1	4-2	1-0	5-1	2-0	5-0
Bristol Rovers FC	4-0	2-1	1-3	0-0	0-5		1-1	1-2	4-1	3-1	1-2	2-1	1-1	4-0	5-2	1-0	2-2	4-1	5-1	3-1	0-2	
Charlton Athletic FC	5-1	1-3	1-1	1-0	0-1	3-1		4-2	1-2	1-0	3-0	2-2	3-2	1-1	3-0	5-2	2-0	1-1	2-0	1-0	2-2	2-1
Coventry City FC	1-0	6-2	3-1	1-2	2-5	2-2	1-0		3-1	0-0	0-2	4-1	5-1	1-4	3-1	0-3	1-0	3-3	1-0	1-1	1-3	5-1
Crystal Palace FC	0-0	2-2	4-3	2-0	4-2	7-4	2-1	1-2		1-0	2-2	1-1	1-1	1-6	6-2	3-0	7-1	1-1	2-1	5-3	5-0	0-1
Exeter City FC	2-1	4-0	3-1	0-0	1-1	1-1	1-0	8-1	3-1		5-1	1-2	3-0	1-1	3-2	1-0	0-2	0-2	2-0	3-1		2-1
Gillingham FC	2-1	1-0	1-2	2-3	1-1	2-0	1-1	2-0	2-1	3-2		0-0	0-1	2-1	0-1	1-2	1-0	4-1	2-2	2-3	4-4	3-0
Luton Town FC	3-3	4-0	2-1	4-0	0-0	1-1	1-0	4-1	1-0	2-2	2-1		2-1	6-0	4-1	2-0	2-2	3-3	2-0	0-0	1-1	2-2
Merthyr Town FC	2-2	4-6	1-0	1-0	1-1	3-2	3-0	1-0	1-2	3-3	2-0	4-1		1-0	1-2	2-0	1-1	5-1	4-0	0-1	1-2	1-1
Millwall FC	1-0	1-1	3-0	1-1	0-1	2-3	3-0	1-0	1-0	4-2	2-0	7-0	3-1		4-1	4-2	6-1	1-3	2-1	2-0	4-1	3-1
Newport County AFC	5-2	2-1	0-0	0-1	0-0	1-0	2-1	4-1	2-1	2-0	1-0	3-2	4-3	1-1		1-0	0-0	2-1	0-2	3-0	5-3	2-1
Northampton Town	2-1	2-2	2-3	0-0	2-0	3-0	0-1	2-1	1-1	2-1	2-1	2-0	1-4	1-2			3-0	2-0	1-1	2-1	1-0	3-2
Norwich City FC	2-2	4-1	0-2	1-1	2-0	2-3	3-0	0-1	4-4	3-2	4-0	0-2	1-0	6-1				0-2	0-1	1-1	2-1	4-0
Plymouth Argyle FC	2-0	1-1	2-1	2-0	4-2	3-2	3-1	3-0	7-1	2-0	0-0	1-0	1-1	1-1	4-1	3-0	2-1		2-0	2-1	3-1	4-0
Queen's Park Rangers FC	3-0	1-1	1-1	2-2	1-2	2-2	2-1	1-1	0-2	1-1	1-1	1-0	5-1	1-1	2-0	4-2	4-0	4-2		3-2	0-1	2-4
Southend United FC	5-1	0-3	3-1	0-1	0-1	2-1	5-0	3-1	3-1	1-2	2-1	3-1	1-0	2-1	5-0	2-0	3-3	1-2	0-3		2-2	2-0
Swindon Town FC	3-2	2-0	4-2	2-2	2-2	3-5	2-0	2-2	6-1	4-2	1-0	3-2	3-0	3-1	3-1	3-2	1-2	6-2	5-1			4-2
Watford FC	2-2	1-2	0-0	1-0	0-1	3-3	1-0	1-0	1-2	1-0	4-0	2-1	4-1	2-4	0-0	4-0	1-1	1-4	1-2	4-2	2-2	

Division 3 (South)

		Pd	Wn	Dw	Ls	GF	GA	Pts	
1.	Bristol City FC (Bristol)	42	27	8	7	104	54	62	P
2.	Plymouth Argyle FC (Plymouth)	42	25	10	7	95	61	60	
3.	Millwall FC (London)	42	23	10	9	89	51	56	
4.	Brighton & Hove Albion FC (Hove)	42	21	11	10	79	50	53	
5.	Swindon Town FC (Swindon)	42	21	9	12	100	85	51	
6.	Crystal Palace FC (London)	42	18	9	15	84	81	45	
7.	Bournemouth & Boscombe Athletic FC (Bournemouth)	42	18	8	16	78	66	44	
8.	Luton Town FC (Luton)	42	15	14	13	68	66	44	
9.	Newport County AFC (Newport)	42	19	6	17	57	71	44	
10.	Bristol Rovers FC (Bristol)	42	16	9	17	78	80	41	
11.	Brentford FC (London)	42	13	14	15	70	61	40	
12.	Exeter City FC (Exeter)	42	15	10	17	76	73	40	
13.	Charlton Athletic FC (London)	42	16	8	18	60	61	40	
14.	Queen's Park Rangers FC (London)	42	15	9	18	65	71	39	
15.	Coventry City FC (Coventry)	42	15	7	20	71	86	37	
16.	Norwich City FC (Norwich)	42	12	11	19	59	71	35	
17.	Merthyr Town FC (Merthyr Tydfil)	42	13	9	20	63	80	35	
18.	Northampton Town FC (Northampton)	42	15	5	22	59	87	35	
19.	Southend United FC (Southend-on-Sea)	42	14	6	22	64	77	34	
20.	Gillingham FC (Gillingham)	42	11	10	21	54	72	32	
21.	Watford FC (Watford)	42	12	8	22	57	87	32	
22.	Aberdare Athletic FC (Aberdare)	42	9	7	26	62	101	25	#
		924	363	198	363	1592	1592	924	

\# Aberdare Athletic FC were not re-elected to the league for next season. The club merged pre-season with Welsh League club Aberaman AFC with the 1st XI playing in the Football League as Aberdare Athletic FC and the 2nd XI in the Welsh League as Aberdare & Aberaman AFC.   Elected: Torquay United FC

F.A. CUP FINAL   (Wembley Stadium, London – 23/04/1927 – 91,206)

CARDIFF CITY AFC (CARDIFF)   1-0   The Arsenal FC (London)

Ferguson

Cardiff: Farqurharson, Nelson, Watson, Keenor, Sloan, Hardy, Curtis, Irving, Ferguson, L.Davies, McLachlan.

Arsenal: Lewis, Parker, Kennedy, Baker, Butler, John, Hulme, Buchan, Brain, Blyth, Hoar.

Semi-finals

Cardiff City AFC (Cardiff)	3-0	Reading FC (Reading)
The Arsenal FC (London)	2-1	Southampton FC (Southampton)

Quarter-finals

Chelsea FC (London)	0-0, 2-3	Cardiff City AFC (Cardiff)
Millwall FC (London)	0-0, 0-2	Southampton FC (Southampton)
Swansea Town AFC (Swansea)	1-3	Reading FC (Reading)
The Arsenal FC (London)	2-1	Wolverhampton Wanderers FC (Wolverhampton)

1927-28

Football League Division 1 1927-1928 Season	Arsenal	Aston Villa	Birmingham	Blackburn Rovers	Bolton Wands.	Burnley	Bury	Cardiff City	Derby County	Everton	Huddersfield T.	Leicester City	Liverpool	Man. United	Middlesbrough	Newcastle United	Portsmouth	Sheffield United	Sunderland	The Wednes.	Tottenham H.	West Ham United
Arsenal FC		0-3	2-2	3-2	1-2	4-1	3-1	3-0	3-4	3-2	0-0	2-2	6-3	0-1	3-1	4-1	0-2	6-1	2-1	1-1	1-1	2-2
Aston Villa FC	2-2		1-1	2-0	2-2	3-1	1-0	3-1	0-1	2-3	3-0	0-3	3-4	3-1	5-1	3-0	7-2	1-0	4-2	5-4	1-2	1-0
Birmingham FC	1-1	1-1		2-1	1-1	4-0	2-2	1-3	2-1	2-2	2-1	0-2	2-0	0-0	3-2	0-2	2-0	4-1	1-1	1-0	3-2	1-2
Blackburn Rovers FC	4-1	0-1	4-4		1-6	2-1	0-1	0-0	3-2	4-2	1-1	0-0	2-1	3-0	3-0	1-0	6-0	1-0	0-0	3-1	2-1	1-0
Bolton Wanderers FC	1-1	3-1	3-2	3-1		7-1	2-1	2-1	1-3	1-1	0-1	3-3	2-1	3-2	0-0	1-2	3-1	1-1	1-2	2-0	4-1	4-0
Burnley FC	1-2	4-2	2-1	3-1	2-2		2-3	2-1	4-2	3-5	0-1	5-1	2-2	4-0	1-1	5-1	2-0	5-3	3-0	3-1	2-2	0-0
Bury FC	5-1	0-0	2-3	2-3	1-0	2-0		3-0	3-0	2-3	2-3	2-1	5-2	4-3	1-4	1-4	4-0	1-0	5-3	4-2	1-2	3-1
Cardiff City AFC	2-2	2-1	2-1	1-1	2-1	3-2	0-1		4-4	2-0	4-0	3-0	1-1	2-0	1-1	3-1	3-1	2-2	3-1	1-1	2-1	1-5
Derby County FC	4-0	5-0	4-1	6-0	1-0	3-4	5-2	7-1		0-3	0-0	2-1	2-3	5-0	2-1	1-1	2-2	2-1	1-0	4-6	1-1	2-3
Everton FC	3-3	3-2	5-2	4-1	2-2	4-1	1-1	2-1	2-2		2-2	7-1	1-1	5-2	3-1	3-0	0-0	0-0	0-1	4-0	2-5	7-0
Huddersfield Town AFC	2-1	1-1	2-0	3-1	1-0	1-2	3-0	8-2	2-1	4-1		3-1	2-4	4-2	2-4	1-3	4-1	0-1	4-2	1-0	4-2	5-2
Leicester City FC	3-2	3-0	3-0	6-0	4-2	5-0	2-2	4-1	4-0	1-0	1-2		1-1	1-0	3-3	3-0	6-2	3-1	3-3	2-2	6-1	2-3
Liverpool FC	0-2	0-0	2-3	4-2	4-2	2-2	5-1	1-2	5-2	3-3	4-2	1-1		2-0	1-1	0-0	8-2	2-1	2-5	5-2	2-0	1-3
Manchester United FC	4-1	5-1	1-1	1-1	2-1	4-3	0-1	2-2	5-0	1-0	0-0	5-2	6-1		3-0	1-7	2-0	2-3	2-1	1-1	3-0	1-1
Middlesbrough FC	2-2	0-0	1-1	2-0	2-5	2-3	6-1	1-2	3-3	4-2	3-1	1-1	1-1	1-2		1-1	5-1	3-0	0-3	3-3	3-1	2-2
Newcastle United FC	1-1	7-5	1-1	0-1	2-2	1-1	2-3	2-0	4-3	2-2	2-3	1-5	1-1	4-1	3-3		1-3	1-0	3-1	4-3	4-1	3-1
Portsmouth FC	2-3	3-1	2-2	2-2	1-0	1-0	1-0	3-0	2-2	1-3	2-1	2-0	1-0	1-0	4-1	0-1		4-1	3-5	0-0	3-0	2-1
Sheffield United FC	6-4	0-3	3-1	2-3	4-3	5-2	3-1	3-4	1-0	1-3	1-7	1-1	1-1	2-1	4-1	1-1	3-2		5-1	1-1	3-1	6-2
Sunderland AFC	5-1	2-3	4-2	1-0	1-1	2-3	1-0	0-2	0-1	0-2	3-0	2-2	2-1	4-1	1-0	1-1	3-3	0-1		2-3	0-0	3-2
The Wednesday FC	1-1	2-0	2-3	4-1	3-0	5-0	4-0	3-3	2-2	0-5	1-2	4-0	0-2	2-3	0-0	2-0	3-3	0-0			4-2	2-0
Tottenham Hotspur FC	2-0	2-1	1-0	1-1	1-2	5-0	1-4	1-0	1-2	1-3	2-2	2-1	3-1	4-1	4-2	5-2	0-3	2-2	3-1	1-3		5-3
West Ham United FC	2-2	0-0	3-3	4-3	2-0	2-0	1-2	2-0	2-2	0-0	4-2	4-0	3-1	1-2	4-5	5-2	4-2	1-1	2-4	1-2	1-1	

124

	Division 1	Pd	Wn	Dw	Ls	GF	GA	Pts	
1.	EVERTON FC (LIVERPOOL)	42	20	13	9	102	66	53	
2.	Huddersfield Town AFC (Huddersfield)	42	22	7	13	91	68	51	
3.	Leicester City FC (Leicester)	42	18	12	12	96	72	48	
4.	Derby County FC (Derby)	42	17	10	15	96	83	44	
5.	Bury FC (Bury)	42	20	4	18	80	80	44	
6.	Cardiff City AFC (Cardiff)	42	17	10	15	70	80	44	
7.	Bolton Wanderers FC (Bolton)	42	16	11	15	81	66	43	
8.	Aston Villa FC (Birmingham)	42	17	9	16	78	73	43	
9.	Newcastle United FC (Newcastle-upon-Tyne)	42	15	13	14	79	81	43	
10.	Arsenal FC (London)	42	13	15	14	82	86	41	
11.	Birmingham FC (Birmingham)	42	13	15	14	70	75	41	
12.	Blackburn Rovers FC (Blackburn)	42	16	9	17	66	78	41	
13.	Sheffield United FC (Sheffield)	42	15	10	17	79	86	40	
14.	The Wednesday FC (Sheffield)	42	13	13	16	81	78	39	
15.	Sunderland AFC (Sunderland)	42	15	9	18	74	76	39	
16.	Liverpool FC (Liverpool)	42	13	13	16	84	87	39	
17.	West Ham United FC (London)	42	14	11	17	81	88	39	
18.	Manchester United FC (Manchester)	42	16	7	19	72	80	39	
19.	Burnley FC (Burnley)	42	16	7	19	82	98	39	
20.	Portsmouth FC (Portsmouth)	42	16	7	19	66	90	39	
21.	Tottenham Hotspur FC (London)	42	15	8	19	74	86	38	R
22.	Middlesbrough FC (Middlesbrough)	42	11	15	16	81	88	37	R
		924	348	228	348	1765	1765	924	

Top Goalscorer

1)	William "Dixie" DEAN	(Everton FC)	60

125

Football League Division 2 1927-1928 Season	Barnsley	Blackpool	Bristol City	Chelsea	Clapton Orient	Fulham	Grimsby Town	Hull City	Leeds United	Man. City	Nottingham F.	Notts County	Oldham Ath.	Port Vale	Preston N.E.	Reading	Southampton	South Shields	Stoke City	Swansea Town	W.B.A.	Wolves
Barnsley FC	■	2-1	2-3	3-1	4-2	8-4	1-4	1-1	2-1	0-3	2-1	0-0	0-1	4-2	2-1	2-0	0-1	0-0	3-1	3-3	2-4	2-2
Blackpool FC	1-3	■	6-2	2-4	0-1	4-0	4-5	2-1	0-2	2-2	5-3	3-3	1-2	1-6	4-1	3-1	1-0	4-1	3-1	2-2	4-3	3-0
Bristol City FC	2-0	2-2	■	1-1	5-1	3-0	0-0	0-1	1-2	2-0	0-0	1-2	2-1	4-0	1-3	4-1	3-0	1-1	4-0	2-1	0-1	4-1
Chelsea FC	1-2	3-0	5-2	■	1-0	2-1	4-0	2-0	2-3	0-1	2-1	5-0	2-1	1-0	2-1	0-0	0-2	6-0	4-0	1-1	2-0	2-0
Clapton Orient FC	2-0	2-5	4-2	2-1	■	3-2	1-2	0-0	2-1	0-2	2-2	0-1	2-0	0-1	1-1	3-0	2-0	2-2	3-2	1-1	0-0	0-0
Fulham FC	3-1	2-2	5-0	1-1	2-0	■	2-2	0-2	1-1	1-1	2-0	2-1	1-1	4-0	2-2	1-0	1-0	2-0	1-5	3-2	3-1	7-0
Grimsby Town FC	3-1	3-3	1-4	1-1	2-2	1-0	■	1-1	3-2	4-1	1-1	1-2	3-0	4-6	3-3	2-2	1-1	1-2	0-6	1-2	0-6	1-1
Hull City AFC	2-1	2-2	1-1	0-2	2-2	3-2	0-1	■	3-1	0-0	2-0	1-1	2-2	1-0	0-0	0-1	1-0	1-1	1-0	0-2	1-1	2-0
Leeds United AFC	2-2	4-0	3-2	5-0	4-0	2-1	0-0	2-0	■	0-1	4-0	6-0	1-0	3-0	2-4	6-2	2-0	3-0	5-1	5-0	1-2	3-0
Manchester City FC	7-3	4-1	4-2	0-1	5-3	2-1	2-0	2-1	2-1	■	3-3	3-1	3-1	1-0	2-2	4-1	6-1	3-0	4-0	7-4	3-1	3-0
Nottingham Forest FC	1-1	4-1	1-1	2-2	4-3	7-0	5-2	1-1	2-2	4-5	■	2-1	2-1	0-2	3-1	5-3	1-1	7-2	0-2	0-2	0-2	3-2
Notts County FC	9-0	3-1	1-2	0-1	3-0	0-1	3-2	1-1	2-2	2-1	1-2	■	2-1	2-4	6-2	1-1	0-0	4-1	1-2	2-0	3-0	1-2
Oldham Athletic AFC	0-1	6-0	4-1	2-1	5-0	4-2	1-0	5-0	0-1	3-2	4-1	0-0	■	4-1	0-0	3-2	3-1	2-2	3-1	0-1	3-1	3-0
Port Vale FC	2-1	3-0	5-1	1-1	0-0	4-1	2-2	1-2	1-2	1-2	2-2	3-0	1-0	■	2-0	3-0	4-0	2-3	0-0	2-0	4-1	2-2
Preston North End FC	1-2	2-1	5-1	0-3	0-0	1-0	3-0	4-2	5-1	1-0	5-0	4-0	1-1	4-0	■	4-0	1-2	7-2	2-0	4-2	3-3	5-4
Reading FC	1-1	1-0	3-2	1-2	4-0	2-1	2-2	3-0	0-1	1-0	0-2	2-2	1-0	0-0	2-1	■	0-0	5-1	1-1	0-0	1-4	2-1
Southampton FC	6-1	1-0	3-2	2-4	1-3	5-2	5-0	2-0	1-4	1-1	2-1	5-1	5-2	1-3	0-0	0-0	■	3-5	3-6	0-2	3-2	4-1
South Shields FC	0-0	2-2	1-3	2-1	2-2	1-2	1-0	1-5	0-1	3-4	2-3	0-3	0-1	2-3	0-0	2-1	0-0	■	2-3	3-1	2-3	2-2
Stoke City FC	0-0	2-0	1-0	1-0	2-0	5-1	0-0	3-1	5-1	2-0	1-3	3-0	3-0	0-2	3-2	4-1	2-1	3-1	■	1-1	1-1	2-2
Swansea Town AFC	3-0	1-0	1-1	0-0	5-0	3-1	2-0	1-1	5-3	1-1	0-0	2-0	1-0	2-0	2-0	6-3	1-1	2-0	3-2	■	3-2	6-0
West Bromwich Albion FC	1-1	6-3	0-0	3-0	4-1	4-0	3-1	1-1	0-1	1-1	2-3	2-2	0-0	0-0	2-4	5-3	2-1	3-0	2-4	5-2	■	4-0
Wolverhampton Wanderers FC	2-1	2-4	5-2	1-2	5-3	3-1	0-1	1-1	0-0	2-2	1-0	2-2	3-1	2-1	2-3	2-1	2-1	2-1	1-2	1-1	4-1	■

Division 2

		Pd	Wn	Dw	Ls	GF	GA	Pts	
1.	Manchester City FC (Manchester)	42	25	9	8	100	59	59	P
2.	Leeds United AFC (Leeds)	42	25	7	10	98	49	57	P
3.	Chelsea FC (London)	42	23	8	11	75	45	54	
4.	Preston North End FC (Preston)	42	22	9	11	100	66	53	
5.	Stoke City FC (Stoke-on-Trent)	42	22	8	12	78	59	52	
6.	Swansea Town AFC (Swansea)	42	18	12	12	75	63	48	
7.	Oldham Athletic AFC (Oldham)	42	19	8	15	75	51	46	
8.	West Bromwich Albion FC (West Bromwich)	42	17	12	13	90	70	46	
9.	Port Vale FC (Stoke-on-Trent)	42	18	8	16	68	57	44	
10.	Nottingham Forest FC (Nottingham)	42	15	10	7	83	84	40	
11.	Grimsby Town FC (Cleethorpes)	42	14	12	16	69	83	40	
12.	Bristol City FC (Bristol)	42	15	9	18	76	79	39	
13.	Hull City AFC (Kingston-upon-Hull)	42	12	15	15	41	54	39	
14.	Barnsley FC (Barnsley)	42	14	11	17	65	85	39	
15.	Notts County FC (Nottingham)	42	13	12	17	68	74	38	
16.	Wolverhampton Wanderers FC (Wolverhampton)	42	13	10	19	63	91	36	
17.	Southampton FC (Southampton)	42	14	7	21	68	77	35	
18.	Reading FC (Reading)	42	11	13	18	53	75	35	
19.	Blackpool FC (Blackpool)	42	13	8	21	83	101	34	
20.	Clapton Orient FC (London)	42	11	12	19	55	85	34	
21.	Fulham FC (London)	42	13	7	22	68	89	33	R
22.	South Shields FC (South Shields)	42	7	9	26	56	111	23	R
		924	354	216	354	1607	1607	924	

Football League Division 3 (N) 1927-1928 Season	Accrington St.	Ashington	Barrow	Bradford City	Bradford P.A.	Chesterfield	Crewe Alexandra	Darlington	Doncaster Rovers	Durham City	Halifax Town	Hartlepools Utd.	Lincoln City	Nelson	New Brighton	Rochdale	Rotherham United	Southport	Stockport County	Tranmere Rovers	Wigan Borough	Wrexham
Accrington Stanley FC		3-1	5-1	1-1	2-1	0-0	5-0	0-0	1-3	2-0	3-2	2-2	1-0	7-1	2-1	1-0	3-1	4-1	1-0	2-3	2-4	2-0
Ashington FC	1-1		1-0	2-2	0-3	0-0	0-2	2-3	1-2	2-2	3-3	3-1	4-5	5-1	3-2	5-1	6-0	1-3	4-1	3-0	6-3	2-1
Barrow AFC	1-0	1-1		0-0	0-0	2-0	1-1	2-0	0-0	1-2	6-2	2-0	3-3	3-1	2-1	1-3	1-1	3-1	2-3	2-1	6-2	2-2
Bradford City FC	2-0	5-0	4-1		2-3	3-3	4-1	0-1	1-0	4-0	0-0	2-1	3-1	9-1	3-1	2-2	3-1	2-0	2-2	3-1	3-0	2-0
Bradford Park Avenue	3-3	5-0	1-1	5-0		1-0	2-0	6-3	0-2	4-0	3-2	3-0	3-0	3-2	2-1	4-1	3-1	5-3	2-0	6-2	5-1	2-0
Chesterfield FC	3-1	3-0	6-0	2-0	0-0		3-2	1-3	1-0	4-2	3-0	1-3	0-1	6-0	2-3	1-3	2-5	5-2	1-1	2-2	0-0	0-1
Crewe Alexandra FC	2-3	3-0	4-1	2-1	1-3	4-1		3-3	4-1	5-2	1-1	4-0	0-1	6-1	1-1	1-1	3-2	0-1	3-0	2-3	1-2	1-1
Darlington FC	3-0	5-1	1-1	1-2	1-3	4-2	1-3		3-0	5-0	2-0	5-0	9-2	4-1	3-0	1-0	4-1	3-1	3-1	3-7	1-0	1-3
Doncaster Rovers FC	0-0	3-2	4-0	2-1	2-0	4-0	3-1	5-0		5-0	1-1	1-1	3-0	4-2	5-1	5-2	2-0	0-1	0-2	5-2	4-1	1-1
Durham City FC	2-1	0-0	4-1	3-2	0-1	2-0	5-1	3-3	1-3		1-1	1-0	0-4	3-0	3-2	1-4	0-0	1-2	1-3	3-0	1-1	1-1
Halifax Town AFC	3-1	6-1	5-2	2-1	1-1	1-2	0-0	2-1	0-1	3-1		4-1	3-1	5-1	1-1	1-0	0-0	1-1	1-3	2-2	2-2	1-1
Hartlepools United FC	0-2	4-1	6-2	2-3	1-1	1-0	4-3	0-1	1-0	2-1	0-1		1-2	4-5	3-3	0-2	1-3	2-1	2-1	2-0	1-1	4-2
Lincoln City FC	3-1	3-1	5-0	2-2	2-0	0-0	5-2	1-0	2-0	2-1	5-2	1-5		0-0	1-2	3-1	4-1	2-0	2-0	1-1	4-1	5-0
Nelson FC	1-4	1-5	4-0	0-3	1-2	3-3	3-3	4-0	0-1	2-1	3-2	4-2	1-3		0-3	6-3	6-1	1-1	0-4	3-5	3-3	4-0
New Brighton FC	3-1	6-0	3-3	1-1	1-2	3-3	5-1	0-0	3-1	4-0	3-1	2-3	4-0			2-1	1-1	0-1	0-0	0-1	2-1	0-0
Rochdale AFC	3-2	2-2	3-0	3-3	0-4	5-1	4-0	4-1	1-0	1-0	2-2	0-1	0-3	1-0	0-0		2-1	5-1	2-1	1-2	3-0	3-0
Rotherham United FC	2-1	1-1	3-0	0-0	1-0	1-2	2-0	3-1	2-1	1-1	0-0	5-0	2-4	4-3	0-1	3-1		1-1	2-1	6-0		0-1
Southport FC	5-0	3-3	4-0	5-1	2-1	2-1	3-2	3-1	2-1	3-1	3-1	1-2	4-2	1-1	3-1	1-1			4-0	0-1		5-0
Stockport County FC	3-3	3-0	4-0	2-2	3-0	1-0	4-0	2-1	2-1	3-0	2-2	2-0	8-0	0-0	5-0	2-0	6-3			1-0	1-1	5-0
Tranmere Rovers FC	3-2	5-3	5-0	2-1	2-2	6-3	3-3	3-1	0-0	11-1	2-2	1-2	2-2	1-1	4-0	3-0	2-0	1-0	5-2		5-2	2-1
Wigan Borough FC	2-0	0-0	1-0	2-2	1-3	3-2	2-1	0-3	1-1	3-0	1-3	0-2	1-0	4-2	2-2	1-2	0-0	1-3	1-3	1-0		3-0
Wrexham AFC	0-1	5-1	5-0	1-0	1-1	1-2	2-0	1-2	1-2	4-0	2-0	3-2	1-0	5-2	0-2	2-1	2-1	3-2	3-0	1-0	2-0	

Division 3 (North)

		Pd	Wn	Dw	Ls	GF	GA	Pts	
1.	Bradford Park Avenue FC (Bradford)	42	27	9	6	101	45	63	P
2.	Lincoln City FC (Lincoln)	42	24	7	11	91	64	55	
3.	Stockport County FC (Stockport)	42	23	8	11	89	51	54	
4.	Doncaster Rovers FC (Doncaster)	42	23	7	12	80	44	53	
5.	Tranmere Rovers FC (Birkenhead)	42	22	9	11	105	72	53	
6.	Bradford City AFC (Bradford)	42	18	12	12	85	60	48	
7.	Darlington FC (Darlington)	42	21	5	16	89	74	47	
8.	Southport FC (Southport)	42	20	5	17	79	70	45	
9.	Accrington Stanley FC (Accrington)	42	18	8	16	76	67	44	
10.	New Brighton FC (Wallasey)	42	14	14	14	72	62	42	
11.	Wrexham AFC (Wrexham)	42	18	6	18	64	67	42	
12.	Halifax Town AFC (Halifax)	42	13	15	14	73	71	41	
13.	Rochdale AFC (Rochdale)	42	17	7	18	74	77	41	
14.	Rotherham United FC (Rotherham)	42	14	11	17	65	69	39	
15.	Hartlepools United FC (Hartlepool)	42	16	6	20	69	81	38	
16.	Chesterfield FC (Chesterfield)	42	13	10	19	71	78	36	
17.	Crewe Alexandra FC (Crewe)	42	12	10	20	77	86	34	
18.	Ashington FC (Ashington)	42	11	11	20	77	103	33	
19.	Barrow AFC (Barrow-in-Furness)	42	10	11	21	54	102	31	
20.	Wigan Borough FC (Wigan)	42	10	10	22	56	97	30	
21.	Durham City FC (Durham)	42	11	7	24	53	100	29	#
22.	Nelson FC (Nelson)	42	10	6	26	76	136	26	
		924	365	194	365	1676	1676	924	

Football League Division 3 (S) 1927-1928 Season

	Bournemouth	Brentford	Brighton	Bristol Rovers	Charlton Ath.	Coventry City	Crystal Palace	Exeter City	Gillingham	Luton Town	Merthyr Town	Millwall Ath.	Newport Co.	Northampton	Norwich City	Plymouth A.	Q.P.R.	Southend Utd.	Swindon Town	Torquay United	Walsall	Watford
Bournemouth & B. Athletic	■	1-0	3-1	4-3	3-1	2-3	2-2	2-0	3-0	2-2	2-1	5-0	0-0	1-1	2-1	2-2	1-2	2-3	2-0	1-1	3-1	1-0
Brentford FC	2-1	■	1-3	5-1	1-1	4-1	2-1	1-1	2-0	4-2	4-0	6-1	3-1	3-0	3-1	0-2	0-3	2-2	1-4	1-2	3-2	1-1
Brighton & Hove Albion	3-2	5-2	■	5-0	2-2	3-0	4-2	0-2	0-0	3-1	5-0	3-1	1-4	2-1	1-0	4-1	1-3	1-0	4-2	3-0	0-0	1-1
Bristol Rovers FC	3-0	1-3	1-0	■	2-1	1-1	1-1	1-2	2-4	1-2	2-1	1-6	2-1	2-2	3-0	3-1	0-4	1-3	1-0	5-1	5-2	3-1
Charlton Athletic FC	1-1	3-2	3-0	2-1	■	2-1	0-4	0-0	1-0	4-3	0-0	1-1	3-2	2-2	3-2	2-0	1-0	1-2	3-1	1-0	1-3	0-2
Coventry City FC	3-2	0-0	2-2	2-3	3-3	■	2-2	0-0	1-2	4-2	1-2	0-3	0-2	2-4	2-2	1-1	0-0	6-1	4-0	5-1	0-1	2-3
Crystal Palace FC	6-1	0-2	1-1	3-2	5-0	1-0	■	2-0	2-2	3-2	2-0	0-4	2-0	1-0	2-1	0-2	1-1	4-1	1-0	3-2	5-1	2-1
Exeter City FC	4-1	0-1	0-3	4-1	2-1	0-1	2-2	■	2-2	3-2	2-0	2-4	5-1	1-1	2-2	2-0	4-0	3-2	0-0	5-0	3-0	3-3
Gillingham FC	2-1	2-1	0-1	3-1	1-1	1-2	3-1	1-1	■	0-4	1-1	0-1	4-0	1-3	3-0	3-1	1-2	1-0	0-1	4-1	2-0	0-3
Luton Town FC	3-3	5-2	2-5	2-0	2-1	3-1	6-1	2-1	6-1	■	5-1	1-1	1-1	2-0	1-3	1-1	0-1	0-0	2-1	5-0	4-1	3-2
Merthyr Town FC	1-1	3-1	4-2	2-3	0-0	3-2	2-2	0-3	3-1	0-0	■	0-0	0-2	1-3	1-4	0-4	2-3	8-2	1-3	3-2	3-1	3-1
Millwall FC	2-0	3-0	6-0	1-0	5-0	9-1	1-1	2-0	6-0	3-2	3-0	■	5-1	3-0	2-1	2-0	6-1	5-1	3-3	9-1	7-1	4-2
Newport County AFC	4-3	3-0	3-1	3-1	4-3	3-0	0-3	1-0	1-1	7-2	1-1	1-3	■	4-1	2-2	1-1	1-6	3-2	1-3	2-2	4-1	3-2
Northampton Town	1-1	3-2	1-0	2-1	2-1	2-1	1-1	5-0	1-0	6-5	6-0	5-2	1-2	■	4-2	2-1	1-0	2-1	3-0	4-4	10-0	5-0
Norwich City FC	3-3	1-1	0-0	4-2	0-0	0-2	4-1	2-2	0-0	3-0	4-0	2-0	1-1	3-4	■	2-0	3-1	2-1	1-3	4-0	1-4	1-1
Plymouth Argyle FC	3-1	1-0	2-0	4-1	2-0	4-0	5-1	1-2	2-2	4-0	5-0	3-2	2-0	3-3	4-2	■	3-0	3-2	3-0	4-1	2-1	0-1
Queen's Park Rangers FC	2-0	2-3	5-0	4-2	3-3	1-5	2-0	0-1	3-3	3-2	0-0	0-1	4-2	0-4	0-0	0-1	■	3-2	0-1	2-3	1-1	2-1
Southend United FC	3-0	3-2	0-1	2-1	1-2	3-2	6-1	1-2	1-2	1-0	2-1	0-1	5-1	2-0	1-1	3-0	7-0	■	1-1	1-0	2-1	3-0
Swindon Town FC	3-2	1-1	4-3	2-1	2-2	6-0	3-3	3-0	6-1	4-2	1-2	3-0	4-1	4-0	1-1	2-2	0-2	0-1	■	2-2	5-0	4-0
Torquay United FC	2-2	2-1	1-1	0-0	1-2	2-3	0-2	1-1	1-1	0-4	2-2	0-1	1-1	1-5	4-2	1-2	1-0	3-3	2-1	■	1-1	1-1
Walsall FC	2-3	4-2	3-3	1-2	1-0	7-0	1-1	5-1	7-4	4-1	2-2	2-5	0-3	1-1	1-1	2-2	0-1	1-2	2-2	4-0	■	2-0
Watford FC	2-0	1-1	3-3	2-1	1-2	3-1	2-1	3-2	5-3	1-0	1-1	0-3	2-3	2-0	2-0	1-2	3-3	1-1	2-5	1-2	4-0	■

Division 3 (South)

		Pd	Wn	Dw	Ls	GF	GA	Pts	
1.	Millwall FC (London)	42	30	5	7	127	50	65	P
2.	Northampton Town FC (Northampton)	42	23	9	10	102	64	55	
3.	Plymouth Argyle FC (Plymouth)	42	23	7	12	85	54	53	
4.	Brighton & Hove Albion FC (Hove)	42	19	10	13	81	69	48	
5.	Crystal Palace FC (London)	42	18	12	12	79	72	48	
6.	Swindon Town FC (Swindon)	42	19	9	14	90	69	47	
7.	Southend United FC (Southend-on-Sea)	42	20	6	16	80	64	46	
8.	Exeter City FC (Exeter)	42	17	12	13	70	60	46	
9.	Newport County AFC (Newport)	42	18	9	15	81	84	45	
10.	Queen's Park Rangers FC (London)	42	17	9	16	72	71	43	
11.	Charlton Athletic FC (London)	42	15	13	14	60	70	43	
12.	Brentford FC (London)	42	16	8	18	76	74	40	
13.	Luton Town FC (Luton)	42	16	7	19	94	87	39	
14.	Bournemouth & Boscombe Athletic FC (Bournemouth)	42	13	12	17	72	79	38	
15.	Watford FC (Watford)	42	14	10	18	68	78	38	
16.	Gillingham FC (Gillingham)	42	13	11	18	62	81	37	
17.	Norwich City FC (Norwich)	42	10	16	16	66	70	36	
18.	Walsall FC (Walsall)	42	12	9	21	75	101	33	
19.	Bristol Rovers FC (Bristol)	42	14	4	24	67	93	32	
20.	Coventry City FC (Coventry)	42	11	9	22	67	96	31	
21.	Merthyr Town FC (Merthyr Tydfil)	42	9	13	20	53	91	31	
22.	Torquay United FC (Torquay)	42	8	14	20	53	103	30	
		924	355	214	355	1680	1680	924	

F.A. CUP FINAL   (Wembley Stadium, London – 21/04/1928 – 92,041)

BLACKBURN ROVERS FC (BLACKBURN)   3-1   Huddersfield Town AFC (Huddersfield)

Roscamp 2, McLean   *Jackson*

Blackburn: Crawford, Hutton, Jones, Healless, Rankin, Campbell, Thornewell, Puddefoot, Roscamp, McLean, Rigby.

Huddersfield: Mercer, Goodall, Barkas, Redfern, Wilson, Steele, A.Jackson, Kelly, Brown, Stephenson, WH Smith.

Semi-finals

Blackburn Rovers FC (Blackburn)	1-0	Arsenal FC (London)
Huddersfield Town AFC (Huddersfield)	2-2, 0-0, 1-0	Sheffield United FC (Sheffield)

Quarter-finals

Arsenal FC (London)	4-1	Stoke City FC (Stoke-on-Trent)
Blackburn Rovers FC (Blackburn)	2-0	Manchester United FC (Manchester)
Huddersfield Town AFC (Huddersfield)	6-1	Tottenham Hotspur FC (London)
Sheffield United FC (Sheffield)	3-0	Nottingham Forest FC (Nottingham)

1928-29

Football League Division 1 1928-1929 Season	Arsenal	Aston Villa	Birmingham	Blackburn Rovers	Bolton Wanderers	Burnley	Bury	Cardiff City	Derby County	Everton	Huddersfield Town	Leeds United	Leicester City	Liverpool	Manchester City	Manchester United	Newcastle United	Portsmouth	Sheffield United	Sunderland	Wednesday	West Ham United
Arsenal FC		2-5	0-0	1-0	2-0	3-1	7-1	2-1	1-3	2-0	2-0	1-0	1-1	4-4	0-0	3-1	1-2	4-0	2-0	1-1	2-2	2-3
Aston Villa FC	4-2		1-2	2-1	3-5	4-2	7-1	1-0	2-3	2-0	4-1	1-0	4-2	3-1	5-1	0-0	1-1	3-2	3-2	3-1	4-1	5-2
Birmingham FC	1-1	2-4		4-0	0-2	3-6	3-2	0-0	1-4	1-3	1-2	5-1	1-0	0-0	4-1	1-1	0-0	1-0	2-2	1-0	4-1	2-
Blackburn Rovers FC	5-2	2-5	4-1		1-3	1-1	1-1	2-0	3-1	2-1	1-0	0-1	1-1	2-1	2-2	0-3	2-0	4-0	1-1	2-0	4-1	2-0
Bolton Wanderers FC	1-2	3-1	6-2	0-3		0-1	0-1	1-0	3-0	2-3	1-1	4-1	5-0	0-0	1-1	1-1	1-0	4-2	3-1	2-2	2-2	4-1
Burnley FC	3-3	4-1	4-0	2-2	3-1		0-0	3-0	2-2	2-0	3-2	5-0	0-1	3-2	2-3	3-4	4-3	4-1	2-1	3-1	0-2	3-3
Bury FC	1-0	2-2	3-1	1-0	3-4	2-1		4-1	3-3	1-2	2-1	2-2	3-1	2-2	1-2	1-3	2-0	0-0	4-0	1-3	0-4	0-3
Cardiff City AFC	1-1	0-2	1-4	1-1	1-1	7-0	4-0		3-0	0-2	0-0	2-1	1-2	1-2	1-3	2-2	2-0	1-1	0-0	0-1	3-1	3-2
Derby County FC	0-0	1-0	2-2	5-1	2-1	4-0	3-1	2-0		3-0	1-2	3-4	5-2	2-5	1-1	6-1	1-2	1-0	2-2	0-0	6-0	6-0
Everton FC	4-2	0-1	0-2	5-2	3-0	2-0	1-0	1-0	4-0		0-3	0-1	3-1	1-0	2-6	2-4	5-2	4-0	1-3	0-0	0-0	0-4
Huddersfield Town AFC	0-1	3-0	0-0	0-2	4-1	7-1	0-2	1-1	0-0	3-1		6-1	1-1	1-3	2-2	2-1	3-1	6-1	1-2	0-0	4-0	0-0
Leeds United AFC	1-1	4-1	0-1	0-1	2-2	2-1	3-1	3-0	1-1	3-1	1-2		4-3	2-2	4-1	3-2	0-0	3-2	2-0	0-3	0-2	4-1
Leicester City FC	1-1	4-1	5-3	2-1	6-1	1-1	5-2	2-0	1-0	4-1	4-1	4-4		2-0	3-2	2-1	1-1	10-0	3-1	1-0	1-1	5-0
Liverpool FC	2-4	4-0	1-2	1-1	3-0	8-0	3-0	2-0	3-0	1-2	2-3	1-1	6-3		1-1	2-3	2-1	0-0	1-2	5-2	3-2	2-1
Manchester City FC	4-1	3-0	2-3	1-2	5-1	4-1	6-4	1-1	2-3	5-1	3-2	3-0	2-3	2-3		2-2	2-4	2-1	3-1	5-3	2-2	4-2
Manchester United FC	4-1	2-2	1-0	1-4	1-1	1-0	1-0	1-1	0-1	1-1	1-0	1-2	1-1	2-2	1-2		5-0	0-0	1-1	3-0	2-1	2-3
Newcastle United FC	0-3	2-1	1-0	0-2	4-1	2-7	2-1	1-1	4-1	2-0	4-1	3-2	1-0	2-2	4-0	5-0		0-1	4-2	4-3	2-1	1-0
Portsmouth FC	2-0	3-2	3-1	2-2	4-4	3-1	4-1	0-1	1-5	0-0	1-0	0-2	1-0	0-1	1-0	3-0	0-1		2-3	4-0	3-2	3-0
Sheffield United FC	2-2	1-3	3-2	2-1	1-1	10-0	6-1	3-1	2-1	2-1	1-0	1-1	1-4	1-3	6-1	3-1	3-0			4-0	1-1	3-3
Sunderland AFC	5-1	1-3	3-4	3-1	4-0	2-1	3-1	1-0	4-0	2-2	4-1	2-1	2-1	3-1	5-1	5-2	5-0	4-4			4-3	4-1
The Wednesday FC	3-2	4-1	3-0	1-0	0-0	1-1	3-1	1-0	5-0	1-0	1-1	4-2	1-0	3-2	4-0	2-1	3-1	2-1	5-2	2-1		6-0
West Ham United FC	3-4	4-1	2-1	3-3	3-0	4-0	2-3	1-1	2-2	2-4	1-1	8-2	2-1	1-1	3-0	3-1	1-0	0-1	4-0	3-3	3-2	

Division 1	Pd	Wn	Dw	Ls	GF	GA	Pts	
1. THE WEDNESDAY FC (SHEFFIELD)	42	21	10	11	86	62	52	*
2. Leicester City FC (Leicester)	42	21	9	12	96	67	51	
3. Aston Villa FC (Birmingham)	42	23	4	15	98	81	50	
4. Sunderland AFC (Sunderland)	42	20	7	15	93	75	47	
5. Liverpool FC (Liverpool)	42	17	12	13	90	64	46	
6. Derby County FC (Derby)	42	18	10	14	86	71	46	
7. Blackburn Rovers FC (Blackburn)	42	17	11	14	72	63	45	
8. Manchester City FC (Manchester)	42	18	9	15	95	86	45	
9. Arsenal FC (London)	42	16	13	13	77	72	45	
10. Newcastle United FC (Newcastle-upon-Tyne)	42	19	6	17	70	72	44	
11. Sheffield United FC (Sheffield)	42	15	11	16	86	85	41	
12. Manchester United FC (Manchester)	42	14	13	15	66	76	41	
13. Leeds United AFC (Leeds)	42	16	9	17	71	84	41	
14. Bolton Wanderers FC (Bolton)	42	14	12	16	73	80	40	
15. Birmingham FC (Birmingham)	42	15	10	17	68	77	40	
16. Huddersfield Town AFC (Huddersfield)	42	14	11	17	70	61	39	
17. West Ham United FC (London)	42	15	9	18	86	96	39	
18. Everton FC (Liverpool)	42	17	4	21	63	75	38	
19. Burnley FC (Burnley)	42	15	8	19	81	103	38	
20. Portsmouth FC (Portsmouth)	42	15	6	21	56	80	36	
21. Bury FC (Bury)	42	12	7	23	62	99	31	R
22. Cardiff City AFC (Cardiff)	42	8	13	21	43	59	29	R
	924	360	204	360	1688	1688	924	

* The Wednesday FC (Sheffield) changed their club name to Sheffield Wednesday FC (Sheffield) from the next season.

Top Goalscorer

1) David HALLIDAY   (Sunderland AFC)   43

Football League Division 2 1928-1929 Season	Barnsley	Blackpool	Bradford P.A.	Bristol City	Chelsea	Clapton Orient	Grimsby Town	Hull City	Middlesbrough	Millwall	Nottingham F.	Notts County	Oldham Ath.	Port Vale	Preston N.E.	Reading	Southampton	Stoke City	Swansea Town	Tottenham H.	W.B.A.	Wolves
Barnsley FC		3-1	1-2	4-2	0-1	2-0	0-2	2-2	2-2	2-2	1-2	2-0	2-1	6-0	4-1	2-3	4-1	4-2	2-1	4-1	2-0	2-2
Blackpool FC	0-1		3-0	2-1	0-1	0-1	1-1	2-1	3-0	3-0	2-2	3-2	4-0	4-0	3-2	7-0	3-0	2-0	2-2	2-2	0-2	3-0
Bradford Park Avenue	2-1	5-2		3-2	1-2	2-1	1-0	5-1	3-2	4-0	1-1	2-2	2-0	7-2	1-0	4-1	2-1	3-1	4-1	4-1	4-1
Bristol City FC	3-1	3-2	1-0		0-0	1-0	2-2	0-0	0-1	5-0	2-5	0-4	6-0	2-1	1-0	0-0	1-1	1-1	2-1	2-1	2-3	3-2
Chelsea FC	1-0	2-3	3-1	3-0		2-2	3-2	0-0	2-0	0-3	3-0	1-1	2-3	3-3	2-1	2-1	1-1	3-1	4-0	1-1	2-5	0-2
Clapton Orient FC	3-1	2-4	1-0	0-1	1-0		3-1	0-2	3-0	1-1	1-4	2-2	0-1	1-1	1-1	1-0	1-2	2-3	0-2	2-1
Grimsby Town FC	2-1	1-4	4-2	3-2	1-0	6-1		0-1	1-4	3-0	2-2	2-1	1-0	3-1	1-0	4-0	2-1	2-1	4-1	2-0	3-1	2-0
Hull City AFC	0-0	1-3	1-0	5-1	2-2	0-0	2-3		1-1	4-0	0-1	1-1	1-0	2-0	5-1	3-0	2-2	1-3	1-1	1-1	4-1	1-3
Middlesbrough FC	1-0	4-1	5-3	3-1	4-5	4-0	3-0	1-1		3-0	1-0	3-1	1-0	5-1	2-3	0-0	1-2	1-0	0-0	3-0	1-1	8-3
Millwall FC	0-2	2-1	1-3	3-1	2-1	2-0	4-1	0-0	2-3		1-1	0-1	3-3	2-1	3-1	5-1	2-4	1-3	3-0	5-1	2-2	0-5
Nottingham Forest FC	1-3	2-0	3-2	1-1	3-0	0-0	0-1	3-1	1-1	0-4		1-2	3-1	2-2	4-1	1-2	1-1	1-5	2-1	2-2	1-2	2-1
Notts County FC	4-1	3-1	3-3	2-0	4-3	2-0	1-2	6-0	0-3	4-5	1-1		2-0	3-0	1-1	1-1	1-0	5-1	2-0	1-1	3-0
Oldham Athletic AFC	1-0	4-2	2-1	1-0	1-0	1-1	0-3	0-1	1-3	4-1	2-0	3-2		1-1	2-1	2-1	1-1	2-1	3-1	3-0	0-4
Port Vale FC	3-0	1-0	0-1	5-0	1-0	3-0	0-3	4-1	2-3	5-2	4-2	3-0	2-1		3-2	4-0	1-2	1-2	0-0	2-1	8-1	1-4
Preston North End FC	2-1	3-1	2-0	2-2	3-0	5-2	5-2	1-0	0-0	3-4	3-2	0-1	3-2	7-1		7-0	0-1	2-2	2-2	2-2	1-1	5-1
Reading FC	1-0	4-1	4-0	2-1	3-3	4-2	1-3	3-0	2-3	0-2	0-3	1-2	6-1	2-1	0-0		0-1	1-1	2-0	4-3	5-3	3-0
Southampton FC	1-2	8-2	2-2	2-1	1-2	2-0	3-1	3-2	1-1	2-1	4-0	1-2	4-0	2-2		0-0	3-0	1-1	1-2
Stoke City FC	0-0	1-1	2-0	2-0	0-1	3-1	1-2	1-1	3-2	0-0	1-1	5-0	1-1	2-1	1-1	5-0	3-0		5-0	2-0	4-1	4-3
Swansea Town AFC	2-1	5-5	3-1	0-2	0-1	0-1	2-1	0-1	2-0	3-5	1-0	3-2	2-0	5-0	0-1	1-1	3-3		4-0	6-1	2-0
Tottenham Hotspur FC	2-0	1-2	3-2	1-1	4-1	2-1	4-1	2-5	2-1	3-0	4-1	4-2	2-2	3-2	1-0	1-1		2-0	3-2
West Bromwich Albion FC	6-2	2-2	1-2	1-1	3-0	3-1	1-0	2-0	1-1	3-2	3-0	1-3	1-0	3-1	1-1	5-0	3-1	2-3	5-1	3-2		0-2
Wolverhampton Wanderers FC	3-1	1-5	3-1	2-1	1-1	3-2	2-2	2-4	3-3	0-1	2-3	3-1	0-0	4-0	1-2	2-0	1-1	4-0	0-0	4-2	0-1	

Division 2

		Pd	Wn	Dw	Ls	GF	GA	Pts	
1.	Middlesbrough FC (Middlesbrough)	42	22	11	9	92	57	55	P
2.	Grimsby Town FC (Cleethorpes)	42	24	5	13	82	61	53	P
3.	Bradford Park Avenue FC (Bradford)	42	22	4	16	88	70	48	
4.	Southampton FC (Southampton)	42	17	14	11	74	60	48	
5.	Notts County FC (Nottingham)	42	19	9	14	78	65	47	
6.	Stoke City FC (Stoke-on-Trent)	42	17	12	13	74	51	46	
7.	West Bromwich Albion FC (West Bromwich)	42	19	8	15	80	79	46	
8.	Blackpool FC (Blackpool)	42	19	7	16	92	76	45	
9.	Chelsea FC (London)	42	17	10	15	64	65	44	
10.	Tottenham Hotspur FC (London)	42	17	9	16	75	81	43	
11.	Nottingham Forest FC (Nottingham)	42	15	12	15	71	70	42	
12.	Hull City AFC (Kingston-upon-Hull)	42	13	14	15	58	63	40	
13.	Preston North End FC (Preston)	42	15	9	18	78	79	39	
14.	Millwall FC (London)	42	16	7	19	71	86	39	
15.	Reading FC (Reading)	42	15	9	18	63	86	39	
16.	Barnsley FC (Barnsley)	42	16	6	20	69	66	38	
17.	Wolverhampton Wanderers FC (Wolverhampton)	42	15	7	20	77	81	37	
18.	Oldham Athletic AFC (Oldham)	42	16	5	21	54	75	37	
19.	Swansea Town AFC (Swansea)	42	13	10	19	58	72	36	
20.	Bristol City FC (Bristol)	42	13	10	19	58	72	36	
21.	Port Vale FC (Stoke-on-Trent)	42	15	4	23	71	86	34	R
22.	Clapton Orient FC (London)	42	12	8	22	45	72	32	R
		924	367	190	367	1576	1576	924	

131

Football League Division 3 (N) 1928-1929 Season	Accrington St.	Ashington	Barrow	Bradford City	Carlisle United	Chesterfield	Crewe Alex.	Darlington	Doncaster R.	Halifax Town	Hartlepools Utd.	Lincoln City	Nelson	New Brighton	Rochdale	Rotherham Utd.	Southport	South Shields	Stockport Co.	Tranmere R.	Wigan Borough	Wrexham
Accrington Stanley FC		0-1	1-0	0-1	2-3	0-0	2-0	4-0	6-0	1-1	2-2	0-1	4-4	3-1	2-2	1-3	2-0	2-0	2-0	2-0	2-0	4-3
Ashington FC	2-2		1-0	2-8	0-4	0-2	0-5	4-2	4-7	0-3	3-1	1-1	3-2	1-1	2-1	0-1	1-3	1-3	0-1	3-2	1-1	2-2
Barrow AFC	2-1	3-0		1-3	1-1	1-2	2-4	3-1	2-2	1-3	2-1	2-3	7-2	0-0	3-3	4-0	1-2	1-1	2-4	1-2	1-0	2-2
Bradford City AFC	4-1	2-0	8-0		4-2	6-1	4-1	3-0	3-0	2-2	4-1	2-3	0-2	5-2	0-0	11-1	5-0	3-1	2-1	8-0	1-0	5-0
Carlisle United FC	4-3	5-1	4-1	2-2		1-2	1-0	3-0	1-2	2-1	8-0	3-1	4-0	2-1	4-2	1-1	4-2	5-0	0-5	4-1	2-1	1-1
Chesterfield FC	4-1	4-1	3-0	0-5	1-2		1-0	2-1	0-1	3-2	4-1	1-3	2-0	1-2	6-0	3-2	1-2	4-1	3-1	1-2	4-1	1-1
Crewe Alexandra FC	4-0	7-0	3-1	0-0	1-1	6-1		2-0	1-1	3-0	4-2	1-3	1-1	3-0	1-1	3-0	1-1	1-5	2-0	0-1	0-4	3-1
Darlington FC	0-0	4-0	1-2	3-3	0-0	2-2	4-2		1-0	2-0	4-1	2-1	3-2	3-1	5-3	2-1	3-1	2-2	2-3	1-2	3-0	0-0
Doncaster Rovers FC	4-1	2-1	1-0	1-1	3-0	2-0	0-1	3-1		1-0	4-1	0-0	2-2	1-2	4-2	1-0	4-2	0-2	2-1	1-2	1-2	2-0
Halifax Town AFC	4-2	1-0	2-0	1-1	5-2	1-1	2-2	5-1	2-2		2-0	4-2	1-2	1-1	1-1	3-1	2-1	0-2	1-1	2-0	1-0	2-1
Hartlepools United FC	1-3	1-3	1-0	1-3	1-0	0-2	2-1	2-0	2-2	3-1		3-2	2-2	5-2	0-2	1-1	4-2	0-5	1-1	4-1	1-3	2-0
Lincoln City FC	3-1	3-1	5-0	3-4	3-0	1-0	1-0	0-0	2-1	3-0	7-1		5-1	4-0	2-0	1-1	4-1	5-0	1-2	3-1	3-1	3-1
Nelson FC	0-2	5-0	3-4	0-1	1-0	1-0	4-1	2-1	2-4	3-1	1-0	3-4		3-0	3-0	4-1	1-1	1-1	0-0	2-0	2-1	1-3
New Brighton FC	2-1	3-2	1-3	0-3	1-0	2-3	2-3	1-0	1-1	1-0	1-3	6-1	0-1		6-1	0-0	3-1	1-0	4-1	1-2	2-2	2-0
Rochdale AFC	2-1	5-0	4-2	1-3	4-0	2-1	2-1	5-0	1-3	2-2	7-4	0-2	2-1	4-2		2-1	1-1	1-2	1-3	5-1	0-0	4-4
Rotherham United FC	2-1	0-0	2-1	2-2	4-0	2-0	1-2	2-0	1-2	0-0	3-2	3-2	4-0	3-1	5-0		0-2	1-1	3-3	0-1	4-2	2-1
Southport FC	3-1	2-1	2-2	0-3	4-3	1-0	6-2	3-1	3-3	1-0	6-2	2-1	5-1	0-0	1-1	2-0		5-0	1-1	1-2	3-0	1-3
South Shields FC	3-0	0-0	2-2	1-1	5-0	6-3	3-0	1-3	1-0	2-1	1-1	1-0	3-2	0-2	5-2	10-1	4-0		0-1	4-1	2-2	3-2
Stockport County FC	6-1	4-0	3-2	2-1	2-2	3-1	2-2	7-3	4-1	3-0	7-3	3-0	2-1	4-0	1-0	2-1	7-1	4-0		4-1	2-1	6-2
Tranmere Rovers FC	1-1	3-2	2-1	1-0	1-2	3-1	1-2	4-0	1-1	2-1	3-0	2-1	6-1	1-3	5-1	4-0	6-1	4-0	2-1		3-2	1-1
Wigan Borough FC	5-2	5-1	2-1	2-0	2-2	5-1	4-2	2-0	4-2	1-1	2-0	4-0	1-0	1-1	4-1	1-0	1-0	4-0	4-0	0-1		1-1
Wrexham AFC	4-1	4-0	5-0	2-1	5-1	4-3	1-2	4-3	4-2	2-2	3-1	2-1	3-1	1-1	3-0	2-0	3-1	1-0	2-1	3-1	1-3	

Division 3 (North)

		Pd	Wn	Dw	Ls	GF	GA	Pts	
1.	Bradford City AFC (Bradford)	42	27	9	6	128	43	63	P
2.	Stockport County FC (Stockport)	42	28	6	8	111	58	62	
3.	Wrexham AFC (Wrexham)	42	21	10	11	91	69	52	
4.	Wigan Borough FC (Wigan)	42	21	9	12	82	49	51	
5.	Doncaster Rovers FC (Doncaster)	42	20	10	12	76	66	50	
6.	Lincoln City FC (Lincoln)	42	21	6	15	91	67	48	
7.	Tranmere Rovers FC (Birkenhead)	42	22	3	17	79	77	47	
8.	Carlisle United FC (Carlisle)	42	19	8	15	86	77	46	
9.	Crewe Alexandra FC (Crewe)	42	18	8	16	80	68	44	
10.	South Shields FC (South Shields)	42	18	8	16	83	74	44	
11.	Chesterfield FC (Chesterfield)	42	18	5	19	71	77	41	
12.	Southport FC (Southport)	42	16	8	18	75	85	40	
13.	Halifax Town AFC (Halifax)	42	13	13	16	63	62	39	
14.	New Brighton FC (Wallasey)	42	15	9	18	64	71	39	
15.	Nelson FC (Nelson)	42	17	5	20	77	90	39	
16.	Rotherham United FC (Rotherham)	42	15	9	18	60	77	39	
17.	Rochdale AFC (Rochdale)	42	13	10	19	79	96	36	
18.	Accrington Stanley FC (Accrington)	42	13	8	21	68	82	34	
19.	Darlington FC (Darlington)	42	13	7	22	64	88	33	
20.	Barrow AFC (Barrow-in-Furness)	42	10	8	24	64	93	28	
21.	Hartlepools United FC (Hartlepool)	42	10	6	26	59	112	26	
22.	Ashington FC (Ashington)	42	8	7	27	45	115	23	#
		924	376	172	376	1696	1696	924	

132

Ashington FC (Ashington) were not re-elected to the league for the next season.   Elected: York City FC (York)

Football League Division 3 (S) 1928-1929 Season	Bournemouth	Brentford	Brighton	Bristol Rovers	Charlton Ath.	Coventry City	Crystal Palace	Exeter City	Fulham	Gillingham	Luton Town	Merthyr Town	Newport Co.	Northampton	Norwich City	Plymouth Arg.	Q.P.R.	Southend Utd	Swindon T.	Torquay Utd	Walsall	Watford
Bournemouth & B. Athletic		1-1	3-2	6-2	4-2	2-1	2-0	3-1	1-0	4-3	3-3	3-0	0-1	2-0	2-0	4-1	2-3	2-2	2-1	4-3	1-2	3-3
Brentford FC	0-0		5-1	2-0	1-0	1-0	2-4	4-2	1-2	4-1	0-1	2-1	1-3	2-2	4-0	0-2	1-1	1-0	2-0	0-0	1-0	0-1
Brighton & Hove Albion	1-0	3-2		4-0	2-3	0-1	1-5	3-2	2-0	3-1	1-0	2-1	2-1	0-3	3-0	2-1	2-1	2-1	2-2	1-2	2-1	1-1
Bristol Rovers FC	1-2	2-0	3-0		3-0	1-1	1-1	1-1	5-3	2-4	1-1	3-0	0-3	1-2	2-0	0-1	1-1	4-1	1-4	2-1	4-1	1-1
Charlton Athletic FC	6-2	1-0	3-0	1-2		3-1	1-3	3-1	0-0	1-1	4-1	2-2	2-2	3-1	1-0	2-1	2-2	3-2	4-1	2-0	5-0	2-0
Coventry City FC	1-2	1-0	3-0	2-0	0-1		1-3	1-1	1-2	2-0	1-1	6-1	3-1	0-2	3-0	1-4	0-0	1-1	4-1	2-1	1-1	1-1
Crystal Palace FC	1-3	1-0	1-0	5-2	0-2	0-3		1-0	2-1	3-0	3-0	0-1	1-1	1-0	2-1	1-4	1-4	3-2	6-1	0-1	1-1	3-0
Exeter City FC	6-3	2-3	4-1	2-2	2-5	2-3	1-2		1-4	4-2	1-1	5-0	6-1	2-0	3-1	1-2	1-1	1-2	1-1	1-3	1-1	2-2
Fulham FC	3-0	1-0	3-1	6-1	2-5	2-2	2-2	0-0		4-2	4-2	4-0	2-3	2-1	2-1	5-2	5-0	2-4	2-0	2-1	5-1	2-3
Gillingham FC	2-2	1-2	1-1	1-0	1-0	1-1	0-1	1-3	2-2		1-0	1-0	0-4	2-1	4-0	2-0	0-0	0-2	0-0	1-1	1-4	0-0
Luton Town FC	2-1	2-1	1-0	4-2	3-0	1-1	5-3	4-0	1-3	8-0		2-0	5-2	4-0	2-1	2-2	3-2	4-2	5-3	1-2	3-1	2-2
Merthyr Town FC	1-0	2-2	1-0	4-0	2-3	2-2	2-2	2-1	4-1	2-3	3-4		2-1	2-2	2-2	1-2	2-1	0-0	3-0	1-0	2-1	
Newport County AFC	0-2	1-1	1-2	2-0	2-0	2-1	1-3	1-1	3-3	5-0	1-2	6-1		0-3	2-2	1-0	0-0	2-2	0-1	4-1	3-1	0-2
Northampton Town FC	2-0	1-1	1-1	3-1	4-1	3-3	8-1	4-0	3-3	1-0	2-2	4-1	7-0		2-0	3-0	4-2	2-3	1-1	6-1	4-2	3-0
Norwich City FC	5-1	2-4	3-1	2-1	0-1	3-0	0-1	5-0	2-2	1-2	3-0	3-1	3-1	1-1		0-3	3-1	2-5	1-1	3-0	2-1	5-2
Plymouth Argyle FC	2-0	4-0	1-0	2-0	2-2	3-0	1-1	0-0	4-2	3-0	2-0	4-0	5-2	1-1	4-0		1-2	1-1	3-0	4-0	2-2	2-0
Queen's Park Rangers FC	0-0	2-2	3-2	0-3	2-2	2-3	1-1	1-0	2-1	1-1	1-1	8-0	0-0	4-1	3-0	2-0		3-1	4-2	5-1	2-4	1-3
Southend United FC	4-4	1-1	1-1	1-0	1-3	0-0	3-0	1-0	0-1	2-0	5-0	5-1	4-2	2-2	5-3	1-1	0-3		1-1	3-0	3-1	1-3
Swindon Town FC	3-3	3-1	2-2	2-1	1-1	1-2	3-2	2-0	1-2	2-1	4-2	2-1	5-2	0-1	1-2	0-0	2-1	3-1		1-1	5-1	5-0
Torquay United FC	4-1	4-1	5-1	0-1	3-1	0-2	1-2	1-3	1-1	2-1	2-2	6-2	4-1	0-1	0-3	2-2	3-4	2-1	2-4		3-2	1-0
Walsall FC	2-1	2-0	1-2	1-3	0-2	0-1	3-1	7-2	2-2	4-0	0-0	1-1	3-1	4-3	3-3	1-1	3-1	4-1	1-1	1-0		4-0
Watford FC	0-3	2-0	2-1	1-0	3-1	4-2	3-3	3-0	2-6	1-0	3-2	4-0	3-0	1-1	2-2	6-3	4-1	4-1	3-2	0-2	4-1	

Division 3 (South)

		Pd	Wn	Dw	Ls	GF	GA	Pts	
1.	Charlton Athletic FC (London)	42	23	8	11	86	60	54	P
2.	Crystal Palace FC (London)	42	23	8	11	81	67	54	
3.	Northampton Town FC (Northampton)	42	20	12	10	96	57	52	
4.	Plymouth Argyle FC (Plymouth)	42	20	12	10	83	51	52	
5.	Fulham FC (London)	42	21	10	11	107	71	52	
6.	Queen's Park Rangers FC (London)	42	19	14	9	82	61	52	
7.	Luton Town FC (Luton)	42	19	11	12	89	73	49	
8.	Watford FC (Watford)	42	19	10	13	79	74	48	
9.	Bournemouth & Boscombe Athletic FC (Bournemouth)	42	19	9	14	84	77	47	
10.	Swindon Town FC (Swindon)	42	15	13	14	75	72	43	
11.	Coventry City FC (Coventry)	42	14	14	14	62	57	42	
12.	Southend United FC (Southend-on-Sea)	42	15	11	16	80	75	41	
13.	Brentford FC (London)	42	14	10	18	56	60	38	
14.	Walsall FC (Walsall)	42	13	12	17	73	79	38	
15.	Brighton & Hove Albion FC (Hove)	42	16	6	20	58	76	38	
16.	Newport County AFC (Newport)	42	13	9	20	69	86	35	
17.	Norwich City FC (Norwich)	42	14	6	22	69	81	34	
18.	Torquay United FC (Torquay)	42	14	6	22	66	84	34	
19.	Bristol Rovers FC (Bristol)	42	13	7	33	60	79	33	
20.	Merthyr Town FC (Merthyr Tydfil)	42	11	8	23	55	103	30	
21.	Exeter City FC (Exeter)	42	9	11	22	67	88	29	
22.	Gillingham FC (Gillingham)	42	10	9	23	43	83	29	
		924	354	216	354	1614	1614	924	

133

F.A. CUP FINAL (Wembley Stadium, London – 27/03/29 – 92,576)

BOLTON WANDERERS FC (BOLTON)   2-0   Portsmouth FC (Portsmouth)

Butler, Blackmore

Bolton: Pym, Haworth, Finney, Kean, Seddon, Nuttall, Butler, McClelland, Blackmore, Gibson, W.Cook.

Portsmouth: Gilfillan, Mackie, Bell, Nichol, McIlwaine, Thackeray, Forward, J.Smith, Weddle, Watson, F.Cook

Semi-finals

Bolton Wanderers FC (Bolton)	2-1	Huddersfield Town AFC (Huddersfield)
Portsmouth FC (Portsmouth)	1-0	Aston Villa FC (Birmingham)

Quarter-finals

Aston Villa FC (Birmingham)	1-0	Arsenal FC (London)
Blackburn Rovers FC (Blackburn)	1-1, 1-2	Bolton Wanderers FC (Bolton)
Portsmouth FC (Portsmouth)	3-2	West Ham United FC (London)
West Bromwich Albion FC (West Bromwich)	1-1, 1-2	Huddersfield Town AFC (Huddersfield)

1929-30

Football League Division 1 1929-1930 Season

	Arsenal	Aston Villa	Birmingham	Blackburn Rovers	Bolton Wanderers	Burnley	Derby County	Everton	Grimsby Town	Huddersfield Town	Leeds United	Leicester City	Liverpool	Manchester City	Manchester United	Middlesbrough	Newcastle United	Portsmouth	Sheffield United	Sheffield Wednesday	Sunderland	West Ham United
Arsenal FC	■	2-4	1-0	4-0	1-2	6-1	1-1	4-0	4-1	2-0	4-0	1-1	0-1	3-2	4-2	1-2	0-1	1-2	8-1	2-3	0-1	0-1
Aston Villa FC	5-2	■	2-1	3-0	2-0	1-2	2-2	5-2	4-1	5-3	3-4	3-0	2-3	0-2	1-0	4-2	2-0	0-1	5-1	1-3	2-1	2-3
Birmingham FC	2-3	1-1	■	1-2	3-1	2-0	2-4	0-0	0-2	4-1	1-0	3-0	1-0	3-0	0-1	1-1	5-1	1-0	2-1	1-0	3-1	4-2
Blackburn Rovers FC	1-1	2-0	7-5	■	3-1	8-3	0-3	3-1	4-1	5-2	2-1	3-1	1-0	1-3	5-4	7-0	4-2	1-0	0-1	0-1	5-3	3-3
Bolton Wanderers FC	0-0	3-0	0-0	2-1	■	1-1	1-2	5-0	2-3	7-1	4-2	1-0	0-2	1-2	4-1	2-2	1-1	2-1	2-1	1-3	3-0	4-1
Burnley FC	2-2	1-4	3-1	3-2	2-2	■	6-2	1-1	3-1	1-3	0-3	1-1	4-1	4-2	4-0	4-1	0-3	4-0	5-0	2-4	2-0	1-1
Derby County FC	4-1	4-0	3-1	4-3	2-1	1-3	■	2-1	5-4	2-2	3-0	2-2	2-2	4-2	1-1	3-1	3-1	3-2	2-1	4-1	3-0	4-3
Everton FC	1-1	3-4	2-4	2-2	3-3	3-0	4-0	■	2-4	0-2	1-1	4-5	3-3	2-3	0-0	3-2	5-2	1-1	3-2	1-4	4-1	1-2
Grimsby Town FC	1-1	0-2	2-1	5-3	1-1	4-0	2-1	0-3	■	4-2	1-2	1-4	3-2	2-2	2-2	0-3	4-0	1-1	4-1	0-5	0-1	2-2
Huddersfield Town AFC	2-2	1-1	1-1	0-0	0-2	3-0	0-1	1-2	0-1	■	1-0	3-2	3-0	1-1	2-2	1-0	2-0	2-1	2-2	4-1	0-2	3-0
Leeds United AFC	2-0	4-1	1-0	4-2	2-1	3-0	2-1	2-1	6-0	0-1	■	1-2	1-1	3-2	3-1	1-2	5-2	1-0	2-2	3-0	5-0	1-3
Leicester City FC	6-6	4-3	2-1	1-1	5-2	4-3	0-0	5-4	1-0	1-2	2-2	■	2-1	3-1	4-1	4-1	6-1	0-5	3-3	2-1	1-2	1-2
Liverpool FC	1-0	2-0	1-1	1-1	3-0	1-3	2-2	0-3	2-0	3-0	1-0	1-1	■	1-6	1-0	5-2	0-0	2-0	1-3	0-6	3-1	
Manchester City FC	3-1	1-2	1-4	1-1	2-0	2-2	3-0	1-2	3-1	1-1	4-1	3-2	4-3	■	0-1	3-1	3-0	5-2	2-1	3-3	2-2	4-3
Manchester United FC	1-0	2-3	0-0	1-0	1-1	1-0	3-2	3-3	2-5	1-0	3-1	2-1	1-2	1-3	■	0-3	5-0	3-0	1-5	2-2	2-1	4-2
Middlesbrough FC	1-1	2-3	5-1	2-4	3-1	3-1	4-0	1-2	1-5	1-3	1-1	0-2	5-0	1-0	2-3	■	2-2	2-0	3-1	4-1	3-0	2-0
Newcastle United FC	1-1	2-2	1-1	5-1	2-3	2-1	2-3	1-0	3-1	5-2	2-1	2-1	3-1	2-2	4-1	3-2	■	4-1	3-5	1-3	3-0	1-0
Portsmouth FC	0-1	1-2	2-1	4-0	3-0	7-1	3-1	1-4	1-1	0-1	0-0	3-0	3-3	2-2	3-0	1-1	2-0	■	3-1	0-4	1-1	3-1
Sheffield United FC	4-1	3-3	4-2	5-7	2-3	3-1	2-0	2-0	2-3	0-1	3-2	7-1	4-0	1-2	3-1	1-3	1-0	2-3	■	2-2	4-2	4-2
Sheffield Wednesday FC	0-2	3-0	1-1	4-0	1-0	4-1	6-3	4-0	1-0	3-1	1-2	4-0	2-1	5-1	7-2	1-0	4-2	1-1	1-1	■	1-1	2-1
Sunderland AFC	0-1	4-1	2-0	3-1	4-1	3-3	3-1	2-2	2-0	1-0	1-4	2-1	2-3	5-2	2-4	3-2	1-0	1-1	3-2	2-4	■	4-2
West Ham United FC	3-2	5-2	0-1	2-3	5-3	1-0	2-0	3-1	2-0	2-3	3-0	1-2	4-1	3-0	2-1	5-3	5-1	0-1	1-0	1-1		■

	Division 1	Pd	Wn	Dw	Ls	GF	GA	Pts	
1.	SHEFFIELD WEDNESDAY FC (SHEFFIELD)	42	26	8	8	105	57	60	
2.	Derby County FC (Derby)	42	21	8	13	90	82	50	
3.	Manchester City FC (Manchester)	42	19	9	14	91	81	47	
4.	Aston Villa FC (Birmingham)	42	21	5	16	92	83	47	
5.	Leeds United AFC (Leeds)	42	20	6	16	79	63	46	
6.	Blackburn Rovers FC (Blackburn)	42	19	7	16	99	93	45	
7.	West Ham United FC (London)	42	19	5	18	86	79	43	
8.	Leicester City FC (Leicester)	42	17	9	16	86	90	43	
9.	Sunderland AFC (Sunderland)	42	18	7	17	76	80	43	
10.	Huddersfield Town AFC (Huddersfield)	42	17	9	16	63	69	43	
11.	Birmingham FC (Birmingham)	42	16	9	17	67	62	41	
12.	Liverpool FC (Liverpool)	42	16	9	17	63	79	41	
13.	Portsmouth FC (Portsmouth)	42	15	10	17	66	62	40	
14.	Arsenal FC (London)	42	14	11	17	78	66	39	
15.	Bolton Wanderers FC (Bolton)	42	15	9	18	74	74	39	
16.	Middlesbrough FC (Middlesbrough)	42	16	6	20	82	84	38	
17.	Manchester United FC (Manchester)	42	15	8	19	67	88	38	
18.	Grimsby Town FC (Cleethorpes)	42	15	7	20	73	89	37	
19.	Newcastle United FC (Newcastle-upon-Tyne)	42	15	7	20	71	92	37	
20.	Sheffield United FC (Sheffield)	42	15	6	21	91	96	36	
21.	Burnley FC (Burnley)	42	14	8	20	79	97	36	R
22.	Everton FC (Liverpool)	42	12	11	19	80	92	35	R
		924	375	174	375	1758	1758	924	

Top Goalscorer

1)	Victor WATSON	(West Ham United FC)	41

Football League Division 2 — 1929-1930 Season

	Barnsley	Blackpool	Bradford City	Bradford P.A.	Bristol City	Bury	Cardiff City	Charlton Ath.	Chelsea	Hull City	Millwall	Nottingham F.	Notts County	Oldham Ath.	Preston N.E.	Reading	Southampton	Stoke City	Swansea Town	Tottenham H.	W.B.A.	Wolves
Barnsley FC		2-4	2-1	1-1	3-1	2-1	2-2	2-0	1-1	3-0	1-2	1-1	2-2	2-1	0-0	1-0	3-1	3-1	1-0	2-0	2-2	3-1
Blackpool FC	2-1		3-0	1-0	7-1	2-1	3-0	6-0	1-1	1-2	4-3	5-1	1-2	3-0	5-1	4-2	5-1	0-2	3-0	3-2	1-0	3-2
Bradford City AFC	0-1	1-1		1-2	3-0	2-1	0-1	4-1	0-1	2-1	1-1	1-2	2-0	2-4	1-1	1-0	2-5	3-0	3-3	0-2	2-2	2-2
Bradford Park Avenue	4-4	5-0	0-2		3-1	2-1	2-0	4-0	1-3	4-2	6-0	5-1	3-3	2-2	5-2	5-2	1-1	3-2	3-0	2-1	5-1	0-0
Bristol City FC	2-1	0-1	1-3	0-0		1-2	2-0	1-1	2-1	4-0	1-0	4-1	0-0	0-4	2-2	5-3	3-1	2-6	2-1	1-0	2-1	1-2
Bury FC	2-1	0-1	2-4	5-1	2-0		4-2	2-2	1-0	2-1	5-1	0-0	2-0	0-2	1-2	2-4	4-2	2-0	1-0	2-1	3-2	3-1
Cardiff City AFC	1-0	4-2	0-1	2-0	1-1	5-1		1-0	1-0	0-1	3-1	1-3	5-0	2-0	2-1	5-2	1-2	0-0	1-0	3-2	1-0	2-0
Charlton Athletic FC	2-0	1-4	1-3	2-0	3-1	1-2	4-1		1-1	4-0	1-1	5-0	1-0	1-1	1-1	0-0	4-1	4-4	0-2	1-0	0-1	2-0
Chelsea FC	2-0	4-0	3-2	1-2	2-1	5-3	1-0	1-1		3-0	3-0	2-0	3-1	1-1	5-0	1-0	2-0	3-2	1-0	3-0	2-0	1-1
Hull City AFC	2-0	0-3	0-0	0-2	0-1	1-3	2-2	0-2	1-3		3-2	1-2	0-0	1-0	2-0	4-2	3-1	3-0	1-0	2-0	3-2	2-0
Millwall FC	2-1	3-1	2-2	1-2	1-1	2-4	2-0	1-1	0-0	0-0		2-2	2-0	2-1	2-0	3-1	1-1	2-1	0-2	2-5	2-1	4-0
Nottingham Forest FC	4-0	0-0	2-1	1-1	5-2	1-2	3-1	0-2	0-0	2-1	1-1		1-1	1-2	2-4	5-0	0-5	2-2	1-0	0-2	2-4	5-2
Notts County FC	3-0	0-2	2-0	1-1	3-1	1-3	2-1	4-0	2-2	4-1	1-1	0-0		1-1	0-3	3-0	1-2	3-3	0-0	1-1	0-1	0-3
Oldham Athletic AFC	3-2	1-2	6-1	5-1	2-2	2-0	4-1	1-0	4-2	3-1	2-2	0-0	2-2		0-2	0-0	3-2	5-0	4-1	0-1	5-0	6-0
Preston North End FC	3-1	4-6	2-2	4-1	2-2	1-1	2-3	0-3	1-2	1-2	3-1	1-2	3-1	0-3		2-1	1-1	5-1	0-0	4-0	2-2	1-1
Reading FC	1-0	1-1	1-1	1-0	1-6	0-1	2-0	3-1	3-1	1-1	0-1	0-1	2-0	1-1	2-0		1-1	0-0	3-1	3-0	2-2	3-1
Southampton FC	4-0	4-2	2-1	2-2	3-0	0-0	1-1	2-0	4-2	2-2	0-0	2-0	2-2	2-0	1-2	4-3		2-1	2-1	1-0	2-0	1-0
Stoke City FC	3-0	0-1	2-0	1-1	6-2	1-0	1-1	1-1	3-1	1-0	6-0	1-1	0-2	2-3	2-2	4-0	2-1		0-1	1-0	0-3	3-0
Swansea Town AFC	0-2	3-0	5-0	2-4	1-1	2-4	1-0	2-0	3-0	2-0	3-1	1-1	3-2	3-0	4-0	0-1	2-2	2-2		0-1	1-0	2-2
Tottenham Hotspur FC	2-1	6-1	1-1	1-1	2-1	2-2	1-2	3-0	3-3	2-2	1-1	2-0	1-1	0-0	3-2	3-1	3-0	2-0	3-0		0-2	4-2
West Bromwich Albion FC	4-2	5-1	4-2	5-0	2-0	5-1	0-2	1-1	2-0	7-1	6-1	1-3	4-2	0-3	2-0	1-0	5-1	2-3	6-2	4-3		7-3
Wolverhampton Wanderers FC	3-0	1-2	6-0	4-4	1-0	2-0	4-0	0-4	0-1	4-2	1-1	2-1	5-1	1-1	4-0	2-1	2-0	2-1	4-1	3-0	2-4	

Division 2

		Pd	Wn	Dw	Ls	GF	GA	Pts	
1.	Blackpool FC (Blackpool)	42	27	4	11	98	67	58	P
2.	Chelsea FC (London)	42	22	11	9	74	46	55	P
3.	Oldham Athletic AFC (Oldham)	42	21	11	10	90	51	53	
4.	Bradford Park Avenue FC (Bradford)	42	19	12	11	91	70	50	
5.	Bury FC (Bury)	42	22	5	15	78	67	49	
6.	West Bromwich Albion FC (West Bromwich)	42	21	5	16	105	73	47	
7.	Southampton FC (Southampton)	42	17	11	14	77	76	45	
8.	Cardiff City AFC (Cardiff)	42	18	8	16	61	59	44	
9.	Wolverhampton Wanderers FC (Wolverhampton)	42	16	9	17	77	79	41	
10.	Nottingham Forest FC (Nottingham)	42	13	15	14	55	69	41	
11.	Stoke City FC (Stoke-on-Trent)	42	16	8	18	74	72	40	
12.	Tottenham Hotspur FC (London)	42	15	9	18	59	61	39	
13.	Charlton Athletic FC (London)	42	14	11	17	59	63	39	
14.	Millwall FC (London)	42	12	15	15	57	73	39	
15.	Swansea Town AFC (Swansea)	42	14	9	19	57	61	37	
16.	Preston North End FC (Preston)	42	13	11	19	65	80	37	
17.	Barnsley FC (Barnsley)	42	14	8	20	56	71	36	
18.	Bradford City AFC (Bradford)	42	12	12	18	60	77	36	
19.	Reading FC (Reading)	42	12	11	19	54	67	35	
20.	Bristol City FC (Bristol)	42	13	9	20	61	83	35	
21.	Hull City AFC (Kingston-upon-Hull)	42	14	7	21	51	78	35	R
22.	Notts County FC (Nottingham)	42	9	15	18	54	70	33	R
		924	354	216	354	1513	1513	924	

Football League Division 3 (N) 1929-1930 Season	Accrington St.	Barrow	Carlisle United	Chesterfield	Crewe Alexandra	Darlington	Doncaster R.	Halifax Town	Hartlepools Utd.	Lincoln City	Nelson	New Brighton	Port Vale	Rochdale	Rotherham Utd.	Southport	South Shields	Stockport Co.	Tranmere Rovers	Wigan Borough	Wrexham	York City
Accrington Stanley FC		3-1	7-2	3-0	0-3	3-1	3-3	7-1	3-0	0-3	3-0	5-0	0-2	6-2	2-0	1-1	1-2	0-1	3-3	3-1	1-3	1-1
Barrow AFC	3-1		0-2	0-1	1-0	0-1	1-0	0-4	3-0	2-1	0-2	3-0	1-1	2-0	5-1	0-2	1-3	1-4	1-1	4-1	3-3	0-0
Carlisle United FC	2-1	7-1		6-0	2-0	1-4	1-1	2-0	5-2	2-4	2-2	2-2	1-4	2-0	3-1	4-0	4-1	1-5	4-3	5-0	5-1	2-2
Chesterfield FC	4-2	2-1	3-1		5-1	4-1	2-1	2-0	2-1	3-0	1-0	1-1	2-0	2-1	2-0	1-2	1-3	1-0	5-0	5-0	5-0	3-0
Crewe Alexandra FC	2-1	0-0	1-2	2-1		1-2	4-0	4-1	5-2	1-1	4-0	2-3	0-2	6-1	6-1	5-4	2-2	1-1	3-1	2-1	2-0	2-2
Darlington FC	2-4	4-0	3-0	1-4	3-0		6-2	3-2	0-0	1-1	6-1	1-2	0-1	3-0	8-1	2-1	8-3	1-2	7-2	2-0	5-1	5-2
Doncaster Rovers FC	3-1	4-0	1-4	2-1	2-1	3-1		1-0	0-0	3-0	1-1	0-2	3-1	2-0	3-1	1-0	1-1	1-1	4-2	4-2	0-3
Halifax Town AFC	1-1	0-1	1-0	3-2	1-3	3-1	1-0		0-0	1-1	1-1	4-0	1-2	2-3	1-1	0-2	0-3	0-1	1-2	2-0	2-0
Hartlepools United FC	2-2	2-0	1-0	0-0	5-1	2-5	3-0	3-0		4-0	1-2	1-1	2-0	2-8	1-1	2-1	0-1	2-0	4-0	5-0	3-1
Lincoln City FC	3-3	3-0	4-1	2-1	2-2	2-2	3-1	0-1	2-2		4-1	5-3	3-2	0-0	1-1	1-1	2-2	1-0	8-0	2-0	3-0	3-0
Nelson FC	2-1	2-0	2-2	0-2	1-1	0-1	4-1	1-0	3-2	0-0		2-1	2-3	1-0	0-1	2-2	0-1	1-2	0-1	1-3	4-0	3-1
New Brighton FC	5-0	5-0	2-1	1-1	3-1	1-3	4-0	0-0	1-4	2-1		0-1	2-2	1-3	4-1	3-2	3-0	5-0	2-1	1-1
Port Vale FC	5-2	5-0	4-0	4-1	2-0	0-2	2-1	3-0	2-1	5-2	3-1	5-1		3-3	7-1	1-0	3-0	1-2	1-0	4-0	3-0	1-1
Rochdale AFC	4-0	6-1	2-0	2-1	3-1	4-1	2-4	0-3	1-1	3-4	4-1	5-0	0-0		1-2	2-2	2-0	3-1	2-1	2-1	5-4	4-2
Rotherham United FC	2-4	7-0	4-1	1-1	1-4	1-4	1-0	2-0	0-4	1-0	1-2	2-2	2-2	0-4		6-3	0-1	2-2	5-0	4-1	1-3	2-5
Southport FC	2-0	0-2	4-3	5-1	0-3	3-0	1-1	4-0	1-1	3-2	0-0	1-1	1-2	2-3	7-1		2-1	1-2	4-4	1-1	5-3	1-0
South Shields FC	2-2	2-0	5-2	3-1	1-0	3-3	2-1	1-0	3-5	3-1	2-1	1-2	0-0	2-2	5-0	4-0		2-3	1-5	2-2	1-1	4-1
Stockport County FC	1-0	5-0	7-1	1-0	2-3	4-0	3-0	6-0	5-1	1-1	6-1	2-0	4-2	4-2	6-1	2-2	2-0		3-1	1-1	0-1	2-3
Tranmere Rovers FC	2-2	5-2	3-0	1-2	1-2	3-2	1-3	7-1	0-1	2-3	1-1	3-1	1-5	5-4	3-1	3-0	2-0		3-0	2-1	4-4
Wigan Borough FC	2-1	2-0	8-0	2-1	2-2	3-2	3-2	2-1	1-3	4-1	2-0	5-0	0-3	3-1	1-1	1-1	1-1	0-1	0-2		2-1	0-2
Wrexham AFC	0-1	3-0	3-3	1-1	1-0	2-2	0-2	2-1	3-5	3-1	5-1	2-1	0-2	8-0	1-0	1-2	1-3	1-1	2-0	2-1		1-1
York City FC	2-0	3-1	2-2	1-1	4-2	1-1	2-2	3-0	4-1	1-0	1-0	3-0	0-2	6-0	3-0	0-4	2-2	1-2	4-0	4-0	0-0	

Division 3 (North)

		Pd	Wn	Dw	Ls	GF	GA	Pts	
1.	Port Vale FC (Stoke-on-Trent)	42	30	7	5	103	37	67	P
2.	Stockport County FC (Stockport)	42	28	7	7	106	44	63	
3.	Darlington FC (Darlington)	42	22	6	14	108	73	50	
4.	Chesterfield FC (Chesterfield)	42	22	6	14	76	56	50	
5.	Lincoln City FC (Lincoln)	42	17	14	11	83	61	48	
6.	York City FC (York)	42	15	16	11	77	64	46	
7.	South Shields FC (South Shields)	42	18	10	14	77	74	46	*
8.	Hartlepools United FC (Hartlepool)	42	17	11	14	81	74	45	
9.	Southport FC (Southport)	42	15	13	14	81	74	43	
10.	Rochdale AFC (Rochdale)	42	18	7	17	89	91	43	
11.	Crewe Alexandra FC (Crewe)	42	17	8	17	82	71	42	
12.	Tranmere Rovers FC (Birkenhead)	42	16	9	17	83	86	41	
13.	New Brighton FC (Wallasey)	42	16	8	18	69	79	40	
14.	Doncaster Rovers FC (Doncaster)	42	15	9	18	62	69	39	
15.	Carlisle United FC (Carlisle)	42	16	7	19	90	101	39	
16.	Accrington Stanley FC (Accrington)	42	14	9	19	84	81	37	
17.	Wrexham AFC (Wrexham)	42	13	8	21	67	88	34	
18.	Wigan Borough FC (Wigan)	42	13	7	22	60	88	33	
19.	Nelson FC (Nelson)	42	13	7	22	51	80	33	
20.	Rotherham United FC (Rotherham)	42	11	8	23	67	113	30	
21.	Halifax Town AFC (Halifax)	42	10	8	24	44	79	28	
22.	Barrow AFC (Barrow-in-Furness)	42	11	5	26	41	98	27	
		924	367	190	367	1681	1681	924	

* South Shields FC (South Shields) moved to the town of Gateshead and changed their name to Gateshead FC.

Football League Division 3 (S) — 1929-1930 Season

	Bournemouth	Brentford	Brighton	Bristol Rovers	Clapton Orient	Coventry City	Crystal Palace	Exeter City	Fulham	Gillingham	Luton Town	Merthyr Town	Newport County	Northampton	Norwich City	Plymouth Arg.	Q.P.R.	Southend Utd.	Swindon Town	Torquay United	Walsall	Watford
Bournemouth & B. Athletic	■	1-2	1-1	3-1	5-1	1-0	2-1	3-0	5-0	1-2	5-1	4-2	1-1	3-1	2-3	1-1	0-0	0-0	1-3	4-1	1-1	3-2
Brentford FC	1-0	■	5-2	2-1	3-1	3-1	2-0	2-0	5-1	2-1	2-0	6-0	1-0	2-0	3-0	3-0	3-0	2-1	3-2	5-0	6-2	5-0
Brighton & Hove Albion	4-3	2-0	■	1-0	1-0	1-1	1-2	1-1	5-0	2-0	4-1	4-1	3-2	2-1	6-3	0-1	2-3	1-0	3-0	5-0	4-0	2-1
Bristol Rovers FC	2-1	4-1	1-0	■	0-0	1-3	2-3	1-0	4-1	3-0	2-2	2-2	2-3	2-3	0-1	2-3	4-1	4-2	3-2	2-0	3-1	1-2
Clapton Orient FC	0-0	1-1	4-1	3-0	■	3-1	2-1	3-0	2-4	2-0	6-1	1-0	3-1	0-0	0-0	0-2	2-4	1-1	2-1	1-1	1-1	1-1
Coventry City FC	0-2	2-1	0-2	1-0	5-2	■	1-0	3-3	3-1	5-0	5-1	2-2	2-0	2-2	3-1	1-0	2-3	5-1	1-2	4-1	4-0	3-1
Crystal Palace FC	1-1	2-1	2-2	3-0	3-0	4-3	■	1-1	4-3	5-1	4-1	6-1	1-0	1-3	3-2	3-0	1-1	1-2	1-0	4-2	5-1	1-1
Exeter City FC	1-2	0-0	1-4	5-2	4-0	1-1	6-1	■	2-1	3-0	2-2	1-1	0-4	6-4	3-0	1-1	0-2	3-1	5-1	0-0	0-2	1-0
Fulham FC	3-3	2-0	5-1	6-2	2-2	2-0	1-2	2-2	■	2-1	1-1	5-4	2-1	1-0	3-3	1-3	0-2	2-2	4-1	1-0	3-2	6-1
Gillingham FC	1-5	1-3	2-2	3-3	2-0	0-3	1-1	2-0	0-1	■	2-0	6-0	5-0	5-2	1-2	0-0	3-1	1-0	0-0	0-0	2-1	1-2
Luton Town FC	1-0	2-1	1-0	3-0	1-2	2-2	2-2	0-4	4-1	2-0	■	4-0	4-2	1-0	1-1	5-2	2-1	0-3	1-1	3-1	2-3	2-2
Merthyr Town FC	0-1	2-3	2-8	1-1	0-1	2-2	5-2	0-2	3-4	1-1	3-1	■	5-1	1-0	1-5	0-3	1-4	2-2	3-3	3-0	2-3	2-1
Newport County AFC	1-1	1-3	2-2	2-2	0-0	4-2	0-0	4-1	1-1	5-1	0-0	10-0	■	2-1	4-4	0-2	4-5	0-0	2-1	2-1	3-2	1-1
Northampton Town FC	2-0	1-1	1-3	6-1	3-0	2-2	2-0	2-2	3-1	3-1	4-1	2-0	2-0	■	4-0	1-1	2-1	5-1	3-3	2-2	1-0	2-1
Norwich City FC	1-0	2-2	2-0	4-2	1-0	10-2	2-2	3-1	0-4	2-0	1-1	5-1	4-1	4-3	■	1-2	3-0	1-1	1-5	2-0	3-0	3-1
Plymouth Argyle FC	2-1	1-1	1-1	3-0	3-0	3-0	6-1	4-1	3-0	6-1	2-1	3-1	1-0	4-1		■	4-0	1-0	5-0	5-0	1-1	2-1
Queen's Park Rangers FC	3-1	2-1	3-1	2-1	1-1	3-1	4-1	20	0-0	2-1	1-0	2-0	4-1	0-2	3-2	1-2	■	2-5	8-3	1-1	2-2	0-0
Southend United FC	4-1	2-0	0-0	6-0	4-1	1-2	3-2	1-0	1-2	0-0	1-1	6-0	2-1	1-2	1-1	1-1	1-0	■	3-1	1-1	1-0	1-3
Swindon Town FC	1-1	0-2	0-1	2-2	0-0	1-1	3-1	1-0	1-1	3-0	1-1	6-3	5-1	2-0	2-1	1-2	2-2	5-1	■	2-1	3-1	1-3
Torquay United FC	7-0	2-1	5-2	2-1	0-5	1-3	2-2	2-1	2-4	1-1	2-2	4-0	3-2	0-1	2-2	3-4	1-3	1-1	1-1	■	5-2	4-0
Walsall FC	2-2	1-2	2-0	0-0	0-1	3-2	0-0	5-2	2-2	1-2	1-0	6-0	2-1	1-2	1-0	1-3	4-0	1-3	4-0	7-0	■	1-2
Watford FC	0-0	1-2	3-0	4-3	3-0	1-3	1-1	2-1	0-0	4-1	0-4	2-3	2-3	1-2	2-1	0-2	1-1	2-1	4-1	2-0	2-1	■

Division 3 (South)

		Pd	Wn	Dw	Ls	GF	GA	Pts	
1.	Plymouth Argyle FC (Plymouth)	42	30	8	4	98	38	68	P
2.	Brentford FC (London)	42	28	5	9	94	44	61	
3.	Queen's Park Rangers FC (London)	42	21	9	12	80	68	51	
4.	Northampton Town FC (Northampton)	42	21	8	13	82	58	50	
5.	Brighton & Hove Albion FC (Hove)	42	21	8	13	87	63	50	
6.	Coventry City FC (Coventry)	42	19	9	14	88	73	47	
7.	Fulham FC (London)	42	18	11	13	87	83	47	
8.	Norwich City FC (Norwich)	42	18	10	14	88	77	46	
9.	Crystal Palace FC (London)	42	17	12	13	81	74	46	
10.	Bournemouth & Boscombe Athletic FC (Bournemouth)	42	15	13	14	72	61	43	
11.	Southend United FC (Southend-on-Sea)	42	15	13	14	69	59	43	
12.	Clapton Orient FC (London)	42	14	13	15	55	62	41	
13.	Luton Town FC (Luton)	42	14	12	16	64	78	40	
14.	Swindon Town FC (Swindon)	42	13	12	17	73	83	38	
15.	Watford FC (Watford)	42	15	8	19	60	73	38	
16.	Exeter City FC (Exeter)	42	12	11	19	67	73	35	
17.	Walsall FC (Walsall)	42	13	8	21	71	78	34	
18.	Newport County AFC (Newport)	42	12	10	20	74	85	34	
19.	Torquay United FC (Torquay)	42	10	11	21	64	94	31	
20.	Bristol Rovers FC (Bristol)	42	11	8	23	67	93	30	
21.	Gillingham FC (Gillingham)	42	11	8	23	51	80	30	
22.	Merthyr Town FC (Merthyr Tydfil)	42	6	9	27	60	135	21	#
		924	354	216	354	1632	1632	924	

\# Merthyr Town FC (Merthyr Tydfil) were not re-elected to the league for the next season.

Elected: Thames FC (London)

F.A. CUP FINAL   (Wembley Stadium, London – 26/04/1930 – 92,448)

ARSENAL FC (LONDON)   2-0   Huddersfield Town AFC (Huddersfield)

James, Lambert

Arsenal: Preedy, Parker, Hapgood, Baker, Seddon, John, Hulme, Jack, Lambert, James, Bastin.

Huddersfield: Turner, Goodall, Spence, Naylor, Wilson, Campbell, A.Jackson, Kelly, Davies, Raw, WH Smith.

Semi-finals

Arsenal FC (London)	2-2, 1-0	Hull City AFC (Kingston-upon-Hull)
Huddersfield Town AFC (Huddersfield)	2-1	Sheffield Wednesday FC (Sheffield)

Quarter-finals

Aston Villa FC (Birmingham)	1-2	Huddersfield Town AFC (Huddersfield)
Newcastle United FC (Newcastle-upon-Tyne)	1-1, 0-1	Hull City AFC (Kingston-upon-Hull)
Nottingham Forest FC (Nottingham)	2-2, 1-3	Sheffield Wednesday FC (Sheffield)
West Ham United FC (London)	0-3	Arsenal FC (London)

1930-31

Football League Division 1 1930-1931 Season	Arsenal	Aston Villa	Birmingham	Blackburn Rovers	Blackpool	Bolton Wanderers	Chelsea	Derby County	Grimsby Town	Huddersfield Town	Leeds United	Leicester City	Liverpool	Manchester City	Manchester United	Middlesbrough	Newcastle United	Portsmouth	Sheffield United	Sheffield Wednesday	Sunderland	West Ham United
Arsenal FC		5-2	1-1	3-2	7-1	5-0	2-1	6-3	9-1	0-0	3-1	4-1	3-1	3-1	4-1	5-3	1-2	1-1	1-1	2-0	1-3	1-1
Aston Villa FC	5-1		1-1	5-2	4-1	3-1	3-3	4-6	2-0	6-1	4-3	4-2	4-2	4-2	7-0	8-1	4-3	2-2	4-0	2-0	42	6-1
Birmingham FC	2-4	0-4		4-1	1-1	0-2	6-2	1-2	4-1	2-0	0-1	2-1	2-0	3-2	0-0	1-2	1-1	2-1	3-1	2-0	1-0	0-2
Blackburn Rovers FC	2-2	0-2	2-1		5-0	2-2	2-0	1-0	5-2	5-3	3-1	3-0	3-3	0-1	4-1	4-5	1-0	1-2	2-1	5-2	3-0	1-0
Blackpool FC	1-4	2-2	0-1	1-1		3-3	2-1	1-0	3-1	1-1	3-7	5-4	1-3	2-2	5-1	3-2	0-0	2-2	2-1	0-4	3-1	1-3
Bolton Wanderers FC	1-4	1-1	2-0	1-1	1-0		1-1	1-2	4-2	1-0	2-0	4-1	2-0	1-1	3-1	3-0	0-3	3-1	6-2	2-2	2-2	4-2
Chelsea FC	1-5	0-2	1-0	3-2	3-0	0-1		1-1	5-0	1-2	1-0	1-0	2-2	2-0	6-2	4-0	1-1	2-0	1-0	0-0	5-0	2-1
Derby County FC	4-2	1-1	0-0	1-1	3-2	4-1	6-2		1-0	4-1	4-1	1-0	2-2	1-1	6-1	1-2	1-5	5-1	4-3	2-3	4-1	1-1
Grimsby Town FC	0-1	1-2	4-1	2-0	6-2	4-1	0-1	5-3		2-1	2-0	8-2	0-0	3-5	2-1	4-1	2-2	0-3	2-1	2-3	2-1	4-0
Huddersfield Town AFC	1-1	1-6	1-0	1-1	10-1	3-2	1-1	3-0	2-2		3-0	4-1	2-1	1-1	3-0	2-2	0-3	1-3	1-1	1-1	2-0	2-0
Leeds United AFC	1-2	0-2	3-1	4-2	2-2	3-1	2-3	3-1	0-0	1-2		1-3	1-2	4-2	5-0	7-0	1-0	2-2	4-0	2-3	0-3	3-0
Leicester City FC	2-7	4-1	2-1	3-1	6-0	2-1	2-1	1-1	0-1	1-2	4-0		3-2	3-2	5-4	0-3	3-1	3-1	2-2	2-5	1-1	1-1
Liverpool FC	1-1	1-1	0-0	2-1	5-2	7-2	3-1	0-0	1-1	1-4	2-0	3-1		0-2	1-1	3-4	2-1	6-1	1-2	2-4	2-0	
Manchester City FC	1-4	3-1	4-2	3-0	2-4	3-0	2-0	4-3	1-0	0-1	1-0	0-2	1-1		4-1	4-2	2-0	1-3	0-4	2-0	2-0	1-1
Manchester United FC	1-2	3-4	2-0	0-1	0-0	1-1	1-0	2-1	0-2	0-6	0-0	0-0	4-1	1-3		4-4	4-7	0-1	1-2	4-1	1-1	1-0
Middlesbrough FC	2-5	3-1	1-1	4-1	5-1	3-0	2-2	4-1	2-1	-3	5-0	2-2	3-3	4-1	3-1		3-1	0-1	4-1	2-0	1-0	2-2
Newcastle United FC	1-3	2-0	2-2	2-3	0-2	4-0	1-0	2-5	1-2	1-1	4-1	5-2	0-4	0-1	4-3	0-5		4-7	1-0	1-2	2-0	4-2
Portsmouth FC	1-1	5-0	2-2	3-0	4-3	1-0	1-1	2-0	4-3	2-2	1-1	2-1	4-0	1-1	4-1	1-0	1-2		2-3	2-4	1-1	2-0
Sheffield United FC	1-1	3-4	3-1	1-1	5-1	2-0	4-0	3-3	2-1	0-2	1-1	0-2	4-1	2-2	3-1	4-2	3-1	3-1		1-1	3-3	1-2
Sheffield Wednesday FC	1-2	3-3	9-1	1-3	7-1	1-0	1-1	3-2	4-1	2-1	4-0	3-5	1-3	3-0	3-2	2-2	1-3				7-2	5-3
Sunderland AFC	1-4	1-1	1-0	8-2	2-4	3-1	2-0	1-3	3-2	4-2	4-0	2-5	6-5	3-3	1-2	1-1	5-0	0-0	2-1	5-1		6-1
West Ham United FC	2-4	5-5	1-2	4-3	3-2	1-4	4-1	0-1	3-4	2-1	1-1	2-0	7-0	2-0	5-1	0-3	3-2	4-3	4-1	3-3	0-3	

	Division 1	Pd	Wn	Dw	Ls	GF	GA	Pts	
1.	ARSENAL FC (LONDON)	42	28	10	4	127	59	66	
2.	Aston Villa FC (Birmingham)	42	25	9	8	128	78	59	
3.	Sheffield Wednesday FC (Sheffield)	42	22	8	12	102	75	52	
4.	Portsmouth FC (Portsmouth)	42	18	13	11	84	67	49	
5.	Huddersfield Town AFC (Huddersfield)	42	18	12	12	81	65	48	
6.	Derby County FC (Derby)	42	18	10	14	94	79	46	
7.	Middlesbrough FC (Middlesbrough)	42	19	8	15	98	90	46	
8.	Manchester City FC (Manchester)	42	18	10	14	75	70	46	
9.	Liverpool FC (Liverpool)	42	15	12	15	86	85	42	
10.	Blackburn Rovers FC (Blackburn)	42	17	8	17	83	84	42	
11.	Sunderland AFC (Sunderland)	42	16	9	17	89	85	41	
12.	Chelsea FC (London)	42	15	10	17	64	67	40	
13.	Grimsby Town FC (Cleethorpes)	42	17	5	20	82	87	39	
14.	Bolton Wanderers FC (Bolton)	42	15	9	18	68	81	39	
15.	Sheffield United FC (Sheffield)	42	14	10	18	78	84	38	
16.	Leicester City FC (Leicester)	42	16	6	20	80	95	38	
17.	Newcastle United FC (Newcastle-upon-Tyne)	42	15	6	21	78	87	36	
18.	West Ham United FC (London)	42	14	8	20	79	94	36	
19.	Birmingham FC (Birmingham)	42	13	10	19	55	70	36	
20.	Blackpool FC (Blackpool)	42	11	10	21	71	125	32	
21.	Leeds United AFC (Leeds)	42	12	7	23	68	81	31	R
22.	Manchester United FC (Manchester)	42	7	8	27	53	115	22	R
		924	363	198	363	1823	1823	924	

Top Goalscorer

1)	Tom WARING	(Aston Villa FC)	49

Football League Division 2 1930-1931 Season	Barnsley	Bradford City	Bradford P.A.	Bristol City	Burnley	Bury	Cardiff City	Charlton Ath.	Everton	Millwall	Nottingham F.	Oldham Ath.	Plymouth Arg.	Port Vale	Preston N.E.	Reading	Southampton	Stoke City	Swansea T.	Tottenham H.	W.B.A.	Wolves
Barnsley FC	■	2-1	1-0	1-0	0-1	2-1	4-0	5-0	1-1	2-3	3-1	1-2	0-4	5-2	1-1	3-2	3-1	4-2	1-0	0-1	0-0	3-0
Bradford City AFC	1-0	■	0-4	1-1	2-3	3-1	2-1	3-2	0-3	0-0	1-0	0-0	1-0	2-1	0-0	6-1	4-3	2-2	3-0	2-0	2-3	4-1
Bradford Park Avenue	1-0	1-2	■	5-2	4-1	5-1	3-0	3-2	4-1	6-0	4-1	4-0	7-1	5-1	5-2	1-3	1-1	2-2	5-1	4-1	3-1	1-1
Bristol City FC	2-1	0-1	2-0	■	1-1	4-2	1-0	3-0	0-1	1-2	1-4	1-0	2-1	1-1	1-0	2-1	1-1	2-1	2-1	1-1	1-1	0-3
Burnley FC	2-2	1-1	3-2	4-2	■	0-2	1-0	1-1	5-2	2-1	5-2	6-1	2-2	1-2	1-0	8-1	3-2	1-2	2-2	1-0	2-1	4-2
Bury FC	3-1	3-1	3-1	6-0	2-1	■	3-0	0-1	2-2	5-0	1-0	1-3	2-0	0-3	3-0	2-2	1-0	3-0	2-0	2-0	2-2	1-0
Cardiff City AFC	2-0	1-1	0-3	0-1	4-0	1-3	■	0-2	1-2	4-4	1-1	0-0	4-1	2-1	0-0	5-0	0-1	3-2	1-1	0-3	3-6	0-3
Charlton Athletic FC	1-1	2-1	3-1	0-0	2-1	3-2	4-1	■	0-7	2-0	1-1	1-1	1-3	3-1	1-3	2-1	3-1	1-2	3-0	1-0	0-4	1-2
Everton FC	5-2	4-2	4-2	1-3	3-2	3-2	1-1	7-1	■	2-0	2-0	6-4	9-1	2-3	2-1	3-2	2-1	5-0	5-1	4-2	2-1	4-0
Millwall FC	4-1	1-1	1-1	2-1	1-0	0-0	6-0	1-3	0-1	■	5-1	4-0	1-0	5-7	4-0	1-0	1-3	1-0	2-0	2-3	2-0	1-1
Nottingham Forest FC	3-3	4-1	1-0	6-1	3-3	3-0	3-1	4-3	2-2	2-1	■	4-1	1-1	1-0	1-4	1-1	3-1	3-0	3-0	2-2	1-6	3-4
Oldham Athletic AFC	0-0	3-0	2-0	1-3	3-1	3-2	4-2	0-3	3-3	3-1	3-1	■	2-1	3-3	2-0	1-1	2-1	1-3	1-1	1-2	2-2	2-0
Plymouth Argyle FC	4-0	0-2	0-0	5-3	1-2	3-6	5-1	1-3	2-3	5-0	1-0	1-1	■	2-1	1-2	3-1	2-3	1-2	0-0	2-0	0-5	3-2
Port Vale FC	5-2	1-0	8-2	1-0	0-0	0-1	2-0	1-1	1-3	3-2	3-2	2-0	2-1	■	1-0	2-1	1-0	0-0	2-0	3-0	1-0	0-1
Preston North End FC	1-1	4-2	1-1	2-2	2-0	3-0	7-0	4-1	2-1	1-3	2-4	1-0	2-1	1-3	■	3-3	5-0	5-1	0-0	2-1	2-3	5-4
Reading FC	6-1	0-0	3-0	4-1	3-1	3-4	3-0	2-0	0-2	5-2	1-3	1-2	0-3	1-4	1-3	■	1-1	7-3	1-0	1-2	0-3	3-0
Southampton FC	4-0	4-1	2-3	5-1	5-0	1-0	0-1	3-0	2-1	3-1	3-1	2-1	3-3	2-0	2-1	3-2	■	2-1	1-2	0-3	1-2	2-1
Stoke City FC	0-0	1-1	1-1	3-1	1-1	3-1	1-0	0-0	2-0	2-3	1-0	4-0	0-0	1-0	3-1	2-1	1-3	■	5-0	2-1	0-1	1-2
Swansea Town AFC	1-0	1-2	2-1	5-2	1-1	5-2	3-2	1-1	2-5	4-1	3-2	0-0	2-0	2-1	2-1	2-1	0-1	1-2	■	1-2	1-1	1-1
Tottenham Hotspur FC	4-2	3-1	3-2	4-1	8-1	3-1	2-2	5-0	1-0	4-1	2-1	4-0	1-1	5-0	0-0	7-1	1-3	3-0	1-1	■	2-2	1-0
West Bromwich Albion FC	5-0	1-0	1-1	3-0	2-0	2-0	3-2	3-2	1-2	0-0	2-1	2-0	1-2	4-1	2-0	1-0	4-0	0-0	0-2	1-1	■	2-1
Wolverhampton Wanderers FC	2-0	0-1	1-1	0-1	2-4	7-0	4-1	1-1	3-1	2-0	4-2	3-0	4-3	3-0	2-0	3-1	3-2	5-1	3-1	3-1	1-4	■

Division 2

		Pd	Wn	Dw	Ls	GF	GA	Pts	
1.	Everton FC (Liverpool)	42	28	5	9	121	66	61	P
2.	West Bromwich Albion FC (West Bromwich)	42	22	10	10	83	49	54	P
3.	Tottenham Hotspur FC (London)	42	22	7	13	88	55	51	
4.	Wolverhampton Wanderers FC (Wolverhampton)	42	21	5	16	84	67	47	
5.	Port Vale FC (Stoke-on-Trent)	42	21	5	16	67	61	47	
6.	Bradford Park Avenue FC (Bradford)	42	18	10	14	97	66	46	
7.	Preston North End FC (Preston)	42	17	11	14	83	64	45	
8.	Burnley FC (Burnley)	42	17	11	14	81	77	45	
9.	Southampton FC (Southampton)	42	19	6	17	74	62	44	
10.	Bradford City AFC (Bradford)	42	17	10	15	61	63	44	
11.	Stoke City FC (Stoke-on-Trent)	42	17	10	15	64	71	44	
12.	Oldham Athletic AFC (Oldham)	42	16	10	16	61	72	42	
13.	Bury FC (Bury)	42	19	3	20	75	82	41	
14.	Millwall FC (London)	42	16	7	19	71	80	39	
15.	Charlton Athletic FC (London)	42	15	9	18	59	86	39	
16.	Bristol City FC (Bristol)	42	15	8	19	54	82	38	
17.	Nottingham Forest FC (Nottingham)	42	14	9	19	80	85	37	
18.	Plymouth Argyle FC (Plymouth)	42	14	8	20	76	84	36	
19.	Barnsley FC (Barnsley)	42	13	9	20	59	79	35	
20.	Swansea Town AFC (Swansea)	42	12	10	20	51	74	34	
21.	Reading FC (Reading)	42	12	6	24	72	96	30	R
22.	Cardiff City AFC (Cardiff)	42	8	9	25	47	87	25	R
		924	373	178	373	1608	1608	924	

Football League Division 3 (N) 1930-1931 Season

	Accrington St.	Barrow	Carlisle United	Chesterfield	Crewe Alex.	Darlington	Doncaster R.	Gateshead	Halifax Town	Hartlepools Utd.	Hull City	Lincoln City	Nelson	New Brighton	Rochdale	Rotherham Utd.	Southport	Stockport Co.	Tranmere R.	Wigan Borough	Wrexham	York City
Accrington Stanley FC		3-1	3-0	1-3	3-1	2-1	2-0	2-1	1-1	0-2	1-3	5-3	3-1	3-0	2-3	3-2	2-0	2-2	5-2	3-0	1-3	4-2
Barrow AFC	0-0		7-2	0-3	2-0	3-2	3-1	0-0	3-1	4-0	3-0	3-2	2-1	4-1	0-0	1-0	1-1	1-0	1-3	4-1	2-3	1-2
Carlisle United FC	7-3	0-1		0-0	4-1	2-1	1-1	2-2	6-2	3-0	1-5	3-6	8-1	2-0	7-1	1-2	4-3	5-1	3-0	6-1	1-1	2-0
Chesterfield FC	7-3	3-1	2-1		2-0	2-1	2-1	8-1	7-0	3-0	0-4	3-2	2-1	1-0	4-1	2-1	1-1	5-1	3-1	4-0	3-1	2-1
Crewe Alexandra FC	2-1	6-2	3-5	2-1		2-2	2-1	6-2	0-1	2-1	3-4	2-0	4-2	1-3	3-1	2-3	0-0	1-0	1-2	3-2	2-1	5-1
Darlington FC	1-1	3-2	3-0	5-1	1-2		0-0	2-2	4-1	4-2	2-4	0-1	2-1	3-1	1-1	2-2	2-3	1-2	2-0	2-3	1-1	3-0
Doncaster Rovers FC	6-1	0-0	2-0	1-0	2-0	1-2		1-1	3-3	1-1	0-2	0-1	2-0	0-0	4-0	3-3	0-0	2-0	6-0	5-1	1-1	0-2
Gateshead FC	4-0	4-1	1-0	3-3	2-2	1-1	2-1		3-1	0-0	1-0	1-0	2-0	4-0	0-2	2-0	2-3	2-1	3-0	4-2	4-3	2-1
Halifax Town AFC	1-1	4-0	1-5	1-1	4-0	1-0	0-2	3-0		3-1	1-1	3-2	1-0	1-0	1-0	0-0	3-0	2-1	0-1	0-0	0-0	2-1
Hartlepools United FC	3-3	3-2	3-5	1-3	2-0	1-1	0-2	2-3	2-1		1-3	0-3	4-0	4-1	4-2	1-2	1-2	1-2	6-1	2-1	3-0	2-1
Hull City AFC	1-1	1-1	1-1	3-1	5-1	4-1	8-2	4-0	10-0	5-0		1-3	4-0	3-0	3-1	2-2	5-1	1-1	1-0	0-0	2-3	3-1
Lincoln City FC	5-2	5-0	5-1	1-1	3-1	1-0	1-0	0-0	4-1	3-1	3-1		2-0	4-0	5-0	1-3	3-3	6-1	1-3	2-0	3-2	4-1
Nelson FC	4-2	0-3	1-2	0-5	1-1	3-1	2-0	2-2	3-2	1-1	0-2	1-2		2-2	1-1	0-4	1-1	0-4	2-1	2-0	2-0	2-5
New Brighton FC	0-0	3-1	2-0	3-1	3-0	1-5	2-1	0-0	3-0	1-0	1-1	2-1	2-0		2-1	3-1	1-2	0-2	1-3	0-2	1-1	5-3
Rochdale AFC	1-6	4-2	1-3	2-3	1-0	1-2	3-5	0-1	2-3	1-2	1-0	4-2	5-4	2-0		6-1	0-4	1-0	1-3	0-4	4-3	2-2
Rotherham United FC	8-1	6-0	1-0	0-1	1-1	0-2	3-0	1-1	2-1	1-1	1-2	3-0	2-0	1-3	2-1		3-3	3-4	4-6	5-2	1-4	2-1
Southport FC	3-3	3-2	1-2	3-0	3-1	0-1	2-1	1-0	5-2	2-0	1-0	1-2	8-1	3-0	4-0	4-1		2-0	1-1	3-1	1-1	1-0
Stockport County FC	4-1	6-0	3-0	2-1	2-0	0-1	2-2	3-1	3-0	3-1	3-2	4-2	1-0	2-0	2-2	5-2	2-0		1-1	4-1	2-2	0-0
Tranmere Rovers FC	8-0	5-0	2-0	2-0	0-0	1-2	1-2	2-2	2-2	6-4	3-3	7-1	3-0	7-3	4-2	3-1	3-0	3-1		5-1	2-0	4-1
Wigan Borough FC	3-2	2-1	1-2	1-5	6-0	2-0	3-0	3-3	3-0	3-1	0-1	3-1	1-1	0-1	3-1	0-0	1-0	4-3	1-1		1-1	3-1
Wrexham AFC	6-1	1-1	2-1	2-1	7-0	2-0	4-1	5-1	3-2	2-0	2-0	2-2	5-1	2-1	1-1	3-2	2-4	3-2	2-2	2-0		3-2
York City FC	3-1	4-2	4-0	2-2	4-3	2-1	4-2	4-3	4-1	4-2	3-2	1-1	3-0	4-1	3-0	1-1	3-1	1-2	3-1	2-3	0-1	

Division 3 (North)

		Pd	Wn	Dw	Ls	GF	GA	Pts	
1.	Chesterfield FC (Chesterfield)	42	26	6	10	102	57	58	P
2.	Lincoln City FC (Lincoln)	42	25	7	10	102	59	57	
3.	Tranmere Rovers FC (Birkenhead)	42	24	6	12	111	74	54	
4.	Wrexham AFC (Wrexham)	42	21	12	9	94	62	54	
5.	Southport FC (Southport)	42	22	9	11	88	56	53	
6.	Hull City AFC (Kingston-upon-Hull)	42	20	10	12	99	55	50	
7.	Stockport County FC (Stockport)	42	20	9	13	77	61	49	
8.	Carlisle United FC (Carlisle)	42	20	5	17	98	81	45	
9.	Gateshead FC (Gateshead)	42	16	13	13	71	73	45	
10.	Wigan Borough FC (Wigan)	42	19	5	18	76	86	43	
11.	Darlington FC (Darlington)	42	16	10	16	71	59	42	
12.	York City FC (York)	42	18	6	18	85	82	42	
13.	Accrington Stanley FC (Accrington)	42	15	9	18	84	108	39	
14.	Rotherham United FC (Rotherham)	42	13	12	17	81	83	38	
15.	Doncaster Rovers FC (Doncaster)	42	13	11	18	65	65	37	
16.	Barrow AFC (Barrow-in-Furness)	42	15	7	20	68	89	37	
17.	Halifax Town AFC (Halifax)	42	13	9	20	55	89	35	
18.	Crewe Alexandra FC (Crewe)	42	14	6	22	66	93	34	
19.	New Brighton FC (Wallasey)	42	13	7	22	49	76	33	
20.	Hartlepools United FC (Hartlepool)	42	12	6	24	67	86	30	
21.	Rochdale AFC (Rochdale)	42	12	6	24	62	107	30	
22.	Nelson FC (Nelson)	42	6	7	29	43	113	19	#
		924	373	178	373	1714	1714	924	

Nelson FC (Nelson) were not re-elected to the league for the next season.   Elected: Chester FC (Chester)

Football League Division 3 (S) 1930-1931 Season	Bournemouth	Brentford	Brighton	Bristol Rovers	Clapton Orient	Coventry City	Crystal Palace	Exeter City	Fulham	Gillingham	Luton Town	Newport Co.	Northampton	Norwich City	Notts County	Q.P.R.	Southend Utd.	Swindon Town	Thames	Torquay United	Walsall	Watford
Bournemouth & B. Athletic	■	1-0	1-2	4-0	1-1	2-0	0-0	3-1	2-1	2-1	0-0	4-2	1-3	4-1	2-1	2-0	0-0	4-1	3-3	2-2	0-2	1-1
Brentford FC	1-2	■	3-2	4-0	3-0	1-2	8-2	2-1	4-1	1-1	0-1	3-2	0-4	3-1	2-2	5-3	3-1	5-2	6-1	0-0	6-1	2-1
Brighton & Hove Albion	3-1	1-0	■	4-0	3-1	2-0	1-1	3-2	1-1	5-0	2-0	5-0	1-1	1-0	1-3	1-1	1-2	1-0	2-4	3-0	3-3	1-0
Bristol Rovers FC	2-5	2-5	3-3	■	4-1	1-0	2-1	1-1	2-1	1-0	5-1	2-0	1-4	3-0	2-2	3-0	2-3	4-1	4-1	3-1	1-2	1-5
Clapton Orient FC	0-0	3-0	1-0	3-1	■	3-3	3-2	2-3	2-0	0-2	3-2	3-1	2-2	2-0	1-4	2-3	3-1	2-3	2-1	4-0	2-5	4-0
Coventry City FC	3-3	0-1	0-0	5-1	4-0	■	3-5	3-1	2-1	1-2	1-2	6-4	0-1	3-0	1-2	2-0	0-0	4-0	7-1	6-1	2-1	2-2
Crystal Palace FC	1-0	5-1	0-1	0-2	3-1	1-0	■	7-2	5-2	5-0	5-1	7-1	0-0	2-1	1-1	4-0	3-1	3-1	2-1	5-0	6-3	6-1
Exeter City FC	4-1	4-0	2-2	0-3	6-1	2-3	4-3	■	3-2	3-0	1-1	3-0	3-3	1-0	3-3	2-0	1-1	3-1	4-3	2-2	2-5	2-1
Fulham FC	1-0	1-1	0-1	6-2	2-0	0-0	2-0	4-2	■	1-1	2-1	0-1	4-2	1-0	0-2	1-0	6-1	4-2	3-0	5-2		3-2
Gillingham FC	0-0	1-1	0-0	1-1	2-0	6-2	3-5	3-2		■	4-0	4-1	0-2	2-1	0-5	2-2	1-0	3-1	2-3	2-0		4-2
Luton Town FC	2-3	1-1	2-2	4-1	0-1	2-0	1-2	3-1	5-0	4-1	■	3-1	4-0	1-0	3-0	5-1	2-1	4-0	8-0	3-1	0-0	4-1
Newport County AFC	7-3	0-2	2-0	1-1	1-1	1-1	2-1	4-0	1-3	1-3	3-1	■	5-2	3-0	2-3	2-3	3-1	3-1	1-1	2-1	1-1	0-2
Northampton Town FC	2-2	1-2	2-1	1-1	0-0	0-3	0-0	1-0	4-2	0-1	0-0	1-0	■	3-1	0-0	6-0	4-0	3-0	4-1	0-3	3-0	2-3
Norwich City FC	2-1	3-0	2-2	1-3	2-0	2-2	2-1	1-2	1-1	4-0	1-0	4-1	1-1	■	2-2	1-1	0-1	2-0	0-0	3-0	3-1	0-1
Notts County FC	2-0	1-0	2-2	3-0	5-0	4-1	2-2	1-2	6-1	2-1	1-0	5-0	2-2	4-0	■	2-0	1-1	2-0	4-0	2-0	6-1	1-0
Queen's Park Rangers FC	3-0	3-1	4-1	2-0	4-2	2-0	4-0	7-2	0-2	1-0	3-1	7-1	0-2	3-1	4-1	■	0-2	1-3	2-0	1-2	3-0	2-3
Southend United FC	4-0	0-1	0-2	4-0	2-0	2-0	5-1	2-4	3-2	0-2	6-2	2-1	2-0	2-1	2-0	2-0	■	5-3	1-0	6-3	2-0	1-0
Swindon Town FC	4-1	3-2	1-1	3-1	5-1	4-0	4-4	2-1	4-1	5-2	0-0	4-4	5-1	5-2	1-2	4-1	1-1	■	3-0	4-0	4-3	2-1
Thames FC	1-4	2-0	0-0	1-2	3-0	1-2	0-2	1-0	0-0	2-2	1-0	3-1	2-1	2-0	0-0	1-0	3-0	3-2	■	1-1	4-1	3-2
Torquay United FC	4-4	0-3	3-1	3-3	5-2	0-0	3-1	0-0	3-1	3-0	3-0	2-0	1-4	6-2	3-1	5-0	5-1			■	0-1	3-1
Walsall FC	3-3	1-4	0-0	4-2	4-2	1-2	2-1	2-1	2-0	2-2	0-1	1-0	2-6	7-0	2-1	0-2	1-3	2-2	6-0	0-4	■	2-2
Watford FC	2-0	1-3	5-0	2-2	1-2	4-1	0-2	0-1	2-2	1-0	1-0	6-2	1-2	2-2	0-1	0-4	1-3	3-0	1-0	1-0	6-0	■

Division 3 (South)

		Pd	Wn	Dw	Ls	GF	GA	Pts	
1.	Notts County FC (Nottingham)	42	24	11	7	97	46	59	P
2.	Crystal Palace FC (London)	42	22	7	13	107	71	51	
3.	Brentford FC (London)	42	22	6	14	90	64	50	
4.	Brighton & Hove Albion FC (Hove)	42	17	15	10	68	53	49	
5.	Southend United FC (Southend-on-Sea)	42	22	5	15	76	60	49	
6.	Northampton Town FC (Northampton)	42	18	12	12	77	59	48	
7.	Luton Town FC (Luton)	42	19	8	15	76	51	46	
8.	Queen's Park Rangers FC (London)	42	20	3	19	82	75	43	
9.	Fulham FC (London)	42	18	7	17	77	75	43	
10.	Bournemouth & Boscombe Athletic FC (Bournemouth)	42	15	13	14	72	73	43	
11.	Torquay United FC (Torquay)	42	17	9	16	80	84	43	
12.	Swindon Town FC (Swindon)	42	18	6	18	89	94	42	
13.	Exeter City FC (Exeter)	42	17	8	17	84	90	42	
14.	Coventry City FC (Coventry)	42	16	9	17	75	65	41	
15.	Bristol Rovers FC (Bristol)	42	16	8	18	75	92	40	
16.	Gillingham FC (Gillingham)	42	14	10	18	61	76	38	
17.	Walsall FC (Walsall)	42	14	9	19	78	95	37	T
18.	Watford FC (Watford)	42	14	7	21	72	75	35	
19.	Clapton Orient FC (London)	42	14	7	21	63	91	35	
20.	Thames FC (London)	42	13	8	21	54	93	34	
21.	Norwich City FC (Norwich)	42	10	8	24	47	76	28	
22.	Newport County AFC (Newport)	42	11	6	25	69	111	28	#
		924	371	182	371	1669	1669	924	

T: Walsall FC (Walsall) were transferred to Division 3 (North) from the next season.

Newport County AFC were not re-elected to the league for the next season.   Elected: Mansfield Town FC

F.A. CUP FINAL   (Wembley Stadium, London – 25/04/1931 – 92,406)

WEST BROMWICH ALBION FC   2-1   Birmingham FC (Birmingham)
WG Richardson 2   *Bradford*

West Bromwich: Pearson, Shaw, Trentham, Magee, W.Richardson, Edwards, Glidden, Carter, W.G. Richardson, Sandford, Wood.

Birmingham: Hibbs, Liddell, Barkas, Cringan, Morrall, Leslie, Briggs, Crosbie, Bradford, Gregg, Curtis.

Semi-finals

Birmingham FC (Birmingham)	2-0	Sunderland AFC (Sunderland)
Everton FC (Liverpool)	0-1	West Bromwich Albion FC (West Bromwich)

Quarter-finals

Birmingham FC (Birmingham)	2-2, 3-0	Chelsea FC (London)
Everton FC (Liverpool)	9-1	Southport FC (Southport)
Sunderland AFC (Sunderland)	1-1, 4-2	Exeter City FC (Exeter)
West Bromwich Albion FC (West Bromwich)	1-1, 2-1	Wolverhampton Wanderers FC (Wolverhampton)

1931-32

Football League Division 1 1931-1932 Season	Arsenal	Aston Villa	Birmingham	Blackburn R.	Blackpool	Bolton Wands.	Chelsea	Derby County	Everton	Grimsby Town	Huddersfield T.	Leicester City	Liverpool	Manchester C.	Middlesbrough	Newcastle Utd.	Portsmouth	Sheffield Utd.	Sheffield Wed.	Sunderland	W.B.A.	West Ham Utd.
Arsenal FC		1-1	3-0	4-0	2-0	1-1	1-1	2-1	3-2	4-0	1-1	2-1	6-0	4-0	5-0	1-0	3-3	0-2	3-1	2-0	0-1	4-1
Aston Villa FC	1-1		3-2	1-5	5-1	2-1	1-3	2-0	2-3	7-0	2-3	3-2	6-1	2-1	7-1	3-0	0-1	5-0	3-1	2-0	2-0	5-1
Birmingham FC	2-2	1-1		2-1	3-0	2-2	4-0	1-1	4-0	2-1	5-0	2-0	3-1	1-5	3-0	4-1	2-1	1-3	1-2	0-0	1-0	4-1
Blackburn Rovers FC	1-1	2-0	1-2		5-1	3-1	2-2	3-2	5-3	3-2	3-0	6-0	1-3	2-2	4-2	0-3	5-3	1-2	1-6	5-2	2-0	2-4
Blackpool FC	1-5	1-3	1-1	2-1		0-3	2-4	2-1	2-0	4-3	2-0	2-3	2-2	2-2	1-2	3-1	1-1	2-0	1-2	3-2	1-2	7-2
Bolton Wanderers FC	1-0	2-1	5-1	3-1	1-2		1-0	1-2	2-1	5-3	1-2	1-0	8-1	1-1	4-2	2-1	4-0	3-1	2-4	3-1	1-0	0-1
Chelsea FC	2-1	3-6	2-1	1-2	4-1	3-0		2-1	0-0	4-1	0-1	1-0	2-0	3-2	4-0	4-1	0-0	1-1	2-3	2-2	0-2	3-2
Derby County FC	1-1	3-1	2-1	1-1	5-0	5-1	1-0		3-0	3-3	3-2	1-1	1-2	2-1	5-2	1-1	2-1	1-3	0-1	3-1	3-1	5-1
Everton FC	1-3	4-2	3-2	5-0	3-2	1-0	7-2	2-1		4-2	4-1	9-2	2-1	0-1	5-1	8-1	0-1	5-1	9-3	4-2	2-1	6-1
Grimsby Town FC	3-1	2-2	1-1	4-3	0-0	2-0	1-2	2-1	1-2		1-4	3-0	5-1	2-1	2-0	1-2	3-1	0-2	3-1	1-3	0-0	2-1
Huddersfield Town AFC	1-2	1-1	1-1	1-1	5-0	2-0	2-1	6-0	0-0	1-1		2-1	4-3	1-0	1-1	1-2	1-0	2-2	6-1	4-1	2-2	3-1
Leicester City FC	1-2	3-8	3-1	1-0	2-2	1-3	1-0	1-1	0-1	1-2	2-4		2-1	4-0	2-2	4-2	2-1	4-3	3-2	5-0	2-3	2-1
Liverpool FC	2-1	2-0	4-3	4-2	3-2	2-2	2-1	1-1	1-3	4-0	0-3	3-3		4-3	7-2	4-2	1-3	2-1	3-1	1-2	4-1	2-2
Manchester City FC	1-3	3-3	2-1	3-1	7-1	2-1	1-1	3-0	1-0	4-1	3-0	5-1	0-1		1-2	5-1	3-3	1-1	2-2	1-1	2-5	0-1
Middlesbrough FC	2-5	1-1	2-0	0-2	0-3	3-1	0-2	5-2	1-0	4-0	1-0	1-1	4-1	3-3		2-1	0-1	4-3	4-0	0-1	1-0	3-2
Newcastle United FC	3-2	3-1	0-3	5-3	2-2	3-1	4-1	3-3	0-0	2-0	2-1	3-2	0-1	2-1	3-1		0-0	5-3	4-1	1-2	5-1	2-2
Portsmouth FC	0-3	0-3	2-1	2-0	2-2	3-2	1-0	2-0	0-3	2-0	3-2	0-1	2-0	3-2	2-0	6-0		2-1	2-0	0-0	0-1	3-0
Sheffield United FC	4-1	5-4	1-0	3-2	1-3	4-0	4-2	3-1	1-5	2-1	0-2	2-2	3-0	2-1	2-1	0-3	1-2		1-1	1-1	1-0	6-0
Sheffield Wednesday FC	1-3	1-0	5-1	5-1	3-0	7-1	2-2	3-1	1-3	4-1	4-1	3-1	1-1	1-1	1-1	2-0	3-1	2-1		3-2	2-5	6-1
Sunderland AFC	2-0	1-1	2-3	2-2	4-0	3-0	2-1	0-0	2-3	2-0	1-3	4-1	1-3	2-5	0-0	1-4	5-1	1-1	3-1		2-1	2-0
West Bromwich Albion FC	1-0	3-0	0-1	4-1	4-0	3-0	4-0	4-0	1-1	5-6	3-2	1-2	1-2	1-1	1-1	2-1	3-0	0-1	1-1	1-0		3-1
West Ham United FC	1-1	2-1	2-4	1-3	1-1	3-1	3-1	2-1	4-2	3-1	1-1	1-4	1-0	1-1	0-2	2-1	2-1	1-2	1-2	2-2	1-5	

	Division 1	Pd	Wn	Dw	Ls	GF	GA	Pts	
1.	EVERTON FC (LIVERPOOL)	42	26	4	12	116	64	56	
2.	Arsenal FC (London)	42	22	10	10	90	48	54	
3.	Sheffield Wednesday FC (Sheffield)	42	22	6	14	96	82	50	
4.	Huddersfield Town AFC (Huddersfield)	42	19	10	13	80	63	48	
5.	Aston Villa FC (Birmingham)	42	19	8	15	104	72	46	
6.	West Bromwich Albion FC (West Bromwich)	42	20	6	16	77	55	46	
7.	Sheffield United FC (Sheffield)	42	20	6	16	80	75	46	
8.	Portsmouth FC (Portsmouth)	42	19	7	16	62	62	45	
9.	Birmingham FC (Birmingham)	42	18	8	16	78	67	44	
10.	Liverpool FC (Liverpool)	42	19	6	17	81	93	44	
11.	Newcastle United FC (Newcastle-upon-Tyne)	42	18	6	18	80	87	42	
12.	Chelsea FC (London)	42	16	8	18	69	73	40	
13.	Sunderland AFC (Sunderland)	42	15	10	17	67	73	40	
14.	Manchester City FC (Manchester)	42	13	12	17	83	73	38	
15.	Derby County FC (Derby)	42	14	10	18	71	75	38	
16.	Blackburn Rovers FC (Blackburn)	42	16	6	20	89	95	38	
17.	Bolton Wanderers FC (Bolton)	42	17	4	21	72	80	38	
18.	Middlesbrough FC (Middlesbrough)	42	15	8	19	64	89	38	
19.	Leicester City FC (Leicester)	42	15	7	20	74	94	37	
20.	Blackpool FC (Blackpool)	42	12	9	21	65	102	33	
21.	Grimsby Town FC (Cleethorpes)	42	13	6	23	67	98	32	R
22.	West Ham United FC (London)	42	12	7	23	62	107	31	R
		924	380	164	380	1727	1727	924	

Top Goalscorer

1) William "Dixie" DEAN   (Everton FC)   44

Football League Division 2 1931-1932 Season	Barnsley	Bradford City	Bradford P.A.	Bristol City	Burnley	Bury	Charlton Ath.	Chesterfield	Leeds United	Man. United	Millwall	Nottingham F.	Notts County	Oldham Ath.	Plymouth Arg.	Port Vale	Preston N.E.	Southampton	Stoke City	Swansea Town	Tottenham H.	Wolves
Barnsley FC		1-2	2-2	1-1	0-1	0-1	1-4	3-1	0-2	0-0	2-1	3-1	1-1	3-1	0-0	3-0	4-2	3-3	1-0	2-3	3-2	2-2
Bradford City AFC	9-1		0-0	3-0	1-2	1-3	1-1	3-0	4-1	4-3	0-0	2-2	0-2	2-0	3-3	4-0	0-1	5-2	2-2	5-1	2-0	2-2
Bradford Park Avenue	1-0	1-0		2-0	2-0	2-1	3-0	1-0	3-0	3-1	1-2	4-1	1-1	5-0	2-0	2-2	1-5	2-1	2-1	2-1	2-1	2-1
Bristol City FC	4-0	0-1	0-0		1-6	1-3	1-2	1-1	0-2	2-1	1-4	1-1	3-2	1-1	0-2	0-2	4-2	0-1	0-0	1-1	1-1	0-4
Burnley FC	5-3	1-1	3-2	1-2		2-2	0-1	2-2	0-5	2-0	1-1	1-0	1-1	1-4	1-1	2-2	2-2	1-3	3-0	4-1	2-0	1-3
Bury FC	7-1	0-2	4-2	2-1	1-0		6-0	0-1	1-4	0-0	2-0	2-2	2-1	2-1	2-2	2-0	4-1	3-0	0-1	2-1	1-1	1-0
Charlton Athletic FC	3-1	1-0	2-2	2-0	0-1	3-0		0-0	0-1	1-0	1-3	3-1	2-2	2-0	2-1	2-1	3-1	3-3	1-1	3-3	2-5	3-2
Chesterfield FC	2-2	2-2	3-2	3-1	5-1	4-1	3-2		1-1	1-3	1-0	1-0	1-4	0-2	1-2	4-0	3-1	1-0	1-3	1-2	4-2	1-1
Leeds United AFC	0-1	1-1	3-2	1-0	3-1	1-0	2-0	3-3		1-4	0-1	1-1	2-2	5-0	0-0	4-1	1-0	2-0	3-2	1-0	2-1	2-1
Manchester United FC	3-0	1-0	0-2	0-1	5-1	1-2	0-2	3-1	2-5		2-0	3-2	3-3	5-1	2-1	2-0	3-2	2-3	1-1	2-1	1-1	3-2
Millwall FC	2-0	6-1	3-0	1-0	2-0	2-1	1-0	5-0	2-3	1-1		1-0	4-3	0-0	1-3	2-2	4-1	0-1	1-3	1-1	1-2	1-2
Nottingham Forest FC	1-2	2-1	6-1	3-1	1-2	0-2	3-2	4-0	3-3	2-1	1-1		2-1	3-0	3-2	2-1	2-2	2-1	1-1	6-1	1-3	2-0
Notts County FC	2-3	1-1	0-2	3-0	5-0	1-1	2-2	1-1	1-1	1-2	2-0	2-6		1-0	3-0	4-2	1-4	5-0	2-1	1-2	3-1	3-1
Oldham Athletic AFC	2-2	1-1	2-1	2-1	3-1	1-2	1-0	6-1	2-1	1-5	1-1	2-4	5-2		1-3	3-0	2-2	2-0	1-3	1-2	0-2	1-2
Plymouth Argyle FC	3-0	3-3	4-1	2-1	4-0	5-1	1-1	4-0	3-2	3-1	8-1	5-1	3-4	5-0		1-3	2-1	1-2	1-1	4-2	4-1	3-3
Port Vale FC	3-0	2-0	1-3	4-2	1-3	1-1	0-1	2-1	1-2	1-2	2-2	2-0	2-0	1-1	2-0		0-1	0-0	3-0	0-4	1-3	1-7
Preston North End FC	1-2	5-2	1-0	1-1	2-1	0-2	3-2	2-2	0-0	0-0	2-0	1-1	0-0	2-3	5-2	1-4		2-1	2-0	1-0	2-0	4-2
Southampton FC	2-0	0-1	0-3	1-1	3-0	2-1	1-1	1-2	2-1	1-1	3-1	4-0	3-1	1-1	0-6	5-1	3-3		1-2	3-0	2-1	1-3
Stoke City FC	2-0	3-1	1-0	1-1	3-0	3-2	4-0	2-1	3-4	3-0	0-0	2-1	2-2	1-1	3-2	4-0	4-1	2-0		0-0	2-2	1-1
Swansea Town AFC	3-0	0-1	1-0	2-0	5-1	2-0	2-0	1-0	0-2	3-4	4-0	4-1	5-1	1-0	4-1	2-3	0-3	3-4	1-1		1-1	1-1
Tottenham Hotspur FC	4-2	1-5	3-3	2-1	1-1	0-0	0-1	3-3	3-1	4-1	1-0	1-3	2-0	3-2	2-1	2-0	9-3	4-0	5-2	3-3		3-3
Wolverhampton Wanderers FC	2-0	3-1	6-0	4-2	3-1	6-0	3-1	6-0	1-1	7-0	5-0	0-0	0-0	7-1	2-0	2-0	3-2	5-1	0-1	2-0	4-0	

Division 2

		Pd	Wn	Dw	Ls	GF	GA	Pts	
1.	Wolverhampton Wanderers FC (Wolverhampton)	42	24	8	10	115	49	56	P
2.	Leeds United AFC (Leeds)	42	22	10	10	78	54	54	P
3.	Stoke City FC (Stoke-on-Trent)	42	19	14	9	69	48	52	
4.	Plymouth Argyle FC (Plymouth)	42	20	9	13	100	66	49	
5.	Bury FC (Bury)	42	21	7	14	70	58	49	
6.	Bradford Park Avenue FC (Bradford)	42	21	7	14	72	63	49	
7.	Bradford City AFC (Bradford)	42	16	13	13	80	61	45	
8.	Tottenham Hotspur FC (London)	42	16	11	15	87	78	43	
9.	Millwall FC (London)	42	17	9	16	61	61	43	
10.	Charlton Athletic FC (London)	42	17	9	16	61	66	43	
11.	Nottingham Forest FC (Nottingham)	42	16	10	16	77	72	42	
12.	Manchester United FC (Manchester)	42	17	8	17	71	72	42	
13.	Preston North End FC (Preston)	42	16	10	16	75	77	42	
14.	Southampton FC (Southampton)	42	17	7	18	66	77	41	
15.	Swansea Town AFC (Swansea)	42	16	7	19	73	75	39	
16.	Notts County FC (Nottingham)	42	13	12	17	75	75	38	
17.	Chesterfield FC (Chesterfield)	42	13	11	18	64	86	37	
18.	Oldham Athletic AFC (Oldham)	42	13	10	19	62	84	36	
19.	Burnley FC (Burnley)	42	13	9	20	59	87	35	
20.	Port Vale FC (Stoke-on-Trent)	42	13	7	22	58	89	33	
21.	Barnsley FC (Barnsley)	42	12	9	21	55	91	33	R
22.	Bristol City FC (Bristol)	42	6	11	25	39	78	23	R
		924	358	208	358	1567	1567	924	

Football League — Division 3 (N) — 1931-1932 Season

	Accrington St.	Barrow	Carlisle United	Chester	Crewe Alexandra	Darlington	Doncaster R.	Gateshead	Halifax Town	Hartlepools Utd.	Hull City	Lincoln City	New Brighton	Rochdale	Rotherham Utd.	Southport	Stockport Co.	Tranmere Rovers	Walsall	Wigan Borough	Wrexham	York City
Accrington Stanley FC	■	2-0	5-3	2-3	2-0	4-0	3-2	1-2	4-0	5-0	1-1	2-2	4-1	3-0	5-2	1-1	2-0	2-2	1-0	---	5-0	2-1
Barrow AFC	3-0	■	4-1	4-0	2-1	3-4	3-2	3-1	3-1	4-1	0-2	0-2	4-1	4-1	3-0	1-1	4-2	3-1	7-1	---	1-0	3-1
Carlisle United FC	3-0	3-1	■	4-3	2-1	0-2	5-1	0-0	4-0	3-2	0-1	0-3	0-0	4-0	1-2	2-2	1-1	1-1	4-0	---	2-2	1-1
Chester FC	1-0	4-2	4-1	■	1-0	3-1	1-1	1-1	3-1	2-3	2-0	2-1	2-0	7-2	2-1	4-0	2-1	3-1	5-1	4-0	2-5	3-0
Crewe Alexandra FC	3-1	3-2	5-1	1-0	■	0-1	2-0	3-5	4-3	6-0	4-3	8-1	3-2	1-0	5-0	1-1	2-2	0-0	2-1	4-3	3-0	8-1
Darlington FC	4-1	0-2	0-1	4-1	1-0	■	2-3	1-2	3-0	6-3	2-1	0-6	3-0	3-1	2-1	0-1	2-0	1-2	2-0	5-0	1-1	4-1
Doncaster Rovers FC	3-1	0-1	3-3	3-0	2-1	3-2	■	1-2	3-1	1-3	0-1	0-3	2-1	2-0	0-3	3-0	1-1	2-2		---	2-4	1-0
Gateshead FC	4-0	4-0	4-0	1-2	3-3	3-2	2-1	■	1-1	3-1	2-1	2-3	4-0	3-1	4-1	2-0	3-3	2-2		---	4-0	6-0
Halifax Town AFC	1-0	1-0	1-1	2-1	4-1	0-3	4-0	1-2	■	2-0	2-2	3-0	0-0	3-2	1-1	3-0	2-2	0-0	1-2	---	1-0	4-1
Hartlepools United FC	1-0	0-2	2-2	2-2	3-1	3-3	5-0	1-2	4-1	■	2-3	4-3	1-0	3-0	1-4	2-2	0-5	4-3		---	0-1	7-2
Hull City AFC	3-0	3-0	2-0	0-2	2-4	4-1	4-1	0-1	1-0	3-1	■	4-1	4-1	4-1	0-1	1-0	4-4	3-0	3-0	---	5-0	2-3
Lincoln City FC	5-1	3-1	3-1	4-0	5-1	2-0	1-2	1-0	9-1	6-0	1-0	■	3-0	3-0	3-1	7-0	1-2	4-2	3-0	3-0		1-1
New Brighton FC	2-1	0-3	4-1	0-1	0-1	0-0	1-0	1-3	2-0	1-1	1-2	2-1	■	1-1	3-1	2-1	1-1	0-1	1-1	---	1-1	0-2
Rochdale AFC	2-2	0-6	4-3	0-3	2-3	1-1	3-1	0-3	1-4	1-3	3-6	3-5	3-2	■	1-4	0-1	1-0	3-6	0-1	---	2-4	3-5
Rotherham United FC	2-3	0-2	4-1	3-0	0-2	2-4	6-3	2-1	5-0	1-2	0-1	2-2	5-0	2-0	■	1-0	1-0	5-1	2-0	---	0-0	0-1
Southport FC	4-2	3-1	2-0	1-1	1-1	3-0	5-0	1-1	2-2	1-2	1-1	1-1	1-0	3-1	3-2	■	1-0	1-0	5-1	---	2-0	3-0
Stockport County FC	3-0	2-0	0-0	0-0	1-2	1-0	1-0	1-0	2-1	3-2	2-0	0-1	3-1	3-1	1-0	0-1	■	0-1	0-1	---	5-1	3-2
Tranmere Rovers FC	8-1	6-1	3-0	2-2	4-1	3-1	0-1	4-3	5-2	0-2	1-0	5-1	9-1	6-1	2-0	2-2		■	4-1	---	3-1	2-2
Walsall FC	5-5	1-2	3-1	1-1	2-1	1-0	2-0	1-2	4-2	2-3	1-4	3-0	2-1	3-0	2-1	3-0	2-1	3-1	■	3-0	2-0	2-2
Wigan Borough FC	---	---	3-2	---	---	---	---	2-1	0-1	1-1	3-1	0-3	---	---	---	---	---	---	---	■	---	---
Wrexham AFC	2-1	0-1	1-0	1-1	2-4	3-0	2-1	2-3	5-3	2-1	1-3	2-1	4-0	0-1	1-1	2-1	2-1	5-1	5-0	5-0	■	2-1
York City FC	1-0	1-0	2-4	3-1	3-3	3-0	1-2	3-2	7-2	3-1	0-0	1-1	4-0	5-2	2-0	1-2	1-0	3-2	2-0	---	3-2	■

Division 3 (North)

		Pd	Wn	Dw	Ls	GF	GA	Pts	
1.	Lincoln City FC (Lincoln)	40	26	5	9	106	47	57	P
2.	Gateshead FC (Gateshead)	40	25	7	8	94	48	57	
3.	Chester FC (Chester)	40	21	8	11	78	60	50	
4.	Tranmere Rovers FC (Birkenhead)	40	19	11	10	107	58	49	
5.	Barrow AFC (Barrow-in-Furness)	40	24	1	15	86	59	49	
6.	Crewe Alexandra FC (Crewe)	40	21	6	13	95	66	48	
7.	Southport FC (Southport)	40	18	10	12	58	53	46	
8.	Hull City AFC (Kingston-upon-Hull)	40	20	5	15	82	53	45	
9.	York City FC (York)	40	18	7	15	76	81	43	
10.	Wrexham AFC (Wrexham)	40	18	7	15	64	69	43	
11.	Darlington FC (Darlington)	40	17	4	19	66	69	38	
12.	Stockport County FC (Stockport)	40	13	11	16	55	53	37	
13.	Hartlepools United FC (Hartlepool)	40	16	5	19	78	100	37	
14.	Accrington Stanley FC (Accrington)	40	15	6	19	75	80	36	
15.	Doncaster Rovers FC (Doncaster)	40	16	4	20	59	80	36	
16.	Walsall FC (Walsall)	40	16	3	21	57	85	35	
17.	Halifax Town AFC (Halifax)	40	13	8	19	61	87	34	
18.	Carlisle United FC (Carlisle)	40	11	11	18	64	79	33	
19.	Rotherham United FC (Rotherham)	40	14	4	22	63	72	32	
20.	New Brighton FC (Wallasey)	40	8	8	24	38	76	24	
21.	Rochdale AFC (Rochdale)	40	4	3	33	48	135	11	
---.	Wigan Borough FC (Wigan)	12	3	1	8	12	33	7	#
		840	353	134	353	1510	1510	840	

Wigan Borough FC (Wigan) resigned from the league on 26th October 1931 and their playing record was deleted.

Football League Division 3 (S) 1931-1932 Season	Bournemouth	Brentford	Brighton	Bristol Rovers	Cardiff City	Clapton Orient	Coventry City	Crystal Palace	Exeter City	Fulham	Gillingham	Luton Town	Mansfield T.	Northampton	Norwich City	Q.P.R.	Reading	Southend Utd	Swindon T.	Thames	Torquay Utd.	Watford
Bournemouth & B. Athletic	■	1-3	1-2	2-2	3-0	0-1	2-2	4-1	5-2	0-3	0-2	1-1	3-2	1-1	1-0	2-2	2-2	0-0	2-1	4-2	5-0	3-3
Brentford FC	4-2	■	2-2	4-2	2-3	3-0	4-2	1-1	2-2	0-0	1-1	1-0	1-1	2-0	0-1	1-0	3-0	2-3	2-0	1-0	3-0	1-2
Brighton & Hove Albion	4-1	1-2	■	2-0	0-0	1-1	4-1	0-3	1-1	2-3	7-0	3-2	4-0	0-0	2-1	1-0	2-0	1-2	1-0	4-1	0-2	2-1
Bristol Rovers FC	4-1	2-0	0-4	■	2-2	2-1	3-1	6-1	2-4	2-2	5-2	3-1	1-1	3-2	0-1	1-1	2-0	0-0	0-2	4-1	1-1	3-2
Cardiff City AFC	0-0	3-2	1-1	3-1	■	5-0	6-1	1-3	5-2	0-3	1-0	4-1	2-0	5-0	0-2	0-4	5-1	2-3	3-0	9-2	5-2	2-1
Clapton Orient FC	1-2	2-2	2-2	1-0	1-1	■	5-2	1-3	2-2	0-1	3-1	0-0	4-0	3-2	1-3	3-0	2-2	2-4	4-2	1-1	1-3	2-2
Coventry City FC	6-1	0-1	4-3	1-1	2-1	4-2	■	8-0	4-0	5-5	6-4	3-2	5-1	4-1	3-0	1-0	5-1	0-2	3-2	2-0	3-1	5-0
Crystal Palace FC	1-1	1-0	2-0	5-0	5-0	0-0	2-2	■	3-0	2-0	1-0	1-1	2-1	4-0	3-1	1-1	1-1	3-2	0-0	2-1	7-0	2-1
Exeter City FC	1-0	4-1	3-1	1-0	3-1	4-3	3-0	0-1	■	0-3	4-0	1-1	3-0	0-0	3-0	6-2	4-0	3-0	1-1	4-1	3-1	2-0
Fulham FC	3-0	2-1	3-0	3-2	4-0	5-1	5-3	4-0	3-1	■	0-2	3-2	2-1	1-3	4-0	1-3	3-3	1-1	2-2	8-0	10-2	5-0
Gillingham FC	1-4	0-2	0-0	1-0	1-1	0-2	1-3	0-0	0-1	2-1	■	1-3	2-0	3-2	3-3	1-0	1-1	4-0	2-1	2-0	1-0	0-1
Luton Town FC	1-0	1-1	3-2	3-0	2-1	1-5	3-1	3-0	6-3	1-3	2-0	■	3-1	1-0	7-1	4-1	6-1	1-3	6-0	2-0	6-1	0-1
Mansfield Town FC	2-1	2-0	3-3	0-3	1-2	4-3	3-3	1-1	3-1	1-2	3-1	5-2	■	2-0	5-2	2-2	1-7	4-4	3-2	4-0	2-4	3-2
Northampton Town FC	1-1	3-0	0-1	6-0	1-0	4-3	3-2	5-0	2-1	0-1	1-0	1-2	3-0	■	2-2	6-1	2-4	1-2	4-1	0-4	2-0	1-1
Norwich City FC	1-2	1-0	2-1	6-0	2-0	3-2	6-2	3-2	0-1	2-2	1-1	3-3	1-1	0-0	■	2-1	0-0	1-1	4-2	7-0	2-0	4-1
Queen's Park Rangers FC	0-3	1-2	1-1	2-1	2-3	3-2	1-1	2-2	1-0	3-1	7-0	3-1	1-1	3-2	2-2	■	2-0	2-1	1-2	6-0	3-1	4-4
Reading FC	3-1	1-2	3-1	3-0	5-1	5-0	2-1	3-0	2-0	4-2	2-0	2-1	4-1	3-2	1-1	3-2	■	3-1	5-2	5-1	4-1	2-1
Southend United FC	1-3	1-0	2-0	4-1	1-1	1-3	4-0	1-0	0-1	4-1	2-0	1-1	5-2	0-1	2-0	0-0	1-1	■	3-0	1-1	4-2	3-0
Swindon Town FC	3-0	1-3	1-2	2-1	1-4	2-3	2-2	3-2	2-1	2-2	4-0	3-2	5-2	3-0	2-0	1-2	0-2	1-2	■	2-0	3-0	4-1
Thames FC	4-2	1-1	1-2	0-2	1-2	3-3	5-2	1-3	0-0	0-0	3-0	2-4	6-3	0-2	1-0	3-2	0-0	1-3	1-1	■	1-1	1-2
Torquay United FC	1-1	1-1	1-1	8-1	2-2	3-0	3-3	3-1	2-1	2-3	1-0	1-2	2-2	4-1	2-4	2-3	1-4	2-1	2-1	3-1	■	3-6
Watford FC	4-2	1-4	2-2	5-2	3-0	2-1	2-0	1-2	1-0	3-1	2-0	3-1	4-1	1-2	1-1	2-2	3-2	1-1	4-1	3-2	1-0	■

	Division 3 (South)	**Pd**	**Wn**	**Dw**	**Ls**	**GF**	**GA**	**Pts**	
1.	Fulham FC (London)	42	24	9	9	111	62	57	P
2.	Reading FC (Reading)	42	23	9	10	97	67	55	
3.	Southend United FC (Southend-on-Sea)	42	21	11	10	77	53	53	
4.	Crystal Palace FC (London)	42	20	11	11	74	63	51	
5.	Brentford FC (London)	42	19	10	13	68	52	48	
6.	Luton Town FC (Luton)	42	20	7	15	95	70	47	
7.	Exeter City FC (Exeter)	42	20	7	15	77	62	47	
8.	Brighton & Hove Albion FC (Hove)	42	17	12	13	73	58	46	
9.	Cardiff City AFC (Cardiff)	42	19	8	15	87	73	46	
10.	Norwich City FC (Norwich)	42	17	12	13	76	67	46	
11.	Watford FC (Watford)	42	19	8	15	81	79	46	
12.	Coventry City FC (Coventry)	42	18	8	16	108	97	44	
13.	Queen's Park Rangers FC (London)	42	15	12	15	79	73	42	
14.	Northampton Town FC (Northampton)	42	16	7	19	69	69	39	
15.	Bournemouth & Boscombe Athletic FC (Bournemouth)	42	13	12	17	70	78	38	
16.	Clapton Orient FC (London)	42	12	11	19	77	90	35	
17.	Swindon Town FC (Swindon)	42	14	6	22	70	84	34	
18.	Bristol Rovers FC (Bristol)	42	13	8	21	65	92	34	
19.	Torquay United FC (Torquay)	42	12	9	21	72	106	33	
20.	Mansfield Town FC (Mansfield)	42	11	10	21	75	108	32	T
21.	Gillingham FC (Gillingham)	42	10	8	24	40	82	28	
22.	Thames FC (London)	42	7	9	26	53	109	23	#
		924	360	204	360	1694	1694	924	

148

did Thames FC (London) did not seek re-election at the end of the season and were thus relegated from the league.

T: Mansfield Town FC (Mansfield) were transferred to Division 3 (North) from the next season.

Elected: Aldershot FC (Aldershot) and Newport County AFC (Newport)

F.A. CUP FINAL   (Wembley Stadium, London – 23/04/1932 – 92,298)

NEWCASTLE UNITED FC	2-1	Arsenal FC (London)
Allen 2		*John*

Newc.: McInroy, Nelson, Fairhurst, McKenzie, Davidson, Weaver, Boyd, Richardson, Allen, McMenemy, Lang.
Arsenal: Moss, Parker, Hapgood, C.Jones, Roberts, Male, Hulme, Jack, Lambert, Bastin, John.

Semi-finals

Arsenal FC (London)	1-0	Manchester City FC (Manchester)
Chelsea FC (London)	1-2	Newcastle United FC (Newcastle-upon-Tyne)

Quarter-finals

Bury FC (Bury)	3-4	Manchester City FC (Manchester)
Huddersfield Town AFC (Huddersfield)	0-1	Arsenal FC (London)
Liverpool FC (Liverpool)	0-2	Chelsea FC (London)
Newcastle United FC (Newcastle-upon-Tyne)	5-0	Watford FC (Watford)

1932-33

Football League Division 1 1932-1933 Season	Arsenal	Aston Villa	Birmingham	Blackburn R.	Blackpool	Bolton Wands.	Chelsea	Derby County	Everton	Huddersfield T.	Leeds United	Leicester City	Liverpool	Man. City	Middlesbro'	Newcastle Utd.	Portsmouth	Sheffield Utd.	Sheffield Wed.	Sunderland	W.B.A.	Wolves
Arsenal FC		5-0	3-0	8-0	1-1	3-2	4-1	3-3	2-1	2-2	1-2	8-2	0-1	2-1	4-2	1-0	2-0	9-2	4-2	6-1	1-2	1-2
Aston Villa FC	5-3		1-0	4-0	6-2	6-1	3-1	2-0	2-1	0-3	0-0	4-2	5-2	1-1	3-1	3-0	4-1	3-0	3-6	1-0	3-2	1-3
Birmingham FC	0-1	3-2		3-1	2-1	2-1	0-0	3-1	4-0	0-2	2-1	0-4	3-0	3-0	1-4	1-2	4-0	4-1	2-1	2-0	1-1	0-0
Blackburn Rovers FC	2-3	0-5	2-0		6-5	3-2	1-3	3-3	3-1	4-2	1-1	1-1	2-2	1-0	4-2	2-1	3-2	3-0	1-1	1-3	4-4	1-0
Blackpool FC	1-2	6-2	0-1	3-0		1-3	4-0	4-1	2-1	1-1	2-1	2-1	4-1	1-0	3-1	0-4	0-2	0-3	3-4	3-1	2-4	2-2
Bolton Wanderers FC	0-4	0-1	2-2	4-2	1-0		2-3	1-1	2-4	2-1	5-0	5-0	3-3	2-1	4-3	2-2	4-1	3-3	3-0	0-0	2-2	2-0
Chelsea FC	1-3	0-1	4-2	2-2	1-0	1-1		1-3	1-0	0-1	6-0	4-1	0-2	3-1	2-1	0-1	4-4	3-0	0-2	1-1	1-2	3-1
Derby County FC	2-2	0-0	2-2	2-1	1-1	4-1	0-1		2-0	2-3	5-1	3-2	1-1	4-0	2-2	3-2	2-0	3-0	2-0	3-0	2-2	4-4
Everton FC	1-1	3-3	4-1	6-1	2-0	2-2	3-2	4-2		2-0	0-1	6-3	3-1	2-1	0-0	0-0	1-1	1-0	2-1	6-1	1-2	5-1
Huddersfield Town AFC	0-1	0-0	0-0	0-3	0-1	2-1	2-0	0-0	0-0		2-2	4-1	3-1	1-0	0-1	4-0	2-2	1-0	4-0	2-1	2-1	3-2
Leeds United AFC	0-0	1-1	1-1	3-1	3-1	4-3	2-0	0-2	1-0	1-1		1-1	5-0	2-1	0-1	6-1	0-1	1-3	3-2	2-3	1-1	2-0
Leicester City FC	1-1	3-0	2-2	1-1	3-0	2-0	1-1	4-0	2-2	3-1	3-1		1-2	1-2	1-1	0-3	2-1	1-1	0-0	4-2	6-2	2-2
Liverpool FC	2-3	0-0	1-0	2-2	4-3	0-1	3-0	6-1	7-4	2-2	0-1	1-2		1-1	1-3	3-0	4-3	2-2	4-1	3-3	2-0	5-1
Manchester City FC	2-3	5-2	1-0	2-3	5-1	2-1	1-4	2-1	3-0	3-0	0-0	4-1	1-1		2-3	1-2	3-1	1-0	2-2	2-4	1-0	4-1
Middlesbrough FC	3-4	0-2	2-2	4-0	2-0	2-1	2-1	0-3	0-2	1-1	0-1	1-1	0-1	2-0		2-3	5-4	2-2	1-1	1-2	3-1	2-1
Newcastle United FC	2-1	3-1	2-1	2-1	1-2	3-1	2-0	0-0	1-2	0-4	3-1	2-1	4-3	2-0	5-1		1-1	2-0	3-1	0-1	3-0	3-2
Portsmouth FC	1-3	2-4	1-1	2-0	2-1	2-1	2-0	2-0	2-2	1-0	3-3	2-1	2-1	1-2	2-0	2-0		1-0	3-0	1-3	3-0	2-0
Sheffield United FC	3-1	1-0	2-1	2-1	1-0	3-2	4-1	4-3	3-2	1-2	0-0	5-2	6-2	2-5	2-0	3-1	2-3		2-3	3-0	1-1	0-0
Sheffield Wednesday FC	3-2	0-2	1-1	1-1	4-1	2-0	2-2	0-0	3-1	2-1	2-0	4-1	3-0	2-1	2-1	2-0	2-1	3-3		3-1	3-1	2-0
Sunderland AFC	3-2	1-1	1-0	4-2	1-1	7-4	2-1	0-2	3-1	1-2	0-0	2-1	0-0	3-2	0-0	0-2	0-3	2-2	1-2		2-2	0-1
West Bromwich Albion FC	1-1	3-1	1-0	1-3	2-1	4-0	3-2	2-0	3-1	2-1	0-1	4-3	2-1	4-0	0-1	3-2	4-2	0-1	2-0	5-1		4-1
Wolverhampton Wanderers FC	1-7	2-4	1-0	5-3	2-3	4-1	1-2	3-1	4-2	6-4	3-3	1-1	3-1	1-2	2-0	1-1	5-2	5-1	3-5	0-2	3-3	

	Division 1	Pd	Wn	Dw	Ls	GF	GA	Pts	
1.	ARSENAL FC (LONDON)	42	25	8	9	118	61	58	
2.	Aston Villa FC (Birmingham)	42	23	8	11	92	67	54	
3.	Sheffield Wednesday FC (Sheffield)	42	21	9	12	80	68	51	
4.	West Bromwich Albion FC (West Bromwich)	42	20	9	13	83	70	49	
5.	Newcastle United FC (Newcastle-upon-Tyne)	42	22	5	15	71	63	49	
6.	Huddersfield Town AFC (Huddersfield)	42	18	11	13	66	53	47	
7.	Derby County FC (Derby)	42	15	14	13	76	69	44	
8.	Leeds United AFC (Leeds)	42	15	14	13	59	62	44	
9.	Portsmouth FC (Portsmouth)	42	18	7	17	74	76	43	
10.	Sheffield United FC (Sheffield)	42	17	9	16	74	80	43	
11.	Everton FC (Liverpool)	42	16	9	17	81	74	41	
12.	Sunderland AFC (Sunderland)	42	15	10	17	63	80	40	
13.	Birmingham FC (Birmingham)	42	14	11	17	57	57	39	
14.	Liverpool FC (Liverpool)	42	14	11	17	79	84	39	
15.	Blackburn Rovers FC (Blackburn)	42	14	10	18	76	102	38	
16.	Manchester City FC (Manchester)	42	16	5	21	68	71	37	
17.	Middlesbrough FC (Middlesbrough)	42	14	9	19	63	73	37	
18.	Chelsea FC (London)	42	14	7	21	63	73	35	
19.	Leicester City FC (Leicester)	42	11	13	18	75	89	35	
20.	Wolverhampton Wanderers FC (Wolverhampton)	42	13	9	20	80	96	35	
21.	Bolton Wanderers FC (Bolton)	42	12	9	21	78	92	33	R
22.	Blackpool FC (Blackpool)	42	14	5	23	69	85	33	R
		924	361	202	361	1645	1645	924	

Top Goalscorer

1)	Jack BOWERS	(Derby County FC)	35

Football League — Division 2 — 1932-1933 Season

	Bradford City	Bradford P.A.	Burnley	Bury	Charlton Ath.	Chesterfield	Fulham	Grimsby Town	Lincoln City	Man. United	Millwall	Nottingham F.	Notts County	Oldham Ath.	Plymouth Arg.	Port Vale	Preston N.E.	Southampton	Stoke City	Swansea Town	Tottenham H.	West Ham Utd.
Bradford City AFC	■	1-0	2-1	3-0	3-0	4-2	2-0	2-2	2-2	1-2	1-5	2-2	1-2	3-0	2-3	7-0	0-0	1-0	1-1	1-1	0-1	5-1
Bradford Park Avenue	2-0	■	0-4	4-0	3-0	5-1	1-4	1-1	6-0	1-1	3-0	3-1	3-4	1-3	1-0	4-2	2-0	2-1	2-2	1-0	3-3	3-0
Burnley FC	0-0	2-0	■	1-0	0-1	1-1	3-3	2-0	0-0	2-3	3-0	3-3	2-1	1-1	1-1	1-1	4-0	2-0	1-2	1-2	1-1	4-0
Bury FC	1-1	0-0	5-3	■	3-1	6-0	1-1	4-1	2-2	2-2	3-0	5-2	3-1	3-3	2-1	0-0	1-2	1-0	3-2	3-0	1-0	6-1
Charlton Athletic FC	0-0	0-2	2-2	1-3	■	2-5	1-2	2-3	4-2	0-1	1-4	3-0	3-3	1-0	4-1	2-1	0-1	2-0	1-0	3-1	0-3	3-1
Chesterfield FC	1-2	2-1	6-0	1-3	2-3	■	3-2	1-2	3-0	1-1	1-0	0-1	0-0	3-1	1-0	2-2	4-3	1-0	1-2	1-0	1-1	1-0
Fulham FC	1-0	5-2	2-1	3-3	3-1	2-2	■	0-1	3-2	3-1	1-1	3-4	1-0	3-1	1-1	1-0	4-2	1-3	3-1	2-2		4-2
Grimsby Town FC	1-1	5-1	1-2	1-0	5-5	1-1	1-0	■	3-3	1-1	1-1	1-1	1-1	5-1	2-3	6-1	5-5	2-2	0-1	2-1	3-2	2-1
Lincoln City FC	0-0	2-2	1-4	2-1	1-1	5-3	3-0	6-3	■	3-2	3-0	1-1	1-1	1-3	0-1	2-1	1-0	2-3	2-0	2-2	6-0	—
Manchester United FC	0-1	2-1	2-1	1-3	1-1	2-1	4-3	1-1	4-1	■	7-1	2-1	2-0	2-0	4-0	1-1	0-0	1-2	0-2	1-1	1-1	1-2
Millwall FC	3-3	1-1	4-1	5-2	2-1	0-0	2-1	0-1	2-0	2-0	■	1-1	1-1	6-1	1-1	3-0	0-0	1-1	1-4	1-0		
Nottingham Forest FC	3-1	1-1	1-1	0-2	0-1	2-3	3-0	3-2	2-2	3-2	0-0	■	3-0	2-3	1-1	1-1	2-1	4-2	1-0	2-2	3-1	2-2
Notts County FC	2-0	1-4	4-2	2-2	3-2	1-1	1-2	1-3	1-1	1-0	1-0	2-4	■	2-1	4-1	5-0	1-1	3-4	1-2	3-0	2-0	
Oldham Athletic AFC	6-1	1-3	2-2	2-1	0-0	2-0	1-3	0-1	5-2	1-1	1-0	1-2	5-0	■	3-1	2-1	0-2	2-0	0-4	0-0	1-5	3-2
Plymouth Argyle FC	2-1	3-2	4-0	1-0	6-1	1-0	2-3	4-0	0-3	2-3	0-0	1-1	0-2	2-1	■	3-1	5-0	1-1	1-0	1-0	2-2	4-1
Port Vale FC	2-0	3-1	1-1	1-0	2-1	9-1	1-2	4-2	3-2	3-3	2-0	0-1	4-0	2-4	4-1	■	0-1	0-2	1-3	2-1	1-1	4-0
Preston North End FC	1-4	2-3	6-1	1-3	4-2	2-0	1-2	4-2	5-0	3-3	0-1	2-1	3-0	2-2	3-0	3-1	■	3-1	1-3	1-3	2-6	4-1
Southampton FC	3-1	2-0	3-1	1-0	3-0	2-1	2-2	3-0	4-0	4-2	2-3	0-2	6-2	0-2	2-2	1-0		■	1-0	2-0	1-1	4-3
Stoke City FC	4-1	4-0	3-0	2-3	2-0	2-1	0-1	2-0	5-2	0-0	1-2	0-1	0-2	4-0	2-0	1-0	1-1	3-1	■	2-0		0-0
Swansea Town AFC	2-0	3-1	2-0	2-1	2-0	3-0	3-0	1-0	3-1	2-1	1-0	0-1	2-0	2-0	0-1	2-0	3-1	2-1	0-2	■	0-2	1-0
Tottenham Hotspur FC	1-1	2-0	4-1	2-1	4-1	4-1	0-0	4-3	3-2	6-1	2-1	0-0	3-1	1-1	0-0	4-0	1-1	5-0	3-2	7-0	■	2-2
West Ham United FC	2-4	2-1	4-4	0-1	7-3	3-1	1-1	5-2	0-0	3-1	3-0	4-3	1-1	5-2	2-2	5-0	1-1	3-1	1-2	3-1	1-0	■

Division 2

		Pd	Wn	Dw	Ls	GF	GA	Pts	
1.	Stoke City FC (Stoke-on-Trent)	42	25	6	11	78	39	56	P
2.	Tottenham Hotspur FC (London)	42	20	15	7	96	51	55	P
3.	Fulham FC (London)	42	20	10	12	78	65	50	
4.	Bury FC (Bury)	42	20	9	13	84	59	49	
5.	Nottingham Forest FC (Nottingham)	42	17	15	10	67	59	49	
6.	Manchester United FC (Manchester)	42	15	13	14	71	68	43	
7.	Millwall FC (London)	42	16	11	15	59	57	43	
8.	Bradford Park Avenue FC (Bradford)	42	17	8	17	77	71	42	
9.	Preston North End FC (Preston)	42	16	10	16	74	70	42	
10.	Swansea Town AFC (Swansea)	42	19	4	19	50	54	42	
11.	Bradford City AFC (Bradford)	42	14	13	15	65	61	41	
12.	Southampton FC (Southampton)	42	18	5	19	66	66	41	
13.	Grimsby Town FC (Cleethorpes)	42	14	13	15	79	84	41	
14.	Plymouth Argyle FC (Plymouth)	42	16	9	17	63	67	41	
15.	Notts County FC (Nottingham)	42	15	10	17	67	78	40	
16.	Oldham Athletic AFC (Oldham)	42	15	8	19	67	80	38	
17.	Port Vale FC (Stoke-on-Trent)	42	14	10	18	66	79	38	
18.	Lincoln City FC (Lincoln)	42	12	13	17	72	87	37	
19.	Burnley FC (Burnley)	42	11	14	17	67	79	36	
20.	West Ham United FC (London)	42	13	9	20	75	93	35	
21.	Chesterfield FC (Chesterfield)	42	12	10	20	61	84	34	R
22.	Charlton Athletic FC (London)	42	12	7	23	60	91	31	R
		924	351	222	351	1542	1542	924	

Football League Division 3 (N) 1932-1933 Season

	Accrington Stan.	Barnsley	Barrow	Carlisle United	Chester	Crewe Alexandra	Darlington	Doncaster Rovers	Gateshead	Halifax Town	Hartlepools United	Hull City	Mansfield Town	New Brighton	Rochdale	Rotherham United	Southport	Stockport County	Tranmere Rovers	Walsall	Wrexham	York City
Accrington Stanley FC	■	2-0	0-0	3-1	1-4	2-0	2-0	1-1	0-3	4-1	7-1	1-2	6-0	5-4	0-3	5-1	1-1	1-1	3-0	1-3	5-3	5-0
Barnsley FC	4-0	■	3-0	4-1	0-3	7-1	6-2	2-3	2-4	1-1	3-2	1-0	6-2	1-2	3-1	3-1	2-0	2-2	2-1	2-1	5-3	1-1
Barrow AFC	5-0	2-3	■	2-1	2-3	3-0	4-0	3-0	1-2	3-3	3-1	0-2	1-0	2-1	1-1	2-1	2-0	0-3	2-0	1-2	1-1	1-0
Carlisle United FC	2-2	0-1	0-1	■	1-1	2-0	3-0	0-2	1-2	5-3	3-1	1-1	3-1	1-3	2-2	0-0	0-0	2-1	1-1	2-1	1-1	5-1
Chester FC	4-2	3-1	2-1	4-0	■	3-1	5-2	2-0	3-1	6-3	3-3	1-1	5-2	3-0	2-0	1-0	1-1	2-2	1-2	1-0	0-3	5-0
Crewe Alexandra FC	3-1	2-2	2-0	1-0	0-1	■	2-4	4-0	2-0	2-1	6-2	1-1	7-0	4-0	3-1	8-0	1-1	2-1	2-0	2-1	2-0	1-0
Darlington FC	2-2	1-1	1-2	5-2	1-1	3-4	■	2-2	1-3	1-2	3-2	1-3	2-1	5-1	4-1	1-1	1-1	1-0	1-1	1-1	1-1	3-0
Doncaster Rovers FC	2-2	3-1	1-1	4-2	3-3	5-1	3-1	■	3-1	5-1	4-1	1-1	2-2	2-0	1-0	0-1	2-1	1-1	2-2	3-2	1-1	3-2
Gateshead FC	1-0	1-1	2-3	1-0	3-0	2-1	3-0	4-0	■	3-0	3-1	2-3	3-2	2-0	3-0	1-1	4-1	0-3	0-2	1-1	4-4	2-2
Halifax Town AFC	0-0	2-1	2-0	0-1	0-2	1-5	4-2	0-0	1-0	■	4-0	1-3	5-1	3-3	2-0	2-1	1-0	1-3	4-1	4-0	0-0	2-0
Hartlepools United FC	3-1	6-4	0-1	2-1	3-1	3-2	2-1	4-0	2-2	1-1	■	0-1	6-3	3-2	3-0	2-0	4-2	1-1	2-3	2-3	3-1	4-2
Hull City AFC	4-2	5-1	3-0	6-1	2-0	3-0	3-1	6-1	1-1	3-1	3-0	■	4-1	5-0	1-1	4-2	4-0	3-0	3-0	0-1	4-1	2-1
Mansfield Town FC	1-3	0-1	2-1	3-1	1-0	4-0	3-3	2-2	1-2	2-2	7-1	2-1	■	5-0	4-1	9-2	4-0	1-2	2-0	0-0	2-0	2-0
New Brighton FC	2-2	3-5	1-2	2-0	3-1	1-2	7-1	4-4	3-0	5-2	1-0	1-0	1-0	■	0-3	5-2	2-1	1-1	1-1	2-2	0-2	0-1
Rochdale AFC	2-0	2-3	0-0	0-1	2-0	1-4	1-1	2-3	1-0	1-0	6-2	3-2	2-1	1-0	■	2-2	1-3	0-3	1-1	3-1	3-1	1-4
Rotherham United FC	2-3	0-0	1-0	1-0	0-5	5-0	3-1	1-1	1-2	6-1	1-1	3-2	3-0	1-0	2-0	■	3-1	2-1	2-0	4-1	0-2	1-0
Southport FC	2-3	2-0	3-0	4-0	2-1	4-1	5-1	1-0	4-1	1-2	6-3	0-1	5-2	1-1	2-0	2-0	■	2-1	1-1	2-1	1-0	5-1
Stockport County FC	2-0	5-4	4-1	8-5	1-0	5-1	5-1	5-4	4-3	6-0	2-3	2-2	1-1	2-3	2-2	1-0	3-1	■	3-0	5-0	1-0	2-0
Tranmere Rovers FC	4-0	3-0	1-3	1-2	2-2	5-0	3-1	3-2	4-2	3-3	2-3	3-0	2-3	3-1	1-0	2-1	2-2	2-2	■	1-3	0-0	2-3
Walsall FC	1-0	1-1	1-1	5-0	3-1	2-1	4-0	2-0	2-0	4-0	4-1	1-0	8-1	0-0	2-1	1-1	3-1	0-0	3-2	■	2-3	4-2
Wrexham AFC	1-0	3-0	4-1	2-1	1-2	7-0	3-1	3-0	5-1	5-2	8-1	3-1	1-1	5-0	4-1	5-1	6-0	2-1	1-1	3-0	■	3-1
York City FC	0-0	3-2	3-1	0-1	3-1	4-0	6-1	2-3	2-2	5-3	1-1	1-2	4-3	3-0	2-6	4-3	0-1	2-2	0-1	4-2	2-3	■

Division 3 (North)

		Pd	Wn	Dw	Ls	GF	GA	Pts	
1.	Hull City AFC (Kingston-upon-Tyne)	42	26	7	9	100	45	59	P
2.	Wrexham AFC (Wrexham)	42	24	9	9	106	51	57	
3.	Stockport County FC (Stockport)	42	21	12	9	99	58	54	
4.	Chester FC (Chester)	42	22	8	12	94	66	52	
5.	Walsall FC (Walsall)	42	19	10	13	75	58	48	
6.	Doncaster Rovers FC (Doncaster)	42	17	14	11	77	79	48	
7.	Gateshead FC (Gateshead)	42	19	9	14	78	67	47	
8.	Barnsley FC (Barnsley)	42	19	8	15	92	80	46	
9.	Barrow AFC (Barrow-in-Furness)	42	18	7	17	60	60	43	
10.	Crewe Alexandra FC (Crewe)	42	20	3	19	80	84	43	
11.	Tranmere Rovers FC (Birkenhead)	42	17	8	17	70	66	42	
12.	Southport FC (Southport)	42	17	7	18	70	67	41	
13.	Accrington Stanley FC (Accrington)	42	15	10	17	78	76	40	
14.	Hartlepools United FC (Hartlepool)	42	16	7	19	87	116	39	
15.	Halifax Town AFC (Halifax)	42	15	8	19	71	90	38	
16.	Mansfield Town FC (Mansfield)	42	14	7	21	84	100	35	
17.	Rotherham United FC (Rotherham)	42	14	6	22	60	84	34	
18.	Rochdale AFC (Rochdale)	42	13	7	22	58	80	33	
19.	Carlisle United FC (Carlisle)	42	13	7	22	51	75	33	
20.	York City FC (York)	42	13	6	23	72	92	32	
21.	New Brighton FC (Wallasey)	42	11	10	21	63	88	32	
22.	Darlington FC (Darlington)	42	10	8	24	66	109	28	
		924	373	178	373	1691	1691	924	

Football League Division 3 (S) — 1932-1933 Season

Home \ Away	Ald	Bmth	Bfd	Bton	BCi	BRo	Car	Cla	Cov	CPa	Exe	Gil	Lut	New	Nmp	NwC	QPR	Rea	Sou	Swi	Tor	Wat
Aldershot FC	■	1-1	1-1	1-1	1-0	1-0	1-0	4-0	1-1	3-1	4-1	3-0	2-2	2-1	0-1	1-3	2-0	4-4	1-2	0-1	2-0	2-1
Bournemouth & B. Athletic	1-0	■	1-1	1-1	6-1	2-2	3-2	4-2	3-1	3-2	1-1	1-0	0-2	1-2	1-1	1-1	3-0	0-3	4-0	5-1	1-2	2-2
Brentford FC	2-0	1-1	■	2-1	2-1	0-0	7-3	4-2	2-1	2-0	0-2	1-2	1-0	6-0	1-0	2-2	2-0	1-1	3-1	1-0	3-1	2-1
Brighton & Hove Albion	0-2	3-0	1-2	■	7-0	0-3	1-0	0-0	1-0	1-2	2-1	1-0	2-0	1-0	2-1	1-1	4-1	5-3	1-2	5-1	1-1	3-0
Bristol City FC	2-2	1-1	1-2	3-4	■	3-1	3-1	3-0	5-3	3-3	0-1	1-1	5-2	3-2	5-4	1-1	2-3	4-1	5-1	5-1	2-0	2-3
Bristol Rovers FC	4-1	1-0	2-4	5-3	1-1	■	0-0	2-0	1-0	2-3	1-0	1-0	0-0	2-2	4-3	1-1	4-1	1-0	3-1	1-0	0-2	2-0
Cardiff City AFC	2-1	3-0	2-1	1-2	1-1	4-3	■	6-1	2-2	1-1	1-3	1-0	3-2	1-3	6-0	4-2	2-5	0-1	2-0	3-0	2-1	1-1
Clapton Orient FC	2-3	1-1	1-5	2-0	2-2	0-3	3-0	■	2-1	4-1	2-2	1-2	0-0	3-1	2-2	0-0	2-2	2-5	0-0	7-1	1-4	2-0
Coventry City FC	3-0	3-0	2-3	2-2	6-0	2-0	5-0	5-0	■	6-2	4-2	4-0	3-1	3-1	3-5	7-0	3-1	2-3	2-1	5-0	1-3	4-1
Crystal Palace FC	3-0	3-0	2-1	5-0	2-2	2-0	4-1	2-1	1-3	■	2-2	5-1	3-0	0-0	2-0	4-0	0-1	1-1	4-1	4-3	2-1	0-3
Exeter City FC	0-0	2-3	1-2	4-1	2-0	1-0	1-0	3-0	5-0	1-1	■	2-1	2-0	4-0	3-1	2-1	2-0	4-1	3-0	5-0	5-0	5-2
Gillingham FC	5-2	4-0	1-3	2-0	4-2	2-0	1-1	3-1	3-0	2-0	1-2	■	1-1	2-0	5-1	0-2	3-1	6-1	1-1	2-2	3-1	1-3
Luton Town FC	2-1	1-2	5-5	0-0	5-4	1-1	8-1	4-1	4-1	1-1	4-0	2-1	■	2-2	2-1	1-1	3-1	1-1	3-3	6-2	2-1	3-2
Newport County AFC	2-1	1-1	1-6	5-2	1-1	3-1	4-2	0-2	2-1	1-3	1-1	0-2	3-2	■	0-3	3-4	5-1	3-3	1-3	1-2	3-1	2-0
Northampton Town FC	5-2	6-0	1-0	0-0	2-1	1-1	2-0	3-0	5-1	5-3	1-0	1-0	1-2	8-0	■	2-2	2-1	1-0	0-0	6-0	0-0	6-0
Norwich City FC	3-2	6-0	3-0	1-0	3-0	1-1	3-1	2-1	2-1	3-0	0-0	2-1	3-1	2-0	4-0	■	3-2	2-2	1-0	5-2	1-2	1-2
Queen's Park Rangers FC	2-2	3-1	2-3	0-1	1-1	1-1	5-1	2-1	3-3	2-1	1-3	1-1	3-1	6-1	1-1	2-2	■	0-3	6-1	4-2	1-1	2-1
Reading FC	2-2	6-2	1-3	3-0	2-2	3-1	4-2	3-3	2-3	2-2	4-0	4-1	4-1	4-0	3-2	3-1	3-1	■	1-1	7-1	5-2	1-1
Southend United FC	5-1	2-1	0-1	2-1	3-1	2-2	2-2	3-3	1-3	1-3	2-2	2-2	1-1	2-2	2-1	1-0	3-1	2-3	■	0-0	2-2	1-1
Swindon Town FC	3-2	2-0	0-0	5-1	1-4	1-1	6-2	3-3	1-2	1-0	2-1	1-1	2-0	2-1	2-4	0-0	0-1	2-2	2-2	■	0-0	1-2
Torquay United FC	1-0	2-1	1-1	1-0	0-0	1-1	4-1	1-1	3-3	2-1	1-3	1-2	3-1	4-0	5-1	2-2	3-1	1-1	8-1	4-3	■	3-2
Watford FC	2-0	2-1	1-1	0-4	1-0	3-1	2-1	1-1	3-1	1-0	0-0	2-0	4-1	3-2	4-0	1-2	2-2	1-1	2-2	2-2	0-0	■

Division 3 (South)

		Pd	Wn	Dw	Ls	GF	GA	Pts	
1.	Brentford FC (London)	42	26	10	6	90	49	62	P
2.	Exeter City FC (Exeter)	42	24	10	8	88	48	58	
3.	Norwich City FC (Norwich)	42	22	13	7	88	55	57	
4.	Reading FC (Reading)	42	19	13	10	103	71	51	
5.	Crystal Palace FC (London)	42	19	8	15	78	64	46	
6.	Coventry City FC (Coventry)	42	19	6	17	106	77	44	
7.	Gillingham FC (Gillingham)	42	18	8	16	72	61	44	
8.	Northampton Town FC (Northampton)	42	18	8	16	76	66	44	
9.	Bristol Rovers FC (Bristol)	42	15	14	13	61	56	44	
10.	Torquay United FC (Torquay)	42	16	12	14	72	67	44	
11.	Watford FC (Watford)	42	16	12	14	66	63	44	
12.	Brighton & Hove Albion FC (Hove)	42	17	8	17	66	65	42	
13.	Southend United FC (Southend-on-Sea)	42	15	11	16	65	82	41	
14.	Luton Town FC (Luton)	42	13	13	16	78	78	39	
15.	Bristol City FC (Bristol)	42	12	13	17	83	90	37	
16.	Queen's Park Rangers FC (London)	42	13	11	18	72	87	37	
17.	Aldershot FC (Aldershot)	42	13	10	19	61	72	36	
18.	Bournemouth & Boscombe Athletic FC (Bournemouth)	42	12	12	18	60	81	36	
19.	Cardiff City AFC (Cardiff)	42	12	7	23	69	99	31	
20.	Clapton Orient FC (London)	42	8	13	21	59	93	29	
21.	Newport County AFC (Newport)	42	11	7	24	61	105	29	
22.	Swindon Town FC (Swindon)	42	9	11	22	60	105	29	
		924	347	230	347	1634	1634	924	

F.A. CUP FINAL   (Wembley Stadium, London – 29/04/1933 – 92,950)

EVERTON FC (LIVERPOOL)   3-0   Manchester City FC (Manchester)

Stein, Dean, Dunn

Everton: Sagar, Cook, Cresswell, Britton, White, Thompson, Geldard, Dunn, Dean, Johnson, Stein.

Man. City: Langford, Cann, Dale, Busby, Cowan, Bray, Toseland, Marshall, Herd, McMullan, Brook.

Semi-finals

Everton FC (Liverpool)	2-1	West Ham United FC (London)
Manchester City FC (Manchester)	3-2	Derby County FC (Derby)

Quarter-finals

Burnley FC (Burnley)	0-1		Manchester City FC (Manchester)
Derby County FC (Derby)	4-4,	1-0 (aet)	Sunderland AFC (Sunderland)
Everton FC (Liverpool)	6-0		Luton Town FC (Luton)
West Ham United FC (London)	4-0		Birmingham FC (Birmingham)

1933-34

Football League Division 1, 1933-1934 Season

	Arsenal	Aston Villa	Birmingham	Blackburn Rovers	Chelsea	Derby County	Everton	Huddersfield Town	Leeds United	Leicester City	Liverpool	Manchester City	Middlesbrough	Newcastle United	Portsmouth	Sheffield United	Sheffield Wednesday	Stoke City	Sunderland	Tottenham Hotspur	W.B.A.	Wolves
Arsenal FC	■	3-2	1-1	2-1	2-1	1-0	1-2	3-1	2-0	2-0	2-1	1-1	6-0	3-0	1-1	2-0	1-1	3-0	2-1	1-3	3-1	3-2
Aston Villa FC	2-3	■	1-1	1-1	2-0	0-2	2-1	4-3	3-0	2-3	4-2	0-0	3-0	2-3	1-1	3-0	1-0	1-2	2-1	1-5	4-4	6-2
Birmingham FC	0-0	0-0	■	2-0	0-3	2-1	2-2	1-3	4-0	3-0	1-2	0-1	0-0	1-2	3-1	4-2	3-0	0-1	1-1	2-0	0-1	0-0
Blackburn Rovers FC	2-2	2-1	3-1	■	4-2	2-1	1-1	2-2	4-2	3-0	3-1	3-0	0-0	3-2	3-2	3-1	3-1	4-1	0-0	1-0	4-0	7-1
Chelsea FC	2-2	1-0	1-1	3-0	■	0-2	2-0	2-3	1-1	2-0	2-0	1-2	2-3	2-1	4-0	5-0	0-1	2-0	4-0	0-4	3-2	5-2
Derby County FC	2-4	1-1	4-0	1-1	1-0	■	1-1	1-1	3-1	2-1	3-1	4-1	2-0	1-1	0-1	5-1	1-1	5-1	0-0	4-3	1-1	3-1
Everton FC	3-1	2-2	2-0	7-1	2-1	0-3	■	0-1	2-0	1-1	0-0	2-0	1-1	3-7	1-1	4-0	2-3	2-1	1-1	1-0	1-1	1-2
Huddersfield Town AFC	0-1	2-1	0-0	5-3	6-1	2-0	1-0	■	0-0	5-1	0-2	1-0	2-1	4-1	4-0	6-1	3-2	2-2	2-1	2-0	3-1	3-1
Leeds United AFC	0-1	2-4	1-0	4-0	3-1	0-2	2-2	1-1	■	8-0	5-1	3-1	5-2	3-0	1-0	1-1	2-1	2-0	3-1	0-0	3-0	3-3
Leicester City FC	4-1	1-1	3-7	1-2	1-1	2-0	3-1	1-0	2-2	■	1-0	0-0	1-2	3-2	2-1	4-0	2-0	3-1	0-0	1-3	0-1	1-1
Liverpool FC	2-3	2-3	4-1	4-0	3-0	4-2	3-2	2-2	4-3	1-3	■	3-2	6-2	1-2	3-2	1-3	1-1	1-1	3-1	1-1	1-1	1-1
Manchester City FC	2-1	1-0	1-0	3-1	4-2	2-0	2-2	2-2	0-1	1-1	2-1	■	5-2	1-1	2-1	4-1	2-3	4-2	4-1	2-0	2-7	4-0
Middlesbrough FC	0-2	1-2	0-3	3-1	2-2	3-1	2-0	3-0	2-1	4-1	2-1		■	1-0	2-0	10-3	2-3	6-1	0-4	1-1	3-0	0-0
Newcastle United FC	0-1	1-1	0-0	3-1	2-2	1-1	1-2	3-3	2-0	1-0	9-2	2-2	1-1	■	2-2	3-1	0-0	2-2	2-1	1-3	1-2	5-1
Portsmouth FC	1-0	3-2	0-2	2-0	0-2	1-0	0-0	3-0	2-1	3-5	1-0	2-0	4-1	2-0	■	1-1	0-2	3-1	0-0	0-1	2-2	1-1
Sheffield United FC	1-3	3-3	2-1	1-0	4-1	2-0	1-1	1-4	2-1	2-1	2-2	1-1	3-1	4-0	0-1	■	5-1	1-2	2-0	0-0	1-1	3-1
Sheffield Wednesday FC	1-2	1-2	2-1	4-0	2-1	1-1	0-0	1-2	0-2	1-1	1-2	3-0	3-1	1-2	0-1		■	2-2	2-0	2-1	3-1	
Stoke City FC	1-1	1-1	1-1	2-0	1-0	0-4	1-2	3-0	1-2	2-1	1-1	0-1	2-0	2-1	2-1	3-0	0-1	■	3-0	2-0	4-1	1-1
Sunderland AFC	3-0	5-1	4-1	3-0	0-0	0-0	3-2	1-1	4-2	2-1	4-1	0-0	2-0	2-0	0-2	5-0	4-0	4-1	■	6-0	2-2	3-3
Tottenham Hotspur FC	1-1	3-2	3-2	4-1	2-1	1-2	3-0	1-3	5-1	0-1	0-3	5-1	2-0	4-0	0-0	4-1	4-3	0-0	3-1	■	2-1	4-0
West Bromwich Albion FC	1-0	2-1	1-2	0-1	3-1	5-1	3-3	2-3	0-3	2-0	2-2	4-0	3-0	1-1	3-0	1-1	5-1	6-5	1-2		■	2-0
Wolverhampton Wanderers FC	0-1	4-3	2-0	5-3	1-1	3-0	2-0	5-2	2-0	1-1	3-2	8-0	0-1	2-1	1-1	3-2	6-2	0-2	1-6	1-0	0-0	■

	Division 1	Pd	Wn	Dw	Ls	GF	GA	Pts	
1.	ARSENAL FC (LONDON)	42	25	9	8	75	47	59	
2.	Huddersfield Town AFC (Huddersfield)	42	23	10	9	90	61	56	
3.	Tottenham Hotspur FC (London)	42	21	7	14	79	56	49	
4.	Derby County FC (Derby)	42	17	11	14	68	54	45	
5.	Manchester City FC (Manchester)	42	17	11	14	65	72	45	
6.	Sunderland AFC (Sunderland)	42	16	12	14	81	56	44	
7.	West Bromwich Albion FC (West Bromwich)	42	17	10	15	78	70	44	
8.	Blackburn Rovers FC (Blackburn)	42	18	7	17	74	81	43	
9.	Leeds United AFC (Leeds)	42	17	8	17	75	66	42	
10.	Portsmouth FC (Portsmouth)	42	15	12	15	52	55	42	
11.	Sheffield Wednesday FC (Sheffield)	42	16	9	17	62	67	41	
12.	Stoke City FC (Stoke-on-Trent)	42	15	11	16	58	71	41	
13.	Aston Villa FC (Birmingham)	42	14	12	16	78	75	40	
14.	Everton FC (Liverpool)	42	12	16	14	62	63	40	
15.	Wolverhampton Wanderers FC (Wolverhampton)	42	14	12	16	74	86	40	
16.	Middlesbrough FC (Middlesbrough)	42	16	7	19	68	80	39	
17.	Leicester City FC (Leicester)	42	14	11	17	59	74	39	
18.	Liverpool FC (Liverpool)	42	14	10	18	79	87	38	
19.	Chelsea FC (London)	42	14	8	20	67	69	36	
20.	Birmingham FC (Birmingham)	42	12	12	18	54	56	36	
21.	Newcastle United FC (Newcastle-upon-Tyne)	42	10	14	18	68	77	34	R
22.	Sheffield United FC (Sheffield)	42	12	7	23	58	101	31	R
		924	349	226	349	1524	1524	924	

Top Goalscorer

1)   Jack BOWERS   (Derby County FC)   34

155

Football League Division 2 1933-1934 Season	Blackpool	Bolton Wands.	Bradford City	Bradford P.A.	Brentford	Burnley	Bury	Fulham	Grimsby Town	Hull City	Lincoln City	Man. United	Millwall	Nottingham F.	Notts County	Oldham Athletic	Plymouth Arg.	Port Vale	Preston N.E.	Southampton	Swansea Town	West Ham Utd.
Blackpool FC		1-1	3-2	1-1	3-1	1-1	2-0	4-3	3-4	0-0	2-0	3-1	2-2	2-3	2-1	0-0	1-1	1-0	1-2	4-2	2-1	1-1
Bolton Wanderers FC	1-2		3-0	0-1	3-2	4-1	2-0	3-1	0-4	3-3	1-2	3-1	5-0	1-1	1-0	1-0	2-0	3-0	0-2	2-0	2-1	5-1
Bradford City AFC	1-0	5-1		3-0	2-1	2-1	2-2	1-0	2-1	1-2	3-0	1-1	1-0	3-2	3-1	5-2	3-4	1-2	1-0	2-2	2-1	2-2
Bradford Park Avenue	1-2	1-4	2-1		5-2	5-0	0-1	3-1	2-1	3-1	2-1	6-1	4-0	6-2	3-2	4-2	4-1	2-2	2-1	3-1	5-1	0-0
Brentford FC	1-0	3-1	2-1	2-0		5-2	2-3	1-2	1-2	2-2	5-0	3-4	3-0	2-1	2-2	2-1	3-0	0-2	3-2	2-0	2-0	4-1
Burnley FC	3-2	1-3	4-2	1-0	3-1		1-2	2-1	2-0	3-1	3-1	1-4	2-1	1-0	1-0	0-1	2-2	0-1	1-4	2-1	3-1	4-2
Bury FC	2-5	1-1	1-0	2-1	1-2	1-1		3-3	1-3	3-1	0-2	2-1	5-1	4-2	3-1	1-1	4-0	0-3	2-1	1-0	4-1	2-1
Fulham FC	1-0	0-2	0-1	0-2	1-1	1-1	2-1		1-0	1-1	1-0	0-2	2-0	3-1	3-0	1-2	3-2	3-0	1-0	1-0	1-0	3-1
Grimsby Town FC	7-0	2-3	1-4	3-2	2-2	1-0	2-0	3-1		4-1	3-0	7-3	5-2	2-2	2-1	5-1	1-2	3-0	3-1	3-1	3-1	1-1
Hull City AFC	3-0	1-0	2-2	1-2	0-1	0-1	3-1	0-0	0-1		2-0	4-1	3-2	2-2	0-0	5-4	2-1	1-0	0-0	2-0	0-0	2-0
Lincoln City FC	2-2	2-2	0-1	2-1	0-2	4-0	1-2	5-0	3-3	2-1		5-1	0-1	0-0	1-1	1-1	1-0	0-1	1-1	1-0	1-0	0-2
Manchester United FC	2-0	1-5	2-1	0-4	1-3	5-2	2-1	1-0	1-3	4-1	1-1		1-1	0-1	1-2	2-3	0-3	2-0	1-0	2-0	1-0	0-1
Millwall FC	0-0	2-1	1-1	1-0	2-0	0-0	0-0	0-1	2-0	4-1	0-2	0-0		3-2	1-0	0-0	0-3	1-1	1-0	0-3	1-1	1-2
Nottingham Forest FC	0-0	2-2	1-2	3-0	1-1	0-2	7-2	2-0	4-2	0-1	6-2	1-1	2-0		2-0	1-3	2-1	6-1	2-3	4-1	4-2	0-1
Notts County FC	1-1	1-2	3-0	1-0	1-2	3-1	2-1	4-1	1-2	0-0	2-0	0-0	0-0	0-1		1-1	2-1	3-2	2-2	2-2	1-1	1-2
Oldham Athletic AFC	2-0	1-3	4-3	1-3	1-4	1-0	2-2	2-2	1-5	7-0	3-0	2-0	1-0	4-1	2-0		1-1	5-1	3-1	1-1	0-0	4-1
Plymouth Argyle FC	0-3	3-0	3-0	4-1	1-1	1-0	3-3	0-0	0-2	1-1	3-0	4-0	1-0	4-3	1-0	1-0		3-0	0-0	2-2	1-0	4-4
Port Vale FC	1-0	0-0	3-1	3-1	1-0	0-2	4-1	2-2	0-1	3-0	1-0	2-3	5-1	3-1	0-0	2-0	4-0		2-0	2-1	1-0	0-0
Preston North End FC	3-0	1-1	0-1	0-1	3-2	3-2	0-3	2-0	1-2	5-0	2-1	3-2	4-2	4-0	2-0	1-0	1-1	0-0		3-1	3-0	3-1
Southampton FC	3-2	1-0	4-1	5-0	0-0	2-1	1-0	2-0	4-2	1-1	3-1	1-0	2-3	2-0	3-2	1-0	0-1	1-4	0-1		1-0	3-2
Swansea Town AFC	2-2	0-0	2-1	5-1	2-3	3-0	1-1	1-1	1-1	1-0	2-1	2-0	1-1	1-1	2-2	2-1	4-0	1-2	1-0	1-0		1-1
West Ham United FC	1-2	4-2	1-2	0-1	3-2	1-2	3-1	5-1	3-1	2-1	4-1	2-1	1-1	2-1	5-3	1-4	5-1	1-0	6-0	0-0	1-1	

Division 2

		Pd	Wn	Dw	Ls	GF	GA	Pts	
1.	Grimsby Town FC (Cleethorpes)	42	27	5	10	103	59	59	P
2.	Preston North End FC (Preston)	42	23	6	13	71	52	52	P
3.	Bolton Wanderers FC (Bolton)	42	21	9	12	79	55	51	
4.	Brentford FC (London)	42	22	7	13	85	60	51	
5.	Bradford Park Avenue FC (Bradford)	42	23	3	16	86	67	49	
6.	Bradford City AFC (Bradford)	42	20	6	16	73	67	46	
7.	West Ham United FC (London)	42	17	11	14	78	70	45	
8.	Port Vale FC (Stoke-on-Trent)	42	19	7	16	60	55	45	
9.	Oldham Athletic AFC (Oldham)	42	17	10	15	72	60	44	
10.	Plymouth Argyle FC (Plymouth)	42	15	13	14	69	70	43	
11.	Blackpool FC (Blackpool)	42	15	13	14	62	64	43	
12.	Bury FC (Bury)	42	17	9	16	70	73	43	
13.	Burnley FC (Burnley)	42	18	6	18	60	72	42	
14.	Southampton FC (Southampton)	42	15	8	19	54	58	38	
15.	Hull City AFC (Kingston-upon-Hull)	42	13	12	17	52	68	38	
16.	Fulham FC (London)	42	15	7	20	48	67	37	
17.	Nottingham Forest FC (Nottingham)	42	13	9	20	73	74	35	
18.	Notts County FC (Nottingham)	42	12	11	19	53	62	35	
19.	Swansea Town AFC (Swansea)	42	10	15	17	51	60	35	
20.	Manchester United FC (Manchester)	42	14	6	22	50	85	34	
21.	Millwall FC (London)	42	11	11	20	39	68	33	R
22.	Lincoln City FC (Lincoln)	42	9	8	25	44	75	26	R
		924	366	192	366	1441	1441	924	

Football League Division 3 (N) — 1933-1934 Season

	Accrington Stan.	Barnsley	Barrow	Carlisle United	Chester	Chesterfield	Crewe Alexandra	Darlington	Doncaster Rovers	Gateshead	Halifax Town	Hartlepools United	Mansfield Town	New Brighton	Rochdale	Rotherham United	Southport	Stockport County	Tranmere Rovers	Walsall	Wrexham	York City
Accrington Stanley FC	■	0-9	0-4	2-1	4-1	1-0	0-2	2-0	4-1	5-2	1-1	2-2	1-1	8-0	1-3	2-2	3-2	0-3	2-2	1-0	1-1	4-1
Barnsley FC	6-0	■	3-1	1-0	2-0	3-2	5-2	4-0	2-2	0-0	1-0	5-4	6-1	2-0	4-1	5-1	3-2	2-0	5-1	1-1	3-0	1-0
Barrow AFC	2-6	3-4	■	2-0	9-0	2-0	0-3	5-2	2-1	12-1	5-2	2-2	6-3	3-3	5-3	4-1	3-3	2-0	1-3	5-5	3-1	2-2
Carlisle United FC	3-0	1-4	0-0	■	1-0	1-1	6-1	3-3	0-1	6-0	1-0	4-1	3-2	1-2	3-0	0-1	0-0	2-2	2-1	3-2	0-0	3-2
Chester FC	7-0	4-2	1-3	3-3	■	3-2	1-0	8-0	3-1	4-0	1-2	3-3	1-1	0-0	7-1	5-1	1-0	1-1	4-2	0-1	1-2	1-1
Chesterfield FC	1-0	3-0	2-1	4-0	6-1	■	3-2	0-1	1-1	6-2	4-2	3-1	3-2	4-0	3-0	2-1	2-1	1-0	1-0	1-2	4-0	2-0
Crewe Alexandra FC	4-2	4-2	1-3	4-0	3-5	1-2	■	2-3	4-0	3-2	1-1	1-0	2-1	6-2	4-1	0-2	2-2	2-2	3-1	1-4	1-0	5-3
Darlington FC	3-1	0-4	4-1	1-2	0-4	1-1	1-1	■	4-0	3-3	4-2	5-3	1-4	1-0	1-1	4-1	4-0	1-2	1-3	2-1	2-1	4-0
Doncaster Rovers FC	5-1	4-4	3-2	2-1	3-1	1-3	4-0	3-2	■	5-2	3-0	3-0	1-0	1-0	5-0	2-1	3-0	0-2	2-0	4-0	1-4	3-1
Gateshead FC	2-0	1-4	0-0	2-3	1-3	2-1	2-1	2-2	2-4	■	4-0	6-3	5-3	6-0	2-1	4-1	2-2	0-4	1-2	2-1	0-3	0-2
Halifax Town AFC	2-1	1-1	4-1	3-2	1-0	5-0	3-2	2-0	0-1	2-4	■	6-2	4-2	1-4	3-2	6-2	0-2	2-1	1-3	3-0		
Hartlepools United FC	3-0	0-2	7-0	3-2	1-0	0-3	2-1	6-2	2-2	3-3	5-0	■	3-1	2-1	4-0	1-2	3-1	1-1		0-1	4-1	2-0
Mansfield Town FC	5-0	1-5	0-5	6-0	2-1	0-3	4-1	4-0	1-1	1-1	6-1	1-1	■	5-2	5-0	3-0	2-2	1-1	0-0	1-2	1-1	0-2
New Brighton FC	0-3	0-1	2-2	2-1	0-2	0-0	2-1	3-2	2-1	3-0	4-1	5-1	0-2	■	3-1	5-2	2-1	1-0	2-0	0-1	2-1	
Rochdale AFC	0-1	3-1	1-2	0-1	6-0	0-1	2-0	1-0	0-2	2-0	1-2	3-0	2-2	1-1	■	0-2	3-3	1-1		3-3	1-2	3-6
Rotherham United FC	3-1	0-2	1-1	0-1	0-3	1-3	3-4	0-0	0-0	3-2	1-2	4-2	1-2	2-2	4-0	■	0-1	1-1	2-2	1-1	1-3	3-2
Southport FC	1-1	2-2	1-3	1-1	3-1	0-0	1-1	3-2	1-0	0-1	4-0	0-2	3-3	4-0	4-0		■	1-4	2-2	3-1	1-0	1-1
Stockport County FC	3-0	1-1	4-1	4-0	4-2	0-0	1-0	6-0	4-3	1-0	13-0	3-1	5-1	3-1	9-2			■	2-1	3-2	7-3	2-1
Tranmere Rovers FC	2-0	5-2	4-1	3-1	6-1	0-1	5-1	2-2	2-0	2-1	3-2	3-2	1-0	4-0	1-2	5-0	1-1		■	1-0	1-2	3-0
Walsall FC	5-0	5-1	2-4	3-2	5-0	2-2	5-1	3-0	0-0	5-1	2-0	5-0	0-0	2-1	2-0	3-1	4-1	2-0	5-3	■	3-1	1-0
Wrexham AFC	3-2	4-2	3-2	8-1	0-3	2-3	5-1	6-1	1-1	2-3	0-2	3-1	5-0	5-4	4-0	0-1	5-1	4-2			■	2-3
York City FC	3-2	1-1	6-1	4-1	3-2	1-2	4-1	1-1	1-2	1-1	1-0	1-3	1-0	2-1	6-1	0-1	1-0	2-2	1-0	2-2	2-4	■

Division 3 (North)

		Pd	Wn	Dw	Ls	GF	GA	Pts	
1.	Barnsley FC (Barnsley)	42	27	8	7	118	61	62	P
2.	Chesterfield FC (Chesterfield)	42	27	7	8	86	43	61	
3.	Stockport County FC (Stockport)	42	24	11	7	115	52	59	
4.	Walsall FC (Walsall)	42	23	7	12	97	60	53	
5.	Doncaster Rovers FC (Doncaster)	42	22	9	11	83	61	53	
6.	Wrexham AFC (Wrexham)	42	23	5	14	102	73	51	
7.	Tranmere Rovers FC (Birkenhead)	42	20	7	15	84	63	47	
8.	Barrow AFC (Barrow-in-Furness)	42	19	9	14	116	94	47	
9.	Halifax Town AFC (Halifax)	42	20	4	18	80	91	44	
10.	Chester FC (Chester)	42	17	6	19	89	86	40	
11.	Hartlepools United FC (Hartlepool)	42	16	7	19	89	93	39	
12.	York City FC (York)	42	15	8	19	71	74	38	
13.	Carlisle United FC (Carlisle)	42	15	8	19	66	81	38	
14.	Crewe Alexandra FC (Crewe)	42	15	6	21	81	97	36	
15.	New Brighton FC (Wallasey)	42	14	8	20	62	87	36	
16.	Darlington FC (Darlington)	42	13	9	20	70	101	35	
17.	Mansfield Town FC (Mansfield)	42	11	12	19	81	88	34	
18.	Southport FC (Southport)	42	8	17	17	63	90	33	
19.	Gateshead FC (Gateshead)	42	12	9	21	76	110	33	
20.	Accrington Stanley FC (Accrington)	42	13	7	22	65	101	33	
21.	Rotherham United FC (Rotherham)	42	10	8	24	53	91	28	
22.	Rochdale AFC (Rochdale)	42	9	6	27	53	103	24	
		924	373	178	373	1800	1800	924	

Football League Division 3 (S) — 1933-1934 Season

	Aldershot	Bournemouth	Brighton	Bristol City	Bristol Rovers	Cardiff City	Charlton Athletic	Clapton Orient	Coventry City	Crystal Palace	Exeter City	Gillingham	Luton Town	Newport County	Northampton	Norwich City	Q.P.R.	Reading	Southend United	Swindon Town	Torquay United	Watford
Aldershot FC		0-0	0-1	2-2	0-1	1-3	3-2	0-0	1-1	0-4	0-2	0-2	0-0	3-2	1-1	2-1	3-1	3-0	2-0	1-2	3-0	3-2
Bournemouth & B. Athletic	1-2		1-1	5-0	2-0	1-3	1-2	2-0	3-3	1-1	1-3	1-1	4-3	0-0	4-0	2-4	3-2	1-1	1-4	1-1	3-4	3-2
Brighton & Hove Albion	3-1	6-0		5-1	0-2	4-0	1-0	1-1	1-1	4-1	2-1	5-2	1-1	1-1	3-3	1-1	0-1	1-1	1-0	3-0	3-1	2-0
Bristol City FC	1-1	3-1	5-0		0-3	3-0	0-1	3-0	0-0	2-2	1-1	1-1	0-0	1-1	2-3	0-1	0-2	1-2	5-1	2-2	2-0	1-0
Bristol Rovers FC	4-1	3-0	1-1	5-1		3-1	2-5	2-2	4-1	0-1	1-1	4-2	0-1	2-0	1-1	3-0	4-1	1-0	3-1	3-0	3-0	1-0
Cardiff City AFC	1-2	4-2	1-4	1-5	1-5		1-1	1-2	3-3	4-0	2-1	1-3	0-4	1-3	0-2	3-1	2-0	1-1	0-1	0-1	0-1	4-1
Charlton Athletic FC	1-0	4-3	4-3	2-1	2-1	2-0		1-1	2-0	4-2	4-1	2-2	2-0	6-1	1-1	3-3	1-2	0-1	1-3	1-0	6-0	4-3
Clapton Orient FC	9-2	4-1	2-1	4-0	0-0	4-2	1-3		0-0	2-0	4-0	2-1	1-1	3-0	5-1	3-2	2-2	2-3	5-2	1-0	4-1	2-3
Coventry City FC	5-1	4-1	2-0	9-0	5-3	4-1	3-2	3-1		5-1	1-3	7-1	2-2	5-2	1-1	2-0	5-1	3-1	2-0	5-1	5-1	2-0
Crystal Palace FC	4-1	4-1	2-1	0-1	1-2	3-2	1-0	3-2	2-1		0-0	3-2	2-2	1-1	1-2	0-1	4-1	0-0	1-1	0-0	4-1	4-3
Exeter City FC	0-0	4-0	3-0	2-0	0-0	4-0	2-0	0-3	1-0	1-2		2-0	4-2	1-0	0-2	3-4	1-1	4-1	2-0	2-2	4-0	3-1
Gillingham FC	1-2	5-1	3-0	2-1	3-2	6-2	1-1	1-1	3-7	0-5	1-1		1-1	5-1	1-2	1-4	5-1	0-0	3-3	3-3	3-3	3-3
Luton Town FC	1-1	2-0	1-2	3-0	2-2	3-1	2-1	2-0	0-1	2-1	3-2	4-2		1-1	3-1	2-3	4-2	3-1	3-1	2-3	10-2	2-1
Newport County AFC	1-2	1-1	2-2	2-2	1-0	2-2	1-1	1-1	0-0	1-0	1-0	3-1	1-2		2-0	0-0	1-2	1-2	3-0	1-2	0-0	0-3
Northampton Town FC	0-0	4-1	1-1	2-3	1-2	2-0	1-2	3-0	2-2	4-2	5-3	1-0	2-3	5-3		2-2	2-1	2-4	2-2	2-2	1-1	1-0
Norwich City FC	2-2	6-1	4-3	7-2	0-0	2-0	3-0	3-0	3-1	2-0	1-1	4-0	2-1	2-0	2-0		1-0	2-0	3-1	2-2	3-1	3-1
Queen's Park Rangers FC	2-4	1-0	2-0	1-0	1-0	4-0	2-1	2-0	0-1	2-1	2-0	5-0	2-1	2-1	2-1	5-2		0-0	4-0	1-0	2-0	0-0
Reading FC	3-2	4-0	2-0	1-1	2-2	3-1	4-0	1-0	0-0	3-1	2-0	4-1	4-0	2-2	1-0	5-0	5-2		5-0	2-0	5-2	6-1
Southend United FC	1-0	1-2	0-0	3-0	2-2	1-1	1-0	2-1	0-4	3-1	1-2	0-1	3-5	2-0	0-0	0-2	2-2	0-2		4-1	3-1	3-1
Swindon Town FC	1-0	3-2	1-1	4-2	1-0	6-3	1-3	3-0	0-1	3-2	1-1	3-1	3-1	1-1	1-1	0-0	3-1	3-1	1-4		2-0	1-0
Torquay United FC	0-0	1-0	3-0	2-2	2-1	3-1	1-4	2-1	1-3	2-1	0-2	2-1	0-1	1-2	3-2	1-2	1-1	1-1	3-0	2-0		1-3
Watford FC	3-0	1-2	2-0	1-1	0-0	1-2	0-1	6-0	3-3	3-1	2-0	2-1	0-1	3-0	1-0	1-3	0-0	2-0	2-1	4-0	5-0	

Division 3 (South)

		Pd	Wn	Dw	Ls	GF	GA	Pts	
1.	Norwich City FC (Norwich)	42	25	11	6	88	49	61	P
2.	Coventry City FC (Coventry)	42	21	12	9	100	54	54	
3.	Reading FC (Reading)	42	21	12	9	82	50	54	
4.	Queen's Park Rangers FC (London)	42	24	6	12	70	51	54	
5.	Charlton Athletic FC (London)	42	22	8	12	83	56	52	
6.	Luton Town FC (Luton)	42	21	10	11	83	61	52	
7.	Bristol Rovers FC (Bristol)	42	20	11	11	77	47	51	
8.	Swindon Town FC (Swindon)	42	17	11	14	64	68	45	
9.	Exeter City FC (Exeter)	42	16	11	15	68	57	43	
10.	Brighton & Hove Albion FC (Hove)	42	15	13	14	68	60	43	
11.	Clapton Orient FC (London)	42	16	10	16	75	69	42	
12.	Crystal Palace FC (London)	42	16	9	17	71	67	41	
13.	Northampton Town FC (Northampton)	42	14	12	16	71	78	40	
14.	Aldershot FC (Aldershot)	42	13	12	17	52	71	38	
15.	Watford FC (Watford)	42	15	7	20	71	63	37	
16.	Southend United FC (Southend-on-Sea)	42	12	10	20	51	74	34	
17.	Gillingham FC (Gillingham)	42	11	11	20	75	96	33	
18.	Newport County AFC (Newport)	42	8	17	17	49	70	33	
19.	Bristol City FC (Bristol)	42	10	13	19	58	85	33	
20.	Torquay United FC (Torquay)	42	13	7	22	53	93	33	
21.	Bournemouth & Boscombe Athletic FC (Bournemouth)	42	9	9	24	60	102	27	
22.	Cardiff City AFC (Cardiff)	42	9	6	27	57	105	24	
		924	348	228	348	1526	1526	924	

F.A. CUP FINAL   (Wembley Stadium, London – 28/04/1934 – 93,258)

MANCHESTER CITY FC (MANCHESTER)   2-1   Portsmouth FC (Portsmouth)
Tilson 2   *Rutherford*

Man. City: Swift, Barnett, Dale, Busby, Cowan, Bray, Toseland, Marshall, Tilson, Herd, Brook.

Portsmouth: Gilfillan, Mackie, W.Smith, Nichol, Allen, Thackeray, Worrall, J.Smith, Weddle, Easson, Rutherford.

Semi-finals

Manchester City FC (Manchester)	6-1	Aston Villa FC (Birmingham)
Portsmouth FC (Portsmouth)	4-1	Leicester City FC (Leicester)

Quarter-finals

Arsenal FC (London)	1-2	Aston Villa FC (Birmingham)
Bolton Wanderers FC (Bolton)	0-3	Portsmouth FC (Portsmouth)
Manchester City FC (Manchester)	1-0	Stoke City FC (Stoke-on-Trent)
Preston North End FC (Preston)	0-1	Leicester City FC (Leicester)

1934-35

Football League Division 1 — 1934-1935 Season

	Arsenal	Aston Villa	Birmingham	Blackburn Rovers	Chelsea	Derby County	Everton	Grimsby Town	Huddersfield Town	Leeds United	Leicester City	Liverpool	Manchester City	Middlesbrough	Portsmouth	Preston North End	Sheffield Wednesday	Stoke City	Sunderland	Tottenham Hotspur	W.B.A.	Wolves
Arsenal FC	■	1-2	5-1	4-0	2-2	0-1	2-0	1-1	1-0	3-0	8-0	8-1	3-0	8-0	1-1	5-3	4-1	2-0	0-0	5-1	4-3	7-0
Aston Villa FC	1-3	■	2-2	1-1	0-3	3-2	2-2	3-2	1-1	1-1	5-0	4-2	4-2	0-3	5-4	42	4-0	4-1	1-1	1-0	2-3	2-1
Birmingham FC	3-0	2-1	■	1-0	0-1	3-2	2-3	3-2	0-4	3-1	2-3	1-3	1-3	4-2	2-1	3-0	0-4	0-0	2-2	2-1	1-2	1-1
Blackburn Rovers FC	2-0	5-0	3-1	■	1-2	2-5	6-2	2-2	4-2	1-1	0-0	0-2	1-0	3-2	0-0	1-0	2-1	0-1	0-0	2-0	3-0	4-2
Chelsea FC	2-5	2-0	2-2	4-2	■	1-1	3-0	2-0	2-1	7-1	3-1	4-1	4-2	2-1	1-1	0-0	1-2	0-2	2-2	1-3	2-3	4-2
Derby County FC	3-1	1-1	1-1	1-1	3-0	■	4-1	1-4	4-1	1-2	1-1	1-2	1-2	2-0	0-1	0-3	4-0	0-2	3-1	2-1	9-3	2-0
Everton FC	0-2	2-2	2-0	5-2	3-2	2-2	■	3-1	4-2	4-4	2-1	1-0	1-2	1-1	3-2	4-1	2-2	5-0	6-2	5-2	4-0	5-2
Grimsby Town FC	2-2	5-1	4-3	1-2	3-1	1-3	0-0	■	1-1	3-2	3-1	3-2	1-1	2-2	3-0	3-1	3-1	3-1	0-0	3-0	3-0	2-1
Huddersfield Town AFC	1-1	1-1	2-2	6-0	3-0	1-0	1-1	1-5	■	3-1	2-3	8-0	3-0	3-1	2-0	3-4	4-0	1-4	0-3	0-0	3-0	4-1
Leeds United AFC	1-1	1-1	1-1	5-1	5-2	4-2	2-0	3-1	2-0	■	0-2	0-3	1-2	2-4	3-3	0-0	4-2	2-4	4-3	4-1	1-1	
Leicester City FC	3-5	5-0	2-1	0-1	1-0	0-1	5-2	2-2	0-3	1-0	■	3-1	1-3	3-1	6-3	0-0	0-1	0-3	0-2	6-0	0-1	1-1
Liverpool FC	0-2	3-1	5-4	2-0	6-0	1-3	2-1	1-1	3-2	4-2	5-1	■	2-1	2-2	0-0	1-2	5-0	2-2	4-1	3-2	2-1	
Manchester City FC	1-1	4-1	0-0	3-3	2-0	0-1	2-2	1-0	0-0	3-0	6-3	3-1	■	6-2	2-4	1-2	4-1	3-1	1-0	3-1	3-2	5-0
Middlesbrough FC	0-1	4-1	0-1	3-3	2-2	1-1	3-2	0-2	2-1	3-3	1-0	2-0	1-2	■	1-1	3-3	5-3	2-0	0-0	2-2		
Portsmouth FC	3-3	0-1	2-1	3-1	1-1	5-1	5-1	1-0	5-0	0-0	1-1	1-2	4-2	1-0	■	4-0	2-1	0-1	2-4	1-1	0-2	0-1
Preston North End FC	2-1	0-0	0-1	3-1	2-0	0-1	2-2	1-0	2-0	0-2	2-0	2-2	2-4	2-0	1-1	■	2-1	5-2	1-1	1-0	1-2	2-1
Sheffield Wednesday FC	0-0	2-1	2-1	2-2	3-1	1-0	0-0	1-0	1-1	1-0	1-1	4-1	1-0	3-3	3-0	2-1	■	4-1	2-2	4-0	2-1	3-1
Stoke City FC	2-2	4-1	2-0	3-1	0-1	1-1	3-2	0-2	8-1	3-0	1-1	2-0	2-0	1-2	3-1	1-1	■	0-3	4-1	3-0	1-2	
Sunderland AFC	2-1	3-3	5-1	3-0	4-0	1-4	7-0	3-0	4-1	3-0	2-0	2-3	3-2	1-1	4-1	3-1	2-2	4-1	■	1-2	0-1	0-0
Tottenham Hotspur FC	0-6	0-2	1-1	1-0	1-3	2-2	1-1	2-1	0-0	1-1	2-2	5-1	0-0	3-1	4-1	1-2	3-2	3-2	1-1	■	0-1	3-1
West Bromwich Albion FC	0-3	2-2	1-2	2-2	2-2	4-3	0-1	4-2	4-1	6-3	1-1	1-1	6-3	4-2	0-0	1-1	3-0	1-1	4-0		■	5-2
Wolverhampton Wanderers FC	1-1	5-2	3-1	2-1	6-1	5-1	4-2	0-3	2-3	1-2	3-1	5-3	5-0	5-3	2-3	2-2	2-2	2-1	1-2	6-2	3-2	■

	Division 1	Pd	Wn	Dw	Ls	GF	GA	Pts	
1.	ARSENAL FC (LONDON)	42	23	12	7	115	46	58	
2.	Sunderland AFC (Sunderland)	42	19	16	7	90	51	54	
3.	Sheffield Wednesday FC (Sheffield)	42	18	13	11	70	64	49	
4.	Manchester City FC (Manchester)	42	20	8	14	82	67	48	
5.	Grimsby Town FC (Cleethorpes)	42	17	11	14	78	60	45	
6.	Derby County FC (Derby)	42	18	9	15	81	66	45	
7.	Liverpool FC (Liverpool)	42	19	7	16	85	88	45	
8.	Everton FC (Liverpool)	42	16	12	14	89	88	44	
9.	West Bromwich Albion FC (West Bromwich)	42	17	10	15	83	83	44	
10.	Stoke City FC (Stoke-on-Trent)	42	18	6	18	71	70	42	
11.	Preston North End FC (Preston)	42	15	12	15	62	67	42	
12.	Chelsea FC (Chelsea)	42	16	9	17	73	82	41	
13.	Aston Villa FC (Birmingham)	42	14	13	15	74	88	41	
14.	Portsmouth FC (Portsmouth)	42	15	10	17	71	72	40	
15.	Blackburn Rovers FC (Blackburn)	42	14	11	17	66	78	39	
16.	Huddersfield Town AFC (Huddersfield)	42	14	10	18	76	71	38	
17.	Wolverhampton Wanderers FC (Wolverhampton)	42	15	8	19	88	94	38	
18.	Leeds United AFC (Leeds)	42	13	12	17	75	92	38	
19.	Birmingham FC (Birmingham)	42	13	10	19	63	81	36	
20.	Middlesbrough FC (Middlesbrough)	42	10	14	18	70	90	34	
21.	Leicester City FC (Leicester)	42	12	9	21	61	86	33	R
22.	Tottenham Hotspur FC (London)	42	10	10	22	54	93	30	R
		924	346	232	346	1677	1677	924	

Top Goalscorer

1)   Ted DRAKE   (Arsenal FC)   42

Football League Division 2 — 1934-1935 Season

	Barnsley	Blackpool	Bolton Wands.	Bradford City	Bradford P.A.	Brentford	Burnley	Bury	Fulham	Hull City	Man. United	Newcastle Utd.	Norwich City	Nottingham F.	Notts County	Oldham Athletic	Plymouth Arg.	Port Vale	Sheffield United	Southampton	Swansea Town	West Ham Utd.
Barnsley FC		2-2	1-1	2-0	1-1	3-3	0-0	3-0	2-0	2-2	0-2	2-1	2-1	1-2	1-1	4-0	1-4	2-0	0-0	1-1	1-0	1-1
Blackpool FC	3-0		1-1	2-1	1-0	2-2	1-0	1-1	1-1	2-1	1-2	4-1	2-1	1-0	3-1	4-0	4-1	3-1	1-0	4-1	2-1	3-2
Bolton Wanderers FC	8-0	4-2		3-0	1-2	2-0	7-0	2-0	4-0	1-2	3-1	1-0	4-0	2-3	5-1	2-0	3-2	2-0	1-1	4-0	1-0	3-1
Bradford City AFC	1-0	0-2	1-1		3-1	3-0	1-1	0-0	0-0	3-2	2-0	3-3	1-1	4-0	2-0	2-0	0-1	3-0	2-5	1-1	2-0	0-2
Bradford Park Avenue	3-2	0-0	4-0	2-1		2-3	1-1	2-1	0-0	1-2	1-2	1-3	1-1	1-1	2-0	2-2	1-1	1-3	3-1	3-1	3-1	1-3
Brentford FC	8-1	2-1	1-0	2-0	1-0		6-1	2-1	1-0	2-1	3-1	3-0	2-1	1-1	4-1	2-1	1-0	8-0	3-1	3-2	1-0	2-0
Burnley FC	4-1	1-2	2-1	1-2	1-2	0-3		3-3	3-1	1-3	1-3	1-0	2-1	4-0	4-2	1-2	2-2	0-2	3-0	3-0	3-0	5-2
Bury FC	4-1	1-5	2-1	2-1	2-4	4-1	0-0		2-0	0-1	0-1	0-2	1-0	1-0	2-0	2-1	3-1	3-1	4-1	2-1	2-1	2-4
Fulham FC	1-3	4-1	2-1	3-1	2-2	2-2	2-0	1-2		4-0	3-1	3-2	1-3	2-1	7-0	3-1	3-0	2-0	7-2	3-3	4-1	3-0
Hull City AFC	1-1	2-2	0-2	1-0	2-1	1-3	0-1	1-2	1-2		3-2	1-1	5-0	5-1	1-1	1-1	0-3	0-0	0-3	0-0	0-0	4-0
Manchester United FC	4-1	3-2	0-3	2-0	2-0	0-0	3-4	1-0	1-0	3-0		0-1	5-0	3-2	2-1	4-1	3-1	2-1	3-3	3-1	3-1	3-1
Newcastle United FC	4-1	4-1	1-3	4-2	0-1	2-5	2-0	5-1	1-1	6-2	0-1		2-0	2-0	1-4	2-3	1-2	4-1	1-0	1-2	5-1	3-0
Norwich City FC	0-1	1-1	2-3	6-1	3-0	2-1	2-3	4-1	0-4	2-0	3-2	2-0		3-3	7-2	0-0	1-1	4-0	2-2	1-2	2-2	1-2
Nottingham Forest FC	4-1	0-0	2-0	2-0	2-2	0-0	5-0	1-4	1-1	2-1	2-1	5-1	5-2		2-3	4-1	1-3	2-0	2-1	3-1	1-0	2-0
Notts County FC	1-4	3-2	0-2	2-3	1-1	0-1	1-0	1-2	1-1	1-1	1-0	0-1	1-0	3-5		2-1	1-3	3-2	0-1	3-1	4-0	0-2
Oldham Athletic AFC	1-4	2-3	1-4	3-1	1-1	1-3	1-2	7-2	2-1	5-0	3-1	3-2	4-2	0-5	1-0		1-1	2-0	3-2	0-2	2-2	1-2
Plymouth Argyle FC	3-1	1-2	1-0	3-1	2-2	1-1	2-2	3-0	3-1	6-4	1-3	0-1	5-2	4-0	2-0	1-0		2-1	2-0	4-0	3-2	0-1
Port Vale FC	4-0	2-2	1-3	1-1	1-1	2-2	3-1	0-1	1-1	1-2	3-2	1-3	1-1	2-0	5-3	2-2	2-2		2-0	4-1	2-1	2-2
Sheffield United FC	2-1	1-1	6-2	1-2	3-1	1-2	0-0	5-3	1-2	3-4	3-1	5-1	1-1	2-1	3-0	1-2	3-0	1-2		6-1	1-1	1-2
Southampton FC	0-1	2-0	1-1	4-1	1-0	0-0	2-1	1-1	3-0	1-0	1-4	1-1	1-2	2-2	0-0	1-1	0-0	1-1	1-1		1-0	2-2
Swansea Town AFC	1-1	2-1	2-1	3-1	0-0	2-4	2-0	1-0	2-0	2-1	1-0	3-4	1-1	3-0	2-1	5-1	3-0	1-1	0-0	0-1		5-4
West Ham United FC	4-3	2-1	4-1	1-0	2-1	2-0	1-2	3-0	2-1	1-2	0-0	3-2	1-0	3-1	4-0	2-0	2-1	3-1	1-2	2-0	2-1	

Division 2

		Pd	Wn	Dw	Ls	GF	GA	Pts	
1.	Brentford FC (London)	42	26	9	7	93	48	61	P
2.	Bolton Wanderers FC (Bolton)	42	26	4	12	96	48	56	P
3.	West Ham United FC (London)	42	26	4	12	80	63	56	
4.	Blackpool FC (Blackpool)	42	21	11	10	79	57	53	
5.	Manchester United FC (Manchester)	42	23	4	15	76	55	50	
6.	Newcastle United FC (Newcastle-upon-Tyne)	42	22	4	16	89	68	48	
7.	Fulham FC (London)	42	17	12	13	76	56	46	
8.	Plymouth Argyle FC (Plymouth)	42	19	8	15	75	64	46	
9.	Nottingham Forest FC (Nottingham)	42	17	8	17	76	70	42	
10.	Bury FC (Bury)	42	19	4	19	62	73	42	
11.	Sheffield United FC (Sheffield)	42	16	9	17	79	70	41	
12.	Burnley FC (Burnley)	42	16	9	17	63	73	41	
13.	Hull City AFC (Kingston-upon-Hull)	42	16	8	18	63	74	40	
14.	Norwich City FC (Norwich)	42	14	11	17	71	61	39	
15.	Bradford Park Avenue FC (Bradford)	42	11	16	15	55	63	38	
16.	Barnsley FC (Barnsley)	42	13	12	17	60	83	38	
17.	Swansea Town AFC (Swansea)	42	14	8	20	56	67	36	
18.	Port Vale FC (Stoke-on-Trent)	42	11	12	19	55	74	34	
19.	Southampton FC (Southampton)	42	11	12	19	46	75	34	
20.	Bradford City AFC (Bradford)	42	12	8	22	50	68	32	
21.	Oldham Athletic AFC (Oldham)	42	10	6	26	56	95	26	R
22.	Notts County FC (Nottingham)	42	9	7	26	46	97	25	R
		924	369	186	369	1502	1502	924	

Football League Division 3 (N) — 1934-1935 Season

Team	Acc	Bar	Car	Che	Chf	Cre	Dar	Don	Gat	Hal	Har	Lin	Man	NB	Roc	Rot	Sou	Sto	Tra	Wal	Wre	Yor
Accrington Stanley FC	■	5-2	1-0	1-1	1-0	3-0	2-1	1-5	4-2	1-1	0-4	3-0	2-0	1-3	2-5	2-3	1-1	3-1	1-0	3-3	2-2	5-2
Barrow AFC	0-2	■	2-1	4-2	1-1	1-1	4-4	2-1	3-2	2-0	2-0	1-1	3-0	1-2	1-1	2-1	2-1	1-4	1-0	3-1	1-3	0-3
Carlisle United FC	2-0	0-0	■	1-3	3-1	1-3	1-2	1-1	5-4	2-4	2-2	2-1	1-1	4-1	0-0	2-1	0-1	1-2	1-1	1-6	0-2	4-0
Chester FC	4-0	6-2	3-0	■	1-1	2-2	3-1	1-3	2-2	5-0	4-1	0-1	3-2	5-4	1-0	4-1	0-2	5-1	0-0	2-1	6-2	5-1
Chesterfield FC	0-0	3-0	3-0	1-2	■	1-2	2-2	3-2	3-1	4-0	4-0	3-1	0-0	1-0	2-1	2-1	3-3	5-0	0-2	2-0	1-4	3-1
Crewe Alexandra FC	4-2	4-3	1-1	1-1	1-0	■	4-1	1-1	2-1	3-1	1-1	1-0	1-1	2-3	4-1	0-0	2-1	2-3	1-2	1-0	2-0	3-2
Darlington FC	5-0	3-1	5-0	1-0	2-1	6-2	■	1-1	2-1	0-1	3-0	4-1	1-0	1-0	2-2	4-0	0-0	0-0	2-2	3-2	3-1	2-0
Doncaster Rovers FC	2-1	2-0	3-0	3-0	0-2	2-0	2-0	■	5-0	0-1	3-1	1-3	2-1	7-1	1-0	3-5	2-0	3-4	2-0	4-0	2-1	4-1
Gateshead FC	1-1	1-0	3-2	2-4	1-4	5-2	3-0	0-0	■	3-1	2-1	0-2	2-2	2-1	2-0	1-1	1-2	3-2	0-2	1-0	1-0	2-1
Halifax Town AFC	2-1	2-1	4-0	1-0	0-2	1-0	2-1	1-0	4-0	■	4-1	2-1	2-1	6-2	1-1	2-1	4-3	1-1	1-2	1-1	3-2	5-3
Hartlepools United FC	4-2	5-2	5-2	0-2	1-1	4-2	0-1	2-1	1-2	0-3	■	1-5	1-1	2-2	0-0	3-1	4-1	4-0	6-1	2-1	4-3	3-1
Lincoln City FC	1-0	6-0	4-2	0-0	2-0	1-1	2-4	0-2	5-0	2-3	2-1	■	4-0	1-0	3-0	4-0	4-1	3-0	2-2	5-1	1-3	3-1
Mansfield Town FC	2-1	3-2	3-0	1-1	1-0	4-1	2-2	2-0	1-1	4-0	2-1	3-4	■	2-1	1-0	2-1	2-3	3-2	4-2	4-2	4-0	5-1
New Brighton FC	2-1	3-1	5-1	0-2	3-1	1-1	0-1	1-1	3-0	0-0	1-4	0-2	2-1	■	1-0	3-2	0-0	1-2	0-1	2-2	0-0	4-2
Rochdale AFC	2-2	0-1	3-1	3-3	0-2	3-0	1-3	0-1	6-1	2-4	3-2	2-0	1-0	3-1	■	1-3	2-2	0-5	1-1	1-0	3-3	2-0
Rotherham United FC	2-0	0-0	4-1	6-1	2-2	2-2	2-1	1-3	3-0	2-2	0-1	5-0	3-0	1-2	4-0	■	4-2	2-0	3-1	4-2	2-0	4-1
Southport FC	0-0	0-2	0-3	1-1	1-1	2-1	1-4	1-2	1-1	1-2	1-1	3-3	1-2	2-1	2-1	0-3	■	1-2	4-0	3-2	2-1	0-3
Stockport County FC	5-1	4-1	2-0	0-1	4-2	3-0	3-2	3-2	5-1	3-2	1-2	0-2	1-1	3-1	4-0	6-1	1-0	■	0-3	6-1		
Tranmere Rovers FC	2-1	2-1	3-1	1-1	2-1	5-1	1-1	0-2	2-2	1-0	2-1	3-0	0-1	4-1	3-3	4-1	3-1	4-1	■	4-0	1-1	4-0
Walsall FC	6-0	5-0	1-0	1-1	2-1	4-0	0-0	0-2	5-0	4-1	1-2	0-0	2-2	5-1	0-0	5-2	2-2	3-1	3-0	■	0-0	2-3
Wrexham AFC	2-2	1-1	4-2	2-2	2-1	2-1	4-0	1-2	3-1	5-0	0-2	2-2	1-3	3-0	2-0	0-1	3-0	2-1	2-2	4-2	■	2-0
York City FC	5-2	1-1	7-0	1-1	1-1	7-3	2-1	1-2	3-0	0-1	3-1	1-2	2-1	1-0	0-1	5-0	3-1	3-1	0-0	4-1	0-0	■

Division 3 (North)

		Pd	Wn	Dw	Ls	GF	GA	Pts	
1.	Doncaster Rovers FC (Doncaster)	42	26	5	11	87	44	57	P
2.	Halifax Town AFC (Halifax)	42	25	5	12	76	67	55	
3.	Chester FC (Chester)	42	20	14	8	91	58	54	
4.	Lincoln City FC (Lincoln)	42	22	7	13	87	58	51	
5.	Darlington FC (Darlington)	42	21	9	12	80	59	51	
6.	Tranmere Rovers FC (Birkenhead)	42	20	11	11	74	55	51	
7.	Stockport County FC (Stockport)	42	22	3	17	90	72	47	
8.	Mansfield Town FC (Mansfield)	42	19	9	14	75	62	47	
9.	Rotherham United FC (Rotherham)	42	19	7	16	86	73	45	
10.	Chesterfield FC (Chesterfield)	42	17	10	15	71	52	44	
11.	Wrexham AFC (Wrexham)	42	16	11	15	76	69	43	
12.	Hartlepools United FC (Hartlepool)	42	17	7	18	80	78	41	
13.	Crewe Alexandra FC (Crewe)	42	14	11	17	66	86	39	
14.	Walsall FC (Walsall)	42	13	10	19	81	72	36	
15.	York City FC (York)	42	15	6	21	76	82	36	
16.	New Brighton FC (Wallasey)	42	14	8	20	59	76	36	
17.	Barrow AFC (Barrow-in-Furness)	42	13	9	20	58	87	35	
18.	Accrington Stanley FC (Accrington)	42	12	10	20	63	89	34	
19.	Gateshead FC (Gateshead)	42	13	8	21	58	96	34	
20.	Rochdale AFC (Rochdale)	42	11	11	20	53	71	33	
21.	Southport FC (Southport)	42	10	12	20	55	85	32	
22.	Carlisle United FC (Carlisle)	42	8	7	27	51	102	23	
		924	367	190	367	1593	1593	924	

Football League Division 3 (S) 1934-1935 Season	Aldershot	Bournemouth	Brighton	Bristol City	Bristol Rovers	Cardiff City	Charlton Athletic	Clapton Orient	Coventry City	Crystal Palace	Exeter City	Gillingham	Luton Town	Millwall	Newport County	Northampton	Q.P.R.	Reading	Southend United	Swindon Town	Torquay United	Watford
Aldershot FC	■	1-1	1-0	1-0	1-2	2-0	3-2	1-1	3-1	2-2	0-0	4-1	0-1	0-0	3-2	2-0	1-0	2-5	3-2	3-0	2-0	0-0
Bournemouth & B. Athletic	4-1	■	1-0	1-1	3-0	3-1	2-2	1-0	0-2	1-1	3-2	1-1	1-3	3-1	3-1	0-1	0-2	4-1	2-1	1-1	1-2	1-2
Brighton & Hove Albion	3-0	2-0	■	2-0	3-1	3-1	2-1	3-0	2-0	3-0	6-0	1-1	4-1	0-2	3-1	2-3	5-1	1-0	2-2	2-2	0-0	2-0
Bristol City FC	2-0	2-1	1-0	■	1-1	4-0	1-4	0-0	0-2	0-1	2-0	3-1	0-2	4-2	2-1	1-1	5-1	1-0	2-0	2-0	1-0	3-1
Bristol Rovers FC	1-0	4-1	0-0	2-2	■	3-2	0-0	1-2	2-1	5-3	5-5	4-3	1-1	2-0	5-3	7-1	2-0	3-0	2-1	2-2	1-0	2-0
Cardiff City AFC	1-1	2-1	0-0	3-3	4-1	■	2-1	3-0	2-4	2-0	5-0	0-2	1-0	3-1	3-4	2-2	2-1	1-1	2-0	1-3	1-1	2-1
Charlton Athletic FC	4-0	0-1	3-1	4-1	2-0	3-1	■	2-1	3-3	2-2	1-0	2-0	4-2	3-1	6-0	0-1	3-1	3-1	3-0	6-0	3-2	5-2
Clapton Orient FC	3-1	0-1	6-0	4-0	5-2	0-1	1-2	■	0-1	2-0	0-3	2-2	1-1	2-1	4-0	3-2	3-1	2-1	3-0	2-0	3-1	1-1
Coventry City FC	0-0	4-1	0-2	1-1	1-0	2-0	4-0	4-0	■	1-1	1-1	4-0	1-0	5-1	5-0	2-0	4-1	1-2	6-3	3-0	6-0	1-1
Crystal Palace FC	3-0	1-0	3-0	3-1	2-0	6-1	1-2	1-0	3-1	■	0-1	2-0	2-1	1-1	6-0	2-0	2-3	3-1	1-0	7-0	2-2	0-0
Exeter City FC	8-1	4-1	3-1	3-0	2-2	2-1	3-1	1-1	2-0	0-6	■	2-0	1-2	0-1	3-0	3-0	2-3	4-3	3-3	1-1	1-1	
Gillingham FC	1-1	3-1	0-0	1-0	1-1	1-0	3-6	1-0	2-5	2-0	2-1	■	1-1	1-3	5-0	3-1	1-0	1-1	2-2	2-0	3-0	1-2
Luton Town FC	6-1	4-0	4-0	1-1	6-2	4-0	1-2	3-0	4-0	2-2	4-0	2-2	■	2-1	4-1	2-2	1-1	2-4	1-1	3-0	3-1	2-2
Millwall FC	3-0	2-0	3-1	0-1	0-2	2-2	1-3	1-1	1-3	3-2	1-0	3-2	1-4	■	2-0	0-1	2-0	2-2	1-0	1-0	4-2	0-0
Newport County AFC	2-0	6-1	1-0	2-0	1-1	4-0	0-2	3-3	2-1	2-3	1-3	2-2	2-4	1-2	■	1-3	2-1	2-2	0-5	1-2	1-4	0-1
Northampton Town FC	0-0	0-1	4-1	2-2	1-0	3-0	1-1	3-1	3-4	3-2	2-1	2-1	1-0	2-0		■	1-0	1-3	1-1	4-2	3-0	1-0
Queen's Park Rangers FC	2-0	2-1	2-1	4-1	2-0	2-2	0-3	6-3	1-1	3-3	1-1	2-0	3-0	1-0	4-1	3-1	■	2-0	1-1	1-1	5-1	2-1
Reading FC	5-4	4-1	4-4	2-0	5-1	1-1	2-2	0-0	2-0	6-1	2-0	3-0	1-0	2-1	6-1	3-1	0-0	■	3-2	2-1	3-1	3-2
Southend United FC	2-1	0-0	3-2	6-0	5-1	2-1	0-3	0-2	1-1	1-4	1-2	0-0	3-3	1-2	2-1	2-1	2-0	6-1	■	2-0	2-3	0-2
Swindon Town FC	3-2	0-2	4-4	1-0	1-0	2-1	2-2	1-1	0-0	1-1	6-1	3-0	0-1	0-1	0-0	5-3	3-1	1-1	5-0	■	5-0	2-1
Torquay United FC	2-1	1-2	3-0	3-1	1-2	5-2	1-2	4-2	1-0	7-1	3-0	5-0	6-2	1-1	2-1	2-0	7-0	1-1	2-0	2-1	■	1-3
Watford FC	0-1	3-1	0-1	4-0	3-0	1-3	2-0	5-0	2-0	0-1	3-1	2-2	2-3	7-0	1-1	2-0	1-0	3-1	7-4	3-0		■

Division 3 (South)

		Pd	Wn	Dw	Ls	GF	GA	Pts	
1.	Charlton Athletic FC (London)	42	27	7	8	103	52	61	P
2.	Reading FC (Reading)	42	21	11	10	89	65	53	
3.	Coventry City FC (Coventry)	42	21	9	12	86	50	51	
4.	Luton Town FC (Luton)	42	19	12	11	92	60	50	
5.	Crystal Palace FC (London)	42	19	10	13	86	64	48	
6.	Watford FC (Watford)	42	19	9	14	76	49	47	
7.	Northampton Town FC (Northampton)	42	19	8	15	65	67	46	
8.	Bristol Rovers FC (Bristol)	42	17	10	15	73	77	44	
9.	Brighton & Hove Albion FC (Hove)	42	17	9	16	69	62	43	
10.	Torquay United FC (Torquay)	42	18	6	18	81	75	42	
11.	Exeter City FC (Exeter)	42	16	9	17	70	75	41	
12.	Millwall FC (London)	42	17	7	18	57	62	41	
13.	Queen's Park Rangers FC (London)	42	16	9	17	63	72	41	
14.	Clapton Orient FC (London)	42	15	10	17	65	65	40	
15.	Bristol City FC (Bristol)	42	15	9	18	52	68	39	
16.	Swindon Town FC (Swindon)	42	13	12	17	67	78	38	
17.	Bournemouth & Boscombe Athletic FC (Bournemouth)	42	15	7	20	54	71	37	
18.	Aldershot FC (Aldershot)	42	13	10	19	50	75	36	
19.	Cardiff City AFC (Cardiff)	42	13	9	20	62	82	35	
20.	Gillingham FC (Gillingham)	42	11	13	18	55	75	35	
21.	Southend United FC (Southend-on-Sea)	42	11	9	22	65	78	31	
22.	Newport County AFC (Newport)	42	10	5	27	54	112	25	
		924	362	200	362	1534	1534	924	

F.A. CUP FINAL (Wembley Stadium, London – 27/04/1935 – 93,204)

SHEFFIELD WEDNESDAY FC (SHEFFIELD)   4-2   West Bromwich Albion FC (West Bromwich)

Palethorpe, Hooper, Rimmer 2   *Boyes, Sandford*

Wednesday: Brown, Nibloe, Catlin, Sharp, Millership, Burrows, Hooper, Surtees, Palethorpe, Starling, Rimmer.

West Bromwich: Pearson, Shaw, Trentham, Murphy, W.Richardson, Edwards, Glidden, Carter, W.G. Richardson, Sandford, Boyes.

Semi-finals

Bolton Wanderers FC (Bolton)	1-1, 0-2	West Bromwich Albion FC (West Bromwich)
Sheffield Wednesday FC (Sheffield)	3-0	Burnley FC (Burnley)

Quarter-finals

Burnley FC (Burnley)	3-2	Birmingham FC (Birmingham)
Everton FC (Liverpool)	1-2	Bolton Wanderers FC (Bolton)
Sheffield Wednesday FC (Sheffield)	2-1	Arsenal FC (London)
West Bromwich Albion FC (West Bromwich)	1-0	Preston North End FC (Preston)

1935-36

Football League Division 1 — 1935-1936 Season

	Arsenal	Aston Villa	Birmingham	Blackburn Rovers	Bolton Wanderers	Brentford	Chelsea	Derby County	Everton	Grimsby Town	Huddersfield Town	Leeds United	Liverpool	Manchester City	Middlesbrough	Portsmouth	Preston North End	Sheffield Wednesday	Stoke City	Sunderland	W.B.A.	Wolves
Arsenal FC		1-0	1-1	5-1	1-1	1-1	1-1	1-1	1-1	6-0	1-1	2-2	1-2	2-3	2-0	2-3	2-1	2-2	1-0	3-1	4-0	4-0
Aston Villa FC	1-7		2-1	2-4	1-2	2-2	2-2	0-2	1-1	2-6	4-1	3-3	3-0	2-2	2-7	4-2	5-1	1-2	4-0	2-2	0-7	4-2
Birmingham FC	1-1	2-2		4-2	0-0	2-1	2-1	2-3	4-2	1-1	4-1	2-0	2-0	0-1	1-0	4-0	0-0	4-1	0-5	2-7	1-3	0-0
Blackburn Rovers FC	0-1	5-1	1-2		0-3	1-0	1-0	0-0	1-1	1-0	2-1	0-3	2-2	4-1	2-2	3-1	1-1	3-2	0-1	1-1	3-1	1-0
Bolton Wanderers FC	2-1	4-3	2-0	3-1		0-2	2-3	0-2	2-0	4-0	1-2	3-0	0-0	3-3	3-1	4-0	1-1	1-1	1-2	2-1	3-1	0-3
Brentford FC	2-1	1-2	0-1	3-1	4-0		2-1	6-0	4-1	3-0	1-2	2-2	1-2	0-0	1-0	3-1	5-2	2-2	0-0	1-5	2-2	5-0
Chelsea FC	1-1	1-0	0-0	5-1	2-1	2-1		1-1	2-2	0-2	1-0	1-0	2-2	2-1	2-1	1-0	5-2	1-2	3-5	3-1	2-2	2-2
Derby County FC	0-4	1-3	2-2	1-0	4-0	2-1	1-1		3-3	2-0	2-0	2-1	2-2	3-0	3-2	1-1	2-0	3-1	0-1	4-0	2-0	3-1
Everton FC	0-2	2-2	4-3	4-0	3-3	1-2	5-1	4-0		4-0	1-3	0-0	0-0	2-2	5-2	3-0	5-0	4-3	5-1	0-3	5-3	4-1
Grimsby Town FC	1-0	4-1	1-0	1-1	3-1	6-1	1-3	4-1	0-4		1-1	0-1	0-0	1-1	1-0	1-2	0-0	4-0	3-0	4-0	4-2	2-1
Huddersfield Town AFC	0-0	4-1	1-0	1-1	0-0	2-2	2-0	1-1	2-1	1-0		1-2	1-0	1-1	4-1	1-0	1-0	2-1	0-0	2-3		3-0
Leeds United AFC	1-1	4-2	0-0	1-4	5-2	1-2	2-0	1-0	3-1	1-2	2-2		1-0	1-1	0-1	1-0	0-1	7-2	4-1	3-0	1-1	2-0
Liverpool FC	0-1	3-2	1-2	4-1	1-1	0-0	2-3	0-0	6-0	7-2	3-0	2-1		0-2	2-2	2-0	2-1	1-0	2-0	0-3	5-0	0-2
Manchester City FC	1-0	5-0	3-1	2-0	7-0	2-1	0-0	1-0	1-0	0-3	1-2	1-3	6-0		6-0	0-0	1-3	3-0	1-2	0-1	1-0	2-1
Middlesbrough FC	2-2	1-2	0-2	6-1	0-0	0-0	4-1	0-3	6-1	5-1	4-2	1-1	2-2	2-0		3-2	2-0	5-0	0-0	6-0	3-1	4-2
Portsmouth FC	2-1	3-0	0-3	3-1	2-1	1-3	2-0	3-0	2-0	3-2	0-0	2-2	2-1	1-2	1-0		1-1	3-2	2-0	2-2	3-1	1-0
Preston North End FC	1-0	3-0	3-1	2-0	1-0	2-4	2-0	1-0	2-2	1-0	4-0	5-0	3-1	4-0	0-5	1-1		0-1	1-1	3-2	3-0	2-0
Sheffield Wednesday FC	3-2	5-2	3-1	0-0	2-2	3-3	4-1	1-0	3-3	3-0	1-2	3-0	0-0	0-0	1-1	0-0	1-0		0-1	0-0	2-5	0-0
Stoke City FC	0-3	2-3	3-1	2-0	1-2	2-2	3-0	0-0	2-1	1-0	1-0	3-1	2-1	1-0	1-1	2-0	2-1	0-3		0-2	3-2	4-1
Sunderland AFC	5-4	1-3	2-1	7-2	7-2	1-3	3-3	3-1	3-3	3-1	4-3	2-1	2-0	2-0	2-1	5-0	4-2	5-1	1-0		6-1	3-1
West Bromwich Albion FC	1-0	0-3	0-0	8-1	2-2	1-0	1-2	0-3	6-1	4-1	1-2	3-2	6-1	5-1	5-2	2-0	2-4	2-2	2-0	1-3		2-1
Wolverhampton Wanderers FC	2-2	2-2	3-1	8-1	3-3	3-2	3-3	0-0	4-0	1-0	2-2	3-0	3-1	4-3	4-0	2-0	4-2	2-1	1-1	3-4	2-0	

Division 1	Pd	Wn	Dw	Ls	GF	GA	Pts	
1. SUNDERLAND AFC (SUNDERLAND)	42	25	6	11	109	74	56	
2. Derby County FC (Derby)	42	18	12	12	61	52	48	
3. Huddersfield Town AFC (Huddersfield)	42	18	12	12	59	56	48	
4. Stoke City FC (Stoke-on-Trent)	42	20	7	15	57	57	47	
5. Brentford FC (London)	42	17	12	13	81	60	46	
6. Arsenal FC (London)	42	15	15	12	78	48	45	
7. Preston North End FC (Preston)	42	18	8	16	67	64	44	
8. Chelsea FC (London)	42	15	13	14	65	72	43	
9. Manchester City FC (Manchester)	42	17	8	17	68	60	42	
10. Portsmouth FC (Portsmouth)	42	17	8	17	54	67	42	
11. Leeds United AFC Leeds)	42	15	11	16	66	64	41	
12. Birmingham FC (Birmingham)	42	15	11	16	61	63	41	
13. Bolton Wanderers FC (Bolton)	42	14	13	15	67	76	41	
14. Middlesbrough FC (Middlesbrough)	42	15	10	17	84	70	40	
15. Wolverhampton Wanderers FC (Wolverhampton)	42	15	10	17	77	76	40	
16. Everton FC (Liverpool)	42	13	13	16	89	89	39	
17. Grimsby Town FC (Cleethorpes)	42	17	5	20	65	73	39	
18. West Bromwich Albion FC (West Bromwich)	42	16	6	20	89	88	38	
19. Liverpool FC (Liverpool)	42	13	12	17	60	64	38	
20. Sheffield Wednesday FC (Sheffield)	42	13	12	17	63	77	38	
21. Aston Villa FC (Birmingham)	42	13	9	20	81	110	35	R
22. Blackburn Rovers FC (Blackburn)	42	12	9	21	55	96	33	R
	924	351	122	351	1556	1556	924	

Top Goalscorers

1)	W.G. RICHARDSON	(West Bromwich Albion FC)	39
2)	Raich CARTER	(Sunderland AFC)	31
	Pat GLOVER	(Grimsby Town FC)	31
	Robert GURNEY	(Sunderland AFC)	31

Football League Division 2 — 1935-1936 Season

	Barnsley	Blackpool	Bradford City	Bradford P.A.	Burnley	Bury	Charlton Ath.	Doncaster R.	Fulham	Hull City	Leicester City	Man. United	Newcastle Utd.	Norwich City	Nottingham F.	Plymouth Arg.	Port Vale	Sheffield United	Southampton	Swansea Town	Tottenham H.	West Ham Utd.
Barnsley FC	■	1-2	0-1	5-1	3-1	1-1	1-2	2-1	2-0	5-1	3-3	0-3	3-2	2-3	0-2	1-2	4-2	3-2	3-1	0-0	0-0	1-2
Blackpool FC	3-0	■	3-3	4-2	2-0	2-3	6-1	5-2	1-1	4-1	3-5	4-1	6-0	2-1	1-4	3-1	3-1	3-0	2-1	1-1	2-4	4-1
Bradford City AFC	1-1	2-1	■	2-1	0-0	2-0	2-1	3-1	1-0	1-1	2-0	1-0	3-2	0-1	0-0	2-2	1-1	2-1	2-1	2-2	0-1	3-1
Bradford Park Avenue	3-0	3-2	1-1	■	2-0	1-1	3-0	3-1	1-1	2-1	3-1	1-0	3-2	1-0	1-4	22	3-0	3-3	1-1	1-1	2-5	2-0
Burnley FC	3-0	3-2	3-0	1-1	■	1-1	0-2	1-1	0-2	2-0	2-2	2-2	1-2	1-1	1-0	0-1	5-1	1-1	2-0	5-2	0-0	1-0
Bury FC	3-0	1-1	1-1	1-0	0-4	■	1-1	5-1	0-0	3-1	3-0	2-3	3-4	0-1	2-6	2-0	5-0	3-2	0-0	2-1	1-1	3-0
Charlton Athletic FC	3-0	1-1	2-1	3-1	4-0	5-2	■	3-0	2-1	4-1	1-0	0-0	4-2	4-1	4-1	1-1	1-1	2-0	4-1	2-1	2-2	
Doncaster Rovers FC	1-1	0-3	2-1	3-2	1-0	1-0	2-0	■	0-0	6-1	1-0	0-0	2-2	3-0	0-0	1-2	2-0	0-0	0-1	1-1	2-1	0-2
Fulham FC	1-1	4-2	5-1	4-1	2-2	7-0	0-0	1-3	■	3-0	2-0	2-2	3-1	1-1	6-0	2-2	7-0	3-1	0-2	0-1	1-2	4-2
Hull City AFC	1-3	0-3	2-5	1-1	1-2	2-3	2-4	2-3	1-1	■	3-3	1-1	2-3	0-2	2-1	1-2	2-2	2-2	3-2	1-0		2-3
Leicester City FC	2-0	4-1	2-1	5-0	2-0	1-2	4-1	60	5-2	2-2	■	1-1	1-0	1-1	2-1	2-0	2-0	1-3	1-1	4-1	4-1	1-1
Manchester United FC	1-1	3-2	3-1	4-0	4-0	2-1	3-0	0-0	1-0	2-0	0-1	■	3-1	2-1	5-0	3-2	7-2	3-1	4-0	3-0	0-0	2-3
Newcastle United FC	3-0	1-0	3-2	3-3	1-1	3-0	1-2	2-1	6-2	4-1	3-1	0-2	■	1-1	5-1	5-0	2-2	3-0	4-1	2-0	1-4	3-3
Norwich City FC	3-1	0-1	1-1	4-1	2-0	5-3	3-1	2-1	1-0	3-0	1-2	3-5	1-0	■	4-0	0-0	4-2	0-1	5-1	0-1	1-4	4-3
Nottingham Forest FC	6-0	2-2	1-0	2-0	2-0	2-2	0-0	6-2	1-1	0-0	0-1	1-1	1-2	2-2	■	0-1	9-2	0-1	2-0	2-2	4-1	0-2
Plymouth Argyle FC	7-1	3-2	0-1	2-0	2-0	3-0	4-2	1-3	2-0	0-1	2-1	3-1	1-0	5-1	3-1	■	4-1	1-1	0-0	1-2	2-1	4-1
Port Vale FC	0-4	2-2	2-1	3-2	1-1	2-2	2-1	2-0	4-0	1-1	0-3	3-0	3-1	2-0	1-1	0-2	■	1-1	0-2	0-1	1-5	2-3
Sheffield United FC	2-0	1-0	3-0	2-1	2-0	3-0	2-0	3-0	0-1	7-0	1-1	1-1	5-1	3-2	1-0	0-0	4-0	■	2-1	4-1	1-1	4-2
Southampton FC	0-1	1-0	0-0	3-0	1-0	0-0	2-5	1-0	1-2	1-0	2-1	1-3	1-1	0-1	0-1	1-1	7-2	2-0	■	4-3	2-0	2-4
Swansea Town AFC	0-0	1-0	8-1	1-2	1-3	4-1	1-2	2-0	0-2	6-1	2-1	1-2	4-3	2-1	2-0	3-2	1-3	0-0		■	1-1	0-1
Tottenham Hotspur FC	3-0	3-1	4-0	4-0	5-1	4-3	1-1	3-1	2-2	3-1	1-1	0-0	1-2	2-1	1-2	5-2	1-1	8-0	7-2		■	1-3
West Ham United FC	2-0	2-1	1-1	1-0	0-0	6-0	1-3	1-2	0-0	4-1	3-2	1-2	4-1	3-2	5-2	4-2	4-0	3-2	0-0	4-0	2-2	■

Division 2

		Pd	Wn	Dw	Ls	GF	GA	Pts	
1.	Manchester United FC (Manchester)	42	22	12	8	85	43	56	P
2.	Charlton Athletic FC (London)	42	22	11	9	85	58	55	P
3.	Sheffield United FC (Sheffield)	42	20	12	10	79	50	52	
4.	West Ham United FC (London)	42	22	8	12	90	68	52	
5.	Tottenham Hotspur FC (London)	42	18	13	11	91	55	49	
6.	Leicester City FC (Leicester)	42	19	10	13	79	57	48	
7.	Plymouth Argyle FC (Plymouth)	42	20	8	14	71	57	48	
8.	Newcastle United FC (Newcastle-upon-Tyne)	42	20	6	16	88	79	46	
9.	Fulham FC (London)	42	15	14	13	76	52	44	
10.	Blackpool FC (Blackpool)	42	18	7	17	93	72	43	
11.	Norwich City FC (Norwich)	42	17	9	16	72	65	43	
12.	Bradford City AFC (Bradford)	42	15	13	14	55	65	43	
13.	Swansea Town AFC (Swansea)	42	15	9	18	67	76	39	
14.	Bury FC (Bury)	42	13	12	17	66	84	38	
15.	Burnley FC (Burnley)	42	12	13	17	50	59	37	
16.	Bradford Park Avenue FC (Bradford)	42	14	9	19	62	84	37	
17.	Southampton FC (Southampton)	42	14	9	19	47	65	37	
18.	Doncaster Rovers FC (Doncaster)	42	14	9	19	51	71	37	
19.	Nottingham Forest FC (Nottingham)	42	12	11	19	69	76	35	
20.	Barnsley FC (Barnsley)	42	12	9	21	54	80	33	
21.	Port Vale FC (Stoke-on-Trent)	42	12	8	22	56	106	32	R
22.	Hull City AFC (Kingston-upon-Hull)	42	5	10	27	47	111	20	R
		924	351	222	351	1533	1533	924	

Football League Division 3 (N) 1935-1936 Season

	Accrington Stan.	Barrow	Carlisle United	Chester	Chesterfield	Crewe Alexandra	Darlington	Gateshead	Halifax Town	Hartlepools Utd.	Lincoln City	Mansfield Town	New Brighton	Oldham Athletic	Rochdale	Rotherham Utd.	Southport	Stockport Co.	Tranmere R.	Walsall	Wrexham	York City
Accrington Stanley FC	■	2-0	0-0	0-3	0-1	2-1	1-0	6-1	2-0	3-2	2-2	1-1	5-2	1-0	2-4	1-1	1-0	1-1	3-1	3-1	0-1	7-2
Barrow AFC	0-1	■	1-1	2-4	1-1	1-1	2-0	3-0	0-0	1-1	0-0	2-2	3-0	3-0	6-2	3-0	0-1	1-0	0-0	1-0	2-1	1-1
Carlisle United FC	3-1	2-2	■	1-3	2-1	1-2	3-0	2-0	0-0	0-0	4-1	3-0	3-0	2-1	4-3	1-1	4-0	2-1	0-1	2-1	5-1	0-0
Chester FC	4-0	1-2	3-2	■	1-1	0-1	4-1	4-0	3-1	4-0	4-2	4-0	8-2	1-1	5-2	0-0	5-1	2-0	1-1	2-0	1-1	12-0
Chesterfield FC	0-3	6-1	5-0	1-0	■	6-0	5-1	2-0	3-1	2-0	0-1	2-1	3-1	3-0	2-2	5-0	5-0	0-0	0-1	3-0	5-0	2-2
Crewe Alexandra FC	4-0	3-1	2-0	1-1	5-6	■	2-0	2-4	3-2	3-2	2-1	1-1	5-1	2-2	3-1	4-1	4-1	0-1	0-0	4-3	3-2	2-1
Darlington FC	2-1	4-1	4-1	1-1	1-2	2-2	■	5-2	3-2	4-2	1-0	2-1	4-1	5-0	4-0	3-1	3-2	3-1	1-3	1-1	4-2	3-0
Gateshead FC	0-0	4-3	1-1	2-0	3-3	2-1	1-1	■	2-2	1-0	4-0		3-1	0-0	1-0	1-1	3-1	1-0	1-1	2-2	2-0	0-0
Halifax Town AFC	1-0	3-2	1-0	2-3	2-3	2-4	0-1	1-1	■	0-1	2-1	1-0	3-0	4-2	1-0	1-2	0-0	1-0	1-1	4-1	2-0	
Hartlepools United FC	2-1	0-0	1-1	0-2	2-1	1-0	2-1	2-0	1-0	■	1-1	4-1	4-1	0-1	1-0	5-1	2-1	1-1	2-2	5-0	1-1	4-2
Lincoln City FC	6-0	2-0	2-0	1-1	0-1	6-2	2-1	5-0	3-1	1-0	■	1-2	2-0	2-1	5-1	4-0	4-0	3-0	5-0	4-1	3-1	3-2
Mansfield Town FC	3-1	1-3	1-1	1-1	1-1	1-1	4-2	3-2	3-2	4-0	2-2	■	2-0	1-0	3-0	8-2	5-1	2-1	2-3	3-2	3-2	5-0
New Brighton FC	2-3	2-3	3-0	3-3	1-2	3-1	1-1	1-0	1-4	0-0	0-5	1-0	■	1-3	2-0	3-0	2-1	2-0	0-0	1-1	0-4	0-2
Oldham Athletic AFC	3-0	3-1	1-3	0-0	0-0	2-0	2-2	3-0	2-2	2-3	4-1	6-0	3-3	■	4-1	4-0	1-3	4-1	2-1	5-2	6-2	
Rochdale AFC	2-2	1-1	0-0	1-1	1-1	2-1	1-1	5-0	2-0	1-0	0-0	3-1	1-0	2-6	■	1-1	2-1	1-1	0-0	6-4	2-1	2-3
Rotherham United FC	1-3	1-0	4-0	1-2	0-0	3-1	4-0	3-0	2-0	3-0	1-1	2-1	5-0	1-0	6-0	■	5-0	1-1	1-2	2-0	1-2	5-0
Southport FC	2-1	3-1	0-3	2-1	1-0	1-1	4-1	1-1	2-0	1-1	0-3	3-3	2-1	1-1	1-1	2-1	■	2-3	1-1	1-0	1-1	0-1
Stockport County FC	1-2	2-1	2-0	2-0	2-2	0-1	2-0	3-1	1-0	2-1	4-0	6-1	1-1	2-0	4-0	1-2	2-0	■	2-1	0-1	3-2	3-2
Tranmere Rovers FC	6-0	2-1	4-1	3-1	1-3	4-2	2-0	0-2	3-1	1-1	4-2	3-1	13-4	5-2	2-2	5-2	4-1	3-1	■	3-1	6-1	3-1
Walsall FC	2-0	5-1	3-0	1-0	1-1	4-1	4-1	2-0	2-1	6-0	4-1	7-0	1-2	1-2	1-0	0-1	3-1	0-1	0-0	■	5-0	6-0
Wrexham AFC	3-0	2-0	1-1	1-0	0-1	3-1	3-1	2-4	1-3	1-0	5-1	3-0	0-1	0-1	2-0	4-2	4-0	4-0	1-1		■	1-0
York City FC	1-1	1-2	2-0	1-2	1-1	4-1	4-1	2-2	2-2	2-1	7-5	2-0	3-1	2-1	2-1	0-0	0-4	2-0	0-0	1-1		■

Division 3 (North)

		Pd	Wn	Dw	Ls	GF	GA	Pts	
1.	Chesterfield FC (Chesterfield)	42	24	12	6	92	39	60	P
2.	Chester FC (Chester)	42	22	11	9	100	45	55	
3.	Tranmere Rovers FC (Birkenhead)	42	22	11	9	93	58	55	
4.	Lincoln City FC (Lincoln)	42	22	9	11	91	51	53	
5.	Stockport County FC (Stockport)	42	20	8	14	65	49	48	
6.	Crewe Alexandra FC (Crewe)	42	19	9	14	80	76	47	
7.	Oldham Athletic AFC (Oldham)	42	18	9	15	86	73	45	
8.	Hartlepools United FC (Hartlepool)	42	15	12	15	57	61	42	
9.	Accrington Stanley FC (Accrington)	42	17	8	17	63	72	42	
10.	Walsall FC (Walsall)	42	16	9	17	79	59	41	T
11.	Rotherham United FC (Rotherham)	42	16	9	17	69	66	41	
12.	Darlington FC (Darlington)	42	17	6	19	74	79	40	
13.	Carlisle United FC (Carlisle)	42	14	12	16	56	62	40	
14.	Gateshead FC (Gateshead)	42	13	14	15	56	76	40	
15.	Barrow AFC (Barrow-in-Furness)	42	13	12	17	58	65	38	
16.	York City FC (York)	42	13	12	17	62	95	38	
17.	Halifax Town AFC (Halifax)	42	15	7	20	57	61	37	
18.	Wrexham AFC (Wrexham)	42	15	7	20	66	75	37	
19.	Mansfield Town FC (Mansfield)	42	14	9	19	80	91	37	
20.	Rochdale AFC (Rochdale)	42	10	13	19	58	88	33	
21.	Southport FC (Southport)	42	11	9	22	48	90	31	
22.	New Brighton FC (Wallasey)	42	9	6	27	43	102	24	
		924	355	214	355	1533	1533	924	

T: Walsall FC (Walsall) were transferred to Division 3 (South) from the next season.

Football League Division 3 (S) 1935-1936 Season	Aldershot	Bournemouth	Brighton	Bristol City	Bristol Rovers	Cardiff City	Clapton Orient	Coventry City	Crystal Palace	Exeter City	Gillingham	Luton Town	Millwall	Newport County	Northampton	Notts County	Q.P.R.	Reading	Southend United	Swindon Town	Torquay United	Watford
Aldershot FC	■	2-0	1-0	0-0	6-1	1-1	1-0	1-2	1-3	3-0	0-2	0-1	1-1	1-1	2-0	3-1	1-3	1-0	1-1	1-3	1-0	1-1
Bournemouth & B. Athletic	0-0	■	1-2	3-0	2-1	4-4	2-0	1-1	2-5	1-1	1-2	2-1	1-2	2-0	4-0	0-1	0-1	4-1	2-1	1-0	1-1	2-2
Brighton & Hove Albion	2-1	0-1	■	3-0	4-1	1-0	1-3	2-1	2-1	3-1	1-1	1-1	0-0	7-1	5-1	5-1	1-1	4-2	1-3	0-2	3-2	2-1
Bristol City FC	1-0	1-0	0-3	■	0-2	0-2	2-0	0-0	2-0	2-1	2-1	1-2	4-1	1-2	3-2	1-1	0-0	1-1	2-1	5-0	2-0	2-2
Bristol Rovers FC	2-2	2-1	5-2	1-1	■	1-1	1-1	3-2	2-4	6-1	4-3	2-2	2-0	3-0	5-2	0-0	1-1	1-4	3-2	2-1	3-0	0-1
Cardiff City AFC	0-1	1-1	1-0	1-0	0-0	■	4-1	1-0	1-1	5-2	4-0	2-3	3-1	2-0	0-2	3-2	3-2	2-3	1-1	2-1	1-2	0-2
Clapton Orient FC	0-1	1-1	3-1	2-0	2-0	2-1	■	0-1	1-0	1-2	3-1	3-0	1-0	4-0	0-2	1-0	1-0	3-0	1-2	1-1	0-2	
Coventry City FC	0-2	2-0	5-0	3-1	3-1	5-1	2-0	■	8-1	3-0	4-0	0-0	5-0	7-1	4-0	5-1	6-1	3-1	3-0	3-1	2-1	2-0
Crystal Palace FC	2-1	2-0	4-0	6-1	5-3	3-2	2-2	3-1	■	2-2	1-1	5-1	5-0	6-0	6-1	0-2	0-2	3-0	5-1	1-0	1-2	
Exeter City FC	5-1	1-3	3-3	0-1	3-1	2-0	2-3	1-3	1-0	■	2-5	1-2	4-3	3-3	3-1	0-0	0-0	4-5	1-0	0-3	1-1	1-3
Gillingham FC	4-2	1-2	1-2	2-1	1-2	3-0	3-0	1-1	0-2	2-2	■	0-1	1-3	3-0	2-3	0-0	2-2	2-0	2-1	3-1	1-0	0-0
Luton Town FC	2-2	0-0	2-1	1-0	12-0	2-2	5-3	1-1	6-0	1-2	1-2	■	0-0	7-0	3-3	1-0	2-0	2-1	1-2	2-1	1-0	1-2
Millwall FC	1-2	3-0	0-0	1-1	2-1	2-4	1-0	2-2	4-0	2-2	4-1	0-0	■	2-2	2-1	2-1	2-0	0-1	1-2	1-0	1-1	1-1
Newport County AFC	1-1	0-0	0-2	2-0	1-0	0-0	2-3	2-1	2-5	2-1	4-2	0-2	4-1	■	5-1	1-2	3-4	1-5	3-1	2-2	1-6	0-5
Northampton Town FC	3-0	2-1	1-0	0-2	3-3	2-0	2-4	3-1	1-1	0-0	0-0	2-4	3-0		■	3-1	1-4	4-2	2-0	0-0	2-1	0-0
Notts County FC	1-2	1-3	1-1	3-2	6-0	2-0	0-2	0-0	3-1	3-3	0-3	0-0	6-2	3-0		■	3-0	1-3	1-0	0-2	1-0	0-2
Queen's Park Rangers FC	5-0	2-0	3-2	4-1	4-0	5-1	4-0	0-0	3-0	3-1	5-2	0-0	2-3	1-1	0-0	2-2	■	0-1	2-1	5-1	2-1	3-1
Reading FC	3-1	0-2	3-0	5-2	3-2	4-1	4-1	2-1	0-1	2-0	1-0	2-1	3-1	5-2	3-1	1-2		■	2-1	2-0	2-0	3-0
Southend United FC	2-2	3-3	0-0	0-1	1-1	3-1	2-1	0-0	7-1	4-0	4-2	0-1	6-0	1-1	2-1	0-0	0-0	1-2	■	1-0	2-1	1-1
Swindon Town FC	3-2	2-3	1-2	1-1	3-0	2-1	2-2	1-2	0-2	1-1	3-0	3-0	3-1	1-1	3-1	2-1	2-2	4-1	1-3	■	4-1	1-6
Torquay United FC	3-1	0-2	1-0	2-0	2-0	2-1	1-0	3-3	3-2	2-1	4-2	2-1	1-3	3-2	3-3	0-1	4-2	0-0	1-1	2-1	■	2-1
Watford FC	0-0	4-1	2-1	0-2	1-2	4-0	1-1	5-0	3-2	1-0	1-2	1-3	2-1	2-5	4-1	1-2	2-1	4-2	5-0	2-1	2-2	■

	Division 3 (South)	**Pd**	**Wn**	**Dw**	**Ls**	**GF**	**GA**	**Pts**	
1.	Coventry City FC (Coventry)	42	24	9	9	102	45	57	P
2.	Luton Town FC (Luton)	42	22	12	8	81	45	56	
3.	Reading FC (Reading)	42	26	2	14	87	62	54	
4.	Queen's Park Rangers FC (London)	42	22	9	11	84	53	53	
5.	Watford FC (Watford)	42	20	9	13	80	54	49	
6.	Crystal Palace FC (London)	42	22	5	15	96	74	49	
7.	Brighton & Hove Albion FC (Hove)	42	18	8	16	70	63	44	
8.	Bournemouth & Boscombe Athletic FC (Bournemouth)	42	16	11	15	60	56	43	
9.	Notts County FC (Nottingham)	42	15	12	15	60	57	42	
10.	Torquay United FC (Torquay)	42	16	9	17	62	62	41	
11.	Aldershot FC (Aldershot)	42	14	12	16	53	61	40	
12.	Millwall FC (London)	42	14	12	16	58	71	40	
13.	Bristol City FC (Bristol)	42	15	10	17	48	59	40	
14.	Clapton Orient FC (London)	42	16	6	20	55	61	38	
15.	Northampton Town FC (Northampton)	42	15	8	19	62	90	38	
16.	Gillingham FC (Gillingham)	42	14	9	19	66	77	37	
17.	Bristol Rovers FC (Bristol)	42	14	9	19	69	95	37	
18.	Southend United FC (Southend-on-Sea)	42	13	10	19	61	62	36	
19.	Swindon Town FC (Swindon)	42	14	8	20	64	73	36	
20.	Cardiff City AFC (Cardiff)	42	13	10	19	60	73	36	
21.	Newport County AFC (Newport)	42	11	9	22	60	111	31	
22.	Exeter City FC (Exeter)	42	8	11	23	59	93	27	
		924	362	200	362	1497	1497	924	

F.A. CUP FINAL   (Wembley Stadium, London – 25/04/1936 – 93,384)

ARSENAL FC (LONDON)	1-0	Sheffield United FC (Sheffield)

Drake

Arsenal: Wilson, Male, Hapgood, Crayston, Roberts, Copping, Hulme, Bowden, Drake, James, Bastin.

Sheffield United: Smith, Hooper, Wilkinson, Jackson, Johnson, McPherson, Barton, Barclay, Dodds, Pickering, Williams.

Semi-finals

Arsenal FC (London)	1-0	Grimsby Town FC (Cleethorpes)
Fulham FC (London)	1-2	Sheffield United FC (Sheffield)

Quarter-finals

Arsenal FC (London)	4-1	Barnsley FC (Barnsley)
Fulham FC (London)	3-0	Derby County FC (Derby)
Grimsby Town FC (Cleethorpes)	3-1	Middlesbrough FC (Middlesbrough)
Sheffield United FC (Sheffield)	3-1	Tottenham Hotspur FC (London)

1936-37

Football League Division 1 1936-1937 Season	Arsenal	Birmingham	Bolton Wanderers	Brentford	Charlton Athletic	Chelsea	Derby County	Everton	Grimsby Town	Huddersfield Town	Leeds United	Liverpool	Manchester City	Manchester United	Middlesbrough	Portsmouth	Preston North End	Sheffield Wednesday	Stoke City	Sunderland	W.B.A.	Wolves
Arsenal FC	■	1-1	0-0	1-1	1-1	4-1	2-2	3-2	0-0	1-1	4-1	1-0	1-3	1-1	5-3	4-0	4-1	1-1	0-0	4-1	2-0	3-0
Birmingham FC	1-3	■	1-1	4-0	1-2	0-0	0-1	2-0	2-3	4-2	2-1	5-0	2-2	2-2	0-0	2-1	1-0	1-1	2-4	2-0	1-1	1-0
Bolton Wanderers FC	0-5	0-0	■	2-2	2-1	2-1	1-3	1-2	1-2	2-2	2-1	0-1	0-2	0-4	1-3	1-0	0-0	1-0	0-0	1-1	4-1	1-2
Brentford FC	2-0	2-1	2-2	■	4-2	1-0	6-2	2-2	2-3	1-1	4-1	5-2	2-6	4-0	4-1	4-0	1-1	2-1	2-1	3-3	2-1	3-2
Charlton Athletic FC	0-2	2-2	1-0	2-1	■	1-0	2-0	2-0	1-0	1-0	1-0	1-1	1-1	3-0	2-2	0-0	3-1	1-0	2-0	3-1	4-2	4-0
Chelsea FC	2-0	1-3	0-1	2-1	3-0	■	1-1	4-0	3-2	0-0	2-1	2-0	4-4	4-2	1-0	1-1	0-0	1-1	1-0	1-3	3-0	0-1
Derby County FC	5-4	3-1	3-0	2-3	5-0	1-1	■	3-1	3-1	3-3	5-3	4-1	0-5	5-4	0-2	1-3	1-2	3-2	2-2	3-0	1-0	5-1
Everton FC	1-1	3-3	3-2	3-0	2-2	0-0	7-0	■	3-0	2-1	7-1	2-0	1-1	2-3	2-3	4-0	2-2	3-1	1-1	3-0	4-2	1-0
Grimsby Town FC	1-3	1-1	3-1	2-0	0-1	3-0	3-4	1-0	■	2-2	4-1	2-1	5-3	6-2	5-1	1-0	6-4	5-1	1-3	6-0	2-3	1-1
Huddersfield Town AFC	0-0	1-1	2-0	1-1	1-2	4-2	2-0	0-3	0-3	■	3-0	4-0	1-1	3-1	2-0	1-2	4-2	1-0	2-1	2-1	1-1	4-0
Leeds United AFC	3-4	0-2	2-2	3-1	2-0	2-3	2-0	3-0	2-0	2-1	■	2-0	1-1	2-1	5-0	3-1	1-0	1-1	3-0	3-1	0-1	
Liverpool FC	2-1	2-0	0-0	2-2	1-2	1-1	3-3	3-2	7-1	1-1	3-0	■	0-5	2-0	0-2	0-0	1-1	2-2	2-1	4-0	1-2	1-0
Manchester City FC	2-0	1-1	2-2	2-1	1-1	0-0	3-2	4-1	1-1	3-0	4-0	5-1	■	1-0	3-1	4-1	4-1	2-4	6-2	4-1		
Manchester United FC	2-0	1-2	1-0	1-3	0-0	0-0	2-2	2-1	1-1	3-1	0-0	2-5	3-2	■	2-1	0-1	1-1	1-1	2-1	2-2	1-1	
Middlesbrough FC	1-1	3-1	2-0	3-0	1-1	2-0	1-3	2-0	0-0	5-0	4-2	3-3	2-0	3-2	■	2-2	2-1	2-0	1-0	5-5	4-1	1-0
Portsmouth FC	1-5	2-1	1-1	1-3	0-1	4-1	1-2	2-2	2-1	1-0	3-0	6-2	2-1	2-1	2-1	■	0-1	1-0	1-0	3-2	5-3	1-1
Preston North End FC	1-3	2-2	1-2	1-1	0-0	1-0	5-2	1-0	3-2	1-1	1-0	3-1	2-5	3-1	2-0	1-1	■	1-1	0-1	2-0	3-2	1-3
Sheffield Wednesday FC	0-0	0-3	2-0	0-2	3-1	1-1	2-3	6-4	2-1	2-2	1-2	1-2	5-1	1-0	1-0	0-0	0-1	■	0-0	2-0	2-3	1-3
Stoke City FC	0-0	2-0	2-2	5-1	1-1	2-0	1-2	2-1	2-0	1-1	2-1	1-1	2-2	3-0	6-2	2-4	0-2	1-0	■	5-3	10-3	2-1
Sunderland AFC	1-1	4-0	3-0	4-1	1-0	2-3	3-2	3-1	5-1	3-2	2-1	4-2	1-3	1-1	4-1	3-2	3-0	2-1	3-0	■	1-0	6-2
West Bromwich Albion FC	2-4	3-2	0-2	1-0	1-2	2-0	1-3	2-1	4-2	2-1	3-0	3-1	2-2	1-0	3-1	0-0	2-3	2-2	6-4		■	2-1
Wolverhampton Wanderers FC	2-0	2-1	2-3	4-0	6-1	1-2	3-1	7-2	5-2	3-1	3-0	2-0	2-1	3-1	0-1	1-1	5-0	4-3	2-1	1-1	5-2	■

	Division 1	Pd	Wn	Dw	Ls	GF	GA	Pts	
1.	MANCHESTER CITY FC (MANCHESTER)	42	22	13	7	107	61	57	
2.	Charlton Athletic FC (London)	42	21	12	9	58	49	54	
3.	Arsenal FC (London)	42	18	16	8	80	49	52	
4.	Derby County FC (Derby)	42	21	7	14	96	90	49	
5.	Wolverhampton Wanderers FC (Wolverhampton)	42	21	5	16	84	67	47	
6.	Brentford FC (London)	42	18	10	14	82	78	46	
7.	Middlesbrough FC (Middlesbrough)	42	19	8	15	74	71	46	
8.	Sunderland AFC (Sunderland)	42	19	6	17	89	87	44	
9.	Portsmouth FC (Portsmouth)	42	17	10	15	62	66	44	
10.	Stoke City FC (Stoke-on-Trent)	42	15	12	15	72	57	42	
11.	Birmingham FC (Birmingham)	42	13	15	14	64	60	41	
12.	Grimsby Town FC (Cleethorpes)	42	17	7	18	86	81	41	
13.	Chelsea FC (London)	42	14	13	15	52	55	41	
14.	Preston North End FC (Preston)	42	14	13	15	56	67	41	
15.	Huddersfield Town AFC (Huddersfield)	42	12	15	15	62	64	39	
16.	West Bromwich Albion FC (West Bromwich)	42	16	6	20	77	98	38	
17.	Everton FC (Liverpool)	42	14	9	19	81	78	37	
18.	Liverpool FC (Liverpool)	42	12	11	19	62	84	35	
19.	Leeds United AFC (Leeds)	42	15	4	23	60	80	34	
20.	Bolton Wanderers FC (Bolton)	42	10	14	18	43	66	34	
21.	Manchester United FC (Manchester)	42	10	12	20	55	78	32	R
22.	Sheffield Wednesday FC (Sheffield)	42	9	12	21	53	69	30	R
		924	347	230	347	1555	1555	924	

Top Goalscorer

1)	Freddie STEELE	(Stoke City FC)	33

Football League Division 2 1936-1937 Season	Aston Villa	Barnsley	Blackburn R.	Blackpool	Bradford City	Bradford P.A.	Burnley	Bury	Chesterfield	Coventry City	Doncaster R.	Fulham	Leicester City	Newcastle Utd.	Norwich City	Nottingham F.	Plymouth Arg.	Sheffield United	Southampton	Swansea Town	Tottenham H.	West Ham Utd.
Aston Villa FC		4-2	2-2	4-0	5-1	4-1	0-0	0-4	6-2	0-0	1-1	0-3	1-3	0-2	3-0	1-1	5-4	2-1	4-0	4-0	1-1	0-2
Barnsley FC	0-4		3-2	2-1	1-1	2-1	1-1	2-2	1-1	3-0	4-1	1-0	1-2	1-0	2-1	1-0	1-3	1-1	2-1	0-1	1-0	0-0
Blackburn Rovers FC	3-4	1-1		2-0	3-0	1-1	3-1	2-3	5-2	2-5	0-2	0-0	6-1	1-0	9-1	2-3	3-1	1-0	2-1	0-4		1-2
Blackpool FC	2-3	1-1	2-0		4-2	6-0	2-0	1-2	0-1	3-0	1-1	3-1	6-2	3-0	0-2	7-1	1-1	1-0	2-0	3-2	0-0	1-0
Bradford City AFC	2-2	3-2	2-2	1-4		2-3	1-3	0-1	2-2	1-0	0-0	1-1	1-2	2-0	2-0	2-1	1-1	3-2	2-2	4-0	2-2	2-1
Bradford Park Avenue	3-3	2-1	1-2	2-1	2-1		2-0	0-1	4-5	1-3	1-0	1-1	1-2	0-3	1-0	3-2	0-0	0-3	3-1	1-1	3-2	2-1
Burnley FC	1-2	3-0	0-0	3-0	3-0	2-2		1-2	3-1	3-3	0-2	0-0	0-3	3-0	3-0	2-0	1-0	1-3	0-0	3-1	2-1	
Bury FC	2-1	2-1	1-1	2-3	5-0	3-1	3-1		4-0	0-4	4-2	1-1	0-1	1-2	3-2	1-1	2-0	2-0	2-1	2-0	5-3	1-1
Chesterfield FC	1-0	2-1	0-4	0-4	7-1	4-2	4-1	1-1		2-3	5-1	4-1	2-5	4-0	3-1	4-2	0-1	2-2	3-0	4-0	1-3	1-1
Coventry City FC	1-0	3-0	0-1	1-2	3-1	4-0	0-1	1-3	2-1		1-1	1-1	1-0	2-2	1-1	2-2	2-0	2-0	2-1	1-0	2-1	4-0
Doncaster Rovers FC	1-0	0-1	0-0	0-4	1-1	1-3	2-0	1-0	0-4	1-1		2-1	0-0	1-2	1-2	0-2	2-1	1-1	2-0	0-0	1-1	1-4
Fulham FC	3-2	1-0	1-1	0-3	0-1	0-0	2-0	1-1	1-0	0-2	1-0		2-0	3-4	2-3	5-2	2-2	4-0	2-0	5-0	3-3	5-0
Leicester City FC	1-0	5-1	1-0	1-2	4-1	5-0	7-3	0-3	3-1	1-0	7-1	2-0		3-2	2-2	2-1	3-2	1-2	2-2	0-0	4-1	2-2
Newcastle United FC	0-2	0-1	2-0	1-2	2-0	1-1	3-0	1-3	1-2	4-2	7-0	1-1	1-0		0-1	3-2	1-1	4-0	3-0	5-1	0-1	5-3
Norwich City FC	5-1	0-1	0-0	1-2	0-0	3-1	2-2	0-0	2-0	0-3	2-1	3-0	1-2	1-5		4-0	1-2	1-1	4-2	3-0	2-3	3-3
Nottingham Forest FC	1-1	4-1	2-0	1-1	2-1	3-2	1-2	1-0	2-2	1-1	2-1	5-3	0-3	0-2	3-4		2-3	1-1	1-1	6-1	3-0	1-0
Plymouth Argyle FC	2-2	1-2	2-0	1-3	4-4	2-0	0-1	3-0	1-1	1-0	7-0	0-3	2-1	1-1	2-0	4-1		2-0	3-1	0-0	0-0	2-2
Sheffield United FC	5-1	2-0	0-1	2-2	3-1	3-0	1-1	1-0	5-0	2-2	2-3	2-0	3-1	2-1	2-0	4-1	2-0		0-0	1-0	3-2	2-0
Southampton FC	2-2	1-3	2-2	5-2	2-0	0-0	1-1	4-1	3-2	1-1	1-0	3-3	1-1	2-0	3-1	0-3	0-0	4-0		2-1	1-0	0-2
Swansea Town AFC	1-2	3-1	1-0	1-1	3-0	3-0	3-0	2-0	4-1	2-0	1-0	3-0	1-3	1-2	2-1	1-0	0-1	2-1	5-1		2-1	0-0
Tottenham Hotspur FC	2-2	3-0	5-1	1-2	5-1	5-1	3-0	2-0	5-1	3-1	2-0	1-1	4-2	0-1	2-3	2-1	1-3	2-2	4-0	3-1		2-3
West Ham United FC	2-1	0-0	3-1	3-0	4-1	1-0	0-2	5-1	1-1	4-0	3-3	4-1	0-2	4-1	2-2	1-1	1-0	4-0	2-0	2-1		

	Division 2	Pd	Wn	Dw	Ls	GF	GA	Pts	
1.	Leicester City FC (Leicester)	42	24	8	10	89	57	56	P
2.	Blackpool FC (Blackpool)	42	24	7	11	88	53	55	P
3.	Bury FC (Bury)	42	22	8	12	74	55	52	
4.	Newcastle United FC (Newcastle-upon-Tyne)	42	22	5	15	80	56	49	
5.	Plymouth Argyle FC (Plymouth)	42	18	13	11	71	53	49	
6.	West Ham United FC (London)	42	19	11	12	73	55	49	
7.	Sheffield United FC (Sheffield)	42	18	10	14	66	54	46	
8.	Coventry City FC (Coventry)	42	17	11	14	66	54	45	
9.	Aston Villa FC (Birmingham)	42	16	12	14	82	70	44	
10.	Tottenham Hotspur FC (London)	42	17	9	16	88	66	43	
11.	Fulham FC (London)	42	15	13	14	71	61	43	
12.	Blackburn Rovers FC (Blackburn)	42	16	10	16	70	62	42	
13.	Burnley FC (Burnley)	42	16	10	16	57	61	42	
14.	Barnsley FC (Barnsley)	42	16	9	17	50	64	41	
15.	Chesterfield FC (Chesterfield)	42	16	8	18	84	89	40	
16.	Swansea Town AFC (Swansea)	42	15	7	20	50	65	37	
17.	Norwich City FC (Norwich)	42	14	8	20	63	71	36	
18.	Nottingham Forest FC (Nottingham)	42	12	10	20	68	90	34	
19.	Southampton FC (Southampton)	42	11	12	19	53	77	34	
20.	Bradford Park Avenue FC (Bradford)	42	12	9	21	52	88	33	
21.	Bradford City AFC (Bradford)	42	9	12	21	54	94	30	R
22.	Doncaster Rovers FC (Doncaster)	42	7	10	25	30	84	24	R
		924	356	212	356	1479	1479	924	

Football League Division 3 (N) 1936-1937 Season

	Accrington St.	Barrow	Carlisle United	Chester	Crewe Alex.	Darlington	Gateshead	Halifax Town	Hartlepools Utd.	Hull City	Lincoln City	Mansfield Town	New Brighton	Oldham Athletic	Port Vale	Rochdale	Rotherham Utd.	Southport	Stockport Co.	Tranmere R.	Wrexham	York City
Accrington Stanley FC	■	5-0	2-1	2-1	4-1	1-0	2-1	3-2	1-2	0-1	1-2	0-3	5-0	1-1	2-3	3-1	3-0	6-3	2-1	4-0	2-2	2-1
Barrow AFC	1-0	■	5-0	1-2	2-2	1-0	3-0	1-2	3-1	2-3	0-4	2-2	2-1	1-2	3-1	3-0	5-1	2-1	0-0	2-0	1-1	2-2
Carlisle United FC	2-0	2-2	■	1-1	4-0	2-0	2-1	1-2	2-0	1-1	3-1	1-2	1-1	2-1	5-2	10	4-1	1-1	1-0	3-1	2-1	1-1
Chester FC	1-1	6-0	4-0	■	5-0	2-1	6-0	1-1	3-0	3-1	7-3	5-1	4-1	2-1	0-0	2-2	2-1	2-3	1-1	5-2	4-1	3-1
Crewe Alexandra FC	2-2	4-1	1-2	1-1	■	1-1	3-1	0-1	1-1	2-1	2-1	2-1	0-2	1-2	0-1	2-2	0-2	3-2	1-2	2-2	1-1	2-2
Darlington FC	4-1	2-4	1-5	1-3	0-3	■	0-2	3-3	5-5	2-2	2-2	0-0	1-2	0-3	1-0	4-1	6-3	4-2	1-1	3-2	1-1	1-1
Gateshead FC	1-1	1-1	1-0	1-1	2-0	5-0	■	0-2	2-2	6-3	0-5	3-3	1-1	0-3	0-1	3-1	2-1	5-4	0-0	4-0	-00	3-2
Halifax Town AFC	3-0	2-1	6-1	1-0	4-1	4-1	2-1	■	2-0	1-0	2-3	0-0	0-0	0-1	0-1	3-2	4-1	1-1	1-1	2-1	1-2	1-2
Hartlepools United FC	1-0	3-1	3-0	0-1	4-1	1-3	6-1	5-3	■	2-2	3-1	3-0	5-0	1-0	2-0	0-2	2-0	2-4	2-1	2-0	2-0	
Hull City AFC	0-3	3-2	1-1	1-1	2-0	4-3	3-2	0-0	1-0	■	1-1	3-0	4-1	2-0	1-1	1-1	2-1	3-2	0-1	5-2	1-0	1-0
Lincoln City FC	3-3	6-0	3-0	3-0	2-4	4-3	4-0	4-1	3-0	5-0	■	2-0	1-0	2-0	1-0	5-3	3-0	4-1	0-2	1-0	6-2	3-1
Mansfield Town FC	2-1	2-1	1-4	5-0	1-4	3-1	3-2	3-0	8-2	5-2	2-2	■	2-3	1-2	7-1	6-2	4-1	3-0	2-3	3-0	1-2	
New Brighton FC	1-1	1-1	1-1	1-0	1-0	2-0	1-1	1-1	4-0	1-1	1-2	0-0	■	0-2	2-0	5-0	4-0	3-1	1-1	1-2	1-0	4-1
Oldham Athletic AFC	3-1	4-3	2-1	1-0	1-1	1-1	4-4	1-0	2-0	3-1	1-0	1-1	3-1	■	5-1	3-0	4-1	3-3	0-2	3-0	2-2	2-2
Port Vale FC	1-1	3-2	1-0	4-0	0-0	2-2	4-2	3-1	1-0	1-3	1-1	5-1	3-1	1-0	■	1-1	2-1	0-2	3-0	2-1	0-3	1-1
Rochdale AFC	4-1	3-1	3-0	0-1	2-0	4-0	0-2	3-5	1-1	4-0	2-3	1-3	4-0	3-0	0-0	■	1-0	2-1	2-2	0-6	3-0	
Rotherham United FC	2-2	4-1	0-1	2-1	3-2	2-4	3-0	6-0	2-4	0-0	3-1	4-1	3-0	4-4	2-0	1-1	■	3-0	1-1	3-1	2-2	2-2
Southport FC	3-1	3-3	2-1	1-2	1-1	0-0	3-0	2-1	1-1	1-4	2-1	3-2	3-0	2-0	3-3	1-1	4-1	■	1-1	1-0	1-1	1-4
Stockport County FC	3-2	4-1	1-2	4-0	1-0	3-3	4-2	0-0	1-1	3-1	0-2	3-1	4-1	1-0	3-0	4-2	2-1		■	5-0	2-0	6-0
Tranmere Rovers FC	1-2	0-0	5-1	5-0	6-1	1-1	6-1	2-1	1-0	2-1	2-2	0-2	3-2	3-3	4-2	4-3	1-2	3-3	2-2	■	1-1	0-0
Wrexham AFC	1-0	2-1	1-0	1-2	5-0	4-0	6-0	0-2	0-1	2-1	0-3	2-3	4-1	1-0	0-1	4-2	3-3	0-0	2-0		■	2-0
York City FC	4-2	1-2	5-2	0-2	2-3	3-0	2-0	4-0	4-1	1-1	0-0	1-1	2-1	3-1	1-2	4-1	4-3	4-0	2-1	4-0	3-4	■

Division 3 (North)

		Pd	Wn	Dw	Ls	GF	GA	Pts	
1.	Stockport County FC (Stockport)	42	23	14	5	84	39	60	P
2.	Lincoln City FC (Lincoln)	42	25	7	10	103	57	57	
3.	Chester FC (Chester)	42	22	9	11	87	57	53	
4.	Oldham Athletic AFC (Oldham)	42	20	11	11	77	59	51	
5.	Hull City AFC (Kingston-upon-Hull)	42	17	12	13	68	69	46	
6.	Hartlepools United FC (Hartlepool)	42	19	7	16	75	69	45	
7.	Halifax Town AFC (Halifax)	42	18	9	15	68	63	45	
8.	Wrexham AFC (Wrexham)	42	16	12	14	71	57	44	
9.	Mansfield Town FC (Mansfield)	42	18	8	16	91	76	44	T
10.	Carlisle United FC (Carlisle)	42	18	8	16	65	68	44	
11.	Port Vale FC (Stoke-on-Trent)	42	17	10	15	58	64	44	
12.	York City FC (York)	42	16	11	15	79	70	43	
13.	Accrington Stanley FC (Accrington)	42	16	9	17	76	69	41	
14.	Southport FC (Southport)	42	12	13	17	73	87	37	
15.	New Brighton FC (Wallasey)	42	13	11	18	55	70	37	
16.	Barrow AFC (Barrow-in-Furness)	42	13	10	19	70	86	36	
17.	Rotherham United FC (Rotherham)	42	14	7	21	78	91	35	
18.	Rochdale AFC (Rochdale)	42	13	9	20	69	86	35	
19.	Tranmere Rovers FC (Birkenhead)	42	12	9	21	71	88	33	
20.	Crewe Alexandra FC (Crewe)	42	10	12	20	55	83	32	
21.	Gateshead FC (Gateshead)	42	11	10	21	63	98	32	
22.	Darlington FC (Darlington)	42	8	14	20	66	96	30	
		924	351	222	351	1602	1602	924	

T: Mansfield Town FC (Mansfield) were transferred to Division 3 (South) from the next season.

Football League Division 3 (S) 1936-1937 Season

	Aldershot	Bournemouth	Brighton	Bristol City	Bristol Rovers	Cardiff City	Clapton Orient	Crystal Palace	Exeter City	Gillingham	Luton Town	Millwall	Newport County	Northampton	Notts County	Q.P.R.	Reading	Southend United	Swindon Town	Torquay United	Walsall	Watford
Aldershot FC		1-3	0-1	3-0	4-0	0-1	1-1	2-2	1-1	3-0	2-3	1-2	2-0	0-2	0-1	0-0	0-2	1-2	2-1	0-1	4-4	2-2
Bournemouth & B. Athletic	2-1		1-0	0-0	3-0	0-2	2-1	3-1	0-0	1-0	2-1	2-1	5-0	3-2	1-0	3-1	2-1	1-0	5-2	3-3	3-2	3-2
Brighton & Hove Albion	1-0	1-0		2-0	5-2	7-2	1-1	1-0	1-0	4-0	2-1	2-2	2-0	1-2	2-2	4-1	1-1	1-0	2-0	5-1	3-0	1-1
Bristol City FC	3-0	4-1	1-0		4-1	2-1	4-0	1-0	2-1	2-0	2-3	2-0	3-1	0-1	1-1	3-2	1-2	0-1	1-2	4-1	0-0	2-2
Bristol Rovers FC	1-0	4-0	2-0	3-1		5-1	4-0	1-0	4-2	0-3	4-0	2-1	1-1	2-0	2-3	1-1	2-2	1-2	2-1	5-1	3-0	0-1
Cardiff City AFC	4-1	2-1	1-2	3-1	3-1		2-1	1-1	3-1	2-0	3-0	0-1	0-1	2-1	0-2	2-0	1-1	1-1	1-2	0-2	2-2	2-2
Clapton Orient FC	1-1	2-1	2-0	0-0	2-1	0-1		1-1	1-0	2-0	0-2	1-0	1-2	3-1	1-1	0-0	3-2	3-0	1-1	2-0	2-2	1-1
Crystal Palace FC	3-0	2-2	2-0	1-0	3-0	2-2	2-3		8-0	1-1	0-4	1-0	6-1	2-2	1-2	0-0	3-1	1-1	2-0	0-0	3-1	2-0
Exeter City FC	1-2	1-1	0-4	3-0	3-2	3-1	0-2	3-2		1-1	2-4	1-1	3-1	2-5	1-3	0-3	2-0	2-2	1-1	2-1	3-0	2-1
Gillingham FC	1-2	1-0	1-0	5-3	1-0	0-0	0-2	2-0	2-2		1-0	1-0	4-4	2-0	3-0	0-0	2-1	1-0	4-1	1-0	2-2	2-1
Luton Town FC	5-2	1-0	2-1	4-0	2-0	8-1	2-0	5-2	2-2	5-2		5-0	5-0	3-2	2-1	0-1	4-0	1-0	5-1	2-0	2-0	4-1
Millwall FC	4-2	0-2	3-0	3-1	1-2	3-1	2-1	3-0	3-3	3-3	0-2		7-2	1-0	2-0	0-2	0-2	1-1	3-1	1-1	3-1	1-1
Newport County AFC	4-0	4-0	1-4	0-0	2-2	2-3	1-1	1-1	2-0	0-0	2-1	1-2		1-3	0-1	1-2	3-0	6-2	1-1	1-1	1-2	1-3
Northampton Town FC	5-3	0-0	2-0	5-1	4-1	2-0	1-1	2-0	2-1	5-0	3-1	2-2	3-2		1-1	0-1	2-1	4-3	4-0	3-0	6-3	0-1
Notts County FC	3-0	4-3	0-1	1-0	4-3	4-0	0-0	0-1	3-1	2-0	2-1	1-1	3-1	3-2		1-2	1-0	2-1	3-2	3-3	2-2	3-1
Queen's Park Rangers FC	3-0	-2	2-3	5-0	2-1	6-0	2-1	1-3	4-0	1-1	0-1	6-2	3-2	0-2			0-0	7-2	1-1	3-0	2-0	1-2
Reading FC	2-0	3-2	2-0	2-1	2-0	3-0	1-1	1-1	1-0	6-2	2-2	3-0	4-4	3-1	4-1	2-0		2-3	2-2	5-1	0-2	3-0
Southend United FC	2-2	0-0	2-1	3-0	2-3	8-1	0-0	2-1	4-4	0-2	3-0	0-0	9-2	2-3	2-3	3-2	1-1		2-0	0-0	3-0	1-1
Swindon Town FC	5-1	3-1	1-2	0-1	4-1	4-2	1-3	4-0	3-1	3-0	2-2	3-0	1-2	2-2	2-1	1-2	4-0			4-2	3-0	1-1
Torquay United FC	5-1	0-0	0-2	5-2	1-0	1-0	4-1	3-0	0-1	0-2	2-2	0-2	1-2	5-0	2-1	2-2	1-4	2-0			3-1	4-7
Walsall FC	0-0	1-1	1-4	1-5	5-2	1-0	3-2	1-0	4-2	2-1	0-1	0-3	1-2	2-2	2-1	2-4	0-1	3-0	5-2	1-0		3-1
Watford FC	5-3	4-0	1-0	1-0	3-0	2-0	2-1	3-1	1-1	6-1	1-3	2-2	3-0	4-1	0-2	6-1	1-3	2-2	4-0	0-0		

Division 3 (South)

		Pd	Wn	Dw	Ls	GF	GA	Pts	
1.	Luton Town FC (Luton)	42	27	4	11	103	53	58	P
2.	Notts County FC (Nottingham)	42	23	10	9	74	52	56	
3.	Brighton & Hove Albion FC (Hove)	42	24	5	13	74	43	53	
4.	Watford FC (Watford)	42	19	11	12	85	60	49	
5.	Reading FC (Reading)	42	19	11	12	76	60	49	
6.	Bournemouth & Boscombe Athletic FC (Bournemouth)	42	20	9	13	65	59	49	
7.	Northampton Town FC (Northampton)	42	20	6	16	85	68	46	
8.	Millwall FC (London)	42	18	10	14	64	54	46	
9.	Queen's Park Rangers FC (London)	42	18	9	15	73	52	45	
10.	Southend United FC (Southend-on-Sea)	42	17	11	14	78	67	45	
11.	Gillingham FC (Gillingham)	42	18	8	16	52	66	44	
12.	Clapton Orient FC (London)	42	14	15	13	52	52	43	
13.	Swindon Town FC (Swindon)	42	14	11	17	75	73	39	
14.	Crystal Palace FC (London)	42	13	12	17	62	61	38	
15.	Bristol Rovers FC (Bristol)	42	16	4	22	71	80	36	
16.	Bristol City FC (Bristol)	42	15	6	21	58	70	36	
17.	Walsall FC (Walsall)	42	13	10	19	62	84	36	
18.	Cardiff City AFC (Cardiff)	42	14	7	21	54	87	35	
19.	Newport County AFC (Newport)	42	12	10	20	67	98	34	
20.	Torquay United FC (Torquay)	42	11	10	21	57	80	32	
21.	Exeter City FC (Exeter)	42	10	12	20	59	88	32	
22.	Aldershot FC (Aldershot)	42	7	9	26	50	89	23	
		924	362	200	362	1496	1496	924	

F.A. CUP FINAL   (Wembley Stadium, London – 01/05/1937 – 93,495)

SUNDERLAND AFC (SUNDERLAND)   3-1   Preston North End FC (Preston)
Gurney, Carter, Burbanks   *F.O'Donnell*

Sunderland: Mapson, Gorman, Hall, Thomson, Johnson, McNab, Duns, Carter, Gurney, Gallacher, Burbanks.

Preston: Burns, Gallimore, A.Beattie, Shankly, Tremelling, Milne, Dougal, Beresford, F.O'Donnell, Fagan, H.O'Donnell.

Semi-finals

Preston North End FC (Preston)	4-1	West Bromwich Albion FC (West Bromwich)
Sunderland AFC (Sunderland)	2-1	Millwall FC (London)

Quarter-finals

Millwall FC (London)	2-0	Manchester City FC (Manchester)
Tottenham Hotspur FC (London)	1-3	Preston North End FC (Preston)
West Bromwich Albion FC (West Bromwich)	3-1	Arsenal FC (London)
Wolverhampton Wanderers FC	1-1, 2-2 (aet), 0-4 (aet)	Sunderland AFC (Sunderland)

1937-38

Football League Division 1 1937-1938 Season	Arsenal	Birmingham	Blackpool	Bolton Wanderers	Brentford	Charlton Athletic	Chelsea	Derby County	Everton	Grimsby Town	Huddersfield Town	Leeds United	Leicester City	Liverpool	Manchester City	Middlesbrough	Portsmouth	Preston North End	Stoke City	Sunderland	W.B.A.	Wolves
Arsenal FC	█	0-0	2-1	5-0	0-2	2-2	2-0	3-0	2-1	5-1	3-1	4-1	3-1	1-0	2-1	1-2	1-1	2-0	4-0	4-1	1-1	5-0
Birmingham FC	1-2	█	1-1	2-0	0-0	1-1	1-1	1-0	0-3	2-2	2-2	3-2	4-1	2-2	2-2	3-1	2-2	0-2	1-1	2-2	2-1	2-0
Blackpool FC	2-1	0-3	█	2-2	1-1	1-0	0-2	1-1	1-0	2-2	4-0	5-2	2-4	0-1	2-1	4-2	2-0	1-0	0-1	0-0	3-1	0-2
Bolton Wanderers FC	1-0	1-1	3-0	█	2-0	1-0	5-5	0-2	1-2	3-1	2-0	0-0	6-1	0-0	2-1	3-1	1-1	1-4	1-0	1-1	3-0	1-2
Brentford FC	3-0	1-2	2-4	1-1	█	5-2	1-1	2-3	3-0	6-1	2-0	1-1	1-1	1-3	2-1	3-3	2-0	2-1	0-0	4-0	0-2	2-1
Charlton Athletic FC	0-3	2-0	4-1	1-1	1-0	█	3-1	1-2	3-1	0-0	4-0	1-1	2-0	3-0	0-0	1-0	5-1	0-0	3-0	2-1	3-1	4-1
Chelsea FC	2-2	2-0	1-3	0-0	2-1	1-1	█	3-0	2-0	1-0	3-1	4-1	4-1	6-1	2-2	0-1	3-1	0-2	2-1	0-0	2-2	0-2
Derby County FC	2-0	0-0	3-1	4-2	1-3	3-2	4-0	█	2-1	1-2	0-4	2-2	0-1	4-1	1-7	1-1	1-0	1-1	4-1	2-2	5-3	1-2
Everton FC	1-4	1-1	3-1	4-1	3-0	3-0	4-1	1-1	█	3-2	1-2	1-1	3-0	1-3	4-1	2-2	5-2	3-5	3-0	3-3	5-3	0-1
Grimsby Town FC	2-1	4-0	1-0	0-1	0-1	1-1	2-0	0-0	2-1	█	4-2	1-1	2-1	0-0	3-1	2-1	1-0	1-1	1-5	0-2	1-4	1-0
Huddersfield Town AFC	2-1	2-1	3-1	1-0	0-3	1-1	1-2	2-0	1-3	1-2	█	0-3	0-0	1-2	1-0	3-0	2-0	1-3	3-0	1-1	2-1	1-0
Leeds United AFC	0-1	1-0	1-1	1-1	4-0	2-2	2-0	0-0	4-4	1-1	2-1	█	0-2	2-0	2-1	5-3	3-1	0-0	2-1	4-3	1-0	1-2
Leicester City FC	1-1	1-4	0-1	1-1	0-1	1-0	1-0	0-0	3-1	1-0	2-1	2-4	█	2-2	1-4	0-1	3-3	1-0	2-0	4-0	4-1	1-1
Liverpool FC	2-0	3-2	4-2	2-1	3-4	1-2	2-2	3-4	1-2	2-1	0-1	1-1	1-1	█	2-0	1-1	3-2	2-2	3-0	4-0	0-1	0-1
Manchester City FC	1-2	2-0	2-1	1-2	0-2	5-3	1-0	6-1	2-0	3-1	3-2	6-2	3-0	1-3	█	1-6	2-1	1-2	0-0	0-0	7-1	2-4
Middlesbrough FC	2-1	1-1	2-2	1-2	0-1	3-1	4-3	4-2	1-2	1-0	0-1	2-0	4-2	1-1	4-0	█	0-0	2-1	2-1	4-1	0-3	
Portsmouth FC	0-0	1-1	1-2	1-1	4-1	2-1	2-4	4-0	3-1	3-0	3-0	4-0	1-1	1-1	2-2	0-2	█	3-2	2-0	1-0	2-3	1-0
Preston North End FC	1-3	2-1	2-0	2-2	1-1	0-1	0-0	4-1	2-1	4-1	1-1	3-1	0-0	4-1	2-2	0-2	1-1	█	2-1	0-0	1-1	2-0
Stoke City FC	1-1	2-2	1-3	3-2	3-0	2-0	2-1	8-1	1-1	1-1	0-1	0-1	1-2	2-0	3-2	3-0	3-1	1-1	█	0-0	4-0	1-0
Sunderland AFC	1-1	1-0	2-1	3-1	1-0	1-1	1-1	2-0	2-0	2-2	2-1	0-0	1-0	2-3	3-1	3-1	0-2	0-2	1-1	█	3-0	1-0
West Bromwich Albion FC	0-0	4-3	1-2	2-4	4-3	0-0	4-0	4-2	3-1	2-1	5-1	2-1	1-3	5-1	1-1	3-1	1-2	1-1	0-1	1-6	█	2-2
Wolverhampton Wanderers FC	3-1	3-2	1-0	1-1	2-1	1-1	1-1	2-2	2-0	1-1	1-4	1-1	10-1	2-0	3-1	0-1	5-0	0-0	2-2	4-0	2-1	█

	Division 1	Pd	Wn	Dw	Ls	GF	GA	Pts	
1.	ARSENAL FC (LONDON)	42	21	10	11	77	44	52	
2.	Wolverhampton Wanderers FC (Wolverhampton)	42	20	11	11	72	49	51	
3.	Preston North End FC (Preston)	42	16	17	9	64	44	49	
4.	Charlton Athletic FC (London)	42	16	14	12	65	51	46	
5.	Middlesbrough FC (Middlesbrough)	42	19	8	15	72	65	46	
6.	Brentford FC (London)	42	18	9	15	69	59	45	
7.	Bolton Wanderers FC (Bolton)	42	15	15	12	64	60	45	
8.	Sunderland AFC (Sunderland)	42	14	16	12	55	57	44	
9.	Leeds United AFC (Leeds)	42	14	15	13	64	69	43	
10.	Chelsea FC (London)	42	14	13	15	65	65	41	
11.	Liverpool FC (Liverpool)	42	15	11	16	65	71	41	
12.	Blackpool FC (Blackpool)	42	16	8	18	61	66	40	
13.	Derby County FC (Derby)	42	15	10	17	66	87	40	
14.	Everton FC (Liverpool)	42	16	7	19	79	75	39	
15.	Huddersfield Town AFC (Huddersfield)	42	17	5	20	55	68	39	
16.	Leicester City FC (Leicester)	42	14	11	17	54	75	39	
17.	Stoke City FC (Stoke-on-Trent)	42	13	12	17	58	59	38	
18.	Birmingham FC (Birmingham)	42	10	18	14	58	62	38	
19.	Portsmouth FC (Portsmouth)	42	13	12	17	62	68	38	
20.	Grimsby Town FC (Cleethorpes)	42	13	12	17	51	68	38	
21.	Manchester City FC (Manchester)	42	14	8	20	80	77	36	R
22.	West Bromwich Albion FC (West Bromwich)	42	14	8	20	74	91	36	R
		924	337	250	337	1430	1430	924	

Top Goalscorer

1) Tommy LAWTON   (Everton FC)   28

Football League Division 2 1937-1938 Season	Aston Villa	Barnsley	Blackburn R.	Bradford P.A.	Burnley	Bury	Chesterfield	Coventry City	Fulham	Luton Town	Man. United	Newcastle Utd.	Norwich City	Nottingham F.	Plymouth Arg.	Sheffield United	Sheffield Wed.	Southampton	Stockport Co.	Swansea Town	Tottenham H.	West Ham Utd.
Aston Villa FC	■	3-0	2-1	2-0	0-0	2-1	0-2	1-1	2-0	4-1	3-0	2-0	2-0	1-2	3-0	1-0	4-3	3-0	7-1	4-0	2-0	2-0
Barnsley FC	0-1	■	0-0	0-1	2-2	2-2	1-1	1-1	0-0	3-1	2-2	3-0	0-0	2-2	3-2	1-1	4-1	0-2	2-0	2-0	1-1	1-0
Blackburn Rovers FC	1-0	5-3	■	0-0	3-3	2-1	3-3	1-3	2-2	2-2	1-1	2-1	5-3	5-1	2-1	2-3	1-0	4-0	3-0	3-1	2-1	2-1
Bradford Park Avenue	1-2	4-3	7-1	■	3-1	1-1	3-2	0-1	1-2	1-1	4-0	2-0	3-0	2-2	2-0	5-1	1-1	2-0	4-1	0-1	3-1	2-1
Burnley FC	3-0	1-0	3-1	1-1	■	2-0	0-2	2-0	1-0	3-2	1-0	2-1	3-0	0-0	0-2	2-0	1-1	4-0	0-0	2-0	2-1	2-0
Bury FC	1-1	0-2	2-1	5-1	4-0	■	4-0	0-2	4-2	3-4	1-2	1-1	3-1	2-0	1-0	2-0	2-1	1-3	0-0	1-2		4-3
Chesterfield FC	0-1	0-0	3-0	0-3	0-1	1-2	■	4-0	0-2	5-2	1-7	6-2	1-0	0-2	1-0	5-0	1-0	4-1			2-2	
Coventry City FC	0-1	1-0	3-2	0-0	1-0	0-2	2-2	■	0-1	2-1	1-0	1-0	2-0	1-1	4-0	2-2	0-1	2-0	1-0	5-0	2-1	1-1
Fulham FC	1-1	0-0	3-1	1-1	2-1	4-0	1-1	3-4	■	4-1	1-0	1-2	3-4	2-0	2-3	1-1	0-0	1-0	2-0	8-1	3-1	1-1
Luton Town FC	3-2	4-0	4-1	4-2	3-1	0-1	1-1	1-4	4-0	■	1-0	4-1	1-1	2-2	1-1	2-3	2-2	1-3	6-4	5-1	2-4	2-2
Manchester United FC	3-1	4-1	2-1	3-1	4-0	2-0	4-1	2-2	1-0	4-2	■	3-0	0-0	4-3	0-0	1-0	3-1	5-1	0-1			4-0
Newcastle United FC	2-0	0-1	2-0	3-0	2-2	1-0	3-1	1-2	1-2	1-3	2-2	■	0-1	3-1	6-0	3-0		1-0	1-0		1-0	2-2
Norwich City FC	1-0	1-0	3-2	1-1	1-0	1-2	2-1	0-2	1-2	0-4	2-3	1-1	■	2-0	4-0	2-3	4-3	1-0	1-1	1-1		2-2
Nottingham Forest FC	0-2	2-1	3-1	1-0	1-1	1-0	4-2	2-1	0-1	1-0	2-3	0-0	1-2	■	1-0	0-1	2-1	1-2	2-1	3-1		0-0
Plymouth Argyle FC	0-3	2-2	2-2	1-0	2-3	2-1	1-1	3-1	4-0	2-4	1-1	2-1	1-1	1-0	■	2-0	2-4	4-0	2-1	2-2	2-2	2-1
Sheffield United FC	0-0	6-3	1-1	3-1	2-1	2-1	0-2	3-2	2-1	2-0	1-2	4-0	4-1	2-1	0-0	■	2-1	5-0	2-0	1-1	1-0	3-1
Sheffield Wednesday FC	1-2	0-1	1-1	1-0	2-1	2-0	1-0	2-1	2-1	4-3	3-0	1-0	0-2	1-1	0-1		■	0-0	3-3	1-1	0-0	1-0
Southampton FC	0-0	2-0	1-0	2-1	0-0	4-1	0-1	4-0	3-6	3-3	1-0	3-1	0-2	0-2	3-1	1-0	0-1	■	5-2	4-1	1-1	3-3
Stockport County FC	1-3	1-2	0-1	1-2	3-1	0-1	1-1	1-1	2-0	2-1	1-0	1-3	1-1	1-0	1-3	1-1	2-1	0-0	■	1-0	3-2	0-0
Swansea Town AFC	2-1	1-0	3-2	0-1	3-1	1-0	1-0	3-3	2-0	1-1	2-2	2-0	1-0	1-0	1-1	0-0	3-5	1-1	0-0	■	3-2	0-0
Tottenham Hotspur FC	2-1	3-0	3-1	2-1	4-0	1-3	2-0	0-0	1-1	3-0	0-1	2-2	4-0	3-0	3-2	1-2	1-2	5-0	2-0	2-0	■	2-0
West Ham United FC	1-1	4-1	2-0	3-1	1-0	3-1	5-0	0-0	0-0	0-0	1-0	3-3	2-1	0-1	0-2	1-0	3-1	1-0	2-1	1-0	1-3	■

Division 2

		Pd	Wn	Dw	Ls	GF	GA	Pts	
1.	Aston Villa FC (Birmingham)	42	25	7	10	73	35	57	P
2.	Manchester United FC (Manchester)	42	22	9	11	82	50	53	P
3.	Sheffield United FC (Sheffield)	42	22	9	11	73	56	53	
4.	Coventry City FC (Coventry)	42	20	12	10	66	45	52	
5.	Tottenham Hotspur FC (London)	42	19	6	17	76	54	44	
6.	Burnley FC (Burnley)	42	17	10	15	54	54	44	
7.	Bradford Park Avenue FC (Bradford)	42	17	9	16	69	56	43	
8.	Fulham FC (London)	42	16	11	15	61	57	43	
9.	West Ham United FC (London)	42	14	14	14	53	52	42	
10.	Bury FC (Bury)	42	18	5	19	63	60	41	
11.	Chesterfield FC (Chesterfield)	42	16	9	17	63	63	41	
12.	Luton Town FC (Luton)	42	15	10	17	89	86	40	
13.	Plymouth Argyle FC (Plymouth)	42	14	12	16	57	65	40	
14.	Norwich City FC (Norwich)	42	14	11	17	56	75	39	
15.	Southampton FC (Southampton)	42	15	9	18	55	77	39	
16.	Blackburn Rovers FC (Blackburn)	42	14	10	18	71	80	38	
17.	Sheffield Wednesday FC (Sheffield)	42	14	10	18	49	56	38	
18.	Swansea Town AFC (Swansea)	42	13	12	17	45	73	38	
19.	Newcastle United FC (Newcastle-upon-Tyne)	42	14	8	20	51	58	36	
20.	Nottingham Forest FC (Nottingham)	42	14	8	20	47	60	36	
21.	Barnsley FC (Barnsley)	42	11	14	17	50	64	36	R
22.	Stockport County FC (Stockport)	42	11	9	22	43	70	31	R
		924	355	214	355	1346	1346	924	

Football League Division 3 (N) — 1937-1938 Season

Football League Division 3 (N) 1937-1938 Season	Accrington St.	Barrow	Bradford City	Carlisle United	Chester	Crewe Alex.	Darlington	Doncaster R.	Gateshead	Halifax Town	Hartlepools Utd.	Hull City	Lincoln City	New Brighton	Oldham Athletic	Port Vale	Rochdale	Rotherham Utd.	Southport	Tranmere R.	Wrexham	York City
Accrington Stanley FC	■	2-0	3-1	1-4	0-0	3-2	2-1	0-1	1-5	3-4	2-1	0-2	0-3	3-1	1-2	2-1	0-1	0-0	3-0	0-1	4-0	1-2
Barrow AFC	0-0	■	0-0	4-2	0-2	1-0	1-1	1-1	1-3	2-1	0-0	1-0	4-1	3-0	2-1	3-0	0-1	1-0	1-2	2-2	0-1	1-2
Bradford City AFC	2-2	1-0	■	4-0	2-2	3-1	2-1	2-0	1-1	3-0	4-1	1-2	2-0	3-0	1-1	5-0	3-1	3-2	1-1	1-3	2-2	0-1
Carlisle United FC	3-1	2-1	2-0	■	1-3	5-1	3-0	2-2	1-0	5-2	3-1	0-1	0-1	1-1	1-1	3-1	0-1	0-1	1-0	0-0	0-0	2-1
Chester FC	3-1	3-1	3-1	1-0	■	0-3	3-2	4-0	2-1	1-1	6-0	1-3	1-1	1-2	3-3	7-2	4-1	2-3	2-1	1-1	2-1	4-3
Crewe Alexandra FC	3-1	4-0	3-1	4-1	1-0	■	2-2	0-0	1-3	4-0	2-0	0-1	2-0	1-0	0-1	1-2	5-1	3-1	5-0	1-0	1-1	4-2
Darlington FC	3-0	0-1	4-2	3-1	2-1	0-1	■	1-1	1-2	3-0	2-0	1-3	1-4	1-0	2-2	2-4	2-1	1-1	0-2	5-3	2-2	
Doncaster Rovers FC	5-1	1-0	4-0	1-3	2-1	0-0	4-0	■	1-0	2-2	3-3	2-1	3-0	3-0	1-1	5-0	0-1	3-0	1-1	2-0	2-1	
Gateshead FC	1-0	6-0	3-0	2-1	3-1	2-0	5-2	2-3	■	4-1	2-1	3-2	1-1	3-1	2-1	3-1	0-0	5-0	2-1	2-2	2-2	
Halifax Town AFC	1-2	1-1	0-2	0-0	1-1	1-2	1-0	0-1	2-0	■	0-0	1-0	2-0	2-0	1-1	2-3	1-3	1-1	1-0	0-0		2-2
Hartlepools United FC	2-0	1-1	1-1	4-1	0-1	2-2	2-1	0-0	1-3	2-0	■	2-2	2-0	0-1	2-1	3-3	4-0	1-2	2-2	2-0	0-0	
Hull City AFC	0-0	4-0	2-2	2-1	2-2	1-1	4-0	2-1	3-1	0-1	4-0	■	1-1	1-1	4-1	0-0	4-1	1-1	10-1	1-1	3-2	3-1
Lincoln City FC	2-0	5-0	4-0	0-1	1-1	3-2	0-0	2-2	3-2	2-0	2-1	2-1	■	4-1	0-1	1-0	2-0	5-0	1-3	0-1	7-1	2-0
New Brighton FC	2-1	2-1	1-1	5-1	4-0	4-0	3-0	1-2	4-1	2-0	4-1	0-0	0-1	■	1-0	1-1	2-0	2-3	2-2	0-1	1-1	1-2
Oldham Athletic AFC	1-0	0-0	1-2	3-0	3-2	0-0	3-0	2-3	3-1	2-1	3-1	1-1	2-2	2-1	■	3-0	4-2	3-1	2-0	2-0	2-0	6-2
Port Vale FC	4-1	4-0	4-3	2-2	2-2	1-1	1-0	1-1	2-2	0-2	5-1	2-4	1-0	3-2	2-2	■	4-1	0-0	1-1	1-0	2-0	3-2
Rochdale AFC	0-1	3-3	2-0	3-1	4-0	1-4	1-1	4-5	2-2	1-1	2-2	0-0	0-1	2-1	1-1	1-1	■	2-0	3-2	0-0	6-1	0-0
Rotherham United FC	1-1	3-0	2-1	0-1	4-1	1-0	4-2	2-2	1-1	4-1	3-1	2-2	4-0	1-2	2-1	3-2	1-0	■	1-1	2-1	1-1	3-0
Southport FC	2-1	2-0	2-0	1-1	2-2	3-1	1-1	1-3	0-0	2-2	2-1	1-1	0-0	2-2	1-1	0-0	2-2	0-3	■	1-3	1-2	2-3
Tranmere Rovers FC	5-0	3-0	2-1	5-0	0-0	2-2	1-1	2-0	4-2	2-0	4-0	3-1	2-0	5-2	1-1	2-1	3-2	0-2	7-2	■	3-2	1-2
Wrexham AFC	2-0	3-2	2-1	0-0	3-1	1-0	4-0	0-0	0-0	2-0	1-0	0-1	1-0	1-0	2-1	2-0	4-1	1-3			■	1-1
York City FC	1-1	1-2	3-1	3-1	4-0	1-2	1-2	2-0	5-1	1-1	1-0	0-1	3-1	3-1	0-0	2-2	0-5	4-1	1-2	2-0	2-1	■

Division 3 (North)

		Pd	Wn	Dw	Ls	GF	GA	Pts	
1.	Tranmere Rovers FC (Birkenhead)	42	23	10	9	81	41	56	P
2.	Doncaster Rovers FC (Doncaster)	42	21	12	9	74	49	54	
3.	Hull City AFC (Kingston-upon-Hull)	42	20	13	9	80	43	53	
4.	Oldham Athletic AFC (Oldham)	42	19	13	10	67	46	51	
5.	Gateshead FC (Gateshead)	42	20	11	11	84	59	51	
6.	Rotherham United FC (Rotherham)	42	20	10	12	68	56	50	
7.	Lincoln City FC (Lincoln)	42	19	8	15	66	50	46	
8.	Crewe Alexandra FC (Crewe)	42	18	9	15	71	53	45	
9.	Chester FC (Chester)	42	16	12	14	77	72	44	
10.	Wrexham AFC (Wrexham)	42	16	11	15	58	63	43	
11.	York City FC (York)	42	16	10	16	70	68	42	
12.	Carlisle United FC (Carlisle)	42	15	9	18	57	67	39	
13.	New Brighton FC (Wallasey)	42	15	8	19	60	61	38	
14.	Bradford City AFC (Bradford)	42	14	10	18	66	69	38	
15.	Port Vale FC (Stoke-on-Trent)	42	12	14	16	65	73	38	T
16.	Southport FC (Southport)	42	12	14	16	53	82	38	
17.	Rochdale AFC (Rochdale)	42	13	11	18	67	78	37	
18.	Halifax Town AFC (Halifax)	42	12	12	18	44	66	36	
19.	Darlington FC (Darlington)	42	11	10	21	54	79	32	
20.	Hartlepools United FC (Hartlepool)	42	10	12	20	53	80	32	
21.	Barrow AFC (Barrow-in-Furness)	42	11	10	21	41	71	32	
22.	Accrington Stanley FC (Accrington)	42	11	7	24	45	75	29	
		924	344	236	344	1401	1401	924	

T: Port Vale FC (Stoke-on-Trent) were transferred to Division 3 (South) from the next season.

Football League — Division 3 (S) — 1937-1938 Season

	Aldershot	Bournemouth	Brighton	Bristol City	Bristol Rovers	Cardiff City	Clapton Orient	Crystal Palace	Exeter City	Gillingham	Mansfield Town	Millwall	Newport County	Northampton	Notts County	Q.P.R.	Reading	Southend United	Swindon Town	Torquay United	Walsall	Watford
Aldershot FC	■	2-0	1-2	1-1	0-2	1-1	1-2	1-0	0-1	2-0	1-0	2-1	5-0	0-2	0-1	1-0	0-0	1-0	1-1	1-0	1-0	1-0
Bournemouth & B. Athletic	3-0	■	0-0	0-0	1-3	3-0	2-1	1-0	2-2	2-0	5-4	0-3	1-1	0-0	1-1	1-1	1-1	7-1	1-2	0-0	5-0	0-0
Brighton & Hove Albion	2-1	3-1	■	1-1	3-0	2-1	2-1	2-1	6-0	1-0	2-0	1-0	1-0	1-2	0-1	3-1	1-1	3-1	3-1	1-1	1-0	1-2
Bristol City FC	3-1	2-1	1-1	■	0-0	0-1	2-0	0-0	4-1	3-1	2-1	0-0	0-0	1-0	3-1	2-0	1-0	4-2	1-1	2-0	3-1	3-1
Bristol Rovers FC	0-1	2-1	0-0	1-0	■	2-1	3-2	1-0	2-1	0-0	0-2	2-0	1-1	1-1	2-2	2-1	1-2	1-2	0-2	5-2	0-2	0-2
Cardiff City AFC	0-1	3-0	4-1	0-0	1-1	■	2-0	4-2	1-1	4-0	4-1	3-2	3-1	4-1	2-2	2-2	4-1	5-0	2-2	5-2	3-1	1-1
Clapton Orient FC	2-1	3-0	0-3	0-0	1-0	1-1	■	0-2	2-1	3-0	1-2	2-1	0-2	2-0	1-1	1-1	1-0	1-0	2-0	2-2	1-1	1-1
Crystal Palace FC	1-1	0-1	3-2	1-1	3-2	1-0	1-0	■	2-2	3-0	4-0	0-0	3-0	0-1	3-1	3-0	4-1	2-1	0-1	4-1	3-1	4-1
Exeter City FC	0-1	3-1	4-0	3-2	0-0	2-1	2-0	2-2	■	3-5	4-0	1-5	2-0	4-1	0-3	0-4	0-2	1-1	4-0	3-2	3-2	1-2
Gillingham FC	2-0	0-2	1-1	1-0	0-1	1-0	1-2	2-4	2-1	■	0-0	2-3	1-0	2-1	1-1	1-5	1-2	2-1	0-0	1-1	3-0	0-0
Mansfield Town FC	2-0	3-2	1-1	3-5	1-0	3-0	3-1	2-0	2-3	3-1	■	1-1	1-1	4-1	1-2	3-2	5-1	2-2	2-0	1-1	3-1	0-1
Millwall FC	4-0	4-0	2-0	0-3	2-1	2-1	2-1	2-1	5-0	1-0	4-0	■	4-0	3-0	5-0	1-0	1-0	0-2	7-0	4-0	4-0	1-1
Newport County AFC	4-0	1-1	1-0	0-0	2-2	1-1	3-1	0-0	2-2	2-0	1-0	3-1	■	0-0	3-0	1-1	2-2	2-0	2-0	0-2	1-2	1-2
Northampton Town FC	1-0	1-3	3-1	1-0	2-0	0-0	2-0	1-1	1-0	4-1	3-0	0-1	2-0	■	2-0	0-2	2-2	0-2	1-0	0-3	1-1	3-2
Notts County FC	1-0	1-2	0-3	2-0	1-1	2-0	1-0	0-1	0-0	1-1	1-1	5-0	2-2	2-1	■	2-2	3-0	3-0	0-0	3-0	1-2	1-2
Queen's Park Rangers FC	3-0	1-2	2-1	0-2	4-0	2-1	3-2	1-0	4-0	2-0	1-1	0-0	1-1	2-1	2-1	■	3-0	1-0	3-0	6-3	3-1	3-1
Reading FC	3-2	4-1	2-1	0-1	4-0	0-0	2-0	3-2	1-0	2-0	3-2	1-0	2-1	4-3	0-2	1-0	■	3-2	2-1	1-1	2-1	4-1
Southend United FC	4-1	1-0	2-1	5-0	1-1	3-1	1-2	2-2	1-1	0-0	1-2	0-2	4-2	2-1	2-1	4-2	4-2	■	0-0	5-1	1-0	2-2
Swindon Town FC	2-0	1-0	0-1	2-3	2-1	2-0	1-0	4-0	3-0	3-3	1-2	3-2	1-0	1-0	1-3	0-0	1-1	1-1	■	1-0	1-1	0-2
Torquay United FC	1-5	0-0	0-1	1-3	4-1	0-1	3-1	0-0	2-1	1-0	1-0	0-0	1-2	0-3	0-2	3-2	3-3	1-0	1-0	■	1-0	0-1
Walsall FC	2-0	2-0	0-3	2-8	5-2	1-0	2-0	1-1	0-2	3-1	2-0	1-1	3-1	1-1	1-0	0-3	2-5	1-5	2-3	0-0	■	3-1
Watford FC	5-1	0-2	1-1	3-1	4-0	4-0	2-0	1-2	0-0	1-1	3-1	1-3	2-0	3-1	4-0	3-1	4-0	3-1	4-0	4-0	2-1	■

Division 3 (South)

		Pd	Wn	Dw	Ls	GF	GA	Pts	
1.	Millwall FC (London)	42	23	10	9	83	37	56	P
2.	Bristol City FC (Bristol)	42	21	13	8	68	40	55	
3.	Queen's Park Rangers FC (London)	42	22	9	11	80	47	53	
4.	Watford FC (Watford)	42	21	11	10	73	43	53	
5.	Brighton & Hove Albion FC (Hove)	42	21	9	12	64	44	51	
6.	Reading FC (Reading)	42	20	11	11	71	63	51	
7.	Crystal Palace FC (London)	42	18	12	12	67	47	48	
8.	Swindon Town FC (Swindon)	42	17	10	15	49	49	44	
9.	Northampton Town FC (Northampton)	42	17	9	16	51	57	43	
10.	Cardiff City AFC (Cardiff)	42	15	12	15	67	54	42	
11.	Notts County FC (Nottingham)	42	16	9	17	50	50	41	
12.	Southend United FC (Southend-on-Sea)	42	15	10	17	70	68	40	
13.	Bournemouth & Boscombe Athletic FC (Bournemouth)	42	14	12	16	56	57	40	
14.	Mansfield Town FC (Mansfield)	42	15	9	18	62	67	39	
15.	Bristol Rovers FC (Bristol)	42	13	13	16	46	61	39	
16.	Newport County AFC (Newport)	42	11	16	15	43	52	38	
17.	Exeter City FC (Exeter)	42	13	12	17	57	70	38	
18.	Aldershot FC (Aldershot)	42	15	5	22	39	59	35	
19.	Clapton Orient FC (London)	42	13	7	22	42	61	33	
20.	Torquay United FC (Torquay)	42	9	12	21	38	73	30	
21.	Walsall FC (Walsall)	42	11	7	24	52	88	29	
22.	Gillingham FC (Gillingham)	42	10	6	26	36	77	26	#
		924	350	224	350	1264	1264	924	

Gillingham FC were not re-elected to the league for next season.   Elected: Ipswich Town FC (Ipswich)

F.A. CUP FINAL   (Wembley Stadium, London – 30/04/1938 – 93,497)

PRESTON NORTH END FC (PRESTON)   1-0 (aet)   Huddersfield Town AFC (Huddersfield)
Mutch pen.

Preston: Holdcroft, Gallimore, A.Beattie, Shankly, Smith, Batey, Watmough, Mutch, Maxwell, R.Beattie, H.O'Donnell.

Huddersfield: Hesford, Craig, Mountford, Willingham, Young, Boot, Hulme, Isaac, McFadyen, Barclay, Beasley.

Semi-finals

Preston North End FC (Preston)	2-1	Aston Villa FC (Birmingham)
Sunderland AFC (Sunderland)	1-3	Huddersfield Town AFC (Huddersfield)

Quarter-finals

Aston Villa FC (Birmingham)	3-2	Manchester City FC (Manchester)
Brentford FC (London)	0-3	Preston North End FC (Preston)
Tottenham Hotspur FC (London)	0-1	Sunderland AFC (Sunderland)
York City FC (York)	0-0, 1-2	Huddersfield Town AFC (Huddersfield)

1938-39

Football League Division 1 1938-1939 Season	Arsenal	Aston Villa	Birmingham	Blackpool	Bolton Wands.	Brentford	Charlton Athletic	Chelsea	Derby County	Everton	Grimsby Town	Huddersfield T.	Leeds United	Leicester City	Liverpool	Man. United	Middlesbrough	Portsmouth	Preston N.E.	Stoke City	Sunderland	Wolves
Arsenal FC	■	0-0	3-1	2-1	3-1	2-0	2-0	1-0	1-2	1-2	2-0	1-0	2-3	0-0	2-0	2-1	1-2	2-0	1-0	4-1	2-0	0-0
Aston Villa FC	1-3	■	5-1	3-1	1-3	5-0	2-0	6-2	0-1	0-3	0-2	4-0	2-1	1-2	2-0	0-2	1-1	2-0	3-0	3-0	1-1	2-2
Birmingham FC	1-2	3-0	■	2-1	0-2	5-1	3-4	1-1	3-0	1-0	1-1	1-1	4-0	2-1	0-0	3-3	2-1	2-0	1-3	1-2	1-2	3-2
Blackpool FC	1-0	2-4	2-1	■	0-0	4-1	0-0	5-1	2-2	0-2	3-1	1-1	1-2	1-1	1-1	3-5	4-0	2-1	2-1	1-1	1-1	1-0
Bolton Wanderers FC	1-1	1-2	3-0	0-1	■	1-1	2-1	0-2	2-1	4-2	1-1	3-2	2-2	4-0	3-1	0-0	4-1	5-1	0-2	1-3	2-1	0-0
Brentford FC	1-0	2-4	0-1	1-1	2-2	■	1-0	1-0	1-3	2-0	1-2	2-1	0-1	2-0	2-5	2-1	2-0	3-0	1-0	1-0	2-3	0-1
Charlton Athletic FC	1-0	1-0	4-4	3-1	2-1	1-1	■	2-0	1-0	2-1	3-1	2-1	2-0	1-0	1-3	7-1	3-0	3-3	3-1	4-2	3-0	0-4
Chelsea FC	4-2	2-1	2-2	1-1	1-1	1-3	1-3	■	0-2	0-2	5-1	3-0	2-2	3-0	4-1	0-1	4-2	1-0	3-1	1-1	4-0	1-3
Derby County FC	1-2	2-1	0-1	2-1	3-0	1-2	3-1	0-1	■	2-1	4-1	1-0	1-0	1-1	1-2	5-1	1-4	0-1	2-0	5-0	1-0	2-2
Everton FC	2-0	3-0	4-2	4-0	2-1	2-1	1-4	4-1	2-2	■	3-0	3-2	4-0	4-0	3-0	4-0	5-1	0-0	1-1	6-2	1-0	
Grimsby Town FC	2-1	1-2	1-0	2-0	1-1	0-0	1-1	2-1	1-1	3-0	■	3-3	3-2	6-1	2-1	1-0	0-2	2-1	1-1	3-1	1-3	2-4
Huddersfield Town AFC	1-1	1-1	3-1	3-0	2-1	1-2	4-0	3-1	3-0	3-0	2-0	■	0-1	2-0	1-1	1-1	0-1	3-0	3-0	1-4	0-1	1-2
Leeds United AFC	4-2	2-0	2-0	1-0	1-2	3-2	2-1	1-1	1-4	1-2	0-1	2-1	■	8-2	1-1	3-1	0-1	2-2	0-0	3-3	1-0	
Leicester City FC	0-2	1-1	2-1	3-4	0-0	1-1	1-5	3-2	2-3	3-0	0-2	0-1	2-0	■	2-2	1-1	5-3	5-0	2-2	2-2	0-2	0-2
Liverpool FC	2-2	3-0	4-0	1-0	1-2	1-0	1-0	2-1	2-1	0-3	2-2	3-3	3-0	1-1	■	1-0	3-1	4-4	4-1	1-0	1-1	0-2
Manchester United FC	1-0	1-1	4-1	0-0	2-2	3-0	0-2	5-1	1-1	0-2	3-1	1-1	0-0	3-0	2-0	■	1-1	1-1	1-1	0-1	0-1	1-3
Middlesbrough FC	1-1	1-1	2-2	9-2	1-2	3-1	4-0	1-1	2-0	4-4	3-2	4-1	3-2	3-0	3-1	8-2	■	2-2	5-1	3-0	1-0	
Portsmouth FC	0-0	0-0	2-0	1-0	2-1	2-2	0-2	2-1	1-3	0-1	2-1	4-0	2-0	0-1	1-1	0-0	1-1	■	0-0	2-0	2-1	1-0
Preston North End FC	2-1	3-2	5-0	1-1	2-2	2-0	2-0	1-1	4-1	0-1	1-1	3-0	2-0	2-1	1-0	1-1	3-1	2-2	■	1-1	2-1	4-2
Stoke City FC	1-0	3-1	6-3	1-1	4-1	3-2	1-0	6-1	3-0	0-0	1-2	2-2	1-1	1-0	3-1	1-1	1-3	1-1	3-1	■	3-1	5-3
Sunderland AFC	0-0	1-5	1-0	1-2	2-2	1-1	1-1	3-2	1-0	1-2	1-1	0-0	2-1	2-0	2-3	5-2	1-2	0-2	1-2	3-0	■	1-1
Wolverhampton Wanderers FC	0-1	2-1	2-1	1-1	1-1	5-2	3-1	2-0	0-0	7-0	5-0	3-0	4-1	0-0	2-2	3-0	6-1	3-0	3-0	3-0	0-0	■

	Division 1	Pd	Wn	Dw	Ls	GF	GA	Pts	
1.	EVERTON FC (LIVERPOOL)	42	27	5	10	88	52	59	
2.	Wolverhampton Wanderers FC (Wolverhampton)	42	22	11	9	88	39	55	
3.	Charlton Athletic FC (London)	42	22	6	14	75	59	50	
4.	Middlesbrough FC (Middlesbrough)	42	20	9	13	93	74	49	
5.	Arsenal FC (London)	42	19	9	14	55	41	47	
6.	Derby County FC (Derby)	42	19	8	15	66	55	46	
7.	Stoke City FC (Stoke-on-Trent)	42	17	12	13	71	68	46	
8.	Bolton Wanderers FC (Bolton)	42	15	15	12	67	58	45	
9.	Preston North End FC (Preston)	42	16	12	14	63	59	44	
10.	Grimsby Town FC (Cleethorpes)	42	16	11	15	61	69	43	
11.	Liverpool FC (Liverpool)	42	14	14	14	62	63	42	
12.	Aston Villa FC (Birmingham)	42	16	9	17	71	60	41	
13.	Leeds United AFC (Leeds)	42	16	9	17	59	67	41	
14.	Manchester United FC (Manchester)	42	11	16	15	57	65	38	
15.	Blackpool FC (Blackpool)	42	12	14	16	56	68	38	
16.	Sunderland AFC (Sunderland)	42	13	12	17	54	67	38	
17.	Portsmouth FC (Portsmouth)	42	12	13	17	47	70	37	
18.	Brentford FC (London)	42	14	8	20	53	74	36	
19.	Huddersfield Town AFC (Huddersfield)	42	12	11	19	58	64	35	
20.	Chelsea FC (London)	42	12	9	21	64	80	33	
21.	Birmingham FC (Birmingham)	42	12	8	22	62	84	32	R
22.	Leicester City FC (Leicester)	42	9	11	22	48	82	29	R
		924	345	234	345	1418	1418	924	

Top Goalscorer

1) Tommy LAWTON   (Everton FC)   35

Football League Division 2 — 1938-1939 Season

	Blackburn Rovers	Bradford P.A.	Burnley	Bury	Chesterfield	Coventry City	Fulham	Luton Town	Manchester City	Millwall	Newcastle United	Norwich City	Nottingham F.	Plymouth Argyle	Sheffield United	Sheffield Wed.	Southampton	Swansea Town	Tottenham H.	Tranmere Rovers	W.B.A.	West Ham United
Blackburn Rovers FC		6-4	1-0	1-0	3-0	0-2	2-1	2-0	3-3	3-1	3-0	6-0	3-2	4-0	1-2	2-4	3-0	4-0	3-1	3-2	3-0	3-1
Bradford Park Avenue	0-4		2-2	3-2	0-0	0-2	1-5	2-1	4-2	1-0	0-1	3-0	1-2	2-2	0-3	3-1	2-1	1-1	0-0	3-0	4-4	1-2
Burnley FC	3-2	0-0		0-1	1-2	1-0	2-0	3-2	1-1	2-0	2-0	3-0	2-1	1-0	2-3	1-2	2-1	1-1	1-0	3-1	0-3	1-0
Bury FC	2-4	0-1	1-0		3-1	5-0	0-2	2-5	1-5	1-1	1-1	2-3	2-1	3-0	2-2	2-3	5-2	4-0	3-1	5-0	3-3	1-1
Chesterfield FC	0-2	2-2	3-2	2-1		3-0	0-1	1-2	0-3	3-0	2-0	2-0	7-1	3-1	1-0	3-1	6-1	6-1	3-1	3-0	3-1	1-0
Coventry City FC	0-1	3-1	1-1	0-0	2-0		3-1	1-0	0-1	2-1	1-0	2-0	5-1	1-2	0-3	1-0	3-0	3-0	4-0	2-0	1-1	0-0
Fulham FC	2-3	4-0	0-0	1-2	2-0	1-0		2-1	2-1	2-1	1-2	0-0	2-2	1-2	1-2	2-2	1-1	1-0	1-0	1-0	0-3	3-2
Luton Town FC	1-1	2-2	1-0	2-1	5-0	1-3	2-1		3-0	0-0	2-1	2-1	1-0	3-4	2-0	1-5	6-2	6-3	0-0	3-1	3-1	1-2
Manchester City FC	3-2	5-1	2-0	0-0	3-1	3-0	3-5	1-2		1-6	4-1	4-1	3-0	1-3	3-2	1-1	2-1	5-0	2-0	5-2	3-3	2-4
Millwall FC	4-1	3-1	1-1	0-0	3-1	0-0	1-1	2-1	3-1		1-1	6-0	5-0	3-0	4-0	2-0	0-1	1-1	2-0	2-1	1-5	0-2
Newcastle United FC	2-2	1-0	3-2	6-0	0-1	0-4	2-0	2-0	0-2	2-2		4-0	4-0	2-1	0-0	2-1	1-0	0-1	0-1	5-1	5-1	2-0
Norwich City FC	4-0	1-3	4-0	3-1	2-0	1-1	3-3	2-1	0-0	0-2	1-1		1-0	2-1	1-2	2-2	2-1	3-0	1-2	2-0	2-3	2-6
Nottingham Forest FC	1-3	2-0	2-2	1-1	0-1	3-0	1-1	2-4	3-4	3-0	2-0	1-0		2-1	0-2	3-3	0-2	1-2	2-2	2-0	0-0	
Plymouth Argyle FC	1-0	4-1	1-0	0-0	0-0	0-2	0-0	4-1	0-4	2-2	0-1	1-0	3-0		0-1	1-1	1-2	2-0	0-0	3-1	1-2	
Sheffield United FC	0-0	3-1	1-1	1-1	1-1	0-0	2-0	2-2	1-0	2-1	4-0	0-1	0-1			0-0	5-1	1-2	6-1	1-1	1-1	3-1
Sheffield Wednesday FC	3-0	2-0	4-1	2-0	0-0	2-2	5-1	4-1	3-1	3-1	0-2	7-0	1-1	1-2	1-0		2-0	1-1	1-0	2-0	2-1	1-4
Southampton FC	1-3	3-2	2-1	0-0	2-2	0-2	2-1	0-4	1-2	1-1	0-0	3-1	2-2	2-1	2-2	4-3		4-1	1-2	3-1	0-2	
Swansea Town AFC	2-1	2-2	4-0	3-3	1-1	2-4	1-1	2-3	2-0	1-1	0-1	3-0	1-2	1-2	1-0	1-1	1-3		1-0	1-3	3-2	3-2
Tottenham Hotspur FC	4-3	2-2	1-0	4-3	2-2	2-1	1-0	1-0	2-3	4-0	4-1	4-1	1-0	2-2	3-3	1-1	3-0			3-1	2-2	2-1
Tranmere Rovers FC	1-1	2-1	0-3	3-0	0-1	1-2	0-1	2-3	3-9	0-3	0-1	1-1	2-0	0-2	1-4	1-1	2-0	0-2			3-1	2-2
West Bromwich Albion FC	2-0	0-2	1-2	6-0	1-0	3-1	3-0	3-0	0-0	5-2	4-2	0-0	4-2	3-4	5-1	2-0	0-0	4-3	2-0			3-2
West Ham United FC	1-2	0-2	1-0	0-0	1-1	4-1	1-0	0-1	2-1	0-0	1-1	2-0	5-0	2-1	0-0	2-3	1-2	5-2	0-2	6-1	2-1	

Division 2

		Pd	Wn	Dw	Ls	GF	GA	Pts	
1.	Blackburn Rovers FC (Blackburn)	42	25	5	12	94	60	55	P
2.	Sheffield United FC (Sheffield)	42	20	14	8	69	41	54	P
3.	Sheffield Wednesday FC (Sheffield)	42	21	11	10	88	59	53	
4.	Coventry City FC (Coventry)	42	21	8	13	62	45	50	
5.	Manchester City FC (Manchester)	42	21	7	14	96	72	49	
6.	Chesterfield FC (Chesterfield)	42	20	9	13	69	52	49	
7.	Luton Town FC (Luton)	42	22	5	15	82	66	49	
8.	Tottenham Hotspur FC (London)	42	19	9	14	67	62	47	
9.	Newcastle United FC (Newcastle-upon-Tyne)	42	18	10	14	61	48	46	
10.	West Bromwich Albion FC (West Bromwich)	42	18	9	15	89	72	45	
11.	West Ham United FC (London)	42	17	10	15	70	52	44	
12.	Fulham FC (London)	42	17	10	15	61	55	44	
13.	Millwall FC (London)	42	14	14	14	64	53	42	
14.	Burnley FC (Burnley)	42	15	9	18	50	56	39	
15.	Plymouth Argyle FC (Plymouth)	42	15	8	19	49	55	38	
16.	Bury FC (Bury)	42	12	13	17	65	74	37	
17.	Bradford Park Avenue FC (Bradford)	42	12	11	19	61	82	35	
18.	Southampton FC (Southampton)	42	13	9	20	56	82	35	
19.	Swansea Town AFC (Swansea)	42	11	12	19	50	83	34	
20.	Nottingham Forest FC (Nottingham)	42	10	11	21	49	82	31	
21.	Norwich City FC (Norwich)	42	13	5	24	50	91	31	R
22.	Tranmere Rovers FC (Birkenhead)	42	6	5	31	39	99	17	R
		924	360	204	360	1441	1441	924	

Football League Division 3 (N) — 1938-1939 Season — Results Grid

	Accrington Stanley	Barnsley	Barrow	Bradford City	Carlisle United	Chester	Crewe Alexandra	Darlington	Doncaster Rovers	Gateshead	Halifax Town	Hartlepools United	Hull City	Lincoln City	New Brighton	Oldham Athletic	Rochdale	Rotherham United	Southport	Stockport County	Wrexham	York City
Accrington Stanley FC		0-2	0-2	2-3	1-1	2-3	2-1	3-0	0-0	1-1	1-2	0-0	1-1	3-4	1-2	1-3	0-5	2-1	1-4	3-2	3-1	3-1
Barnsley FC	4-1		4-0	5-2	3-0	3-0	5-2	7-1	1-1	2-0	1-0	2-0	5-1	4-0	1-1	3-0	2-0	2-0	3-1	0-1	2-1	1-0
Barrow AFC	2-3	1-2		2-1	5-0	0-1	1-2	2-0	4-4	1-1	0-0	1-1	3-1	2-2	3-0	2-0	3-1	4-1	4-0	0-2	4-0	2-0
Bradford City AFC	2-1	0-2	3-0		2-0	1-0	4-1	6-2	2-1	1-1	1-0	0-1	6-2	3-0	3-3	1-4	3-0	5-2	2-1	4-0	4-0	6-0
Carlisle United FC	6-4	3-1	3-0	0-2		1-3	1-0	1-1	2-3	2-2	1-2	2-0	1-2	4-3	1-1	2-0	5-1	3-1	1-1	3-2	1-1	1-3
Chester FC	1-0	2-1	1-2	3-2	6-1		4-0	0-0	0-4	2-2	5-1	8-2	1-1	0-0	1-3	4-2	0-0	1-4	2-0	4-3	4-2	5-1
Crewe Alexandra FC	2-1	0-0	1-1	0-0	7-1	0-2		2-0	1-2	3-2	2-2	3-2	1-0	6-0	7-1	1-2	4-1	0-0	4-2	2-1	1-0	8-2
Darlington FC	3-0	0-1	3-1	0-4	2-1	1-3	1-0		1-2	5-2	3-0	0-1	3-1	3-0	3-3	1-2	3-1	1-0	2-4	4-3	3-1	3-1
Doncaster Rovers FC	7-1	1-3	1-1	1-2	1-0	4-1	1-2	4-1		2-3	0-0	3-1	1-0	4-1	4-1	3-2	5-0	1-1	0-0	3-1	0-0	1-0
Gateshead FC	4-1	1-1	2-1	0-0	1-1	3-0	0-5	0-2	2-0		2-0	2-0	2-2	2-0		3-0	2-2	7-1	0-0	4-1	5-1	2-3
Halifax Town AFC	2-0	1-4	1-0	2-2	5-1	1-1	0-0	1-1	3-3	2-0		2-0	2-0	0-1	2-1	1-1	1-1	3-3	0-2	2-1		
Hartlepools United FC	2-1	0-1	1-2	1-3	2-1	2-5	0-1	1-3	3-1	1-0	1-0		3-3	2-1	2-0	0-4	2-1	1-1	5-1	0-2	1-3	3-2
Hull City AFC	6-1	0-1	4-0	3-2	11-1	3-0	2-1	3-2	0-0	1-0	1-1	4-1		4-2	3-0	0-2	3-3	0-2	2-1	4-4	1-1	2-0
Lincoln City FC	3-0	2-4	1-1	4-0	2-1	0-3	3-2	0-0	2-5	0-0	2-2	0-3		0-0	1-0	2-0	0-1	3-2	8-3	3-3		
New Brighton FC	4-1	1-2	2-0	2-1	2-3	1-3	1-2	3-6	0-1	5-2	6-1	3-2		0-1		3-1	3-1	1-1	0-0	2-3	3-2	
Oldham Athletic AFC	2-0	4-2	1-0	2-1	6-0	1-3	3-0	2-0	0-0	1-3	1-0	4-2	4-1	1-0	1-0		1-2	2-0	2-4	3-1	4-2	6-0
Rochdale AFC	4-1	2-1	2-2	1-1	2-3	5-2	5-0	6-1	1-1	5-2	4-5	3-4	4-0	4-0	2-0	1-2		0-1	5-0	0-1	0-2	2-2
Rotherham United FC	2-1	0-1	1-2	2-0	4-0	2-0	4-1	3-3	2-2	0-1	5-1	0-2	1-3	0-0	3-1		7-1		1-0	3-2	2-0	
Southport FC	1-0	0-0	4-1	2-2	7-1	2-0	1-2	1-0	0-4	2-0	4-1	1-1	4-0	4-1	1-1	0-1	4-1	1-0		3-0	3-1	1-1
Stockport County FC	3-0	1-1	3-1	2-0	3-0	0-0	5-1	5-2	1-2	3-2	3-3	5-0	2-2	3-3	1-1	3-1	1-2	5-0	3-1		2-1	3-1
Wrexham AFC	2-0	1-1	3-0	1-1	2-5	3-2	0-4	3-1	3-0	2-0	3-2	3-0	4-2	1-0	1-2	4-1	1-0	2-0	4-3	2-1		1-3
York City FC	2-2	2-3	2-3	0-1	4-1	2-2	4-1	1-1	2-2	1-1	3-0	2-0	1-0	1-3	2-0	4-1	0-7	0-1	2-3	1-2	1-0	

Division 3 (North)

		Pd	Wn	Dw	Ls	GF	GA	Pts	
1.	Barnsley FC (Barnsley)	42	30	7	5	94	34	67	P
2.	Doncaster Rovers FC (Doncaster)	42	21	14	7	87	47	56	
3.	Bradford City AFC (Bradford)	42	22	8	12	89	56	52	
4.	Southport FC (Southport)	42	20	10	12	75	54	50	
5.	Oldham Athletic AFC (Oldham)	42	22	5	15	76	59	49	
6.	Chester FC (Chester)	42	20	9	13	88	70	49	
7.	Hull City AFC (Kingston-upon-Hull)	42	18	10	14	83	74	46	
8.	Crewe Alexandra FC (Crewe)	42	19	6	17	82	70	44	
9.	Stockport County FC (Stockport)	42	17	9	16	91	77	43	
10.	Gateshead FC (Gateshead)	42	14	14	14	74	67	42	
11.	Rotherham United FC (Rotherham)	42	17	8	17	64	64	42	
12.	Halifax Town AFC (Halifax)	42	13	16	13	52	54	42	
13.	Barrow AFC (Barrow-in-Furness)	42	16	9	17	66	65	41	
14.	Wrexham AFC (Wrexham)	42	17	7	18	66	79	41	
15.	Rochdale AFC (Rochdale)	42	15	9	18	92	82	39	
16.	New Brighton FC (Wallasey)	42	15	9	18	68	73	39	
17.	Lincoln City FC (Lincoln)	42	12	9	21	66	92	33	
18.	Darlington FC (Darlington)	42	13	7	22	62	92	33	
19.	Carlisle United FC (Carlisle)	42	13	7	22	64	111	33	
20.	York City FC (York)	42	12	8	22	66	92	32	
21.	Hartlepools United FC (Hartlepool)	42	12	7	23	55	94	31	
22.	Accrington Stanley FC (Accrington)	42	7	6	29	49	103	20	
		924	365	194	365	1609	1609	924	

Football League Division 3 (S) — 1938-1939 Season

	Aldershot	Bournemouth	Brighton	Bristol City	Bristol Rovers	Cardiff City	Clapton Orient	Crystal Palace	Exeter City	Ipswich Town	Mansfield Town	Newport County	Northampton	Notts County	Port Vale	Q.P.R.	Reading	Southend United	Swindon Town	Torquay United	Walsall	Watford
Aldershot FC		2-1	1-1	0-1	1-0	1-1	1-0	2-1	2-0	3-1	3-0	1-0	3-0	0-3	2-0	1-1	1-0	1-0	1-0	1-1	3-3	1-1
Bournemouth & B. Athletic	4-0		2-0	4-0	5-2	0-0	0-0	1-1	2-0	0-0	1-1	0-1	3-1	3-2	1-1	4-2	0-0	0-4	2-0	2-5	3-1	1-1
Brighton & Hove Albion	0-3	1-1		1-0	6-3	1-2	2-0	0-0	6-1	2-0	3-0	0-0	1-0	2-0	1-0	3-1	2-2	3-0	4-0	2-0	3-1	0-0
Bristol City FC	1-0	2-0	2-0		2-1	1-1	3-1	1-1	4-1	3-2	2-0	0-2	0-0	2-1	5-1	2-2	5-1	1-0	1-1	1-3	2-1	2-0
Bristol Rovers FC	0-0	1-0	0-1	1-1		1-1	1-0	1-2	4-1	3-3	3-0	0-0	1-0	0-0	0-1	0-0	2-4	4-1	5-0	0-1	2-0	1-1
Cardiff City AFC	2-4	5-0	4-1	2-1	0-2		1-2	0-1	1-2	2-1	0-0	1-2	2-0	4-1	2-4	1-0	0-1	1-0	2-1	3-1	2-1	5-3
Clapton Orient FC	2-0	1-1	2-0	1-1	2-1	1-1		4-0	3-3	1-1	0-0	1-3	3-0	1-1	0-0	2-1	1-2	5-0	5-0	3-0	1-1	0-0
Crystal Palace FC	3-0	3-0	1-0	3-2	0-0	2-0	4-2		3-2	3-0	6-2	1-1	2-0	5-1	0-0	0-0	4-3	1-1	1-3	4-0	2-0	2-0
Exeter City FC	3-3	0-0	2-2	2-1	1-1	2-1	4-4	4-2		3-0	2-0	3-1	3-2	1-0	1-3	1-1	3-2	3-3	0-0	1-2	3-2	1-3
Ipswich Town FC	7-2	0-2	0-0	4-0	0-0	1-2	3-0	2-1	2-2		5-1	1-4	2-0	0-2	1-0	2-1	4-2	3-1	1-0	1-0	1-0	5-1
Mansfield Town FC	1-0	2-0	4-2	3-2	1-3	2-2	0-0	0-0	4-2	0-1		0-2	1-1	2-0	2-2	0-0	3-1	1-1	4-0	0-0	0-0	0-0
Newport County AFC	1-0	2-2	2-0	0-2	3-0	2-1	2-0	0-0	3-2	0-0	1-1		2-1	0-2	2-0	3-0	6-4	1-0	2-1	2-1	2-1	2-1
Northampton Town FC	5-0	2-0	1-4	2-2	2-1	2-1	3-0	0-0	0-0	2-0	3-4	1-0		2-1	1-0	1-1	2-2	0-2	4-1	4-1	2-0	2-0
Notts County FC	1-1	0-1	4-3	0-0	3-1	1-1	1-0	0-0	3-1	2-1	1-1	2-0	1-0		4-0	0-0	2-0	4-1	2-0	5-1	0-0	0-3
Port Vale FC	1-3	2-0	1-1	4-0	2-1	1-1	1-1	3-2	3-0	2-1	0-2	3-1	2-0	2-1		1-2	0-2	2-2	2-0	0-1	5-1	1-2
Queen's Park Rangers FC	7-0	1-0	1-2	3-1	1-1	5-0	1-1	1-2	5-0	0-0	3-0	0-1	2-2	3-0	2-2		2-2	1-1	2-1	1-1	3-1	1-1
Reading FC	5-0	1-0	3-0	2-2	2-0	0-0	2-2	3-1	1-1	2-1	0-0	0-1	5-1	3-1	2-1	2-4		3-0	3-0	3-5	1-1	3-2
Southend United FC	2-1	2-2	1-1	2-0	3-2	2-0	1-0	3-1	0-1	0-1	5-0	2-0	1-0	0-0	2-1	2-0	*		2-3	1-1	2-0	3-0
Swindon Town FC	2-1	4-2	3-2	1-0	2-1	4-1	2-2	2-2	1-1	1-2	8-0	4-1	1-2	2-2	4-2	2-1	2-2	2-1		3-1	1-4	3-0
Torquay United FC	1-1	2-0	0-2	3-1	2-2	1-3	2-1	1-2	0-1	1-1	3-0	1-1	1-2	0-2	1-2	0-2	2-3	1-1	2-0		0-1	2-1
Walsall FC	2-2	1-2	0-2	5-0	2-2	6-3	5-1	1-1	1-2	0-1	0-0	1-1	1-0	3-3	4-0	0-1	3-0	0-2	5-0	5-0		2-0
Watford FC	1-1	1-0	1-1	2-2	4-1	1-0	1-0	4-1	4-2	0-0	1-1	0-1	2-0	0-1	2-0	4-1	3-1	3-0	4-1	0-0	4-2	

Division 3 (South)

		Pd	Wn	Dw	Ls	GF	GA	Pts	
1.	Newport County AFC (Newport)	42	22	11	9	58	45	55	P
2.	Crystal Palace FC (London)	42	20	12	10	71	52	52	
3.	Brighton & Hove Albion FC (Hove)	42	19	11	12	68	49	49	
4.	Watford FC (Watford)	42	17	12	13	62	51	46	
5.	Reading FC (Reading)	42	16	14	12	69	59	46	
6.	Queen's Park Rangers FC (London)	42	15	14	13	68	49	44	
7.	Ipswich Town FC (Ipswich)	42	16	12	14	62	52	44	
8.	Bristol City FC (Bristol)	42	16	12	14	61	63	44	
9.	Swindon Town FC (Swindon)	42	18	8	16	72	77	44	
10.	Aldershot FC (Aldershot)	42	16	12	14	53	66	44	
11.	Notts County FC (Nottingham)	42	17	9	16	59	54	43	
12.	Southend United FC (Southend-on-Sea)	42	16	9	17	61	64	41	
13.	Cardiff City AFC (Cardiff)	42	15	11	16	61	65	41	
14.	Exeter City FC (Exeter)	42	13	14	15	65	82	40	
15.	Bournemouth & Boscombe Athletic FC (Bournemouth)	42	13	13	16	52	58	39	
16.	Mansfield Town FC (Mansfield)	42	12	15	15	44	62	39	
17.	Northampton Town FC (Northampton)	42	15	8	19	51	58	38	
18.	Port Vale FC (Stoke-on-Trent)	42	14	9	19	52	58	37	
19.	Torquay United FC (Torquay)	42	14	9	19	54	70	37	
20.	Clapton Orient FC (London)	42	11	13	18	53	55	35	
21.	Walsall FC (Walsall)	42	11	11	20	68	69	33	
22.	Bristol Rovers FC (Bristol)	42	10	13	19	55	61	22	
		924	336	252	336	1319	1319	924	

F.A. CUP FINAL   (Wembley Stadium, London – 29/04/1939 – 99,370)

PORTSMOUTH FC (PORTSMOUTH)   4-1   Wolverhampton Wanderers FC

Barlow 2, Anderson, Parker   *Dorsett*

Portsmouth: Walker, Morgan, Rochford, Guthrie, Rowe, Wharton, Worrall, McAlinden, Anderson, Barlow, Parker.

Wolves: Scott, Morris, Taylor, Galley, Cullis, Gardiner, Burton, McIntosh, Westcott, Dorsett, Maguire.

Semi-finals

Portsmouth FC (Portsmouth)	2-1	Huddersfield Town AFC (Huddersfield)
Wolverhampton Wanderers FC (Wolverhampton)	5-0	Grimsby Town AFC (Cleethorpes)

Quarter-finals

Chelsea FC (London)	0-1	Grimsby Town FC (Cleethorpes)
Huddersfield Town AFC (Huddersfield)	1-1, 2-1	Blackburn Rovers FC (Blackburn)
Portsmouth FC (Portsmouth)	1-0	Preston North End FC (Preston)
Wolverhampton Wanderers FC (Wolverhampton)	2-0	Everton FC (Liverpool)

1939-40

Football League Division 1 1939-1940 Season	Arsenal	Aston Villa	Blackburn Rovers	Blackpool	Bolton Wanderers	Brentford	Charlton Athletic	Chelsea	Derby County	Everton	Grimsby Town	Huddersfield Town	Leeds United	Liverpool	Manchester United	Middlesbrough	Portsmouth	Preston North End	Sheffield United	Stoke City	Sunderland	Wolves
Arsenal FC		--	1-0	--	--	--	--	--	--	--	--	--	--	--	--	--	--	--	--	--	5-2	--
Aston Villa FC	--		--	--	--	--	--	--	--	1-2	--	--	--	--	--	2-0	--	--	--	--	--	--
Blackburn Rovers FC	--	--		--	--	--	--	--	--	2-2	--	--	--	--	--	--	--	--	--	--	--	--
Blackpool FC	--	--	--		--	2-1	--	--	--	--	--	--	--	--	--	--	--	--	--	--	--	2-1
Bolton Wanderers FC	--	--	--	--		--	--	--	--	--	--	--	--	--	--	--	2-1	--	--	--	--	--
Brentford FC	--	--	--	--	--		--	--	--	--	--	1-0	--	--	--	--	--	--	--	--	--	--
Charlton Athletic FC	--	--	--	--	--	--		--	--	--	--	--	--	--	2-0	--	--	--	--	--	--	--
Chelsea FC	--	--	--	--	3-2	--	--		--	--	--	--	--	--	1-1	--	--	--	--	--	--	--
Derby County FC	--	1-0	--	--	--	--	--	--		--	--	--	--	--	--	--	2-0	--	--	--	--	--
Everton FC	--	--	--	--	1-1	--	--	--	--		--	--	--	--	--	--	--	--	--	--	--	--
Grimsby Town FC	--	--	--	--	--	--	--	--	--	--		--	--	--	--	--	--	2-0	--	--	--	0-0
Huddersfield Town AFC	--	--	--	0-1	--	--	--	--	--	--	--		--	--	--	--	--	--	--	--	--	--
Leeds United AFC	--	--	--	--	--	--	0-1	--	--	--	--	--		--	--	--	--	--	0-1	--	--	--
Liverpool FC	--	--	--	--	--	--	--	1-0	--	--	--	--	--		4-1	--	--	--	--	--	--	--
Manchester United FC	--	--	--	--	--	--	--	--	--	--	4-0	--	--	--		--	--	--	--	--	--	--
Middlesbrough FC	--	--	--	--	--	--	--	--	--	--	--	--	--	--	--		--	--	--	2-2	--	--
Portsmouth FC	--	--	2-1	--	--	--	--	--	--	--	--	--	--	--	--	--		--	--	--	--	--
Preston North End FC	--	--	--	--	--	--	--	--	--	--	--	--	0-0	--	--	--	--		0-0	--	--	--
Sheffield United FC	--	--	--	--	--	--	--	--	--	--	--	--	--	2-1	--	--	--	--		--	--	--
Stoke City FC	--	--	--	--	1-2	--	4-0	--	--	--	--	--	--	--	--	--	--	--	--		--	--
Sunderland AFC	--	--	--	--	--	--	--	--	--	3-0	--	1-2	--	--	--	--	--	--	--	--		--
Wolverhampton Wanderers FC	2-2	--	--	--	--	--	--	--	--	--	--	--	--	--	--	--	--	--	--	--	--	

Division 1	Pd	Wn	Dw	Ls	GF	GA	Pts
1. Blackpool FC (Blackpool)	3	3	-	-	5	2	6
2. Sheffield United FC (Sheffield)	3	2	1	-	3	1	5
3. Arsenal FC (London)	3	2	1	-	8	4	5
4. Liverpool FC (Liverpool)	3	2	-	1	6	3	4
5. Everton FC (Liverpool)	3	1	2	-	5	4	4
6. Bolton Wanderers FC (Bolton)	3	2	-	1	6	5	4
7. Derby County FC (Derby)	3	2	-	1	3	3	4
7. Charlton Athletic FC (London)	3	2	-	1	3	3	4
9. Stoke City FC (Stoke-on-Trent)	3	1	1	1	7	4	3
10. Manchester United FC (Manchester)	3	1	1	1	5	3	3
11. Chelsea FC (London)	3	1	1	1	4	4	3
11. Brentford FC (London)	3	1	1	1	3	3	3
13. Grimsby Town FC (Cleethorpes)	3	1	1	1	2	4	3
14. Aston Villa FC (Birmingham)	3	1	-	2	3	3	2
15. Sunderland AFC (Sunderland)	3	1	-	2	6	7	2
16. Wolverhampton Wanderers FC (Wolverhampton)	3	-	2	1	3	4	2
17. Huddersfield Town AFC (Huddersfield)	3	1	-	2	2	3	2
18. Portsmouth FC (Portsmouth)	3	1	-	2	3	5	2
19. Preston North End FC (Preston)	3	-	2	1	-	2	2
20. Blackburn Rovers FC (Blackburn)	3	-	1	2	3	5	1
21. Middlesbrough FC (Middlesbrough)	3	-	1	2	3	8	1
22. Leeds United AFC (Leeds)	3	-	1	2	-	2	1
	66	25	16	25	83	83	66

The League was suspended due to World War 2 conditions and did not resume until the 1946-47 season. However, regional competitions were played during the intervening years.

Football League Division 2 — 1939-1940 Season

	Barnsley	Birmingham	Bradford Park Avenue	Burnley	Bury	Chesterfield	Coventry City	Fulham	Leicester City	Luton Town	Manchester City	Millwall	Newcastle United	Newport County	Nottingham Forest	Plymouth Argyle	Sheffield Wednesday	Southampton	Swansea Town	Tottenham Hotspur	W.B.A.	West Ham United
Barnsley FC	■	--	--	--	--	--	--	--	--	--	--	--	--	--	4-1	--	--	--	--	--	--	--
Birmingham FC	--	■	--	2-0	--	--	--	2-0	--	--	--	--	--	--	--	--	--	--	--	--	--	--
Bradford Park Avenue	--	--	■	--	--	--	--	--	--	0-3	--	2-2	--	--	--	--	--	--	--	--	--	--
Burnley FC	--	--	--	■	--	--	1-1	--	--	--	--	--	--	--	--	--	--	--	--	--	--	--
Bury FC	--	--	--	--	■	--	--	--	3-1	--	--	--	--	--	--	--	--	--	--	--	--	--
Chesterfield FC	--	--	2-0	--	--	■	--	--	--	--	--	--	--	--	--	--	--	--	--	--	--	--
Coventry City FC	4-2	--	--	--	--	--	■	--	--	--	--	--	--	--	--	--	--	--	--	--	3-3	--
Fulham FC	--	--	--	--	--	--	--	■	--	1-1	--	--	--	--	--	--	--	--	--	--	--	--
Leicester City FC	--	--	--	--	--	--	--	--	■	--	4-3	--	--	--	--	--	--	--	--	--	--	--
Luton Town FC	--	--	--	--	--	--	--	--	--	■	--	--	--	--	--	--	3-0	--	--	--	--	--
Manchester City FC	--	--	--	--	1-1	2-0	--	--	--	--	■	--	--	--	--	--	--	--	--	--	--	--
Millwall FC	--	--	--	--	--	--	--	--	--	--	--	■	3-0	--	0-2	--	--	--	--	--	--	--
Newcastle United FC	--	--	--	--	--	--	--	--	--	--	--	--	■	--	--	--	--	--	8-1	--	--	--
Newport County AFC	--	--	--	--	--	--	--	--	--	--	--	--	--	■	--	--	--	3-1	--	1-1	--	--
Nottingham Forest FC	--	--	--	--	--	--	--	--	--	--	--	2-0	2-1	--	■	--	--	--	--	--	--	--
Plymouth Argyle FC	--	--	--	--	--	--	--	--	--	--	--	--	--	--	--	■	--	--	--	--	--	1-3
Sheffield Wednesday FC	3-1	--	--	--	--	--	--	--	--	--	--	--	--	--	0-1	--	■	--	--	--	--	--
Southampton FC	--	--	--	--	3-0	--	--	--	--	--	--	--	--	--	--	--	--	■	1-3	--	--	--
Swansea Town AFC	--	--	--	--	--	--	--	--	--	--	--	--	--	--	--	--	--	--	■	--	1-2	--
Tottenham Hotspur FC	--	1-1	--	--	--	--	--	--	--	--	--	--	--	--	--	--	--	--	--	■	--	--
West Bromwich Albion FC	--	--	--	--	--	--	--	--	--	--	--	--	--	--	--	--	--	--	--	3-4	■	--
West Ham United FC	--	--	--	--	--	--	--	--	2-1	0-2	--	--	--	--	--	--	--	--	--	--	--	■

Division 2

		Pd	Wn	Dw	Ls	GF	GA	Pts
1.	Luton Town FC (Luton)	3	2	1	-	7	1	5
2.	Birmingham FC (Birmingham)	3	2	1	-	5	1	5
3.	Coventry City FC (Coventry)	3	1	2	-	8	6	4
3.	Plymouth Argyle FC (Plymouth)	3	2	-	1	4	3	4
5.	West Ham United FC (London)	3	2	-	1	5	4	4
6.	Leicester City FC (Leicester)	3	2	-	1	6	5	4
6.	Tottenham Hotspur FC (London)	3	1	2	-	6	5	4
8.	Nottingham Forest FC (Nottingham)	3	2	-	1	5	5	4
9.	Millwall FC (London)	3	1	1	1	5	4	3
9.	Newport County AFC (Newport)	3	1	1	1	5	4	3
11.	Manchester City FC (Manchester)	3	1	1	1	6	5	3
12.	West Bromwich Albion FC (West Bromwich)	3	1	1	1	8	8	3
13.	Bury FC (Bury)	3	1	1	1	4	5	3
14.	Newcastle United FC (Newcastle-upon-Tyne)	3	1	-	2	8	6	2
15.	Chesterfield FC (Chesterfield)	2	1	-	1	2	2	2
16.	Barnsley FC (Barnsley)	3	1	-	2	7	8	2
17.	Southampton FC (Southampton)	3	1	-	2	5	6	2
18.	Sheffield Wednesday FC (Sheffield)	3	1	-	2	3	5	2
19.	Swansea Town AFC (Swansea)	3	1	-	2	5	11	2
20.	Fulham FC (London)	3	-	1	2	3	6	1
21.	Burnley FC (Burnley)	2	-	1	1	1	3	1
22.	Bradford Park Avenue FC (Bradford)	3	-	1	2	2	7	1
		64	25	14	25	110	110	64

186

Football League Division 3 (N) 1939-1940 Season	Accrington Stanley	Barrow	Bradford City	Carlisle United	Chester	Crewe Alexandra	Darlington	Doncaster Rovers	Gateshead	Halifax Town	Hartlepools United	Hull City	Lincoln City	New Brighton	Oldham Athletic	Rochdale	Rotherham United	Southport	Stockport County	Tranmere Rovers	Wrexham	York City
Accrington Stanley FC	■	--	--	--	--	--	--	--	--	--	--	--	--	--	2-0	--	--	--	--	--	--	--
Barrow AFC	1-2	■	2-2	--	--	--	--	--	--	--	--	--	--	--	--	--	--	--	--	--	--	--
Bradford City AFC	0-2	--	■	--	--	--	--	--	--	--	--	--	--	--	--	--	--	--	--	--	--	--
Carlisle United FC	--	--	--	■	--	--	--	--	--	--	--	--	--	--	--	--	--	--	2-0	--	--	--
Chester FC	--	--	--	--	■	--	--	1-0	--	--	--	--	--	--	--	--	--	--	--	2-0	--	--
Crewe Alexandra FC	--	--	--	--	--	■	--	--	--	--	0-0	--	--	--	--	--	--	--	--	--	--	--
Darlington FC	--	--	--	--	--	--	■	--	--	--	--	--	--	--	--	--	--	1-0	--	--	--	--
Doncaster Rovers FC	--	--	--	--	--	--	--	■	--	--	--	--	--	--	--	2-0	--	--	--	--	--	--
Gateshead FC	--	--	--	--	--	0-3	--	--	■	--	3-0	--	--	--	--	--	--	--	--	--	--	--
Halifax Town AFC	--	--	--	--	--	--	--	--	--	■	--	--	--	--	2-0	--	--	--	--	--	1-1	--
Hartlepools United FC	--	1-1	--	--	--	--	--	--	--	--	■	--	--	--	--	--	--	--	--	--	--	--
Hull City AFC	--	--	--	--	--	--	--	--	--	--	--	■	2-2	--	--	--	--	--	--	--	--	--
Lincoln City FC	--	--	--	--	--	--	0-2	--	4-3	--	--	--	■	--	--	--	--	--	--	--	--	--
New Brighton FC	--	--	2-1	--	--	--	--	4-2	--	--	--	--	--	■	--	--	--	--	--	--	--	--
Oldham Athletic AFC	--	--	--	3-1	--	--	--	--	--	--	--	--	--	--	■	--	--	--	--	--	--	--
Rochdale AFC	--	--	--	--	--	--	--	--	--	--	--	--	--	--	--	■	--	--	--	--	1-0	1-0
Rotherham United FC	--	--	--	--	--	--	2-2	--	--	--	--	--	--	--	--	--	■	--	--	--	--	2-1
Southport FC	--	--	--	--	--	--	--	--	--	--	--	--	1-1	--	--	--	--	■	--	3-3	--	--
Stockport County FC	--	--	--	--	--	--	--	--	0-3	--	--	--	--	--	--	--	--	--	■	--	--	--
Tranmere Rovers FC	--	--	--	--	--	--	--	--	--	--	--	--	--	--	--	--	3-1	--	--	■	--	--
Wrexham AFC	--	--	--	--	--	--	--	--	--	--	--	--	--	--	2-0	--	--	--	--	--	■	--
York City FC	--	--	--	--	2-2	--	--	--	--	--	--	--	--	--	--	--	--	--	--	--	--	■

Division 3 (North)

		Pd	Wn	Dw	Ls	GF	GA	Pts
1.	Accrington Stanley FC (Accrington)	3	3	-	-	6	1	6
2.	Halifax Town AFC (Halifax)	3	2	1	-	6	1	5
3.	Darlington FC (Darlington)	3	2	1	-	5	2	5
3.	Chester FC (Chester)	3	2	1	-	5	2	5
5.	New Brighton FC (Wallasey)	3	2	-	1	6	5	4
6.	Rochdale AFC (Rochdale)	3	2	-	1	2	2	4
7.	Crewe Alexandra FC (Crewe)	2	1	1	-	3	-	3
8.	Wrexham AFC (Wrexham)	3	1	1	1	3	2	3
9.	Tranmere Rovers FC (Birkenhead)	3	1	1	1	6	6	3
10.	Lincoln City FC (Lincoln)	3	1	1	1	6	7	3
11.	Rotherham United FC (Rotherham)	3	1	1	1	5	6	3
12.	Carlisle United FC (Carlisle)	2	1	-	1	3	3	2
12.	Hull City AFC (Kingston-upon-Hull)	2	-	2	-	3	3	2
14.	Gateshead FC (Gateshead)	3	1	-	2	6	7	2
15.	Barrow AFC (Barrow-in-Furness)	3	-	2	1	4	5	2
15.	Doncaster Rovers FC (Doncaster)	3	1	-	2	4	5	2
15.	Southport FC (Southport)	3	-	2	1	4	5	2
18.	Oldham Athletic AFC (Oldham)	3	1	-	2	3	5	2
19.	Hartlepools United FC (Hartlepool)	3	-	2	1	1	4	2
20.	York City FC (York)	3	-	1	2	3	5	1
21.	Bradford City AFC (Bradford)	3	-	1	2	3	6	1
22.	Stockport County FC (Stockport)	2	-	-	2	-	5	1
		62	22	18	22	87	87	62

Football League Division 3 (S) 1939-1940 Season	Aldershot	Bournemouth	Brighton	Bristol City	Bristol Rovers	Cardiff City	Clapton Orient	Crystal Palace	Exeter City	Ipswich Town	Mansfield Town	Northampton	Norwich City	Notts County	Port Vale	Q.P.R.	Reading	Southend United	Swindon Town	Torquay United	Walsall	Watford
Aldershot FC	■	--	--	0-1	--	--	--	--	--	--	--	--	--	--	--	--	--	--	--	--	--	--
Bournemouth & B. Athletic	--	■	--	--	--	--	--	--	--	--	10-0	--	--	--	--	2-2	--	--	--	--	--	--
Brighton & Hove Albion	2-1	--	■	--	--	--	--	--	--	--	--	--	--	--	--	0-0	--	--	--	--	--	--
Bristol City FC	--	--	3-3	■	--	--	--	--	--	--	--	--	--	1-2	--	--	--	--	--	--	--	--
Bristol Rovers FC	--	--	--	--	■	--	--	--	--	--	--	--	--	--	--	--	--	2-2	--	--	--	--
Cardiff City AFC	--	--	--	--	--	■	--	--	--	--	--	--	--	2-4	--	--	--	--	--	--	--	--
Clapton Orient FC	--	--	--	--	--	--	■	--	--	2-2	--	--	--	--	--	--	--	0-0	--	--	--	--
Crystal Palace FC	--	--	--	3-0	--	--	--	■	--	--	--	--	--	--	--	--	--	--	--	--	--	--
Exeter City FC	--	--	--	--	--	--	--	--	■	--	--	--	--	--	--	--	--	--	--	2-2	--	--
Ipswich Town FC	--	--	--	2-0	--	--	--	--	--	■	--	1-1	--	--	--	--	--	--	--	--	--	--
Mansfield Town FC	--	--	--	--	--	--	--	4-5	--	--	■	--	--	--	--	--	--	--	--	--	--	--
Northampton Town FC	--	--	--	--	--	--	--	1-2	--	--	--	■	--	--	--	--	--	--	1-0	--	--	--
Norwich City FC	--	--	--	--	--	1-2	--	--	--	--	--	--	■	--	--	--	--	--	--	--	--	--
Notts County FC	--	2-1	--	--	--	--	--	--	--	--	--	--	--	■	--	--	--	--	--	--	--	--
Port Vale FC	--	--	--	--	--	--	--	0-1	--	--	--	--	--	--	■	--	--	--	--	--	--	--
Queen's Park Rangers FC	--	--	--	--	--	--	--	--	--	--	--	--	--	--	--	■	--	--	--	--	--	2-2
Reading FC	--	--	--	--	--	--	--	5-0	--	--	--	--	--	--	--	--	■	1-0	--	--	--	--
Southend United FC	--	--	--	--	--	--	--	--	--	--	--	--	--	--	--	--	--	■	--	--	3-2	--
Swindon Town FC	2-2	--	--	--	--	0-1	--	--	--	--	--	--	--	--	--	--	--	--	■	--	--	--
Torquay United FC	--	--	--	--	--	--	--	--	--	2-2	--	--	--	--	--	--	--	--	--	■	0-0	--
Walsall FC	--	--	--	--	--	--	--	--	--	--	--	--	--	--	--	1-0	--	--	--	--	■	--
Watford FC	--	--	--	--	--	--	1-1	--	--	--	1-2	--	--	--	--	--	--	--	--	--	--	■

Division 3 (South)

		Pd	Wn	Dw	Ls	GF	GA	Pts
1.	Reading FC (Reading)	3	2	1	-	8	2	5
2.	Exeter City FC (Exeter)	3	2	1	-	5	3	5
3.	Notts County FC (Nottingham)	2	2	-	-	6	3	4
4.	Ipswich Town FC (Ipswich)	3	1	2	-	5	3	4
5.	Brighton & Hove Albion FC (Hove)	3	1	2	-	5	4	4
6.	Cardiff City AFC (Cardiff)	3	2	-	1	5	5	4
7.	Crystal Palace FC (London)	3	2	-	1	8	9	4
8.	Bournemouth & Boscombe Athletic FC (Bournemouth)	3	1	1	1	13	4	3
9.	Mansfield Town FC (Mansfield)	3	1	1	1	8	8	3
9.	Bristol City FC (Bristol)	3	1	1	1	5	5	3
9.	Norwich City FC (Norwich)	3	1	1	1	4	4	3
9.	Torquay United FC (Torquay)	3	-	3	-	4	4	3
9.	Clapton Orient FC (London)	3	-	3	-	3	3	3
9.	Southend United FC (Southend-on-Sea)	3	1	1	1	3	3	3
9.	Walsall FC (Walsall)	3	1	1	1	3	3	3
16.	Queen's Park Rangers FC (London)	3	-	2	1	4	5	2
16.	Watford FC (Watford)	3	-	2	1	4	5	2
18.	Northampton Town FC (Northampton)	3	1	-	2	2	12	2
19.	Aldershot FC (Aldershot)	3	-	1	2	3	5	1
20.	Swindon Town FC (Swindon)	3	-	1	2	2	4	1
21.	Bristol Rovers FC (Bristol)	3	-	1	2	2	7	1
22.	Port Vale FC (Stoke-on-Trent)	2	-	1	1	-	1	1
		64	19	26	19	102	102	64

South League (Group "A")

		Pd	Wn	Dw	Ls	GF	GA	Pts
1.	Arsenal FC (London)	18	13	4	1	62	22	30
2.	West Ham United FC (London)	18	12	1	5	57	33	25
3.	Millwall FC (London)	18	8	5	5	46	38	21
4.	Watford FC (Watford)	18	9	3	6	44	38	21
5.	Norwich City FC (Norwich)	18	7	6	5	41	36	20
6.	Charlton Athletic FC (London)	18	8	1	9	61	58	17
7.	Crystal Palace FC (London)	18	5	3	10	39	56	13
8.	Clapton Orient FC (London)	18	5	3	10	28	60	13
9.	Tottenham Hotspur FC (London)	18	5	2	11	37	43	12
10.	Southend United FC (Southend-on-Sea)	18	4	-	14	30	61	8
		180	76	28	76	445	445	180

South League (Group "B")

		Pd	Wn	Dw	Ls	GF	GA	Pts
1.	Queen's Park Rangers FC (London)	18	12	2	4	49	26	26
2.	Bournemouth & Boscombe Athletic FC (Bournemouth)	18	11	2	5	52	37	24
3.	Chelsea FC (London)	18	9	5	4	43	37	23
4.	Reading FC (Reading)	18	10	2	6	47	42	22
5.	Fulham FC (London)	18	7	4	7	42	41	18
6.	Portsmouth FC (Portsmouth)	18	7	2	9	37	42	16
7.	Aldershot FC (Aldershot)	18	5	4	9	38	49	14
8.	Brighton & Hove Albion FC (Hove)	18	5	1	12	42	53	11
9.	Southampton FC (Southampton)	18	4	-	14	41	63	8
		162	70	22	70	391	390	162

South League (Group "C")

		Pd	Wn	Dw	Ls	GF	GA	Pts
1.	Tottenham Hotspur FC (London)	18	11	4	3	43	30	26
2.	West Ham United FC (London)	18	10	4	4	53	28	24
3.	Arsenal FC (London)	18	9	5	4	41	26	23
4.	Brentford FC (London)	18	8	4	6	42	34	20
5.	Millwall FC (London)	18	7	5	6	36	30	19
6.	Charlton Athletic FC (London)	18	7	4	7	39	56	18
7.	Fulham FC (London)	18	8	1	9	38	42	17
8.	Southampton FC (Southampton)	18	5	3	10	28	55	13
9.	Chelsea FC (London)	18	4	3	11	33	53	11
10.	Portsmouth FC (Portsmouth)	18	3	3	12	26	45	9
		180	72	36	72	379	399	180

South League (Group "D")

		Pd	Wn	Dw	Ls	GF	GA	Pts
1.	Crystal Palace FC (London)	18	13	1	4	64	30	27
2.	Queen's park Rangers FC (London)	18	10	3	5	38	28	23
3.	Watford FC (Watford)	18	7	7	4	41	29	21
4.	Southend United FC (Southend-on-Sea)	18	8	3	7	41	37	19
5.	Aldershot FC (Aldershot)	18	7	3	8	38	36	17
6.	Clapton Orient FC (London)	18	7	3	8	33	45	17
7.	Norwich City FC (Norwich)	17	6	4	7	31	31	16
8.	Bournemouth & Boscombe Athletic FC (Bournemouth)	17	7	2	8	38	40	16
9.	Reading FC (Reading)	18	6	2	10	31	42	14
10.	Brighton & Hove Albion FC (Hove)	18	2	4	12	30	65	8
		178	73	32	73	385	383	178

West League

		Pd	Wn	Dw	Ls	GF	GA	Pts
1.	Stoke City FC (Stoke-on-Trent)	22	13	5	4	57	41	31
2.	Liverpool FC (Liverpool)	22	12	5	5	66	40	29
3.	Everton FC (Liverpool)	22	12	4	6	64	33	28
4.	Manchester United FC (Manchester)	22	14	-	8	74	41	28
5.	Manchester City FC (Manchester)	22	12	4	6	73	41	28
6.	Wrexham AFC (Wrexham)	22	10	5	7	45	50	25
7.	New Brighton FC (Wallasey)	22	10	3	9	55	52	23
8.	Port Vale FC (Stoke-on-Trent)	22	10	2	10	52	56	22
9.	Chester FC (Chester)	22	7	5	10	40	51	19
10.	Crewe Alexandra FC (Crewe)	22	6	1	15	44	79	13
11.	Stockport County FC (Stockport)	22	4	3	15	45	79	11
12.	Tranmere Rovers FC (Birkenhead)	22	2	3	17	41	93	7
		264	112	40	112	656	656	264

North-East League

		Pd	Wn	Dw	Ls	GF	GA	Pts
1.	Huddersfield Town AFC (Huddersfield)	20	15	4	1	54	22	34
2.	Newcastle United FC (Newcastle-upon-Tyne)	20	12	1	7	59	42	25
3.	Bradford Park Avenue FC (Bradford)	19	10	2	7	47	38	22
4.	Middlesbrough FC (Middlesbrough)	20	9	4	7	49	42	22
5.	Leeds United AFC (Leeds)	18	9	3	6	36	27	21
6.	Bradford City AFC (Bradford)	19	8	4	7	41	37	20
7.	Hull City AFC (Kingston-upon-Hull)	20	8	1	11	35	41	17
8.	York City FC (York)	20	8	1	11	36	51	17
9.	Darlington FC (Darlington)	19	6	3	10	44	56	15
10.	Hartlepools United FC (Hartlepool)	20	6	1	13	27	47	13
11.	Halifax Town AFC (Halifax)	19	3	2	14	28	53	8
		214	94	26	94	456	456	214

North-West League

		Pd	Wn	Dw	Ls	GF	GA	Pts
1.	Bury FC (Bury)	22	16	2	4	64	30	34
2.	Preston North End FC (Preston)	22	15	2	5	63	27	32
3.	Blackpool FC (Blackpool)	22	13	6	3	75	36	32
4.	Bolton Wanderers FC (Bolton)	22	13	4	5	55	30	30
5.	Oldham Athletic AFC (Oldham)	22	11	2	9	55	61	24
6.	Burnley FC (Burnley)	22	9	5	8	48	43	23
7.	Barrow AFC (Barrow-in-Furness)	22	8	4	10	54	57	20
8.	Blackburn Rovers FC (Blackburn)	22	7	4	11	37	40	18
9.	Rochdale AFC (Rochdale)	22	5	5	12	38	58	15
10.	Southport FC (Southport)	22	5	4	13	34	62	14
11.	Carlisle United FC (Carlisle)	22	4	4	14	38	68	12
12.	Accrington Stanley FC (Accrington)	22	2	6	14	31	78	10
		264	108	48	108	592	590	264

South-West League

		Pd	Wn	Dw	Ls	GF	GA	Pts
1.	Plymouth Argyle FC (Plymouth)	28	16	4	8	72	41	36
2.	Torquay United FC (Torquay)	28	14	6	8	73	62	34
3.	Bristol Rovers FC (Bristol)	28	9	10	9	62	55	28
4.	Newport County AFC (Newport)	28	12	4	12	70	63	28
5.	Swindon Town FC (Swindon)	28	10	8	10	66	63	28
6.	Swansea Town AFC (Swansea)	28	10	6	12	54	60	26
7.	Cardiff City AFC (Cardiff)	28	6	13	9	45	63	25
8.	Bristol City FC (Bristol)	28	7	5	16	57	92	19
		224	84	56	84	499	499	224

Midlands League	Pd	Wn	Dw	Ls	GF	GA	Pts
1. Wolverhampton Wanderers FC (Wolverhampton)	28	19	3	6	76	44	41
2. West Bromwich Albion FC (West Bromwich)	28	18	4	6	87	51	40
3. Birmingham FC (Birmingham)	28	12	5	11	56	60	29
4. Coventry City FC (Coventry)	28	13	3	12	68	57	29
5. Luton Town FC (Luton)	28	10	4	14	76	88	24
6. Northampton Town FC (Northampton)	28	7	8	13	48	59	22
7. Leicester City FC (Leicester)	28	7	6	15	51	71	20
8. Walsall FC (Walsall)	28	7	5	16	51	83	19
	224	93	38	93	513	513	224

East Midlands League	Pd	Wn	Dw	Ls	GF	GA	Pts
1. Chesterfield FC (Chesterfield)	20	14	2	4	69	23	30
2. Sheffield United FC (Sheffield)	20	12	1	7	46	34	25
3. Barnsley FC (Barnsley)	20	10	5	5	43	39	25
4. Grimsby Town FC (Cleethorpes)	20	10	2	8	40	44	22
5. Mansfield Town FC (Mansfield)	20	9	3	8	49	48	21
6. Doncaster Rovers FC (Doncaster)	20	7	4	9	37	45	18
7. Lincoln City FC (Lincoln)	20	9	-	11	42	53	18
8. Rotherham United FC (Rotherham)	20	7	4	9	24	42	18
9. Sheffield Wednesday FC (Sheffield)	20	5	5	10	33	42	15
10. Nottingham Forest FC (Nottingham)	20	5	4	11	37	43	14
11. Notts County FC (Nottingham)	20	6	2	12	40	57	14
	220	94	32	94	460	470	220

1940-41

North	Pd	Wn	Dw	Ls	GF	GA	Pts	Gl. Av.
1. Preston North End FC (Preston)	29	18	7	4	81	37	43	2.189
2. Chesterfield FC (Chesterfield)	35	20	6	9	76	40	46	1.900
3. Manchester City FC (Manchester)	35	18	10	7	104	55	46	1.890
4. Barnsley FC (Barnsley)	30	18	4	8	86	49	40	1.775
5. Everton FC (Liverpool)	34	19	7	8	85	51	45	1.666
6. Blackpool FC (Blackpool)	20	13	3	4	56	34	29	1.646
7. Halifax Town AFC (Halifax)	30	10	13	7	64	51	33	1.254
8. Manchester United FC (Manchester)	35	14	8	13	80	65	36	1.249
9. Lincoln City FC (Lincoln)	27	13	7	7	65	53	33	1.226
10. Newcastle United FC (Newcastle-upon-Tyne)	23	12	-	11	49	41	24	1.195
11. Huddersfield Town AFC (Huddersfield)	33	11	6	16	69	58	28	1.189
12. Middlesbrough FC (Middlesbrough)	27	16	1	10	84	71	33	1.183
13. New Brighton FC (Wallasey)	26	15	1	10	97	82	31	1.182
14. Burnley FC (Burnley)	35	17	7	11	62	53	41	1.169
15. Leeds United AFC (Leeds)	30	13	8	9	62	54	34	1.148
16. Liverpool FC (Liverpool)	37	15	6	16	91	82	36	1.102
17. Wrexham AFC (Wrexham)	29	15	5	9	78	71	35	1.098
18. Chester FC (Chester)	35	14	6	15	94	89	34	1.056
19. Doncaster Rovers FC (Doncaster)	32	15	7	10	77	74	37	1.040
20. Oldham Athletic AFC (Oldham)	37	17	4	16	78	77	38	1.012
21. Grimsby Town FC (Cleethorpes)	27	12	2	13	60	63	26	.952

		Pd	Wn	Dw	Ls	GF	GA	Pts	Gl. Av.
22.	Bradford Park Avenue FC (Bradford)	31	9	7	15	64	74	25	.864
23.	Rotherham United FC (Rotherham)	29	12	5	12	48	57	29	.842
24.	Blackburn Rovers FC (Blackburn)	32	9	10	13	49	60	28	.816
25.	Bury FC (Bury)	38	10	9	19	80	100	29	.800
26.	Bolton Wanderers FC (Bolton)	16	6	2	8	31	40	14	.775
27.	Tranmere Rovers FC (Birkenhead)	25	9	5	11	67	90	23	.744
28.	Sheffield United FC (Sheffield)	25	6	6	13	44	60	18	.733
29.	Bradford City AFC (Bradford)	24	8	3	13	71	99	19	.727
30.	Rochdale AFC (Rochdale)	32	12	5	15	64	92	29	.695
31.	Southport FC (Southport)	28	7	2	19	61	88	16	.693
32.	York City FC (York)	25	7	4	14	49	71	18	.690
33.	Hull City AFC (Kingston-upon-Hull)	23	8	3	12	44	67	19	.656
34.	Sheffield Wednesday FC (Sheffield)	30	9	6	15	50	78	24	.641
35.	Stockport County FC (Stockport)	29	9	5	15	54	93	23	.580
36.	Crewe Alexandra FC (Crewe)	24	2	3	19	32	84	7	.380

South

		Pd	Wn	Dw	Ls	GF	GA	Pts	Gl. Av.
1.	Crystal Palace FC (London)	27	16	4	7	86	44	36	1.954
2.	West Ham United FC (London)	25	14	6	5	70	39	34	1.794
3.	Coventry City FC (Coventry)	10	5	3	2	28	16	13	1.750
4.	Arsenal FC (London)	19	10	5	4	66	38	25	1.736
5.	Cardiff City AFC (Cardiff)	24	12	5	7	75	50	29	1.500
6.	Reading FC (Reading)	26	14	5	7	73	51	33	1.431
7.	Norwich City FC (Norwich)	19	9	2	8	73	55	20	1.327
8.	Watford FC (Watford)	35	15	6	14	96	73	36	1.315
9.	Portsmouth FC (Portsmouth)	31	16	2	13	92	71	34	1.296
10.	Tottenham Hotspur FC (London)	23	9	5	9	53	41	23	1.292
11.	Millwall FC (London)	31	16	5	10	73	57	37	1.280
12.	Walsall FC (Walsall)	32	14	7	11	100	80	35	1.250
13.	West Bromwich Albion FC (West Bromwich)	28	13	5	10	83	69	31	1.202
14.	Leicester City FC (Leicester)	33	17	5	11	87	73	39	1.191
15.	Northampton Town FC (Northampton)	30	14	3	13	84	71	31	1.183
16.	Bristol City FC (Bristol)	20	10	2	8	55	48	22	1.145
17.	Mansfield Town FC (Mansfield)	29	12	6	11	77	68	30	1.132
18.	Charlton Athletic FC (London)	19	7	4	8	37	34	18	1.088
19.	Aldershot FC (Aldershot)	24	14	2	8	73	68	30	1.073
20.	Brentford FC (London)	23	9	3	11	51	51	21	1.000
21.	Chelsea FC (London)	23	10	4	9	57	58	24	.981
22.	Birmingham FC (Birmingham)	16	7	1	8	38	43	15	.883
23.	Fulham FC (London)	30	10	7	13	62	73	27	.849
24.	Luton Town FC (Luton)	35	11	7	17	82	100	29	.820
25.	Stoke City FC (Stoke-on-Trent)	36	9	9	18	76	96	27	.791
26.	Queen's Park Rangers FC (London)	23	8	3	12	47	60	19	.783
27.	Brighton & Hove Albion FC (Hove)	25	8	7	10	51	75	23	.680
28.	Nottingham Forest FC (Nottingham)	25	7	3	15	50	77	17	.649
29.	Bournemouth & Boscombe Athletic FC	27	9	3	15	59	92	21	.641
30.	Notts County FC (Nottingham)	21	8	3	10	42	66	19	.636
31.	Southend United FC (Southend-on-Sea)	29	12	4	13	64	101	28	.633
32.	Southampton FC (Southampton)	31	4	4	23	53	111	12	.477
33.	Swansea Town AFC (Swansea)	10	2	1	7	12	33	5	.363
34.	Clapton Orient FC (London)	15	1	3	11	19	66	5	.287

1941-42

London League	Pd	Wn	Dw	Ls	GF	GA	Pts
1. Arsenal FC (London)	30	23	2	5	108	43	48
2. Portsmouth FC (Portsmouth)	30	20	2	8	105	59	42
3. West Ham United FC (London)	30	17	5	8	81	44	39
4. Aldershot FC (Aldershot)	30	17	5	8	85	56	39
5. Tottenham Hotspur FC (London)	30	15	8	7	61	41	38
6. Crystal Palace FC (London)	30	14	6	10	70	53	34
7. Reading FC (Reading)	30	13	8	9	76	58	34
8. Charlton Athletic FC (London)	30	14	5	11	72	64	33
9. Brentford FC (London)	30	14	2	14	80	76	30
10. Queen's Park Rangers FC (London)	30	11	3	16	52	59	25
11. Fulham FC (London)	30	10	4	16	79	99	24
12. Brighton & Hove Albion FC (Hove)	30	9	4	17	71	108	22
13. Chelsea FC (London)	30	8	4	18	56	88	20
14. Millwall FC (London)	30	7	5	18	53	82	19
15. Clapton Orient FC (London)	30	5	7	18	42	94	17
16. Watford FC (Watford)	30	6	4	20	47	114	16
	480	203	74	203	1138	1138	480

North Regional Championship	Pd	Wn	Dw	Ls	GF	GA	Pts
1. Blackpool FC (Blackpool)	18	14	1	3	75	19	29
2. Lincoln City FC (Lincoln)	18	13	3	2	54	28	29
3. Preston North End FC (Preston)	18	13	1	4	58	18	27
4. Manchester United FC (Manchester)	18	10	6	2	79	27	26
5. Stoke City FC (Stoke-on-Trent)	18	12	2	4	75	36	26
6. Everton FC (Liverpool)	18	12	2	4	61	31	26
7. Blackburn Rovers FC (Blackburn)	18	10	6	2	40	24	26
8. Liverpool FC (Liverpool)	18	11	4	3	66	44	26
9. Gateshead FC (Gateshead)	18	9	5	4	39	35	23
10. Sunderland AFC (Sunderland)	18	9	4	5	50	30	22
11. Huddersfield Town AFC (Huddersfield)	18	10	1	7	48	33	21
12. Bradford Park Avenue FC (Bradford)	18	8	5	5	33	28	21
13. Grimsby Town FC (Cleethorpes)	18	7	6	5	41	31	20
14. Barnsley FC (Barnsley)	18	8	4	6	39	31	20
15. Newcastle United FC (Newcastle-upon-Tyne)	18	7	6	5	46	39	20
16. Sheffield Wednesday FC (Sheffield)	18	8	3	7	48	54	19
16. Manchester City FC (Manchester)	18	8	3	7	48	54	19
18. Sheffield United FC (Sheffield)	18	7	4	7	39	38	18
19. Burnley FC (Burnley)	18	6	6	6	36	40	18
20. Halifax Town AFC (Halifax)	18	7	3	8	29	41	17
21. Oldham Athletic AFC (Oldham)	18	6	4	8	40	49	16
22. Rochdale AFC (Rochdale)	18	6	4	8	28	52	16
23. Chesterfield FC (Chesterfield)	18	5	5	8	27	31	15
24. Chester FC (Chester)	18	6	3	9	45	53	15
25. Middlesbrough FC (Middlesbrough)	18	6	3	9	44	56	15
26. Leeds United AFC (Leeds)	18	7	1	10	36	46	15
27. Doncaster Rovers FC (Doncaster)	18	6	2	10	39	46	14
28. Bradford City AFC (Bradford)	18	5	4	9	32	42	14
29. Rotherham United FC (Rotherham)	18	6	2	10	33	47	14
30. New Brighton FC (Wallasey)	18	4	6	8	39	75	14
31. Tranmere Rovers FC (Birkenhead)	18	5	3	10	35	60	13

North Regional Championship (continued)	Pd	Wn	Dw	Ls	GF	GA	Pts
32. York City FC (York)	18	4	4	10	41	55	12
33. Mansfield Town FC (Mansfield)	18	6	-	12	29	50	12
34. Bolton Wanderers FC (Bolton)	18	3	5	10	35	48	11
35. Southport FC (Southport)	18	5	1	12	33	61	11
36. Bury FC (Bury)	18	3	3	12	37	59	9
37. Wrexham AFC (Wrexham)	18	2	5	11	40	69	9
38. Stockport County FC (Stockport)	18	2	2	14	34	73	6

The North Regional Championship was played between August 1941 and 25th December 1941.

In the South Regional Championship, the "Average" was calculated over 18 matches.

The "League Championship" was played between 27/12/41 and 30/05/42. The "Average" was based on 23 matches but clubs which had not played a minimum of 18 matches were not included in the classification (i.e. clubs from positions 23 – 51).

South Regional League	Pd	Wn	Dw	Ls	GF	GA	Pts	Average
1. Leicester City FC (Leicester)	17	11	3	3	40	17	25	26.471
2. West Bromwich Albion FC (West Bromwich)	13	9	1	3	62	26	19	26.308
3. Cardiff City AFC (Cardiff)	15	9	1	5	43	28	19	22.800
4. Norwich City FC (Norwich)	8	4	2	2	20	13	10	22.500
5. Bournemouth & Boscombe Athletic FC (B'mouth)	10	6	-	4	26	18	12	21.600
5. Bristol City FC (Bristol)	15	9	-	6	46	45	18	21.600
7. Walsall FC (Walsall)	18	9	1	8	49	45	19	19.000
8. Northampton Town FC (Northampton)	16	7	2	7	39	38	16	18.000
9. Wolverhampton Wanderers FC (Wolverhampton)	16	6	2	8	27	36	14	15.750
10. Southampton FC (Southampton)	10	4	-	6	27	32	8	14.400
11. Luton Town FC (Luton)	18	5	1	12	34	73	11	11.000
12. Nottingham Forest FC (Nottingham)	13	2	1	10	18	39	5	6.923
13. Swansea Town AFC (Swansea)	9	1	-	8	18	39	2	4.000
	178	82	14	82	449	449	178	

"League Championship"	Pd	Wn	Dw	Ls	GF	GA	Pts	Average
1. Manchester United FC (Manchester)	19	12	4	3	44	25	28	33.895
2. Blackpool FC (Blackpool)	22	14	4	4	108	34	32	33.455
3. Northampton Town FC (Northampton)	21	14	2	5	70	31	30	32.857
3. Liverpool FC (Liverpool)	21	14	2	5	57	39	30	32.857
5. Wolverhampton Wanderers FC	20	13	1	6	52	29	27	31.050
6. Huddersfield Town AFC (Huddersfield)	20	9	6	5	42	33	24	27.600
7. Blackburn Rovers FC (Blackburn)	22	10	6	6	40	31	26	27.182
8. West Bromwich Albion FC (West Bromwich)	18	9	3	6	53	43	21	26.833
8. Grimsby Town FC (Cleethorpes)	18	8	5	5	31	22	21	26.833
10. Sunderland AFC (Sunderland)	22	9	7	6	53	42	25	26.136
11. Cardiff City AFC (Cardiff)	20	9	4	7	59	38	22	25.300
12. Preston North End FC (Preston)	19	6	7	6	41	30	19	23.000
12. Chesterfield FC (Chesterfield)	18	8	2	8	32	31	18	23.000
12. Middlesbrough FC (Middlesbrough)	18	7	4	7	37	36	18	23.000
12. Everton FC (Liverpool)	23	9	5	9	37	41	23	23.000
12. Stoke City FC (Stoke-on-Trent)	20	9	2	9	41	49	20	23.000
17. Leicester City FC (Leicester)	18	6	4	8	39	38	16	20.444

	"League Championship" (continued)	Pd	Wn	Dw	Ls	GF	GA	Pts	Average
18.	Bradford Park Avenue FC (Bradford)	19	5	6	8	35	40	16	19.368
19.	Halifax Town AFC (Halifax)	19	4	7	8	30	40	15	18.158
19.	Burnley FC (Burnley)	19	7	1	11	29	53	15	18.158
21.	Chester FC (Chester)	20	6	3	11	34	41	15	17.250
22.	Oldham Athletic AFC (Oldham)	18	4	3	11	30	43	11	14.056
23.	Barnsley FC (Barnsley)	15	9	3	3	48	23	21	32.200
24.	Norwich City FC (Norwich)	12	7	1	4	27	19	15	28.750
25.	Bristol City FC (Bristol)	17	9	3	5	55	29	21	28.412
26.	Sheffield United FC (Sheffield)	17	8	4	5	39	33	20	27.059
27.	Lincoln City FC (Lincoln)	13	7	1	5	45	33	15	26.538
28.	Manchester City FC (Manchester)	17	9	1	7	33	26	19	25.706
28.	York City FC (York)	17	6	7	4	39	37	19	25.706
30.	Nottingham Forest FC (Nottingham)	16	8	1	7	32	30	17	24.438
31.	Southampton FC (Southampton)	12	5	2	5	27	32	12	23.000
32.	Newcastle United FC (Newcastle-upon-Tyne)	17	5	6	6	33	40	16	21.647
33.	Bury FC (Bury)	15	6	2	7	46	39	14	21.467
33.	Rotherham United FC (Rotherham)	15	6	2	7	32	34	14	21.467
33.	Bolton Wanderers FC (Bolton)	15	5	4	6	26	33	14	21.467
36.	Bradford City AFC (Bradford)	14	6	1	7	28	25	13	21.357
37.	New Brighton FC (Wallasey)	11	5	-	6	23	38	10	20.909
38.	Southport FC (Southport)	16	6	2	8	30	38	14	20.125
39.	Wrexham AFC (Wrexham)	12	4	2	6	26	32	10	19.167
40.	Leeds United AFC (Leeds)	17	7	-	10	33	33	14	18.941
41.	Sheffield Wednesday FC (Sheffield)	15	5	2	8	22	36	12	18.400
42.	Gateshead FC (Gateshead)	13	4	2	7	23	36	10	17.692
43.	Rochdale AFC (Rochdale)	13	5	-	8	23	39	10	17.692
44.	Bournemouth & Boscombe Athletic FC	8	2	2	4	11	21	6	17.250
45.	Tranmere Rovers FC (Birkenhead)	15	4	3	8	24	55	11	16.867
46.	Luton Town FC (Luton)	16	4	2	10	20	54	10	14.375
47.	Walsall FC (Walsall)	13	4	-	9	14	34	8	14.154
48.	Swansea Town AFC (Swansea)	11	1	4	6	11	39	6	12.545
49.	Stockport County FC (Stockport)	10	1	3	6	12	38	5	11.500
50.	Doncaster Rovers FC (Doncaster)	9	2	-	7	10	30	4	10.222
51.	Mansfield Town FC (Mansfield)	11	1	2	8	15	36	4	8.364

1942-43

	North Regional (1st Championship)	Pd	Wn	Dw	Ls	GF	GA	Pts
1.	Blackpool FC (Blackpool)	18	16	1	1	93	28	33
2.	Liverpool FC (Liverpool)	18	14	1	3	70	34	29
3.	Sheffield Wednesday FC (Sheffield)	18	12	3	3	61	26	27
4.	Manchester United FC (Manchester)	18	12	2	4	58	26	26
5.	Huddersfield Town AFC (Huddersfield)	18	10	6	2	52	32	26
6.	Stoke City FC (Stoke-on-Trent)	18	11	3	4	46	25	25
7.	Coventry City FC (Coventry)	18	10	5	3	28	16	25
8.	Southport FC (Southport)	18	11	3	4	64	42	25
9.	Derby County FC (Derby)	18	11	2	5	51	37	24
10.	Bradford Park Avenue FC (Bradford)	18	8	7	3	46	21	23
11.	Lincoln City FC (Lincoln)	18	9	5	4	58	36	23
12.	Halifax Town AFC (Halifax)	18	10	3	5	39	27	23
13.	Gateshead FC (Gateshead)	18	10	3	5	52	45	23
14.	Aston Villa FC (Birmingham)	18	10	2	6	47	33	23

		Pd	Wn	Dw	Ls	GF	GA	Pts
15.	Everton FC (Liverpool)	18	10	2	6	52	41	22
16.	Grimsby Town FC (Cleethorpes)	17	8	5	4	42	31	21
17.	York City FC (York)	18	9	3	6	47	36	21
18.	Blackburn Rovers FC (Blackburn)	18	9	3	6	56	43	21
19.	Barnsley FC (Barnsley)	18	8	5	5	39	30	21
20.	Sheffield United FC (Sheffield)	18	7	6	5	45	35	20
21.	Birmingham FC (Birmingham)	18	9	2	7	27	30	20
22.	Sunderland AFC (Sunderland)	18	8	3	7	46	40	19
23.	Chester FC (Chester)	18	7	4	7	43	40	18
24.	Walsall FC (Walsall)	18	6	5	7	33	31	17
25.	Northampton Town FC (Northampton)	18	8	1	9	38	44	17
26.	Newcastle United FC (Newcastle-upon-Tyne)	18	6	4	8	51	52	16
27.	Chesterfield FC (Chesterfield)	18	5	6	7	30	34	16
28.	West Bromwich Albion FC (West Bromwich)	18	6	4	8	35	43	16
29.	Notts County FC (Nottingham)	18	7	2	9	34	57	16
30.	Manchester City FC (Manchester)	18	7	1	10	46	47	15
31.	Nottingham Forest FC (Nottingham)	18	6	3	9	38	39	15
32.	Burnley FC (Burnley)	18	5	5	8	35	45	15
33.	Leicester City FC (Leicester)	18	5	4	9	32	37	14
34.	Bury FC (Bury)	18	6	2	10	53	81	14
35.	Stockport County FC (Stockport)	18	5	3	10	34	55	13
36.	Rotherham United FC (Rotherham)	18	4	5	9	28	48	13
37.	Tranmere Rovers FC (Birkenhead)	18	5	3	10	36	63	13
38.	Wolverhampton Wanderers FC (Wolverhampton)	18	5	2	11	28	41	12
39.	Crewe Alexandra FC (Crewe)	18	5	2	11	43	64	12
40.	Middlesbrough FC (Middlesbrough)	18	4	4	10	30	50	12
41.	Rochdale AFC (Rochdale)	18	5	2	11	34	57	12
42.	Wrexham AFC (Wrexham)	18	5	1	12	43	67	11
43.	Leeds United AFC (Leeds)	18	3	4	11	28	45	10
44.	Oldham Athletic AFC (Oldham)	18	4	2	12	29	54	10
45.	Bradford City AFC (Bradford)	18	4	2	12	30	63	10
46.	Bolton Wanderers FC (Bolton)	18	3	3	12	31	52	9
47.	Doncaster Rovers FC (Doncaster)	17	3	3	11	23	41	9
48.	Mansfield Town FC (Mansfield)	18	2	4	12	25	65	8

London & South League

		Pd	Wn	Dw	Ls	GF	GA	Pts
1.	Arsenal FC (London)	28	21	1	6	102	40	43
2.	Tottenham Hotspur FC (London)	28	16	6	6	68	28	38
3.	Queen's Park Rangers FC (London)	28	18	2	8	64	49	38
4.	Portsmouth FC (Portsmouth)	28	16	3	9	66	52	35
5.	Southampton FC (Southampton)	28	14	5	9	86	58	33
6.	West Ham United FC (London)	28	14	5	9	80	66	33
7.	Chelsea FC (London)	28	14	4	10	52	45	32
8.	Aldershot FC (Aldershot)	28	14	2	12	87	77	30
9.	Brentford FC (London)	28	12	5	11	64	63	29
10.	Charlton Athletic FC (London)	28	13	3	12	68	75	29
11.	Clapton Orient FC (London)	28	11	5	12	54	72	27
12.	Brighton & Hove Albion FC (Hove)	28	10	5	13	65	73	25
13.	Reading FC (Reading)	28	9	6	13	67	74	24
14.	Fulham FC (London)	28	10	2	16	69	78	22
15.	Crystal Palace FC (London)	28	7	5	16	49	75	19
16.	Millwall FC (London)	28	6	5	17	66	88	17
17.	Watford FC (Watford)	28	7	2	19	51	88	16
18.	Luton Town FC (Luton)	28	4	6	18	43	100	14

North Regional (2nd Championship)

		Pd	Wn	Dw	Ls	GF	GA	Pts
1.	Liverpool FC (Liverpool)	20	15	2	3	64	32	32
2.	Lovell's Athletic FC (Newport)	20	11	5	4	63	32	27
3.	Manchester City FC (Manchester)	19	11	5	4	43	24	27
4.	Aston Villa FC (Birmingham)	20	13	1	6	44	30	27
5.	Sheffield Wednesday FC (Sheffield)	20	9	8	3	43	26	26
6.	Manchester United FC (Manchester)	19	11	3	5	52	26	25
7.	York City FC (York)	18	11	3	4	52	30	25
8.	Huddersfield Town AFC (Huddersfield)	19	11	3	5	48	28	25
9.	Coventry City FC (Coventry)	20	11	3	6	33	21	25
10.	Stoke City FC (Stoke-on-Trent)	20	10	4	6	42	34	24
11.	West Bromwich Albion FC (West Bromwich)	20	11	7	2	49	40	24
12.	Notts County FC (Nottingham)	20	9	6	5	37	34	24
13.	Blackpool FC (Blackpool)	19	8	7	4	49	31	23
14.	Newcastle United FC (Newcastle-upon-Tyne)	19	10	3	6	62	42	23
15.	Blackburn Rovers FC (Blackburn)	18	9	4	5	45	35	22
16.	Bristol City FC (Bristol)	19	8	6	5	41	33	22
17.	Chesterfield FC (Chesterfield)	20	9	4	7	35	30	22
18.	Derby County FC (Derby)	20	8	5	7	41	34	21
19.	Aberaman AFC (Aberaman)	18	10	1	7	39	41	21
20.	Sunderland AFC (Sunderland)	19	8	4	7	58	40	20
21.	Rochdale AFC (Rochdale)	16	9	2	5	39	26	20
22.	Leicester City FC (Leicester)	20	9	2	9	40	37	20
23.	Sheffield United FC (Sheffield)	19	8	4	7	43	42	20
24.	Bradford Park Avenue FC (Bradford)	19	7	5	7	35	31	19
25.	Everton FC (Liverpool)	19	9	1	9	51	46	19
26.	Bath City FC (Bath)	18	7	4	7	49	46	18
27.	Birmingham FC (Birmingham)	20	8	2	10	32	29	18
28.	Barnsley FC (Barnsley)	17	8	2	7	34	37	18
29.	Nottingham Forest FC (Nottingham)	18	7	4	7	30	34	18
30.	Crewe Alexandra FC (Crewe)	20	7	4	9	44	57	18
31.	Bradford City AFC (Bradford)	16	7	2	7	29	29	16
32.	Wrexham AFC (Wrexham)	17	7	3	7	36	37	17
33.	Bolton Wanderers FC (Bolton)	17	7	2	8	34	42	16
34.	Tranmere Rovers FC (Birkenhead)	20	6	4	10	37	48	16
35.	Halifax Town AFC (Halifax)	18	7	2	9	30	39	16
36.	Chester FC (Chester)	20	6	3	11	40	49	15
37.	Northampton Town FC (Northampton)	17	6	2	9	30	37	14
38.	Wolverhampton Wanderers FC (Wolverhampton)	17	5	4	8	38	45	14
39.	Swansea Town AFC (Swansea)	18	4	6	8	36	52	14
40.	Grimsby Town FC (Cleethorpes)	13	4	4	5	30	27	12
41.	Bury FC (Bury)	16	5	3	8	44	42	13
42.	Doncaster Rovers FC (Doncaster)	17	5	3	9	27	41	13
43.	Rotherham United FC (Rotherham)	18	4	5	9	28	43	13
44.	Gateshead FC (Gateshead)	13	6	-	7	29	36	12
45.	Stockport County FC (Stockport)	19	4	4	11	37	76	12
46.	Southport FC (Southport)	18	4	3	11	38	58	11
47.	Leeds United AFC (Leeds)	16	5	1	10	32	50	11
48.	Oldham Athletic AFC (Oldham)	18	4	3	11	28	47	11
49.	Middlesbrough FC (Middlesbrough)	18	5	-	13	31	69	10
50.	Lincoln City FC (Lincoln)	10	4	1	5	23	18	9
51.	Burnley FC (Burnley)	14	3	3	8	17	31	9
52.	Walsall FC (Walsall)	16	3	2	11	22	35	8
53.	Cardiff City AFC (Cardiff)	17	2	3	12	22	47	7
54.	Mansfield Town FC (Mansfield)	10	1	1	8	12	41	3

West Regional League	Pd	Wn	Dw	Ls	GF	GA	Pts
1. Lovell's Athletic FC (Newport)	18	14	2	2	59	21	30
2. Bath City FC (Bath)	18	14	-	4	66	26	28
3. Cardiff City AFC (Cardiff)	18	8	3	7	41	45	19
4. Bristol City FC (Bristol)	17	7	3	7	59	37	17
5. Swansea Town AFC (Swansea)	18	3	1	14	27	77	7
6. Aberaman AFC (Aberaman)	17	2	1	14	29	75	5

1943-44

North Regional (1st Championship)	Pd	Wn	Dw	Ls	GF	GA	Pts
1. Blackpool FC (Blackpool)	18	12	4	2	56	20	28
2. Manchester United FC (Manchester)	18	13	2	3	56	30	28
3. Liverpool FC (Liverpool)	18	13	1	4	72	26	27
4. Doncaster Rovers FC (Doncaster)	18	11	5	2	45	25	27
5. Bradford Park Avenue FC (Bradford)	18	11	4	3	65	28	26
6. Huddersfield Town AFC (Huddersfield)	18	12	2	4	48	25	26
7. Northampton Town FC (Northampton)	18	10	5	3	43	25	25
8. Aston Villa FC (Birmingham)	18	11	3	4	43	27	25
9. Sunderland AFC (Sunderland)	18	10	3	5	46	30	23
10. Hartlepools United FC (Hartlepool)	18	10	3	5	44	31	23
11. Everton FC (Liverpool)	18	9	4	5	60	34	22
12. Blackburn Rovers FC (Blackburn)	18	10	2	6	47	32	22
13. Rochdale AFC (Rochdale)	18	10	2	6	43	41	22
14. Sheffield United FC (Sheffield)	18	8	5	5	30	26	21
15. Lincoln City FC (Lincoln)	18	8	4	6	51	40	20
16. Birmingham FC (Birmingham)	18	8	4	6	38	31	20
17. Manchester City FC (Manchester)	18	9	2	7	38	35	20
18. Mansfield Town FC (Mansfield)	18	9	2	7	32	33	20
19. Derby County FC (Derby)	18	8	4	6	43	45	20
20. Chester FC (Chester)	18	9	2	7	40	43	20
21. Grimsby Town FC (Cleethorpes)	18	8	3	7	32	36	19
22. West Bromwich Albion FC (West Bromwich)	18	8	3	7	42	44	19
23. Gateshead FC (Gateshead)	18	8	2	8	40	51	18
24. Burnley FC (Burnley)	18	5	7	6	24	22	17
25. Walsall FC (Walsall)	18	5	7	6	27	31	17
26. Nottingham Forest FC (Nottingham)	18	6	5	7	33	39	17
27. Leeds United AFC (Leeds)	18	6	5	7	38	50	17
28. Leicester City FC (Leicester)	18	6	4	8	33	30	16
29. Darlington FC (Darlington)	18	6	4	8	49	48	16
30. Rotherham United FC (Rotherham)	18	7	2	9	38	42	16
31. York City FC (York)	18	7	2	9	35	40	16
32. Halifax Town AFC (Halifax)	18	6	4	8	27	36	16
33. Southport FC (Southport)	18	7	2	9	33	51	16
34. Stoke City FC (Stoke-on-Trent)	18	6	3	9	40	35	15
35. Chesterfield FC (Chesterfield)	18	7	1	10	29	31	15
36. Oldham Athletic AFC (Oldham)	18	7	1	10	30	44	15
37. Stockport County FC (Stockport)	18	5	5	8	24	43	15
38. Coventry City FC (Coventry)	18	4	6	8	25	23	14
39. Newcastle United FC (Newcastle-upon-Tyne)	18	5	4	9	32	37	14
40. Sheffield Wednesday FC (Sheffield)	18	5	4	9	29	34	14
41. Middlesbrough FC (Middlesbrough)	18	4	6	8	35	52	14

		Pd	Wn	Dw	Ls	GF	GA	Pts
42.	Wolverhampton Wanderers FC (Wolverhampton)	18	5	3	10	30	42	13
43.	Bury FC (Bury)	18	6	1	11	31	44	13
44.	Barnsley FC (Barnsley)	18	5	2	11	32	42	12
45.	Bradford City AFC (Bradford)	18	4	3	11	27	47	11
46.	Wrexham AFC (Wrexham)	18	5	1	12	43	63	11
47.	Notts County FC (Nottingham)	18	4	3	11	26	53	11
48.	Bolton Wanderers FC (Bolton)	18	5	-	13	24	46	10
49.	Tranmere Rovers FC (Birkenhead)	18	4	1	13	39	71	9
50.	Crewe Alexandra FC (Crewe)	18	4	1	13	29	62	9

London & South League

		Pd	Wn	Dw	Ls	GF	GA	Pts
1.	Tottenham Hotspur FC (London)	30	19	8	3	71	36	46
2.	West Ham United FC (London)	30	17	7	6	74	39	41
3.	Queen's Park Rangers FC (London)	30	14	12	4	69	54	40
4.	Arsenal FC (London)	30	14	10	6	72	42	38
5.	Crystal Palace FC (London)	30	16	5	9	75	53	37
6.	Portsmouth FC (Portsmouth)	30	16	5	9	68	59	37
7.	Brentford FC (London)	30	14	7	9	71	51	35
8.	Chelsea FC (London)	30	16	2	12	79	55	34
9.	Fulham FC (London)	30	11	9	10	80	73	31
10.	Millwall FC (London)	30	13	4	13	70	66	30
11.	Aldershot FC (Aldershot)	30	12	6	12	64	73	30
12.	Reading FC (Reading)	30	12	3	15	73	62	27
13.	Southampton FC (Southampton)	30	10	7	13	67	88	27
14.	Charlton Athletic FC (London)	30	9	7	14	57	73	25
15.	Watford FC (Watford)	30	6	8	16	58	80	20
16.	Brighton & Hove Albion FC (Hove)	30	9	2	19	55	82	20
17.	Luton Town FC (Luton)	30	3	5	22	41	104	11
18.	Clapton Orient FC (London)	30	4	3	23	32	87	11

North Regional (2nd Championship)

		Pd	Wn	Dw	Ls	GF	GA	Pts
1.	Bath City FC (Bath)	21	16	2	3	78	26	34
2.	Wrexham AFC (Wrexham)	21	15	4	2	62	29	34
3.	Liverpool FC (Liverpool)	21	14	2	5	71	38	30
4.	Birmingham FC (Birmingham)	20	12	5	3	47	19	29
5.	Rotherham United FC (Rotherham)	21	12	5	4	54	30	29
6.	Aston Villa FC (Birmingham)	21	13	3	5	50	34	29
7.	Blackpool FC (Blackpool)	20	12	3	5	53	27	27
8.	Cardiff City AFC (Cardiff)	21	13	1	7	53	28	27
9.	Manchester United FC (Manchester)	21	10	7	4	55	38	27
10.	Bradford Park Avenue FC (Bradford)	20	11	4	5	50	30	26
11.	Newcastle United FC (Newcastle-upon-Tyne)	20	13	-	7	47	36	26
12.	Everton FC (Liverpool)	21	12	1	8	73	39	25
13.	Stoke City FC (Stoke-on-Trent)	21	10	5	6	66	45	25
14.	Leicester City FC (Leicester)	21	10	5	6	40	32	25
15.	Darlington FC (Darlington)	21	11	2	8	50	30	24
16.	Nottingham Forest FC (Nottingham)	20	9	6	5	32	20	24
17.	Sheffield United FC (Sheffield)	21	11	2	8	53	35	24
18.	Coventry City FC (Coventry)	21	10	4	7	48	37	24
19.	Manchester City FC (Manchester)	21	9	6	6	42	35	24
20.	Lovell's Athletic FC (Newport)	20	10	2	8	48	30	22
21.	Gateshead FC (Gateshead)	21	9	4	8	45	53	22
22.	Doncaster Rovers FC (Doncaster)	17	9	3	5	42	33	21
23.	Derby County FC (Derby)	21	8	5	8	33	28	21

North Regional (2nd Championship) (cont.)	Pd	Wn	Dw	Ls	GF	GA	Pts
24. Rochdale AFC (Rochdale)	20	8	5	7	40	36	21
25. Barnsley FC (Barnsley)	17	8	4	5	34	30	20
26. Halifax Town AFC (Halifax)	20	8	4	8	44	42	20
27. Chester FC (Chester)	20	9	2	9	65	65	20
28. Hartlepools United FC (Hartlepool)	20	8	4	8	49	50	20
29. Stockport County FC (Stockport)	19	10	-	9	44	49	20
30. Sheffield Wednesday FC (Sheffield)	20	8	4	8	32	36	20
31. Blackburn Rovers FC (Blackburn)	16	8	3	5	30	27	19
32. Huddersfield Town AFC (Huddersfield)	21	8	3	10	41	40	19
33. West Bromwich Albion FC (West Bromwich)	21	5	9	7	46	48	19
34. Bolton Wanderers FC (Bolton)	21	8	3	10	42	49	19
35. Leeds United AFC (Leeds)	18	8	3	7	34	40	19
36. Northampton Town FC (Northampton)	19	9	-	10	37	39	18
37. Burnley FC (Burnley)	18	6	6	6	39	42	18
38. Bristol City FC (Bristol)	20	6	5	9	38	42	17
39. York City FC (York)	20	7	11	2	37	40	16
40. Middlesbrough FC (Middlesbrough)	21	6	4	11	41	51	16
41. Swansea Town AFC (Swansea)	20	7	2	11	42	67	16
42. Grimsby Town FC (Cleethorpes)	15	6	3	6	23	28	15
43. Bury FC (Bury)	20	6	3	11	38	55	15
44. Oldham Athletic AFC (Oldham)	18	5	4	9	28	36	14
45. Sunderland AFC (Sunderland)	19	6	2	11	44	58	14
46. Chesterfield FC (Chesterfield)	19	5	4	10	31	41	14
47. Mansfield Town FC (Mansfield)	14	6	1	7	23	25	13
48. Wolverhampton Wanderers FC (Wolverhampton)	20	3	6	11	28	56	12
49. Walsall FC (Walsall)	17	3	6	8	17	35	12
50. Tranmere Rovers FC (Birkenhead)	20	6	-	14	29	62	12
51. Bradford City AFC (Bradford)	18	4	2	12	27	47	10
52. Southport FC (Southport)	20	3	3	14	35	67	9
53. Lincoln City FC (Lincoln)	18	3	2	13	25	56	8
54. Notts County FC (Nottingham)	20	3	-	17	23	68	6
55. Crewe Alexandra FC (Crewe)	18	2	1	15	31	83	5
56. Aberaman AFC (Aberaman)	18	1	1	16	20	87	3

West Regional League	Pd	Wn	Dw	Ls	GF	GA	Pts
1. Lovell's Athletic FC (Newport)	18	12	6	6	62	30	24
2. Cardiff City AFC (Cardiff)	18	11	1	6	45	28	23
3. Bath City FC (Bath)	18	9	1	8	41	42	19
4. Aberaman AFC (Aberaman)	18	8	2	8	32	35	18
5. Bristol City FC (Bristol)	18	8	1	9	32	36	17
6. Swansea Town AFC (Swansea)	18	3	1	14	25	66	7

1944-45

North Regional (1st Championship)	Pd	Wn	Dw	Ls	GF	GA	Pts
1. Huddersfield Town AFC (Huddersfield)	18	14	3	1	50	22	31
2. Derby County FC (Derby)	18	14	1	3	54	19	29
3. Sunderland AFC (Sunderland)	18	12	4	2	52	25	28
4. Aston Villa FC (Birmingham)	18	12	3	3	54	19	27
5. Everton FC (Liverpool)	18	12	2	4	58	25	26
6. Wrexham AFC (Wrexham)	18	11	3	4	40	18	25
7. Doncaster Rovers FC (Doncaster)	18	12	-	6	48	27	24
8. Bradford Park Avenue FC (Bradford)	18	10	4	4	45	31	24

North Regional (1st Championship) (cont.)

		Pd	Wn	Dw	Ls	GF	GA	Pts	
9.	Bolton Wanderers FC (Bolton)	18	9	6	3	34	22	24	
10.	Manchester City FC (Manchester)	18	9	4	5	53	31	22	
11.	Stoke City FC (Stoke-on-Trent)	18	9	4	5	37	25	22	
12.	Birmingham FC (Birmingham)	18	8	4	6	30	21	22	*
13.	Barnsley FC (Barnsley)	18	10	2	6	42	32	22	
14.	Rotherham United FC (Rotherham)	18	9	4	5	31	25	22	
15.	West Bromwich Albion FC (West Bromwich)	18	9	4	5	36	30	22	
16.	Liverpool FC (Liverpool)	18	9	3	6	41	30	21	
17.	Grimsby Town FC (Cleethorpes)	18	9	3	6	37	29	21	
18.	Halifax Town AFC (Halifax)	18	8	5	5	30	29	21	
19.	Chester FC (Chester)	18	9	3	6	45	45	21	
20.	Blackpool FC (Blackpool)	18	9	2	7	53	38	20	
21.	Burnley FC (Burnley)	18	8	4	6	39	27	20	
22.	Leeds United AFC (Leeds)	18	9	2	7	53	42	20	
23.	Sheffield Wednesday FC (Sheffield)	18	9	2	7	34	30	20	
24.	Chesterfield FC (Chesterfield)	18	8	3	7	30	19	19	
25.	Darlington FC (Darlington)	18	9	1	8	52	45	19	
26.	Wolverhampton Wanderers FC (Wolverhampton)	18	7	5	6	31	27	19	
27.	Rochdale AFC (Rochdale)	18	7	5	6	35	33	19	
28.	Crewe Alexandra FC (Crewe)	18	9	1	8	43	41	19	
29.	Blackburn Rovers FC (Blackburn)	18	7	4	7	30	29	18	
30.	Manchester United FC (Manchester)	18	8	2	8	40	40	18	
31.	Preston North End FC (Preston)	18	7	4	7	26	28	18	
32.	Walsall FC (Walsall)	18	5	6	7	27	29	16	
33.	Gateshead FC (Gateshead)	18	7	2	9	45	53	16	
34.	Northampton Town FC (Northampton)	18	5	6	7	30	38	16	
35.	Newcastle United FC (Newcastle-upon-Tyne)	18	7	1	10	51	38	15	
36.	Sheffield United FC (Sheffield)	18	6	3	9	27	25	15	
37.	Hartlepools United FC (Hartlepool)	18	7	1	10	41	47	15	
38.	Oldham Athletic AFC (Oldham)	18	7	1	10	28	36	15	
39.	Mansfield Town FC (Mansfield)	18	6	3	9	31	40	15	
40.	Nottingham Forest FC (Nottingham)	18	5	5	8	22	34	15	
41.	Coventry City FC (Coventry)	18	6	2	10	23	42	14	
42.	York City FC (York)	18	6	1	11	49	52	13	
43.	Middlesbrough FC (Middlesbrough)	18	5	3	10	34	57	13	
44.	Bradford City AFC (Bradford)	18	6	1	11	35	60	13	
45.	Accrington Stanley FC (Accrington)	18	5	2	11	29	46	12	
46.	Port Vale FC (Stoke-on-Trent)	18	5	2	11	22	36	12	
47.	Bury FC (Bury)	18	5	2	11	28	48	12	
48.	Stockport County FC (Stockport)	18	5	1	12	33	70	11	
49.	Hull City AFC (Kingston-upon-Hull)	18	4	3	11	23	60	11	
50.	Southport FC (Southport)	18	3	4	11	32	55	10	
51.	Lincoln City FC (Lincoln)	18	4	2	14	32	56	10	
52.	Leicester City FC (Leicester)	18	3	4	11	23	46	10	
53.	Tranmere Rovers FC (Birkenhead)	18	2	1	15	20	53	5	
54.	Notts County FC (Nottingham)	18	2	1	15	19	62	5	

West Regional League

		Pd	Wn	Dw	Ls	GF	GA	Pts
1.	Cardiff City AFC (Cardiff)	18	12	3	3	54	24	27
2.	Bristol City FC (Bristol)	18	13	1	4	59	30	27
3.	Lovell's Athletic FC (Newport)	18	10	3	5	40	31	23
4.	Bath City FC (Bath)	18	8	3	7	47	46	19
5.	Aberaman AFC (Aberaman)	18	3	1	14	34	71	7
6.	Swansea Town AFC (Swansea)	18	2	1	15	32	63	5

* Birmingham FC (Birmingham) changed their club name to Birmingham City FC from the next season.

North Regional (2nd Championship)	Pd	Wn	Dw	Ls	GF	GA	Pts	
1. Derby County FC (Derby)	26	19	3	4	78	28	41	
2. Everton FC (Liverpool)	27	17	3	7	79	43	37	
3. Liverpool FC (Liverpool)	24	16	3	5	67	26	35	
4. Burnley FC (Burnley)	26	15	3	8	56	36	33	
5. Newcastle United FC (Newcastle-upon-Tyne)	23	15	1	7	71	38	31	
6. Aston Villa FC (Birmingham)	25	14	2	9	70	45	30	
7. Chesterfield FC (Chesterfield)	24	10	9	5	40	24	29	
8. Wolverhampton Wanderers FC (Wolverhampton)	24	11	7	6	45	31	29	
9. Manchester United FC (Manchester)	22	13	3	6	47	33	29	
10. Darlington FC (Darlington)	24	13	3	8	61	45	29	
11. Bristol City FC (Bristol)	22	13	7	2	55	33	28	
12. Blackburn Rovers FC (Blackburn)	24	13	2	9	62	51	28	
13. Huddersfield Town AFC (Huddersfield)	27	12	4	11	52	49	28	
14. Wrexham AFC (Wrexham)	22	10	7	5	55	36	27	
15. Bolton Wanderers FC (Bolton)	23	11	5	7	52	35	27	
16. Blackpool FC (Blackpool)	24	12	3	9	58	42	27	
17. Stoke City FC (Stoke-on-Trent)	23	12	2	9	67	42	26	
18. Lovell's Athletic FC (Newport)	19	12	2	5	44	27	26	
19. Cardiff City AFC (Cardiff)	20	12	2	6	41	27	26	
20. Grimsby Town FC (Cleethorpes)	21	10	6	5	51	37	26	
21. Birmingham FC (Birmingham)	24	9	7	8	38	34	25	*
22. Crewe Alexandra FC (Crewe)	23	11	3	9	50	50	25	
23. Doncaster Rovers FC (Doncaster)	20	11	2	7	44	26	24	
24. Bradford Park Avenue FC (Bradford)	22	10	4	8	49	39	24	
25. Accrington Stanley FC (Accrington)	24	9	6	9	39	41	24	
26. Barnsley FC (Barnsley)	24	11	2	11	39	42	24	
27. Rotherham United FC (Rotherham)	20	10	3	7	41	37	23	
28. Gateshead FC (Gateshead)	21	9	5	7	46	42	23	
29. Preston North End FC (Preston)	25	9	4	12	41	56	22	
30. Sheffield United FC (Sheffield)	24	9	3	12	56	48	21	
31. Sunderland AFC (Sunderland)	25	9	3	13	53	54	21	
32. Leeds United AFC (Leeds)	22	9	3	10	53	55	21	
33. Sheffield Wednesday FC (Sheffield)	25	8	5	12	53	56	21	
34. Leicester City FC (Leicester)	21	7	6	8	40	38	20	
35. Bath City FC (Bath)	20	10	-	10	50	48	20	
36. Bury FC (Bury)	20	8	4	8	38	43	20	
37. York City FC (York)	22	8	4	10	48	56	20	
38. Chester FC (Chester)	22	9	2	11	49	61	20	
39. Bradford City AFC (Bradford)	20	8	3	9	43	46	19	
40. West Bromwich Albion FC (West Bromwich)	22	6	7	9	39	44	19	
41. Hartlepools United FC (Hartlepool)	21	8	3	10	34	54	19	
42. Coventry City FC (Coventry)	21	6	6	9	36	53	18	
43. Nottingham Forest FC (Nottingham)	17	5	7	5	23	25	17	
44. Tranmere Rovers FC (Birkenhead)	23	8	1	14	40	56	17	
45. Halifax Town AFC (Halifax)	18	6	5	7	22	35	17	
46. Lincoln City FC (Lincoln)	17	6	4	7	42	51	16	
47. Manchester City FC (Manchester)	19	7	2	10	32	43	16	
48. Northampton Town FC (Northampton)	14	6	3	5	23	30	15	
49. Oldham Athletic AFC (Oldham)	21	7	1	13	39	56	15	
50. Stockport County FC (Stockport)	19	7	-	12	31	50	14	
51. Middlesbrough FC (Middlesbrough)	24	6	2	16	40	73	14	
52. Walsall FC (Walsall)	18	5	3	10	24	33	13	
53. Swansea Town AFC (Swansea)	20	6	1	13	42	63	13	
54. Port Vale FC (Stoke-on-Trent)	21	5	2	14	27	60	12	
55. Mansfield Town FC (Mansfield)	12	5	6	1	22	38	11	
56. Hull City AFC (Kingston-upon-Hull)	18	5	1	12	30	54	11	

North Regional (2nd Championship) (cont.)	Pd	Wn	Dw	Ls	GF	GA	Pts
57. Rochdale AFC (Rochdale)	20	4	3	13	17	49	11
58. Southport FC (Southport)	22	3	3	16	33	82	9
59. Notts County FC (Nottingham)	21	4	-	17	29	62	8
60. Aberaman AFC (Aberaman)	17	2	2	13	36	69	6

London & South League	Pd	Wn	Dw	Ls	GF	GA	Pts
1. Tottenham Hotspur FC (London)	30	23	6	1	81	30	52
2. West Ham United FC (London)	30	22	3	5	96	47	47
3. Brentford FC (London)	30	17	4	9	87	57	38
4. Chelsea FC (London)	30	16	5	9	100	55	37
5. Southampton FC (Southampton)	30	17	3	10	96	69	37
6. Crystal Palace FC (London)	30	15	5	10	74	70	35
7. Reading FC (Reading)	30	14	6	10	78	68	34
8. Arsenal FC (London)	30	14	3	13	77	67	31
9. Queen's Park Rangers FC (London)	30	10	10	10	70	61	30
10. Watford FC (Watford)	30	11	6	13	66	84	28
11. Fulham FC (London)	30	11	4	15	79	83	26
12. Portsmouth FC (Portsmouth)	30	11	4	15	56	61	26
13. Charlton Athletic FC (London)	30	12	2	16	72	81	26
14. Brighton & Hove Albion FC (Hove)	30	10	2	18	66	95	22
15. Luton Town FC (Luton)	30	6	7	17	56	104	19
16. Aldershot FC (Aldershot)	30	7	4	19	44	85	18
17. Millwall FC (London)	30	5	7	18	50	84	17
18. Clapton Orient FC (London)	30	5	7	18	39	86	17

1945-46

North League	Pd	Wn	Dw	Ls	GF	GA	Pts
1. Sheffield United FC (Sheffield)	42	27	6	9	112	62	60
2. Everton FC (Liverpool)	42	23	9	10	88	54	55
3. Bolton Wanderers FC (Bolton)	42	20	11	11	67	45	51
4. Manchester United FC (Manchester)	42	19	11	12	98	62	49
5. Sheffield Wednesday FC (Sheffield)	42	20	8	14	67	60	48
6. Newcastle United FC (Newcastle-upon-Tyne)	42	21	5	16	106	70	47
7. Chesterfield FC (Chesterfield)	42	17	12	13	68	49	46
8. Barnsley FC (Barnsley)	42	17	11	14	76	68	45
9. Blackpool FC (Blackpool)	42	18	9	15	94	92	45
10. Manchester City FC (Manchester)	42	20	4	18	78	75	44
11. Liverpool FC (Liverpool)	42	17	9	16	80	70	43
12. Middlesbrough FC (Middlesbrough)	42	17	9	16	75	87	43
13. Stoke City FC (Stoke-on-Trent)	42	18	6	18	88	79	42
14. Bradford Park Avenue FC (Bradford)	42	17	6	19	71	84	40
15. Huddersfield Town AFC (Huddersfield)	42	17	4	21	90	89	38
16. Burnley FC (Burnley)	42	13	10	19	63	84	36
17. Grimsby Town FC (Cleethorpes)	42	13	9	20	61	89	35
18. Sunderland AFC (Sunderland)	42	15	5	22	55	83	35
19. Preston North End FC (Preston)	42	14	6	22	70	77	34
20. Bury FC (Bury)	42	12	10	20	60	85	34
21. Blackburn Rovers FC (Blackburn)	42	11	7	24	60	111	29
22. Leeds United AFC (Leeds)	42	9	7	26	66	118	25
	924	375	174	375	1693	1693	924

Division 3 (North – East Region)

		Pd	Wn	Dw	Ls	GF	GA	Pts
1.	Rotherham United FC (Rotherham)	18	12	2	4	56	28	26
2.	Darlington FC (Darlington)	18	12	2	4	61	36	26
3.	Gateshead FC (Gateshead)	18	11	2	5	51	34	24
4.	Doncaster Rovers FC (Doncaster)	18	8	4	6	34	35	20
5.	York City FC (York)	18	6	6	6	34	34	18
6.	Halifax Town AFC (Halifax)	18	7	4	7	39	46	18
7.	Bradford City AFC (Bradford)	18	6	4	8	45	40	16
8.	Carlisle United FC (Carlisle)	18	5	3	10	34	58	13
9.	Lincoln City FC (Lincoln)	18	4	2	12	34	54	10
10.	Hartlepools United FC (Hartlepool)	18	3	3	12	22	45	9
		180	74	32	74	410	410	180

Division 3 (North – West Region)

		Pd	Wn	Dw	Ls	GF	GA	Pts
1.	Accrington Stanley FC (Accrington)	18	10	4	4	37	19	24
2.	Rochdale AFC (Rochdale)	18	10	2	6	43	35	22
3.	Crewe Alexandra FC (Crewe)	18	9	3	6	43	31	21
4.	Chester FC (Chester)	18	8	5	5	44	38	21
5.	Wrexham AFC (Wrexham)	18	8	4	6	30	25	20
6.	Tranmere Rovers FC (Birkenhead)	18	9	2	7	33	31	20
7.	Stockport County FC (Stockport)	18	6	3	9	38	38	15
8.	Oldham Athletic AFC (Oldham)	18	5	5	8	29	32	15
9.	Barrow AFC (Barrow-in-Furness)	18	4	4	10	21	44	12
10.	Southport FC (Southport)	18	3	4	11	22	47	10
		180	72	36	72	340	340	180

South League

		Pd	Wn	Dw	Ls	GF	GA	Pts
1.	Birmingham City FC (Birmingham)	42	28	5	9	96	45	61
2.	Aston Villa FC (Birmingham)	42	25	11	6	106	58	61
3.	Charlton Athletic FC (London)	42	25	10	7	92	45	60
4.	Derby County FC (Derby)	42	24	7	11	101	62	55
5.	West Bromwich Albion FC (West Bromwich)	42	22	8	12	104	69	52
6.	Wolverhampton Wanderers FC (Wolverhampton)	42	20	11	11	75	48	51
7.	West Ham United FC (London)	42	20	11	11	94	76	51
8.	Fulham FC (London)	42	20	10	12	93	73	50
9.	Tottenham Hotspur FC (London)	42	22	3	17	78	81	47
10.	Chelsea FC (London)	42	19	6	17	92	80	44
11.	Arsenal FC (London)	42	16	11	15	76	73	43
12.	Millwall FC (London)	42	17	8	17	79	105	42
13.	Coventry City FC (Coventry)	42	15	10	17	70	69	40
14.	Brentford FC (London)	42	14	10	18	82	72	38
15.	Nottingham Forest FC (Nottingham)	42	12	13	17	72	73	37
16.	Southampton FC (Southampton)	42	14	9	19	97	105	37
17.	Swansea Town AFC (Swansea)	42	15	7	20	90	112	37
18.	Luton Town FC (Luton)	42	13	7	22	60	92	33
19.	Portsmouth FC (Portsmouth)	42	11	6	25	66	87	28
20.	Leicester City FC (Leicester)	42	8	7	27	57	101	23
21.	Newport County AFC (Newport)	42	9	2	31	52	125	20
22.	Plymouth Argyle FC (Plymouth)	42	3	8	31	39	120	14
		924	372	180	372	1771	1771	924

Division 3 (South – North Region)	Pd	Wn	Dw	Ls	GF	GA	Pts	
1. Queen's Park Rangers FC (London)	20	14	4	2	50	15	32	
2. Norwich City FC (Norwich)	20	11	4	5	54	31	26	
3. Port Vale FC (Stoke-on-Trent)	20	9	6	5	34	25	24	
4. Watford FC (Watford)	20	10	2	8	42	47	22	
5. Ipswich Town FC (Ipswich)	20	8	4	8	33	36	20	
6. Notts County FC (Nottingham)	20	8	4	8	39	47	20	
7. Northampton Town FC (Northampton)	20	8	3	9	37	34	19	
8. Clapton Orient FC (London)	20	5	6	9	28	42	16	*
9. Walsall FC (Walsall)	20	6	3	11	31	42	15	
10. Southend United FC (Southend-on-Sea)	20	5	5	10	33	49	15	
11. Mansfield Town FC (Mansfield)	20	3	5	12	29	42	11	
	220	87	46	87	410	410	220	

Division 3 (South – South Region)	Pd	Wn	Dw	Ls	GF	GA	Pts
1. Crystal Palace FC (London)	20	13	3	4	55	31	29
2. Cardiff City AFC (Cardiff)	20	13	2	5	69	31	28
3. Bristol City FC (Bristol)	20	11	2	7	51	40	24
4. Brighton & Hove Albion FC (Hove)	20	10	1	9	49	50	21
5. Bristol Rovers FC (Bristol)	20	7	6	7	44	44	20
6. Swindon Town FC (Swindon)	20	8	3	9	35	47	19
7. Bournemouth & Boscombe Athletic FC (Bournemouth)	20	7	3	10	52	50	17
8. Aldershot FC (Aldershot)	20	6	5	9	38	56	17
9. Exeter City FC (Exeter)	20	6	4	10	33	41	16
10. Reading FC (Reading)	20	5	5	10	43	49	15
11. Torquay United FC (Torquay)	20	5	4	11	22	52	14
	220	91	38	91	491	491	220

* Clapton Orient FC (London) changed their club name to Leyton Orient FC (London) from the next season.

F.A. CUP FINAL   (Wembley Stadium, London – 27/04/1946 – 98,215)

DERBY COUNTY FC (DERBY)   4-1   Charlton Athletic FC (London)

H.Turner o.g., Doherty, Stamps 2   *H.Turner*

Derby: Woodley, Nicholas, Howe, Bullions, Leuty, Musson, Harrison, Carter, Stamps, Doherty, Duncan.

Charlton: Bartram, Phipps, Shreeve, H.Turner, Oakes, Johnson, Fell, Brown, AA Turner, Welsh, Duffy.

Semi-finals

Bolton Wanderers FC (Bolton)	0-2	Charlton Athletic FC (London)
Derby County FC (Derby)	1-1, 4-0	Birmingham City FC (Birmingham)

Quarter-finals

Aston Villa FC (Birmingham)	3-4, 1-1	Derby County FC (Derby)
Bradford Park Avenue FC (Bradford)	2-2, 0-6	Birmingham City FC (Birmingham)
Charlton Athletic FC (London)	6-3, 3-1	Brentford FC (London)
Stoke City FC (Stoke-on-Trent)	0-2, 0-0	Bolton Wanderers FC (Bolton)

Football League Division 1 1946-1947 Season	Arsenal	Aston Villa	Blackburn Rovers	Blackpool	Bolton Wanderers	Brentford	Charlton Athletic	Chelsea	Derby County	Everton	Grimsby Town	Huddersfield Town	Leeds United	Liverpool	Manchester United	Middlesbrough	Portsmouth	Preston North End	Sheffield United	Stoke City	Sunderland	Wolves
Arsenal FC	■	0-2	1-3	1-1	2-2	2-2	1-0	1-2	0-1	2-1	5-3	1-2	4-2	1-2	6-2	4-0	21	4-1	2-3	1-0	2-2	1-1
Aston Villa FC	0-2	■	2-1	1-1	1-1	5-2	4-0	2-0	2-0	0-1	3-3	2-2	2-1	1-2	0-0	0-1	1-1	4-2	2-3	0-1	4-0	3-0
Blackburn Rovers FC	1-2	0-1	■	1-1	2-1	0-3	1-0	1-2	1-1	4-1	1-1	2-2	1-0	0-0	2-1	1-2	0-1	1-2	2-0	0-2	1-2	1-2
Blackpool FC	2-1	1-0	1-0	■	0-1	4-2	0-0	1-0	2-1	0-3	2-3	2-1	3-0	3-2	3-1	0-5	4-3	4-0	4-2	0-2	0-5	2-0
Bolton Wanderers FC	1-3	2-1	0-0	1-1	■	1-0	0-1	1-1	5-1	0-2	1-2	4-0	2-0	1-3	2-2	1-1	1-0	1-2	3-2	3-2	0-1	0-3
Brentford FC	0-1	0-2	0-3	2-1	1-0	■	1-4	0-2	0-3	1-1	0-1	2-0	1-1	1-1	0-0	0-0	1-3	2-3	2-1	1-4	0-3	4-1
Charlton Athletic FC	2-2	1-1	0-2	0-1	2-0	3-0	■	2-3	2-4	4-1	0-0	0-3	5-0	1-3	1-3	3-3	0-0	0-0	1-2	1-0	5-0	1-4
Chelsea FC	2-1	1-3	0-2	1-4	4-3	3-2	2-2	■	3-0	1-1	0-0	1-0	3-0	3-1	0-3	0-3	1-2	1-4	2-5	2-1	1-2
Derby County FC	0-1	1-2	2-1	1-2	1-3	2-1	1-0	3-1	■	5-1	4-1	1-0	2-1	1-4	4-3	1-1	2-0	2-2	1-2	3-0	5-1	2-1
Everton FC	3-2	2-0	1-0	1-1	2-1	0-2	1-1	2-0	4-1	■	3-3	1-0	4-1	1-0	2-2	2-1	1-0	2-0	2-3	2-2	4-2	0-2
Grimsby Town FC	0-0	0-3	2-1	2-3	2-2	2-2	3-1	2-1	2-0	2-2	■	1-0	4-1	1-6	0-0	4-0	3-2	2-3	2-1	2-5	1-2	
Huddersfield Town AFC	0-0	1-0	0-1	1-3	1-0	3-0	5-1	1-4	5-2	1-0	3-2	■	1-0	1-4	2-2	3-1	1-2	3-0	1-1	1-0	0-0	0-1
Leeds United AFC	1-1	1-1	0-1	4-2	4-0	1-2	0-2	2-1	1-2	2-1	1-0	5-0	■	1-2	0-2	3-3	0-1	0-3	2-2	1-2	1-1	0-1
Liverpool FC	4-2	4-1	2-1	2-3	0-3	1-0	1-1	7-4	1-1	0-0	5-0	1-0	2-0	■	1-0	0-1	3-0	3-0	1-2	2-0	1-0	1-5
Manchester United FC	5-2	2-1	4-0	3-0	1-0	4-1	4-1	1-1	4-1	3-0	2-1	5-2	3-1	5-0	■	1-0	3-0	1-1	6-2	1-1	0-3	3-1
Middlesbrough FC	2-0	1-2	0-1	1-2	3-1	2-0	1-2	3-2	1-0	4-0	3-0	4-1	3-0	2-2	2-4	■	3-3	2-0	2-4	5-4	1-3	1-1
Portsmouth FC	0-2	3-2	3-1	0-1	2-0	3-0	3-0	0-2	1-2	2-1	4-1	3-1	4-1	1-2	0-1	3-1	■	4-4	0-0	1-3	4-1	1-1
Preston North End FC	2-0	3-1	4-0	2-0	0-4	5-2	5-1	1-1	1-1	2-1	3-0	6-2	3-2	0-0	1-1	0-1	1-1	■	1-2	1-3	2-2	2-2
Sheffield United FC	2-1	1-2	0-1	4-2	4-2	6-1	1-3	2-2	3-2	2-0	1-1	2-2	6-2	0-1	2-2	3-1	2-3		■	2-1	4-2	2-0
Stoke City FC	3-1	0-0	0-0	4-1	1-2	3-1	2-2	6-1	3-2	2-1	3-0	3-0	5-2	2-1	3-2	3-1	1-1	5-0	3-0	■	0-0	0-3
Sunderland AFC	1-4	4-1	1-0	3-2	3-1	2-1	1-1	1-2	3-2	4-1	1-2	3-0	1-0	1-4	1-1	1-0	0-0	0-2	2-1	0-1	■	0-1
Wolverhampton Wanderers FC	6-1	1-2	3-3	3-1	5-0	1-2	2-0	6-4	7-2	2-3	2-0	6-1	1-0	1-2	3-2	2-4	3-1	4-1	3-1	3-0	2-1	■

	Division 1	Pd	Wn	Dw	Ls	GF	GA	Pts	
1.	LIVERPOOL FC (LIVERPOOL)	42	25	7	10	84	52	57	
2.	Manchester United FC (Manchester)	42	22	12	8	95	54	56	
3.	Wolverhampton Wanderers FC (Wolverhampton)	42	25	6	11	98	56	56	
4.	Stoke City FC (Stoke-on-Trent)	42	24	7	11	90	53	55	
5.	Blackpool FC (Blackpool)	42	22	6	14	71	70	50	
6.	Sheffield United FC (Sheffield)	42	21	7	14	89	75	49	
7.	Preston North End FC (Preston)	42	18	11	13	76	74	47	
8.	Aston Villa FC (Birmingham)	42	18	9	15	67	53	45	
9.	Sunderland AFC (Sunderland)	42	18	8	16	65	66	44	
10.	Everton FC (Liverpool)	42	17	9	16	62	67	43	
11.	Middlesbrough FC (Middlesbrough)	42	17	8	17	73	68	42	
12.	Portsmouth FC (Portsmouth)	42	16	9	17	66	60	41	
13.	Arsenal FC (London)	42	16	9	17	72	70	41	
14.	Derby County FC (Derby)	42	18	5	19	73	79	41	
15.	Chelsea FC (London)	42	16	7	19	69	84	39	
16.	Grimsby Town FC (Cleethorpes)	42	13	12	17	61	82	38	
17.	Blackburn Rovers FC (Blackburn)	42	14	8	20	45	53	36	
18.	Bolton Wanderers FC (Bolton)	42	13	8	21	57	69	34	
19.	Charlton Athletic FC (London)	42	11	12	19	57	71	34	
20.	Huddersfield Town AFC (Huddersfield)	42	13	7	22	53	79	33	
21.	Brentford FC (London)	42	9	7	26	45	88	25	R
22.	Leeds United AFC (Leeds)	42	6	6	30	45	90	18	R
		924	372	180	372	1513	1513	924	

Top Goalscorer

1)   Dennis WESTCOTT   (Wolverhampton Wanderers FC)   37

Football League Division 2 — 1946-1947 Season

	Barnsley	Birmingham City	Bradford P.A.	Burnley	Bury	Chesterfield	Coventry City	Fulham	Leicester City	Luton Town	Manchester City	Millwall	Newcastle United	Newport County	Nottingham F.	Plymouth Argyle	Sheffield Wed.	Southampton	Swansea Town	Tottenham H.	W.B.A.	West Ham United
Barnsley FC	■	3-1	3-1	1-0	4-0	1-2	0-2	4-1	1-0	4-0	0-2	4-1	1-1	3-1	3-2	1-3	4-1	4-4	3-1	1-3	2-1	1-2
Birmingham City FC	1-2	■	4-0	0-2	3-0	0-0	2-0	2-1	4-0	1-0	3-1	4-0	2-0	1-1	4-0	6-1	3-1	3-1	3-1	1-0	1-0	3-0
Bradford Park Avenue	1-3	2-0	■	0-1	2-2	0-0	5-1	1-2	1-2	2-1	1-1	0-0	2-1	2-1	0-1	3-2	1-1	2-3	0-0	2-1	2-4	0-1
Burnley FC	2-2	1-0	1-2	■	1-1	1-1	1-1	2-0	0-0	1-1	0-0	3-0	3-0	3-2	3-0	2-1	2-0	1-0	1-0	0-0	0-2	2-1
Bury FC	4-4	2-0	6-3	2-2	■	0-2	1-0	7-2	2-3	3-0	2-2	5-2	2-2	0-1	5-0	3-3	4-2	2-1	3-3	1-2	4-0	4-0
Chesterfield FC	2-1	0-1	1-1	0-0	3-1	■	2-1	1-1	2-0	2-1	0-1	2-3	1-0	2-0	1-1	4-1	4-2	5-0	1-0	0-0	1-1	3-1
Coventry City FC	1-1	0-0	0-0	0-3	3-1	1-1	■	1-0	2-1	0-1	4-0	1-1	6-0	1-1	1-0	5-1	2-3	3-2	3-1	3-2	1-1	1-2
Fulham FC	6-1	0-1	0-3	1-0	2-0	2-1	2-0	■	4-2	2-1	2-2	3-2	0-3	4-1	1-1	3-1	1-2	0-0	3-0	1-1	0-1	3-2
Leicester City FC	6-0	2-1	2-1	1-4	0-0	0-1	1-0	2-0	■	2-1	0-3	5-0	2-4	3-0	1-1	4-1	3-5	2-0	0-1	1-1	1-1	4-0
Luton Town FC	3-1	1-3	3-0	1-3	2-0	1-1	1-1	2-0	1-2	■	0-0	3-0	4-3	6-3	3-2	3-4	4-1	2-2	3-0	3-2	2-0	2-1
Manchester City FC	5-1	1-0	7-2	1-0	3-1	0-0	4-0	1-0	2-0	2-0	■	1-0	0-2	5-1	4-3	2-1	1-1	1-1	1-1	5-0	2-0	2-0
Millwall FC	3-1	0-2	0-1	1-1	1-0	1-1	3-5	1-1	1-0	2-0	1-3	■	1-4	3-1	4-0	1-1	2-2	3-1	1-1	0-3	1-2	1-2
Newcastle United FC	4-2	2-2	5-0	1-2	1-1	2-1	3-1	1-3	1-1	7-2	3-2	0-2	■	13-0	3-0	3-2	4-0	1-3	1-1	1-1	0-2	2-3
Newport County AFC	2-1	0-3	1-3	0-3	2-0	3-0	4-2	4-2	2-3	1-3	0-3	3-1	4-2	■	2-5	1-0	4-3	1-2	2-4	2-4	2-7	1-1
Nottingham Forest FC	2-1	1-1	4-0	1-0	2-0	1-0	1-0	2-1	2-0	4-2	0-1	1-2	0-2	6-1	■	5-1	2-2	6-0	1-1	1-1	1-1	4-3
Plymouth Argyle FC	3-2	0-2	2-4	2-2	3-1	1-0	2-2	2-2	4-0	2-1	2-3	0-2	0-1	4-1	2-0	■	4-1	2-3	2-1	3-4	2-1	3-1
Sheffield Wednesday FC	2-4	1-0	1-2	1-2	2-5	0-1	4-2	1-1	1-3	1-1	3-0	1-1	2-1	2-1	2-1	2-1	■	3-0	3-0	5-1	2-2	1-1
Southampton FC	1-1	0-0	3-2	0-1	1-1	1-1	5-2	2-0	0-1	1-1	1-2	1-1	5-1	5-2	5-1	3-1	3-1	■	4-0	1-0	0-1	4-2
Swansea Town AFC	2-2	1-0	1-6	0-2	1-0	1-2	2-3	0-2	3-4	2-0	1-0	0-3	1-2	5-1	3-2	3-1	2-0	4-2	■	0-2	2-3	2-1
Tottenham Hotspur FC	1-1	1-2	3-3	1-1	2-1	3-4	1-1	1-2	1-1	1-1	0-0	2-1	1-3	2-0	2-1	2-1	3-1	2-1	3-1	■	2-0	0-0
West Bromwich Albion FC	2-5	3-0	1-1	1-1	3-0	3-2	1-1	6-1	4-2	1-2	31	2-4	3-2	2-2	5-1	2-5	1-2	2-0	2-1	3-2	■	2-3
West Ham United FC	4-0	0-4	1-1	0-5	3-3	5-0	1-2	3-2	0-2	2-1	1-0	3-1	0-2	3-0	2-2	4-1	2-1	4-0	3-0	2-2	3-2	■

Division 2

		Pd	Wn	Dw	Ls	GF	GA	Pts	
1.	Manchester City FC (Manchester)	42	26	10	6	78	35	62	P
2.	Burnley FC (Burnley)	42	22	14	6	65	29	58	P
3.	Birmingham City FC (Birmingham)	42	25	5	12	74	33	55	
4.	Chesterfield FC (Chesterfield)	42	18	14	10	58	44	50	
5.	Newcastle United FC (Newcastle-upon-Tyne)	42	19	10	13	95	62	48	
6.	Tottenham Hotspur FC (London)	42	17	14	11	65	53	48	
7.	West Bromwich Albion FC (West Bromwich)	42	20	8	14	88	75	48	
8.	Coventry City FC (Coventry)	42	16	13	13	66	59	45	
9.	Leicester City FC (Leicester)	42	18	7	17	69	64	43	
10.	Barnsley FC (Barnsley)	42	17	8	17	84	86	42	
11.	Nottingham Forest FC (Nottingham)	42	15	10	17	69	74	40	
12.	West Ham United FC (London)	42	16	8	18	70	76	40	
13.	Luton Town FC (Luton)	42	16	7	19	71	73	39	
14.	Southampton FC (Southampton)	42	15	9	18	69	76	39	
15.	Fulham FC (London)	42	15	9	18	63	74	39	
16.	Bradford Park Avenue FC (Bradford)	42	14	11	17	65	77	39	
17.	Bury FC (Bury)	42	12	12	18	80	78	36	
18.	Millwall FC (London)	42	14	8	20	56	79	36	
19.	Plymouth Argyle FC (Plymouth)	42	14	5	23	79	96	33	
20.	Sheffield Wednesday FC (Sheffield)	42	12	8	22	67	88	32	
21.	Swansea Town AFC (Swansea)	42	11	7	24	55	83	29	R
22.	Newport County AFC (Newport)	42	10	3	29	61	133	23	R
		924	362	200	362	1547	1547	924	

Football League Division 3 (N) 1946-1947 Season	Accrington Stanley	Barrow	Bradford City	Carlisle United	Chester	Crewe Alexandra	Darlington	Doncaster Rovers	Gateshead	Halifax Town	Hartlepools United	Hull City	Lincoln City	New Brighton	Oldham Athletic	Rochdale	Rotherham United	Southport	Stockport County	Tranmere	Wrexham	York City
Accrington Stanley FC		1-3	0-0	4-3	1-4	2-3	3-0	0-1	0-3	1-1	2-1	0-0	8-4	3-1	2-3	2-3	2-3	1-0	2-1	2-1	0-1	1-2
Barrow AFC	1-3		0-0	3-1	1-0	0-2	2-3	0-1	1-0	3-0	2-0	1-0	1-3	0-1	5-2	2-2	2-3	2-1	1-0	0-1	1-0	0-1
Bradford City AFC	3-1	5-0		2-2	0-0	1-0	2-0	0-1	2-2	3-1	1-2	1-1	3-0	2-1	1-0	0-1	2-0	5-1	0-2	2-2	2-1	3-2
Carlisle United FC	4-2	4-1	4-3		3-2	3-3	1-5	2-3	3-1	1-0	5-1	0-2	1-0	3-2	1-2	1-3	1-1	1-1	1-1	4-2	1-1	1-2
Chester FC	3-1	3-0	3-0	4-0		2-0	1-1	1-3	0-1	2-0	2-1	5-1	3-0	2-1	2-0	1-0	2-2	2-1	3-0	4-1	2-0	6-0
Crewe Alexandra FC	5-0	0-1	2-2	2-0	0-2		3-2	0-3	1-1	2-1	1-1	2-0	0-5	3-0	2-2	1-2	2-0	3-2	4-3	1-0	2-0	
Darlington FC	5-0	0-1	0-1	2-1	3-3	4-0		1-1	2-0	0-1	0-2	4-3	4-0	1-1	4-1	4-3	4-2	1-2	1-2	1-1	1-1	3-1
Doncaster Rovers FC	5-0	8-0	4-3	9-2	3-0	1-1	5-0		3-0	2-0	5-1	4-1	1-1	0-0	4-2	2-1	1-1	2-0	1-3	2-0	5-0	0-0
Gateshead FC	2-1	0-5	1-2	1-3	3-4	2-1	1-0	1-3		6-1	0-1	1-0	3-0	3-0	1-1	2-2	2-2	1-2	3-1	3-3	1-2	
Halifax Town AFC	2-1	3-2	1-2	0-1	1-2	1-2	0-2	4-2	2-1		1-4	2-0	2-3	0-1	1-1	3-0	2-3	1-1	1-2	1-3	0-0	0-3
Hartlepools United FC	0-2	1-1	0-0	4-1	5-1	5-2	4-1	0-2	1-3	1-4		0-0	2-0	3-0	1-0	0-3	2-1	3-0	1-0	1-0	1-3	1-1
Hull City AFC	3-0	1-0	0-2	2-0	1-0	2-2	2-1	0-1	1-2	3-0	1-1		0-0	1-1	0-1	0-1	0-2	4-0	0-3	1-0	1-0	2-2
Lincoln City FC	1-1	1-0	0-0	3-1	2-2	1-3	2-0	3-5	4-0	3-1	5-2	0-3		5-1	1-3	3-4	4-2	4-0	2-1	3-1	2-2	
New Brighton FC	4-0	0-1	0-1	2-2	0-3	4-0	4-1	2-5	2-3	1-1	2-1	1-5	4-2		4-0	1-2	1-0	1-0	1-0	2-1	1-0	0-3
Oldham Athletic AFC	1-2	0-1	0-1	0-2	1-0	3-1	2-0	0-1	1-1	6-1	0-0	1-2	3-1	2-2		3-2	0-1	2-4	0-0	1-2	1-5	2-2
Rochdale AFC	5-1	1-1	1-1	6-0	2-1	1-1	3-0	2-3	2-3	1-0	1-0	5-2	2-0	2-2	1-3		1-1	0-0	1-4	3-0	0-1	0-1
Rotherham United FC	4-1	4-3	2-1	4-0	3-1	5-1	4-1	3-2	4-0	6-1	4-0	2-0	3-0	3-0	8-0	3-3		2-1	2-1	6-0	3-2	6-1
Southport FC	0-1	2-2	0-1	0-2	2-4	2-2	2-2	0-5	2-1	6-1	3-3	3-1	1-3	2-0	2-4	0-2	2-0		4-1	1-2	1-1	0-3
Stockport County FC	2-0	2-0	4-0	2-0	0-3	3-2	1-0	1-3	2-0	4-1	1-2	0-2	3-2	2-0	4-0	5-2	1-2	2-0		4-0	1-0	4-2
Tranmere Rovers FC	0-1	1-1	2-0	1-1	3-2	3-2	2-0	3-5	1-0	1-1	4-1	1-3	5-2	3-3	4-2	2-3	1-4	2-0	2-1		0-0	2-1
Wrexham AFC	4-0	1-1	2-0	2-1	0-4	1-0	7-1	0-2	2-0	2-0	4-1	0-1	4-1	3-2	2-1	2-2	1-1	1-1	2-1	0-0		3-1
York City FC	0-1	0-2	0-3	2-2	4-4	2-3	3-0	1-4	3-1	2-0	1-4	3-0	2-4	1-2	1-0	2-3	2-3	1-1	3-2	0-1	2-2	

Division 3 (North)

		Pd	Wn	Dw	Ls	GF	GA	Pts	
1.	Doncaster Rovers FC (Doncaster)	42	33	6	3	123	40	72	P
2.	Rotherham United FC (Rotherham)	42	29	6	7	114	53	64	
3.	Chester FC (Chester)	42	25	6	11	95	51	56	
4.	Stockport County FC (Stockport)	42	24	2	16	78	53	50	
5.	Bradford City AFC (Bradford)	42	20	10	12	62	47	50	
6.	Rochdale AFC (Rochdale)	42	19	10	13	80	64	48	
7.	Wrexham AFC (Wrexham)	42	17	12	13	65	51	46	
8.	Crewe Alexandra FC (Crewe)	42	17	8	16	70	74	43	
9.	Barrow AFC (Barrow-in-Furness)	42	17	7	18	54	62	41	
10.	Tranmere Rovers FC (Birkenhead)	42	17	7	18	66	77	41	
11.	Hull City AFC (Kingston-upon-Hull)	42	16	8	18	49	53	40	
12.	Lincoln City FC (Lincoln)	42	17	5	20	86	87	39	
13.	Hartlepools United FC (Hartlepool)	42	15	9	18	64	73	39	
14.	Gateshead FC (Gateshead)	42	16	6	20	62	72	38	
15.	York City FC (York)	42	14	9	19	67	81	37	
16.	Carlisle United FC (Carlisle)	42	14	9	19	70	93	37	
17.	Darlington FC (Darlington)	42	15	6	21	68	80	36	
18.	New Brighton FC (Wallasey)	42	14	8	20	57	77	36	
19.	Oldham Athletic AFC (Oldham)	42	12	8	22	55	80	32	
20.	Accrington Stanley FC (Accrington)	42	14	4	24	56	92	32	
21.	Southport FC (Southport)	42	7	11	24	53	85	25	
22.	Halifax Town AFC (Halifax)	42	8	6	28	43	92	22	
		924	380	164	380	1537	1537	924	

Football League Division 3 (S) 1946-1947 Season	Aldershot	Bournemouth	Brighton	Bristol City	Bristol Rovers	Cardiff City	Crystal Palace	Exeter City	Ipswich Town	Leyton Orient	Mansfield T.	Northampton	Norwich City	Notts County	Port Vale	Q.P.R.	Reading	Southend Utd.	Swindon Town	Torquay United	Walsall	Watford
Aldershot FC	■	2-1	1-3	4-3	0-2	0-1	0-2	2-0	4-1	0-0	1-1	1-1	3-1	1-1	0-0	1-2	1-3	0-0	2-0	0-0	1-2	1-2
Bournemouth & B. Athletic	2-2	■	1-0	0-0	1-3	2-0	4-0	4-1	1-1	2-0	3-1	2-1	0-1	1-2	3-0	1-1	1-0	3-1	5-2	5-0	2-3	0-1
Brighton & Hove Albion	2-1	1-1	■	1-1	1-2	0-4	1-0	1-6	0-0	2-1	5-0	2-2	3-3	3-2	0-0	0-2	1-4	2-1	1-4	2-0	2-0	1-1
Bristol City FC	9-0	1-0	0-0	■	4-0	2-1	3-0	2-2	1-2	3-0	5-2	2-3	2-1	1-1	3-0	1-1	5-2	2-0	3-1	5-0	1-2	1-2
Bristol Rovers FC	0-0	0-2	0-0	0-3	■	1-0	2-1	1-0	1-1	6-1	1-0	0-3	1-2	4-1	0-0	3-1	2-2	1-3	3-0	3-0	2-2	3-4
Cardiff City AFC	2-1	2-0	4-0	1-1	4-0	■	0-0	5-0	3-2	1-0	5-0	6-2	6-1	2-1	1-0	2-2	3-0	3-1	5-0	1-0	3-0	1-0
Crystal Palace FC	0-0	0-1	1-0	0-0	2-1	1-2	■	1-0	1-1	2-0	2-1	2-2	0-1	2-1	1-2	0-0	2-1	0-3	4-1	6-1	1-1	2-0
Exeter City FC	4-1	4-1	2-1	1-3	3-2	0-2	2-1	■	0-0	3-1	1-0	1-0	3-0	2-2	1-1	3-0	1-3	1-5	1-1	1-1	2-2	1-0
Ipswich Town FC	1-1	2-1	1-2	3-2	0-2	0-1	1-1	2-1	■	0-0	2-1	1-1	5-2	0-1	2-1	1-2	1-0	3-1	1-1	2-1	2-0	2-0
Leyton Orient FC	1-3	2-3	2-1	4-1	3-0	0-1	0-1	3-1	2-2	■	3-1	2-1	3-0	1-3	5-3	1-1	3-3	1-1	0-0	0-1	1-0	3-1
Mansfield Town FC	1-3	1-1	0-3	1-3	3-1	1-3	3-1	1-0	4-3	1-3	■	3-2	4-4	1-0	0-3	0-3	2-2	0-1	1-1	1-0	1-1	2-0
Northampton Town FC	2-2	2-1	6-1	2-2	1-2	0-2	1-0	1-2	2-2	4-1	3-0	■	1-0	2-1	1-0	4-4	4-0	2-3	4-1	1-0	0-8	4-1
Norwich City FC	2-3	1-6	2-3	4-3	3-3	2-1	2-3	1-3	0-1	5-0	3-1	2-3	■	2-2	3-0	0-2	1-5	1-5	2-0	0-2	4-2	2-2
Notts County FC	2-0	1-0	2-0	0-3	6-0	1-1	0-0	0-0	1-2	1-2	5-1	1-0	3-0	■	3-2	1-2	1-0	0-2	0-0	0-2	3-1	4-1
Port Vale FC	4-2	1-0	4-1	2-1	2-1	0-4	4-2	1-2	1-0	2-1	1-1	1-3	4-1	4-1	■	2-2	5-1	5-1	1-1	2-1	2-2	3-0
Queen's Park Rangers FC	4-1	3-0	2-0	1-0	0-2	2-3	1-2	2-0	1-3	2-0	1-1	1-1	4-1	2-0	2-0	■	2-0	1-0	7-0	0-0	1-0	2-1
Reading FC	1-0	3-2	2-0	2-5	1-1	0-0	10-2	4-0	1-3	2-0	3-0	3-0	4-3	1-1	0-2	1-0	■	7-2	3-3	2-2	1-1	2-3
Southend United FC	2-1	2-2	0-0	4-1	2-3	0-2	0-2	2-2	1-1	4-0	3-0	3-0	1-1	1-3	0-2	2-0	0-2	■	2-0	3-1	5-0	2-1
Swindon Town FC	7-0	1-3	2-2	1-1	1-0	3-2	1-2	2-0	2-1	2-0	6-1	3-1	1-1	4-2	3-2	2-2	2-1	2-1	■	2-4	4-1	2-3
Torquay United FC	0-1	2-2	3-1	2-3	3-0	0-0	2-1	2-1	0-0	3-2	2-2	2-1	2-1	1-2	1-0	2-1	3-0	0-1	1-5	■	2-0	2-0
Walsall FC	2-0	3-0	1-1	3-0	2-0	2-3	3-3	2-1	4-2	3-1	0-0	2-0	2-2	2-0	4-1	0-2	2-2	2-2	0-1	2-1	■	1-3
Watford FC	4-1	0-2	1-4	2-3	1-0	2-0	1-0	3-1	2-0	3-1	1-2	1-1	4-1	2-2	2-0	0-2	2-1	4-0	1-1	3-3	0-2	■

Division 3 (South)

		Pd	Wn	Dw	Ls	GF	GA	Pts	
1.	Cardiff City AFC (Cardiff)	42	30	6	6	93	30	66	P
2.	Queen's Park Rangers FC (London)	42	23	11	8	74	40	57	
3.	Bristol City FC (Bristol)	42	20	11	11	94	56	51	
4.	Swindon Town FC (Swindon)	42	19	11	12	84	73	49	
5.	Walsall FC (Walsall)	42	17	12	13	74	59	46	
6.	Ipswich Town FC (Ipswich)	42	16	14	12	61	53	46	
7.	Bournemouth & Boscombe Athletic FC (Bournemouth)	42	18	8	16	72	54	44	
8.	Southend United FC (Southend-on-Sea)	42	17	10	15	71	60	44	
9.	Reading FC (Reading)	42	16	11	15	83	74	43	
10.	Port Vale FC (Stoke-on-Trent)	42	17	9	16	68	63	43	
11.	Torquay United FC (Torquay)	42	15	12	15	52	61	42	
12.	Notts County FC (Nottingham)	42	15	10	17	63	63	40	
13.	Northampton Town FC (Northampton)	42	15	10	17	72	75	40	
14.	Bristol Rovers FC (Bristol)	42	16	8	18	59	69	40	
15.	Exeter City FC (Exeter)	42	15	9	18	60	69	39	
16.	Watford FC (Watford)	42	17	5	20	61	76	39	
17.	Brighton & Hove Albion FC (Hove)	42	13	12	17	54	72	38	
18.	Crystal Palace FC (London)	42	13	11	18	49	62	37	
19.	Leyton Orient FC (London)	42	12	8	22	54	75	32	
20.	Aldershot FC (Aldershot)	42	10	12	20	48	78	32	
21.	Norwich City FC (Norwich)	42	10	8	24	64	100	28	
22.	Mansfield Town FC (Mansfield)	42	9	10	23	48	96	28	T
		924	353	218	353	1458	1458	924	

T: Mansfield Town FC (Mansfield) were transferred to Division 3 (North) from the next season.

F.A. CUP FINAL   (Wembley Stadium, London – 26/04/1947 – 99,000)

CHARLTON ATHLETIC FC (LONDON)   1-0 (aet)   Burnley FC (Burnley)

Duffy

Charlton: Bartram, Croker, Shreeve, Johnson, Phipps, Whittaker, Hurst, Dawson, W.Robinson, Welsh, Duffy.

Burnley: Strong, Woodruff, Mather, Attwell, Brown, Bray, Chew, Morris, Harrison, Potts, Kippax.

Semi-finals

Charlton Athletic FC (London)	4-0	Newcastle United FC (Newcastle-upon-Tyne)
Liverpool FC (Liverpool)	0-0, 0-1	Burnley FC (Burnley)

Quarter-finals

Charlton Athletic FC (London)	2-1	Preston North End FC (Preston)
Liverpool FC (Liverpool)	4-1	Birmingham City FC (Birmingham)
Middlesbrough FC (Middlesbrough)	1-1, 0-1	Burnley FC (Burnley)
Sheffield United FC (Sheffield)	0-2	Newcastle United FC (Newcastle-upon-Tyne)

1947-48

Football League Division 1 1947-1948 Season	Arsenal	Aston Villa	Blackburn Rovers	Blackpool	Bolton Wanderers	Burnley	Charlton Athletic	Chelsea	Derby County	Everton	Grimsby Town	Huddersfield Town	Liverpool	Manchester City	Manchester United	Middlesbrough	Portsmouth	Preston North End	Sheffield United	Stoke City	Sunderland	Wolves
Arsenal FC		1-0	2-0	2-1	2-0	3-0	6-0	0-2	1-2	1-1	8-0	2-0	1-2	1-1	2-1	7-0	0-0	3-0	3-2	3-0	3-1	5-2
Aston Villa FC	4-2		3-2	0-1	3-1	2-2	2-1	3-0	2-2	3-0	2-2	2-1	2-1	1-1	0-1	1-1	2-1	4-1	2-0	1-0	2-0	1-2
Blackburn Rovers FC	0-1	0-0		1-1	4-0	1-2	0-0	1-1	3-4	2-3	4-0	1-2	1-2	1-0	1-1	1-7	1-0	2-3	4-0	2-0	4-3	1-0
Blackpool FC	3-0	1-0	1-0		1-1	0-1	3-1	3-0	2-2	5-0	3-1	4-0	2-0	1-1	1-0	1-0	1-0	0-1	2-1	1-2	0-1	2-2
Bolton Wanderers FC	0-1	1-0	1-0	1-0		1-1	1-0	2-1	0-3	0-0	2-0	1-5	3-0	2-1	0-1	1-3	4-0	1-2	2-3	0-1	3-1	3-2
Burnley FC	0-1	1-0	0-0	1-0	2-0		0-2	1-0	0-2	0-1	4-1	2-1	3-0	1-1	0-0	3-0	3-2	1-0	0-0	4-0	4-0	1-1
Charlton Athletic FC	2-4	1-1	0-1	2-0	2-1	1-1		3-1	1-5	2-3	2-3	0-0	2-0	0-1	1-2	1-0	2-2	1-2	0-0	0-1	1-0	5-1
Chelsea FC	0-0	4-2	1-0	2-2	1-1	0-2	3-0		1-0	3-1	2-3	2-4	3-1	2-2	0-4	4-2	1-0	2-0	1-0	4-1	1-1	1-1
Derby County FC	1-0	1-3	5-0	1-0	2-1	1-1	0-3	5-1		1-0	4-1	0-0	0-4	0-0	1-1	4-2	2-1	2-1	1-1	1-1	5-1	1-2
Everton FC	0-2	3-0	4-1	1-2	2-0	0-3	0-1	2-3	1-3		3-1	1-1	0-3	1-0	2-0	2-1	0-2	2-1	0-1	3-0	1-1	1-1
Grimsby Town FC	0-4	3-0	2-2	0-1	0-2	1-2	1-3	0-0	2-3	3-0		3-0	0-2	1-0	1-1	0-5	1-0	1-1	0-3	0-0	1-2	0-4
Huddersfield Town AFC	1-1	0-1	1-1	2-0	1-2	0-1	0-1	3-1	2-1	1-3	5-1		1-1	1-1	0-2	2-1	0-2	1-0	2-1	0-0	2-2	0-1
Liverpool FC	1-3	3-3	2-1	2-0	0-0	1-1	2-3	3-0	2-2	4-0	3-1	4-0		1-1	2-2	0-1	0-3	3-1	4-0	0-0	0-0	2-1
Manchester City FC	0-0	0-2	1-3	1-0	0-2	4-1	4-0	1-0	0-1	3-1	1-1	2-0			0-0	2-0	1-0	0-3	4-3	3-0	4-3	
Manchester United FC	1-1	2-0	4-1	1-1	0-2	5-0	6-2	5-0	1-0	2-2	3-4	4-4	2-0	1-1		2-1	3-2	1-1	0-1	1-1	3-1	3-2
Middlesbrough FC	1-1	1-3	1-1	4-0	4-1	1-2	1-2	0-0	1-1	0-1	4-1	1-0	3-1	2-1	2-2		1-2	1-1	3-0	2-1	2-2	2-4
Portsmouth FC	0-0	2-4	1-1	1-1	2-0	0-1	3-1	2-1	0-0	3-0	4-0	3-2	1-0	1-0	1-3	6-1		1-0	6-0	3-0	2-2	2-0
Preston North End FC	0-0	3-0	2-1	0-7	1-0	3-2	2-1	7-4	3-0	2-1	2-1	3-3	2-1	2-1	1-2	1-2			3-3	2-1	2-2	1-3
Sheffield United FC	1-2	3-1	4-1	2-1	2-1	1-1	1-1	3-1	1-2	2-1	4-0	0-1	3-1	2-1	2-1	1-1	1-2	3-1		3-0	3-2	2-2
Stoke City FC	0-0	1-2	2-1	1-1	2-0	3-0	0-1	2-0	1-0	1-1	1-1	1-1	1-1	0-2	3-0	2-4	2-1	0-1	1-1		3-1	2-3
Sunderland AFC	1-1	0-0	0-1	1-0	1-2	2-0	0-1	2-3	1-1	2-0	4-2	2-0	5-1	0-1	1-0	3-0	4-1	0-2	1-1	1-0		2-1
Wolverhampton Wanderers FC	1-1	4-1	5-1	1-1	1-0	1-1	2-0	1-0	1-0	2-4	8-1	2-1	1-2	1-0	2-6	1-3	3-1	4-2	1-1	1-2	2-1	

Division 1	Pd	Wn	Dw	Ls	GF	GA	Pts	
1. ARSENAL FC (LONDON)	42	23	13	6	81	32	59	
2. Manchester United FC (Manchester)	42	19	14	9	81	48	52	
3. Burnley FC (Burnley)	42	20	12	10	56	43	52	
4. Derby County FC (Derby)	42	19	12	11	77	57	50	
5. Wolverhampton Wanderers FC (Wolverhampton)	42	19	9	14	83	70	47	
6. Aston Villa FC (Birmingham)	42	19	9	14	65	57	47	
7. Preston North End FC (Preston)	42	20	7	15	67	68	47	
8. Portsmouth FC (Portsmouth)	42	19	7	16	68	50	45	
9. Blackpool FC (Blackpool)	42	17	10	15	57	41	44	
10. Manchester City FC (Manchester)	42	15	12	15	52	47	42	
11. Liverpool FC (Liverpool)	42	16	10	16	65	61	42	
12. Sheffield United FC (Sheffield)	42	16	10	16	65	70	42	
13. Charlton Athletic FC (London)	42	17	6	19	57	66	40	
14. Everton FC (Liverpool)	42	17	6	19	52	66	40	
15. Stoke City FC (Stoke-on-Trent)	42	14	10	18	41	55	38	
16. Middlesbrough FC (Middlesbrough)	42	14	9	19	71	73	37	
17. Bolton Wanderers FC (Bolton)	42	16	5	21	46	58	37	
18. Chelsea FC (London)	42	14	9	19	53	71	37	
19. Huddersfield Town AFC (Huddersfield)	42	12	12	18	51	60	36	
20. Sunderland AFC (Sunderland)	42	13	10	19	56	67	36	
21. Blackburn Rovers FC (Blackburn)	42	11	10	21	54	72	32	R
22. Grimsby Town FC (Cleethorpes)	42	8	6	28	45	111	22	R
	924	358	208	358	1343	1343	924	

Top Goalscorer

1) Ronnie ROOKE   (Arsenal FC)   33

Football League Division 2 — 1947-1948 Season

	Barnsley	Birmingham City	Bradford P.A.	Brentford	Bury	Cardiff City	Chesterfield	Coventry City	Doncaster Rovers	Fulham	Leeds United	Leicester City	Luton Town	Millwall	Newcastle United	Nottingham Forest	Plymouth Argyle	Sheffield Wed.	Southampton	Tottenham H.	W.B.A.	West Ham United
Barnsley FC		0-1	2-2	1-1	2-1	1-2	0-3	0-1	2-0	1-2	3-0	2-0	3-0	1-0	1-1	2-2	2-1	3-1	2-1	2-1	0-1	1-1
Birmingham City FC	2-3		4-3	0-0	2-0	2-0	0-0	1-1	3-0	3-1	5-1	1-0	2-1	1-0	0-0	2-1	1-1	1-0	0-0	0-0	4-0	0-1
Bradford Park Avenue	3-2	1-2		1-1	5-3	0-1	1-3	2-2	4-0	3-0	3-1	0-2	2-2	4-0	0-3	3-1	3-0	2-0	1-3	0-2	3-1	4-1
Brentford FC	3-3	1-2	2-1		4-1	0-0	0-3	1-4	2-0	0-2	3-0	2-2	0-3	2-1	1-0	3-1	0-0	1-0	2-2	2-0	1-0	1-1
Bury FC	1-1	1-1	0-4	2-2		1-2	2-0	0-0	4-2	1-0	1-1	0-2	2-2	0-0	3-5	1-0	0-0	1-2	3-0	2-0	1-2	1-2
Cardiff City AFC	1-0	2-0	1-0	1-0	2-2		0-0	1-1	3-0	1-0	3-0	1-0	6-0	1-1	4-1	3-0	2-1	5-1	0-3	0-5	0-3	3-0
Chesterfield FC	1-1	0-3	0-1	4-0	1-2	2-2		4-3	0-3	1-0	3-0	2-3	2-0	2-0	0-0	1-1	0-2	0-1	3-1	0-2	6-0	2-1
Coventry City FC	3-2	0-1	5-0	3-0	0-0	1-0	3-0		1-0	5-2	1-2	0-1	4-1	0-1	1-1	1-1	0-0	3-1	0-1	1-1	1-0	0-1
Doncaster Rovers FC	1-2	0-0	3-0	0-0	1-3	2-2	1-0	0-0		0-1	3-0	1-1	0-2	2-2	3-0	2-0	2-0	0-1	1-1	1-1	2-1	1-0
Fulham FC	0-1	1-1	0-0	5-0	1-1	4-1	0-0	0-2	0-0		3-2	3-1	1-1	3-0	0-1	0-2	0-2	0-1	0-2	0-1	0-1	1-1
Leeds United AFC	4-1	0-1	2-0	1-1	5-1	4-0	3-0	2-1	0-0	0-1		3-1	0-2	2-1	3-1	2-2	5-0	2-2	0-0	1-3	3-1	2-1
Leicester City FC	4-1	0-0	2-0	1-2	2-1	2-1	1-2	2-2	3-2	0-2	2-0		3-2	3-0	2-2	3-1	2-1	2-3	0-0	0-3	1-1	1-3
Luton Town FC	2-1	0-1	3-3	3-0	1-1	1-1	2-1	2-3	2-1	0-3	6-1	2-1		1-2	2-1	2-1	1-0	3-1	1-1	0-3	1-1	1-1
Millwall FC	3-3	0-0	0-1	0-1	1-7	0-1	0-2	6-2	1-0	1-2	1-1	0-4	3-1		2-1	2-0	2-0	0-0	3-0	0-0	1-1	1-1
Newcastle United FC	1-0	1-0	2-0	1-0	1-0	4-1	2-3	0-0	2-0	1-0	4-2	2-0	4-1	1-0		0-2	6-1	4-2	5-0	1-0	3-1	3-1
Nottingham Forest FC	1-1	0-2	1-2	2-0	2-1	1-2	1-3	4-0	4-2	0-2	1-0	1-0	1-2	5-2	0-0		1-1	0-0	1-1	1-1	3-1	2-1
Plymouth Argyle FC	1-0	0-3	2-2	0-0	0-0	3-0	1-2	1-0	2-2	0-2	0-0	1-3	1-1	3-0	1-1	2-1		0-2	3-1	1-1	2-1	1-1
Sheffield Wednesday FC	5-2	0-0	3-1	1-1	2-2	2-1	1-0	1-1	2-0	2-0	3-1	1-0	1-0	3-2	1-0	2-1	1-1		1-2	1-0	1-2	5-3
Southampton FC	4-1	2-0	1-2	2-1	1-0	2-2	3-0	3-1	6-1	1-0	1-2	3-1	3-1	5-1	4-2	2-1	2-3	3-1		1-1	1-1	3-1
Tottenham Hotspur FC	0-3	1-2	3-1	4-0	2-2	2-1	3-0	2-1	0-2	0-2	1-1	3-2	1-0	0-3	2-0	5-1	0-0	1-1	0-1		1-1	2-2
West Bromwich Albion FC	0-2	1-1	6-0	3-2	3-3	2-3	1-0	3-1	1-3	2-1	3-2	1-3	1-0	2-1	0-1	3-2	1-1	1-1	1-0	1-0		1-2
West Ham United FC	2-1	0-0	0-0	0-1	2-0	4-2	4-0	1-0	2-1	3-0	2-1	1-1	0-0	1-1	0-2	2-1	1-1	1-4	2-0	1-1	0-2	

Division 2

		Pd	Wn	Dw	Ls	GF	GA	Pts	
1.	Birmingham City FC (Birmingham)	42	22	15	5	55	24	59	P
2.	Newcastle United FC (Newcastle-upon-Tyne)	42	24	8	10	72	41	56	P
3.	Southampton FC (Southampton)	42	21	10	11	71	53	52	
4.	Sheffield Wednesday FC (Sheffield)	42	20	11	11	66	53	51	
5.	Cardiff City AFC (Cardiff)	42	18	11	13	61	58	47	
6.	West Ham United FC (London)	42	16	14	12	55	53	46	
7.	West Bromwich Albion FC (West Bromwich)	42	18	9	15	63	58	45	
8.	Tottenham Hotspur FC (London)	42	15	14	13	56	43	44	
9.	Leicester City FC (Leicester)	42	16	11	15	60	57	43	
10.	Coventry City FC (Coventry)	42	14	13	15	59	52	41	
11.	Fulham FC (London)	42	15	10	17	47	46	40	
12.	Barnsley FC (Barnsley)	42	15	10	17	62	64	40	
13.	Luton Town FC (Luton)	42	14	12	16	56	59	40	
14.	Bradford Park Avenue FC (Bradford)	42	16	8	18	68	72	40	
15.	Brentford FC (London)	42	13	14	15	44	61	40	
16.	Chesterfield FC (Chesterfield)	42	16	7	19	54	55	39	
17.	Plymouth Argyle FC (Plymouth)	42	9	20	13	40	58	38	
18.	Leeds United AFC (Leeds)	42	14	8	20	62	72	36	
19.	Nottingham Forest FC (Nottingham)	42	12	11	19	54	60	35	
20.	Bury FC (Bury)	42	9	16	17	58	68	34	
21.	Doncaster Rovers FC (Doncaster)	42	9	11	22	40	66	29	R
22.	Millwall FC (London)	42	9	11	22	44	74	29	R
		924	335	254	335	1247	1247	924	

Football League Division 3 (N) 1947-1948 Season	Accrington Stanley	Barrow	Bradford City	Carlisle United	Chester	Crewe Alexandra	Darlington	Gateshead	Halifax Town	Hartlepools United	Hull City	Lincoln City	Mansfield Town	New Brighton	Oldham Athletic	Rochdale	Rotherham United	Southport	Stockport County	Tranmere Rovers	Wrexham	York City
Accrington Stanley FC		0-1	2-0	1-2	1-0	2-1	3-0	1-0	2-0	4-2	2-4	2-1	1-0	5-3	2-3	1-2	0-1	0-0	5-2	1-0	0-2	1-0
Barrow AFC	3-0		0-1	2-0	1-0	2-0	0-0	1-2	2-1	1-2	0-2	0-1	1-0	1-1	2-4	0-1	1-3	2-0	0-0	3-0	1-1	1-0
Bradford City AFC	1-2	1-1		1-1	3-2	1-2	4-0	2-2	2-1	3-1	2-0	2-4	0-1	1-1	0-2	4-0	0-1	4-2	1-0	4-1	1-0	1-3
Carlisle United FC	2-3	1-2	1-2		2-0	5-2	4-1	1-1	5-2	1-1	1-0	0-0	2-5	3-1	2-1	4-1	5-0	0-3	2-3	4-3	1-2	1-1
Chester FC	1-0	0-0	2-1	4-1		4-2	1-1	2-3	0-0	2-0	4-1	1-1	1-2	4-2	2-1	2-1	2-3	0-0	2-2	4-0	4-1	2-3
Crewe Alexandra FC	0-0	1-2	3-2	0-2	1-0		4-1	0-1	0-1	2-0	3-1	3-0	0-0	4-0	2-2	2-1	3-3	4-1	4-2	3-2	1-0	1-3
Darlington FC	3-1	2-2	1-1	4-3	1-1	0-1		1-1	4-1	1-0	2-0	1-3	1-2	3-1	0-6	0-0	1-3	0-0	0-2	3-1	1-1	
Gateshead FC	4-2	0-2	2-2	1-3	2-1	2-0	1-2		3-0	7-0	0-1	3-2	2-1	3-1	3-5	5-0	1-1	3-2	1-1	3-0	2-2	0-1
Halifax Town AFC	3-3	1-1	0-0	2-1	1-1	4-1	1-1	0-0		0-0	0-2	0-1	1-1	1-2	1-5	2-3	2-1	0-0	4-0	2-2	0-1	0-1
Hartlepools United FC	4-0	0-3	0-2	1-1	2-1	0-1	3-0	3-2	1-1		3-1	1-2	1-0	1-0	3-1	4-1	2-2	2-0	1-1	0-0	0-2	2-2
Hull City AFC	4-2	0-0	2-1	3-1	2-1	2-1	0-3	2-3	1-2	5-0		0-1	1-0	3-0	1-0	0-0	5-3	1-0				
Lincoln City FC	2-3	2-1	3-0	3-0	4-2	0-0	3-1	3-0	3-1	5-0	2-3		0-0	1-2	2-0	3-0	3-1	3-1	3-0	2-0	2-1	1-0
Mansfield Town FC	1-0	1-0	1-1	2-3	2-1	3-1	4-0	1-2	3-1	3-2	1-1	0-2		5-0	1-1	1-2	2-0	1-2	1-3	1-0	1-2	
New Brighton FC	0-1	1-1	0-2	1-3	0-1	1-2	2-1	1-2	1-0	1-2	1-0	0-1	2-2		2-2	0-0	1-2	2-2	1-0	0-1	2-1	2-1
Oldham Athletic AFC	1-0	2-1	3-0	2-1	3-1	0-0	3-3	0-1	1-1	0-2	0-0	0-0	1-1	3-0		1-1	1-5	1-1	0-0	0-1	1-4	2-2
Rochdale AFC	1-3	2-2	2-0	2-1	2-2	1-2	2-1	2-1	2-1	1-1	1-1	1-2	1-0	2-0			1-0	2-1	1-2	1-1	2-1	3-0
Rotherham United FC	1-0	0-0	4-1	7-2	5-1	0-0	0-0	3-0	3-2	0-0	0-2	2-1	6-1	4-1	4-1			0-2	4-1	2-0	6-0	3-2
Southport FC	1-1	1-2	1-2	0-4	3-0	2-0	2-0	2-0	1-2	0-1	1-1	4-0	4-0	2-2	1-2				0-4	1-4	1-0	2-1
Stockport County FC	1-1	2-3	3-3	2-3	4-1	2-1	1-3	1-1	2-1	0-0	1-1	0-1	5-0	1-2	3-0	4-0	2-2	0-3		2-0	0-1	4-2
Tranmere Rovers FC	0-1	1-0	2-1	0-3	2-3	0-0	3-0	0-1	1-0	2-1	1-4	1-0	1-0	4-1	0-1	2-2	2-3				2-3	4-2
Wrexham AFC	1-1	3-1	4-2	2-1	2-1	1-1	1-2	0-3	6-3	3-1	1-0	3-0	2-1	0-0	1-2	5-1	1-3	2-0	6-0			3-0
York City FC	1-2	0-0	3-3	2-2	2-0	0-1	0-2	3-1	6-0	4-0	2-2	0-1	1-2	3-1	1-0	0-0	2-0	3-3	3-2	1-2	1-1	

Division 3 (North)

		Pd	Wn	Dw	Ls	GF	GA	Pts	
1.	Lincoln City FC (Lincoln)	42	26	8	8	81	40	60	P
2.	Rotherham United FC (Rotherham)	42	25	9	8	95	49	59	
3.	Wrexham AFC (Wrexham)	42	21	8	13	74	54	50	
4.	Gateshead FC (Gateshead)	42	19	11	12	75	57	49	
5.	Hull City AFC (Kingston-upon-Hull)	42	18	11	13	59	48	47	
6.	Accrington Stanley FC (Accrington)	42	20	6	16	62	59	46	
7.	Barrow AFC (Barrow-in-Furness)	42	16	13	13	49	40	45	
8.	Mansfield Town FC (Mansfield)	42	17	11	14	57	51	45	
9.	Carlisle United FC (Carlisle)	42	18	7	17	88	77	43	
10.	Crewe Alexandra FC (Crewe)	42	18	7	17	61	63	43	
11.	Oldham Athletic AFC (Oldham)	42	14	13	15	63	64	41	
12.	Rochdale AFC (Rochdale)	42	15	11	16	48	72	41	
13.	York City FC (York)	42	13	14	15	65	60	40	
14.	Bradford City AFC (Bradford)	42	15	10	17	65	66	40	
15.	Southport FC (Southport)	42	14	11	17	60	63	39	
16.	Darlington FC (Darlington)	42	13	13	16	54	70	39	
17.	Stockport County FC (Stockport)	42	13	12	17	63	67	38	
18.	Tranmere Rovers FC (Birkenhead)	42	16	4	22	54	72	36	
19.	Hartlepools United FC (Hartlepool)	42	14	8	20	51	73	36	
20.	Chester FC (Chester)	42	13	9	20	64	67	35	
21.	Halifax Town AFC (Halifax)	42	7	13	22	43	76	27	
22.	New Brighton FC (Wallasey)	42	8	9	25	38	81	25	
		924	353	218	353	1369	1369	924	

Football League Division 3 (S) 1947-1948 Season	Aldershot	Bournemouth	Brighton	Bristol City	Bristol Rovers	Crystal Palace	Exeter City	Ipswich Town	Leyton Orient	Newport County	Northampton	Norwich City	Notts County	Port Vale	Q.P.R.	Reading	Southend United	Swansea Town	Swindon Town	Torquay United	Walsall	Watford
Aldershot FC	■	0-3	1-1	1-1	2-0	2-0	0-0	0-1	0-0	1-2	1-1	2-2	1-0	1-1	1-4	1-2	1-1	0-3	2-2	1-0	3-1	1-1
Bournemouth & B. Athletic	1-1	■	4-1	2-0	3-0	0-0	2-1	4-0	1-1	5-0	2-0	1-3	2-0	3-0	0-1	2-0	0-1	1-0	1-0	6-2	1-1	1-1
Brighton & Hove Albion	1-1	0-2	■	0-2	3-1	1-1	0-1	4-1	0-0	3-0	2-3	2-0	1-3	2-2	0-5	2-0	1-0	0-1	1-0	2-1	0-4	1-3
Bristol City FC	2-4	0-4	1-2	■	5-2	2-0	1-1	4-0	6-0	1-0	1-1	6-0	1-0	2-1	2-1	0-2	6-0	3-2	2-2	1-2	0-0	1-2
Bristol Rovers FC	7-1	1-2	4-1	0-2	■	1-1	2-2	2-0	0-2	2-3	1-2	2-3	2-0	2-1	0-1	2-3	1-2	2-2	3-1	0-2	2-3	3-0
Crystal Palace FC	1-0	2-0	0-0	4-0	0-0	■	1-2	2-1	2-0	2-1	1-0	2-0	1-1	2-0	0-1	2-1	0-0	4-0	1-1	2-1	2-3	1-2
Exeter City FC	4-0	1-1	1-0	3-1	4-0	2-0	■	1-0	1-1	4-4	1-1	2-0	0-1	1-2	0-0	3-1	3-1	2-1	0-2	0-6	3-1	
Ipswich Town FC	2-0	1-1	4-0	1-0	0-4	3-0	2-0	■	1-0	3-0	5-2	1-2	2-0	2-1	1-0	1-0	4-0	3-2	0-1	2-1	3-1	1-3
Leyton Orient FC	0-3	2-0	2-1	0-2	2-4	1-1	2-4	1-1	■	2-2	5-0	2-1	2-1	0-0	1-3	2-2	2-0	1-0	0-3	4-1	0-1	0-2
Newport County AFC	2-2	2-2	1-1	1-0	2-2	3-1	3-0	3-1	3-2	■	1-2	1-1	3-1	0-0	0-0	2-0	1-5	1-1	2-0	0-1	4-2	3-4
Northampton Town FC	2-1	3-6	4-0	0-4	1-3	3-1	3-1	4-2	1-1	1-1	■	1-0	1-2	4-1	1-1	1-1	2-0	0-1	0-0	1-0	2-1	0-1
Norwich City FC	0-1	0-1	2-2	2-3	1-5	3-1	3-0	1-5	3-0	1-2	2-3	■	0-1	1-2	5-2	2-1	1-0	1-2	2-2	1-1	1-0	1-0
Notts County FC	0-2	1-2	4-0	3-1	4-2	1-0	1-1	0-1	1-4	4-1	3-2	1-2	■	2-1	1-1	5-1	2-1	5-1	2-1	1-0	1-0	3-3
Port Vale FC	6-4	2-1	5-0	1-0	1-1	4-1	1-1	4-1	3-0	4-1	2-0	1-2		■	0-2	2-1	2-1	1-1	1-0	1-1	0-1	7-0
Queen's Park Rangers FC	0-0	1-0	2-0	2-0	5-2	1-0	3-1	2-0	1-2	1-0	2-0	3-1	4-1	2-1	■	2-0	3-2	0-0	0-2	3-3	2-1	5-1
Reading FC	0-0	3-0	1-0	2-7	0-0	0-0	2-1	1-2	6-2	0-0	1-1	2-4	3-1	2-0	3-2	■	1-3	4-1	2-3	2-0	0-1	2-0
Southend United FC	4-0	0-2	2-2	4-0	1-0	2-1	2-0	3-2	2-1	1-0	3-1	0-0	1-2	1-1	0-0	1-1	■	1-1	1-0	1-0	1-1	1-1
Swansea Town AFC	2-1	3-2	0-0	6-1	0-1	2-0	2-0	1-5	5-0	3-0	5-1	3-2	1-1	2-0	3-1	1-1	3-0	■	1-0	1-1	1-1	3-0
Swindon Town FC	1-0	0-1	1-1	2-2	1-1	0-0	3-2	0-1	0-1	1-2	0-0	3-2	1-1	1-0	0-0	1-1	0-0	1-0	■	2-2	0-3	1-1
Torquay United FC	2-0	0-1	1-2	2-3	1-2	3-3	1-2	3-0	0-1	4-1	4-2	1-1	2-2	5-0	1-1	1-2	4-1	1-1	1-1	■	3-2	0-1
Walsall FC	3-0	0-0	0-0	2-0	2-0	1-1	4-0	1-2	3-1	1-1	0-0	2-1	1-2	0-0	0-0	6-0	2-1	1-0	1-0	3-2	■	2-0
Watford FC	1-2	0-3	2-3	1-1	3-2	0-5	3-1	2-3	2-1	1-2	1-1	2-2	1-3	1-1	0-1	0-1	2-2	4-1	1-0	2-2	2-0	■

Division 3 (South)

		Pd	Wn	Dw	Ls	GF	GA	Pts	
1.	Queen's Park Rangers FC (London)	42	26	9	7	74	37	61	P
2.	Bournemouth & Boscombe Athletic FC (Bournemouth)	42	24	9	9	76	35	57	
3.	Walsall FC (Walsall)	42	21	9	12	70	40	51	
4.	Ipswich Town FC (Ipswich)	42	23	3	16	67	61	49	
5.	Swansea Town AFC (Swansea)	42	18	12	12	70	52	48	
6.	Notts County FC (Nottingham)	42	19	8	15	68	59	46	
7.	Bristol City FC (Bristol)	42	18	7	17	77	65	43	
8.	Port Vale FC (Stoke-on-Trent)	42	16	11	15	63	54	43	
9.	Southend United FC (Southend-on-Sea)	42	15	13	14	51	58	43	
10.	Reading FC (Reading)	42	15	11	16	56	58	41	
11.	Exeter City FC (Exeter)	42	15	11	16	55	63	41	
12.	Newport County AFC (Newport)	42	14	13	15	61	73	41	
13.	Crystal Palace FC (London)	42	13	13	16	49	49	39	
14.	Northampton Town FC (Northampton)	42	14	11	17	58	72	39	
15.	Watford FC (Watford)	42	14	10	18	57	79	38	
16.	Swindon Town FC (Swindon)	42	10	16	16	41	46	36	
17.	Leyton Orient FC (London)	42	13	10	19	51	73	36	
18.	Torquay United FC (Torquay)	42	11	13	18	63	62	35	
19.	Aldershot FC (Aldershot)	42	10	15	17	45	67	35	
20.	Bristol Rovers FC (Bristol)	42	13	8	21	71	75	34	
21.	Norwich City FC (Norwich)	42	13	8	21	61	76	34	
22.	Brighton & Hove Albion FC (Hove)	42	11	12	19	43	73	34	
		924	346	232	346	1327	1327	924	

F.A. CUP FINAL   (Wembley Stadium, London – 24/04/1948 – 99,000)

MANCHESTER UNITED FC (MANCHESTER)   4-2   Blackpool FC (Blackpool)

Rowley 2, Pearson, Anderson   *Shimwell pen., Mortensen*

Man. United: Crompton, Carey, Aston, Anderson, Chilton, Cockburn, Delaney, Morris, Rowley, Pearson, Mitten.

Blackburn: Robinson, Shimwell, Crosland, Johnston, Hayward, Kelly, Matthews, Munro, Mortensen, Dick, Rickett.

Semi-finals

Blackpool FC (Blackpool)	3-1	Tottenham Hotspur FC (London)
Derby County FC (Derby)	1-3	Manchester United FC (Manchester)

Quarter-finals

Fulham FC (London)	0-2	Blackpool FC (Blackpool)
Manchester United FC (Manchester)	4-1	Preston North End FC (Preston)
Queen's Park Rangers FC (London)	1-1, 0-5	Derby County FC (Derby)
Southampton FC (Southampton)	0-1	Tottenham Hotspur FC (London)

1948-49

Football League Division 1 1948-1949 Season	Arsenal	Aston Villa	Birmingham City	Blackpool	Bolton Wanderers	Burnley	Charlton Athletic	Chelsea	Derby County	Everton	Huddersfield Town	Liverpool	Manchester City	Manchester United	Middlesbrough	Newcastle United	Portsmouth	Preston North End	Sheffield United	Stoke City	Sunderland	Wolves
Arsenal FC		3-1	2-0	2-0	5-0	3-1	2-0	1-2	3-3	5-0	3-0	1-1	1-1	0-1	1-1	0-1	3-2	0-0	5-3	3-0	5-0	3-1
Aston Villa FC	1-0		0-3	2-5	2-4	3-1	4-3	1-1	1-1	0-1	3-3	2-1	1-0	2-1	1-1	2-4	1-1	2-0	4-3	2-1	1-1	5-1
Birmingham City FC	1-1	0-1		1-1	0-0	0-0	1-0	1-0	0-1	1-0	1-0	0-1	4-1	1-0	0-0	2-0	3-0	1-0	1-2	2-1	0-0	0-1
Blackpool FC	1-1	1-0	1-0		1-0	1-1	0-1	2-1	1-1	3-0	0-0	1-0	1-1	0-3	1-1	1-3	1-0	2-2	0-3	2-1	3-3	1-3
Bolton Wanderers FC	1-0	3-0	0-0	2-2		0-1	2-2	1-1	4-0	1-0	1-2	0-3	5-1	0-1	4-1	1-5	1-2	5-3	6-1	2-1	4-1	0-5
Burnley FC	1-1	1-1	2-2	2-0	3-0		0-0	3-0	3-1	1-0	1-2	0-2	1-0	0-2	0-0	0-3	2-1	1-0	2-0	1-3	3-1	0-0
Charlton Athletic FC	4-3	0-2	1-1	0-0	1-4	3-1		1-1	1-5	3-1	3-1	2-1	3-2	2-3	2-0	0-0	0-1	0-0	2-1	4-1	4-0	2-3
Chelsea FC	0-1	2-1	2-0	3-3	2-2	1-0	2-2		0-3	6-0	5-0	2-1	1-1	1-1	1-0	2-3	1-2	5-3	1-0	2-2	0-1	4-1
Derby County FC	2-1	2-2	1-0	3-1	1-0	2-0	5-1	2-1		3-2	4-1	3-0	2-0	1-3	2-0	2-4	1-0	1-0	2-1	4-1	2-2	3-2
Everton FC	0-0	1-3	0-5	5-0	1-1	2-1	1-1	0-1	0-1		2-0	1-1	0-0	2-0	3-1	3-3	0-5	4-1	2-1	2-1	1-0	1-0
Huddersfield Town AFC	1-1	0-1	0-0	1-0	0-2	1-0	1-2	3-4	1-1	1-1		0-4	1-0	2-1	0-0	0-2	0-0	0-2	0-0	1-3	2-0	4-0
Liverpool FC	0-1	1-1	1-0	1-1	0-1	1-1	1-1	1-1	0-0	0-0	0-1		0-1	0-2	4-0	1-1	3-1	0-2	3-3	4-0	4-0	0-0
Manchester City FC	0-3	4-1	1-0	1-1	1-0	2-2	0-1	1-0	2-1	2-4	2-0	2-0		0-0	1-0	1-0	1-1	3-2	1-0	0-0	1-1	3-3
Manchester United FC	2-0	3-1	3-0	3-4	3-0	1-1	1-1	1-1	1-2	2-0	4-1	0-0	0-0		1-0	1-1	3-2	2-2	3-2	3-0	1-2	2-0
Middlesbrough FC	0-1	6-0	1-1	1-0	5-0	4-1	2-4	1-1	1-0	1-0	1-0	0-1	0-1	1-4		3-2	1-1	1-0	3-1	1-1	0-0	4-4
Newcastle United FC	3-2	2-1	1-0	3-1	1-1	1-1	2-0	2-2	3-0	1-0	2-4	1-0	0-0	0-1	1-0		0-5	2-5	3-2	2-2	2-1	3-1
Portsmouth FC	4-1	3-0	3-1	1-1	0-0	1-0	3-1	5-2	1-0	4-0	2-0	3-2	3-1	2-2	1-0	1-0		3-1	3-0	1-0	3-0	5-0
Preston North End FC	1-1	0-1	0-0	1-3	1-1	0-3	2-3	3-2	0-0	3-1	2-0	3-2	1-3	1-6	6-1	2-1	2-2		4-1	2-1	1-3	1-1
Sheffield United FC	1-1	0-1	4-0	3-2	1-1	0-0	2-0	2-1	3-1	1-1	0-0	1-2	0-2	2-2	1-0	0-0	3-1	3-2		2-2	2-5	1-1
Stoke City FC	1-0	4-2	2-1	3-2	4-0	2-1	2-2	4-3	4-2	1-0	1-2	3-0	2-3	2-1	3-0	1-1	0-1	2-0	0-1		0-0	2-1
Sunderland AFC	1-1	0-0	1-1	2-2	2-0	0-0	1-0	3-0	2-1	1-1	0-1	0-2	3-0	2-1	1-0	1-1	1-4	0-0	2-0	1-1		3-3
Wolverhampton Wanderers FC	1-3	4-0	2-2	2-1	2-0	3-0	2-0	1-1	2-2	1-0	7-1	0-0	1-1	3-2	0-3	3-0	3-0	2-1	6-0	3-1	0-1	

	Division 1	Pd	Wn	Dw	Ls	GF	GA	Pts	
1.	PORTSMOUTH FC (PORTSMOUTH)	42	25	8	9	84	42	58	
2.	Manchester United FC (Manchester)	42	21	11	10	77	44	53	
3.	Derby County FC (Derby)	42	22	9	11	74	55	53	
4.	Newcastle United FC (Newcastle-upon-Tyne)	42	20	12	10	70	56	52	
5.	Arsenal FC (London)	42	18	13	11	74	44	49	
6.	Wolverhampton Wanderers FC (Wolverhampton)	42	17	12	13	79	66	46	
7.	Manchester City FC (Manchester)	42	15	15	12	47	51	45	
8.	Sunderland AFC (Sunderland)	42	13	17	12	49	58	43	
9.	Charlton Athletic FC (London)	42	15	12	15	63	67	42	
10.	Aston Ville FC (Birmingham)	42	16	10	16	60	76	42	
11.	Stoke City FC (Stoke-on-Trent)	42	16	9	17	66	68	41	
12.	Liverpool FC (Liverpool)	42	13	14	15	53	43	40	
13.	Chelsea FC (Chelsea)	42	12	14	16	69	68	38	
14.	Bolton Wanderers FC (Bolton)	42	14	10	18	59	68	38	
15.	Burnley FC (Burnley)	42	12	14	16	43	50	38	
16.	Blackpool FC (Blackpool)	42	11	16	15	54	67	38	
17.	Birmingham City FC (Birmingham)	42	11	15	16	36	38	37	
18.	Everton FC (Liverpool)	42	13	11	18	41	63	37	
19.	Middlesbrough FC (Middlesbrough)	42	11	12	19	46	57	34	
20.	Huddersfield Town AFC (Huddersfield)	42	12	10	20	40	69	34	
21.	Preston North End FC (Preston)	42	11	11	20	62	75	33	R
22.	Sheffield United FC (Sheffield)	42	11	11	20	57	78	33	R
		924	329	266	329	1303	1303	924	

Top Goalscorer

1)   William MOIR   (Bolton Wanderers FC)   25

Football League Division 2 1948-1949 Season	Barnsley	Blackburn Rovers	Bradford P.A.	Brentford	Bury	Cardiff City	Chesterfield	Coventry City	Fulham	Grimsby Town	Leeds United	Leicester City	Lincoln City	Luton Town	Nottingham Forest	Plymouth Argyle	Q.P.R.	Sheffield Wed.	Southampton	Tottenham Hotspur	W.B.A.	West Ham United
Barnsley FC		1-1	0-0	1-2	3-2	1-1	0-1	1-1	1-1	2-1	1-1	3-1	2-0	1-2	4-0	0-0	4-0	4-0	3-0	4-1	2-0	2-3
Blackburn Rovers FC	5-3		2-3	2-1	1-2	2-1	0-2	2-0	1-0	3-3	0-0	2-0	7-1	4-1	2-1	2-1	2-0	2-1	1-2	1-1	0-0	0-0
Bradford Park Avenue	0-2	2-0		3-1	4-1	3-0	1-1	2-1	1-1	0-1	1-1	3-3	0-3	4-1	1-2	2-2	0-0	1-1	2-0	1-1	4-1	2-3
Brentford FC	0-0	0-1	1-0		8-2	1-1	1-1	2-2	0-0	2-0	1-3	1-2	2-1	2-0	2-1	2-2	0-3	2-2	0-3	0-0	0-0	0-0
Bury FC	4-2	3-1	2-1	1-2		0-3	2-2	0-2	2-0	5-1	3-1	1-2	3-1	3-1	1-1	1-1	0-0	2-1	1-0	1-1	4-0	2-0
Cardiff City AFC	0-3	1-0	6-1	2-0	2-1		3-4	3-0	2-1	3-0	2-1	1-1	3-1	3-3	1-0	3-0	1-1	2-1	0-1	2-2	4-0	4-0
Chesterfield FC	3-2	2-1	2-3	0-1	4-0	0-2		0-0	0-1	0-3	1-1	3-1	1-1	2-0	0-1	2-1	1-1	1-0	0-0	1-0	0-0	0-0
Coventry City FC	4-0	0-1	2-0	2-1	2-1	0-1	0-2		1-0	4-1	4-1	1-2	1-0	2-0	1-2	1-1	1-1	3-4	2-2	2-0	1-0	1-0
Fulham FC	1-1	1-1	2-0	2-1	7-2	4-0	2-1	1-0		3-1	1-0	2-1	4-1	4-0	6-1	5-0	1-1	1-1	1-1	1-2	2-0	2-0
Grimsby Town AFC	3-0	1-2	0-3	3-0	2-3	2-2	3-3	4-1	2-3		5-1	1-0	2-2	2-1	1-2	2-2	4-1	2-0	0-1	1-1	1-0	3-0
Leeds United AFC	4-1	1-0	4-2	0-0	0-1	0-0	1-0	4-1	1-1	6-3		3-1	3-1	2-0	1-0	1-2	1-1	1-1	1-1	0-0	1-3	1-3
Leicester City FC	1-1	3-1	2-2	0-0	3-2	2-2	2-2	3-1	0-3	1-1	6-2		5-3	1-1	4-2	1-1	2-3	2-2	1-3	1-2	0-3	1-1
Lincoln City FC	0-1	3-0	3-6	3-1	1-1	0-0	2-2	1-0	0-3	2-3	0-0	2-0		4-4	1-3	1-2	0-0	3-1	1-2	0-0	0-3	4-3
Luton Town FC	1-0	2-0	0-1	2-1	1-0	3-0	1-0	2-0	1-3	1-4	1-0	1-1	6-0		4-3	3-1	0-0	2-1	1-1	1-0	0-1	0-1
Nottingham Forest FC	0-1	1-0	2-0	1-2	1-0	0-0	0-1	3-0	0-2	0-0	0-0	2-1	1-1	2-0		1-0	0-0	1-2	2-1	2-2	0-1	3-0
Plymouth Argyle FC	3-1	3-0	3-0	1-0	1-0	0-1	2-2	2-3	3-1	0-2	2-1	1-1	0-0	1-1	1-0		3-1	3-2	1-2	0-5	1-2	2-0
Queen's Park Rangers FC	2-2	4-2	1-0	2-0	3-1	0-0	1-1	0-3	1-0	2-0	4-1	2-0	0-3	2-1	0-3	2-1		1-3	1-3	0-0	0-2	2-1
Sheffield Wednesday FC	1-1	3-0	2-1	0-0	1-2	1-1	0-0	2-1	1-2	4-1	3-1	0-0	2-2	0-0	2-1	2-0	2-0		2-0	3-1	2-1	3-0
Southampton FC	3-0	3-0	2-2	2-0	2-0	2-0	1-0	5-2	3-0	0-0	2-1	6-0	4-0	1-1	2-1	3-0	1-0	1-0		3-1	1-1	0-1
Tottenham Hotspur FC	4-1	4-0	5-1	2-0	3-1	1-4	4-0	4-0	1-1	5-2	2-2	1-1	2-1	2-1	1-0	3-2	0-1	3-2	0-1		2-0	1-1
West Bromwich Albion FC	2-0	2-1	7-1	2-0	2-3	2-0	0-0	1-0	1-2	5-2	1-0	2-1	5-0	2-1	3-0	1-1	1-0	2-0	2-2	2-2		2-1
West Ham United FC	2-0	2-1	4-1	1-1	2-1	3-1	1-2	2-2	1-0	1-0	3-2	4-1	2-2	0-1	0-5	3-0	2-0	2-2	1-1	1-0	1-0	

Division 2

		Pd	Wn	Dw	Ls	GF	GA	Pts	
1.	Fulham FC (London)	42	24	9	9	77	37	57	P
2.	West Bromwich Albion FC (West Bromwich)	42	24	8	10	69	39	56	P
3.	Southampton FC (Southampton)	42	23	9	10	69	36	55	
4.	Cardiff City AFC (Cardiff)	42	19	13	10	62	47	51	
5.	Tottenham Hotspur FC (London)	42	17	16	9	72	44	50	
6.	Chesterfield FC (Chesterfield)	42	15	17	10	51	45	47	
7.	West Ham United FC (London)	42	18	10	14	56	58	46	
8.	Sheffield Wednesday FC (Sheffield)	42	15	13	14	63	56	43	
9.	Barnsley FC (Barnsley)	42	14	12	16	62	61	40	
10.	Luton Town FC (Luton)	42	14	12	16	55	57	40	
11.	Grimsby Town FC (Cleethorpes)	42	15	10	17	72	76	40	
12.	Bury FC (Bury)	42	17	6	19	67	76	40	
13.	Queen's Park Rangers FC (London)	42	14	11	17	44	62	39	
14.	Blackburn Rovers FC (Blackburn)	42	15	8	19	53	63	38	
15.	Leeds United AFC (Leeds)	42	12	13	17	55	63	37	
16.	Coventry City FC (Coventry)	42	15	7	20	55	64	37	
17.	Bradford Park Avenue FC (Bradford)	42	13	11	18	65	78	37	
18.	Brentford FC (London)	42	11	14	17	42	53	36	
19.	Leicester City FC (Leicester)	42	10	16	16	62	79	36	
20.	Plymouth Argyle FC (Plymouth)	42	12	12	18	49	64	36	
21.	Nottingham Forest FC (Nottingham)	42	14	7	21	50	54	35	R
22.	Lincoln City FC (Lincoln)	42	8	12	22	53	91	28	R
		924	339	246	339	1303	1303	924	

Football League Division 3 (N) — 1948-1949 Season

	ASt	Bar	BrC	CaU	Che	CrA	Dar	DoR	Gat	HfT	HaU	HuC	MaT	NwB	OlA	Roc	RoU	Sou	StC	TrR	Wre	YoC
Accrington Stanley FC	■	1-1	6-0	2-1	3-1	2-0	3-2	2-0	1-2	1-0	1-2	1-2	1-1	5-1	1-1	0-0	2-3	3-1	2-1	0-2	0-1	2-1
Barrow AFC	0-0	■	0-0	0-0	1-1	1-0	1-1	3-1	3-0	0-0	2-0	1-2	1-0	2-1	2-1	0-1	0-2	2-1	2-1	0-0	1-1	5-0
Bradford City AFC	2-2	0-2	■	1-2	3-2	1-2	0-2	0-1	1-1	2-1	0-0	4-2	1-0	1-1	2-1	1-0	1-2	4-2	1-1	1-3	1-2	2-2
Carlisle United FC	4-1	2-0	3-2	■	2-1	6-2	0-2	3-0	2-1	0-0	1-1	3-1	2-2	2-0	1-1	1-8	4-2	2-1	2-2		3-2	3-3
Chester FC	3-0	4-1	3-0	2-1	■	1-1	1-2	1-2	1-1	0-1	0-0	0-2	1-1	2-0	2-2	2-1	1-1	2-0	2-0	2-2	2-0	4-1
Crewe Alexandra FC	2-0	0-1	2-1	3-0	1-0	■	3-1	0-0	2-1	0-0	3-0	0-0	3-1	2-1	0-4	1-2	0-3	1-0	3-3	2-0	1-0	2-0
Darlington FC	3-0	2-3	1-5	2-2	3-3	4-1	■	1-5	1-3	2-1	2-0	1-2	0-2	2-1	6-1	2-0	0-1	1-1	3-2		3-1	3-1
Doncaster Rovers FC	0-0	0-0	2-0	2-0	0-0	0-1	1-1	■	2-1	1-2	0-0	0-0	1-1	2-1	3-0	0-0	1-2	3-1	2-0		4-2	1-0
Gateshead FC	1-1	3-0	6-2	3-0	2-1	4-1	1-3	0-3	■	1-2	2-1	0-2	0-0	3-0	2-1	3-2	2-0	0-1	3-3		2-0	1-1
Halifax Town AFC	1-0	1-0	1-1	3-4	1-2	0-0	0-3	1-0	2-2	■	2-0	2-4	2-2	0-2	0-1	1-1	0-1	0-1	0-0	0-1	0-1	1-2
Hartlepools United FC	1-0	1-0	1-0		2-1	4-1	0-1	2-1	1-3	0-0	■	0-2	1-1	3-1	1-2	1-4	2-2	0-0	3-6	2-2		2-3
Hull City AFC	3-1	3-0	2-0	3-0	3-2	5-0	0-1	2-0	6-0	2-0		■	4-0	4-1	6-0	1-1	3-2	5-1	6-1	2-0	3-0	2-3
Mansfield Town FC	2-0	2-0	1-0	2-0	1-0	5-1	2-2	2-2	1-1	2-1	1-0	1-1	■	2-0	3-2	2-0	1-2	1-1	4-0	0-0	1-2	3-0
New Brighton FC	1-3	3-1	1-1	2-1	1-1	2-1	1-0	0-1	2-2	2-1	1-0	0-0	1-0	■	0-1	1-2	0-1	0-1	0-2	2-1	2-0	3-1
Oldham Athletic AFC	4-3	2-1	1-2	1-0	2-1	3-2	7-1	0-2	0-0	2-2	5-1	1-1	4-0	4-2	■	0-1	1-3	2-1	5-2	0-2	1-1	4-0
Rochdale AFC	4-1	3-0	1-1	1-0	3-1	3-0	3-4	0-2	3-0	1-0	1-1	1-0	1-1	1-2		■	2-0	1-0	2-1	2-1	2-1	
Rotherham United FC	1-0	2-2	2-0	1-1	2-1	6-1	4-3	2-0	4-0	2-1	0-0	0-1	1-1	2-1	3-1		■	1-0	2-1	7-0	1-3	1-3
Southport FC	3-0	0-0	2-1	2-1	2-1	0-1	3-0	0-2	0-3	2-3	1-2	0-0	1-1	0-1	0-1	1-3		■	1-0	2-3	3-0	0-2
Stockport County FC	2-1	1-2	5-2	2-0	1-1	4-0	2-0	5-1	3-1	3-1	4-0	2-0	1-0	1-2	2-2	0-1	0-0		■	4-1	1-0	1-1
Tranmere Rovers FC	2-2	2-0	1-1	1-1	2-2	2-1	2-0	1-1	2-2	0-2	1-2	0-1	1-1	1-1	2-1	1-0	0-0	2-1	1-0	■	0-2	0-0
Wrexham AFC	1-0	1-0	5-0	4-0	1-0	2-2	4-3	1-0	1-4		1-1	0-2	1-1	2-0	1-1	2-0	0-4	2-0	0-0	0-0	■	3-3
York City FC	1-1	2-0	0-2	6-0	2-0	1-3	2-5	2-3	0-1	2-2	4-0	1-3	2-1	2-1	4-0	1-1	6-1	1-3	4-0	1-0	5-1	■

Division 3 (North)

		Pd	Wn	Dw	Ls	GF	GA	Pts	
1.	Hull City AFC (Kingston-upon-Hull)	42	27	11	4	93	28	65	P
2.	Rotherham United FC (Rotherham)	42	28	6	8	90	46	62	
3.	Doncaster Rovers FC (Doncaster)	42	20	10	12	53	40	50	
4.	Darlington FC (Darlington)	42	20	6	16	83	74	46	
5.	Gateshead FC (Gateshead)	42	16	13	13	69	58	45	
6.	Oldham Athletic AFC (Oldham)	42	18	9	15	75	67	45	
7.	Rochdale AFC (Rochdale)	42	18	9	15	55	53	45	
8.	Stockport County FC (Stockport)	42	16	11	15	61	56	43	
9.	Wrexham AFC (Wrexham)	42	17	9	16	56	62	43	
10.	Mansfield Town FC (Mansfield)	42	14	14	14	52	48	42	
11.	Tranmere Rovers FC (Birkenhead)	42	13	15	14	46	57	41	
12.	Crewe Alexandra FC (Crewe)	42	16	9	17	52	74	41	
13.	Barrow AFC (Barrow-in-Furness)	42	14	12	16	41	48	40	
14.	York City FC (York)	42	15	9	18	74	74	39	
15.	Carlisle United FC (Carlisle)	42	14	11	17	60	77	39	
16.	Hartlepools United FC (Hartlepool)	42	14	10	18	45	58	38	
17.	New Brighton FC (Wallasey)	42	14	8	20	46	58	36	
18.	Chester FC (Chester)	42	11	13	18	57	56	35	
19.	Halifax Town AFC (Halifax)	42	12	11	19	45	62	35	
20.	Accrington Stanley FC (Accrington)	42	12	10	20	55	64	34	
21.	Southport FC (Southport)	42	10	9	22	45	64	31	
22.	Bradford City AFC (Bradford)	42	10	9	23	48	77	29	
		924	350	224	350	1301	1301	924	

Football League Division 3 (S) — 1948-1949 Season

	Aldershot	Bournemouth	Brighton	Bristol City	Bristol Rovers	Crystal Palace	Exeter City	Ipswich Town	Leyton Orient	Millwall	Newport County	Northampton	Norwich City	Notts County	Port Vale	Reading	Southend United	Swansea Town	Swindon Town	Torquay United	Walsall	Watford
Aldershot FC	■	0-0	1-1	0-0	1-5	3-0	1-2	2-0	1-1	5-0	1-2	3-1	4-1	0-1	0-1	0-6	1-0	1-2	1-2	1-3	0-1	0-0
Bournemouth & B. Athletic	1-0	■	0-1	0-0	1-0	2-0	1-0	4-2	3-0	2-0	1-2	5-2	1-2	2-1	2-0	1-3	3-2	1-1	3-0	5-0	2-0	2-1
Brighton & Hove Albion	0-4	1-6	■	0-0	2-1	1-1	2-0	6-1	3-1	1-2	3-2	0-0	1-0	3-2	1-0	2-0	1-0	0-2	1-1	3-1	1-2	0-0
Bristol City FC	1-1	2-1	1-1	■	1-1	2-0	1-0	2-0	3-0	0-0	1-1	3-0	1-6	3-1	1-1	0-2	2-1	0-0	1-3	0-2	2-2	1-1
Bristol Rovers FC	0-2	4-0	0-0	3-1	■	1-0	3-1	1-6	2-3	2-0	3-1	1-0	2-2	3-2	4-1	4-1	0-0	1-1	1-1	1-1	3-0	3-1
Crystal Palace FC	2-1	2-1	0-2	4-0	1-0	■	1-1	1-1	2-1	1-1	0-1	2-2	1-1	1-5	1-1	0-1	2-1	1-1	1-1	1-1	1-3	3-1
Exeter City FC	3-3	2-3	1-1	1-1	2-1	3-1	■	1-3	3-1	3-0	1-2	5-1	4-1	3-1	2-1	1-2	0-0	1-1	3-1	2-0	2-1	2-1
Ipswich Town FC	4-1	1-0	2-2	2-0	0-1	3-2	2-2	■	2-2	1-0	5-1	4-2	1-2	3-2	4-1	3-2	1-3	0-4	4-2	5-1	3-2	1-2
Leyton Orient FC	1-2	1-2	0-3	3-1	1-1	1-1	5-2	1-1	■	2-2	5-2	0-3	0-3	3-1	2-1	1-0	2-0	3-1	1-1	3-1	1-1	1-0
Millwall FC	1-1	4-0	6-2	4-1	1-1	1-0	2-1	0-0	0-0	■	3-1	3-2	1-3	3-2	1-1	1-1	1-0	2-0	3-1	1-3	2-1	2-2
Newport County AFC	0-2	1-2	1-1	0-2	2-1	5-0	0-2	3-0	3-2	1-2	■	2-0	4-3	3-3	2-2	1-1	4-2	2-5	4-1	1-2	1-1	1-1
Northampton Town FC	2-0	1-1	1-1	3-1	0-1	3-2	4-0	1-1	4-1	4-0	2-1	■	1-0	1-2	2-2	1-2	3-2	0-1	2-0	1-1	0-1	1-1
Norwich City FC	0-0	1-1	2-1	4-0	3-0	3-0	3-0	2-0	0-0	1-2	0-0	2-1	■	3-0	1-0	1-2	3-0	1-0	0-0	0-0	1-2	0-1
Notts County FC	2-0	2-3	1-1	2-1	4-1	5-1	9-0	9-2	2-1	1-3	11-1	2-0	2-1	■	2-1	1-0	0-0	1-1	1-2	5-0	2-0	4-0
Port Vale FC	3-0	0-2	3-4	4-2	2-0	0-0	1-1	1-2	3-0	1-0	1-2	1-0	0-0	1-0	■	3-0	0-2	0-2	2-0	3-1	0-2	3-1
Reading FC	2-0	4-2	6-1	2-1	1-0	5-1	2-0	2-1	3-0	2-0	4-1	2-1	1-4	1-2	4-1	■	2-1	1-0	2-1	1-0	1-0	3-1
Southend United FC	1-0	0-0	0-0	1-0	0-1	0-1	0-0	1-1	2-2	2-1	0-1	0-1	2-2	3-2	0-0	0-0	■	0-0	3-4	1-1	2-0	1-1
Swansea Town AFC	2-1	2-0	3-0	2-0	5-0	1-0	6-0	0-1	2-1	2-0	2-1	1-0	2-1	3-1	3-1	2-1	2-2	■	4-0	6-1	3-1	2-0
Swindon Town FC	3-1	1-1	2-0	2-1	1-1	1-0	1-1	4-0	1-1	2-0	5-2	3-3	2-2	1-2	2-0	1-1	2-1	1-0	■	1-1	1-2	1-0
Torquay United FC	2-2	1-1	1-1	0-2	0-2	2-0	2-1	1-1	7-1	2-1	4-0	3-0	2-1	3-1	0-0	4-2	0-3	0-4	3-1	■	5-1	3-1
Walsall FC	0-0	0-0	0-0	0-1	0-1	3-1	4-3	2-1	2-3	5-6	3-1	2-0	4-1	3-2	1-1	2-0	0-3	2-1	0-1	1-1	■	0-1
Watford FC	0-1	0-1	0-0	1-1	0-0	2-0	0-1	1-2	2-1	1-1	2-2	0-1	1-1	2-1	4-1	0-0	4-2	0-3	1-1	2-0	1-1	■

Division 3 (South)

		Pd	Wn	Dw	Ls	GF	GA	Pts	
1.	Swansea Town AFC (Swansea)	42	27	8	7	87	34	62	P
2.	Reading FC (Reading)	42	25	5	12	77	50	55	
3.	Bournemouth & Boscombe Athletic FC (Bournemouth)	42	22	8	12	69	48	52	
4.	Swindon Town FC (Swindon)	42	18	15	9	64	56	51	
5.	Bristol Rovers FC (Bristol)	42	19	10	13	61	51	48	
6.	Brighton & Hove Albion FC (Hove)	42	15	18	9	55	55	48	
7.	Ipswich Town FC (Ipswich)	42	18	9	15	78	77	45	
8.	Millwall FC (London)	42	17	11	14	63	64	45	
9.	Torquay United FC (Torquay)	42	17	11	14	65	70	45	
10.	Norwich City FC (Norwich)	42	16	12	14	67	49	44	
11.	Notts County FC (Nottingham)	42	19	5	18	102	68	43	
12.	Exeter City FC (Exeter)	42	15	10	17	63	76	40	
13.	Port Vale FC (Stoke-on-Trent)	42	14	11	17	51	54	39	
14.	Walsall FC (Walsall)	42	15	8	19	56	64	38	
15.	Newport County AFC (Newport)	42	14	9	19	68	92	37	
16.	Bristol City FC (Bristol)	42	11	14	17	44	62	36	
17.	Watford FC (Watford)	42	10	15	17	41	54	35	
18.	Southend United FC (Southend-on-Sea)	42	9	16	17	41	46	34	
19.	Leyton Orient FC (London)	42	11	12	19	58	80	34	
20.	Northampton Town FC (Northampton)	42	12	9	21	51	62	33	
21.	Aldershot FC (Aldershot)	42	11	11	20	48	59	33	
22.	Crystal Palace FC (London)	42	8	11	23	38	76	27	
		924	343	238	343	1347	1347	924	

F.A. CUP FINAL   (Wembley Stadium, London – 30/04/1949 – 99,500)

WOLVERHAMPTON WANDERERS FC   3-1   Leicester City FC (Leicester)

Pye 2, Smyth   *Griffiths*

Wolves: Williams, Pritchard, Springthorpe, Crook, Shorthouse, Wright, Hancocks, Smyth, Pye, Dunn, Mullen.

Leicester: Bradley, Jelly, Scott, W.Harrison, Plummer, King, Griffiths, Lee, J.Harrison, Chisholm, Adam.

Semi-finals

Leicester City FC (Leicester)	3-1	Portsmouth FC Portsmouth)
Manchester United FC (Manchester)	1-1, 0-1	Wolverhampton Wanderers FC (Wolverhampton)

Quarter-finals

Hull City AFC (Kingston-upon-Hull)	0-1	Manchester United FC (Manchester)
Leicester City FC (Leicester)	2-0	Brentford FC (London)
Portsmouth FC (Portsmouth)	2-1	Derby County FC (Derby)
Wolverhampton Wanderers FC (Wolverhampton)	1-0	West Bromwich Albion FC (West Bromwich)

1949-50

Football League Division 1 1949-1950 Season	Arsenal	Aston Villa	Birmingham City	Blackpool	Bolton Wanderers	Burnley	Charlton Athletic	Chelsea	Derby County	Everton	Fulham	Huddersfield Town	Liverpool	Manchester City	Manchester United	Middlesbrough	Newcastle United	Portsmouth	Stoke City	Sunderland	W.B.A.	Wolves
Arsenal FC		1-3	4-2	1-0	1-1	0-1	2-3	2-3	1-0	5-2	2-1	1-0	1-2	4-1	0-0	1-1	4-2	2-0	6-0	5-0	4-1	1-1
Aston Villa FC	1-1		1-1	0-0	3-0	0-1	1-1	4-0	1-1	2-2	3-1	2-1	2-0	1-0	0-4	4-0	0-1	1-0	1-1	2-0	1-0	1-4
Birmingham City FC	2-1	2-2		0-2	0-0	0-1	2-0	0-3	2-2	0-0	1-1	2-1	2-3	1-0	0-0	0-2	0-3	1-0	1-2	2-0		1-1
Blackpool FC	2-1	1-0	1-1		2-0	2-0	2-0	0-0	1-0	0-1	0-0	4-1	0-0	0-0	3-3	1-1	0-0	2-1	4-2	0-1	3-0	1-2
Bolton Wanderers FC	2-2	1-1	1-0	0-0		0-1	3-0	1-0	0-0	1-2	2-1	1-2	3-2	3-0	1-2	1-2	2-2	1-0	4-0	2-1	3-0	2-4
Burnley FC	0-0	1-0	1-1	0-0	2-1		1-0	1-2	0-1	5-1	1-0	1-0	0-0	1-0	3-2	1-2	2-1	2-1	2-2	0-0	0-1	
Charlton Athletic FC	1-1	1-4	2-0	1-2	0-0	1-1		1-0	1-3	2-0	2-1	2-2	1-3	3-1	1-2	0-3	6-3	1-2	2-0	2-2	1-2	2-3
Chelsea FC	1-2	1-3	3-0	1-1	1-1	0-1	1-3		1-2	3-2	0-0	3-1	1-1	3-0	1-1	2-1	1-3	1-4	2-2	3-1	2-1	0-0
Derby County FC	1-2	3-2	4-1	0-0	4-0	1-1	1-2	2-2		2-0	2-1	4-2	2-2	7-0	0-1	1-0	1-1	2-3	2-3	3-2	3-1	1-2
Everton FC	0-1	1-1	0-0	3-0	0-0	1-1	0-1	1-1	1-2		1-1	3-0	3-0	0-0	3-1	2-1	1-2	2-1	0-2	1-1	0-2	
Fulham FC	2-2	3-0	0-0	1-0	3-0	1-0	1-2	1-1	0-0	0-0		4-1	0-1	1-0	1-0	2-1	2-1	2-0	1-1			
Huddersfield Town AFC	2-2	1-0	1-0	0-1	2-0	1-2	2-1	1-2	2-0	1-2	2-2		3-2	1-0	3-1	2-2	1-2	0-1	4-0	3-1	1-1	1-0
Liverpool FC	2-0	2-1	2-0	0-1	1-1	0-1	1-0	2-2	3-1	3-1	1-1	2-3		4-0	1-0	2-0	2-2	2-2	1-1	4-2	2-1	0-2
Manchester City FC	0-2	3-3	4-0	0-3	1-1	1-0	2-0	1-1	2-2	0-0	2-0	1-2	1-2		1-2	1-0	2-1	1-1	2-1	1-1	2-1	
Manchester United FC	2-0	7-0	0-2	1-2	3-0	3-2	3-2	1-0	0-1	1-1	3-0	6-0	0-0	2-1		2-0	1-1	0-2	2-2	1-3	1-1	3-0
Middlesbrough FC	1-1	0-2	1-0	2-0	2-0	4-1	1-0	2-1	3-1	0-1	1-2	3-0	4-1	0-0	2-3		1-0	1-5	2-0	2-0	3-0	2-0
Newcastle United FC	0-3	3-2	3-1	3-0	3-1	0-0	1-0	2-2	2-1	4-0	3-1	0-0	5-1	4-2	2-1	0-1		1-3	4-1	2-2	5-1	2-0
Portsmouth FC	2-1	5-1	2-0	2-3	1-1	2-1	1-0	4-0	3-1	7-0	3-0	4-0	2-1	1-1	0-0	1-1	1-0		0-0	2-2	0-1	1-1
Stoke City FC	2-5	1-0	3-1	1-1	3-2	1-1	0-3	2-3	1-3	1-0	0-2	0-0	0-0	2-0	3-1	1-0	1-0	0-1		2-1	1-3	2-1
Sunderland AFC	4-2	2-1	1-1	1-1	2-0	1-1	2-1	4-1	6-1	4-2	2-0	1-1	3-2	2-2	1-2	2-0	2-2	1-1	3-0		2-1	3-1
West Bromwich Albion FC	1-2	1-1	3-0	1-0	2-1	3-0	1-0	1-1	1-0	4-0	4-1	0-0	0-0	1-2	0-3	1-1	3-0	0-0	0-2			1-1
Wolverhampton Wanderers FC	3-0	2-3	6-1	3-0	1-1	0-0	2-1	2-2	4-1	1-1	1-1	7-1	1-1	3-0	1-1	3-1	2-1	1-0	2-1	1-3	1-1	

	Division 1	Pd	Wn	Dw	Ls	GF	GA	Pts	
1.	PORTSMOUTH FC (PORTSMOUTH)	42	22	9	11	74	38	52	
2.	Wolverhampton Wanderers FC (Wolverhampton)	42	20	13	9	76	49	53	
3.	Sunderland AFC (Sunderland)	42	21	10	11	83	62	52	
4.	Manchester United FC (Manchester)	42	18	14	10	69	44	50	
5.	Newcastle United FC (Newcastle-upon-Tyne)	42	19	12	11	77	55	50	
6.	Arsenal FC (London)	42	19	11	12	79	55	49	
7.	Blackpool FC (Blackpool)	42	17	15	10	46	35	49	
8.	Liverpool FC (Liverpool)	42	17	14	11	64	54	48	
9.	Middlesbrough FC (Middlesbrough)	42	20	7	15	59	48	47	
10.	Burnley FC (Burnley)	42	16	13	13	40	40	45	
11.	Derby County FC (Derby)	42	17	10	15	69	61	44	
12.	Aston Villa FC (Birmingham)	42	15	12	15	61	61	42	
13.	Chelsea FC (London)	42	12	16	14	58	65	40	
14.	West Bromwich Albion FC (West Bromwich)	42	14	12	16	47	53	40	
15.	Huddersfield Town AFC (Huddersfield)	42	14	9	19	52	73	37	
16.	Bolton Wanderers FC (Bolton)	42	10	14	18	45	59	34	
17.	Fulham FC (London)	42	10	14	18	41	54	34	
18.	Everton FC (Liverpool)	42	10	14	18	42	66	34	
19.	Stoke City FC (Stoke-on-Trent)	42	11	12	19	45	75	34	
20.	Charlton Athletic FC (London)	42	13	6	23	53	65	32	
21.	Manchester City FC (Manchester)	42	8	13	21	36	68	29	R
22.	Birmingham City FC (Birmingham)	42	7	14	21	31	67	28	R
		924	330	264	330	1247	1247	924	

Top Goalscorer

1)	Richard DAVIS	(Sunderland AFC)	25

Football League Division 2 1949-1950 Season	Barnsley	Blackburn Rovers	Bradford P.A.	Brentford	Bury	Cardiff City	Chesterfield	Coventry City	Grimsby Town	Hull City	Leeds United	Leicester City	Luton Town	Plymouth Argyle	Preston N.E.	Q.P.R.	Sheffield United	Sheffield Wed.	Southampton	Swansea Town	Tottenham H.	West Ham United
Barnsley FC	■	1-1	3-2	0-1	1-0	1-0	1-2	4-3	7-2	1-1	1-1	2-2	1-0	4-1	0-1	3-1	2-2	3-4	2-1	5-2	2-0	1-1
Blackburn Rovers FC	4-0	■	0-1	4-1	2-1	1-0	1-1	0-1	3-0	4-2	0-1	3-0	0-0	1-0	2-3	0-0	0-2	0-0	0-0	2-0	1-2	2-0
Bradford Park Avenue	1-3	2-2	■	0-2	1-2	3-3	2-0	2-2	4-1	5-1	1-2	2-2	1-0	3-2	1-2	1-0	1-1	1-3	0-0	0-2	1-3	2-1
Brentford FC	3-0	2-0	2-0	■	2-0	1-0	0-0	2-0	1-0	3-1	0-0	0-1	1-0	0-0	1-0	0-2	1-0	1-1	0-1	0-0	1-4	0-2
Bury FC	2-0	3-0	1-0	1-2	■	2-2	2-0	0-0	3-1	0-0	2-0	3-0	5-2	5-1	1-1	0-0	1-5	0-0	1-1	1-1	1-2	3-1
Cardiff City AFC	3-0	2-1	1-2	0-0	1-0	■	2-0	1-0	1-0	2-0	1-0	2-4	0-0	1-0	3-2	4-0	1-2	1-0	1-1	1-0	0-1	0-1
Chesterfield FC	1-0	2-1	1-1	3-1	2-1	0-1	■	0-1	2-1	0-1	3-1	1-0	0-1	2-0	2-0	2-1	0-1	1-2	0-0	4-1	1-1	1-0
Coventry City FC	1-1	1-1	3-1	1-1	1-2	2-1	3-0	■	1-1	2-0	0-4	1-2	1-0	3-0	0-0	0-0	2-4	3-0	1-2	1-2	0-1	5-1
Grimsby Town AFC	2-2	1-2	4-0	4-1	4-2	0-0	5-2	3-2	■	1-0	2-0	2-1	6-1	2-2	1-3	1-1	4-0	4-1	1-1	2-1	2-3	2-0
Hull City AFC	2-0	3-1	3-3	2-0	3-2	1-1	1-0	2-1	2-2	■	1-0	4-0	1-1	4-2	4-2	1-1	0-4	1-1	1-2	0-0	1-0	2-2
Leeds United AFC	1-0	2-1	0-0	1-0	4-1	2-0	0-0	3-3	1-0	3-0	■	1-1	2-1	1-1	3-1	1-1	0-1	1-1	1-0	1-1	3-0	2-2
Leicester City FC	2-2	3-3	4-1	1-1	0-2	1-0	0-1	1-0	1-0	1-2	1-1	■	3-2	0-0	1-0	3-2	1-1	2-2	2-2	0-1	0-2	2-1
Luton Town FC	3-1	5-2	3-1	1-0	2-1	0-0	1-1	2-0	0-0	0-3	1-0	1-0	■	1-1	1-1	1-2	1-3	0-1	1-1	1-2	1-1	2-2
Plymouth Argyle FC	2-2	0-0	1-1	2-0	2-0	0-0	2-1	1-2	4-2	1-3	1-2	2-1	0-0	■	1-0	0-2	0-1	0-0	0-1	0-1	0-2	1-0
Preston North End FC	1-1	3-1	3-0	2-0	3-1	3-0	0-0	1-1	2-0	4-2	1-1	0-1	0-1	0-0	■	3-2	4-1	0-1	0-3	2-1	1-3	2-1
Queen's Park Rangers FC	0-5	2-3	0-1	3-3	1-0	0-1	3-2	2-0	1-2	1-4	1-1	2-0	3-0	0-2	0-0	■	1-3	0-0	1-0	0-0	0-2	0-1
Sheffield United FC	1-1	4-0	2-1	1-1	4-4	2-0	1-0	1-1	3-1	5-0	1-1	2-2	2-2	1-1	1-0	1-1	■	2-0	0-1	1-1	2-1	0-0
Sheffield Wednesday FC	2-0	2-0	1-1	3-3	1-0	1-1	1-1	4-2	1-1	4-0	6-2	5-2	3-1	1-1	2-4	0-1	2-1	■	2-2	3-0	0-0	2-1
Southampton FC	0-0	3-1	3-1	2-3	4-1	3-1	1-0	1-1	1-2	5-0	2-1	5-3	2-1	3-3	1-0	1-2	1-0	1-0	■	1-2	1-1	3-2
Swansea Town AFC	4-0	2-0	2-0	3-0	1-2	5-1	0-2	1-2	2-1	1-2	1-2	0-0	0-0	2-2	2-1	0-1	1-0	1-2	4-0	■	1-0	1-0
Tottenham Hotspur FC	2-0	2-3	5-0	1-1	3-1	2-0	1-0	3-1	1-2	0-0	2-0	0-2	0-2	4-1	3-2	3-0	7-0	1-0	4-0	3-1	■	4-1
West Ham United FC	2-1	0-2	1-0	2-2	4-0	0-1	1-1	0-1	4-3	2-1	3-1	2-2	0-0	2-2	0-3	1-0	0-0	2-2	1-2	3-0	0-1	■

	Division 2	Pd	Wn	Dw	Ls	GF	GA	Pts	
1.	Tottenham Hotspur FC (London)	42	27	7	8	81	35	61	P
2.	Sheffield Wednesday FC (Sheffield)	42	18	16	8	67	48	52	P
3.	Sheffield United FC (Sheffield)	42	19	14	9	68	49	52	
4.	Southampton FC (Southampton)	42	19	14	9	64	48	52	
5.	Leeds United AFC (Leeds)	42	17	13	12	54	45	47	
6.	Preston North End FC (Preston)	42	18	9	15	60	49	45	
7.	Hull City AFC (Kingston-upon-Tyne)	42	17	11	14	64	72	45	
8.	Swansea Town AFC (Swansea)	42	17	9	16	53	49	43	
9.	Brentford FC (London)	42	15	13	14	44	49	43	
10.	Cardiff City AFC (Cardiff)	42	16	10	16	41	44	42	
11.	Grimsby Town FC (Cleethorpes)	42	16	8	18	74	73	40	
12.	Coventry City FC (Coventry)	42	13	13	16	55	55	39	
13.	Barnsley FC (Barnsley)	42	13	13	16	64	67	39	
14.	Chesterfield FC (Chesterfield)	42	15	9	18	43	47	39	
15.	Leicester City FC (Leicester)	42	12	15	15	55	65	39	
16.	Blackburn Rovers FC (Blackburn)	42	14	10	18	55	60	38	
17.	Luton Town FC (Luton)	42	10	18	14	41	51	38	
18.	Bury FC (Bury)	42	14	9	19	60	65	37	
19.	West Ham United FC (London)	42	12	12	18	53	61	36	
20.	Queen's Park Rangers FC (London)	42	11	12	19	40	57	34	
21.	Plymouth Argyle FC (Plymouth)	42	8	16	18	44	65	32	R
22.	Bradford Park Avenue FC (Bradford)	42	10	11	21	51	77	31	R
		924	331	262	331	1231	1231	924	

Football League — Division 3 (N) — 1949-1950 Season

	Accrington Stanley	Barrow	Bradford City	Carlisle United	Chester	Crewe Alexandra	Darlington	Doncaster Rovers	Gateshead	Halifax Town	Hartlepools United	Lincoln City	Mansfield Town	New Brighton	Oldham Athletic	Rochdale	Rotherham United	Southport	Stockport County	Tranmere Rovers	Wrexham	York City
Accrington Stanley FC	■	1-0	3-2	1-1	4-0	1-1	3-0	2-2	0-1	1-0	1-2	2-0	2-2	3-0	3-4	1-0	1-4	4-0	4-2	2-0	2-0	0-0
Barrow AFC	2-1	■	1-0	1-3	3-1	0-1	2-1	1-1	1-1	4-0	-0	0-0	0-1	1-1	3-1	0-1	1-1	1-0	0-1	1-2	2-1	3-2
Bradford City AFC	5-2	3-2	■	3-2	1-0	0-2	4-1	1-2	2-1	1-3	1-3	0-1	2-1	2-1	1-1	2-1	1-2	6-0	0-1	2-4	1-0	0-2
Carlisle United FC	2-1	2-0	3-0	■	5-1	2-2	0-1	0-0	4-2	0-2	2-1	0-2	1-1	0-0	3-0	2-0	3-1	3-3	2-0	0-0	1-1	4-3
Chester FC	1-0	1-0	4-1	2-4	■	0-1	4-4	3-1	0-3	5-1	3-0	3-1	6-3	2-0	1-0	0-2	4-2	4-1	0-4	0-0	2-1	2-3
Crewe Alexandra FC	2-1	1-1	2-2	2-1	1-2	■	2-0	0-2	3-1	6-3	1-0	3-2	1-1	1-2	1-1	0-1	4-1	1-2	1-0	2-0	1-1	3-3
Darlington FC	0-2	1-1	4-3	1-1	2-1	1-1	■	2-1	2-3	5-1	1-0	2-0	2-2	3-1	1-1	1-1	2-1	0-2	1-1	0-2	3-1	1-1
Doncaster Rovers FC	4-1	1-0	1-1	0-0	2-0	0-2	2-1	■	1-1	4-0	0-0	1-4	0-1	2-0	1-1	0-1	1-0	5-1	3-0	1-1	2-0	1-1
Gateshead FC	5-0	3-1	4-2	2-1	4-0	1-1	3-3	1-1	■	7-1	2-0	2-1	0-1	2-1	2-0	1-3	2-2	3-2	1-0	5-1	0-1	1-1
Halifax Town AFC	1-4	0-1	3-1	1-1	2-1	3-1	1-3	2-2	5-2	■	1-2	0-1	0-3	3-0	1-1	3-2	4-3	0-0	3-1	0-1	0-0	1-2
Hartlepools United FC	0-0	2-3	3-0	1-5	5-1	1-6	2-0	1-1	3-5	3-3	■	2-1	1-3	0-2	1-2	1-2	1-0	1-2	0-0	2-0	3-1	0-2
Lincoln City FC	1-0	4-0	2-2	2-1	2-0	2-0	2-0	1-0	2-0	1-0	6-0	■	1-0	1-2	2-0	0-0	1-1	1-1	0-0	1-0	2-0	1-0
Mansfield Town FC	2-0	1-1	0-2	4-1	0-2	3-0	2-1	1-2	1-0	1-0	7-1	2-1	■	2-2	3-1	1-1	0-2	1-2	3-0	1-1	1-0	1-0
New Brighton FC	3-0	2-0	1-0	3-2	3-3	0-2	1-0	2-2	0-1	1-1	1-0	1-0	1-2	■	0-0	0-4	0-3	1-1	1-3	0-0	3-1	3-1
Oldham Athletic AFC	0-1	1-3	2-1	1-1	0-2	2-1	2-0	1-4	1-0	2-1	3-1	0-2	1-0	3-0	■	0-0	2-2	2-5	3-3	2-1	2-3	2-0
Rochdale AFC	2-0	2-1	2-2	1-0	0-1	2-1	2-0	0-1	1-3	1-0	4-0	2-0	7-1	4-0	1-0	■	1-0	2-0	1-1	3-0	1-1	3-1
Rotherham United FC	6-0	1-2	5-2	1-1	3-2	0-0		1-1	0-2	1-2	5-1	1-3	2-2	3-0	0-1	4-3	■	4-0	2-1	1-1	2-2	1-1
Southport FC	1-0	0-1	1-1	1-2	1-1	2-1	1-1	3-3	0-3						3-2	3-2	4-0	■	1-0	2-1	0-0	1-0
Stockport County FC	1-0	1-3	1-0	2-0	3-0	4-1	2-1	0-1	2-1	2-0	1-1	1-0	0-2	1-3	1-1	0-2	3-2		■	2-1	2-1	3-1
Tranmere Rovers FC	0-1	2-1	1-0	0-0	2-1	2-2	2-1	2-4	1-0	2-1	2-1	2-2	2-1	4-2	1-0	0-2	2-0		2-0	■	2-1	1-0
Wrexham AFC	1-1	1-0	0-0	1-1	1-1	1-2	2-1	0-1	0-1	2-3	1-0	4-0	0-0	2-2	2-1	3-0	0-1	1-0	0-2	0-0	■	2-0
York City FC	2-1	2-0	1-1	1-1	2-3	1-1	1-1	0-3	1-5	3-1	0-2	1-2	3-3	2-1	0-1	2-2	0-3	0-1	1-1	1-0	5-0	■

Division 3 (North)

		Pd	Wn	Dw	Ls	GF	GA	Pts	
1.	Doncaster Rovers FC (Doncaster)	42	19	17	6	66	38	55	P
2.	Gateshead FC (Gateshead)	42	23	7	12	87	54	53	
3.	Rochdale AFC (Rochdale)	42	21	9	12	68	41	51	
4.	Lincoln City FC (Lincoln)	42	21	9	12	60	39	51	
5.	Tranmere Rovers FC (Tranmere)	42	19	11	12	51	48	49	
6.	Rotherham United FC (Rotherham)	42	19	10	13	80	59	48	
7.	Crewe Alexandra FC (Crewe)	42	17	14	11	68	55	48	
8.	Mansfield Town FC (Mansfield)	42	18	12	12	66	54	48	
9.	Carlisle United FC (Carlisle)	42	16	15	11	68	51	47	
10.	Stockport County FC (Stockport)	42	19	7	16	55	52	45	
11.	Oldham Athletic AFC (Oldham)	42	16	11	15	58	63	43	
12.	Chester FC (Chester)	42	17	6	19	70	79	40	
13.	Accrington Stanley FC (Accrington)	42	16	7	19	57	62	39	
14.	New Brighton FC (Wallasey)	42	14	10	18	45	63	38	
15.	Barrow AFC (Barrow-in-Furness)	42	14	9	19	47	53	37	
16.	Southport FC (Southport)	42	12	13	17	51	71	37	
17.	Darlington FC (Darlington)	42	11	13	18	56	69	35	
18.	Hartlepools United FC (Hartlepool)	42	14	5	23	52	79	33	
19.	Bradford City AFC (Bradford)	42	12	8	22	61	76	32	
20.	Wrexham AFC (Wrexham)	42	10	12	20	39	54	32	
21.	Halifax Town AFC (Halifax)	42	12	8	22	58	85	32	
22.	York City FC (York)	42	9	13	20	52	70	31	
		924	349	226	349	1315	1315	924	

Elected: Scunthorpe & Lindsey United FC (Scunthorpe) and Shrewsbury Town FC (Shrewsbury)

Division 3 (North) was extended to 24 clubs from the next season

Football League Division 3 (S) 1949-1950 Season	Aldershot	Bournemouth	Brighton	Bristol City	Bristol Rovers	Crystal Palace	Exeter City	Ipswich Town	Leyton Orient	Millwall	Newport County	Northampton	Norwich City	Nottingham Forest	Notts County	Port Vale	Reading	Southend United	Swindon Town	Torquay United	Walsall	Watford
Aldershot FC	■	0-1	0-1	0-1	3-1	0-0	1-2	5-0	2-0	2-1	4-1	0-0	2-0	1-1	2-0	1-0	2-0	1-1	0-0	3-5	1-0	0-1
Bournemouth & B. Athletic	2-1	■	2-2	3-1	0-2	2-0	2-0	4-0	4-1	1-0	1-1	1-2	2-0	1-2	3-0	2-2	2-1	3-0	1-1	1-2	1-1	0-0
Brighton & Hove Albion	1-1	1-1	■	2-1	1-2	0-0	0-0	2-1	2-2	1-0	5-0	1-1	1-3	2-2	2-3	2-1	2-1	2-1	0-1	2-1	1-1	2-1
Bristol City FC	2-0	3-2	1-2	■	1-2	2-0	1-0	4-2	0-0	2-1	6-0	3-1	1-2	0-2	4-0	2-0	2-2	1-1	1-0	0-0	2-1	0-1
Bristol Rovers FC	2-1	0-0	3-0	2-3	■	0-0	1-0	2-0	3-0	3-1	3-0	0-0	5-1	0-3	0-3	2-1	2-1	1-1	2-0	2-0	1-1	0-2
Crystal Palace FC	2-1	1-0	6-0	1-1	1-0	■	5-3	2-0	1-1	1-0	1-0	0-4	2-0	1-1	1-2	0-1	1-1	2-1	2-2	1-3	2-0	2-0
Exeter City FC	1-0	1-2	2-3	0-0	2-0	2-1	■	1-1	1-1	2-1	3-3	1-3	3-1	0-0	2-2	3-1	3-4	1-1	3-0	1-1	2-1	3-1
Ipswich Town FC	1-0	1-2	2-2	0-0	3-1	4-4	1-0	■	4-4	0-3	1-0	2-2	3-0	1-2	0-4	2-1	2-0	1-3	3-1	3-1	1-5	1-1
Leyton Orient FC	2-7	2-1	0-1	1-0	1-0	2-2	4-1	4-0	■	1-1	2-1	1-0	1-2	1-1	1-4	1-0	2-1	2-2	1-3	2-1	2-2	0-0
Millwall FC	3-0	1-0	5-1	3-1	0-1	2-3	3-1	3-1	3-1	■	1-2	0-2	1-2	2-1	1-3	3-0	3-1	1-2	1-0	1-3	1-1	1-3
Newport County AFC	6-0	5-0	0-1	6-4	2-3	2-2	1-2	1-0	3-2	4-3	■	1-4	3-2	4-1	1-1	1-1	1-1	2-1	1-2	1-0	2-1	3-3
Northampton Town FC	1-1	2-3	2-1	4-2	2-3	2-2	3-3	3-1	3-0	1-0	4-3	■	3-1	0-0	5-1	1-1	2-0	2-0	0-1	3-0	0-0	0-0
Norwich City FC	4-0	0-1	1-2	3-0	4-0	2-0	1-2	1-1	4-0	0-2	4-0	2-1	■	1-1	4-3	0-1	1-1	0-0	4-0	3-3	3-2	2-1
Nottingham Forest FC	3-0	3-0	0-1	3-0	2-0	2-0	5-0	2-0	2-1	3-1	3-0	0-1	0-1	■	1-2	2-0	1-2	1-2	2-1	1-2	1-0	0-1
Notts County FC	3-1	2-0	4-2	4-1	2-0	0-1	3-3	2-0	7-1	2-0	7-0	2-0	5-0	2-0	■	3-1	4-0	2-0	3-0	1-1	1-1	1-0
Port Vale FC	0-1	1-1	3-0	0-2	1-0	2-0	1-0	2-2	2-0	4-0	1-0	3-1	2-2	1-1	3-1	■	1-1	0-0	0-1	2-0	2-0	2-0
Reading FC	1-3	2-1	3-0	1-0	0-1	1-2	3-2	3-1	5-1	2-0	4-1	3-1	4-1	1-1	0-1	2-1	■	5-0	4-3	2-0	1-1	1-0
Southend United FC	3-0	1-0	3-2	2-0	3-1	0-0	1-0	2-2	2-0	3-0	6-0	1-2	1-0	2-3	2-0	1-0	3-2	■	2-0	2-0	2-2	1-1
Swindon Town FC	2-1	3-1	4-2	1-1	1-0	4-2	7-1	0-3	0-1	1-1	1-1	6-1	1-1	0-5	1-1	0-0	2-0	2-2	■	1-2	4-3	0-1
Torquay United FC	4-0	3-1	0-0	3-3	1-0	1-0	1-4	2-2	4-1	1-0	5-3	1-0	1-1	2-0	0-0	0-0	4-2	2-4	1-0	■	2-1	2-1
Walsall FC	0-0	1-1	4-2	1-1	3-1	3-1	3-0	1-3	1-2	0-1	2-0	1-3	1-1	1-3	3-3	1-0	2-0	1-1	0-0	7-1	■	1-1
Watford FC	1-0	4-1	0-0	2-0	0-2	0-0	1-2	6-0	2-1	0-0	0-1	0-0	0-0	0-1	2-1	0-2	1-1	1-0	1-2	1-0	3-0	■

Division 3 (South)	Pd	Wn	Dw	Ls	GF	GA	Pts	
1. Notts County FC (Nottingham)	42	25	8	9	95	50	58	P
2. Northampton Town FC (Northampton)	42	20	11	11	72	50	51	
3. Southend United FC (Southend-on-Sea)	42	19	13	10	66	48	51	
4. Nottingham Forest FC (Nottingham)	42	20	9	13	67	39	49	
5. Torquay United FC (Torquay)	42	19	10	13	66	63	48	
6. Watford FC (Watford)	42	16	13	13	45	35	45	
7. Crystal Palace FC (London)	42	15	14	13	55	54	44	
8. Brighton & Hove Albion FC (Hove)	42	16	12	14	57	69	44	
9. Bristol Rovers FC (Bristol)	42	19	5	18	51	51	43	
10. Reading FC (Reading)	42	17	8	17	70	64	42	
11. Norwich City FC (Norwich)	42	16	10	16	65	63	42	
12. Bournemouth & Boscombe Athletic FC (Bournemouth)	42	16	10	16	57	56	42	
13. Port Vale FC (Stoke-on-Trent)	42	15	11	16	47	42	41	
14. Swindon Town FC (Swindon)	42	15	11	16	59	62	41	
15. Bristol City FC (Bristol)	42	15	10	17	60	61	40	
16. Exeter City FC (Exeter)	42	14	11	17	63	75	39	
17. Ipswich Town FC (Ipswich)	42	12	11	19	57	86	35	
18. Leyton Orient FC (London)	42	12	11	19	53	85	35	
19. Walsall FC (Walsall)	42	9	16	17	61	62	34	
20. Aldershot FC (Aldershot)	42	13	8	21	48	60	34	
21. Newport County AFC (Newport)	42	13	8	21	67	98	34	
22. Millwall FC (London)	42	14	4	24	55	63	32	
	924	350	224	350	1336	1336	924	

Elected: Colchester United FC (Colchester) and Gillingham FC (Gillingham)

Division 3 (South) was extended to 24 clubs from the next season.

F.A. CUP FINAL   (Wembley Stadium, London – 29/04/1950 – 100,000)

ARSENAL FC (LONDON)	2-0	Liverpool FC (Liverpool)

Lewis 2

Arsenal: Swindin, Scott, Barnes, Forbes, L.Compton, Mercer, Cox, Logie, Goring, Lewis, D.Compton.
Liverpool: Sidlow, Lambert, Spicer, Taylor, Hughes, Jones, Payne, Barron, Stubbins, Fagan, Liddell.

Semi-finals

Arsenal FC (London)	2-2, 1-0	Chelsea FC (London)
Liverpool FC (Liverpool)	2-0	Everton FC (Liverpool)

Quarter-finals

Arsenal FC (London)	1-0	Leeds United AFC (Leeds)
Chelsea FC (London)	2-0	Manchester United FC (Manchester)
Derby County FC (Derby)	1-2	Everton FC (Liverpool)
Liverpool FC (Liverpool)	2-1	Blackpool FC (Blackpool)

Football League Division 1 — 1950-51 Season	Arsenal	Aston Villa	Blackpool	Bolton Wands.	Burnley	Charlton Ath	Chelsea	Derby County	Everton	Fulham	Huddersfield T.	Liverpool	Man. United	Middlesbrough	Newcastle Utd.	Portsmouth	Sheffield Wed.	Stoke City	Sunderland	Tottenham H.	W.B.A.	Wolves
Arsenal FC	█	2-1	4-4	1-1	0-1	2-5	0-0	3-1	2-1	5-1	6-2	1-2	3-0	3-1	0-0	0-1	3-0	0-3	5-1	2-2	3-0	2-1
Aston Villa FC	1-1	█	0-3	0-1	3-2	0-0	4-2	1-1	3-3	3-0	0-1	1-1	1-3	0-1	3-0	3-3	2-1	6-2	3-1	2-3	2-0	1-0
Blackpool FC	0-1	1-1	█	2-0	1-2	0-0	3-2	3-1	4-0	4-0	3-1	3-0	1-1	2-1	2-2	3-0	3-2	3-0	2-2	0-1	2-1	1-1
Bolton Wanderers FC	3-0	1-0	1-2	█	1-1	3-0	1-0	3-0	2-0	0-1	4-0	2-1	1-0	0-2	0-2	4-0	0-1	1-1	1-2	1-4	0-2	2-1
Burnley FC	0-1	2-0	0-0	2-0	█	5-1	2-1	1-0	1-1	0-2	0-1	1-1	1-2	3-1	1-1	1-1	1-0	1-1	1-1	2-0	0-1	2-0
Charlton Athletic FC	1-3	2-2	2-3	4-3	0-0	█	1-2	1-2	2-1	0-0	3-2	1-0	1-2	3-0	1-3	0-1	2-1	2-0	3-0	1-1	2-3	3-2
Chelsea FC	0-1	1-1	0-2	4-0	0-2	2-3	█	1-2	2-1	2-0	1-2	1-0	1-1	3-1	1-4	4-0	1-3	1-0	3-0	0-2	1-1	2-1
Derby County FC	4-2	4-2	4-1	2-2	1-1	5-0	1-0	█	0-1	3-2	3-0	1-2	2-4	6-0	1-2	2-3	4-1	1-1	6-5	1-1	1-1	1-2
Everton FC	1-1	1-2	0-2	1-1	1-0	0-0	3-0	1-2	█	1-0	3-2	1-3	1-4	32	3-1	1-5	0-0	0-3	3-1	1-2	0-3	1-1
Fulham FC	3-2	2-1	2-2	0-1	4-1	1-3	1-2	3-5	1-5	█	1-1	2-1	2-2	2-0	1-1	1-4	4-2	2-0	1-1	0-1	0-1	2-1
Huddersfield Town AFC	2-2	4-2	2-1	0-4	3-1	1-1	2-1	2-0	1-2	1-2	█	2-2	2-3	0-0	2-1	3-4	3-1	3-4	3-2	1-2	1-2	
Liverpool FC	1-3	0-0	1-0	3-3	1-0	1-0	1-0	1-0	0-2	2-0	1-4	█	2-1	0-0	2-4	2-1	2-1	0-0	4-0	1-1	1-1	1-4
Manchester United FC	3-1	0-0	1-0	2-3	1-1	3-0	4-1	2-0	3-0	1-0	6-0	1-0	█	1-0	1-2	0-0	3-1	0-0	3-5	2-1	3-0	2-1
Middlesbrough FC	2-1	2-1	4-3	1-1	3-3	7-3	3-0	1-1	4-0	1-1	8-0	1-1	1-2	█	2-1	3-1	2-1	1-0	1-1	1-1	1-2	1-2
Newcastle United FC	2-1	0-1	4-2	0-1	2-1	3-2	3-1	1-1	1-2	6-0	1-1	0-2	1-0		█	2-0	3-1	2-2	0-1	1-1	1-1	1-1
Portsmouth FC	1-1	3-3	2-0	2-1	2-1	3-3	1-3	2-2	6-3	1-0	1-0	1-3	0-0	1-1	0-0	█	4-1	5-1	0-0	1-1	2-2	1-4
Sheffield Wednesday FC	0-2	3-2	3-1	3-4	0-1	1-2	2-2	4-3	6-0	2-2	3-2	4-1	0-4	0-1	0-0	2-1	█	1-1	3-0	1-1	3-0	2-2
Stoke City FC	1-0	1-0	1-0	2-1	0-0	2-0	2-1	4-1	2-0	0-1	2-3	2-0	2-0	1-2	1-2	1-1		█	2-4	0-0	1-1	0-1
Sunderland AFC	0-2	3-3	0-2	1-2	1-1	4-2	1-1	4-0	0-1	0-1	2-1	2-1	2-1	0-0	5-1	1-1			█	0-0	1-1	0-0
Tottenham Hotspur FC	1-0	3-2	1-4	4-2	1-0	1-0	2-1	2-1	3-0	2-1	0-2	3-1	1-0	3-3	7-0	5-1	1-0	6-1	1-1	█	5-0	2-1
West Bromwich Albion FC	2-0	2-0	1-3	0-1	2-1	3-0	1-1	1-2	0-1	0-0	0-2	1-1	0-1	2-3	1-2	5-0	1-3	1-1	3-1	1-2	█	3-2
Wolverhampton Wanderers FC	0-1	2-3	1-1	7-1	0-1	2-3	2-1	2-3	4-0	1-1	3-1	2-0	0-0	3-4	0-1	2-3	4-0	2-3	2-1	2-1	3-1	█

Division 1

		Pd	Wn	Dw	Ls	GF	GA	Pts	
1.	TOTTENHAM HOTSPUR FC (LONDON)	42	25	10	7	82	44	60	
2.	Manchester United FC (Manchester)	42	24	8	10	74	40	56	
3.	Blackpool FC (Blackpool)	42	20	10	12	79	53	50	
4.	Newcastle United FC (Newcastle-upon-Tyne)	42	18	13	11	62	53	49	
5.	Arsenal FC (London)	42	19	9	14	73	56	47	
6.	Middlesbrough FC (Middlesbrough)	42	18	11	13	76	65	47	
7.	Portsmouth FC (Portsmouth)	42	16	15	11	71	68	47	
8.	Bolton Wanderers FC (Bolton)	42	19	7	16	64	61	45	
9.	Liverpool FC (Liverpool)	42	16	11	15	53	59	43	
10.	Burnley FC (Burnley)	42	14	14	14	48	43	42	
11.	Derby County FC (Derby)	42	16	8	18	81	75	40	
12.	Sunderland AFC (Sunderland)	42	12	16	14	63	73	40	
13.	Stoke City FC (Stoke-on-Trent)	42	13	14	15	50	59	40	
14.	Wolverhampton Wanderers FC (Wolverhampton)	42	15	8	19	74	61	38	
15.	Aston Villa FC (Birmingham)	42	12	13	17	66	68	37	
16.	West Bromwich Albion FC (West Bromwich)	42	13	11	18	53	61	37	
17.	Charlton Athletic FC (London)	42	14	9	19	63	80	37	
18.	Fulham FC (London)	42	13	11	18	52	68	37	
19.	Huddersfield Town AFC (Huddersfield)	42	15	6	21	64	92	36	
20.	Chelsea FC (London)	42	13	8	22	53	65	32	
21.	Sheffield Wednesday FC (Sheffield)	42	12	8	22	64	83	32	R
22.	Everton FC (Liverpool)	42	12	8	22	48	86	32	R
		924	348	228	348	1413	1413	924	

Top Goalscorer

1) Stanley MORTENSEN   (Blackpool FC)   30

Football League Division 2 1950-51 Season	Barnsley	Birmingham City	Blackburn Rovers	Brentford	Bury	Cardiff City	Chesterfield	Coventry City	Doncaster Rovers	Grimsby Town	Hull City	Leeds United	Leicester City	Luton Town	Manchester City	Notts County	Preston North End	Q.P.R.	Sheffield United	Southampton	Swansea Town	West Ham United
Barnsley FC	■	0-2	3-0	2-3	2-3	0-0	0-0	3-0	0-1	3-1	4-2	1-2	0-0	6-1	1-1	2-0	4-1	7-0	1-1	1-2	1-0	1-2
Birmingham City FC	2-0	■	3-2	1-1	3-3	0-0	2-1	1-1	0-2	1-1	2-1	0-1	2-0	3-0	1-0	1-4	1-0	1-1	3-0	2-1	5-0	3-1
Blackburn Rovers FC	3-4	2-3	■	3-2	2-4	2-0	1-1	1-0	4-2	2-0	2-2	2-1	1-0	1-0	4-1	0-0	2-1	2-1	0-2	1-0	3-0	1-3
Brentford FC	0-2	2-1	3-2	■	4-0	4-0	4-0	0-4	1-1	5-1	2-1	1-2	0-0	1-0	2-0	1-3	2-4	2-1	3-1	4-0	2-1	1-1
Bury FC	0-3	4-1	1-3	2-1	■	1-2	2-2	1-0	3-1	2-3	0-2	0-1	2-3	4-1	2-0	0-1	3-1	0-1	1-1	1-0	1-1	3-0
Cardiff City AFC	1-1	2-1	1-0	1-1	2-2	■	1-0	2-1	0-0	5-2	2-1	1-0	2-1	1-1	2-0	1-2	0-1	4-2	2-0	2-2	1-0	2-1
Chesterfield FC	1-2	1-1	4-1	2-2	3-0	0-3	■	1-1	1-4	2-2	0-0	1-0	1-0	3-0	2-0	3-1	2-0	2-0	2-3	2-3	3-1	1-2
Coventry City FC	3-3	3-1	6-1	3-3	5-2	2-1	1-0	■	3-1	1-0	4-1	1-0	2-1	4-1	0-2	1-2	1-0	3-0	2-3	2-2	3-1	1-0
Doncaster Rovers FC	3-2	0-1	0-1	0-3	1-1	0-0	1-2	2-1	■	3-1	2-4	4-4	2-2	5-2	4-3	3-2	2-0	0-2	1-1	0-0	1-0	3-0
Grimsby Town AFC	3-1	1-1	1-1	7-2	2-1	0-0	1-2	1-2	1-0	■	1-1	2-2	0-2	0-2	4-4	1-0	0-4	2-2	4-2	4-2	4-2	0-1
Hull City AFC	3-3	3-2	2-2	3-0	4-0	2-0	2-1	0-2	1-2	2-1	■	2-0	1-3	5-3	3-3	1-0	0-0	5-1	1-1	4-1	2-1	1-2
Leeds United AFC	2-2	3-0	0-1	1-0	1-1	2-0	2-0	1-0	3-1	1-0	3-0	■	2-1	1-1	0-1	0-3	0-3	2-2	3-5	5-3	2-0	2-0
Leicester City FC	1-2	1-3	2-0	1-2	4-0	1-1	1-0	3-0	2-0	0-0	4-0	1-5	■	3-1	1-2	1-1	2-3	6-2	2-2	3-1	2-3	1-1
Luton Town FC	1-1	1-1	1-1	2-0	4-2	1-1	3-0	1-1	3-1	4-0	1-2	2-3	0-2	■	2-2	1-1	1-2	2-0	0-0	0-1	3-1	1-1
Manchester City FC	6-0	3-1	1-0	4-0	5-1	2-1	5-1	1-0	3-3	2-2	0-0	4-1	1-1	1-1	■	0-0	0-3	5-2	5-3	2-3	1-2	2-0
Notts County FC	2-1	0-1	1-1	2-3	4-2	1-2	1-0	0-2	1-2	3-2	2-2	0-0	2-3	2-2	0-0	■	1-3	3-3	3-0	2-2	3-2	4-1
Preston North End FC	7-0	1-0	3-0	4-2	2-0	1-1	4-1	1-1	6-1	0-1	3-1	0-0	3-2	1-0	2-4	3-1	■	1-0	1-1	3-2	5-1	0-1
Queen's Park Rangers FC	2-1	2-0	3-1	1-1	3-2	3-2	1-1	3-1	1-2	7-1	3-1	3-0	3-0	1-1	1-2	1-0	1-4	■	2-1	2-0	1-1	3-3
Sheffield United FC	0-2	3-2	0-3	5-1	3-0	1-2	4-1	2-0	0-0	4-2	3-2	2-1	2-1	0-0	1-2	2-3	2-0	1-2	■	1-2	6-1	1-1
Southampton FC	1-0	0-2	1-1	2-1	1-0	1-1	1-1	5-4	1-1	5-1	2-3	2-0	2-2	2-1	2-1	2-1	1-0	3-3	2-2	■	2-1	2-2
Swansea Town AFC	1-0	0-1	1-2	2-1	2-0	1-0	2-0	1-1	2-2	1-3	1-0	4-2	0-2	2-3	2-1	2-1	1-0	1-2	2-1	2-1	■	3-2
West Ham United FC	4-2	1-2	2-3	1-2	2-3	0-0	2-0	3-2	0-0	2-1	3-3	3-1	0-0	2-1	2-4	4-2	2-0	4-1	3-5	3-0	1-1	■

	Division 2	**Pd**	**Wn**	**Dw**	**Ls**	**GF**	**GA**	**Pts**	
1.	Preston North End FC (Preston)	42	26	5	11	91	49	57	P
2.	Manchester City FC (Manchester)	42	19	14	9	89	61	52	P
3.	Cardiff City AFC (Cardiff)	42	17	16	9	53	45	50	
4.	Birmingham City FC (Birmingham)	42	20	9	13	64	53	49	
5.	Leeds United AFC (Leeds)	42	20	8	14	63	55	48	
6.	Blackburn Rovers FC (Blackburn)	42	19	8	15	65	66	46	
7.	Coventry City FC (Coventry)	42	19	7	16	75	59	45	
8.	Sheffield United FC (Sheffield)	42	16	12	14	72	62	44	
9.	Brentford FC (London)	42	18	8	16	75	74	44	
10.	Hull City AFC (Kingston-upon-Hull)	42	16	11	15	74	70	43	
11.	Doncaster Rovers FC (Doncaster)	42	15	13	14	64	68	43	
12.	Southampton FC (Southampton)	42	15	13	14	66	73	43	
13.	West Ham United FC (London)	42	16	10	16	68	69	42	
14.	Leicester City FC (Leicester)	42	15	11	16	68	58	41	
15.	Barnsley FC (Barnsley)	42	15	10	17	74	68	40	
16.	Queen's Park Rangers FC (London)	42	15	10	17	71	82	40	
17.	Notts County FC (Nottingham)	42	13	13	16	61	60	39	
18.	Swansea Town AFC (Swansea)	42	16	4	22	54	77	36	
19.	Luton Town FC (Luton)	42	9	14	19	57	70	32	
20.	Bury FC (Bury)	42	12	8	22	60	86	32	
21.	Chesterfield FC (Chesterfield)	42	9	12	21	44	69	30	R
22.	Grimsby Town FC (Cleethorpes)	42	8	12	22	61	95	28	R
		924	348	228	348	1469	1469	924	

Football League Division 3 (N) 1950-51 Season	Accrington St.	Barrow	Bradford City	Bradford P.A.	Carlisle United	Chester	Crewe Alex.	Darlington	Gateshead	Halifax Town	Hartlepools	Lincoln City	Mansfield T.	New Brighton	Oldham Ath.	Rochdale	Rotherham U.	Scunthorpe U.	Shrewsbury T.	Southport	Stockport Co.	Tranmere R.	Wrexham	York City
Accrington Stanley	■	1-0	0-2	3-3	0-4	1-2	1-0	1-0	2-2	1-0	2-0	3-1	0-2	1-1	1-2	1-2	0-2	0-0	2-0	3-1	2-3	0-2	1-0	2-0
Barrow AFC	4-0	■	1-3	2-3	1-2	2-0	0-1	0-3	1-1	2-0	3-0	3-1	2-3	1-1	2-1	4-3	0-2	1-0	0-0	3-1	1-0	1-2	2-0	2-0
Bradford City AFC	7-0	5-1	■	4-1	2-4	0-1	1-1	0-3	2-2	2-0	3-1	0-0	2-3	3-0	1-0	2-1	3-4	2-0	1-0	3-0	0-1	2-2	5-3	5-2
Bradford Park Ave.	3-0	5-0	3-1	■	0-2	2-0	1-1	2-1	2-0	2-1	1-1	2-1	1-0	2-1	3-1	0-1	0-4	2-2	2-4	2-0	3-0	4-1	0-1	4-0
Carlisle United FC	3-1	1-1	2-1	1-0	■	2-1	2-1	2-1	3-0	1-0	1-0	2-0	2-0	1-0	1-0	4-0	0-1	3-1	2-2	3-1	2-2	3-1	0-2	3-2
Chester FC	2-2	1-2	2-2	2-0	1-1	■	1-1	3-1	2-2	2-1	2-1	2-1	0-1	3-1	3-1	1-3	1-2	4-1	3-1	0-2	3-0	1-3	0-0	3-1
Crewe Alexandra FC	3-0	2-0	1-1	2-4	1-1	3-0	■	5-0	0-1	0-0	3-1	0-4	2-0	2-1	3-1	1-2	2-0	1-2	1-0	1-2	1-1	1-1	1-1	2-4
Darlington FC	3-0	1-1	2-1	1-4	1-0	0-0	2-0	■	4-2	2-0	0-1	1-1	1-2	5-3	0-0	0-2	2-2	3-2	2-1	1-1	2-1	1-1	1-1	0-3
Gateshead FC	7-0	1-0	2-0	5-0	4-3	2-1	4-0	5-2	■	5-0	0-1	1-3	4-0	3-2	4-1	0-3	1-0	3-0	1-3	2-0	2-0	0-0	1-0	3-0
Halifax Town AFC	2-2	0-0	1-2	2-2	1-0	3-1	1-0	2-2	1-0	■	1-0	4-1	0-1	0-1	3-0	1-0	1-1	3-3	3-1	4-0	1-0	0-1	0-1	1-3
Hartlepools United	1-0	6-1	1-1	3-1	3-3	1-2	0-2	6-1	3-0	5-2	■	2-2	1-1	0-1	0-1	0-0	4-2	1-0	3-2	2-1	2-1	4-1	4-1	4-1
Lincoln City FC	9-1	3-0	1-4	1-3	1-1	2-1	4-1	3-0	2-1	3-1	1-0	■	3-0	3-0	2-0	4-2	0-2	2-1	5-0	1-2	6-0	2-1	2-1	2-1
Mansfield Town FC	5-0	4-0	1-1	3-2	2-1	3-1	4-1	2-1	2-1	3-1	1-0	1-1	■	4-0	3-1	1-0	1-1	1-1	2-2	2-1	2-1	1-1	3-1	2-1
New Brighton FC	1-1	1-2	0-6	3-3	0-1	1-0	0-2	2-2	0-1	1-0	1-0	0-1	0-1	■	2-0	1-5	2-4	1-2	0-0	1-0	1-1	3-0	1-0	1-1
Oldham Athletic AFC	2-1	0-1	2-2	2-3	1-1	1-0	0-2	2-0	2-3	2-0	5-1	0-0	2-0	3-1	■	2-0	4-5	3-4	2-1	4-0	1-3	3-4	2-2	2-2
Rochdale AFC	3-1	1-0	4-0	1-2	4-1	2-3	1-1	0-0	2-0	0-0	3-1	3-0	1-0	0-1	3-1	■	0-2	2-0	5-0	1-1	1-1	2-3	2-0	0-1
Rotherham United FC	6-2	3-0	1-0	2-1	3-0	0-0	2-3	0-1	1-2	2-0	2-1	3-0	5-0	3-1	4-1	3-1	■	4-1	2-0	1-1	0-0	1-2	5-0	0-1
Scunthorpe United	3-0	1-0	0-0	1-1	1-0	2-0	1-1	2-0	2-1	2-2	0-0	1-1	0-0	3-0	0-0	0-0	0-0	■	0-0	0-0	1-1	2-0	1-0	1-0
Shrewsbury Town FC	0-1	1-0	2-0	1-0	0-3	1-0	0-1	2-2	1-0	2-0	1-0	1-2	4-2	2-2	0-2	1-2	3-1	1-56	■	0-3	1-2	2-1	1-0	1-0
Southport FC	3-0	4-1	0-1	2-4	1-0	0-1	2-0	1-0	0-1	1-1	3-0	0-1	1-4	1-1	0-1	2-2	1-2	1-1	2-2	■	2-0	0-1	3-1	1-1
Stockport County FC	0-0	4-1	3-1	2-1	1-2	0-3	3-0	1-0	5-2	2-1	2-0	3-1	4-0	1-1	2-2	1-3	1-2	2-0	3-2	2-0	■	0-0	2-1	1-0
Tranmere Rovers FC	1-1	3-0	3-1	2-2	2-2	3-1	3-0	3-2	2-2	3-2	1-0	0-1	2-1	4-3	1-0	2-1	2-1	1-0	0-1	4-0	1-1	■	1-2	7-2
Wrexham AFC	1-1	1-0	0-3	3-1	2-1	2-0	0-2	3-1	0-0	2-2	1-0	2-3	2-2	0-1	0-2	3-1	0-0	3-1	1-0	3-3	2-0	2-1	■	4-3
York City FC	3-0	0-2	1-2	1-3	1-1	2-2	1-2	1-1	1-1	0-0	3-0	2-2	1-1	2-0	2-2	2-2	3-3	0-0	2-0	2-0	0-0	4-0	3-0	■

Division 3 (North)

		Pd	Wn	Dw	Ls	GF	GA	Pts	
1.	Rotherham United FC (Rotherham)	46	31	9	6	103	41	71	P
2.	Mansfield Town FC (Mansfield)	46	26	12	8	78	48	64	
3.	Carlisle United FC (Carlisle)	46	25	12	9	79	50	62	
4.	Tranmere Rovers FC (Birkenhead)	46	24	11	11	83	62	59	
5.	Lincoln City FC (Lincoln)	46	25	8	13	89	58	58	
6.	Bradford Park Avenue FC (Bradford)	46	23	8	15	90	72	54	
7.	Bradford City AFC (Bradford)	46	21	10	15	90	63	52	
8.	Gateshead FC (Gateshead)	46	21	8	17	84	62	50	
9.	Crewe Alexandra FC (Crewe)	46	19	10	17	61	60	48	
10.	Stockport County FC (Stockport)	46	20	8	18	63	63	48	
11.	Rochdale AFC (Rochdale)	46	17	11	18	69	62	45	
12.	Scunthorpe & Lindsey United FC (Scunthorpe)	46	13	18	15	58	57	44	
13.	Chester FC (Chester)	46	17	9	20	62	64	43	
14.	Wrexham AFC (Wrexham)	46	15	12	19	55	71	42	
15.	Oldham Athletic FC (Oldham)	46	16	8	22	73	73	40	
16.	Hartlepools United FC (Hartlepool)	46	16	7	23	64	66	39	
17.	York City FC (York)	46	12	15	19	66	77	39	
18.	Darlington FC (Darlington)	46	13	13	20	59	77	39	
19.	Barrow AFC (Barrow-in-Furness)	46	16	6	24	51	76	38	
20.	Shrewsbury Town FC (Shrewsbury)	46	15	7	24	43	74	37	T
21.	Southport FC (Southport)	46	13	10	23	56	72	36	
22.	Halifax Town AFC (Halifax)	46	11	12	23	50	69	34	
23.	Accrington Stanley FC (Accrington)	46	11	10	25	42	101	32	
24.	New Brighton FC (Wallasey)	46	11	8	27	40	90	30	#
		1104	431	242	431	1608	1608	1104	

T: Shrewsbury Town FC (Shrewsbury) were transferred to Division 3 (South) for next season.

New Brighton FC (Wallasey) were not re-elected and were replaced by Workington AFC (Workington) for next season.

Football League Division 3 (S) — 1950-51 Season

	ALD	BOU	BRI	BCi	BRo	COL	CRY	EXE	GIL	IPS	LEY	MIL	NEW	Nth	NRW	NOT	PLY	PVl	REA	SOU	SWI	TOR	WAL	WAT
Aldershot Town FC	—	0-1	0-0	0-0	1-1	2-0	3-0	4-2	2-4	0-1	3-1	2-1	3-1	3-0	1-1	1-0	2-2	2-0	1-1	2-2	0-1	1-0	3-0	1-1
Bournemouth & Bos.	4-0	—	2-2	1-0	2-0	2-0	5-0	1-1	3-1	2-1	5-0	1-0	2-0	1-0	0-0	3-2	0-2	3-1	1-0	3-1	2-1	0-0	3-1	3-3
Brighton & Hove Alb.	1-2	2-1	—	1-1	2-2	3-1	1-0	4-1	2-2	4-0	3-0	2-3	9-1	5-1	1-1	1-2	0-6	2-2	1-1	2-1	1-0	2-2	1-0	1-1
Bristol City FC	1-1	2-0	2-0	—	1-0	0-2	2-0	3-1	2-0	2-1	4-1	2-1	1-0	2-2	0-3	1-0	3-1	3-3	0-3	2-0	0-2	3-3	3-0	3-0
Bristol Rovers FC	3-0	2-0	3-2	2-1	—	1-1	1-1	3-1	3-0	1-1	2-1	1-0	1-0	1-1	3-3	0-3	2-1	2-0	4-0	4-1	1-0	1-1	1-1	3-0
Colchester United FC	1-0	4-1	4-1	1-1	0-0	—	1-0	0-1	4-2	2-3	1-0	3-1	2-1	2-3	0-2	3-0	1-1	1-1	1-3	4-1	3-1	0-1	4-1	1-1
Crystal Palace FC	0-2	0-1	0-2	1-0	1-0	1-3	—	0-1	4-3	1-3	1-1	1-1	1-1	0-0	0-5	1-6	0-1	0-2	0-3	0-2	2-0	2-1	1-0	1-1
Exeter City FC	3-0	2-1	4-2	1-0	0-2	5-0	1-2	—	1-2	2-0	0-0	0-1	2-2	1-0	1-2	0-5	3-2	0-3	1-3	1-0	0-0	1-0	3-3	2-2
Gillingham FC	3-0	2-2	1-1	1-2	1-0	0-0	0-0	9-4	—	0-1	1-0	4-3	0-1	3-1	2-2	1-4	2-1	1-1	0-3	0-2	2-1	2-0	4-1	3-1
Ipswich Town FC	5-2	1-0	3-0	2-0	2-3	3-0	1-1	1-0	5-1	—	2-2	2-1	1-1	0-1	1-3	2-0	2-2	0-2	1-0	4-1	3-1	3-1	2-1	2-1
Leyton Orient FC	1-0	2-0	2-1	0-2	1-0	1-1	2-0	1-3	4-0	2-0	—	0-2	0-3	1-0	3-1	1-0	2-3	2-0	1-1	2-1	5-1	2-1	1-2	1-2
Millwall FC	1-0	3-0	1-1	5-3	1-1	5-0	4-0	3-1	4-0	3-1	2-4	—	2-1	1-1	1-1	1-1	2-2	1-3	1-1	4-0	1-4	2-0	4-0	4-0
Newport County AFC	7-0	1-0	3-0	0-1	2-1	2-0	2-4	0-3	1-0	1-2	0-0	2-3	—	2-2	1-1	0-2	2-0	2-1	5-0	6-1	2-1	2-1	3-0	2-2
Northampton Town	1-0	0-1	0-2	2-2	1-1	2-1	2-0	4-1	4-1	2-1	3-3	1-2	1-4	—	1-2	2-2	1-3	1-1	1-1	1-2	1-0	1-0	1-0	6-0
Norwich City FC	2-2	0-1	1-1	0-0	1-1	3-1	3-0	2-0	1-3	2-1	2-1	1-1	0-0	1-0	—	2-0	1-0	2-1	3-0	2-1	1-0	1-1	1-1	1-0
Nottingham Forest	7-0	1-0	4-0	1-0	2-1	0-0	1-0	2-2	9-2	0-0	1-1	2-2	2-2	4-2	1-0	—	4-1	2-1	1-1	3-0	2-1	3-1	4-0	2-1
Plymouth Argyle FC	5-1	3-1	3-3	2-0	0-0	7-1	4-0	0-1	2-0	2-1	2-2	1-1	4-1	2-1	0-2	2-1	—	1-0	2-0	5-1	1-0	1-1	3-1	2-0
Port Vale FC	3-1	3-1	0-1	1-3	0-0	1-1	2-2	2-0	4-3	1-0	0-3	2-1	1-1	2-1	1-1	0-2	0-2	—	0-0	2-1	3-1	1-0	1-0	1-0
Reading FC	7-1	0-0	7-0	4-2	1-0	3-2	1-1	4-2	1-1	4-0	1-1	5-0	2-1	1-1	2-1	1-1	3-0	3-0	—	0-2	3-3	4-1	2-1	2-1
Southend United FC	4-2	6-1	3-1	1-1	1-1	4-2	5-2	5-1	4-0	1-0	0-3	3-0	3-0	0-2	3-2	1-1	1-1	3-3	3-3	—	2-0	8-2	3-0	5-1
Swindon Town FC	4-0	2-1	0-1	1-2	2-1	2-0	1-0	2-0	2-0	1-0	1-0	2-3	1-2	2-1	1-1	4-1	0-2	1-2	2-3	2-1	—	1-1	1-1	3-2
Torquay United FC	1-2	0-2	3-1	4-1	1-2	4-1	4-1	0-1	1-2	0-1	3-4	1-1	1-5	2-1	1-3	3-2	2-2	1-0	1-3	1-3	1-0	—	3-2	3-2
Walsall FC	3-1	0-1	1-0	3-1	1-2	4-2	0-0	0-2	2-1	2-0	1-1	4-0	1-0	0-1	0-2	2-1	2-0	1-2	1-2	1-0	3-1	3-2	—	1-0
Watford FC	1-2	2-1	1-1	1-2	1-0	2-0	1-0	1-2	5-0	0-2	2-0	0-0	0-2	0-1	0-2	1-1	1-1	2-0	3-1	1-3	1-2	2-2	1-3	—

Division 3 (South)

		Pd	Wn	Dw	Ls	GF	GA	Pts	
1.	Nottingham Forest FC (Nottingham)	46	30	10	6	110	40	70	P
2.	Norwich City FC (Norwich)	46	25	14	7	82	45	64	
3.	Reading FC (Reading)	46	21	15	10	88	53	57	
4.	Plymouth Argyle FC (Plymouth)	46	24	9	13	85	55	57	
5.	Millwall FC (London)	46	23	10	13	80	57	56	
6.	Bristol Rovers FC (Bristol)	46	20	15	11	64	42	55	
7.	Southend United FC (Southend-on-Sea)	46	21	10	15	92	69	52	
8.	Ipswich Town FC (Ipswich)	46	23	6	17	69	58	52	
9.	Bournemouth & Boscombe Athletic FC (Bournemouth)	46	22	7	17	65	57	51	
10.	Bristol City FC (Bristol)	46	20	11	15	64	59	51	
11.	Newport County AFC (Newport)	46	19	9	18	77	70	47	
12.	Port Vale FC (Stoke-on-Trent)	46	16	13	17	60	65	45	
13.	Brighton & Hove Albion FC (Hove)	46	13	17	16	71	79	43	
14.	Exeter City FC (Exeter)	46	18	6	22	62	85	42	
15.	Walsall FC (Walsall)	46	15	10	21	52	62	40	
16.	Colchester United FC (Colchester)	46	14	12	20	63	76	40	
17.	Swindon Town FC (Swindon)	46	18	4	24	55	67	40	
18.	Aldershot FC (Aldershot)	46	15	10	21	56	88	40	
19.	Leyton Orient FC (London)	46	15	8	23	53	75	38	
20.	Torquay United FC (Torquay)	46	14	9	23	64	81	37	
21.	Northampton Town FC (Northampton)	46	10	16	20	55	67	36	
22.	Gillingham FC (Gillingham)	46	13	9	24	69	101	35	
23.	Watford FC (Watford)	46	9	11	26	54	88	29	
24.	Crystal Palace FC (London)	46	8	11	27	33	84	27	
		1104	426	252	426	1623	1623	1104	

F.A. CUP FINAL   (Wembley Stadium, London – 28/04/1951 – 100,000)

NEWCASTLE UNITED FC   2-0   Blackpool FC (Blackpool)

Milburn 2

Newcastle: Fairbrother, Cowell, Corbett, Harvey, Brennan, Crowe, Walker, Taylor, Milburn, G.Robledo, Mitchell.

Blackburn: Farm, Shimwell, Garrett, Johnston, Hayward, Kelly, Matthews, Mudie, Mortensen, Slater, Perry.

Semi-finals

Blackpool FC (Blackpool)   2-1   Tottenham Hotspur FC (London)
Bolton Wanderers FC (Bolton)   4-3   Everton FC (Liverpool)

Quarter-finals

Birmingham City FC (Birmingham)   1-0   Manchester United FC (Manchester)
Blackpool FC (Blackpool)   1-0   Fulham FC (London)
Newcastle United FC (Newcastle-upon-Tyne)   0-0, 3-1   Bristol Rovers FC (Bristol)
Sunderland AFC (Sunderland)   1-1, 1-3   Wolverhampton Wanderers FC (Wolverhampton)

1951-52

Football League Division 1 1951-52 Season	Arsenal	Aston Villa	Blackpool	Bolton Wanderers	Burnley	Charlton Athletic	Chelsea	Derby County	Fulham	Huddersfield Town	Liverpool	Manchester City	Manchester United	Middlesbrough	Newcastle United	Portsmouth	Preston North End	Stoke City	Sunderland	Tottenham Hotspur	W.B.A.	Wolves
Arsenal FC		2-1	4-1	4-2	1-0	2-1	2-1	3-1	4-3	2-2	0-0	2-2	1-3	3-1	1-1	4-1	3-3	4-1	3-0	1-1	6-3	2-2
Aston Villa FC	1-0		4-0	1-1	4-1	0-2	7-1	4-1	4-1	1-0	2-0	1-2	2-5	2-0	2-2	2-0	3-2	2-3	2-1	0-3	2-0	3-3
Blackpool FC	0-0	0-3		1-0	1-0	1-2	1-2	2-1	4-2	3-1	2-0	2-2	2-2	2-2	6-3	0-0	0-3	4-2	3-0	1-0	2-0	3-2
Bolton Wanderers FC	2-1	5-2	1-0		1-4	2-1	3-0	1-2	2-1	2-1	1-0	2-1	1-0	3-1	0-0	0-3	1-1	1-1	1-1	1-1	3-2	2-2
Burnley FC	0-1	2-1	2-0	1-3		1-0	1-1	0-1	1-0	0-2	0-0	0-0	1-1	7-1	2-1	1-0	0-2	4-0	0-1	1-1	6-1	2-2
Charlton Athletic FC	1-3	0-1	2-0	1-0	1-0		1-1	3-3	3-0	4-0	2-0	0-0	2-2	4-3	3-0	0-2	4-2	4-0	2-1	0-3	3-3	1-0
Chelsea FC	1-3	2-2	2-1	1-3	4-1	1-0		0-1	2-1	1-3	0-3	4-2	5-0	1-0	1-1	0-0	1-1	0-1	0-2	1-3	1-3	0-1
Derby County FC	1-2	1-1	1-1	5-2	1-1	0-1	3-1		5-0	2-1	1-1	1-3	0-3	1-3	1-3	4-3	4-3	3-4	4-2	2-1	2-1	1-3
Fulham FC	0-0	2-2	1-2	1-2	1-2	3-3	1-2	3-0		1-0	1-1	1-2	3-3	6-0	1-1	2-3	2-3	5-0	0-1	1-2	1-0	2-2
Huddersfield Town AFC	2-3	3-1	1-3	0-2	1-3	1-0	1-0	1-1	1-0		1-2	5-1	3-2	1-0	2-4	0-1	2-0	0-2	2-2	1-1	3-0	1-7
Liverpool FC	0-0	1-2	1-1	1-1	3-1	1-1	1-1	2-0	4-0	2-1		1-2	0-0	1-1	3-0	0-2	2-2	2-1	2-2	1-1	2-5	1-1
Manchester City FC	0-2	2-2	0-0	0-3	0-1	4-2	3-1	4-2	1-1	3-0	1-2		1-2	2-1	2-3	0-1	1-0	0-1	3-1	1-1	1-2	0-0
Manchester United FC	6-1	1-1	3-1	1-0	6-1	3-2	3-0	2-1	3-2	1-1	4-0	1-1		4-2	2-1	1-3	1-2	4-0	0-1	2-0	5-1	2-0
Middlesbrough FC	0-3	2-0	1-0	2-0	5-0	2-1	0-0	0-0	2-0	2-1	3-3	2-2	1-4		2-1	2-1	2-5	3-0	0-2	2-1	0-1	4-0
Newcastle United FC	2-0	6-1	1-3	0-1	7-1	6-0	3-1	6-2	1-1	1-0	2-2	0-2	2-2	3-1		3-3	3-0	6-0	2-2	7-2	1-4	3-1
Portsmouth FC	1-1	2-0	1-3	3-0	2-2	1-0	1-0	3-4	3-1	1-3	1-0	1-0	5-4	3-1	2-1		1-2	4-1	0-2	2-0	1-1	2-3
Preston North End FC	2-0	2-2	3-1	2-2	1-2	3-0	1-0	0-1	0-1	5-2	4-0	1-1	1-2	0-1	1-2	2-2		2-0	4-2	1-1	1-0	3-0
Stoke City FC	2-1	4-1	2-3	1-2	2-1	1-2	1-2	1-1	0-0	1-2	3-1	0-0	3-2	4-5	2-0	0-0	1-1		1-6	1-1	1-0	1-0
Sunderland AFC	4-1	1-3	1-3	0-2	0-0	4-1	4-1	2-2	7-1	3-0	1-2	3-1	1-4	3-1	1-4	4-1	0-0	0-1		0-1	3-3	1-1
Tottenham Hotspur FC	1-2	2-0	2-0	2-1	1-1	2-3	3-2	5-0	1-0	1-0	2-3	1-2	2-0	3-1	2-1	3-1	1-0	2-0	2-0		3-1	4-2
West Bromwich Albion FC	3-1	1-1	1-1	3-2	1-1	1-1	0-1	1-0	0-2	0-0	3-3	3-2	3-3	2-3	3-3	5-0	1-1	1-0	1-1	3-1		2-1
Wolverhampton Wanderers FC	2-1	1-2	3-0	5-1	1-2	2-2	5-3	1-2	2-2	0-0	2-1	2-2	0-2	4-0	3-0	1-1	1-4	3-0	0-3	1-1	1-4	

	Division 1	Pd	Wn	Dw	Ls	GF	GA	Pts	
1.	MANCHESTER UNITED FC (MANCHESTER)	42	23	11	8	95	52	57	
2.	Tottenham Hotspur FC (London)	42	22	9	11	76	51	53	
3.	Arsenal FC (London)	42	21	11	10	80	61	53	
4.	Portsmouth FC (Portsmouth)	42	20	8	14	68	58	48	
5.	Bolton Wanderers FC (Bolton)	42	19	10	13	65	61	48	
6.	Aston Villa FC (Birmingham)	42	19	9	14	79	70	47	
7.	Preston North End FC (Preston)	42	17	12	13	74	54	46	
8.	Newcastle United FC (Newcastle-upon-Tyne)	42	18	9	15	98	73	45	
9.	Blackpool FC (Blackpool)	42	18	9	15	64	64	45	
10.	Charlton Athletic FC (London)	42	17	10	15	68	63	44	
11.	Liverpool FC (Liverpool)	42	12	19	11	57	61	43	
12.	Sunderland AFC (Sunderland)	42	15	12	15	70	61	42	
13.	West Bromwich Albion FC (West Bromwich)	42	14	13	15	74	77	41	
14.	Burnley FC (Burnley)	42	15	10	17	56	63	40	
15.	Manchester City FC (Manchester)	42	13	13	16	58	61	39	
16.	Wolverhampton Wanderers FC (Wolverhampton)	42	12	14	16	73	73	38	
17.	Derby County FC (Derby)	42	15	7	20	63	80	37	
18.	Middlesbrough FC (Middlesbrough)	42	15	6	21	64	88	36	
19.	Chelsea FC (London)	42	14	8	20	52	72	36	
20.	Stoke City FC (Stoke-on-Trent)	42	12	7	23	49	88	31	
21.	Huddersfield Town AFC (Huddersfield)	42	10	8	24	49	82	28	R
22.	Fulham FC (London)	42	8	11	23	58	77	27	R
		924	349	126	349	1490	1490	924	

Top Goalscorer

1) George ROBLEDO   (Newcastle United FC)   33

Football League Division 2 — 1951-52 Season

	Barnsley	Birmingham City	Blackburn Rovers	Brentford	Bury	Cardiff City	Coventry City	Doncaster Rovers	Everton	Hull City	Leeds United	Leicester City	Luton Town	Nottingham Forest	Notts County	Q.P.R.	Rotherham United	Sheffield United	Sheffield Wednesday	Southampton	Swansea Town	West Ham United
Barnsley FC	■	1-2	1-2	0-0	3-3	2-0	1-0	1-1	1-0	2-2	3-1	3-3	1-2	1-1	2-1	3-1	0-1	3-4	5-4	3-1	2-3	1-1
Birmingham City FC	2-1	■	0-1	1-2	2-1	3-2	3-1	2-2	1-2	2-2	1-1	2-0	3-1	0-2	2-0	1-0	4-0	3-0	0-0	1-1	1-1	2-1
Blackburn Rovers FC	2-1	1-4	■	3-0	1-2	0-1	0-1	3-3	1-0	1-0	2-3	2-1	2-1	3-2	2-0	4-2	1-1	1-5	0-0	0-1	3-1	3-1
Brentford FC	1-1	1-0	1-1	■	4-0	1-1	1-0	1-0	1-0	2-1	1-1	1-3	3-3	1-1	1-0	0-0	2-0	4-1	2-3	1-2	3-1	1-1
Bury FC	3-0	3-0	0-2	1-0	■	1-1	0-2	1-1	1-0	3-1	1-2	1-4	0-1	2-0	2-1	3-1	3-1	1-0	1-2	8-2	4-1	4-0
Cardiff City AFC	3-0	3-1	3-1	2-0	3-0	■	4-1	2-1	3-1	1-0	3-1	4-0	3-0	4-1	3-1	2-4	1-1	2-1	1-0	3-0	1-1	1-1
Coventry City FC	0-0	1-1	1-2	2-1	3-0	2-1	■	1-2	2-1	1-4	4-2	1-3	5-2	3-3	0-2	0-0	2-1	1-1	0-2	3-1	3-2	1-2
Doncaster Rovers FC	1-2	0-5	1-0	1-2	1-1	1-0	1-0	■	3-1	0-1	2-0	2-2	1-1	0-1	1-5	4-0	0-3	2-1	1-1	0-1	3-0	4-1
Everton FC	1-1	1-3	0-2	1-0	2-2	3-0	4-1	1-1	■	5-0	2-0	2-0	1-3	1-0	1-5	3-0	3-3	1-0	3-3	3-0	2-1	2-0
Hull City AFC	0-0	0-1	3-0	4-1	5-0	0-0	5-0	2-0	1-0	■	3-2	3-1	1-2	1-4	1-3	4-1	3-3	2-1	0-0	5-2	1-1	1-1
Leeds United AFC	1-0	1-1	1-0	1-1	2-1	1-2	3-1	0-0	1-2	2-0	■	2-1	1-1	0-0	1-0	3-1	3-2	1-1	1-1	1-1	1-1	3-1
Leicester City FC	1-2	4-0	2-1	1-1	1-1	3-0	3-1	2-1	1-2	1-0	1-2	■	3-3	3-1	4-1	2-0	2-0	5-5	3-1	3-0	1-1	3-1
Luton Town FC	4-2	2-4	1-1	0-2	2-1	2-2	2-1	1-4	1-1	1-1	2-1	1-2	■	3-3	6-0	0-1	1-1	2-1	5-3	2-1	2-2	6-1
Nottingham Forest FC	3-3	0-1	1-0	2-0	1-0	2-3	3-1	1-1	2-0	4-0	1-1	2-2	2-0	■	3-2	3-1	4-2	0-2	2-1	3-0	2-2	0-0
Notts County FC	4-0	5-0	0-1	5-2	2-1	1-1	2-1	1-1	0-0	4-0	1-2	2-3	5-4	2-2	■	0-0	0-3	3-1	2-2	3-4	2-0	1-0
Queen's Park Rangers FC	1-1	0-2	2-1	3-1	3-2	1-1	1-4	0-2	4-4	1-1	0-0	1-0	0-0	4-3	1-4	■	2-3	4-2	2-2	2-1	1-1	2-0
Rotherham United FC	4-0	1-2	3-0	1-1	4-3	2-0	0-1	2-0	1-1	4-2	0-2	0-1	1-2	2-0	1-0	2-0	■	3-1	3-3	4-1	1-3	2-1
Sheffield United FC	1-2	4-2	1-1	1-4	1-0	6-1	1-2	2-1	4-1	3-0	5-0	3-0	1-0	1-2	1-0	1-0	1-0	■	7-3	2-2	5-0	6-1
Sheffield Wednesday FC	2-1	1-1	2-0	2-0	2-1	4-2	3-1	3-1	4-0	6-0	1-1	4-0	1-1	6-0	3-5	1-3	1-1	3-1	■	3-1	1-1	2-2
Southampton FC	1-1	2-0	2-1	2-1	4-2	1-1	2-2	2-0	1-0	1-1	0-0	2-0	2-3	5-2	4-0	1-1	3-1	0-1	1-4	■	3-2	1-2
Swansea Town AFC	2-1	4-0	5-1	1-1	0-2	1-1	7-1	1-2	0-2	3-0	4-1	1-0	1-2	1-1	2-3	5-0	3-1	1-2	1-1	1-1	■	2-1
West Ham United FC	2-1	0-1	3-1	1-0	1-1	1-1	3-1	3-3	3-3	2-0	2-0	2-3	3-0	3-1	2-1	4-2	2-1	5-1	0-6	4-0	2-2	■

	Division 2	Pd	Wn	Dw	Ls	GF	GA	Pts	
1.	Sheffield Wednesday FC (Sheffield)	42	21	11	10	100	66	53	P
2.	Cardiff City AFC (Cardiff)	42	20	11	11	72	54	51	P
3.	Birmingham City FC (Birmingham)	42	21	9	12	67	56	51	
4.	Nottingham Forest FC (Nottingham)	42	18	13	11	77	62	49	
5.	Leicester City FC (Leicester)	42	19	9	14	78	64	47	
6.	Leeds United AFC (Leeds)	42	18	11	13	59	57	47	
7.	Everton FC (Liverpool)	42	17	10	15	64	58	44	
8.	Luton Town FC (Luton)	42	16	12	14	77	78	44	
9.	Rotherham United FC (Rotherham)	42	17	8	17	73	71	42	
10.	Brentford FC (London)	42	15	12	15	54	55	42	
11.	Sheffield United FC (Sheffield)	42	18	5	19	90	76	41	
12.	West Ham United FC (London)	42	15	11	16	67	77	41	
13.	Southampton FC (Southampton)	42	15	11	16	61	73	41	
14.	Blackburn Rovers FC (Blackburn)	42	17	6	19	54	63	40	
15.	Notts County FC (Nottingham)	42	16	7	19	71	68	39	
16.	Doncaster Rovers FC (Doncaster)	42	13	12	17	55	60	38	
17.	Bury FC (Bury)	42	15	7	20	67	69	37	
18.	Hull City AFC (Kingston-upon-Hull)	42	13	11	18	60	70	37	
19.	Swansea Town AFC (Swansea)	42	12	12	18	72	76	36	
20.	Barnsley FC (Barnsley)	42	11	14	17	59	72	36	
21.	Coventry City FC (Coventry)	42	14	6	22	59	82	34	R
22.	Queen's Park Rangers FC (London)	42	11	12	19	52	81	34	R
		924	352	220	352	1488	1488	924	

Football League Division 3 (N) 1951-52 Season	Accrington Stanley	Barrow	Bradford City	Bradford Park Avenue	Carlisle United	Chester	Chesterfield	Crewe Alexandra	Darlington	Gateshead	Grimsby Town	Halifax Town	Hartlepools	Lincoln City	Mansfield Town	Oldham Athletic	Rochdale	Scunthorpe United	Southport	Stockport County	Tranmere Rovers	Workington	Wrexham	York City
Accrington Stanley		1-1	0-1	5-1	0-2	4-2	2-0	2-3	1-3	1-2	0-3	2-2	0-0	1-3	1-0	1-2	0-0	2-2	0-0	0-3	1-1	0-0	4-2	2-1
Barrow AFC	3-1		1-0	0-2	0-1	1-0	2-0	2-1	2-2	2-1	3-1	0-0	2-1	1-2	1-1	0-1	4-0	2-1	0-0	1-3	2-0	1-0	3-1	0-0
Bradford City AFC	1-3	2-2		2-2	1-2	1-0	1-0	0-2	3-1	1-1	0-2	3-2	0-2	1-1	2-1	5-2	3-0	1-0	2-1	2-3	2-0	1-0	3-2	3-3
Bradford Park Ave.	1-1	3-1	2-1		0-1	3-0	3-3	3-2	2-0	2-0	3-2	6-1	1-2	1-1	0-1	1-0	1-1	2-2	2-2	4-2	2-3	2-1	5-0	2-1
Carlisle United FC	4-1	0-1	1-0	1-0		0-0	2-3	2-0	1-1	0-0	1-2	2-2	2-1	1-4	0-0	3-1	1-3	0-2	2-1	1-0	0-1	2-0	2-1	1-0
Chester FC	3-1	0-0	1-0	4-2	4-2		3-0	2-0	2-0	0-3	0-3	5-1	3-3	0-1	1-5	1-2	4-0	3-1	2-1	0-0	4-1	2-2	2-1	0-1
Chesterfield FC	2-0	2-0	2-2	0-0	3-0	2-0		0-0	4-2	1-0	3-1	3-1	2-2	2-2	1-1	1-0	5-1	3-0	2-0	1-0	1-1	3-1	3-0	2-1
Crewe Alexandra FC	3-3	1-1	0-1	3-4	1-1	1-2	2-1		3-0	4-2	1-2	4-1	4-2	0-2	1-0	3-1	1-2	1-0	1-0	2-1	2-0	2-2	0-0	1-0
Darlington FC	4-5	1-2	3-1	3-0	1-2	1-1	3-0	0-1		3-2	0-2	0-2	2-1	1-1	2-1	2-2	2-3	1-1	2-2	2-1	2-1	1-0	2-1	1-0
Gateshead FC	1-0	2-0	2-2	0-1	1-1	1-0	1-1	1-0	2-2		1-1	3-0	2-0	3-1	4-1	1-0	2-1	3-0	0-2	4-1	4-1	1-1	1-1	1-1
Grimsby Town FC	2-1	1-0	2-1	3-0	4-1	2-1	2-0	0-1	3-0	2-0		8-1	2-0	2-3	1-1	3-1	4-0	3-2	4-1	4-0	1-0	5-0	0-0	2-1
Halifax Town AFC	0-4	0-1	1-1	0-0	1-2	4-1	0-0	2-3	4-1	3-0	3-0		2-0	1-3	1-0	1-0	2-0	2-1	4-2	1-3	1-2	2-1	0-1	1-1
Hartlepools United	4-2	3-1	2-1	2-1	2-1	2-1	4-1	3-0	2-0	1-0	2-1	6-1		1-1	2-0	1-1	1-3	3-1	0-1	0-1	0-1	1-0	1-0	3-2
Lincoln City FC	2-2	3-0	2-1	2-0	2-2	4-1	5-1	11-1	7-2	1-0	0-2	4-1	4-3		1-2	4-0	2-0	4-1	4-0	2-1	3-0	7-0	3-2	3-1
Mansfield Town FC	3-0	2-1	1-0	1-2	3-1	2-1	2-1	3-2	2-3	2-2	4-2	0-1	1-0	0-1		2-1	1-1	4-1	4-0	3-0	1-1	3-2	3-0	1-1
Oldham Athletic AFC	3-1	3-1	2-1	1-2	2-0	11-2	3-0	5-2	3-2	2-0	1-1	2-0	5-2	4-1	5-3		1-1	2-0	2-1	1-0	3-0	0-1	2-1	2-0
Rochdale AFC	3-1	4-1	1-1	1-1	0-4	0-5	2-0	1-0	6-2	0-3	0-0	0-0	3-0	0-1	1-0	2-2		1-2	1-0	0-3	2-0	1-5	0-2	0-2
Scunthorpe United	3-1	0-0	1-0	0-0	0-1	2-2	1-1	2-0	5-2	1-1	1-3	2-0	1-3	4-1	2-2	3-1	2-2		1-1	2-0	3-1	0-0	3-1	0-0
Southport FC	0-0	2-2	1-1	0-0	2-1	1-0	4-1	3-0	0-2	0-0	0-3	0-0	1-0	0-3	0-0	1-2	5-1	0-1		1-0	4-2	1-1	0-0	1-1
Stockport County FC	6-0	2-2	1-2	1-0	1-1	0-0	2-1	4-2	5-0	0-0	1-1	6-2	0-1	1-1	2-1	0-0	1-0	1-1	3-1		2-0	5-0	0-0	3-1
Tranmere Rovers FC	3-1	3-1	3-1	1-2	3-2	3-1	2-0	1-0	3-0	5-1	2-3	1-2	4-1	2-2	1-1	0-4	4-3	3-1	5-1	2-0		3-1	3-1	2-0
Workington AFC	0-2	3-1	0-1	2-3	1-2	2-2	3-1	3-1	2-1	1-2	2-4	2-1	1-1	0-3	0-1	1-1	0-0	6-1	0-3	1-2	1-2		2-0	1-0
Wrexham AFC	1-0	2-4	3-0	3-2	3-1	3-2	0-3	4-0	1-1	2-1	2-0	2-1	0-0	4-2	3-1	1-0	1-2	3-0	0-0	0-1	0-0	0-0		1-1
York City FC	6-1	2-1	3-1	1-0	0-0	4-2	1-0	3-0	2-1	1-0	1-1	6-2	3-1	1-0	3-0	5-0	1-1	0-1	0-2	0-1	1-1	5-1	4-2	

Division 3 (North)

		Pd	Wn	Dw	Ls	GF	GA	Pts	
1.	Lincoln City FC (Lincoln)	46	30	9	7	121	52	69	P
2.	Grimsby Town FC (Cleethorpes)	46	29	8	9	96	45	66	
3.	Stockport County FC (Stockport)	46	23	13	10	74	40	59	
4.	Oldham Athletic AFC (Oldham)	46	24	9	13	90	61	57	
5.	Gateshead FC (Gateshead)	46	21	11	14	66	49	53	
6.	Mansfield Town FC (Mansfield)	46	22	8	16	73	60	52	
7.	Carlisle United FC (Carlisle)	46	19	13	14	62	57	51	
8.	Bradford Park Avenue FC (Bradford)	46	19	12	15	74	64	50	
9.	Hartlepools United FC (Hartlepool)	46	21	8	17	71	65	50	
10.	York City FC (York)	46	18	13	15	73	52	49	
11.	Tranmere Rovers FC (Birkenhead)	46	21	6	19	76	71	48	
12.	Barrow AFC (Barrow-in-Furness)	46	17	12	17	57	61	46	
13.	Chesterfield FC (Chesterfield)	46	17	11	18	65	66	45	
14.	Scunthorpe & Lindsey United FC (Scunthorpe)	46	14	16	16	65	74	44	
15.	Bradford City AFC (Bradford)	46	16	10	20	61	68	42	
16.	Crewe Alexandra FC (Crewe)	46	17	8	21	63	82	42	
17.	Southport FC (Southport)	46	15	11	20	53	71	41	
18.	Wrexham AFC (Wrexham)	46	15	9	22	63	73	39	
19.	Chester FC (Chester)	46	15	9	22	72	85	39	
20.	Halifax Town AFC (Halifax)	46	14	7	25	61	97	35	
21.	Rochdale AFC (Rochdale)	46	11	13	22	47	79	35	
22.	Accrington Stanley FC (Accrington)	46	10	12	24	61	92	32	
23.	Darlington FC (Darlington)	46	11	9	26	64	103	31	
24.	Workington FC (Workington)	46	11	7	28	50	91	29	
		1104	430	244	430	1658	1658	1104	

234

Football League Division 3 (S) 1951-52 Season	Aldershot Town	Bournemouth	FC	Bristol City	Bristol Rovers	Colchester Utd.	Crystal Palace	Exeter City	Gillingham	Ipswich Town	Leyton Orient	Millwall	Newport County	Northampton T.	Norwich City	Plymouth Argyle	Port Vale	Reading	Shrewsbury T.	Southend Utd.	Swindon Town	Torquay United	Walsall	Watford
Aldershot Town FC	■	1-3	0-2	1-0	1-3	1-1	3-0	4-1	2-1	1-1	0-1	2-1	4-0	0-1	2-0	1-2	4-1	0-2	1-1	2-2	4-0	1-3	3-1	2-0
Bournemouth & Bos.	0-2	■	3-1	0-0	1-0	5-0	1-2	0-4	3-3	2-2	3-2	0-2	5-1	3-0	1-2	1-2	0-1	1-2	2-0	2-1	4-1	3-1	2-1	0-0
Brighton & Hove Alb.	4-2	0-1	■	1-1	1-1	5-1	4-3	2-1	0-0	5-1	3-1	0-0	1-2	2-0	2-0	2-3	2-1	1-0	1-0	5-0	4-0	3-4	5-1	4-1
Bristol City FC	1-1	1-0	4-1	■	1-1	2-0	2-0	1-1	3-2	0-2	1-1	2-1	3-1	2-0	2-5	1-1	1-0	1-3	3-0	6-0	2-1	2-2	2-0	1-3
Bristol Rovers FC	5-1	1-2	5-0	2-0	■	6-0	4-0	2-2	5-0	1-0	1-0	1-1	2-2	1-1	2-1	1-1	4-1	1-2	3-3	2-0	1-0	5-0	5-1	0-1
Colchester United FC	0-2	1-1	0-0	4-1	2-1	■	1-2	1-0	1-0	1-0	0-1	2-2	2-1	2-5	1-1	1-0	0-0	4-1	2-2	1-0	2-0	0-0	3-2	1-0
Crystal Palace FC	0-2	2-2	1-2	2-1	0-1	2-2	■	2-1	0-2	3-1	2-1	1-1	1-1	3-3	2-0	0-1	3-1	1-2	1-1	1-0	1-1	2-1	2-1	2-0
Exeter City FC	0-4	2-2	2-0	0-0	0-1	0-0	0-1	■	4-2	2-1	6-1	0-3	3-4	0-3	2-4	1-0	2-0	1-4	4-2	2-2	1-2	4-0	1-0	1-0
Gillingham FC	3-3	0-2	2-3	5-0	2-1	1-2	4-4	2-1	■	1-1	1-1	2-3	2-1	1-2	1-2	4-2	1-1	0-0	2-0	4-0	3-0	4-1	1-0	1-0
Ipswich Town FC	2-3	3-1	5-0	1-1	1-2	0-2	1-1	2-4	1-1	■	1-0	3-0	3-1	3-2	0-2	2-2	2-0	4-2	1-0	4-1	1-5	2-0	0-1	1-0
Leyton Orient FC	0-1	1-0	2-3	2-0	3-3	7-0	0-4	3-0	1-0	2-0	■	0-0	1-1	2-1	3-3	1-0	0-4	4-1	1-4	1-0	0-1	3-0	1-0	1-0
Millwall FC	3-2	3-1	0-3	3-2	1-1	1-1	3-1	4-0	3-1	4-0	2-0	■	2-0	2-1	0-2	1-1	3-2	0-0	2-0	4-0	1-1	4-1	2-1	1-0
Newport County AFC	4-2	2-0	1-1	1-0	2-2	0-1	1-0	4-0	1-1	2-1	1-0	2-1	■	2-0	2-2	3-3	3-1	3-1	3-0	1-0	1-2	1-1	4-2	2-5
Northampton Town	6-2	5-3	3-0	1-2	2-0	2-0	5-2	3-1	2-1	1-0	4-0	1-1	5-0	■	1-2	3-1	3-1	0-3	6-0	4-3	1-0	2-4	4-1	1-4
Norwich City FC	1-2	2-0	0-1	1-0	1-0	5-2	1-0	1-1	5-0	1-0	1-0	1-2	2-1	3-0	■	2-3	2-1	3-2	1-0	2-0	2-0	7-0	8-0	3-0
Plymouth Argyle FC	2-1	4-1	2-2	2-2	1-2	3-1	5-0	2-1	4-2	2-0	3-0	5-0	5-0	2-0	3-1	■	3-0	3-2	6-1	3-0	3-0	2-2	3-0	3-1
Port Vale FC	4-1	2-2	1-1	1-0	1-1	1-1	2-0	3-0	1-0	0-0	3-0	2-1	4-2	0-0	0-0	1-0	■	0-2	1-0	0-0	2-2	2-2	1-0	1-1
Reading FC	5-1	5-0	1-4	3-0	4-2	4-2	3-1	2-1	2-1	4-0	1-1	2-0	1-1	2-0	2-1	1-1	5-1	■	6-2	5-2	2-0	6-1	3-0	4-1
Shrewsbury Town FC	5-1	1-0	1-0	2-1	1-0	2-1	2-2	0-2	3-0	1-1	4-1	0-2	1-2	0-3	2-1	2-1	2-0	2-1	■	0-1	0-1	0-1	1-1	2-3
Southend United FC	7-1	1-0	2-0	5-1	2-1	3-2	4-0	0-0	3-1	5-0	1-0	0-1	2-1	2-0	2-1	1-1	2-0	2-2	2-2	■	2-2	2-2	3-0	5-1
Swindon Town FC	1-1	2-0	0-2	0-0	0-0	2-1	0-2	3-1	2-1	1-2	2-2	1-1	1-1	1-1	2-2	2-0	1-2	1-0	1-1	2-2	■	2-1	1-1	0-1
Torquay United FC	6-1	2-2	0-1	1-2	4-2	3-1	1-5	5-1	2-1	2-0	1-1	2-5	1-2	1-2	3-2	2-3	0-3	3-2	1-3	9-0	1-2	■	1-1	2-0
Walsall FC	1-0	2-2	1-1	1-0	1-0	1-3	3-0	1-2	1-0	1-3	2-4	1-2	0-1	3-0	4-0	2-5	3-0	2-0	0-4	2-0	0-0	2-3	■	3-1
Watford FC	2-2	1-2	3-1	3-1	0-3	0-1	2-0	1-1	2-2	1-1	0-1	1-2	1-1	2-4	1-1	1-3	2-0	3-1	4-1	0-0	1-7	1-2	2-0	■

Division 3 (South)

		Pd	Wn	Dw	Ls	GF	GA	Pts	
1.	Plymouth Argyle FC (Plymouth)	46	29	8	9	107	53	66	P
2.	Reading FC (Reading)	46	29	3	14	112	60	61	
3.	Norwich City FC (Norwich)	46	26	9	11	89	50	61	
4.	Millwall FC (London)	46	23	12	11	74	53	58	
5.	Brighton & Hove Albion FC (Hove)	46	24	10	12	87	63	58	
6.	Newport County AFC (Newport)	46	21	12	13	77	76	54	
7.	Bristol Rovers FC (Bristol)	46	20	12	14	89	53	52	
8.	Northampton Town FC (Northampton)	46	22	5	19	93	74	49	
9.	Southend United FC (Southend-on-Sea)	46	19	10	17	75	66	48	
10.	Colchester United FC (Colchester)	46	17	12	17	56	77	46	
11.	Torquay United FC (Torquay)	46	17	10	19	86	98	44	
12.	Aldershot FC (Aldershot)	46	18	8	20	78	89	44	
13.	Port Vale FC (Stoke-on-Trent)	46	14	15	17	50	66	43	T
14.	Bournemouth & Boscombe Athletic FC (Bournemouth)	46	16	10	20	69	75	42	
15.	Bristol City FC (Bristol)	46	15	12	19	58	69	42	
16.	Swindon Town FC (Swindon)	46	14	14	18	51	68	42	
17.	Ipswich Town FC (Ipswich)	46	16	9	21	63	74	41	
18.	Leyton Orient FC (London)	46	16	9	21	55	68	41	
19.	Crystal Palace FC (London)	46	15	9	22	61	80	39	
20.	Shrewsbury Town FC (Shrewsbury)	46	13	10	23	62	86	36	
21.	Watford FC (Watford)	46	13	10	23	57	81	36	
22.	Gillingham FC (Gillingham)	46	11	13	22	71	81	35	
23.	Exeter City FC (Exeter)	46	13	9	24	65	86	35	
24.	Walsall FC (Walsall)	46	13	5	28	55	94	31	
		1104	434	236	434	1740	1740	1104	

T: Port Vale FC (Stoke-on-Trent) were transferred to Division 3 (North) for the next season.

F.A. CUP FINAL   (Wembley Stadium, London – 03/05/1952 – 100,000)

NEWCASTLE UNITED FC   1-0   Arsenal FC (London)

G.Robledo

Newcastle: Simpson, Cowell, McMichael, Harvey, Brennan, E.Robledo, Walker, Foulkes, Milburn, G.Robledo, Mitchell.

Arsenal: Swindin, Barnes, L.Smith, Forbes, Daniel, Mercer, Cox, Logie, Holton, Lishman, Roper.

Semi-finals

Arsenal FC (London)	1-1, 3-0	Chelsea FC (London)
Newcastle United FC (Newcastle-upon-Tyne)	0-0, 2-1	Blackburn Rovers FC (Blackburn)

Quarter-finals

Blackburn Rovers FC (Blackburn)	3-1	Burnley FC (Burnley)
Luton Town FC (Luton)	2-3	Arsenal FC (London)
Portsmouth FC (Portsmouth)	2-4	Newcastle United FC (Newcastle-upon-Tyne)
Sheffield United FC (Sheffield)	0-1	Chelsea FC (London)

Football League Division 1 1952-53 Season	Arsenal	Aston Villa	Blackpool	Bolton Wanderers	Burnley	Cardiff City	Charlton Athletic	Chelsea	Derby County	Liverpool	Manchester City	Manchester United	Middlesbrough	Newcastle United	Portsmouth	Preston North End	Sheffield Wed.	Stoke City	Sunderland	Tottenham Hotspur	W.B.A.	Wolves
Arsenal FC	■	3-1	3-1	4-1	3-2	0-1	3-4	2-0	6-2	5-3	3-1	2-1	2-1	3-0	3-1	1-1	2-2	3-1	1-2	4-0	2-2	5-3
Aston Villa FC	1-2	■	1-5	1-1	2-0	2-0	1-1	1-1	3-0	4-0	0-0	3-3	1-0	0-1	6-0	1-0	4-3	1-1	3-0	0-3	1-1	0-1
Blackpool FC	3-2	1-1	■	3-0	4-2	0-1	8-4	3-1	2-1	3-1	4-1	0-0	1-1	0-2	3-2	1-1	0-1	1-1	2-0	2-0	2-0	2-0
Bolton Wanderers FC	4-6	0-0	4-0	■	1-2	0-1	1-2	1-2	2-0	2-2	2-1	5-3	4-2	0-5	0-3	1-1	2-1	5-0	2-3	0-1	2-1	
Burnley FC	1-1	1-0	0-1	0-1	■	0-0	2-0	1-1	1-2	2-0	2-1	2-1	0-1	2-1	3-2	2-2	1-1	3-2	5-1	3-2	5-0	0-0
Cardiff City AFC	0-0	1-2	2-2	1-0	0-0	■	0-1	3-3	2-0	4-0	6-0	1-2	1-1	0-0	0-1	0-2	4-0	2-0	4-1	0-0	1-2	0-0
Charlton Athletic FC	2-2	5-1	2-0	2-0	0-0	3-1	■	2-2	3-1	3-2	1-2	2-2	2-0	0-2	2-1	3-0	5-1	3-1	3-2	0-0	2-2	
Chelsea FC	1-1	4-0	4-0	1-0	0-2	0-2	0-1	■	1-1	3-0	3-1	2-3	1-1	1-2	2-0	5-3	1-0	0-0	3-2	2-1	0-2	1-2
Derby County FC	2-0	0-1	1-1	4-3	1-3	1-1	1-1	3-2	■	3-2	5-0	2-3	3-3	0-2	3-0	0-1	2-1	4-0	3-1	0-0	1-1	2-3
Liverpool FC	1-5	0-2	2-2	0-0	1-1	2-1	1-2	2-0	1-1	■	0-1	1-2	4-1	5-3	1-1	2-2	1-0	3-2	2-0	2-1	3-0	2-1
Manchester City FC	2-4	4-1	5-0	1-2	0-0	2-2	5-1	4-0	1-0	0-2	■	2-1	5-1	2-1	2-1	3-1	2-1	2-5	0-1	0-1	0-1	3-1
Manchester United FC	0-0	3-1	2-1	1-0	1-3	1-4	3-2	2-0	1-0	3-1	1-1	■	3-2	2-2	1-1	5-2	1-1	0-2	1-1	3-2	2-2	0-3
Middlesbrough FC	2-0	1-0	5-1	1-2	2-2	3-0	1-0	4-0	1-0	2-3	5-4	5-0	■	2-1	3-2	1-1	2-2	1-0	1-2	0-4	4-2	1-1
Newcastle United FC	2-2	2-1	0-1	2-3	0-0	3-0	3-2	2-1	1-0	1-2	2-0	1-2	1-0	■	1-0	4-3	1-5	1-2	2-2	1-1	3-5	1-1
Portsmouth FC	2-2	1-1	0-2	3-1	2-1	0-2	1-1	2-0	2-2	3-1	2-1	2-0	1-4	5-1	■	2-5	5-2	1-1	5-2	2-1	1-2	2-2
Preston North End FC	2-0	1-3	4-2	2-2	2-1	2-3	2-1	2-1	3-0	1-1	6-2	0-5	3-0	2-1	4-0	■	1-0	3-0	3-2	1-0	1-0	1-1
Sheffield Wednesday FC	1-4	2-2	2-0	1-1	2-4	2-0	0-3	1-0	2-0	0-2	1-1	0-0	2-0	2-2	3-4	1-1	■	1-0	4-0	2-0	4-5	2-3
Stoke City FC	1-1	1-4	4-0	1-2	1-3	0-0	1-0	1-1	1-2	3-1	2-1	3-1	1-0	1-0	2-4	0-0	1-3	■	3-0	2-0	5-1	1-2
Sunderland AFC	3-1	2-2	1-1	2-0	2-1	4-2	2-1	2-1	2-1	3-2	3-2	2-2	1-1	0-2	1-1	2-2	2-1	1-1	■	1-1	1-0	5-2
Tottenham Hotspur FC	1-3	1-1	4-0	1-1	2-1	2-1	2-0	2-3	5-2	3-1	3-3	1-2	7-1	3-2	3-3	4-4	2-1	1-0	2-2	■	3-4	3-2
West Bromwich Albion FC	2-0	3-2	0-1	0-1	1-2	1-0	3-1	0-1	2-2	3-0	2-1	3-1	3-0	1-0	2-0	2-1	0-1	3-2	1-1	2-1	■	1-1
Wolverhampton Wanderers FC	1-1	2-1	2-5	3-1	5-1	1-0	1-2	2-2	3-1	3-0	7-3	6-2	3-3	2-0	4-1	0-2	3-1	3-0	1-1	0-0	2-0	■

	Division 1	Pd	Wn	Dw	Ls	GF	GA	Pts	
1.	ARSENAL FC (LONDON)	42	21	12	9	97	64	54	
2.	Preston North End FC (Preston)	42	21	12	9	85	60	54	
3.	Wolverhampton Wanderers FC (Wolverhampton)	42	19	13	10	86	63	51	
4.	West Bromwich Albion FC (West Bromwich)	42	21	8	13	66	60	50	
5.	Charlton Athletic FC (London)	42	19	11	12	77	63	49	
6.	Burnley FC (Burnley)	42	18	12	12	67	52	48	
7.	Blackpool FC (Blackpool)	42	19	9	14	71	70	47	
8.	Manchester United FC (Manchester)	42	18	10	14	69	72	46	
9.	Sunderland AFC (Sunderland)	42	15	13	14	68	82	43	
10.	Tottenham Hotspur FC (London)	42	15	11	16	78	69	41	
11.	Aston Villa FC (Birmingham)	42	14	13	15	63	61	41	
12.	Cardiff City AFC (Cardiff)	42	14	12	16	54	46	40	
13.	Middlesbrough FC (Middlesbrough)	42	14	11	17	70	77	39	
14.	Bolton Wanderers FC (Bolton)	42	15	9	18	61	69	39	
15.	Portsmouth FC (Portsmouth)	42	14	10	18	74	83	38	
16.	Newcastle United FC (Newcastle-upon-Tyne)	42	14	9	19	59	70	37	
17.	Liverpool FC (Liverpool)	42	14	8	20	61	82	36	
18.	Sheffield Wednesday FC (Sheffield)	42	12	11	19	62	72	35	
19.	Chelsea FC (London)	42	12	11	19	56	66	35	
20.	Manchester City FC (Manchester)	42	14	7	21	72	87	35	
21.	Stoke City FC (Stoke-on-Trent)	42	12	10	20	53	66	34	R
22.	Derby County FC (Derby)	42	11	10	21	59	74	32	R
		924	346	232	346	1508	1508	924	

Top Goalscorer

1) Charles WAYMAN   (Preston North End FC)   24

	Barnsley	Birmingham City	Blackburn Rovers	Brentford	Bury	Doncaster Rovers	Everton	Fulham	Huddersfield Town	Hull City	Leeds United	Leicester City	Lincoln City	Luton Town	Nottingham Forest	Notts County	Plymouth Argyle	Rotherham United	Sheffield United	Southampton	Swansea Town	West Ham United
Barnsley FC		1-3	1-4	0-2	3-2	2-2	2-3	1-1	2-4	5-1	2-2	0-3	1-1	2-3	0-2	1-2	0-3	2-3	1-3	0-1	3-1	2-0
Birmingham City FC	3-1		1-2	3-1	0-2	2-1	4-2	1-4	0-2	4-3	2-2	3-1	2-2	2-2	0-5	3-2	4-0	4-0	1-2	2-0	1-4	2-0
Blackburn Rovers FC	2-0	1-2		3-0	4-0	2-1	3-1	2-2	1-1	2-0	1-1	2-0	0-2	1-1	2-1	3-2	1-3	0-1	1-2	3-0	3-0	3-0
Brentford FC	4-0	1-2	3-2		2-2	1-0	2-4	2-2	1-3	1-0	3-3	4-2	1-0	1-1	1-1	5-0	1-2	1-1	0-0	3-0	0-0	1-4
Bury FC	5-2	3-0	1-0	3-0		2-1	0-5	1-1	1-1	2-1	2-2	1-4	2-2	1-0	2-0	0-1	3-2	2-0	0-4	0-0	1-3	1-1
Doncaster Rovers FC	1-1	1-0	3-3	0-2	1-1		3-0	0-0	1-1	3-1	0-0	2-0	1-0	1-0	2-0	1-1	2-1	0-2	1-0	2-0	1-2	2-3
Everton FC	2-1	1-1	0-3	5-0	3-0	7-1		3-3	2-1	0-2	2-2	2-2	0-3	1-1	3-0	1-1	2-0	0-1	0-0	2-2	0-0	2-0
Fulham FC	3-1	3-1	2-1	5-0	2-0	1-3	3-0		0-2	2-1	2-1	4-6	4-2	2-0	0-1	6-0	2-1	4-1	1-2	1-1	3-1	2-3
Huddersfield Town AFC	6-0	1-1	0-3	0-0	2-0	3-1	8-2	4-2		1-1	1-0	1-0	5-0	1-2	1-0	4-0	1-0	1-1	1-1	5-0	3-0	0-1
Hull City AFC	2-2	2-0	3-0	2-2	0-2	1-1	1-0	3-1	0-2		1-0	1-1	1-1	0-2	3-1	0-1	3-2	4-0	1-0	1-1	1-1	1-0
Leeds United AFC	4-1	0-1	0-3	3-2	2-0	1-1	2-0	2-0	2-1	3-1		0-1	2-1	2-2	2-1	3-1	1-1	4-0	0-3	1-1	5-1	3-2
Leicester City FC	2-2	3-4	2-1	2-3	3-2	4-2	4-2	6-1	2-1	5-0	3-3		3-2	1-1	3-0	2-0	3-2	0-0	4-1	2-1	4-1	0-0
Lincoln City FC	1-1	1-1	4-1	0-0	4-0	2-0	1-1	2-2	2-2	2-1	1-1	3-2		1-2	2-3	3-0	0-0	1-3	3-2	2-2	3-1	3-1
Luton Town FC	6-0	0-1	6-0	0-1	4-1	1-2	4-2	2-0	0-2	3-2	2-0	2-0	4-0		3-0	5-1	1-0	2-1	4-1	1-2	3-1	0-0
Nottingham Forest FC	3-0	0-2	1-2	3-0	4-1	2-2	3-3	0-1	1-0	4-1	2-1	1-3	1-1	4-3		1-0	3-1	4-3	1-1	2-3	6-4	0-0
Notts County FC	1-0	2-0	5-0	4-0	2-1	4-3	2-2	1-1	1-0	2-0	3-2	2-2	1-1	1-2	3-2		0-4	2-1	0-3	1-2	3-4	1-1
Plymouth Argyle FC	4-0	2-1	3-1	1-0	0-0	0-0	1-0	3-1	0-2	2-1	0-1	2-1	0-0	2-1	0-3	2-2		4-3	5-2	3-1	3-2	1-1
Rotherham United FC	3-1	1-1	0-0	4-1	6-1	4-2	2-2	1-0	0-0	2-1	3-1	0-0	3-2	1-3	2-3	2-3	2-3		0-2	2-2	2-1	1-1
Sheffield United FC	3-0	2-2	3-0	3-2	3-1	2-2	1-0	1-2	0-1	7-2	6-1	1-1	2-0	2-1	5-0	1-4	5-0	1-4		5-3	7-1	3-1
Southampton FC	1-2	1-1	6-1	0-2	1-2	3-3	1-1	5-3	0-2	5-1	2-2	5-2	1-0	3-1	2-2	1-1	2-3	2-3	4-4		1-4	1-2
Swansea Town AFC	3-0	1-1	1-1	3-2	2-0	2-1	2-2	2-2	3-3	3-0	3-2	1-1	1-1	4-2	2-1	5-1	2-2	0-0	1-2	1-2		4-1
West Ham United FC	3-1	1-2	0-0	3-1	3-2	1-3	3-1	1-2	0-1	0-0	2-2	4-1	5-1	0-1	3-2	2-2	0-1	2-4	1-1	1-0	3-0	

	Division 2	Pd	Wn	Dw	Ls	GF	GA	Pts	
1.	Sheffield United FC (Sheffield)	42	25	10	7	97	55	60	P
2.	Huddersfield Town AFC (Huddersfield)	42	24	10	8	84	33	58	P
3.	Luton Town FC (Luton)	42	22	8	12	84	49	52	
4.	Plymouth Argyle FC (Plymouth)	42	20	9	13	65	60	49	
5.	Leicester City FC (Leicester)	42	18	12	12	89	74	48	
6.	Birmingham City FC (Birmingham)	42	19	10	13	71	66	48	
7.	Nottingham Forest FC (Nottingham)	42	18	8	16	77	67	44	
8.	Fulham FC (London)	42	17	10	15	81	71	44	
9.	Blackburn Rovers FC (Blackburn)	42	18	8	16	68	65	44	
10.	Leeds United AFC (Leeds)	42	14	15	13	71	63	43	
11.	Swansea Town AFC (Swansea)	42	15	12	15	78	81	42	
12.	Rotherham United FC (Rotherham)	42	16	9	17	75	74	41	
13.	Doncaster Rovers FC (Doncaster)	42	12	16	14	58	64	40	
14.	West Ham United FC (London)	42	13	13	16	58	60	39	
15.	Lincoln City FC (Lincoln)	42	11	17	14	64	71	39	
16.	Everton FC (Liverpool)	42	12	14	16	71	75	38	
17.	Brentford FC (London)	42	13	11	18	59	76	37	
18.	Hull City AFC (Kingston-upon-Hull)	42	14	8	20	57	69	36	
19.	Notts County FC (Nottingham)	42	14	8	20	60	88	36	
20.	Bury FC (Bury)	42	13	9	20	53	81	35	
21.	Southampton FC (Southampton)	42	10	13	19	68	85	33	R
22.	Barnsley FC (Barnsley)	42	5	8	29	47	108	18	R
		924	343	238	343	1535	1535	924	

Football League Division 3 (N) — 1952-53 Season

Column key: ACC = Accrington Stanley, BAR = Barrow, BCY = Bradford City, BPA = Bradford Park Ave., CAR = Carlisle United, CHE = Chester, CHF = Chesterfield, CRE = Crewe Alexandra, DAR = Darlington, GAT = Gateshead, GRI = Grimsby Town, HAL = Halifax Town, HAR = Hartlepools, MAN = Mansfield Town, OLD = Oldham Athletic, PV = Port Vale, ROC = Rochdale, SCU = Scunthorpe United, SOU = Southport, STK = Stockport County, TRA = Tranmere Rovers, WOR = Workington, WRE = Wrexham, YOR = York City

	ACC	BAR	BCY	BPA	CAR	CHE	CHF	CRE	DAR	GAT	GRI	HAL	HAR	MAN	OLD	PV	ROC	SCU	SOU	STK	TRA	WOR	WRE	YOR
Accrington Stanley		1-0	1-1	3-2	1-0	1-1	1-1	1-1	1-0	1-1	1-2	1-1	1-1	2-2	0-2	1-1	2-1	2-1	1-2	1-4	0-2	0-1	1-2	1-0
Barrow AFC	2-0		5-1	2-0	0-0	3-0	2-1	1-2	2-2	2-2	1-1	5-1	2-1	3-0	4-3	1-2	2-1	1-1	1-0	2-0	3-0	1-1	1-0	
Bradford City AFC	3-2	2-2		2-1	7-2	2-2	2-1	1-3	4-3	3-1	1-0	5-0	1-1	2-1	0-0	1-0	0-3	0-0	2-2	3-0	5-3	4-0	3-1	1-1
Bradford Park Ave.	4-0	1-0	2-2		2-2	1-0	0-1	1-0	3-0	3-0	0-3	1-2	1-1	1-1	0-0	2-2	2-1	1-1	1-0	1-1	1-0	6-1	1-2	2-3
Carlisle United FC	4-4	0-0	4-4	1-3		1-1	3-0	1-2	4-2	2-2	3-0	1-2	4-1	1-0	0-0	2-0	5-0	8-0	2-0	2-1	4-0	3-1	1-0	1-1
Chester FC	1-2	2-1	2-0	0-3	1-2		2-0	2-2	6-3	0-2	0-2	0-1	2-2	0-1	2-3	1-0	1-1	0-0	4-4	1-1	2-1	1-1	1-1	1-2
Chesterfield FC	3-0	1-1	1-1	1-1	4-2	2-1		1-0	3-0	1-1	3-2	2-1	2-0	4-1	1-2	4-0	1-1	1-2	2-1	1-2	1-1	2-1	1-2	
Crewe Alexandra FC	3-2	1-1	1-1	2-3	2-2	4-1	2-1		0-1	4-3	1-2	1-1	1-2	1-0	1-0	1-4	4-2	2-0	2-0	2-0	1-1	4-0	3-3	3-0
Darlington FC	1-0	1-0	4-1	1-3	0-0	3-2	3-1	1-1		1-0	1-1	0-2	3-0	0-5	0-2	3-2	3-1	1-0	1-2	1-0	2-2			0-1
Gateshead FC	5-0	3-1	2-2	3-2	2-0	4-1	2-4	6-1	5-1		2-0	3-1	1-1	1-2	1-0	1-1	3-1	1-1	1-2	0-1	1-1	1-1	1-0	1-1
Grimsby Town FC	3-0	2-1	0-0	2-3	2-3	5-4	0-0	1-0	2-0	0-0		2-0	7-0	5-1	1-1	1-1	3-2	1-1	0-1	3-1	2-0	2-0	0-0	
Halifax Town AFC	3-0	1-0	1-1	2-4	2-1	3-1	3-1	1-3	3-2	1-3	3-2		3-2	1-2	2-2		1-2	3-1		4-1	3-0		5-2	0-0
Hartlepools United	4-1		1-0	1-1	0-2	2-2	2-0	2-1	0-0		2-0	0-0		2-0	4-1	2-1	3-0	0-2	4-2	2-1	2-1			
Mansfield Town FC	0-0	2-2	3-1	1-1	2-2	2-1	1-4	3-0	3-2	2-0	1-1	2-1	2-0		0-2	1-0	1-0	1-0	2-2	2-2	1-0	0-0	0-2	1-1
Oldham Athletic AFC	3-0	3-0	2-0	2-1	2-4	2-1	1-1	0-1	5-0	1-1	1-1	1-0	4-2	1-0		0-1	1-0	3-0	3-1	1-1	5-2	4-1	4-2	1-1
Port Vale FC	0-2	3-0	0-0	1-0	0-0	1-1	3-0	3-1	2-1	1-1	4-0	1-3	1-1	1-1	5-2		4-0	0-0	2-0	2-0	2-0	1-0	2-0	1-0
Rochdale AFC	1-0	6-2	2-1	1-0	1-2	3-1	0-2	1-1	2-3	0-2	1-1	3-1	1-0	3-1	1-1			2-2	0-2	2-0	2-1	2-0	4-1	0-3
Scunthorpe United	5-2	1-2	4-0	1-2	1-2	1-1	1-0	2-0	2-0	0-0	1-1	0-0	0-1	1-1	1-2	5-1			3-0	2-0	2-1	2-1	1-2	0-3
Southport FC	1-0	3-2	3-0	2-2	2-0	2-0	1-0	3-0	3-2	4-3	1-0	3-2	1-0	1-0	1-3	1-0	2-3			3-0	1-1	2-0	2-0	3-1
Stockport County FC	3-1	6-1	6-1	3-0	4-1	4-1	4-2	2-2	3-1	2-2	1-1	2-2	1-1		0-2	2-1	3-0		3-2		6-0	3-1	1-1	
Tranmere Rovers FC	2-0	2-0	3-1	4-0	4-1	4-0	3-1	5-2	2-0	2-1	0-0	0-2	1-0	0-0	1-1	1-1	0-1	1-1	1-0			3-0	4-2	1-3
Workington AFC	3-0	3-1	3-2	2-2	1-1	1-2	2-3	4-0	3-1	0-2	3-1	2-0	1-1	0-1	1-1	1-2	0-3	2-4	0-2	2-0			4-0	1-3
Wrexham AFC	3-1	4-0	2-1	0-3	3-0	7-0	2-2	1-1	4-2	1-0	3-1	3-2	1-0	2-2	3-1	3-0	2-3	3-2	5-2	1-0	3-0			1-1
York City FC	2-0	1-1	0-0	3-1	1-0	0-0	0-0	2-1	3-0	1-2	2-0	2-2	1-0	2-0	1-2	1-0	2-0	0-2	3-1	3-0	2-0	1-3	2-1	

	Division 3 (North)	Pd	Wn	Dw	Ls	GF	GA	Pts	
1.	Oldham Athletic AFC (Oldham)	46	22	15	9	77	45	59	P
2.	Port Vale FC (Stoke-on-Trent)	46	20	18	8	67	35	58	
3.	Wrexham AFC (Wrexham)	46	24	8	14	86	66	56	
4.	York City FC (York)	46	20	13	13	60	45	53	
5.	Grimsby Town FC (Cleethorpes)	46	21	10	15	75	59	52	
6.	Southport FC (Southport)	46	20	11	15	63	60	51	
7.	Bradford Park Avenue FC (Bradford)	46	19	12	15	75	61	50	
8.	Gateshead FC (Gateshead)	46	17	15	14	76	60	49	
9.	Carlisle United FC (Carlisle)	46	18	13	15	82	68	49	
10.	Crewe Alexandra FC (Crewe)	46	20	8	18	70	68	48	
11.	Stockport County FC (Stockport)	46	17	13	16	82	69	47	
12.	Chesterfield FC (Chesterfield)	46	18	11	17	65	63	47	Jt.
12.	Tranmere Rovers FC (Birkenhead)	46	21	5	20	65	63	47	Jt.
14.	Halifax Town AFC (Halifax)	46	16	15	15	68	68	47	
15.	Scunthorpe & Lindsey United FC (Scunthorpe)	46	16	14	16	62	56	46	
16.	Bradford City AFC (Bradford)	46	14	18	14	75	80	46	
17.	Hartlepools United FC (Hartlepool)	46	16	14	16	57	61	46	
18.	Mansfield Town FC (Mansfield)	46	16	14	16	55	62	46	
19.	Barrow AFC (Barrow-in-Furness)	46	16	12	18	66	71	44	
20.	Chester FC (Chester)	46	11	15	20	64	85	37	
21.	Darlington FC (Darlington)	46	14	6	26	58	96	34	
22.	Rochdale AFC (Rochdale)	46	14	5	27	62	83	33	
23.	Workington AFC (Workington)	46	11	10	25	55	91	32	
24.	Accrington Stanley FC (Accrington)	46	8	11	27	39	89	27	
		1104	409	286	409	1604	1604	1104	

Football League Division 3 (S) — 1952-53 Season

Results grid (home team in left column, away team across top). Column order: Aldershot Town, Bournemouth, Brighton & H.A., Bristol City, Bristol Rovers, Colchester United, Coventry City, Crystal Palace, Exeter City, Gillingham, Ipswich Town, Leyton Orient, Millwall, Newport County, Northampton Town, Norwich City, Q.P.R., Reading, Shrewsbury Town, Southend United, Swindon Town, Torquay United, Walsall, Watford.

	Ald	Bou	Brh	BrC	BrR	Col	Cov	Cry	Exe	Gil	Ips	Ley	Mil	New	Nor	Nwc	QPR	Rea	Shr	Sou	Swi	Tor	Wal	Wat
Aldershot Town FC		1-0	1-2	1-2	0-0	0-0	4-1	0-1	1-1	3-2	1-1	2-0	1-2	2-2	2-1	1-2	4-1	2-2	4-2	1-1	2-2	0-2	2-0	1-2
Bournemouth & Bos.	0-3		2-1	4-1	1-2	1-0	3-0	4-2	2-1	4-2	2-1	4-1	1-1	1-2	0-1	0-0	1-0	2-0	2-0	5-1	1-1	0-1	5-1	4-1
Brighton & Hove Alb.	4-2	2-0		0-1	2-1	0-0	1-1	4-1	4-2	5-0	1-4	3-1	1-0	2-2	1-1	2-3	2-0	1-1	3-1	2-2	1-2	2-1	4-2	1-2
Bristol City FC	0-0	1-1	2-2		0-0	3-2	1-0	5-0	4-1	4-0	4-2	2-1	0-0	2-0	2-3	0-1	4-4	1-1	3-2	5-0	4-2	4-4	6-1	5-1
Bristol Rovers FC	4-1	2-1	7-0	0-0		3-1	5-2	2-0	0-0	3-1	3-0	1-1	3-1	1-1	3-1	2-1	4-0	2-1	2-1	1-2	3-0	2-0		0-3
Colchester United FC	1-2	1-1	0-0	3-1	0-3		0-1	3-0	3-1	1-1	0-0	3-1	0-0	3-3	1-2	0-4	1-1	2-1	1-0	3-3	-1	4-1	6-1	1-1
Coventry City FC	3-0	2-3	3-1	2-2	1-1	2-2		4-2	1-0	2-1	2-0	3-0	4-1	0-1	1-1	2-1	2-0	4-0	0-0	2-1	1-2	7-2	3-1	1-0
Crystal Palace FC	3-0	1-0	2-1	1-3	1-0	3-1	2-2		2-0	0-0	1-1	2-2	0-1	2-1	4-3	1-1	4-2	0-3	1-2	0-0	3-0	2-2	4-1	1-0
Exeter City FC	2-2	5-1	1-5	0-0	2-0	1-0	2-0	0-0		1-1	1-0	3-2	2-0	1-0	2-2	2-0	2-2	0-2	1-2	4-1	6-1			
Gillingham FC	2-0	1-2	1-2	0-1	0-4	1-1	0-0	1-0	1-0		1-1	3-2	0-1	1-1	1-1	0-3	3-0	2-1	4-2	1-1	0-0	2-1	3-1	2-1
Ipswich Town FC	2-1	2-1	1-0	1-0	1-5	2-2	3-0	2-0	0-1	1-1		0-1	1-6	3-0	1-1	1-1	0-1	1-2	2-1	0-0	1-1	2-2	5-0	1-1
Leyton Orient FC	4-1	2-2	3-0	1-3	3-3	5-3	1-2	0-0	2-0	1-1	3-1		1-4	2-1	0-1	5-0	1-1	0-0	3-0	2-2	4-1	4-1	2-0	
Millwall FC	0-0	3-1	1-1	1-1	3-0	1-1	2-0	0-0	0-0	3-2	0-0		3-0	1-2	2-3	2-1	1-0	4-1	1-1	3-0	3-0	3-0	1-1	
Newport County AFC	2-1	2-1	0-3	4-3	2-2	0-1	4-4	3-2	1-0	1-2	1-3	0-1	1-3		4-1	1-1	2-0	1-0	4-2	0-1	3-0	3-0	3-2	1-1
Northampton Town	4-0	5-1	5-3	0-2	2-2	2-0	3-1	5-1	3-1	3-1	2-0	3-1	1-1	5-0		3-3	4-2	6-1	3-1	4-3	3-1	3-3	2-1	4-1
Norwich City FC	5-0	1-1	3-2	0-0	0-0	3-0	1-1	5-1	2-0	3-0	1-0	5-1	2-2	2-0	1-2		2-0	3-0	2-1	1-1	3-0			5-2
Queen's Park Rangers	2-2	2-1	3-3	0-1	1-0	0-4	1-1	1-1	1-1	2-2	0-1	1-3	4-2	2-2	3-1			1-0	1-0	3-2	1-1	0-1	4-2	2-2
Reading FC	2-3	1-3	0-0	4-0	2-0	2-0	1-0	4-1	3-1	3-2	1-1	2-0	5-0	2-1	2-0	0-1	2-0		5-3	4-1	4-0	0-0	3-0	
Shrewsbury Town FC	2-1	0-0	0-1	0-1	1-3	1-1	1-3	2-2	2-4	1-1	2-4	1-8	0-3	1-1						7-1	2-1	1-0		3-1
Southend United FC	1-1	0-0	1-2	0-4	4-0	1-0	2-2	1-1	3-0	1-0	2-1	1-0	3-1	1-2	0-1	3-1	2-2				3-0	3-1	2-1	1-0
Swindon Town FC	3-2	1-2	3-0	0-0	1-3	0-1	2-3	3-6	5-2	0-0	2-0	1-1	1-2	2-0	3-0	2-1	1-3	2-0	2-2			1-3	2-0	1-2
Torquay United FC	1-2	5-1	1-2	1-2	1-0	5-1	2-1	1-1	5-2	3-2	4-1	5-0	1-0	3-3	3-0	4-1	1-1	2-0	4-0	4-2	3-1		0-3	2-2
Walsall FC	0-0	2-2	3-0	3-3	3-5	0-3	1-1	2-4	2-2	1-3	1-3	1-0	0-2	1-3	1-5	3-2	1-1	2-0	4-4	1-1	1-2	2-0		0-0
Watford FC	1-1	3-0	2-3	4-1	2-3	2-0	1-1	2-0	3-1	0-0	1-0	1-0	1-1	0-1	2-1	3-2	1-1	2-1	1-1	1-1	2-1	1-1	3-0	

Division 3 (South)

		Pd	Wn	Dw	Ls	GF	GA	Pts	
1.	Bristol Rovers FC (Bristol)	46	26	12	8	92	46	64	P
2.	Millwall FC (London)	46	24	14	8	82	44	62	
3.	Northampton Town FC (Northampton)	46	26	10	10	109	70	62	
4.	Norwich City FC (Norwich)	46	25	10	11	99	55	60	
5.	Bristol City FC (Bristol)	46	22	15	9	95	61	59	
6.	Coventry City FC (Coventry)	46	19	12	15	77	62	50	
7.	Brighton & Hove Albion FC (Hove)	46	19	12	15	81	75	50	
8.	Southend United FC (Southend-on-Sea)	46	18	13	15	69	74	49	
9.	Bournemouth & Boscombe Athletic FC (Bournemouth)	46	19	9	18	74	69	47	
10.	Watford FC (Watford)	46	15	17	14	62	63	47	
11.	Reading FC (Reading)	46	19	8	19	69	64	46	
12.	Torquay United FC (Torquay)	46	18	9	19	87	88	45	
13.	Crystal Palace FC (London)	46	15	13	18	66	82	43	
14.	Leyton Orient FC (London)	46	16	10	20	68	73	42	
15.	Newport County AFC (Newport)	46	16	10	20	70	82	42	
16.	Ipswich Town FC (Ipswich)	46	13	15	18	60	69	41	
17.	Exeter City FC (Exeter)	46	13	14	19	61	71	40	
18.	Swindon Town FC (Swindon)	46	14	12	20	64	79	40	
19.	Aldershot Town FC (Aldershot)	46	12	15	19	61	77	39	
20.	Gillingham FC (Gillingham)	46	12	15	19	55	74	39	
21.	Queen's Park Rangers FC (Glasgow)	46	12	15	19	61	82	39	
22.	Colchester United FC (Colchester)	46	12	14	20	59	76	38	
23.	Shrewsbury Town FC (Shrewsbury)	46	12	12	22	68	91	36	
24.	Walsall FC (Walsall)	46	7	10	29	56	118	24	
		1104	404	296	404	1745	1745	1104	

F.A. CUP FINAL   (Wembley Stadium, London – 02/05/1953 – 100,000)

BLACKPOOL FC (BLACKPOOL)	4-3	Bolton Wanderers FC (Bolton)
Mortensen 3, Perry		*Lofthouse, Moir, Bell*

Blackburn: Farm, Shimwell, Garrett, Fenton, Johnston, Robinson, Matthews, Taylor, Mortensen, Mudie, Perry.

Bolton: Hanson, Ball, R.Banks, Wheeler, Barrass, Bell, Holden, Moir, Lofthouse, Hassall, Langton.

Semi-finals

Blackpool FC (Blackpool)	2-1	Tottenham Hotspur FC (London)
Bolton Wanderers FC (Bolton)	4-3	Everton FC (Liverpool)

Quarter-finals

Arsenal FC (London)	1-2	Blackpool FC (Blackpool)
Aston Villa FC (Birmingham)	0-1	Everton FC (Liverpool)
Birmingham City FC (Birmingham)	1-1, 2-2, 0-1	Tottenham Hotspur FC (London)
Gateshead FC (Gateshead)	0-1	Bolton Wanderers FC (Bolton)

1953-54

Football League Division 1 1953-54 Season	Arsenal	Aston Villa	Blackpool	Bolton Wands.	Burnley	Cardiff City	Charlton Ath.	Chelsea	Huddersfield T.	Liverpool	Manchester City	Man. United	Middlesbrough	Newcastle U.	Portsmouth	Preston N.E.	Sheffield Utd.	Sheffield Wed.	Sunderland	Tottenham H.	W.B.A.	Wolves
Arsenal FC	■	1-1	1-1	4-3	2-5	1-1	3-3	1-2	0-0	3-0	2-2	3-1	3-1	2-1	3-0	3-2	1-1	4-1	1-4	0-3	2-2	2-3
Aston Villa FC	2-1	■	2-1	2-2	5-1	1-2	2-1	2-2	2-2	2-1	3-0	2-2	5-3	1-2	1-1	1-0	4-0	2-1	3-1	1-2	6-1	1-2
Blackpool FC	2-2	3-2	■	0-0	2-0	4-1	3-1	2-1	3-1	3-0	2-0	2-0	0-0	1-3	1-1	4-2	2-2	1-2	3-0	1-0	4-1	0-0
Bolton Wanderers FC	3-1	3-0	3-2	■	0-0	3-0	3-1	2-2	0-0	2-0	3-2	0-0	3-2	2-2	6-1	0-2	2-1	2-1	3-1	2-0	2-1	1-1
Burnley FC	2-1	3-2	2-1	1-1	■	3-0	2-0	1-2	2-1	1-1	3-1	2-0	5-0	1-2	1-0	2-1	2-1	4-1	5-1	4-2	1-4	4-1
Cardiff City AFC	0-3	2-1	0-1	1-1	1-0	■	5-0	0-0	2-1	3-1	0-3	1-6	1-0	2-1	3-2	2-1	2-0	2-2	1-1	1-0	2-0	1-3
Charlton Athletic FC	1-5	1-1	4-2	1-0	3-1	3-2	■	1-1	2-1	6-0	1-0	8-1	0-0	3-1	2-1	3-0	4-2	5-3	0-1	1-1	2-0	
Chelsea FC	0-2	1-2	5-1	2-0	2-1	2-0	3-1	■	2-2	5-2	0-1	3-1	1-1	1-2	4-3	1-0	1-2	0-1	2-2	1-0	5-0	4-2
Huddersfield Town AFC	2-2	4-0	0-0	2-1	3-1	2-0	4-1	3-1	■	2-0	1-1	0-0	2-1	3-2	5-1	2-2	2-2	2-0	2-1	2-5	0-2	2-1
Liverpool FC	1-2	6-1	5-2	1-2	4-0	0-1	2-3	1-1	1-3	■	2-2	4-4	4-1	2-2	3-1	1-5	3-0	2-2	4-3	2-2	0-0	1-1
Manchester City FC	0-0	0-1	1-4	3-0	3-2	1-1	3-0	1-1	0-1	0-2	■	2-0	5-2	0-0	2-1	1-4	2-1	3-2	2-1	4-1	2-3	0-4
Manchester United FC	2-2	1-0	4-1	1-5	1-2	2-3	2-0	1-1	3-1	5-1	1-1	■	2-2	1-1	2-0	1-0	2-2	5-2	1-0	2-0	1-3	1-0
Middlesbrough FC	2-0	2-1	0-1	3-2	1-3	0-2	3-3	0-3	0-1	1-4			■	2-3	2-2	0-4	2-0	4-1	0-0	3-0	1-1	3-3
Newcastle United FC	5-2	0-1	2-1	2-3	3-1	4-0	0-2	1-1	0-2	4-0	4-3	1-2	2-3	■	1-1	0-4	4-1	3-0	2-1	1-3	3-7	1-2
Portsmouth FC	1-1	2-1	4-4	3-2	3-2	1-1	3-1	3-2	5-2	5-1	4-1	1-1	0-2	2-0	■	1-3	3-4	2-1	4-1	1-1	3-0	2-0
Preston North End FC	0-1	1-1	2-3	3-1	2-1	1-2	2-0	1-0	1-2	2-1	4-0	1-3	1-0	2-2	4-0	■	2-1	6-0	6-2	2-1	0-2	0-1
Sheffield United FC	1-0	2-1	3-4	3-0	2-1	0-1	1-1	1-3	3-6	3-1	2-2	1-3	2-2	3-1	3-1	1-1	■	2-0	1-3	5-2	1-2	3-3
Sheffield Wednesday FC	2-1	3-1	1-2	1-2	2-0	2-1	1-2	2-0	1-4	1-1	2-0	4-1	3-0	4-4	4-2	3-2		■	2-2	2-3		0-0
Sunderland AFC	7-1	2-0	3-2	1-2	2-1	5-0	2-1	1-2	1-1	3-2	4-5	0-2	0-2	1-1	3-1	2-2	2-2	2-4	■	4-3	2-1	3-2
Tottenham Hotspur FC	1-4	1-0	2-2	3-2	2-3	0-1	3-1	2-1	1-0	2-1	1-1	4-1	3-0	1-1	2-6	2-1	3-1	0-3		■	0-1	2-3
West Bromwich Albion FC	2-0	1-1	2-1	1-1	0-0	6-1	2-3	5-2	4-0	5-2	1-0	2-0	2-1	2-2	2-3	3-2	2-2	4-2	2-0	3-0	■	0-1
Wolverhampton Wanderers FC	0-2	1-2	4-1	1-1	1-2	3-1	5-0	8-1	4-0	2-1	3-1	3-1	2-4	3-2	4-3	1-0	6-1	4-1	3-1	2-0	1-0	■

	Division 1	Pd	Wn	Dw	Ls	GF	GA	Pts	
1.	WOLVERHAMPTON WANDERERS FC (WOLV'N)	42	25	7	10	96	56	57	
2.	West Bromwich Albion FC (West Bromwich)	42	22	9	11	86	63	53	
3.	Huddersfield Town AFC (Huddersfield)	42	20	11	11	78	61	51	
4.	Manchester United FC (Manchester)	42	18	12	12	73	58	48	
5.	Bolton Wanderers FC (Bolton)	42	18	12	12	75	60	48	
6.	Blackpool FC (Blackpool)	42	19	10	13	80	69	48	
7.	Burnley FC (Burnley)	42	21	4	17	78	67	46	
8.	Chelsea FC (London)	42	16	12	14	74	68	44	
9.	Charlton Athletic FC (London)	42	19	6	17	75	77	44	
10.	Cardiff City AFC (Cardiff)	42	18	8	16	51	71	44	
11.	Preston North End FC (Preston)	42	19	5	18	87	58	43	
12.	Arsenal FC (London)	42	15	13	14	75	73	43	
13.	Aston Villa FC (Birmingham)	42	16	9	17	70	68	41	
14.	Portsmouth FC (Portsmouth)	42	14	11	17	81	89	39	
15.	Newcastle United FC (Newcastle-upon-Tyne)	42	14	10	18	72	77	38	
16.	Tottenham Hotspur FC (London)	42	16	5	21	65	76	37	
17.	Manchester City FC (Manchester)	42	14	9	19	62	77	37	
18.	Sunderland AFC (Sunderland)	42	14	8	20	81	89	36	
19.	Sheffield Wednesday FC (Sheffield)	42	15	6	21	70	91	36	
20.	Sheffield United FC (Sheffield)	42	11	11	20	69	90	33	
21.	Middlesbrough FC (Middlesbrough)	42	10	10	22	60	91	30	R
22.	Liverpool FC (Liverpool)	42	9	10	23	68	97	28	R
		924	363	198	363	1626	1626	924	

Top Goalscorers

1)	James GLAZZARD	(Huddersfield Town AFC)	29
	Johnny NICHOLLS	(West Bromwich Albion FC)	29

Football League Division 2 — 1953-54 Season

	Birmingham City	Blackburn Rovers	Brentford	Bristol Rovers	Bury	Derby County	Doncaster Rovers	Everton	Fulham	Hull City	Leeds United	Leicester City	Lincoln City	Luton Town	Nottingham Forest	Notts County	Oldham Athletic	Plymouth Argyle	Rotherham United	Stoke City	Swansea Town	West Ham United
Birmingham City FC		0-0	5-1	1-1	0-0	3-0	0-1	5-1	2-2	2-0	3-3	1-2	1-0	5-1	2-2	3-0	2-1	3-0	2-3	1-0	6-0	2-0
Blackburn Rovers FC	3-0		2-2	1-1	4-1	0-3	2-0	0-0	5-1	3-1	2-2	3-0	6-0	2-0	2-0	2-0	4-0	2-3	3-0	3-0	1-0	4-1
Brentford FC	2-0	1-4		0-3	2-1	0-0	1-4	1-0	2-1	2-2	2-1	1-3	0-1	0-1	1-1	0-0	3-1	1-0	0-1	0-0	3-1	3-1
Bristol Rovers FC	1-1	1-2	0-0		2-0	3-0	0-1	0-0	2-1	4-2	1-1	3-0	0-1	3-3	1-0	1-1	1-0	3-1	1-0	3-2	0-1	2-2
Bury FC	1-1	0-0	1-1	3-1		4-0	2-1	2-2	1-3	3-0	4-4	2-5	1-1	0-1	2-1	3-3	1-0	3-0	0-6	1-2	2-0	
Derby County FC	2-4	2-2	4-1	0-1	3-1		2-0	2-6	3-3	2-0	0-2	2-1	2-0	1-2	0-0	3-1	1-4	1-1	1-1	1-1	4-2	
Doncaster Rovers FC	3-1	0-2	3-0	1-0	0-1	1-3		2-2	2-2	4-1	0-0	0-2	1-1	1-3	1-3	4-2	1-0	3-3	1-2	1-0	1-0	2-0
Everton FC	1-0	1-1	6-1	4-0	0-0	3-2	4-1		2-2	2-0	2-1	1-2	3-1	2-1	3-3	3-2	3-1	8-4	3-0	1-1	2-2	1-2
Fulham FC	5-2	2-3	4-1	4-4	3-0	5-2	1-2	0-0		5-1	1-3	1-1	4-1	5-1	3-1	4-3	3-1	3-1	2-4	0-1	4-3	3-4
Hull City AFC	3-0	0-2	2-0	4-1	3-0	3-0	3-1	1-3	2-1		1-1	0-3	3-0	1-2	3-0	8-0	2-0	1-0	1-2	4-3	2-1	
Leeds United AFC	1-1	3-2	4-0	3-3	3-4	3-1	3-1	3-1	1-2	0-0		7-1	5-2	2-1	0-2	6-0	2-1	1-1	4-2	1-1	3-2	1-2
Leicester City FC	3-4	4-0	6-0	1-0	2-0	2-2	2-0	2-2	2-2	1-3	5-0		9-2	1-2	1-0	4-2	4-1	4-0	4-1	2-1		
Lincoln City FC	0-1	8-0	2-1	1-2	0-0	2-2	0-2	1-1	4-2	3-0	2-0	3-1		1-1	2-2	3-0	3-1	2-0	4-3	3-1		
Luton Town FC	2-0	2-1	1-1	1-1	3-2	2-1	2-0	1-1	1-2	3-1	1-1	2-2	1-0		0-1	2-1	4-4	2-1	1-1	1-1	2-0	3-1
Nottingham Forest FC	1-1	0-1	2-1	3-1	2-2	4-2	2-2	3-3	4-1	2-0	5-2	3-1	4-2	2-1		5-0	1-1	3-0	4-1	5-4	2-1	4-0
Notts County FC	2-1	0-5	2-0	1-5	0-0	0-1	1-5	0-2	0-0	1-1	2-0	1-1	1-1	1-2	1-1		2-0	2-0	1-2	2-1	3-0	3-1
Oldham Athletic AFC	2-3	1-0	2-0	0-0	0-0	0-0	2-2	0-4	2-3	0-0	4-2	0-2	1-0	1-2	1-3	1-3		1-1	2-3	1-0	2-2	3-1
Plymouth Argyle FC	2-2	1-1	3-2	3-3	1-1	3-2	0-0	4-0	2-2	2-2	1-1	0-3	1-2	2-2	1-0	3-3	5-0		0-2	1-1	1-1	2-1
Rotherham United FC	1-0	1-4	1-1	1-1	1-0	5-2	4-0	1-2	3-2	3-2	2-4	1-1	4-1	1-1	3-0	0-1	7-0	2-1		2-2	2-1	5-0
Stoke City FC	3-2	3-0	1-1	3-2	4-0	2-2	2-2	2-4	1-3	4-0	2-2	4-1	1-1	0-1	0-1	3-2	1-1		5-0	1-1		
Swansea Town AFC	1-3	2-1	1-0	3-1	2-1	2-1	0-1	0-2	2-0	1-0	4-3	0-0	4-2	1-1	2-1	2-2	4-0	0-1	0-2	2-2		1-1
West Ham United FC	1-2	2-1	0-1	1-1	5-0	0-0	2-1	1-1	3-1	1-0	5-2	4-1	5-0	1-0	1-1	1-2	0-1	2-2	3-0	2-2	4-1	

	Division 2	Pd	Wn	Dw	Ls	GF	GA	Pts	
1.	Leicester City FC (Leicester)	42	23	10	9	97	60	56	P
2.	Everton FC (Liverpool)	42	20	16	6	92	58	56	P
3.	Blackburn Rovers FC (Blackburn)	42	23	9	10	86	50	55	
4.	Nottingham Forest FC (Nottingham)	42	20	12	10	86	59	52	
5.	Rotherham United FC (Rotherham)	42	21	7	14	80	67	49	
6.	Luton Town FC (Luton)	42	18	12	12	64	59	48	
7.	Birmingham City FC (Birmingham)	42	18	11	13	78	58	47	
8.	Fulham FC (London)	42	17	10	15	98	85	44	
9.	Bristol Rovers FC (Bristol)	42	14	16	12	64	58	44	
10.	Leeds United AFC (Leeds)	42	15	13	14	89	81	43	
11.	Stoke FC (stoke-on-Trent)	42	12	17	13	71	60	41	
12.	Doncaster Rovers FC (Doncaster)	42	16	9	17	59	63	41	
13.	West Ham United FC (London)	42	15	9	18	67	69	39	
14.	Notts County FC (Nottingham)	42	13	13	16	54	74	39	
15.	Hull City AFC (Kingston-upon-Hull)	42	16	6	20	64	66	38	
16.	Lincoln City FC (Lincoln)	42	14	9	19	65	83	37	
17.	Bury FC (Bury)	42	11	14	17	54	72	36	
18.	Derby County FC (Derby)	42	12	11	19	64	82	35	
19.	Plymouth Argyle FC (Plymouth)	42	9	16	17	65	82	34	
20.	Swansea Town AFC (Swansea)	42	13	8	21	58	82	34	
21.	Brentford FC (London)	42	10	11	21	40	78	31	R
22.	Oldham Athletic AFC (Oldham)	42	8	9	25	40	89	25	R
		924	338	248	338	1535	1535	924	

243

Football League Division 3 (N) — 1953-54 Season

Column key: ACC = Accrington Stanley, BAR = Barnsley, BRW = Barrow, BDC = Bradford City, BPA = Bradford Park Avenue, CAR = Carlisle United, CHE = Chester, CHF = Chesterfield, CRE = Crewe Alexandra, DAR = Darlington, GAT = Gateshead, GRI = Grimsby Town, HAL = Halifax Town, HAR = Hartlepools, MAN = Mansfield Town, PVA = Port Vale, ROC = Rochdale, SCU = Scunthorpe United, SOU = Southport, STK = Stockport County, TRA = Tranmere Rovers, WOR = Workington, WRE = Wrexham, YOR = York City

Home \ Away	ACC	BAR	BRW	BDC	BPA	CAR	CHE	CHF	CRE	DAR	GAT	GRI	HAL	HAR	MAN	PVA	ROC	SCU	SOU	STK	TRA	WOR	WRE	YOR
Accrington Stanley		3-0	3-2	0-1	0-0	2-2	1-0	2-2	2-1	0-0	2-2	3-1	3-0	2-0	5-1	2-2	1-0	0-1	1-1	2-1	0-1	4-2	1-2	2-0
Barnsley FC	5-0		3-2	4-2	2-1	1-1	3-0	4-1	1-1	5-1	0-2	0-0	1-2	3-2	2-1	0-1	2-1	0-1	2-1	4-1	3-0	4-2	3-0	2-1
Barrow AFC	4-3	0-1		3-0	4-1	1-1	2-1	2-2	3-1	2-2	0-0	4-0	1-1	1-1	4-2	0-0	4-2	1-2	2-3	1-0	2-0	0-1	1-0	4-1
Bradford City AFC	1-0	1-0	1-0		3-0	1-0	1-0	2-0	3-0	2-0	2-2	3-0	2-0	1-1	2-2	1-1	4-0	1-3	4-1	1-1	1-0	1-1	1-2	1-0
Bradford Park Ave.	6-4	0-2	2-1	4-0		2-4	5-0	1-1	1-1	2-2	3-1	4-1	4-2	5-0	1-0	1-2	2-2	2-2	1-1	3-2	1-2	3-1	2-0	2-0
Carlisle United FC	2-1	2-4	2-2	2-0	0-1		1-1	2-3	5-0	1-1	1-0	3-3	5-0	2-3	5-0	0-0	7-0	5-1	3-2	2-0	0-2	2-2	0-0	1-1
Chester FC	3-0	1-1	1-1	3-0	2-3	0-1		2-2	2-0	2-2	5-0	1-1	3-1	1-1	0-2	1-1	0-0	0-0	1-0	1-2	1-2	3-0	2-1	3-1
Chesterfield FC	0-0	1-1	1-1	2-3	5-1	5-0	4-0		0-2	1-1	1-1	1-2	2-1	0-0	1-2	2-1	1-0	2-0	4-0	2-1	1-0	1-0	1-0	3-2
Crewe Alexandra FC	0-3	3-2	2-0	1-2	1-1	0-0	1-0	2-0		1-0	3-1	1-3	3-0	0-0	0-0	2-1	1-1	0-0	1-5	1-2	2-3	1-2	1-1	
Darlington FC	4-1	1-1	1-3	1-0	2-1	3-2	1-0	3-2	0-1		0-2	3-0	1-1	0-1	1-2	0-3	0-0	3-0	0-1	1-0	2-1	3-0	0-2	1-3
Gateshead FC	4-0	0-0	1-0	1-0	0-2	2-2	2-1	3-3	2-0	1-2		7-1	4-0	1-3	1-3	1-0	0-0	1-0	4-2	4-1	3-1	3-0		
Grimsby Town FC	2-0	0-1	1-0	1-0	0-2	2-1	1-1	3-1	1-0	2-0	2-1		2-1	0-0	2-2	3-2	1-2	1-0	1-1	0-1	1-0	1-0		3-0
Halifax Town AFC	2-0	1-2	2-0	0-1	2-2	2-0	1-1	2-1	1-0	0-0	0-0	2-0		1-0	2-0	0-1	1-0	0-3	1-2	0-1	1-1	3-0	1-0	2-3
Hartlepools United	0-1	0-1	2-2	1-1	0-2	1-1	2-0	0-1	0-0	1-0	1-0	3-0	2-0		3-1	2-1	6-0	3-2	1-1	6-0	1-2	2-2	1-1	2-2
Mansfield Town FC	1-1	2-0	2-3	0-0	1-1	2-1	2-2	6-0	6-0	1-1	5-1	3-1	1-0			1-2	2-0	4-2	3-1	2-0	0-0	4-0		7-2
Port Vale FC	1-0	0-0	4-0	2-0	1-0	1-0	2-2	1-0	1-0	0-0	2-0	2-0	3-1	1-1			6-0	0-0	7-0	1-0	2-0	2-0		5-0
Rochdale AFC	1-0	1-1	1-0	3-2	1-0	2-1	4-0	0-1	4-1	3-0	4-1	0-1	2-2	1-0	0-0			1-1	2-0	0-0	0-1	4-2	6-2	1-2
Scunthorpe United	1-2	6-0	3-2	4-1	2-1	2-1	2-1	2-2	1-1	2-1	3-2	0-0	2-2	0-2	1-1				1-1	2-0	3-1	4-1	3-1	3-0
Southport FC	5-3	5-2	0-1	1-0	3-0	0-1	1-2	3-0	2-4	2-1	1-0	2-1	0-0	1-1	4-3					1-2	0-0	1-1	4-1	
Stockport County FC	1-1	3-0	5-1	5-0	4-1	3-2	5-0	6-1	1-0	2-0	0-1	3-2	1-1	1-0	3-2	1-1	1-2	1-1	1-1		6-0	2-0	2-2	0-1
Tranmere Rovers FC	1-0	0-1	1-0	0-1	1-1	1-2	2-1	1-2	1-0	1-0	1-4	2-4	1-0	3-2	2-5	1-3	5-1	1-1	2-0	2-2		4-2	6-1	1-1
Workington AFC	3-1	2-0	1-1	2-2	1-1	2-2	2-0	1-2	1-2	1-1	2-0	2-0	3-1	0-0	1-1	2-0	0-1	1-3	0-1	0-0	2-1		1-1	5-2
Wrexham AFC	4-2	1-1	1-2	0-1	4-2	2-1	1-2	1-1	4-2	5-1	4-0	5-0	2-0	2-0	1-2	0-2	3-1	2-1	1-0	3-0	8-0	1-1		1-1
York City FC	1-2	0-2	5-2	3-2	0-0	1-3	2-1	1-3	0-3	3-3	1-1	1-2	1-1	5-0	5-1	0-1	1-2	2-0	2-1	0-0	0-0	0-0	5-2	

Division 3 (North)

		Pd	Wn	Dw	Ls	GF	GA	Pts	
1.	Port Vale FC (Stoke-on-Trent)	46	26	17	3	74	21	69	P
2.	Barnsley FC (Barnsley)	46	24	10	12	77	57	58	
3.	Scunthorpe & Lindsey United FC (Scunthorpe)	46	21	15	10	77	56	57	
4.	Gateshead FC (Gateshead)	46	21	13	12	74	55	55	
5.	Bradford City AFC (Bradford)	46	22	9	15	60	55	53	
6.	Chesterfield FC (Chesterfield)	46	19	14	13	76	64	52	
7.	Mansfield Town FC (Mansfield)	46	20	11	15	88	67	51	
8.	Wrexham AFC (Wrexham)	46	21	9	16	81	68	51	
9.	Bradford Park Avenue FC (Bradford)	46	18	14	14	77	68	50	
10.	Stockport County FC (Stockport)	46	18	11	17	77	67	47	
11.	Southport FC (Southport)	46	17	12	17	63	60	46	
12.	Barrow AFC (Barrow-in-Furness)	46	16	12	18	72	71	44	
13.	Carlisle United FC (Carlisle)	46	14	15	17	83	71	43	
14.	Tranmere Rovers FC (Birkenhead)	46	18	7	21	59	70	43	
15.	Accrington Stanley FC (Accrington)	46	16	10	20	66	74	42	
16.	Crewe Alexandra FC (Crewe)	46	14	13	19	49	67	41	
17.	Grimsby Town FC (Cleethorpes)	46	16	9	21	51	77	41	
18.	Hartlepools United FC (Hartlepool)	46	13	14	19	59	65	40	
19.	Rochdale AFC (Rochdale)	46	15	10	21	59	77	40	
20.	Workington AFC (Workington)	46	13	14	19	59	80	40	
21.	Darlington FC (Darlington)	46	12	14	20	50	71	38	
22.	York City FC (York)	46	12	13	21	64	86	37	
23.	Halifax Town AFC (Halifax)	46	12	10	24	44	73	34	
24.	Chester FC (Chester)	46	11	10	25	48	67	32	
		1104	409	286	409	1587	1587	1104	

Football League Division 3 (S) — 1953-54 Season

	Aldershot Town	Bournemouth	Brighton & H.A.	Bristol City	Colchester United	Coventry City	Crystal Palace	Exeter City	Gillingham	Ipswich Town	Leyton Orient	Millwall	Newport County	Northampton Town	Norwich City	Q.P.R.	Reading	Shrewsbury Town	Southampton	Southend United	Swindon Town	Torquay United	Walsall	Watford
Aldershot Town FC		1-2	2-3	2-5	3-0	4-2	1-2	1-2	1-2	3-0	1-1	1-1	2-0	3-1	0-0	1-4	2-2	1-0	1-1	4-0	1-0	4-1	3-1	3-1
Bournemouth & Bos.	1-1		1-1	5-2	4-2	1-0	2-0	4-1	4-1	2-3	1-2	4-1	1-1	2-1	2-0	0-1	1-1	2-1	3-1	0-1	4-0	1-2	1-1	1-3
Brighton & Hove Alb.	3-2	3-0		2-1	1-0	3-1	3-0	2-1	3-1	1-2	2-1	4-0	4-2	3-2	0-0	3-1	3-2	2-3	2-1	3-2	1-1	1-2	5-3	3-3
Bristol City FC	4-0	1-1	1-1		3-0	1-0	4-0	5-1	1-1	2-3	1-0	2-1	3-0	2-1	3-1	1-2	3-1	3-1	1-0	4-1	5-1	3-0	4-1	2-1
Colchester United FC	3-0	1-1	1-1	0-2		0-3	4-1	0-1	0-1	1-2	1-0	3-0	2-2	1-1	0-1	5-0	2-4	3-1	0-1	2-2	3-1	1-1	2-2	
Coventry City FC	2-1	2-0	1-2	3-0	2-1		0-0	2-0	2-1	1-3	4-0	1-0	0-0	1-0	3-1	1-1	2-1	2-1	1-0	0-1	4-0	2-0	0-1	
Crystal Palace FC	0-0	3-1	1-1	1-2	0-1	3-1		0-0	1-2	1-1	2-2	2-3	3-0	2-2	1-0	0-3	1-0	3-2	4-3	4-2	3-2	4-1	1-0	1-1
Exeter City FC	1-3	1-0	0-1	0-1	1-2	4-0	7-0		1-2	1-2	2-1	4-1	1-0	1-0	0-2	2-0	0-1	4-0	1-1	3-1	1-2	2-1	2-1	
Gillingham FC	1-3	1-0	0-0	2-2	2-0	2-0	3-2	0-1		1-1	1-2	2-0	0-1	3-1	1-0	3-0	2-0	2-1	1-0	0-4	3-0	2-3		
Ipswich Town FC	4-0	2-1	2-3	2-1	3-0	4-1	2-0	1-1	6-1		3-1	1-1	2-1	1-1	2-1	1-1	0-0	2-1	1-1	2-0	2-1	3-0	1-0	
Leyton Orient FC	1-2	5-0	0-2	4-1	3-1	1-0	2-0	3-1	3-1	1-2		2-2	3-0	2-0	3-1	2-2	2-1	2-0	1-4	1-1	1-1	3-2	2-1	1-1
Millwall FC	2-0	2-1	0-2	1-0	0-0	1-2	2-2	2-1	3-1	1-2	0-3		3-1	1-0	1-3	4-0	2-0	3-1	1-1	2-1	1-6	1-2	6-2	3-3
Newport County AFC	2-2	4-0	1-0	3-2	1-1	2-1	1-3	0-3	1-0	1-2	1-1	0-0		2-0	4-1	2-1	2-1	1-0	0-4	3-2	1-0	4-2	0-1	
Northampton Town	6-2	2-1	4-2	3-0	3-0	0-1	6-0	2-2	1-1	1-0	2-2	4-2	1-0		2-0	2-1	1-1	1-0	3-0	5-0	2-0	3-1	5-1	4-1
Norwich City FC	3-3	1-3	0-1	1-1	2-1	2-1	2-1	1-2	0-0	1-2	3-1	4-3	2-0	4-1		2-2	2-3	1-0	1-0	2-2	0-1	2-2	0-1	4-1
Queen's Park Rangers	0-2	2-1	1-2	0-1	0-0	0-3	1-1	0-0	3-1	3-1	2-1	4-0	5-1	1-1	0-2		2-0	0-0	0-1	1-0	0-2	5-1	2-0	0-4
Reading FC	6-1	0-1	2-1	0-2	2-0	4-3	4-1	4-1	0-1	3-1	1-1	2-4	4-1	2-0	4-4	3-1		1-1	4-1	2-0	3-1	2-4	0-2	4-1
Shrewsbury Town FC	0-2	1-1	3-1	4-3	3-1	1-1	1-1	1-1	0-0	1-1	3-3	3-1	2-1	-4	4-0	1-1	0-3		3-2	2-1	1-0	2-1	4-1	6-4
Southampton FC	2-0	2-1	1-0	4-2	2-1	3-1	2-1	4-1	4-2	4-0	1-0	0-0	3-1	1-1	4-2	1-0	0-0	4-2		3-5	3-1	2-2	0-0	2-0
Southend United FC	2-1	2-1	2-1	3-0	2-2	1-2	1-2	1-1	3-1	2-1	2-0	5-2	4-1	1-2	3-0	2-1					3-1	1-0	3-1	3-0
Swindon Town FC	3-1	2-1	0-1	5-0	3-0	1-1	1-1	2-4	2-1	1-2	2-1	7-1	0-0	0-0	0-1	1-0	2-1	0-1	3-0			6-1	3-0	2-2
Torquay United FC	3-0	2-0	2-3	4-0	3-1	1-1	1-0	3-2	3-3	1-1	2-3	2-2	3-2	1-1	2-4	2-2	2-2	2-0	1-1	1-1	2-1		3-1	2-2
Walsall FC	0-2	1-0	3-1	0-0	2-3	1-0	1-1	1-1	1-1	0-2	4-2	0-2	0-1	1-1	1-4	2-0	1-3	0-0	1-0	2-0	0-1	1-3		0-0
Watford FC	6-1	2-3	1-1	2-0	3-0	1-0	4-1	0-2	6-1	1-0	3-1	2-1	1-0	1-1	1-3	0-2	3-0	3-1	2-0	2-2	2-1	3-1	3-1	

Division 3 (South)

		Pd	Wn	Dw	Ls	GF	GA	Pts	
1.	Ipswich Town FC (Ipswich)	46	27	10	9	82	51	64	P
2.	Brighton & Hove Albion FC (Hove)	46	26	9	11	86	61	61	
3.	Bristol City FC (Bristol)	46	25	6	15	88	66	56	
4.	Watford FC (Watford)	46	21	10	15	85	69	52	
5.	Northampton Town FC (Northampton)	46	20	11	15	82	55	51	
6.	Southampton FC (Southampton)	46	22	7	17	76	63	51	
7.	Norwich City FC (Norwich)	46	20	11	15	73	66	51	
8.	Reading FC (Reading)	46	20	9	17	86	73	49	
9.	Exeter City FC (Exeter)	46	20	8	18	68	58	48	
10.	Gillingham FC (Gillingham)	46	19	10	17	61	66	48	
11.	Leyton Orient FC (London)	46	18	11	17	79	73	47	
12.	Millwall FC (London)	46	19	9	18	74	77	47	
13.	Torquay United FC (Torquay)	46	17	12	17	81	88	46	
14.	Coventry City FC (Coventry)	46	18	9	19	61	56	45	
15.	Newport County AFC (Newport)	46	19	6	21	61	81	44	
16.	Southend United FC (Southend-on-Sea)	46	18	7	21	69	71	43	
17.	Aldershot FC (Aldershot)	46	17	9	20	74	86	43	
18.	Queen's Park Rangers FC (London)	46	16	10	20	60	68	42	
19.	Bournemouth & Boscombe Athletic FC (Bournemouth)	46	16	8	22	67	70	40	
20.	Swindon Town FC (Swindon)	46	15	10	21	67	70	40	
21.	Shrewsbury Town FC (Shrewsbury)	46	14	12	20	65	76	40	
22.	Crystal Palace FC (London)	46	14	12	20	60	86	40	
23.	Colchester United FC (Colchester)	46	10	10	26	50	78	30	
24.	Walsall FC (Walsall)	46	9	8	29	40	87	26	
		1104	440	224	440	1695	1695	1104	

F.A. CUP FINAL   (Wembley Stadium, London – 01/05/1954 – 100,000)

WEST BROMWICH ALBION FC   3-2   Preston North End FC (Preston)

Allen 2 (1 pen.), Griffin   *Morrison, Wayman*

West Bromwich: Sanders, Kennedy, Millard, Dudley, Dugdale, Barlow, Griffin, Ryan, Allen, Nicholls, Lee.

Preston: Thompson, Cunningham, Walton, Docherty, Marston, Forbes, Finney, Foster, Wayman, Baxter, Morrison.

Semi-finals

Preston North End FC (Preston)	2-0	Sheffield Wednesday FC (Sheffield)
West Bromwich Albion FC (West Bromwich)	2-1	Port Vale FC (Stoke-on-Trent)

Quarter-finals

Leicester City FC (Leicester)	1-1, 2-2, 1-3	Preston North End FC (Preston)
Leyton Orient FC (London)	0-1	Port Vale FC (Stoke-on-Trent)
Sheffield Wednesday FC (Sheffield)	1-1, 2-0	Bolton Wanderers FC (Bolton)
West Bromwich Albion FC (West Bromwich)	3-0	Tottenham Hotspur FC (London)

Football League Division 1 1954-55 Season	Arsenal	Aston Villa	Blackpool	Bolton Wands.	Burnley	Cardiff City	Charlton Athletic	Chelsea	Everton	Huddersfield T.	Leicester City	Manchester City	Manchester Utd.	Newcastle United	Portsmouth	Preston N.E.	Sheffield United	Sheffield Wed.	Sunderland	Tottenham H.	W.B.A.	Wolves
Arsenal FC	■	2-0	3-0	3-0	4-0	2-0	3-1	1-0	2-0	3-5	1-1	2-3	2-3	1-3	0-1	2-0	4-0	3-2	1-3	2-0	2-2	1-1
Aston Villa FC	2-1	■	3-1	3-0	3-1	0-2	1-2	3-2	0-2	0-0	2-5	2-0	2-1	1-2	1-0	1-3	3-1	0-0	2-2	2-4	3-0	4-2
Blackpool FC	2-2	0-1	■	2-3	1-0	0-0	1-1	1-0	4-0	1-1	2-0	1-3	2-4	2-0	2-2	1-2	1-2	2-1	0-0	5-1	3-1	0-2
Bolton Wanderers FC	2-2	3-3	3-0	■	0-1	0-0	3-2	2-5	2-0	1-0	4-1	2-2	1-1	2-1	3-1	2-1	1-0	2-2	3-0	1-2	2-4	6-1
Burnley FC	3-0	2-0	0-1	2-0	■	1-0	3-0	1-1	0-2	1-1	3-1	2-0	2-4	1-0	1-0	2-2	2-1	2-0	0-1	1-2	1-2	1-0
Cardiff City AFC	1-2	0-1	1-2	2-2	0-3	■	4-3	0-1	4-3	1-1	2-1	3-0	3-0	4-2	1-1	2-5	1-1	5-3	0-1	1-2	3-2	3-2
Charlton Athletic FC	1-1	6-1	3-3	2-0	3-1	4-1	■	0-2	5-0	2-1	2-3	1-1	1-1	1-1	2-2	0-4	3-1	1-3	1-3	1-2	1-3	1-3
Chelsea FC	1-1	4-0	0-0	3-2	1-0	1-1	1-2	■	0-2	4-1	3-1	0-2	5-6	4-3	4-1	0-1	1-1	3-0	2-1	2-1	3-3	1-0
Everton FC	1-0	0-1	0-1	0-0	1-1	3-1	2-2	1-1	■	4-0	2-2	1-0	2-3	1-0	2-3	3-1	1-0	1-2	1-0	1-2	1-2	3-2
Huddersfield Town AFC	0-1	1-2	1-3	2-0	0-1	2-0	0-0	1-0	2-1	■	3-1	0-0	1-3	2-0	0-4	1-2	3-0	1-1	1-0	3-3	2-0	2-0
Leicester City FC	3-3	4-2	2-2	4-0	2-2	2-1	1-1	1-1	2-2	1-3	■	0-2	1-0	3-2	4-0	0-1	0-1	4-3	1-1	2-0	6-3	1-2
Manchester City FC	2-1	2-4	1-6	4-2	0-0	4-1	1-5	1-1	1-0	2-4	2-2	■	3-2	3-1	1-2	3-1	5-2	2-2	1-0	0-0	4-0	3-0
Manchester United FC	2-1	0-1	4-1	1-1	1-0	5-2	2-1	1-2	2-1	3-1	4-1	0-5	■	2-2	3-1	5-0	2-0	2-2	2-1	3-0	2-4	2-4
Newcastle United FC	5-1	5-3	1-1	0-0	2-1	3-0	3-1	1-3	4-0	2-2	2-0	2-0	2-0	■	2-1	3-3	1-2	5-0	1-2	4-4	3-0	2-3
Portsmouth FC	2-1	2-2	3-0	1-0	0-2	1-3	2-0	0-0	5-0	4-2	2-1	1-0	0-0	3-1	■	2-0	6-2	2-1	2-2	0-3	6-1	0-0
Preston North End FC	3-1	0-3	3-1	2-2	1-1	7-1	1-2	1-2	0-0	2-4	5-0	0-2	3-3	1-1	2-0	■	1-2	6-0	3-1	1-0	3-1	3-2
Sheffield United FC	1-1	1-3	2-1	2-0	1-0	1-3	5-0	1-2	2-5	2-2	1-1	0-2	3-0	6-2	5-2	0-5	■	1-0	1-0	4-1	1-2	1-2
Sheffield Wednesday FC	1-2	6-3	2-1	3-2	1-1	2-1	2-2	1-1	2-2	4-1	1-0	2-4	2-4	0-3	1-3	2-0	1-2	■	1-2	2-2	5-0	2-2
Sunderland AFC	0-1	0-0	2-0	1-1	2-2	1-1	1-2	3-3	3-0	1-1	1-1	3-2	4-3	4-2	2-2	2-1	2-2	2-0	■	1-1	4-2	0-0
Tottenham Hotspur FC	0-1	1-1	3-2	2-0	0-3	0-2	1-4	2-4	1-3	5-1	2-2	0-2	2-1	1-1	3-1	5-0	7-2	0-1	1-1	■	3-1	3-2
West Bromwich Albion FC	3-1	2-3	0-1	0-0	2-2	1-0	2-1	2-4	3-3	2-1	6-4	2-1	2-0	4-2	3-1	2-0	3-3	1-2	2-2	1-2	■	1-0
Wolverhampton Wanderers FC	3-1	1-0	1-0	1-2	5-0	1-1	2-1	3-4	1-3	6-4	5-0	2-2	4-2	2-2	2-2	1-1	4-1	4-2	2-0	4-2	4-0	■

	Division 1	Pd	Wn	Dw	Ls	GF	GA	Pts	
1.	CHELSEA FC (LONDON)	42	20	12	10	81	57	52	
2.	Wolverhampton Wanderers FC (Wolverhampton)	42	19	10	13	89	70	48	
3.	Portsmouth FC (Portsmouth)	42	18	12	12	74	62	48	
4.	Sunderland AFC (Sunderland)	42	15	18	9	64	54	48	
5.	Manchester United FC (Manchester)	42	20	7	15	84	74	47	
6.	Aston Villa FC (Birmingham)	42	20	7	15	72	73	47	
7.	Manchester City FC (Manchester)	42	18	10	14	76	69	46	
8.	Newcastle United FC (Newcastle-upon-Tyne)	42	17	9	16	89	77	43	
9.	Arsenal FC (London)	42	17	9	16	69	63	43	
10.	Burnley FC (Burnley)	42	17	9	16	51	48	43	
11.	Everton FC (Liverpool)	42	16	10	16	62	68	42	
12.	Huddersfield Town AFC (Huddersfield)	42	14	13	15	63	68	41	
13.	Sheffield United FC (Sheffield)	42	17	7	18	70	86	41	
14.	Preston North End FC (Preston)	42	16	8	18	83	64	40	
15.	Charlton Athletic FC (London)	42	15	10	17	76	75	40	
16.	Tottenham Hotspur FC (London)	42	16	8	18	72	73	40	
17.	West Bromwich Albion FC (West Bromwich)	42	16	8	18	76	96	40	
18.	Bolton Wanderers FC (Bolton)	42	13	13	16	62	69	39	
19.	Blackpool FC (Blackpool)	42	14	10	18	60	64	38	
20.	Cardiff City AFC (Cardiff)	42	13	11	18	62	76	37	
21.	Leicester City FC (Leicester)	42	12	11	19	74	86	35	R
22.	Sheffield Wednesday FC (Sheffield)	42	8	10	24	63	100	26	R
		924	351	222	351	1572	1572	924	

Top Goalscorer

1) Ronald ALLEN   (West Bromwich Albion FC)   27

Football League — Division 2 — 1954-55 Season

	Bir	Bla	Bri	Bur	Der	Don	Ful	Hul	Ips	Lee	Lin	Liv	Lut	Mid	NoF	NoC	Ply	PoV	Rot	Sto	Swa	WHU
Birmingham City FC	—	3-1	2-1	1-3	1-1	4-1	3-2	0-0	4-0	2-0	3-3	9-1	2-1	3-0	0-1	1-1	3-1	7-2	3-1	2-0	2-0	1-2
Blackburn Rovers FC	3-3	—	8-3	1-1	5-2	7-2	3-1	4-0	4-1	1-2	1-0	4-3	0-0	9-0	0-1	4-5	2-2	2-1	4-1	2-0	4-1	5-2
Bristol Rovers FC	1-1	2-1	—	2-1	4-1	1-0	4-1	1-0	4-0	5-1	2-2	3-0	3-2	2-2	2-1	1-4	3-1	1-0	1-0	1-1	7-0	2-4
Bury FC	0-1	2-1	3-1	—	2-2	1-4	1-3	4-1	2-1	5-3	3-1	3-4	2-1	0-1	1-1	1-2	3-1	2-2	2-2	1-1	2-1	4-1
Derby County FC	0-0	0-3	1-1	2-3	—	5-0	3-4	3-0	2-0	2-4	3-0	3-2	0-0	1-2	1-2	1-1	2-2	6-1	2-3	1-2	1-4	0-0
Doncaster Rovers FC	1-5	1-3	2-2	1-0	2-0	—	4-0	2-2	1-1	0-1	1-1	4-1	0-3	3-1	0-3	4-2	3-2	1-0	0-4	1-1	2-1	2-1
Fulham FC	2-1	5-1	2-3	0-0	2-0	5-2	—	0-1	4-1	1-3	2-1	3-1	1-2	1-1	2-3	3-1	1-1	2-2	2-2	1-1	5-1	0-0
Hull City AFC	0-3	1-4	0-1	1-0	1-1	1-1	0-0	—	4-2	0-2	4-0	2-2	0-4	1-0	2-3	5-2	0-2	2-1	1-2	1-1	4-3	0-1
Ipswich Town FC	1-2	1-1	1-0	2-3	2-1	5-1	2-4	2-0	—	1-2	1-2	2-0	3-1	6-1	0-1	2-1	1-0	2-2	0-1	1-1	1-1	0-3
Leeds United AFC	1-0	2-0	2-0	1-0	1-0	1-1	3-0	4-1	3-0	—	2-3	2-2	4-0	1-1	2-0	3-2	2-4	0-1	5-2	2-2	5-2	2-1
Lincoln City FC	1-1	2-1	0-2	3-2	3-0	5-1	2-2	1-1	2-0	1-1	—	3-3	1-2	3-3	1-2	3-2	0-1	2-3	1-4	2-2	2-2	2-1
Liverpool FC	2-2	4-1	5-3	1-1	2-0	3-2	4-1	2-1	6-2	2-2	2-4	—	4-4	3-1	1-0	3-1	3-3	1-1	3-1	2-4	1-1	1-2
Luton Town FC	1-0	7-3	2-0	3-2	3-2	3-0	3-0	1-1	3-2	0-0	2-1	3-2	—	2-0	3-0	3-1	3-1	4-2	4-0	3-1	1-2	2-0
Middlesbrough FC	2-5	4-3	1-0	1-1	3-1	3-1	4-2	1-2	0-1	1-0	1-2	1-2	0-2	—	1-4	2-0	4-1	2-0	5-1	1-2	4-2	6-0
Nottingham Forest FC	0-2	1-2	1-0	2-3	3-0	3-1	2-0	0-1	2-0	1-1	1-1	3-1	1-5	4-2	—	0-1	2-0	2-3	0-2	0-3	0-0	1-1
Notts County FC	3-2	3-1	2-0	2-1	2-3	4-0	0-0	3-1	2-1	1-2	2-1	0-3	3-3	1-3	4-1	—	2-0	1-1	3-2	1-0	2-1	5-1
Plymouth Argyle FC	1-0	0-2	0-1	2-4	1-0	1-2	3-2	1-2	3-1	1-0	1-0	2-2	1-2	1-3	3-2	2-2	—	0-0	2-1	1-2	2-0	1-1
Port Vale FC	2-0	0-3	1-0	1-0	3-0	1-1	4-0	3-0	3-3	0-1	1-3	4-3	1-1	1-1	1-2	0-1	1-0	—	1-0	1-0	1-0	1-1
Rotherham United FC	0-2	5-1	6-2	4-2	2-1	2-3	2-3	2-0	3-2	3-0	3-0	6-1	2-0	3-0	3-2	2-0	2-0	3-0	—	2-1	2-0	2-2
Stoke City FC	2-1	1-1	2-0	3-2	3-1	3-0	1-1	5-0	0-1	4-2	2-0	0-0	1-2	2-0	3-0	3-1	0-0	1-2	1-0	—	4-1	0-2
Swansea Town AFC	0-3	2-3	1-1	1-1	3-0	3-0	2-2	1-0	6-1	2-0	3-1	3-2	2-1	2-0	3-0	4-2	7-1	2-1	3-5	1-2	—	5-2
West Ham United FC	2-2	2-5	5-2	3-3	1-0	0-1	2-1	1-1	4-0	2-1	0-1	0-3	2-1	2-1	2-0	3-0	6-1	2-0	1-2	3-0	3-3	—

	Division 2	Pd	Wn	Dw	Ls	GF	GA	Pts	
1.	Birmingham City FC (Birmingham)	42	22	10	10	92	47	54	P
2.	Luton Town FC (Luton)	42	23	8	11	88	53	54	P
3.	Rotherham United FC (Rotherham)	42	25	4	13	94	64	54	
4.	Leeds United AFC (Leeds)	42	23	7	12	70	53	53	
5.	Stoke City FC (Stoke-on-Trent)	42	21	10	11	69	46	52	
6.	Blackburn Rovers FC (Blackburn)	42	22	6	14	114	79	50	
7.	Notts County FC (Nottingham)	42	21	6	15	74	71	48	
8.	West Ham United FC (London)	42	18	10	14	74	70	46	
9.	Bristol Rovers FC (Bristol)	42	19	7	16	75	70	45	
10.	Swansea Town AFC (Swansea)	42	17	9	16	86	83	43	
11.	Liverpool FC (Liverpool)	42	16	10	16	92	96	42	
12.	Middlesbrough FC (Middlesbrough)	42	18	6	18	73	82	42	
13.	Bury FC (Bury)	42	15	11	16	77	72	41	
14.	Fulham FC (London)	42	14	11	17	76	79	39	
15.	Nottingham Forest FC (Nottingham)	42	16	7	19	58	62	39	
16.	Lincoln City FC (Lincoln)	42	13	10	19	68	79	36	
17.	Port Vale FC (Stoke-on-Trent)	42	12	11	19	48	71	35	
18.	Doncaster Rovers FC (Doncaster)	42	14	7	21	58	95	35	
19.	Hull City AFC (Kingston-upon-Hull)	42	12	10	20	44	69	34	
20.	Plymouth Argyle FC (Plymouth)	42	12	7	23	57	82	31	
21.	Ipswich Town FC (Ipswich)	42	11	6	25	57	92	28	R
22.	Derby County FC (Derby)	42	7	9	26	53	82	23	R
		924	371	182	371	1597	1597	924	

Football League Division 3 (N) 1954-55 Season	Accrington Stanley	Barnsley	Barrow	Bradford City	Bradford P.A.	Carlisle United	Chester	Chesterfield	Crewe Alexandra	Darlington	Gateshead	Grimsby Town	Halifax Town	Hartlepools	Mansfield Town	Oldham Athletic	Rochdale	Scunthorpe United	Southport	Stockport County	Tranmere Rovers	Workington	Wrexham	York City
Accrington Stanley	■	2-3	6-3	1-0	4-3	3-2	3-0	4-1	1-0	3-0	6-2	3-0	3-1	2-5	3-2	4-0	5-4	2-1	1-1	0-1	3-1	2-0	2-0	2-2
Barnsley FC	1-2	■	3-0	1-0	2-1	3-1	4-2	3-0	3-1	4-1	3-0	1-3	3-0	0-0	1-0	2-2	2-0	1-0	0-0	2-1	4-1	3-1	4-2	1-0
Barrow AFC	1-2	3-1	■	3-2	3-1	2-1	2-0	2-0	0-3	1-1	0-1	2-0	1-3	0-2	2-2	3-1	4-2	1-3	2-1	2-0	1-0	2-2	1-1	1-5
Bradford City AFC	0-3	0-2	2-1	■	1-1	2-0	0-0	1-1	2-0	3-0	1-1	4-0	2-0	0-1	1-0	0-1	1-0	2-4	0-1	2-3	2-1	0-1	2-2	2-3
Bradford Park Ave.	3-2	1-0	3-0	2-0	■	0-2	3-0	1-3	2-1	1-1	2-2	2-1	0-1	1-0	0-0	0-2	1-1	0-0	1-0	0-0	3-1	0-0	3-1	1-3
Carlisle United FC	1-0	2-4	4-0	1-0	3-2	■	1-2	1-2	4-0	0-1	1-2	3-1	4-0	3-2	1-2	5-2	7-2	1-2	2-1	3-3	1-2	0-4	1-0	4-5
Chester FC	1-1	0-2	3-1	1-0	2-0	1-2	■	1-0	3-1	0-2	1-2	1-0	1-3	1-0	1-0	2-4	0-0	1-1	0-2	1-0	0-2	1-0	1-2	
Chesterfield FC	6-1	3-1	4-1	2-1	1-3	2-1	5-3	■	0-0	2-0	1-3	1-0	2-1	3-0	4-1	1-3	3-1	2-0	2-1	3-7	2-1	2-0	3-1	0-3
Crewe Alexandra FC	0-3	1-2	5-1	1-0	2-1	4-1	1-3	2-2	■	2-2	1-1	0-0	1-1	2-1	4-1	2-2	1-1	2-3	4-4	3-0	1-1	2-2	2-3	
Darlington FC	3-3	0-1	3-2	4-0	3-0	1-1	4-1	0-2	2-1	■	5-1	1-3	0-1	3-1	0-2	3-1	1-2	2-0	0-0	2-2	1-2	2-2	1-0	
Gateshead FC	1-1	0-4	3-1	2-1	3-2	0-0	0-0	1-3	1-0	1-1	■	1-0	3-0	4-0	2-2	0-1	0-1	1-0	4-4	3-2	0-1	1-1		
Grimsby Town FC	2-1	1-3	1-0	1-4	2-0	1-2	3-1	1-2	0-2	1-1	0-1	■	1-3	3-2	1-1	1-4	0-1	1-1	2-2	0-1	1-3	2-1		
Halifax Town AFC	1-1	0-1	1-2	0-0	0-0	5-3	3-1	2-0	3-3	4-1	4-0	3-2	■	1-0	1-2	0-0	1-1	1-2	0-0	2-2	2-0	3-3		
Hartlepools United	1-3	0-3	0-0	0-0	1-0	1-0	3-1	1-3	1-0	1-0	3-2	1-0	■	1-2	2-0	4-2	2-1	2-1	4-0	3-2	3-0	1-1		
Mansfield Town FC	2-2	1-1	0-5	1-0	2-1	1-1	2-1	2-0	4-2	3-1	0-1	3-0	2-1	0-2	■	1-3	3-2	2-1	3-0	0-0	3-1	2-0	1-2	
Oldham Athletic AFC	0-1	4-1	3-2	1-1	5-0	2-1	2-1	4-1	4-0	3-1	1-2	4-0	1-2	0-1	1-1	■	0-0	1-1	1-0	1-1	2-1	2-1	2-1	3-2
Rochdale AFC	0-0	3-0	4-1	1-2	3-2	1-2	2-0	0-0	1-1	2-2	4-0	0-3	2-2	2-1	2-0	2-1	■	2-0	1-0	2-2	2-1	2-1	2-1	1-1
Scunthorpe United	4-0	1-0	3-0	1-0	1-1	1-1	1-1	2-1	3-1	1-0	0-1	1-2	5-1	2-0	6-1	2-2	■	2-0	1-2	1-1	1-0	0-1		
Southport FC	1-1	0-2	2-1	1-0	4-1	1-1	0-0	1-2	2-2	1-0	0-0	1-0	1-1	1-0	1-1	1-0	0-1		■	1-2	1-2	2-1		
Stockport County FC	0-0	1-0	1-2	1-1	6-0	5-2	3-0	3-2	6-1	3-0	0-0	0-2	0-2	2-2	3-2	1-4	4-2	0-2	■	2-0	0-1	4-0	1-2	
Tranmere Rovers FC	3-1	0-1	0-4	2-0	3-3	6-1	1-1	0-0	1-2	0-1	1-2	2-2	1-2	3-1	2-1	2-1	3-1	1-2	2-2	1-1	■	1-1	1-2	1-0
Workington AFC	0-1	1-0	0-0	1-1	1-3	1-0	1-1	2-3	3-3	6-1	4-0	2-2	1-0	0-1	2-2	3-0	1-0	1-1	0-1	4-1	1-0	■	2-1	2-1
Wrexham AFC	3-1	3-0	3-0	1-3	1-0	1-1	2-1	0-2	5-0	2-2	2-0	5-0	1-1	1-4	1-3	0-0	0-1	2-2	1-4	1-2	1-1		■	2-6
York City FC	1-1	1-3	1-4	0-1	1-2	2-1	5-0	3-2	3-1	3-1	2-1	0-0	2-1	1-0	3-1	2-1	2-0	2-3	1-1	4-0	1-0	0-0	3-3	■

Division 3 (North)

		Pd	Wn	Dw	Ls	GF	GA	Pts	
1.	Barnsley FC (Barnsley)	46	30	5	11	86	46	65	P
2.	Accrington Stanley FC (Accrington)	46	25	11	10	96	67	61	
3.	Scunthorpe & Lindsey United FC (Scunthorpe)	46	23	12	11	81	53	58	
4.	York City FC (York)	46	24	10	12	92	63	58	
5.	Hartlepools United FC (Hartlepool)	46	25	5	16	64	49	55	
6.	Chesterfield FC (Chesterfield)	46	24	6	16	81	70	54	
7.	Gateshead FC (Gateshead)	46	20	12	14	65	69	52	
8.	Workington AFC (Workington)	46	18	14	14	68	55	50	
9.	Stockport County FC (Stockport)	46	18	12	16	84	70	48	
10.	Oldham Athletic AFC (Oldham)	46	19	10	17	74	68	48	
11.	Southport FC (Southport)	46	16	16	14	47	44	48	
12.	Rochdale AFC (Rochdale)	46	17	14	15	69	66	48	
13.	Mansfield Town FC (Mansfield)	46	18	9	19	65	71	45	
14.	Halifax Town AFC (Halifax)	46	15	13	18	63	67	43	
15.	Darlington FC (Darlington)	46	14	14	18	62	73	42	
16.	Bradford Park Avenue FC (Bradford)	46	15	11	20	56	70	41	
17.	Barrow AFC (Barrow-in-Furness)	46	17	6	23	70	89	40	
18.	Wrexham AFC (Wrexham)	46	13	12	21	65	77	38	
19.	Tranmere Rovers FC (Birkenhead)	46	13	11	22	55	70	37	
20.	Carlisle United FC (Carlisle)	46	15	6	25	78	89	36	
21.	Bradford City AFC (Bradford)	46	13	10	23	47	55	36	
22.	Crewe Alexandra FC (Crewe)	46	10	14	22	68	91	34	
23.	Grimsby Town FC (Cleethorpes)	46	13	8	25	47	78	34	
24.	Chester FC (Chester)	46	12	9	25	44	77	33	
		1104	427	250	427	1627	1627	1104	

Football League — Division 3 (S), 1954-55 Season

(Home \ Away)	Aldershot Town	Bournemouth	Brentford	Brighton & H.A.	Bristol City	Colchester United	Coventry City	Crystal Palace	Exeter City	Gillingham	Leyton Orient	Millwall	Newport County	Northampton Town	Norwich City	Q.P.R.	Reading	Shrewsbury Town	Southampton	Southend United	Swindon Town	Torquay United	Walsall	Watford
Aldershot Town FC		1-1	2-3	2-2	0-2	2-2	1-1	3-0	4-2	0-2	0-1	3-0	0-0	3-4	4-1	2-0	3-1	2-0	2-0	1-0	0-0	2-1	4-0	3-0
Bournemouth & Bos.	4-0		1-2	1-1	0-1	2-0	2-1	4-1	2-0	1-2	0-3	0-1	3-3	0-1	1-3	2-2	0-0	3-1	1-1	2-1	1-1	0-2	1-1	1-1
Brentford FC	1-1	1-3		2-3	2-2	3-2	2-3	3-0	1-0	3-0	2-0	3-1	1-0	1-3	1-0	1-1	2-2	2-2	0-3	2-2	4-2	4-2	0-2	3-2
Brighton & Hove Alb.	5-3	1-1	3-4		0-1	1-1	2-0	1-0	5-3	1-0	1-0	1-2	4-1	2-1	0-1	4-1	3-2	0-0	1-2	3-1	1-1	3-0	3-1	
Bristol City FC	6-1	2-2	2-1	3-2		4-0	2-0	3-0	2-0	1-4	5-0	5-1	0-0	5-1	0-1	1-2	4-1	2-0	3-2	3-0	1-1	5-3	1-0	
Colchester United FC	1-1	3-3	3-2	2-4	0-2		0-1	2-0	1-2	2-2	2-2	1-0	4-1	1-0	0-2	2-4	3-5	2-0	0-0				2-2	1-3
Coventry City FC	2-1	1-0	1-0	2-1	1-3	0-0		4-1	1-1	4-1	2-2	4-1	3-2	0-0	4-0	5-1	3-0	1-1	1-4	1-0	0-1	5-3	3-2	
Crystal Palace FC	3-2	2-1	1-1	1-0	1-2	0-0	1-0		1-1	0-2	1-1	1-1	2-1	3-1	2-0	1-1	2-2	1-2	2-2	0-0	1-1	3-1	1-1	
Exeter City FC	0-1	1-1	3-2	3-1	0-1	2-2	0-0	2-0		1-1	1-7	4-1	1-1	3-1	0-1	2-1	3-1	1-0	0-1	2-1	2-1	1-1	0-0	
Gillingham FC	0-2	0-2	2-1	1-1	1-1	2-1	2-1	2-1	1-1		0-0	1-1	4-2	2-2	2-1	3-1	5-1	3-3	1-0	1-1	2-1	3-1	3-2	0-1
Leyton Orient FC	1-5	3-1	0-1	0-0	4-1	2-0	1-0	2-1	5-0	2-2		1-0	1-2	2-1	1-2	3-0	2-0	5-0	4-1	5-1	1-0	2-1	1-0	0-1
Millwall FC	3-1	1-1	2-2	2-0	1-3	5-2	3-1	5-2	2-2	3-2	1-0		1-1	0-0	0-1	2-2	2-0	2-0	1-0	1-4	4-1	1-0	1-1	
Newport County AFC	2-1	1-1	3-1	1-3	2-2	2-1	2-1	1-3	1-2	2-1				0-1	4-0	3-1	1-1		2-2	2-2	1-1	1-0		0-2
Northampton Town	2-1	5-0	1-2	1-0	2-0	6-1	1-0	1-1	2-0	4-1	2-2	0-1	2-2		1-1	1-3	2-6	3-1	2-1	6-2	1-0	1-0	1-1	1-1
Norwich City FC	4-3	0-1	1-0	0-0	0-2	1-1	2-0	3-0	1-2	1-1	2-1	2-0	3-2			1-1	1-0	2-0	3-3	2-1	5-1	2-1	3-1	
Queen's Park Rangers	5-0	1-1	1-1	3-2	1-1	4-1	3-2	1-0	1-2	1-1	2-0	1-2	2-0	1-0	2-1		2-3	2-0	2-2	1-1	3-1	4-2	1-1	2-1
Reading FC	2-2	1-0	0-0	0-2	0-2	4-0	2-2	5-0	0-0	2-2	0-2	0-1	1-1	3-1				1-2	0-1	1-1	2-1	3-2	2-2	1-1
Shrewsbury Town FC	1-0	3-0	2-2	0-2	0-2	2-0	1-0	1-1	1-1	0-2	3-2	3-0	4-0	2-1	1-0	2-3			3-1	2-3	7-0	3-2	2-2	2-1
Southampton FC	1-1	0-0	6-4	3-2	2-1	0-1	1-0	3-2	1-0	3-0	1-1	1-0	4-1	3-2	2-2	3-1	2-1			3-0	1-1	0-0	2-1	2-0
Southend United FC	0-1	2-2	3-2	4-0	3-2	4-2	1-0	3-2	0-0	1-1	4-1	4-1	2-2	1-1	0-0	4-1	0-1	4-1	0-1		4-1	1-2	2-1	1-3
Swindon Town FC	1-0	0-2	1-1	0-2	2-2	1-1	3-0	0-0	2-0	2-1	0-0	1-1	1-3	0-1	1-0	2-0	0-2	2-1	1-0	0-1		0-0	2-2	6-1
Torquay United FC	2-2	0-1	4-2	2-1	2-2	2-1	1-2	2-2	1-0	1-3	2-7	4-2	2-3	5-2	2-0	3-2	3-1	2-0	2-2	4-1	1-1		2-0	2-2
Walsall FC	2-2	6-1	2-2	0-2	1-3	3-1	1-1	1-4	1-0	0-1	1-4	1-1	3-3	6-1	2-1	4-0	4-0	0-0	4-1	1-2	2-4			0-1
Watford FC	0-0	1-0	2-2	0-0	0-2	2-0	1-0	7-1	1-1	1-1	1-3	5-3	3-2	1-1	2-2	1-1	1-3	2-1	2-1	1-1	3-0	4-1	4-0	

Division 3 (South)

		Pd	Wn	Dw	Ls	GF	GA	Pts	
1.	Bristol City FC (Bristol)	46	30	10	6	101	47	70	P
2.	Leyton Orient FC (London)	46	26	9	11	89	47	61	
3.	Southampton FC (Southampton)	46	24	11	11	75	51	59	
4.	Gillingham FC (Gillingham)	46	20	15	11	77	66	55	
5.	Millwall FC (Millwall)	46	20	11	15	72	68	51	
6.	Brighton & Hove Albion FC (Hove)	46	20	10	16	76	63	50	
7.	Watford FC (Watford)	46	18	14	14	71	62	50	
8.	Torquay United FC (Torquay)	46	18	12	16	82	82	48	
9.	Coventry City FC (Coventry)	46	18	11	17	67	59	47	
10.	Southend United FC (Southend-on-Sea)	46	17	12	17	83	80	46	
11.	Brentford FC (London)	46	16	14	16	82	82	46	
12.	Norwich City FC (Norwich)	46	18	10	18	60	60	46	
13.	Northampton Town FC (Northampton)	46	19	8	19	73	81	46	
14.	Aldershot FC (Aldershot)	46	16	13	17	75	71	45	
15.	Queen's Park Rangers FC (London)	46	15	14	17	69	75	44	
16.	Shrewsbury Town FC (Shrewsbury)	46	16	10	20	70	78	42	
17.	Bournemouth & Boscombe Athletic FC (Bournemouth)	46	12	18	16	57	65	42	
18.	Reading FC (Reading)	46	13	15	18	65	73	41	
19.	Newport County AFC (Newport)	46	11	16	19	60	73	38	
20.	Crystal Palace FC (London)	46	11	16	19	52	80	38	
21.	Swindon Town FC (Swindon)	46	11	15	20	46	64	37	
22.	Exeter City FC (Exeter)	46	11	15	20	47	73	37	
23.	Walsall FC (Walsall)	46	10	14	22	75	86	34	
24.	Colchester United FC (Colchester)	46	9	13	24	53	91	31	
		1104	399	306	399	1677	1677	1104	

F.A. CUP FINAL   (Wembley Stadium, London – 07/05/1955 – 100,000)

NEWCASTLE UNITED FC   3-1   Manchester City FC (Manchester)
Milburn, Mitchell, Hannah   *Johnstone*

Newcastle: Simpson, Cowell, Batty, Scoular, Stokoe, Casey, White, Milburn, Keeble, Hannah, Mitchell.

Man. City: Trautmann, Meadows, Little, Barnes, Ewing, Paul, Spurdle, Hayes, Revie, Johnstone, Fagan.

Semi-finals

Manchester City FC (Manchester)	1-0	Sunderland AFC (Sunderland)
Newcastle United FC (Newcastle-upon-Tyne)	1-1, 2-0	York City FC (York)

Quarter-finals

Birmingham City FC (Birmingham)	0-1	Manchester City FC (Manchester)
Huddersfield Town AFC (Huddersfield)	1-1, 0-2	Newcastle United FC (Newcastle-upon-Tyne)
Notts County FC (Nottingham)	0-1	York City FC (York)
Sunderland AFC (Sunderland)	2-0	Wolverhampton Wanderers FC (Wolverhampton)

Football League Division 1 1955-56 Season	Arsenal	Aston Villa	Birmingham City	Blackpool	Bolton Wands.	Burnley	Cardiff City	Charlton Athletic	Chelsea	Everton	Huddersfield T.	Luton Town	Man. City	Man. United	Newcastle United	Portsmouth	Preston N.E.	Sheffield United	Sunderland	Tottenham H.	W.B.A.	Wolves
Arsenal FC		1-0	1-0	4-1	3-1	0-1	3-1	2-4	1-1	3-2	2-0	3-0	0-0	1-1	1-0	1-3	3-2	2-1	3-1	0-1	2-0	2-2
Aston Villa FC	1-1		0-0	1-1	0-2	2-0	2-0	1-1	1-4	2-0	3-0	1-0	0-3	4-4	3-0	1-3	3-2	3-2	1-4	0-2	3-0	0-0
Birmingham City FC	4-0	2-2		1-2	5-1	1-2	2-1	4-0	3-0	6-2	5-0	0-0	4-3	2-2	3-1	3-2	0-3	0-2	1-2	3-0	2-0	0-0
Blackpool FC	3-1	6-0	2-0		0-0	1-1	2-1	5-0	2-1	4-0	4-2	3-2	0-1	0-0	5-1	2-3	2-6	1-1	7-3	0-2	5-1	2-1
Bolton Wanderers FC	4-1	1-0	6-0	1-3		0-1	4-0	1-3	4-0	1-1	2-2	4-0	1-3	3-1	3-2	4-0	0-0	2-1	0-3	3-2	4-0	2-1
Burnley FC	0-1	2-0	3-2	0-2	2-0		0-2	2-1	5-0	0-1	2-0	3-1	2-2	0-0	3-1	3-0	1-2	1-1	4-0	2-0	1-2	1-2
Cardiff City AFC	1-2	1-0	2-1	1-0	1-0	2-2		3-1	1-1	3-1	1-2	2-0	4-1	0-1	1-1	2-3	3-1	3-2	3-1	0-0	1-3	1-9
Charlton Athletic FC	2-0	3-1	2-0	1-2	3-1	2-1	0-0		1-2	0-2	4-1	2-2	5-2	3-0	0-2	6-1	2-1	3-2	2-1	1-2	5-1	0-2
Chelsea FC	2-0	0-0	1-2	2-1	0-2	0-0	2-1	3-1		6-1	0-0	0-0	2-1	2-4	2-1	1-5	0-1	1-0	2-3	2-0	2-0	2-3
Everton FC	1-1	2-1	5-1	1-0	1-0	1-1	2-0	3-2	3-3		5-1	0-1	1-1	4-2	0-0	0-2	0-4	1-4	1-2	2-1	2-0	2-1
Huddersfield Town AFC	0-1	1-1	1-1	3-1	3-1	1-0	1-2	4-0	1-3	1-0		0-2	3-3	0-2	2-6	1-0	2-2	1-2	4-0	1-0	1-0	1-3
Luton Town FC	0-0	2-0	0-1	3-1	0-0	2-3	3-0	2-1	2-2	2-2	1-2		3-2	0-2	4-2	1-0	2-1	2-1	8-2	1-1	0-2	5-1
Manchester City FC	2-2	2-2	1-1	2-0	2-0	1-3	3-1	0-2	2-2	3-0	1-0	3-2		1-0	1-2	4-1	0-2	3-1	4-2	1-2	2-0	2-2
Manchester United FC	1-1	1-0	2-1	2-1	1-0	2-0	1-1	5-1	3-0	2-1	3-0	3-1	2-1		5-2	1-0	3-2	3-1	2-1	2-2	3-1	4-3
Newcastle United FC	2-0	2-3	2-2	1-2	3-0	3-1	4-0	4-1	1-1	1-2	1-1	4-0	3-1	0-0		2-1	5-0	4-2	3-1	1-2	0-3	3-1
Portsmouth FC	5-2	2-2	0-5	3-3	3-3	3-1	1-1	4-0	4-4	1-0	5-2	0-2	2-4	3-2	0-2		0-2	1-2	1-1	4-1	1-1	2-1
Preston North End FC	0-1	0-1	1-1	3-3	0-1	4-2	1-2	2-2	2-3	0-1	1-2	2-1	0-3	3-1	4-3	2-1		0-2	2-2	3-3	0-1	2-0
Sheffield United FC	0-2	2-2	0-3	2-1	1-3	1-2	0-0	2-1	1-1	3-1	0-4	1-1	1-0	2-1	1-3	3-1	3-1		2-3	2-0	2-2	3-3
Sunderland AFC	3-1	5-1	1-0	0-0	0-0	4-4	1-1	3-2	4-3	0-0	4-1	1-2	0-3	2-1	1-6	4-2	2-2	3-2		3-2	2-1	1-4
Tottenham Hotspur FC	3-1	4-3	0-1	1-1	0-3	0-1	1-1	2-3	4-0	1-1	1-2	2-1	2-1	1-2	3-1	1-0	0-4	3-1	2-3		4-1	2-1
West Bromwich Albion FC	2-1	1-0	0-2	1-2	2-0	1-0	2-1	3-3	3-0	2-0	1-2	3-1	0-4	1-4	1-1	4-0	3-2	2-1	3-0	1-0		1-1
Wolverhampton Wanderers FC	3-3	0-0	1-0	2-3	4-2	3-1	0-2	2-0	2-1	1-0	4-0	1-2	7-2	0-2	2-1	3-1	2-1	3-2	3-1	5-1	3-2	

	Division 1	Pd	Wn	Dw	Ls	GF	GA	Pts	
1.	MANCHESTER UNITED FC (MANCHESTER)	42	25	10	7	83	51	60	
2.	Blackpool FC (Blackpool)	42	20	9	13	86	62	49	
3.	Wolverhampton Wanderers FC (Wolverhampton)	42	20	9	13	89	65	49	
4.	Manchester City FC (Manchester)	42	18	10	14	82	69	46	
5.	Arsenal FC (London)	42	18	10	14	60	61	46	
6.	Birmingham City FC (Birmingham)	42	18	9	15	75	57	45	
7.	Burnley FC (Burnley)	42	18	8	16	64	54	44	
8.	Bolton Wanderers FC (Bolton)	42	18	7	17	71	58	43	
9.	Sunderland AFC (Sunderland)	42	17	9	16	80	95	43	
10.	Luton Town FC (Luton)	42	17	8	17	66	64	42	
11.	Newcastle United FC (Newcastle-upon-Tyne)	42	17	7	18	85	70	41	
12.	Portsmouth FC (Portsmouth)	42	16	9	17	78	85	41	
13.	West Bromwich Albion FC (West Bromwich)	42	18	5	19	58	70	41	
14.	Charlton Athletic FC (London)	42	17	6	19	75	81	40	
15.	Everton FC (Liverpool)	42	15	10	17	55	69	40	
16.	Chelsea FC (London)	42	14	11	17	64	77	39	
17.	Cardiff City AFC (Cardiff)	42	15	9	18	55	69	39	
18.	Tottenham Hotspur FC (London)	42	15	7	20	61	71	37	
19.	Preston North End FC (Preston)	42	14	8	20	73	72	36	
20.	Aston Villa FC (Birmingham)	42	11	13	18	52	69	35	
21.	Huddersfield Town AFC (Huddersfield)	42	14	7	21	54	83	35	R
22.	Sheffield United FC (Sheffield)	42	12	9	21	63	77	33	R
		924	367	190	367	1529	1529	924	

Top Goalscorer

1) Nat LOFTHOUSE   (Bolton Wanderers FC)   33

Football League Division 2 1955-56 Season	Barnsley	Blackburn Rovers	Bristol City	Bristol Rovers	Bury	Doncaster Rovers	Fulham	Hull City	Leeds United	Leicester City	Lincoln City	Liverpool	Middlesbrough	Nottingham Forest	Notts County	Plymouth Argyle	Port Vale	Rotherham United	Sheffield Wednesday	Stoke City	Swansea Town	West Ham United
Barnsley FC	■	2-1	0-0	4-3	3-3	2-2	3-0	2-1	2-1	0-1	1-0	0-5	0-4	1-1	3-1	1-2	1-2	3-2	0-3	1-0	3-2	1-1
Blackburn Rovers FC	5-1	■	4-6	2-0	3-1	1-1	1-0	2-0	2-3	2-3	0-2	3-3	2-1	2-2	2-0	2-1	7-1	3-1	2-2	3-0	3-0	4-1
Bristol City FC	2-0	2-0	■	1-1	3-1	4-1	2-1	5-2	0-1	1-1	5-1	2-1	2-0	0-0	1-3	6-0	0-0	5-2	3-2	0-1	2-1	3-1
Bristol Rovers FC	1-1	1-0	0-3	■	4-2	4-2	2-2	4-2	4-1	2-1	3-0	1-2	7-2	4-1	2-0	2-1	1-2	1-4	4-2	4-2	1-2	1-1
Bury FC	3-0	0-4	1-1	0-1	■	5-1	1-5	3-2	1-0	3-1	3-3	1-4	1-1	1-2	4-0	7-1	2-2	2-1	2-5	1-0	2-4	4-1
Doncaster Rovers FC	1-1	2-2	3-2	2-1	2-3	■	4-2	3-0	1-2	6-2	2-0	1-0	0-1	1-3	1-1	3-1	3-0	1-1	2-2	2-4	3-1	2-1
Fulham FC	5-1	3-0	3-0	3-5	3-1	4-0	■	5-0	1-2	3-0	3-1	4-1	1-1	4-3	1-1	2-1	1-4	1-1	1-2	2-0	4-1	3-1
Hull City AFC	4-1	0-3	1-3	1-2	2-3	1-1	2-2	■	1-4	2-4	2-1	1-2	2-2	1-0	0-1	2-0	0-1	2-0	0-3	2-2	3-2	1-4
Leeds United AFC	3-1	1-2	2-1	2-1	1-0	3-0	6-1	1-0	■	4-0	1-0	4-2	2-0	3-0	1-0	4-2	1-1	4-1	2-1	1-0	2-2	3-3
Leicester City FC	0-0	0-2	2-2	4-2	5-0	3-0	2-1	1-2	5-2	■	4-0	3-1	1-1	5-2	4-0	5-1	4-1	3-1	1-2	3-1	6-1	2-1
Lincoln City FC	4-0	3-0	2-0	2-0	4-2	1-1	6-1	2-0	1-1	7-1	■	2-0	1-2	1-3	2-0	1-0	1-0	1-1	2-2	2-1	3-1	1-0
Liverpool FC	1-1		4-0	4-2	1-2	7-0	3-1	3-1	1-0	3-1	2-1	■	1-1	5-2	1-0	4-1	2-0	4-1	0-1	3-2	4-1	3-1
Middlesbrough FC	1-1	1-0	2-1	0-1	1-3	4-1	1-1	5-1	5-3	4-3	4-2	1-2	■	3-2	1-0	3-1	1-1	0-1	2-2	1-3	4-1	2-0
Nottingham Forest FC	1-0	1-1	0-2	1-1	0-2	5-0	1-0	2-1	2-0	2-0	2-2	1-3	2-4	■	0-2	3-1	2-2	1-0	2-3	2-1		0-0
Notts County FC	2-2	1-2	3-2	5-2	2-1	3-2	3-4	0-2	2-1	1-1	2-2	2-1	5-0	1-3	■	3-0	0-0	1-2	1-1	1-3	1-5	0-1
Plymouth Argyle FC	3-0	1-0	5-0	0-1	1-4	2-2	0-0	1-1	4-3	0-1	1-4	4-0	4-0	1-2	1-1	■	1-1	3-1	1-1	0-1	0-1	0-1
Port Vale FC	1-2	4-1	2-0	1-1	1-1	2-0	2-1	0-1	2-0	2-3	1-1	1-1	3-2	2-1	3-1	1-1	■	4-1	0-1	1-0	3-0	2-1
Rotherham United FC	0-0	3-2	1-3	1-0	1-3	3-3	2-3	0-2	0-2	3-1	2-2	0-1	2-1	2-1	1-1	0-0	1-0	■	2-3	0-1	2-3	3-2
Sheffield Wednesday FC	3-0	2-1	2-1	4-2	3-3	5-2	2-3	4-1	4-0	1-1	3-1	1-1	5-3	1-1	3-1	5-2	4-0	0-2	■	4-0	2-2	1-1
Stoke City FC	2-1	1-2	4-2	1-2	0-2	5-2	1-2	4-1	2-1	2-0	3-0	3-2	2-5	1-1	0-2	4-1	1-1	1-0	2-0	■	5-0	3-0
Swansea Town AFC	3-1	2-1	2-1	1-2	5-3	2-0	2-0	4-1	1-1	6-1	0-2	2-1	2-1	0-1	5-1	2-2	0-0	4-1	2-1	0-0	■	4-2
West Ham United FC	4-0	2-3	3-0	2-1	3-2	6-1	2-1	1-1	1-1	1-3	2-4	2-0	1-0	1-2	6-1	4-0	0-2	1-1	3-3	2-0	5-1	■

	Division 2	Pd	Wn	Dw	Ls	GF	GA	Pts	
1.	Sheffield Wednesday FC (Sheffield)	42	21	13	8	101	62	55	P
2.	Leeds United AFC (Leeds)	42	23	6	13	80	60	52	P
3.	Liverpool FC (Liverpool)	42	21	6	15	85	63	48	
4.	Blackburn Rovers FC (Blackburn)	42	21	6	15	84	65	48	
5.	Leicester City FC (Leicester)	42	21	6	15	94	78	48	
6.	Bristol Rovers FC (Bristol)	42	21	6	15	84	70	48	
7.	Nottingham Forest FC (Nottingham)	42	19	9	14	68	63	47	
8.	Lincoln City FC (Lincoln)	42	18	10	14	79	65	46	
9.	Fulham FC (London)	42	20	6	16	89	79	46	
10.	Swansea Town AFC (Swansea)	42	20	6	16	83	81	46	
11.	Bristol City FC (Bristol)	42	19	7	16	80	64	45	
12.	Port Vale FC (Stoke-on-Trent)	42	16	13	13	60	58	45	
13.	Stoke City FC (Stoke-on-Trent)	42	20	4	18	71	62	44	
14.	Middlesbrough FC (Middlesbrough)	42	16	8	18	76	78	40	
15.	Bury FC (Bury)	42	16	8	18	86	90	40	
16.	West Ham United FC (London)	42	14	11	17	74	69	39	
17.	Doncaster Rovers FC (Doncaster)	42	12	11	19	69	96	35	
18.	Barnsley FC (Barnsley)	42	11	12	19	47	84	34	
19.	Rotherham United FC (Rotherham)	42	12	9	21	56	75	33	
20.	Notts County FC (Nottingham)	42	11	9	22	55	82	31	
21.	Plymouth Argyle FC (Plymouth)	42	10	8	24	54	87	28	R
22.	Hull City AFC (Kingston-upon-Hull)	42	10	6	26	53	97	26	R
		924	372	180	372	1628	1628	924	

Football League Division 3 (N) — 1955-56 Season

Column key: ACC = Accrington Stanley, BAR = Barrow, BCY = Bradford City, BPA = Bradford Park Ave., CAR = Carlisle United, CHE = Chester, CHF = Chesterfield, CRE = Crewe Alexandra, DAR = Darlington, DER = Derby County, GAT = Gateshead, GRI = Grimsby Town, HAL = Halifax Town, HAR = Hartlepools United, MAN = Mansfield Town, OLD = Oldham Athletic, ROC = Rochdale, SCU = Scunthorpe United, SOU = Southport, STK = Stockport County, TRA = Tranmere Rovers, WOR = Workington, WRE = Wrexham, YOR = York City

	ACC	BAR	BCY	BPA	CAR	CHE	CHF	CRE	DAR	DER	GAT	GRI	HAL	HAR	MAN	OLD	ROC	SCU	SOU	STK	TRA	WOR	WRE	YOR
Accrington Stanley		2-0	2-0	7-0	1-0	4-0	5-1	5-1	2-1	2-0	2-2	0-1	2-2	1-0	3-1	2-2	3-0	2-0	4-2	3-1	0-0	5-1	3-1	1-3
Barrow AFC	3-1		3-1	2-2	0-0	1-2	3-1	5-0	0-1	1-2	4-0	0-0	2-2	3-2	4-1	4-1	2-0	2-2	0-2	2-0	1-1	2-0	0-3	0-1
Bradford City AFC	2-1	1-1		5-0	0-0	1-1	3-5	3-1	3-0	2-1	3-1	0-2	2-0	2-0	4-2	0-0	2-2	4-3	2-0	4-1	5-0	2-0	4-3	3-1
Bradford Park Ave.	1-0	3-2	1-1		2-1	1-1	0-5	2-0	3-0	2-4	3-1	2-1	1-1	1-3	0-3	4-1	3-3	2-0	0-3	2-0	4-5	4-0	4-2	2-1
Carlisle United FC	0-4	2-0	0-0	4-1		4-1	1-1	4-1	2-0	0-3	2-1	1-2	2-2	0-3	5-2	3-1	1-2	1-2	4-0	4-1	0-3	2-4	0-1	3-1
Chester FC	1-1	1-0	1-1	0-0	3-3		2-1	0-0	2-1	2-5	3-0	1-0	0-1	4-3	3-2	0-0	3-5	1-3	1-4	0-0	1-0	2-1	2-2	
Chesterfield FC	0-1	2-0	1-1	5-1	2-1	2-1		8-0	2-1	2-0	3-0	1-0	2-3	2-1	1-0	7-2	2-0	5-1	2-3	2-0	2-4	2-0	3-1	
Crewe Alexandra FC	0-3	0-1	1-4	4-2	3-1	0-0	0-3		1-1	2-1	1-0	0-0	1-4	1-3	2-1	1-2	2-0	1-2	1-1	3-1	4-0	2-1	1-1	1-2
Darlington FC	2-0	4-2	1-1	3-5	0-1	2-1	4-1			1-0	0-0	1-2	0-0	3-1	2-1	2-0	0-1	0-0	6-2	2-2	2-2			1-4
Derby County FC	6-2	2-1	4-1	4-0	3-0	3-1	3-0	3-3	6-2		4-1	1-3	4-1	3-2	4-0	2-0	2-2	2-0	2-0	0-0	2-2	2-0	3-2	
Gateshead FC	4-0	3-2	4-1	3-0	2-3	1-1	3-3	4-1	0-1	2-4		2-0	1-2	3-0	1-3	4-1	1-0	2-0	2-1	3-3	4-3	2-1	3-2	
Grimsby Town FC	3-0	3-0	2-0	1-0	6-1	3-1	5-1	1-0	2-1	3-1		4-0	1-0	2-1	1-1	0-1	3-0	1-0	1-2	1-0	2-1		
Halifax Town AFC	2-0	1-0	3-2	6-0	2-2	0-1	3-0	2-0	3-0	2-2	3-3	0-1		0-2	1-1	5-1	1-0	3-0	1-1	0-1	1-0	2-1	2-4	
Hartlepools United	0-0	1-0	1-0	3-1	3-0	3-1	3-0	6-1	3-0	2-1	1-2	3-2			4-2	1-0	1-0	0-2	1-0	0-0	1-0	3-2	0-1	
Mansfield Town FC	3-2	4-0	0-0	5-0	0-1	3-0	0-1	1-1	3-3	1-1	3-0	0-2	3-1	5-1		2-0	6-0	3-2	0-1	1-1	6-0	0-0	6-1	3-1
Oldham Athletic AFC	1-3	6-1	1-1	5-1	2-2	4-1	2-2	1-1	3-3	1-1	1-2	1-1	1-3	3-2	1-1		2-2	2-1	1-1	3-2	4-1	1-1	2-2	
Rochdale AFC	1-5	3-1	4-2	5-2	4-2	1-5	1-4	0-5	1-2	2-0	2-1	1-4	4-4	3-2	1-3	0-0		1-3	1-0	1-0	3-1			
Scunthorpe United	2-3	2-0	2-0	4-2	4-0	2-1	2-0	1-0	0-1	0-2	1-1	1-0	5-1	3-0	1-2				0-1	1-5	2-1	3-1	1-1	1-1
Southport FC	1-1	2-1	3-1	3-0	1-0	1-0	2-5	2-0	2-0	0-0	1-1	1-1	2-0	2-2						1-1	1-1	0-0	1-1	3-3
Stockport County FC	1-2	4-1	1-0	8-1	2-1	2-1	2-1	1-2	1-2	0-0	3-1	4-0	7-2	0-0	0-0	3-2	4-0				7-0	4-5	4-0	4-1
Tranmere Rovers FC	4-1	1-1	1-1	4-1	0-1	4-0	0-1	2-1	0-1	0-1	1-1	1-1	2-2	1-0	0-3	2-1	2-1	1-2	2-1	1-2		2-0	0-2	2-1
Workington AFC	0-0	6-1	2-1	4-0	4-0	0-0	0-1	1-0	2-0	0-3	6-1	0-0	2-0	5-1	2-1	4-3	1-2	2-3	0-1	3-0			3-1	0-0
Wrexham AFC	1-4	0-0	2-1	1-0	5-2	0-0	3-0	4-2	2-1	3-1	1-1	1-0	1-2	1-3	2-0	1-1	0-0	0-1	2-1	0-1	3-1	0-1		4-5
York City FC	0-1	3-2	0-2	5-0	3-1	3-0	3-1	1-1	4-0	1-0	3-4	5-0	3-0	1-1	2-0	1-2	0-0	0-1	1-0	2-4	1-1	1-3		

Division 3 (North)

		Pd	Wn	Dw	Ls	GF	GA	Pts	
1.	Grimsby Town FC (Cleethorpes)	46	31	6	9	76	29	68	P
2.	Derby County FC (Derby)	46	28	7	11	110	55	63	
3.	Accrington Stanley FC (Accrington)	46	25	9	12	92	57	59	
4.	Hartlepools United FC (Hartlepool)	46	26	5	15	81	60	57	
5.	Southport FC (Southport)	46	23	11	12	66	53	57	
6.	Chesterfield FC (Chesterfield)	46	25	4	17	94	66	54	
7.	Stockport County FC (Stockport)	46	21	9	16	90	61	51	
8.	Bradford City AFC (Bradford)	46	18	13	15	78	64	49	
9.	Scunthorpe & Lindsey FC (Scunthorpe)	46	20	8	18	75	63	48	
10.	Workington AFC (Workington)	46	19	9	18	75	63	47	
11.	York City FC (York)	46	19	9	18	85	72	47	
12.	Rochdale AFC (Rochdale)	46	17	13	16	66	84	47	
13.	Gateshead FC (Gateshead)	46	17	11	18	77	84	45	
14.	Wrexham AFC (Wrexham)	46	16	10	20	66	73	42	
15.	Darlington FC (Darlington)	46	16	9	21	60	73	41	
16.	Tranmere Rovers FC (Birkenhead)	46	16	9	21	59	84	41	
17.	Chester FC (Chester)	46	13	14	19	52	82	40	
18.	Mansfield Town FC (Mansfield)	46	14	11	21	84	81	39	
19.	Halifax Town AFC (Halifax)	46	14	11	21	66	76	39	
20.	Oldham Athletic AFC (Oldham)	46	10	18	18	76	86	38	
21.	Carlisle United FC (Carlisle)	46	15	8	23	71	95	38	
22.	Barrow AFC (Barrow-in-Furness)	46	12	9	25	61	83	33	
23.	Bradford Park Avenue FC (Bradford)	46	13	7	26	61	122	33	
24.	Crewe Alexandra FC (Crewe)	46	9	10	27	50	105	28	
		1104	437	230	437	1771	1771	1104	

Football League Division 3 (S) 1955-56 Season

	Aldershot Town	Bournemouth	Brentford	Brighton & H.A.	Colchester United	Coventry City	Crystal Palace	Exeter City	Gillingham	Ipswich Town	Leyton Orient	Millwall	Newport County	Northampton Town	Norwich City	Q.P.R.	Reading	Shrewsbury Town	Southampton	Southend United	Swindon Town	Torquay United	Walsall	Watford
Aldershot Town FC		1-3	4-1	0-3	1-0	2-2	1-1	1-0	2-2	0-3	1-1	2-1	1-0	2-0	0-0	1-2	4-4	2-0	3-2	3-3	1-1	1-2	2-1	1-1
Bournemouth & Bos.	2-2		0-0	2-0	3-1	0-1	1-0	0-0	1-2	1-1	3-1	4-0	0-0	0-0	0-1	1-0	2-1	2-0	1-3	4-1	4-0	2-0	2-0	4-0
Brentford FC	2-0	2-1		4-2	2-2	1-1	3-0	2-0	1-4	3-2	1-0	2-2	1-1	2-1	1-2	2-0	2-2	1-1	2-1	2-1	1-2	1-3	2-2	0-0
Brighton & Hove Alb.	5-2	4-1	3-0		2-0	2-1	5-0	1-0	5-0	3-0	1-1	2-1	4-1	4-0	6-0	1-1	3-1	3-2	5-0	4-0	2-0	3-2	3-0	2-3
Colchester United FC	4-0	1-0	0-3	3-3		2-0	2-4	5-1	1-1	3-3	2-1	1-2	2-1	2-0	3-2	4-1	0-3	2-0	3-2	3-6	5-0	3-2	1-1	4-1
Coventry City FC	1-1	3-1	2-1	3-2	2-0		1-3	2-2	2-0	3-1	3-0	5-1	3-0	0-1	5-3	4-1	0-2	1-0	2-0	0-0	6-0	1-2	1-1	3-0
Crystal Palace FC	1-0	1-3	0-2	1-2	1-1	3-0		0-1	1-3	1-0	1-2	2-2	1-0	2-3	2-0	1-1	2-3	0-1	0-2	1-2	0-2	3-0	2-0	1-2
Exeter City FC	2-1	2-0	2-3	0-5	0-0	2-3	6-1		2-1	2-2	1-1	3-1	2-0	3-1	1-1	0-2	3-0	3-2	0-1	1-2	0-0	1-1	1-1	1-2
Gillingham FC	2-0	2-1	1-2	1-0	2-1	1-1	1-1	2-1		0-0	0-1	4-3	3-2	0-2	3-1	0-2	2-0	3-1	1-2	2-3	4-0	1-3	0-1	3-0
Ipswich Town FC	2-1	1-0	1-1	2-1	3-1	1-0	3-3	2-2	1-1		2-0	6-2	3-2	1-0	4-1	4-1	3-3	2-1	4-2	3-0	6-2	0-2	5-2	0-0
Leyton Orient FC	8-3	4-0	2-1	0-1	6-0	3-1	8-0	1-1	2-0	1-2		2-1	3-1	1-1	2-2	7-1	1-0	5-2	4-0	3-0	4-0	3-2	4-0	3-1
Millwall FC	3-3	4-0	4-0	2-4	0-1	0-2	1-1	2-0	5-0	0-5	5-0		2-4	4-1	1-0	2-0	4-0	1-2	3-2	5-0	1-1	3-2	3-2	1-1
Newport County AFC	0-1	1-0	1-2	1-0	0-1	4-2	0-1	1-2	3-2	2-1	3-0	1-4		0-1	2-2	2-1	2-3	1-2	1-0	2-0	1-1	2-0	2-0	0-1
Northampton Town	3-2	2-1	1-0	3-0	0-2	2-1	1-1	3-0	0-2	0-5	0-1	4-0	5-0		1-1	5-2	1-2	1-0	3-1	1-1	2-0	2-0	3-1	1-3
Norwich City FC	0-1	0-2	1-0	3-3	1-1	1-0	3-1	2-1	5-1	3-2	2-2	4-1	2-3	4-1		1-0	2-1	3-1	1-4	7-2	4-1	0-0	3-2	4-1
Queen's Park Rangers	2-2	0-1	1-1	2-1	6-2	1-2	0-3	1-0	2-2	1-1	0-1	4-0	0-0	3-2	2-3		3-3	1-1	2-0	1-1	3-1	3-2	3-2	3-2
Reading FC	0-5	0-2	5-2	0-2	1-3	1-0	1-0	1-2	1-2	1-5	0-1	4-1	3-0	4-1	2-2	3-1		0-1	1-1	4-1	0-1	0-3	2-0	6-1
Shrewsbury Town FC	3-3	1-1	1-1	2-1	2-1	3-0	2-0	2-0	3-1	1-1	1-4	3-1	5-0	1-1	6-0	1-1	3-0		2-0	1-1	1-1	1-2	2-1	0-0
Southampton FC	3-1	3-2	1-1	1-2	3-0	3-0	3-1	5-0	1-1	2-2	1-2	3-3	2-3	2-5	4-0	5-2	1-1	1-1		0-0	2-1	6-2	4-1	2-0
Southend United FC	3-2	4-1	2-2	1-2	4-0	3-0	4-3	6-0	2-2	2-3	0-0	3-1	4-1	2-0	3-1	5-1	1-0	2-1			0-0	2-3	3-2	1-0
Swindon Town FC	1-1	2-2	0-1	0-0	3-1	1-1	0-0	0-1	0-1	0-1	1-2	1-0	1-2	0-1	1-1	0-1	0-0	2-1	1-1	1-1		2-1	1-2	0-0
Torquay United FC	5-0	0-0	3-1	0-0	1-2	0-0	1-1	3-1	1-1	2-2	1-3	3-0	1-1	3-1	1-1	2-0	0-0	5-0	3-2	2-2	4-0		3-2	4-1
Walsall FC	4-2	0-0	1-2	2-2	0-0	2-0	4-0	1-1	2-1	1-3	0-2	2-1	3-3	2-0	2-0	2-2	1-0	1-1	1-3	3-1	4-0	1-4		2-1
Watford FC	1-1	0-2	0-2	1-3	1-1	2-1	0-2	2-3	0-1	0-2	0-4	4-2	1-1	2-2	1-1	0-1	1-0	3-4	1-0	3-2	2-1	2-1	4-2	

Division 3 (South)

		Pd	Wn	Dw	Ls	GF	GA	Pts	
1.	Leyton Orient FC (London)	46	29	8	9	106	49	66	P
2.	Brighton & Hove Albion FC (Hove)	46	29	7	10	112	50	65	
3.	Ipswich Town FC (Ipswich)	46	25	14	7	106	60	64	
4.	Southend United FC (Southend-on-Sea)	46	21	11	14	88	80	53	
5.	Torquay United FC (Torquay)	46	20	12	14	86	63	52	
6.	Brentford FC (London)	46	19	14	13	69	66	52	
7.	Norwich City FC (Norwich)	46	19	13	14	86	82	51	
8.	Coventry City FC (Coventry)	46	20	9	17	73	60	49	
9.	Bournemouth & Boscombe Athletic FC (Bournemouth)	46	19	10	17	63	51	48	
10.	Gillingham FC (Gillingham)	46	19	10	17	69	71	48	
11.	Northampton Town FC (Northampton)	46	20	7	19	67	71	47	
12.	Colchester United FC (Colchester)	46	18	11	17	76	81	47	
13.	Shrewsbury Town FC (Shrewsbury)	46	17	12	17	69	66	46	
14.	Southampton FC (Southampton)	46	18	8	20	91	81	44	
15.	Aldershot FC (Aldershot)	46	12	16	18	70	90	40	
16.	Exeter City FC (Exeter)	46	15	10	21	58	77	40	
17.	Reading FC (Reading)	46	15	9	22	70	79	39	
18.	Queen's Park Rangers FC (London)	46	14	11	21	64	86	39	
19.	Newport County AFC (Newport)	46	15	9	22	58	79	39	
20.	Walsall FC (Walsall)	46	15	8	23	68	84	38	
21.	Watford FC (Watford)	46	13	11	22	52	85	37	
22.	Millwall FC (London)	46	15	6	25	83	100	36	
23.	Crystal Palace FC (London)	46	12	10	24	54	83	34	
24.	Swindon Town FC (Swindon)	46	8	14	24	34	78	30	
		1104	427	250	427	1772	1772	1104	

F.A. CUP FINAL   (Wembley Stadium, London – 05/05/1956 – 100,000)

MANCHESTER CITY FC (MANCHESTER)   3-1   Birmingham City FC (Birmingham)

Hayes, Dyson, Johnstone   *Kinsey*

Man. City: Trautmann, Leivers, Little, Barnes, Ewing, Paul, Johnstone, Hayes, Revie, Dyson, Clarke.

Birmingham: Merrick, Hall, Green, Newman, Smith, Boyd, Astall, Kinsey, Brown, Murphy, Govan.

Semi-finals

| Birmingham City FC (Birmingham) | 3-0 | Sunderland AFC (Sunderland) |
| Manchester City FC (Manchester) | 1-0 | Tottenham Hotspur FC (London) |

Quarter-finals

Arsenal FC (London)	1-3	Birmingham City FC (Birmingham)
Manchester City FC (Manchester)	2-1	Everton FC (Liverpool)
Newcastle United FC (Newcastle-upon-Tyne)	0-2	Sunderland AFC (Sunderland)
Tottenham Hotspur FC (London)	3-3, 2-1	West Ham United FC (London)

1956-57

Football League Division 1 1956-57 Season	Arsenal	Aston Villa	Birmingham City	Blackpool	Bolton Wands.	Burnley	Cardiff City	Charlton Athletic	Chelsea	Everton	Leeds United	Luton Town	Man. City	Man. United	Newcastle United	Portsmouth	Preston N.E.	Sheffield Wed.	Sunderland	Tottenham H.	W.B.A.	Wolves
Arsenal FC	■	2-1	4-0	1-1	3-0	2-0	0-0	3-1	2-0	2-0	1-0	1-3	7-3	1-2	0-1	1-1	1-2	6-3	1-1	3-1	4-1	0-0
Aston Villa FC	0-0	■	3-1	3-2	0-0	1-0	4-1	3-1	1-1	5-1	1-1	1-3	2-2	1-3	3-1	2-2	2-0	5-0	2-2	2-4	0-0	4-0
Birmingham City FC	4-2	1-2	■	2-2	0-0	2-0	2-1	4-2	0-1	1-3	6-2	3-0	3-3	3-1	6-1	3-1	3-0	4-0	1-2	0-0	2-0	2-2
Blackpool FC	2-4	0-0	3-1	■	4-2	1-0	3-1	3-2	1-0	5-2	1-1	4-0	4-1	2-2	2-3	5-0	4-0	3-1	1-2	4-1	0-1	3-2
Bolton Wanderers FC	2-1	0-0	3-1	4-1	■	3-0	2-0	2-0	2-2	1-1	5-3	2-2	1-0	2-0	3-1	1-1	2-3	3-2	2-1	1-0	1-1	0-3
Burnley FC	3-1	2-1	2-0	2-2	1-0	■	6-2	2-1	2-0	2-1	0-0	1-1	0-3	1-3	3-2	1-1	2-2	4-1	2-0	1-0	1-0	3-0
Cardiff City AFC	2-3	1-0	1-2	3-4	2-0	3-3	■	2-3	1-1	1-0	4-1	0-0	1-1	2-3	5-2	0-2	2-3	2-1	1-0	0-3	0-0	2-2
Charlton Athletic FC	1-3	0-2	1-0	0-4	2-1	1-2	0-2	■	3-1	1-2	1-2	1-2	1-0	1-5	1-1	1-3	3-4	4-4	3-2	1-1	3-2	2-1
Chelsea FC	1-1	1-1	1-0	2-2	2-2	2-0	1-2	1-3	■	5-1	1-1	4-1	4-2	1-2	6-2	3-3	1-0	0-0	0-2	2-4	2-4	3-3
Everton FC	4-0	0-4	2-0	2-3	2-2	1-0	0-0	5-0	0-3	■		2-1	2-1	1-1	1-2	2-2	1-4	0-1	2-1	1-1	0-1	3-1
Leeds United AFC	3-3	1-0	1-1	5-0	3-2	1-1	3-0	4-0	0-0	5-1	■	1-2	2-0	1-0	0-0	4-1	1-3	3-1	1-1	0-0	0-0	
Luton Town FC	1-2	0-0	0-0	0-2	1-0	3-0	4-2	4-0	2-2			■	3-2	0-2	4-1	1-0	1-0	6-2		1-3	0-1	
Manchester City FC	2-3	1-1	3-1	0-3	1-3	0-1	4-1	5-1	5-4	2-4	1-0	3-2	■	2-4	1-2	5-1	0-2	4-2	3-1	2-2	2-1	2-3
Manchester United FC	6-2	1-1	2-2	0-2	0-2	2-0	3-1	4-2	3-0	2-5	3-2	3-1	2-0	■	6-1	3-0	3-2	4-1	4-0	0-0	1-1	3-0
Newcastle United FC	3-1	1-2	3-2	2-1	4-0	1-1	1-0	3-1	1-2	0-0	2-3	2-2	0-3	1-1	■	2-1	1-2	6-2	2-2	5-2	2-1	
Portsmouth FC	2-3	5-1	3-4	0-0	1-1	1-0	1-0	2-2	3-2	2-5	2-2	0-1	1-3	2-2		■	2-2	1-3	2-3	2-0	0-1	1-0
Preston North End FC	3-0	3-3	1-0	0-0	2-2	1-0	6-0	4-3	1-0	3-0	2-0	3-1	1-3	1-0	7-1		■	1-0	6-0	1-4	3-2	1-0
Sheffield Wednesday FC	2-4	2-1	3-0	1-2	1-2	0-0	5-3	3-1	4-0	2-2	2-3	3-0	2-2	2-1	4-0	3-1	3-1	■	3-2	4-1	4-2	2-1
Sunderland AFC	1-0	1-0	0-1	5-2	3-0	2-1	1-1	8-1	1-1	1-1	2-0	1-0	1-3	2-2	1-0	3-3	0-0	5-2	■	0-2	1-4	2-3
Tottenham Hotspur FC	1-3	3-0	5-1	2-1	4-0	2-0	5-0	6-2	3-4	6-0	5-1	5-0	3-2	2-2	3-1	2-0	1-1	1-1	5-2	■	2-2	4-1
West Bromwich Albion FC	0-2	2-0	0-0	1-3	3-2	2-2	1-2	2-2	2-1	3-0	0-0	4-0	1-1	2-3	1-0	2-1	0-0	1-4	2-0	1-1	■	1-1
Wolverhampton Wanderers FC	5-2	3-0	3-0	4-1	3-2	1-2	3-1	7-3	3-1	2-1	1-2	5-4	5-1	1-1	2-0	6-0	4-3	2-1	2-2	3-0	5-2	■

	Division 1	Pd	Wn	Dw	Ls	GF	GA	Pts	
1.	MANCHESTER UNITED FC (MANCHESTER)	42	28	8	6	103	54	64	
2.	Tottenham Hotspur FC (London)	42	22	12	8	104	56	56	
3.	Preston North End FC (Preston)	42	23	10	9	84	56	56	
4.	Blackpool FC (Blackpool)	42	22	9	11	93	65	53	
5.	Arsenal FC (London)	42	21	8	13	85	69	50	
6.	Wolverhampton Wanderers FC (Wolverhampton)	42	20	8	14	94	70	48	
7.	Burnley FC (Burnley)	42	18	10	14	56	50	46	
8.	Leeds United AFC (Leeds)	42	15	14	13	72	63	44	
9.	Bolton Wanderers FC (Bolton)	42	16	12	14	65	65	44	
10.	Aston Villa FC (Birmingham)	42	14	15	13	65	55	43	
11.	West Bromwich Albion FC (West Bromwich)	42	14	14	14	59	61	42	
12.	Birmingham City FC (Birmingham)	42	15	9	18	69	69	39	Jt.
12.	Chelsea FC (London)	42	13	13	16	73	73	39	Jt.
14.	Sheffield Wednesday FC (Sheffield)	42	16	6	20	82	88	38	
15.	Everton FC (Liverpool)	42	14	10	18	61	79	38	
16.	Luton Town FC (Luton)	42	14	9	19	58	76	37	
17.	Newcastle United FC (Newcastle-upon-Tyne)	42	14	8	20	67	87	36	
18.	Manchester City FC (Manchester)	42	13	9	20	78	88	35	
19.	Portsmouth FC (Portsmouth)	42	10	13	19	62	92	33	
20.	Sunderland AFC (Sunderland)	42	12	8	22	67	88	32	
21.	Cardiff City AFC (Cardiff)	42	10	9	23	53	88	29	R
22.	Charlton Athletic FC (London)	42	9	4	29	62	120	22	R
		924	353	218	353	1612	1612	924	

Top Goalscorer

1) John CHARLES (Leeds United AFC) 38

Football League Division 2 1956-57 Season	Barnsley	Blackburn Rovers	Bristol City	Bristol Rovers	Bury	Doncaster Rovers	Fulham	Grimsby Town	Huddersfield Town	Leicester City	Leyton Orient	Lincoln City	Liverpool	Middlesbrough	Nottingham Forest	Notts County	Port Vale	Rotherham United	Sheffield United	Stoke City	Swansea Town	West Ham United
Barnsley FC		3-3	3-0	0-2	1-1	3-1	1-1	2-0	0-5	2-0	3-0	5-2	4-1	1-3	1-1	1-1	2-0	1-1	1-6	2-2	2-3	1-2
Blackburn Rovers FC	2-0		3-1	2-0	6-2	2-2	2-0	2-0	3-2	1-1	3-3	3-4	2-2	1-0	2-2	1-1	2-4	3-2	3-1	1-0	5-3	0-2
Bristol City FC	1-2	3-0		5-3	2-0	4-0	0-3	0-2	2-1	0-2	4-2	5-1	2-1	2-1	1-5	3-0	3-3	2-1	5-1	1-2	3-1	1-1
Bristol Rovers FC	1-1	0-1	0-0		6-1	6-1	4-0	1-0	4-0	1-2	3-2	0-1	0-0	0-2	3-2	3-0	2-1	4-2	3-1	4-0	1-1	1-1
Bury FC	1-2	2-2	2-3	7-2		4-4	0-1	2-3	1-3	4-5	1-3	1-0	0-2	3-2	1-2	2-1	1-0	1-4	0-1	0-1	1-3	3-3
Doncaster Rovers FC	5-2	1-1	4-1	2-4	1-1		4-0	0-1	4-0	0-2	6-1	3-1	1-1	2-1	1-1	4-2	4-0	1-1	1-0	1-0	0-1	3-0
Fulham FC	2-0	7-2	2-1	3-2	1-3	3-0		3-1	1-0	2-2	3-1	0-1	1-2	0-1	5-1	6-3	3-1	1-2	1-0	7-3		1-4
Grimsby Town FC	4-1	1-3	0-3	3-2	0-1	4-2	3-1		1-2	2-2	0-0	2-0	0-0	3-2	0-0	2-1	1-0	3-2	1-2	4-1	5-0	2-1
Huddersfield Town AFC	2-0	0-2	2-1	2-1	1-2	0-1	1-1	2-1		1-2	3-0	0-1	0-3	0-1	1-0	3-0	3-1	1-0	1-4	2-2	2-2	6-2
Leicester City FC	5-2	6-0	1-1	7-2	3-0	3-1	1-3	4-3	2-2		1-4	4-3	3-2	1-1	6-3	2-1	5-2	5-0	3-2	1-1	5-3	
Leyton Orient FC	2-0	1-1	2-2	1-1	4-3	1-1	0-2	1-1	3-1	1-5		2-1	0-4	1-1	1-4	2-2	3-2	1-1	2-2	1-2	3-0	1-2
Lincoln City FC	4-1	1-2	1-1	1-0	2-0	4-1	1-0	1-0	1-2	2-3	0-2		3-3	1-0	0-2	1-0	4-0	3-3	4-1	0-1	0-2	0-2
Liverpool FC	2-1	2-3	2-1	4-1	2-0	2-1	4-3	2-3	2-3	1-0	4-0			1-2	3-3	4-1	4-1	1-7	1-2	2-0	2-0	1-0
Middlesbrough FC	1-2	2-1	4-1	3-2	2-2	3-2	3-1	2-1	7-2	1-3	1-2	3-0	1-1		2-2	0-0	3-1	0-1	3-1	1-1	6-2	3-1
Nottingham Forest FC	7-1	2-1	2-2	1-1	5-1	2-1	3-1	2-1	0-0	1-2	1-2	1-1	1-0	0-4		2-4	4-2	3-1	2-1	4-0	4-3	3-0
Notts County FC	3-2	2-0	1-1	0-2	2-2	1-2	0-0	0-1	1-2	0-0	1-3	3-0	1-1	2-1	1-2		3-1	1-5	2-2	5-0	1-4	4-1
Port Vale FC	0-0	0-3	3-1	2-3	3-2	4-1	2-1	3-0	1-2	3-2	1-2	2-1	1-2	2-1	1-7	1-2		2-1	0-6	2-2	0-2	0-0
Rotherham United FC	0-0	0-2	6-1	0-0	1-1	0-1	4-3	2-1	3-3	1-1	2-0	3-0	2-2	2-3	3-2	0-0	1-0		0-4	1-0	6-1	0-1
Sheffield United FC	5-0	0-2	1-1	0-0	1-1	4-0	5-2	2-0	2-0	1-2	3-0	2-0	0-4	5-1	4-2	2-7				1-1	2-2	1-0
Stoke City FC	3-0	4-1	0-2	2-1	2-0	1-1	0-2	1-0	5-1	3-1	7-1	1-0	3-1	2-1	6-0	3-1	6-0	3-3			4-1	0-1
Swansea Town AFC	2-3	5-1	5-0	2-3	3-0	4-2	4-5	3-1	4-2	2-3	1-0	1-2	1-1	2-2	1-4	2-2	1-0	4-1	1-0			3-1
West Ham United FC	2-0	1-3	3-1	1-2	1-0	1-1	2-1	0-1	0-2	2-1	2-1	2-1	1-1	1-1	2-1	2-1	2-1	1-1	3-2	1-0	1-2	

	Division 2	Pd	Wn	Dw	Ls	GF	GA	Pts	
1.	Leicester City FC (Leicester)	42	25	11	6	109	67	61	P
2.	Nottingham Forest FC (Nottingham)	42	22	10	10	94	55	54	P
3.	Liverpool FC (Liverpool)	42	21	11	10	82	54	53	
4.	Blackburn Rovers FC (Blackburn)	42	21	10	11	83	75	52	
5.	Stoke City FC (Stoke-on-Trent)	42	20	8	14	83	58	48	
6.	Middlesbrough FC (Middlesbrough)	42	19	10	13	84	60	48	
7.	Sheffield United FC (Sheffield)	42	19	8	15	87	76	46	
8.	West Ham United FC (London)	42	19	8	15	59	63	46	
9.	Bristol Rovers FC (Bristol)	42	18	9	15	81	67	45	
10.	Swansea Town AFC (Swansea)	42	19	7	16	90	90	45	
11.	Fulham FC (London)	42	19	4	19	84	76	42	
12.	Huddersfield Town AFC (Huddersfield)	42	18	6	18	68	74	42	
13.	Bristol City FC (Bristol)	42	16	9	17	74	79	41	
14.	Doncaster Rovers FC (Doncaster)	42	15	10	17	77	77	40	
15.	Leyton Orient FC (London)	42	15	10	17	66	84	40	
16.	Grimsby Town FC (Cleethorpes)	42	17	5	20	61	62	39	
17.	Rotherham United FC (Rotherham)	42	13	11	18	74	75	37	
18.	Lincoln City FC (Lincoln)	42	14	6	22	54	80	34	
19.	Barnsley FC (Barnsley)	42	12	10	20	59	89	34	
20.	Notts County FC (Nottingham)	42	9	12	21	58	86	30	
21.	Bury FC (Bury)	42	8	9	25	60	96	25	R
22.	Port Vale FC (Stoke-on-Trent)	42	8	6	28	57	101	22	R
		924	367	190	367	1644	1644	924	

Football League Division 3 (N) — 1956-57 Season

	Accrington Stanley	Barrow	Bradford City	Bradford P.A.	Carlisle United	Chester	Chesterfield	Crewe Alexandra	Darlington	Derby County	Gateshead	Halifax Town	Hartlepools	Hull City	Mansfield Town	Oldham Athletic	Rochdale	Scunthorpe United	Southport	Stockport County	Tranmere Rovers	Workington	Wrexham	York City
Accrington Stanley		4-1	0-2	5-0	1-2	4-0	1-1	5-0	4-2	0-0	2-0	4-0	2-1	0-3	3-3	2-2	2-1	0-1	4-2	4-0	1-0	2-1	1-0	3-0
Barrow AFC	3-1		4-0	1-0	3-0	3-0	2-1	3-0	3-1	2-2	1-2	1-0	3-1	1-2	2-0	2-1	2-0	1-2	1-1	0-3	5-0	5-2	2-1	1-2
Bradford City AFC	1-2	0-2		2-0	3-2	1-0	3-2	5-1	1-2	0-2	3-1	1-0	1-1	2-1	4-3	4-1	1-1	3-1	3-1	1-1	4-1	2-3	2-1	0-2
Bradford Park Ave.	2-0	4-1	2-0		1-3	3-1	2-0	4-3	3-1	3-2	0-1	2-1	0-2	4-1	1-4	2-2	0-0	1-2	2-3	3-2	1-2	1-3	0-4	0-2
Carlisle United FC	2-2	1-1	1-4	2-1		3-0	4-2	2-1	1-2	1-3	3-2	0-0	2-1	1-3	6-1	2-2	2-1	0-0	1-2	3-3	2-2	1-1	2-2	2-0
Chester FC	0-2	2-0	1-2	2-0	1-2		3-4	4-1	0-3	2-2	4-1	1-1	0-1	1-0	6-2	1-0	2-2	2-2	2-0	1-4	1-1	1-0	0-1	3-4
Chesterfield FC	1-0	3-2	1-1	4-1	2-2	3-0		2-0	4-1	2-2	6-0	2-1	5-1	3-1	1-0	1-0	2-2	1-0	6-0	1-0	3-1	2-2	2-1	3-4
Crewe Alexandra FC	3-4	1-1	1-0	2-0	2-2	0-0	0-4		1-3	2-5	0-3	1-3	1-2	2-3	6-4	2-2	1-6	2-1	0-0	0-1	0-0	0-1	3-0	1-1
Darlington FC	0-0	1-1	3-2	0-5	0-1	5-1	4-1	3-0		1-1	7-0	0-1	3-1	1-1	1-3	1-0	4-3	1-2	1-0	3-1	1-1	4-2	1-5	2-4
Derby County FC	2-2	3-3	0-2	6-1	3-0	3-0	7-1	4-0	1-1		5-3	6-0	2-0	1-0	4-0	3-2	3-0	4-0	2-0	2-0	4-0	2-3	1-0	1-0
Gateshead FC	1-1	2-2	1-2	1-3	4-2	4-1	1-3	1-1	1-2	1-1		2-1	4-3	2-0	1-1	2-3	2-1	0-0	3-1	1-5	3-1	1-2	4-2	0-2
Halifax Town AFC	0-1	3-2	1-0	3-1	1-3	2-1	2-1	1-0	3-2	1-0	0-1		2-0	1-0	2-1	1-1	2-1	1-0	3-1	3-2	4-0	4-2	1-2	0-0
Hartlepools United	2-1	2-0	2-0	2-1	2-1	2-2	5-1	2-0	2-1	2-1	4-1	0-1		3-3	2-1	4-1	0-0	1-0	5-2	4-1	5-1	4-1	0-2	1-0
Hull City AFC	2-1	3-0	1-0	2-0	0-0	2-0	3-2	2-0	1-1	3-3	1-1	3-1	2-0		1-2	2-1	2-0	2-2	2-1	5-3	4-1	0-2	1-2	1-1
Mansfield Town FC	1-3	1-3	3-1	5-1	1-1	3-0	2-1	7-3	1-2	2-4	2-0	4-1	2-1	2-1		2-4	2-3	1-1	1-2	4-2	3-0	2-2	3-1	4-1
Oldham Athletic AFC	2-4	0-1	1-1	3-1	2-2	0-0	3-3	2-0	3-2	1-2	1-2	4-3	0-0	1-3	1-1		0-1	1-1	2-2	1-0	1-0	1-0	2-1	3-1
Rochdale AFC	0-2	1-0	4-1	2-1	2-1	1-0	1-1	3-0	3-1	0-0	1-1	1-0	4-3	0-0	0-2	1-1		3-0	6-1	2-2	1-0	0-0	0-2	1-1
Scunthorpe United	2-3	1-1	1-1	2-2	1-2	3-0	5-1	5-1	1-2	1-4	1-2	6-1	1-2	1-1	0-1	0-0	1-0		1-0	2-3	1-4	2-1	4-3	2-1
Southport FC	3-5	0-0	1-5	5-1	4-1	1-1	0-0	1-1	1-0	3-2	2-3	1-1	1-6	1-0	1-0	2-2	0-1	2-2		0-1	1-0	1-1	1-1	1-1
Stockport County FC	2-1	2-1	1-1	4-0	2-0	2-1	2-1	5-2	3-2	1-1	2-2	2-4	1-2	2-1	3-1	1-3	2-0	3-1	3-1		3-1	0-1	4-0	3-0
Tranmere Rovers FC	1-2	0-2	0-0	0-3	0-1	3-1	2-2	3-0	2-2	0-1	0-0	0-2	0-1	2-4	3-1	2-1	2-2	4-2	1-1	2-2		1-1	2-4	3-3
Workington AFC	4-1	0-1	5-1	0-1	2-0	0-1	2-1	4-0	6-2	2-1	2-1	3-1	1-1	4-3	3-3	0-0	5-0	2-2	2-0	4-1	3-2		3-0	3-2
Wrexham AFC	5-2	5-0	1-2	2-0	6-4	2-2	1-3	5-0	5-0	0-2	4-1	3-2	2-2	5-2	0-0	4-4	4-1	1-1	1-1	2-3	1-0	3-0		1-1
York City FC	3-1	1-0	3-1	1-2	2-0	0-1	1-2	2-1	1-0	1-1	1-0	1-2	3-3	2-1	2-0	2-1	4-0	0-2	9-1	0-0	1-0	2-2	1-0	

Division 3 (North)

		Pd	Wn	Dw	Ls	GF	GA	Pts	
1.	Derby County FC (Derby)	46	26	11	9	111	53	63	P
2.	Hartlepools United FC (Hartlepool)	46	25	9	12	90	63	59	
3.	Accrington Stanley FC (Accrington)	46	25	8	13	95	64	58	
4.	Workington AFC (Workington)	46	24	10	12	93	63	58	
5.	Stockport County FC (Stockport)	46	23	8	15	91	75	54	
6.	Chesterfield FC (Chesterfield)	46	22	9	15	96	79	53	
7.	York City FC (York)	46	21	10	15	75	61	52	
8.	Hull City AFC (Kingston-upon-Hull)	46	21	10	15	84	69	52	
9.	Bradford City AFC (Bradford)	46	22	8	16	78	68	52	
10.	Barrow AFC (Barrow-in-Furness)	46	21	9	16	76	62	51	
11.	Halifax Town AFC (Halifax)	46	21	7	18	65	70	49	
12.	Wrexham AFC (Wrexham)	46	19	10	17	97	74	48	
13.	Rochdale AFC (Rochdale)	46	18	12	16	65	65	48	
14.	Scunthorpe & Lindsey FC (Scunthorpe)	46	15	15	16	71	69	45	
15.	Carlisle United FC (Carlisle)	46	16	13	17	76	85	45	
16.	Mansfield Town FC (Mansfield)	46	17	10	19	91	90	44	
17.	Gateshead FC (Gateshead)	46	17	10	19	72	90	44	
18.	Darlington FC (Darlington)	46	17	8	21	82	95	42	
19.	Oldham Athletic AFC (Oldham)	46	12	15	19	66	74	39	
20.	Bradford Park Avenue FC (Bradford)	46	16	3	27	66	93	35	
21.	Chester FC (Chester)	46	10	13	23	55	84	33	
22.	Southport FC (Southport)	46	10	12	24	52	94	32	
23.	Tranmere Rovers FC (Birkenhead)	46	7	13	26	51	91	27	
24.	Crewe Alexandra FC (Crewe)	46	6	9	31	43	110	21	
		1104	431	242	431	1841	1841	1104	

259

Football League Division 3 (S) — 1956-57 Season

(Home \ Away)	Aldershot Town	Bournemouth	Brentford	Brighton & H.A.	Colchester United	Coventry City	Crystal Palace	Exeter City	Gillingham	Ipswich Town	Millwall	Newport County	Northampton Town	Norwich City	Plymouth Argyle	Q.P.R.	Reading	Shrewsbury Town	Southampton	Southend United	Swindon Town	Torquay United	Walsall	Watford
Aldershot Town FC	■	3-2	0-2	1-4	2-1	0-1	2-1	1-4	0-0	3-1	3-0	3-1	4-0	0-0	0-2	4-2	1-4	1-1	1-1	5-3	2-2	0-1	4-1	3-1
Bournemouth & Bos.	3-2	■	3-0	1-1	1-1	1-2	2-2	3-1	3-1	1-0	6-1	2-1	4-1	1-1	2-1	1-0	2-1	6-1	1-0	1-1	7-0	0-0	2-2	4-0
Brentford FC	2-2	2-2	■	2-5	1-1	1-1	1-1	3-0	3-2	1-1	5-0	0-0	2-1	1-1	4-1	2-0	4-0	3-1	4-0	3-2	4-1	0-0	6-2	1-5
Brighton & Hove Alb.	2-2	2-2	1-2	■	0-0	2-1	1-1	3-0	3-1	3-2	3-2	2-0	5-0	3-0	3-1	1-0	8-3	4-3	1-0	1-1	2-0	6-0	1-3	2-2
Colchester United FC	1-1	3-0	1-0	0-0	■	3-2	3-3	4-0	0-0	0-0	2-1	1-0	5-1	1-1	2-1	1-1	3-2	6-0	3-1	3-2	1-1	2-1	2-1	2-0
Coventry City FC	5-1	4-2	1-1	1-2	2-4	■	3-3	1-0	4-1	1-1	1-2	2-0	3-1	3-2	1-4	5-1	0-1	3-3	2-1	2-0	3-2	3-2	2-2	0-2
Crystal Palace FC	2-1	1-1	0-2	2-2	2-4	1-1	■	0-0	1-2	1-3	2-2	2-1	1-1	4-1	2-1	2-1	1-1	0-1	1-2	2-0	0-0	1-1	3-0	0-0
Exeter City FC	1-1	1-2	1-1	1-3	0-2	4-2	2-1	■	4-0	1-2	1-1	2-0	0-0	0-0	2-1	0-0	1-1	5-1	0-4	6-1	3-2	1-1	0-1	1-2
Gillingham FC	6-2	1-0	2-1	0-0	1-2	1-2	4-1	2-1	■	1-1	1-3	1-1	1-2	1-1	0-3	0-1	0-0	1-1	0-0	0-2	3-0	1-1	2-1	0-3
Ipswich Town FC	4-1	1-0	4-0	4-0	3-1	4-0	4-2	3-0	1-1	■	0-2	5-0	0-1	3-1	2-1	4-0	4-2	5-1	2-0	3-3	4-1	6-0	2-2	4-1
Millwall FC	1-5	3-4	1-1	4-3	3-1	3-2	3-0	1-3	2-1	2-2	■	1-0	1-0	5-1	2-2	2-0	1-0	0-0	0-0	0-0	2-1	7-2	1-0	1-1
Newport County AFC	3-0	5-3	3-0	0-0	1-0	3-0	2-2	1-1	4-0	1-0	0-0	■	3-0	3-1	4-1	1-1	1-2	2-0	2-3	2-1	3-0	2-2	3-0	
Northampton Town	4-2	2-2	5-1	1-0	4-0	1-0	1-1	4-1	2-1	2-1	0-3		■	1-1	2-0	3-0	1-1	2-1	2-2	2-2	3-0	3-0	1-2	
Norwich City FC	1-1	1-3	1-1	1-1	1-2	3-0	1-0	1-0	1-3	1-2	2-0	1-1	2-1	■	3-0	1-2	2-5	3-0	0-3	1-2	2-4	1-2	2-2	1-2
Plymouth Argyle FC	2-2	2-0	2-0	2-0	2-2	0-0	0-1	5-0	2-0	1-2	0-0	3-2	4-3	3-2	■	1-2	0-6	1-1	2-1	1-1	1-0	0-0	2-4	3-3
Queen's Park Rangers	0-1	2-1	2-2	0-0	1-1	1-1	4-2	5-3	5-0	0-0	0-0	1-1	1-0	3-0	3-0	■	1-1	2-1	1-2	3-0	3-0	0-1	1-0	3-1
Reading FC	2-1	0-4	2-0	2-2	0-3	3-0	1-2	4-0	1-3	3-0	0-0	1-1	2-1	3-2	1-0		■	2-2	2-4	3-2	1-0	3-1	3-0	1-1
Shrewsbury Town FC	2-2	0-0	3-2	1-3	5-0	1-1	1-2	1-0	1-1	2-0	2-0	2-0	4-5	3-1	0-0	1-1		■	0-0	0-0	7-3	1-1	3-2	1-0
Southampton FC	1-0	3-0	3-3	1-0	2-1	1-1	3-0	2-1	0-1	0-2	4-0	3-0	2-2	2-2	4-1	4-0			■	1-2	2-1	3-1		3-1
Southend United FC	2-4	2-1	1-0	3-1	3-2	1-2	1-1	2-0	5-0	1-0	3-3	0-1	0-0	0-1	3-0	4-0	1-2	1-2		■	1-0	2-0	2-0	
Swindon Town FC	1-2	2-1	1-3	3-0	4-1	2-2	3-1	3-5	2-3	3-1	1-0	4-0	1-1	0-3	1-2	0-0	3-2	1-2	0-0	3-2	■	1-2	1-2	2-0
Torquay United FC	4-2	1-0	2-0	1-0	4-2	3-1	3-0	1-0	3-3	4-1	7-2	4-0	2-0	7-1	1-1	3-0	3-1	1-1	2-0	3-3	7-0	■	2-0	3-0
Walsall FC	5-1	0-0	7-0	3-2	2-1	1-1	1-2	2-0	2-2	2-0	7-1	0-0	2-2	6-3	1-0	0-2	3-2	1-1	1-1	0-1	1-2	0-1	■	2-0
Watford FC	3-0	1-1	1-1	2-1	0-0	1-0	1-4	1-1	2-3	2-1	2-0	5-0	2-1	3-3	0-1	2-4	1-0	2-3	4-2	1-1	3-4	4-1	1-0	■

Division 3 (South)

#	Club	Pd	Wn	Dw	Ls	GF	GA	Pts	
1.	Ipswich Town FC (Ipswich)	46	25	9	12	101	54	59	P
2.	Torquay United FC (Torquay)	46	24	11	11	89	64	59	
3.	Colchester United FC (Colchester)	46	22	14	10	84	56	58	
4.	Southampton FC (Southampton)	46	22	10	14	76	52	54	
5.	Bournemouth & Boscombe Athletic FC (Bournemouth)	46	19	14	13	88	62	52	
6.	Brighton & Hove Albion FC (Hove)	46	19	14	13	86	65	52	
7.	Southend United FC (Southend-on-Sea)	46	18	12	16	73	65	48	
8.	Brentford FC (London)	46	16	16	14	78	76	48	
9.	Shrewsbury Town FC (Shrewsbury)	46	15	18	13	72	79	48	
10.	Queen's Park Rangers FC (London)	46	18	11	17	61	69	47	
11.	Watford FC (Watford)	46	18	10	18	72	75	46	
12.	Newport County AFC (Newport)	46	16	13	17	65	62	45	
13.	Reading FC (Reading)	46	18	9	19	80	81	45	
14.	Northampton Town FC (Northampton)	46	18	9	19	66	73	45	
15.	Walsall FC (Walsall)	46	16	12	18	80	74	44	
16.	Coventry City FC (Coventry)	46	16	12	18	74	84	44	
17.	Millwall FC (London)	46	16	12	18	64	84	44	
18.	Plymouth Argyle FC (Plymouth)	46	16	11	19	68	73	43	
19.	Aldershot FC (Aldershot)	46	15	12	19	79	92	42	
20.	Crystal Palace FC (London)	46	11	18	17	62	75	40	
21.	Exeter City FC (Exeter)	46	12	13	21	61	79	37	
22.	Gillingham FC (Gillingham)	46	12	13	21	54	85	37	
23.	Swindon Town FC (Swindon)	46	15	6	25	66	96	36	
24.	Norwich City FC (Norwich)	46	8	15	23	61	94	31	
		1104	405	294	405	1760	1760	1104	

F.A. CUP FINAL   (Wembley Stadium, London – 04/05/1957 – 100,000)

ASTON VILLA FC (BIRMINGHAM)   2-1   Manchester United FC (Manchester)
McParland 2   *Taylor*

Aston Villa: Sims, Lynn, Aldiss, Crowther, Dugdale, Saward, Smith, Sewell, Myerscough, Dixon, McParland.

Man. United: Wood, Foulkes, Byrne, Colman, Blanchflower, Edwards, Berry, Whelan, Taylor, R.Charlton, Pegg.

Semi-finals

Aston Villa FC (Birmingham)	2-2, 1-0	West Bromwich Albion FC (West Bromwich)
Manchester United FC (Manchester)	2-0	Birmingham City FC (Birmingham)

Quarter-finals

Birmingham City FC (Birmingham)	0-0, 1-0	Nottingham Forest FC (Nottingham)
Bournemouth & Boscombe Athletic FC (B'mouth)	1-2	Manchester United FC (Manchester)
Burnley FC (Burnley)	1-1, 0-2	Aston Villa FC (Birmingham)
West Bromwich Albion FC (West Bromwich)	2-2, 2-1	Arsenal FC (London)

Football League Division 1 1957-58 Season	Arsenal	Aston Villa	Birmingham City	Blackpool	Bolton Wands.	Burnley	Chelsea	Everton	Leeds United	Leicester City	Luton Town	Man. City	Man. United	Newcastle United	Nottingham F.	Portsmouth	Preston N.E.	Sheffield Wed.	Sunderland	Tottenham H.	W.B.A.	Wolves
Arsenal FC		4-0	1-3	2-3	1-2	0-0	5-4	2-3	2-1	3-1	2-0	2-1	4-5	2-3	1-1	3-2	4-2	1-0	3-0	4-4	2-2	0-2
Aston Villa FC	3-0		0-2	1-1	4-0	3-0	1-3	0-1	2-0	5-1	2-0	1-2	3-2	4-3	1-1	2-1	2-2	2-0	5-2	1-1	2-1	2-3
Birmingham City FC	4-1	3-1		0-0	5-1	2-3	3-3	2-1	1-1	0-1	1-1	4-0	3-3	1-4	0-2	4-1	3-1	1-0	2-3	0-0	3-5	1-5
Blackpool FC	1-0	1-1	4-2		2-3	2-4	2-1	0-1	3-0	5-1	1-2	2-5	1-4	3-2	3-0	2-1	1-2	2-2	7-0	0-2	2-0	3-2
Bolton Wanderers FC	0-1	4-0	1-0	3-0		2-1	3-3	1-5	0-2	2-3	1-2	4-0	1-1	2-0	1-0	0-4	5-4	2-2	3-2	2-2	1-1	
Burnley FC	2-1	3-0	3-1	2-1	3-1		2-1	0-2	3-1	7-3	1-2	2-1	3-0	0-2	3-1	3-1	2-0	6-0	2-0	2-2	1-1	
Chelsea FC	0-0	4-2	5-1	1-4	2-2	6-1		3-1	2-1	4-0	1-3	2-3	2-1	0-0	7-4	0-2	1-0	2-3	0-2	4-2	2-2	1-2
Everton FC	2-2	1-2	0-2	0-0	1-1	1-1	3-0		0-1	2-2	0-2	2-5	3-3	1-2	1-1	4-2	4-2	1-1	3-1	3-4	1-1	1-0
Leeds United AFC	2-0	4-0	1-1	2-1	2-1	1-0	0-0	1-0		2-1	0-2	2-4	1-1	3-0	1-2	2-3	2-2	2-1	1-2	1-1	1-1	1-1
Leicester City FC	0-1	6-1	2-2	2-1	2-3	5-3	3-2	2-2	3-0		4-1	8-4	0-3	2-1	1-3	1-2	1-3	4-1	4-1	1-3	3-3	2-3
Luton Town FC	4-0	3-0	3-0	2-0	1-0	3-2	0-2	0-1	1-1	2-1		1-2	2-2	0-3	2-1	1-3	2-0	7-1	0-0	5-1	3-1	
Manchester City FC	2-4	1-2	1-1	4-3	2-1	4-1	5-2	6-2	1-0	4-3	2-2		2-2	2-1	1-0	4-3	3-1	5-1	4-1	3-4		
Manchester United FC	4-2	4-1	0-2	1-2	7-2	1-0	0-1	3-0	5-0	4-0	3-0	4-1		1-1	1-1	0-3	0-0	2-1	2-2	3-4	0-4	0-4
Newcastle United FC	3-3	2-4	1-2	1-2	1-2	1-3	1-3	2-3	1-2	5-3	3-2	4-1	1-2		1-4	0-2	0-0	2-2	3-1	3-0	1-1	
Nottingham Forest FC	4-0	4-1	1-1	1-2	0-0	7-0	1-0	0-3	1-2	3-1	1-0	2-1	1-2	2-3		2-0	2-1	5-2	2-0	1-2		1-4
Portsmouth FC	5-4	1-0	3-2	2-2	2-2	0-0	3-0	1-2	2-0	5-0	2-3	3-3	2-2	1-4			0-2	0-2	5-1	2-2	1-1	
Preston North End FC	3-0	1-1	8-0	2-1	3-0	2-1	5-2	3-1	3-0	4-1	1-0	6-1	1-1	2-1	2-0	4-0		3-0	3-0	3-1	3-1	1-2
Sheffield Wednesday FC	2-0	2-5	5-3	0-3	1-0	1-2	2-3	2-4	3-2	2-1	2-1	4-5	1-0	1-0	1-2	4-2	4-4		3-3	2-0	1-2	2-1
Sunderland AFC	0-1	1-1	1-6	1-4	1-2	2-3	2-2	1-1	2-1	3-2	3-0	0-1	1-0	0-0	3-3	1-1	0-0	3-3		1-1	2-0	0-2
Tottenham Hotspur FC	3-1	6-2	7-1	2-1	4-1	3-1	1-1	1-3	2-0	1-4	3-1	5-1	1-0	3-3	3-4	3-5	3-3	4-2	0-1		0-0	1-0
West Bromwich Albion FC	1-2	3-2	0-0	1-1	2-2	5-1	1-1	4-0	1-0	6-2	4-2	9-2	4-3	2-1	3-2	3-1	4-1	3-1	3-0	0-2		0-3
Wolverhampton Wanderers FC	1-2	2-1	5-1	3-1	6-1	2-1	2-1	2-0	3-2	5-1	1-1	3-3	3-1	3-1	2-0	1-0	2-0	4-3	5-0	4-0	1-1	

	Division 1	Pd	Wn	Dw	Ls	GF	GA	Pts	
1.	WOLVERHAMPTON WANDERERS FC (WOLV.)	42	28	8	6	103	47	64	
2.	Preston North End FC (Preston)	42	26	7	9	100	51	59	
3.	Tottenham Hotspur FC (London)	42	21	9	12	93	77	51	
4.	West Bromwich Albion FC (West Bromwich)	42	18	14	10	92	70	50	
5.	Manchester City FC (Manchester)	42	22	5	15	104	100	49	
6.	Burnley FC (Burnley)	42	21	5	16	80	74	47	
7.	Blackpool FC (Blackpool)	42	19	6	17	80	67	44	
8.	Luton Town FC (Luton)	42	19	6	17	69	63	44	
9.	Manchester United FC (Manchester)	42	16	11	15	85	75	43	
10.	Nottingham Forest FC (Nottingham)	42	16	10	16	69	63	42	
11.	Chelsea FC (London)	42	15	12	15	83	79	42	
12.	Arsenal FC (London)	42	16	7	19	73	85	39	
13.	Birmingham City FC (Birmingham)	42	14	11	17	76	89	39	
14.	Aston Villa FC (Birmingham)	42	16	7	19	73	86	39	
15.	Bolton Wanderers FC (Bolton)	42	14	10	18	65	87	38	
16.	Everton FC (Liverpool)	42	13	11	18	65	75	37	
17.	Leeds United AFC (Leeds)	42	14	9	19	51	63	37	
18.	Leicester City FC (Leicester)	42	14	5	23	91	112	33	
19.	Newcastle United FC (Newcastle-upon-Tyne)	42	12	8	22	73	81	32	
20.	Portsmouth FC (Portsmouth)	42	12	8	22	73	88	32	
21.	Sunderland AFC (Sunderland)	42	10	12	20	54	97	32	R
22.	Sheffield Wednesday FC (Sheffield)	42	12	7	23	69	92	31	R
		924	368	188	368	1721	1721	924	

Top Goalscorer

1) Robert SMITH   (Tottenham Hotspur FC)   36

Football League Division 2 1957-58 Season	Barnsley	Blackburn Rovers	Bristol City	Bristol Rovers	Cardiff City	Charlton Athletic	Derby County	Doncaster Rovers	Fulham	Grimsby Town	Huddersfield Town	Ipswich Town	Leyton Orient	Lincoln City	Liverpool	Middlesbrough	Notts County	Rotherham United	Sheffield United	Stoke City	Swansea Town	West Ham United
Barnsley FC		0-2	4-1	2-2	1-1	4-1	3-0	1-1	1-0	3-3	2-3	5-1	3-0	1-3	2-1	1-1	1-1	3-0	0-2	1-2	1-0	1-0
Blackburn Rovers FC	3-1		5-0	2-0	4-0	1-1	3-1	3-2	1-1	3-0	1-1	0-0	4-1	0-1	3-3	3-3	3-0	5-0	1-0	1-0	2-2	2-1
Bristol City FC	5-0	0-0		3-2	2-0	1-2	2-1	2-2	0-5	3-2	1-3	1-0	2-2	4-0	1-2	0-0	3-1	0-1	1-4	2-1	1-2	1-1
Bristol Rovers FC	1-1	4-0	3-3		0-2	1-0	5-2	2-1	2-2	0-7	1-1	3-1	4-0	3-0	3-1	5-0	5-2	1-3	2-2	2-0	3-0	2-3
Cardiff City AFC	7-0	4-3	2-3	0-2		0-3	3-2	3-1	3-0	1-3	1-0	1-1	1-1	3-2	6-1	0-2	2-0	2-2	0-0	5-2	0-0	0-3
Charlton Athletic FC	4-2	3-4	1-0	2-3	3-1		2-2	2-0	2-2	2-0	7-6	4-1	3-2	4-1	5-1	6-2	4-1	4-0	3-1	3-0	1-1	0 3
Derby County FC	1-4	0-3	5-2	2-1	0-2	1-3		1-0	3-3	1-0	2-4	2-2	2-0	3-2	2-1	2-1	2-1	3-4	2-0	0-0	1-0	2-3
Doncaster Rovers FC	1-1	1-5	2-1	3-2	0-1	1-2	1-2		1-6	3-3	0-3	1-1	2-0	1-3	1-1	3-2	4-0	3-2	2-2	0-1	3-0	1-2
Fulham FC	1-1	1-1	3-4	3-0	2-0	3-1	2-0	4-1		6-0	2-1	0-0	3-1	4-1	2-2	0-1	1-0	3-1	6-3	3-4	2-0	2-1
Grimsby Town FC	2-1	3-4	1-1	3-2	1-1	4-2	3-2	3-1	3-1		4-1	0-2	7-2	4-0	3-1	4-1	2-0	3-1	1-3	0-0	2-2	1-2
Huddersfield Town AFC	0-5	2-1	0-0	0-0	1-1	3-3	0-0	2-2	0-3	1-0		3-0	2-0	0-1	2-1	1-0	3-0	1-3	1-1	1-0	2-2	3-1
Ipswich Town FC	3-0	2-1	4-2	3-2	3-1	1-4	2-2	2-0	1-1	3-2	4-0		5-3	1-1	3-1	1-1	2-1	1-2	1-0	1-3	0-2	1-4
Leyton Orient FC	2-1	5-1	4-0	1-3	4-2	3-2	1-1	2-0	1-3	5-1	3-1	2-0		1-0	4-0	2-2	6-2	0-1	0-2	5-1	1-4	
Lincoln City FC	1-3	1-1	4-0	0-1	3-1	2-3	1-1	1-1	0-1	1-4	1-1	2-1	2-0		0-1	2-3	2-2	2-0	2-2	1-3	4-0	1-6
Liverpool FC	1-1	2-0	4-3	2-0	3-0	3-1	2-0	5-0	2-1	3-2	1-1	3-1	3-0	1-0		0-2	4-0	2-0	1-0	3-0	4-0	1-1
Middlesbrough FC	3-1	2-3	0-0	4-3	4-1	2-0	3-2	5-0	2-0	5-1	0-1	5-2	2-0	3-1	2-2		3-1	2-2	1-2	1-3	2-1	1-3
Notts County FC	2-3	1-1	0-1	0-0	5-2	2-1	1-0	0-5	1-5	2-0	1-1	0-3	0-1	1-0	0-2	2-0		1-0	1-0	1-2	2-4	1-0
Rotherham United FC	4-1	1-2	4-1	2-0	3-1	1-5	0-2	2-1	3-1	2-0	1-1	1-4	2-2	1-2	2-2	1-4	1-3		1-6	0-2	5-2	1-2
Sheffield United FC	0-0	4-2	0-3	2-0	3-0	0-3	0-1	3-0	1-1	3-1	3-2	1-1	0-2	4-0	1-1	3-2	1-0	2-0		3-0	2-2	2-1
Stoke City FC	3-1	2-4	3-0	3-5	3-0	2-2	2-1	0-0	1-2	4-1	1-1	5-1	1-3	1-1	1-2	4-1	0-1	4-1	2-3		6-2	1-4
Swansea Town AFC	4-2	0-4	5-1	6-4	0-1	1-3	7-0	4-3	4-4	0-2	1-1	0-0	1-2	5-1	0-2	1-4	1-3	1-3	0-2	4-1		3-2
West Ham United FC	1-1	1-1	3-2	6-1	1-1	0-0	2-1	1-1	3-2	2-0	5-2	1-1	3-2	2-2	1-1	2-1	3-1	8-0	0-3	5-0	6-2	

Division 2

		Pd	Wn	Dw	Ls	GF	GA	Pts	
1.	West Ham United FC (London)	42	23	11	8	101	54	57	P
2.	Blackburn Rovers FC (Blackburn)	42	22	12	8	93	57	56	P
3.	Charlton Athletic FC (London)	42	24	7	11	107	69	55	
4.	Liverpool FC (Liverpool)	42	22	10	10	79	54	54	
5.	Fulham FC (London)	42	20	12	10	97	59	52	
6.	Sheffield United FC (Sheffield)	42	21	10	11	75	50	52	
7.	Middlesbrough FC (Middlesbrough)	42	19	7	16	83	74	45	
8.	Ipswich Town FC (Ipswich)	42	16	12	14	68	69	44	
9.	Huddersfield Town AFC (Huddersfield)	42	14	16	12	63	66	44	
10.	Bristol Rovers FC (Bristol)	42	17	8	17	85	80	42	
11.	Stoke City FC (Stoke-on-Trent)	42	18	6	18	75	73	42	
12.	Leyton Orient FC (London)	42	18	5	19	77	79	41	
13.	Grimsby Town FC (Cleethorpes)	42	17	6	19	86	83	40	
14.	Barnsley FC (Barnsley)	42	14	12	16	70	74	40	
15.	Cardiff City AFC (Cardiff)	42	14	9	19	63	77	37	
16.	Derby County FC (Derby)	42	14	8	20	60	81	36	
17.	Bristol City FC (Bristol)	42	13	9	20	63	88	35	
18.	Rotherham United FC (Rotherham)	42	14	5	23	65	101	33	
19.	Swansea Town AFC (Swansea)	42	11	9	22	72	99	31	
20.	Lincoln City FC (Lincoln)	42	11	9	22	55	82	31	
21.	Notts County FC (Nottingham)	42	12	6	24	44	80	30	R
22.	Doncaster Rovers FC (Doncaster)	42	8	11	23	56	88	27	R
		924	362	200	362	1637	1637	924	

Football League Division 3 (N) 1957-58 Season

	Accrington St.	Barrow	Bradford City	Bradford P.A.	Bury	Carlisle United	Chester	Chesterfield	Crewe Alex.	Darlington	Grimsby Town	Halifax Town	Hartlepools	Hull City	Mansfield T.	Oldham Ath.	Rochdale	Scunthorpe U.	Southport	Stockport Co.	Tranmere R.	Workington	Wrexham	York City
Accrington Stanley	■	3-2	2-2	5-2	3-0	3-2	1-2	0-4	2-0	0-0	3-0	2-1	1-2	3-0	4-1	1-1	3-2	2-1	2-2	3-2	2-1	3-0	2-1	3-0
Barrow AFC	3-1	■	1-2	0-0	4-2	2-3	4-1	4-1	0-1	2-1	1-2	0-3	3-3	0-0	2-1	2-2	2-1	0-1	1-0	1-1	1-4	0-0	2-2	1-0
Bradford City AFC	1-1	4-1	■	2-1	3-3	1-1	5-0	0-0	2-1	3-1	0-1	3-0	0-1	1-0	1-1	0-0	1-0	2-3	2-0	2-1	3-0	0-0	3-1	3-2
Bradford Park Ave.	1-3	1-1	0-0	■	1-4	4-1	3-0	2-0	3-1	4-1	2-2	0-2	2-3	4-4	0-2	1-3	2-2	1-2	3-5	1-0	1-0	3-3	3-0	0-2
Bury FC	1-1	4-1	1-0	1-0	■	3-0	1-2	1-0	2-0	5-0	4-1	1-0	3-3	1-1	0-2	4-0	4-1	2-1	4-1	1-1	8-2	3-0	3-0	4-1
Carlisle United FC	6-1	2-1	0-3	2-3	0-2	■	3-2	2-2	2-0	5-2	5-1	1-2	0-1	3-4	1-1	1-0	3-4	4-0	1-1	3-1	2-2	4-0	2-1	
Chester FC	5-1	2-2	0-0	1-2	0-0	0-0	■	0-0	3-2	0-1	1-1	2-1	1-1	1-0	2-1	0-0	1-4	2-0	1-0	2-1	4-3	0-1		9-2
Chesterfield FC	1-0	4-3	0-1	1-1	1-1	1-3	2-1	■	1-1	2-0	5-3	1-2	1-0	1-4	2-1	2-1	1-1	0-0	2-1	2-1	3-0	3-2	2-1	
Crewe Alexandra FC	4-1	1-4	2-2	3-0	0-1	0-0	0-3	1-2	■	2-2	2-2	1-2	2-1	1-2	1-0	0-2	3-2	1-2	0-4	0-3	2-0	3-4		
Darlington FC	0-2	3-0	4-0	4-0	3-2	1-2	2-3	2-0	3-0	■	2-2	5-0	1-3	2-2	2-0	3-1	4-2	1-1	1-2	0-1	2-1	3-1	2-1	
Gateshead FC	1-3	0-2	0-0	2-4	1-2	3-2	3-2	3-0	3-1	4-0	■	0-0	0-1	3-1	1-0	3-2	2-1	3-0	2-3	3-0	1-1	0-0		
Halifax Town AFC	0-2	3-1	3-2	2-0	5-0	2-1	3-2	2-0	1-0	4-1		■	3-0	2-2	4-0	4-0	0-1	4-1	1-0	1-1	2-2	0-0	2-1	
Hartlepools United	1-1	4-1	2-0	0-0	2-1	0-1	2-1	0-2	1-1	5-1	2-2	5-0	■	5-1	2-0	4-1	1-3	2-1	1-2	1-1	1-1	1-0	1-2	2-2
Hull City AFC	1-0	1-1	1-3	3-3	2-1	4-0	3-0	1-0	1-0	2-1	1-1	5-2	1-1	■	1-1	9-0	2-1	2-0	3-2	1-0	0-0	3-2	1-0	1-2
Mansfield Town FC	0-2	4-2	5-2	2-1	6-4	2-0	3-1	1-1	2-1	4-2	3-0	2-1	5-1	1-3	■	4-4	2-4	3-5	3-0	2-2	4-1	6-3	2-1	2-1
Oldham Athletic AFC	0-3	1-1	1-1	4-2	1-3	1-0	5-1	2-1	1-0	2-2	0-0	2-4	4-0	1-1	1-1	■	0-0	2-1	3-2	2-4	1-0	4-1	4-1	2-3
Rochdale AFC	3-0	1-1	0-2	1-2	1-1	1-1	3-4	3-0	5-4	0-0	5-1	7-0	2-1	3-0	1-3		■	1-4	2-0	3-0	2-0	1-0	2-0	1-2
Scunthorpe United	1-0	1-0	0-2	6-2	1-0	3-1	2-1	1-1	3-2	5-0	2-1	1-0	2-0	3-3	1-2	2-0		■	1-0	4-0	1-0	2-2	1-0	1-2
Southport FC	3-3	0-4	0-2	2-1	2-2	2-0	2-4	5-2	2-0	0-3	1-0	0-3	1-2	4-1	2-1	0-2	1-2		■	1-0	3-0	0-1	1-3	0-1
Stockport County FC	0-0	2-0	0-4	3-0	4-0	4-1	2-2	4-1	5-1	4-1	5-1	4-2	2-1	1-0	3-3	3-0	0-3	2-1	1-2	■	2-1	0-2	1-1	2-1
Tranmere Rovers FC	0-1	1-1	4-1	5-0	1-1	0-1	2-2	1-2	5-2	2-1	2-0	3-2	4-4	1-2	1-1	3-1	1-4	2-1	3-2	1-0	■	2-1		6-1
Workington AFC	0-1	0-1	1-1	1-2	3-0	2-1	5-3	0-2	3-2	2-2	1-1	4-4	1-0	3-2	4-0	4-2	1-2	3-2	2-0	1-1	1-2	■	4-2	0-0
Wrexham AFC	1-0	0-0	1-1	1-1	2-0	1-0	1-0	2-2	0-1	2-0	1-2	2-1	3-1	6-0	4-2	2-2	2-0	1-0	1-0	1-0	2-2	1-1	■	2-2
York City FC	0-3	0-0	2-0	3-0	2-1	0-5	1-2	3-3	3-1	3-0	2-2	1-1	3-1	3-1	2-2	1-0	0-0	1-0	0-0	4-0	3-0		1-2	■

Division 3 (North)

		Pd	Wn	Dw	Ls	GF	GA	Pts	
1.	Scunthorpe & Lindsey United FC (Scunthorpe)	46	29	8	9	88	50	66	P*
2.	Accrington Stanley FC (Accrington)	46	25	9	12	83	61	59	
3.	Bradford City AFC (Bradford)	46	21	15	10	73	49	57	
4.	Bury FC (Bury)	46	23	10	13	94	62	56	
5.	Hull City AFC (Kingston-upon-Hull)	46	19	15	12	78	67	53	
6.	Mansfield Town FC (Mansfield)	46	22	8	16	100	92	52	
7.	Halifax Town AFC (Halifax)	46	20	11	15	83	69	51	
8.	Chesterfield FC (Chesterfield)	46	18	15	13	71	69	51	
9.	Stockport County FC (Stockport)	46	18	11	17	74	67	47	
10.	Rochdale AFC (Rochdale)	46	19	8	19	79	67	46	
11.	Tranmere Rovers FC (Birkenhead)	46	18	10	18	82	76	46	
12.	Wrexham AFC (Wrexham)	46	17	12	17	71	73	46	
13.	York City FC (York)	46	17	12	17	68	76	46	
14.	Gateshead FC (Gateshead)	46	15	15	16	68	76	45	
15.	Oldham Athletic AFC (Oldham)	46	14	17	15	72	84	45	
16.	Carlisle United FC (Carlisle)	46	19	6	21	80	78	44	
17.	Hartlepools United FC (Hartlepool)	46	16	12	18	73	76	44	
18.	Barrow AFC (Barrow-in-Furness)	46	13	14	18	66	74	41	
19.	Workington AFC (Workington)	46	14	13	19	72	81	41	
20.	Darlington FC (Darlington)	46	17	7	22	78	89	41	
21.	Chester FC (Chester)	46	13	13	20	73	81	39	
22.	Bradford Park Avenue FC (Bradford)	46	13	11	22	68	95	37	
23.	Southport FC (Southport)	46	11	6	29	52	88	28	
24.	Crewe Alexandra FC (Crewe)	46	8	7	31	47	93	23	
		1104	419	166	419	1783	1783	1104	

* Scunthorpe & Lindsey United FC (Scunthorpe) changed their name to Scunthorpe United FC for the next season.

Football League Division 3 (S) — 1957-58 Season

	Aldershot Town	Bournemouth	Brentford	Brighton & H.A.	Colchester United	Coventry City	Crystal Palace	Exeter City	Gillingham	Millwall	Newport County	Northampton T.	Norwich City	Plymouth Argyle	Port Vale	Q.P.R.	Reading	Shrewsbury T.	Southampton	Southend United	Swindon Town	Torquay United	Walsall	Watford
Aldershot Town FC	■	0-0	0-2	2-3	2-1	1-1	4-1	2-2	2-0	2-2	2-1	0-0	2-1	3-3	0-1	1-1	1-0	0-1	1-5	0-2	2-1	1-1	1-3	2-2
Bournemouth & Bos.	5-1	■	1-0	1-3	1-1	0-0	3-1	2-1	2-1	4-0	4-3	1-1	3-1	0-0	3-1	4-1	4-1	3-1	5-2	2-1	1-1	2-0	1-2	2-1
Brentford FC	4-2	4-2	■	1-0	3-3	1-3	0-3	1-0	1-0	4-1	2-1	7-1	7-1	2-0	4-1	1-1	2-1	2-0	0-0	4-2	0-0	0-1	2-1	0-0
Brighton & Hove Alb.	0-1	2-1	1-1	■	5-2	3-0	3-2	2-2	5-2	4-2	5-3	1-4	0-1	3-2	0-0	1-1	1-2	2-1	1-1	3-1	1-0	1-1	2-0	6-0
Colchester United FC	1-1	3-2	1-1	1-2	■	4-1	1-1	3-0	3-2	2-1	1-1	1-0	1-2	1-2	2-1	2-1	1-3	3-0	4-2	1-0	1-3	3-0	1-1	4-0
Coventry City FC	6-0	0-3	0-0	2-2	1-0	■	2-2	6-1	1-1	1-4	1-2	1-1	1-1	1-0	1-1	1-0	5-0	0-0	1-0	0-1	2-1	4-1	2-2	
Crystal Palace FC	1-1	3-0	2-1	2-4	1-1	2-0	■	2-0	3-0	0-1	2-2	1-3	0-3	3-0	1-0	2-3	2-2	3-0	1-4	2-0	4-1	1-1	4-1	4-2
Exeter City FC	3-0	1-2	3-5	2-0	4-3	1-0	0-1	■	1-3	2-0	0-2	0-1	2-2	4-2	1-0	0-0	1-1	2-1	2-2	0-5	0-1	5-1	2-1	1-2
Gillingham FC	1-1	1-1	3-2	0-1	2-3	3-2	3-0	1-1	■	1-0	0-1	1-2	1-0	0-2	1-1	2-1	1-3	2-1	2-0	2-1	1-0	3-0	1-1	
Millwall FC	3-3	0-2	0-1	2-2	1-4	4-1	3-0	3-0	3-1	■	1-2	0-0	2-2	0-1	2-1	5-0	0-0	1-3	1-2	1-1	1-2	1-3	2-3	
Newport County AFC	3-2	3-1	1-2	1-2	2-2	2-2	0-0	0-0	5-0	1-2	■	0-1	1-0	0-2	2-1	4-2	0-0	2-0	1-1	1-0	4-1	3-2	2-0	2-1
Northampton Town	0-0	4-1	3-1	2-4	4-1	4-0	1-2	9-0	3-1	7-2	0-3	■	0-1	5-0	3-2	1-5	1-2	2-0	1-3	1-3	3-0	1-0	3-0	2-3
Norwich City FC	1-3	2-2	3-2	0-0	1-1	1-1	3-2	3-2	1-1	5-2	2-2		■	1-0	3-0	2-2	0-2	0-2	1-1	3-1	1-1	1-1		
Plymouth Argyle FC	4-2	3-1	0-0	2-1	1-1	4-0	1-0	1-0	2-1	1-0	1-0	3-0	0-1	■	1-0	3-1	1-0	2-2	4-0	2-3	2-2	1-0	2-1	2-1
Port Vale FC	6-1	2-3	0-1	2-2	2-0	0-1	4-0	3-2	2-0	1-1	2-2	3-0	2-2	0-0	■	2-1	1-2	0-0	4-0	1-3	3-1	2-1	2-1	5-0
Queen's Park Rangers	0-1	3-0	1-0	0-1	1-0	3-0	4-2	1-1	1-1	3-0	1-1	1-0	1-1	1-0	2-1	■	3-0	3-2	1-1	2-1	1-1	1-0		3-0
Reading FC	3-0	2-0	1-2	1-1	7-0	2-0	2-2	4-0	4-1	1-0	5-2	1-3	3-0	3-0			■	2-2	1-0	0-4	1-1	3-1	1-1	
Shrewsbury Town FC	5-1	0-4	0-2	2-0	0-0	1-3	0-0	0-1	2-1	0-1	1-1	3-1	0-0	2-0	1-0	2-1	0-2	■	1-3	1-1	1-3	3-0	2-0	1-1
Southampton FC	2-2	7-0	4-2	5-0	3-2	7-1	2-1	6-0	5-1	3-2	2-1	2-1	7-3	0-1	0-3	5-0	0-1	2-2	■	2-2	1-3	4-2	4-1	5-0
Southend United FC	1-2	2-0	0-0	0-2	2-3	5-1	1-1	2-0	2-0	1-1	6-3	2-1	1-1	6-0	2-1	5-1	3-2			■	2-3	0-0	2-1	2-1
Swindon Town FC	3-0	1-0	4-1	2-2	4-0	2-1	0-0	5-1	1-1	3-0	4-0	5-1	1-2	1-0	0-0	1-1	1-1	1-0	0-0	1-1	■	3-1	2-3	0-0
Torquay United FC	2-1	3-1	0-1	2-0	1-3	1-0	1-1	1-3	3-2	2-3	2-2	1-0	1-1	0-2	1-1	3-1	1-4	0-2	1-1	2-2	2-2	■	2-1	1-0
Walsall FC	0-0	3-1	0-2	2-3	3-0	4-1	2-1	3-0	1-1	4-2	3-0	2-1	2-1	0-2	3-0	1-2	0-0	0-1	1-1	1-1	1-1	0-0	■	1-3
Watford FC	1-3	1-1	4-1	0-1	1-1	1-0	2-1	5-4	3-0	3-0	2-2	0-2	0-2	0-1	2-0	0-1	3-0	3-0	1-1	0-0	1-0	1-1		■

	Division 3 (South)	Pd	Wn	Dw	Ls	GF	GA	Pts	
1.	Brighton & Hove Albion FC (Hove)	46	24	12	10	88	64	60	P
2.	Brentford FC (London)	46	24	10	12	82	56	58	
3.	Plymouth Argyle FC (Plymouth)	46	25	8	13	67	48	58	
4.	Swindon Town FC (Swindon)	46	21	15	10	79	50	57	
5.	Reading FC (Reading)	46	21	13	12	79	51	55	
6.	Southampton FC (Southampton)	46	22	10	14	112	72	54	
7.	Southend United FC (Southend-on-Sea)	46	21	12	13	90	58	54	
8.	Norwich City FC (Norwich)	46	19	15	12	75	70	53	
9.	Bournemouth & Boscombe Athletic FC (Bournemouth)	46	21	9	16	81	74	51	
10.	Queen's Park Rangers FC (London)	46	18	14	14	64	65	50	
11.	Newport County AFC (Newport)	46	17	14	15	73	67	48	
12.	Colchester United FC (Colchester)	46	17	13	16	77	79	47	
13.	Northampton Town FC (Northampton)	46	19	6	21	87	79	44	
14.	Crystal Palace FC (London)	46	15	13	18	70	72	43	
15.	Port Vale FC (Stoke-on-Trent)	46	16	10	20	67	58	42	
16.	Watford FC (Watford)	46	13	16	17	59	77	42	
17.	Shrewsbury Town FC (Shrewsbury)	46	15	10	21	49	71	40	
18.	Aldershot FC (Aldershot)	46	12	16	18	59	89	40	
19.	Coventry City FC (Coventry)	46	13	13	20	61	81	39	
20.	Walsall FC (Walsall)	46	14	9	23	61	75	37	
21.	Torquay United FC (Torquay)	46	11	13	22	49	74	35	
22.	Gillingham FC (Gillingham)	46	13	9	24	52	81	35	
23.	Millwall FC (London)	46	11	9	26	63	91	31	
24.	Exeter City FC (Exeter)	46	11	9	26	57	99	31	
		1104	413	278	413	1701	1701	1104	

The league was re-structured for the next season with clubs placed 2nd to 12th in Division 3 North and South plus clubs relegated from Division 2 forming a new Division 3. The remaining clubs who finished 13th to 24th in Division 3 North and South formed a new Division 4.

F.A. CUP FINAL   (Wembley Stadium, London – 03/05/1958 – 100,000)

BOLTON WANDERERS FC (BOLTON)   2-0   Manchester United FC (Manchester)

Lofthouse 2

Bolton: Hopkinson, Hartle, Banks, Hennin, Higgins, Edwards, Birch, Stevens, Lofthouse, Parry, Holden.

Man. United: Gregg, Foulkes, Greaves, Goodwin, Cope, Crowther, Dawson, Taylor, R.Charlton, Viollet, Webster.

Semi-finals

Blackburn Rovers FC (Blackburn)	1-2	Bolton Wanderers FC (Bolton)
Manchester United FC (Manchester)	2-2, 5-3	Fulham FC (London)

Quarter-finals

Blackburn Rovers FC (Blackburn)	2-1	Liverpool FC (Liverpool)
Bolton Wanderers FC (Bolton)	2-1	Wolverhampton Wanderers FC (Wolverhampton)
Fulham FC (London)	3-1	Bristol Rovers FC (Bristol)
West Bromwich Albion FC (west Bromwich)	2-2, 0-1	Manchester United FC (Manchester)